To
Christina

Preface for Students

This book is designed to teach you the Java programming language, and even more importantly, to teach you basic programming techniques. This book requires no previous programming experience and no mathematics other than some very simple high school algebra. However, to get the full benefit of the book, you should have a version of Java available on your computer, so that you can practice with the examples and techniques given in the book. You should have a version of Java with a version number of either 1.1.x or higher or 1.2.x or higher. (The exact number that is filled in for the x is not critical. The x need not even be present. If it says only "version 1.1" or "version 1.2," that is fine. If you have an earlier version of Java, numbered 1.0.x, that will not be a problem for most of the book, but it will definitely be a problem for Chapter 7, and, as you will see, the latest version of Java can be obtained easily and inexpensively.)

Copies of the Programs from the Text

This book contains a CD that includes all the programs and other software examples in the book, so that you can practice with these examples without having to type them into your computer.

Obtaining a Copy of Java

The CD that comes with this book also includes a version of Code Warrior, which is an integrated development environment including an editor and other utilities in addition to the Java language. The CD includes a version of Code Warrior for PC Windows environments and a version for Macintosh environments. The version included on the CD is Code Warrior Lite, which allows you to sample Code Warrior on programs from the text to see if you wish to purchase the full version at a special student rate. Your local college or university bookstore should stock the full student version of Code Warrior.

The Code Warrior environment provided on the CD will allow you to run the programs in this book. If you want to write other Java programs, you will need to purchase the full version of Code Warrior or obtain some other version of Java. If you want an alternative to Code Warrior, a version of Java can be obtained free of charge from Sun Microsystems. At the time of printing, a copy of Java version 1.1.x could be downloaded free of charge from the following web site:

```
http://www.java.sun.com/products/jdk/1.1
```

If you have a web browser such as Netscape's Navigator or Microsoft's Internet Explorer, you can use it to go to this web site and download the software you need to install Java on your computer. At the time that this book was sent to press, only preliminary copies of version 1.2 of Java were available. By the time this book comes out there should be more or less final versions of Java 1.2 available. You might want to search the web for the location of the Sun web site that offers version 1.2. At the time this book went to press, preliminary version of Java version 1.2 could be obtained at the following web site:

http://www.java.sun.com/products/jdk/1.2

If you cannot find version 1.2, version 1.1 will do fine for learning Java with this book.

While you are using your web browser to download Java, you can also go to another web site to download an integrated development environment. An integrated development environment includes an editor and other utilities and will make it more convenient to write and run Java programs. One suitable integrated development environment is the WinEdit environment from Wilson Window Ware. It can be downloaded to try for free. The web site is:

http://www.windowware.com

Self-Test Questions

Each chapter contains numerous self-test question. Complete answers for all the self-test questions are given at the end of each chapter. One of the best ways to practice what you are learning is to do the self-test questions, without looking at the answers, and to only look at the answers after you have done the questions and want to check your answers.

This Text Is Also a Reference Book

In addition to using this book as a textbook, you can and should use it as a reference. When you need to check a particular point that you may have forgotten or that you hear mentioned by somebody but have not yet learned yourself, just look in the index. Many index entries give a page number for "quick reference." Turn to this quick reference page. It will contain a short entry, usually set off in a box, that gives all the essential points on that topic. This can be done to check details of the Java language, as well as details on programming techniques.

Boxed sections in every chapter give you a quick summary of the main points in that chapter; you can use these boxes to review the chapter or to preview the chapter or to check details of the Java language.

We Want Your Opinions

This book was written for you, and I would like to hear any comments you have on the book. You can contact me via electronic mail at the following address:

wsavitch@ucsd.edu

Unfortunately, I cannot provide you with answers to the programming exercises. The publisher provides selected answers to these exercises to only those instructors who adopt the book. For help on the programming exercises, you will have to contact your instructor. (If you are not in a class, then, unfortunately, we still cannot provide answers to the programming exercises.) But, remember that there are answers to all the self-test questions at the end of each chapter.

Walter Savitch
http://www-cse.ucsd.edu/users/savitch

PREFACE FOR INSTRUCTORS

This book was designed to be used in a first course in programming and computer science. It covers programming techniques, as well as the basics of the Java programming language. It is suitable for courses as short as one quarter or as long as one full academic year. It requires no previous programming experience and no mathematics other than a little high school algebra. This book can also be used for a course designed to teach Java to students who have already had another programming course, in which case, the first few chapters can be assigned as outside reading. All the code in the book has been tested using both version 1.1 and version 1.2 of Sun Microsystem's Java JDK. The coverage of Java was carefully arrived at by class testing and is a concise, accessible introduction for beginners.

Flexible

If you are an instructor, this book adapts to the way you teach, rather than making you adapt to the book. This book does not tightly prescribe the order in which your course must cover topics. Neither does it prescribe the specialized libraries that must be used in your course. You can easily change the order in which chapters and sections are covered. The details about rearranging material are explained in the section of this preface entitled **Alternative Orderings**.

Since Java does not include any simple console input, most texts, even more advanced texts, provide some class library for console input. This book requires that you add as little input software as possible, since only one simple class is used for console input. Even that one console input class, which is included early in the book, becomes an understandable programming example for students well before the end of the book. All the remaining software is from standard Java libraries that should be part of any Java installation.

Coverage of Problem Solving and Programming Techniques

This book is designed to teach students basic problem-solving and programming techniques and is not simply a Java syntax book. The book contains numerous case studies and programming tips sections, as well as many other sections that explain important problem-solving and programming techniques, such as top-down design, loop design techniques, debugging techniques, style techniques, abstract data types, basic object-oriented programming techniques, and other computer science topics.

Object-Oriented and Traditional Techniques

Any course that really teaches Java must teach classes early, since almost everything in Java involves classes. The behavior of parameters depends on whether they are class parameters. Even the behavior of the equals operator (==) depends on whether it is comparing objects or simpler data items. Classes cannot be avoided, except by means of absurdly long and complicated "magic formulas." This book introduces classes fairly early, specifically in Chapter 4. Moreover, all the basic information about classes, including inheritance, is presented by the end of Chapter 6. However, some topics on classes, including inheritance, can be postponed to later in a course. Although this is an early classes book, it does not neglect traditional programming techniques, such as top-down design and loop design techniques. These older topics may not be current glamour topics, but they are information that all beginning students need.

The AWT and GUIs

Java comes with a library known as the AWT that allows programmers to design portability GUIs (graphical user interfaces). This book uses the AWT to teach students to produce professional looking windowing interfaces. In the process, students learn event-driven programming, as well as receiving a lot of practice with object-oriented programming. As this material was class-tested and views of instructors were gathered, we found that the AWT was a more accessible way to teach students object-oriented programming than either graphics libraries or applets. (We do, however, have a chapter on applets at the end of the book, and that chapter can be covered fairly early if you desire.)

The AWT is introduced fairly early, specifically in Chapter 7. Since the AWT requires a knowledge of inheritance, in addition to the basics of classes, parameters, and flow of control, this is as early as the AWT can be covered in a comprehensive way. You may choose to introduce the AWT early, late, or not at all. Except for some optional sections, the material after Chapter 7 does not use the AWT. However, for those who do cover the AWT early, there are optional sections that give AWT examples and tips. Also, most programming exercises are designed so they can be done either with or without the AWT. This allows you to introduce the AWT when you want and use it from that point on. For those who want to do the AWT early, this may seem like they are not getting as much practice with the AWT as they should. However, after class testing a preliminary version of this book, I found that deemphasizing the AWT within the text is best. Moreover, this is true even with early AWT coverage. Students get plenty of AWT exposure by seeing the AWT in a few examples in optional sections and by using the AWT in programming exercises. Including long AWT code in examples on other topics simply clutters the discussion. After all, the code to add three labeled buttons can be many times longer than the code that illustrates the point at hand. I personally introduce the AWT early, and find this approach to fit in nicely with early treatment of the AWT.

Language Details and Sample Code

This book teaches programming technique and does not simply teach the Java language. However, neither students nor instructors would be satisfied with an introductory programming course that did not also teach the programming language. Until you calm a student's fears about language details, it is often impossible to get her or his attention to discuss bigger issues. For this reason, this book gives complete explanations of Java language features and lots of sample code. Programs are given in their entirety along with sample input and output.

Self-Test Questions

Self-test questions are spread through out each chapter. These questions have a wide range of difficulty levels. Some require only a one-word answer, whereas others require the reader to write an entire, nontrivial program. Complete answers for all the self-test questions, including those requiring full programs, are given at the end of each chapter.

Class Tested

The material in this book has been fully class tested. Much of the material and methods of presentation were revised in response to this class testing.

Support Material

The support materials described below can be obtained from the publisher, obtained over the Internet, or are included with the book.

CD-ROM

Each book contains a CD that includes all the programs and classes in the book. The CD also includes a version of Code Warrior, which is an integrated development environment that runs on both Windows PCs and Macintosh machines. The student version included on the CD is Code Warrior Lite, which allows students to sample Code Warrior on programs from the text to see if they wish to purchase the full version at a special student rate.

Free Software

Instructors who adopt the text with a minimum number of copies can receive a free professional version of the Code Warrior development environment and a free site license for their class laboratory. This is a completely integrated development environment producing platform-independent code for a number of languages including Java. Instructors should contact their Prentice Hall sales representative for details.

If you prefer an alternative to Code Warrior, a version of Java can be obtained from Sun Microsystems. At the time of printing, a version of the Java JDK 1.1 could be downloaded free of charge from the following web site:

```
http://www.java.sun.com/products/jdk/1.1
```

At the time that this book was sent to press only early beta release copies of version 1.2 of Java were available. At the time of publication the latest beta version of JDK 1.2 was available at the following site:

```
http://www.java.sun.com/products/jdk/1.2
```

By the time this book comes out, there should be more or less final versions of Java 1.2 available. You might want to search the web for the location of the Sun web site that offers a final version of JDK 1.2. If you cannot find version 1.2, version 1.1 will do fine for use with this book.

One suitable integrated development environment to use with the JDK is the WinEdit environment from Wilson Window Ware. It is a shareware product which can be downloaded to try for free. The web site is:

```
http://www.windowware.com
```

Instructor's Resource Guide and Companion Web Site
Instructor tools include a chapter-by-chapter Instructor's Resource Guide that contains numerous teaching hints, quiz questions with solutions, and solutions to many programming exercises. The companion web site includes code, transparency masters, and other teaching resources. Instructors should contact their Prentice Hall sales representative to obtain a copy of the Instructor's Resource Guide and receive information on how to access the companion web site. For the name and number of your sales representative, please call Prentice Hall Faculty Services at 1-800-526-0485. Additional information on this book and other Prentice Hall products can be found on Prentice Hall's web site at

```
http://www.prenhall.com/divisions/ecs
```

Alternative Orderings

There are many possible alternative orderings of chapters and sections. A dependency chart that follows this preface will give you a good general idea of what orderings are easily possible. Rearranging the order of smaller sections not shown in the dependency chart are also possible. Each chapter begins with a prerequisite section that tells what parts of the book must be covered before covering each section of the chapter. The easiest way to choose which order to present material is to first decide on the ordering you prefer, and then check the appropriate chapters to see if the order should be varied a little. As a general guideline, you must cover the first five chapters in order, although some variation is possible in the sections of these chapters. After Chapter 5, you have great flexibility in the order in which chapters are covered. To make this versatility possible, there are a few subsections marked "Alternative Ordering." These subsections can be considered ordinary sections if chapters are read in order. However, if the order is varied, the first paragraph of each "Alternative Ordering" subsection explains whether you should skip or cover the subsection. The most common examples of "Alternative Ordering" subsections are programming examples designed to give more practice with the AWT. If you have not yet covered the AWT, then you should delay covering these AWT examples. In these cases, the material other than the AWT is always covered in other examples, so skipping these does not shortchange the chapter.

Acknowledgments

I thank the Computer Science and Engineering Department of the University of California, San Diego (UCSD) which is my home department and the place that I tested much of this material. Many students in my classes were kind enough to helped correct preliminary versions of this text. These student comments and the comments of instructors who class tested this book were a tremendous help in shaping the final book. In particular, I extend a special thanks to Carole McNamee of California State University, Sacramento and to both Paul Kube and Susan Marx of UCSD; their feedback and class testing of earlier drafts of the book was a great help to me when revising drafts of the book.

I thank all the reviewers who took the time to read drafts of the book and provide details comments and suggestions. In alphabetical order they are

>Michael Clancy—University of California, Berkeley
>Michael Godfrey—Cornell University
>Robert Herrmann—Sun Microsystems, Java Soft
>Robert Holloway—University of Wisconsin, Madison
>Lily Hou—Carnegie-Mellon University
>John Motil—California State University, Northridge
>James Roberts—Carnegie-Mellon University
>Nan C. Schaller—Rochester Institute of Technology
>Ryan Shoemaker—Sun Microsystems, Inc.
>Donald E. Smith—Rutgers University

I thank Rick Grehan of Metrowerks for configuring the Code Warrior Lite software on the CD that accompanies this text.

I also thank all the individuals at Prentice Hall who organized the reviewing and production of this book. In particular, I thank Sondra Chavez for coordinating the entire processes including the reviews, Ann Marie Kalajian for managing the production, Eileen Clark for entering corrections, Sophie Papanikolaou for help with production, and Mary Ann Telatnik for checking historical references. All these wonderful people did a great job, did so under pressure to work fast, and did so cheerfully. Finally, I extend a special thanks to my publisher Alan Apt for his invaluable support and advice throughout the writing and production process.

Walter Savitch
wsavitch@ucsd.edu
http://www-cse.ucsd.edu/users/savitch

DEPENDENCY CHART

If there is a line between two boxes, then the material in the higher box should be done before the material in the lower box. Some of the optional sections marked "Alternative Ordering" have not been taken into account in this chart, but those sections can be omitted with no loss of continuity. What is required for these "Alternative Ordering" sections is clearly explained at the start of each such section.

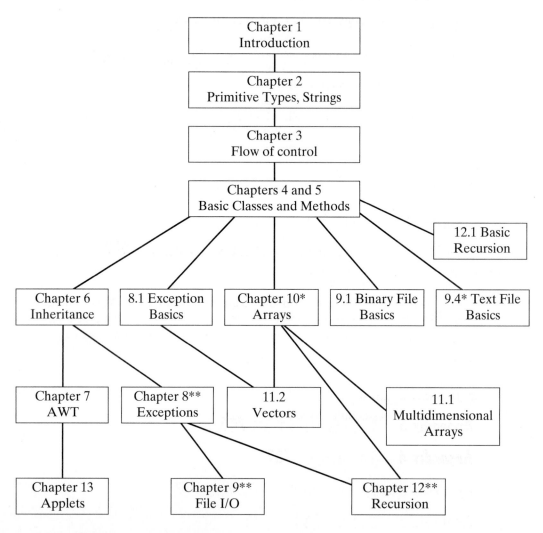

*Some sections require a small amount of material on exceptions, but these sections are clearly marked and can be omitted.

**Note that some sections of these chapters can be covered sooner. Those sections are given in this chart.

BRIEF TABLE OF CONTENTS

Chapter 1   INTRODUCTION AND A TASTE OF JAVA 1

Chapter 2   PRIMITIVE TYPES AND STRINGS 29

Chapter 3   FLOW OF CONTROL 83

Chapter 4   CLASSES, OBJECTS, AND METHODS 155

Chapter 5   PROGRAMMING WITH CLASSES AND METHODS 233

Chapter 6   INHERITANCE 289

Chapter 7   EVENT-DRIVEN PROGRAMMING USING THE AWT 323

Chapter 8   EXCEPTION HANDLING 403

Chapter 9   STREAMS AND FILE I/O 457

Chapter 10   ARRAYS 539

Chapter 11   MULTIDIMENSIONAL ARRAYS AND VECTORS 603

Chapter 12   RECURSION 639

Chapter 13   APPLETS AND HTML 673

Appendix 1   RESERVED WORDS 692

Appendix 2   SavitchIn 693

Appendix 3   ASCII CHARACTER SET 706

Appendix 4   javadoc 707

Appendix 5   BEYOND PUBLIC AND PRIVATE 710

Appendix 6   CLONING 711

Index 714

DETAILED TABLE OF CONTENTS

Chapter 1 INTRODUCTION AND A TASTE OF JAVA 1

Prerequisites 2
1.1 **COMPUTER BASICS 2**
Hardware and Memory 2
Programs 5
Programming Languages and Compilers 6
Java Byte Code 8
Linking 10
Self-Test Questions 10
1.2 **DESIGNING PROGRAMS 10**
Algorithms 11
Object-Oriented Programming 12
Self-Test Questions 13
Reusable Components 13
Testing and Debugging 14
Gotcha Coping with "Gotchas" 15
Gotcha Hidden Errors 15
Self-Test Questions 15
1.3 **A TASTE OF JAVA 15**
History of the Java Language 16
Applets and the World Wide Web 16
A First Java Program 17
Spelling Rules 22
Compiling a Java Program or Class 23
Running a Java Program 24
Self-Test Questions 25

Chapter Summary 25
Answers to Self-Test Questions 26
Programming Exercises 27

Chapter 2 PRIMITIVE TYPES AND STRINGS 29

Prerequisites 30
2.1 **PRIMITIVE TYPES, ASSIGNMENT, AND EXPRESSIONS 30**
Variables and Variable Declarations 30
Primitive Types 34
Assignment Statements 35
Specialized Assignment Operators *(Optional)* 37
Simple Input and Output 38
Number Constants 39
Assignment Compatibilities 40
Type Casting 41

Gotcha Type Casting a Character to an Integer 43
Programming Tip Initialize Variables 43
Gotcha Imprecision in Floating-Point Numbers 44
Self-Test Questions 45
Arithmetic Operators 46
Case Study Vending Machine Change 49
Self-Test Questions 51
Increment and Decrement Operators 53
More About Increment and Decrement Operators *(Optional)* 54

2.2   THE CLASS STRING 55
String Constants and Variables 55
String Methods 55
String Processing 59
Escape Characters 60
The Unicode Character Set 62
Self-Test Questions 63

2.3   DOCUMENTATION AND STYLE 63
Programming Tip Use Meaningful Names for Variables 63
Documentation and Comments 64
Indenting 65
Named Constants 67
Self-Test Questions 70

2.4   KEYBOARD AND SCREEN I/O 71
Screen Output 71
Input Using `SavitchIn` 74
More Input Methods 75
Gotcha `readInt` and `readDouble` 77
Programming Tip Echo Input 78
Self-Test Questions 78

Chapter Summary 79
Answers to Self-Test Questions 79
Programming Exercises 81

Chapter 3   FLOW OF CONTROL 83

Prerequisites 84
3.1   BRANCHING STATEMENTS 84
The `if-else`-Statement 84
Introduction to Boolean Expressions 88
Gotcha Using == with Strings 91
Self-Test Questions 93
Nested Statements and Compound Statements 94
Gotcha Matching `else`'s and `if`'s 95
Multibranch `if-else`-Statements 97
Programming Example Assigning Letter Grades 98

Self-Test Questions 100
The *switch*-Statement 101
Gotcha Omitting a *break*-Statement 104
Self-Test Questions 106

3.2 JAVA LOOP STATEMENTS 107
while-Statements 108
Programming Tip A *while*-Loop Can Perform Zero Iterations 110
The *do-while*-Statement 111
Programming Example Bug Infestation 113
Gotcha Infinite Loops 116
Self-Test Questions 117
The *for*-Statement 118
The Comma in *for*-Statements *(Optional)* 121
Gotcha Extra Semicolon in a Loop Statement 121
Self-Test Questions 123
Choosing a Loop Statement 124
The *break*-Statement in Loops 124
Gotcha Misuse of *break*-Statements 124
The exit Method 126
Self-Test Questions 127

3.3 PROGRAMMING WITH LOOPS 128
The Loop Body 128
Initializing Statements 129
Ending a Loop 130
Programming Example Nested Loops 132
Programming Tip Do Not Declare Variables in a Loop Body 132
Self-Test Questions 132
Loop Bugs 135
Tracing Variables 137
Self-Test Questions 138

3.4 THE TYPE boolean 138
Boolean Expressions and Boolean Variables 139
Precedence Rules 140
Input and Output of Boolean Values 144
Case Study Using a Boolean Variable to End a Loop 144
Self-Test Questions 146

Chapter Summary 146
Answers to Self-Test Questions 148
Programming Exercises 152

Chapter 4 CLASSES, OBJECTS, AND METHODS 155

Prerequisites 156
4.1 CLASS AND METHOD DEFINITIONS 156
Class Files and Separate Compilation 156

Instance Variables 157
Using Methods 161
void-Method Definitions 163
Methods that Return a Value 165
Programming Tip Use of `return` in *void*-Methods 168
The *this* Parameter 169
Self-Test Questions 172
Local Variables 172
Blocks 173
Gotcha Variables Declared in a Block 175
Declaring Variables in a *for*-Statement *(Optional)* 175
Parameters of a Primitive Type 176
Gotcha Use of the Terms "Parameter" and "Argument" 182
Summary of Class and Method Definition Syntax 182
Self-Test Questions 184

4.2 INFORMATION HIDING AND ENCAPSULATION 184
Information Hiding 185
Programming Tip Formal Parameter Names Are Local to the Method 185
Precondition and Postcondition Comments 187
The Public and Private Modifiers 188
Programming Tip Instance Variables Should Be Private 191
Self-Test Questions 191
Programming Example Purchase Class 194
Abstract Data Types (ADTs) 198
Case Study Changing the Implementation of an ADT 202
Self-Test Questions 206

4.3 OBJECTS AND REFERENCE 206
Variables of A Class Type and Objects 207
Gotcha Use of = and == with Variables of A Class Type 209
Programming Tip Define an `equals` Method for Your Classes 210
Programming Example A Species Class 213
Boolean-Valued Methods 213
Self-Test Questions 217
Class Parameters 217
Comparing Class Parameters and Primitive-Type Parameters 220
Programming Tip Make the Compiler Happy 223
Self-Test Questions 224

Chapter Summary 225
Answers to Self-Test Questions 225
Programming Exercises 230

Chapter 5 PROGRAMMING WITH CLASSES AND METHODS 233
Prerequisites 234

5.1 PROGRAMMING WITH METHODS 234
Methods Calling Methods 235
Programming Tip Write Toy Programs 239
Programming Tip Make Helping Methods Private 239
Programming Tip You Can Put a `main` in Any Class 239
Static Methods 240
The `Math` Class 243
Case Study Formatting Output 246
Top–Down Design 252
Testing Methods 252
Self-Test Questions 254
`Integer`, `Double`, and Other Wrapper Classes 255
Gotcha Assigning a Primitive Value to a Wrapper Class 257
Self-Test Questions 257

5.2 POLYMORPHISM 258
Overloading 259
Programming Example A Pet Class 261
Gotcha Overloading and Automatic Type Conversion 261
Gotcha You Cannot Overload Based on the Returned Type 265
Self-Test Questions 266

5.3 CONSTRUCTORS 267
Defining Constructors 268
Gotcha Omitting the Default Constructor 274
Self-Test Questions 275

5.4 INFORMATION HIDING REVISITED 275
Gotcha Instance Variables of a Class Type 275
Self-Test Questions 279

5.5 PACKAGES *(Optional)* 279
Packages and Importing 279
Package Names and Directories 280
Self-Test Questions 282

Chapter Summary 282
Answers to Self-Test Questions 283
Programming Exercises 286

Chapter 6 INHERITANCE 289

Prerequisites 290

6.1 INHERITANCE BASICS 290
Programming Example A Person Class 291
Derived Classes 293
Programming Tip Overriding Method Definitions 295
Gotcha Use of Private Instance Variables from the Base Class 298
Gotcha Private Methods Are Not Inherited 299

Self-Test Questions 299

6.2   PROGRAMMING WITH INHERITANCE 300
Constructors in Derived Classes 300
The `this` Method *(Optional)* 301
Call to an Overridden Method *(Optional)* 302
Programming Tip An Object of a Derived Class Has More than One Type 302
Case Study Character Graphics 304
Dynamic Binding 313
Self-Test Questions 317

Chapter Summary 317
Answers to Self-Test Questions 317
Programming Exercises 321

Chapter 7   EVENT-DRIVEN PROGRAMMING USING THE AWT 323

Prerequisites 324
7.1   SOME BACKGROUND 325
GUIs—Graphical User Interfaces 325
Event-Driven Programming 325
Self-Test Questions 327
7.2   SIMPLE WINDOW INTERFACES 327
Gotcha Save All Your Work Before Running an AWT Program 327
Programming Example A Simple Window 328
Programming Tip Ending an AWT Program 332
More About Window Listeners 333
Gotcha Confusing the Classes Frame and Window 333
Size Units for Screen Objects 334
Coordinate System for Screen Objects 335
More on `paint` and `setVisible` 336
Self-Test Questions 340
Programming Example Another Simple Window 340
Some Methods of the Class `Frame` 343
Self-Test Questions 343
7.3   COMPONENTS, CONTAINERS, AND LAYOUT MANAGERS 345
Programming Example Adding Buttons 346
Adding Components to a Container Class 349
More Layout Managers 351
The `Button` Class 353
Action Events and Action Listeners 354
Programming Tip Copy Other Programmer's Code 356
Programming Tip Guide for Creating Simple Window Interfaces 357
Self-Test Questions·359
The `WindowListener` Interface *(Optional)* 362

7.4 PANELS AND TEXT COMPONENTS 365
The `Panel` Class 365
Text Areas and Text Fields 368
Self-Test Questions 372
Labels for Text Fields and Other Components 372
Inputting and Outputting Numbers 376
Self-Test Questions 379
Case Study A GUI Adding Machine 379
Self-Test Questions 385

7.5 ADDING MENUS 385
Programming Example A GUI with a Menu 385
Menu Bars, Menus, and Menu Items 389
Nested Menus 390
Gotcha Different Events with the Same Labels 392
Additional Examples of Using the AWT 392
Self-Test Questions 392

7.6 INNER CLASSES (Optional) 393
Helping Classes *(Optional)* 393
Self-Test Questions (For the Optional Section) 396

Chapter Summary 396
Answers to Self-Test Questions 397
Programming Exercises 401

Chapter 8 EXCEPTION HANDLING 403

Prerequisites 404
8.1 BASIC EXCEPTION HANDLING 404
Exceptions in Java 405
Predefined Exception Classes 413
Self-Test Questions 414

8.2 DEFINING AND USING EXCEPTION CLASSES 415
Defining Your Own Exception Classes 415
Programming Tip Preserve `getMessage` When You Define
    Exception Classes 417
Programming Tip When to Define an Exception Class 422
Declaring Exceptions (Passing the Buck) 422
Exceptions that Do Not Need to Be Caught 426
Multiple Throws and Catches 427
Programming Tip Catch the More Specific Exception First 430
Programming Example Catching a `NumberFormatException`
    (Alternative Ordering) 431
Self-Test Questions 434
Gotcha Overuse of Exceptions 435
Programming Tip When to Throw An Exception 435

The *finally* Block *(Optional)* 436
Case Study A Line-Oriented Calculator 437
Self-Test Questions 451

Chapter Summary 452
Answers to Self-Test Questions 453
Programming Exercises 454

Chapter 9 STREAMS AND FILE I/O 457

Prerequisites 458
9.1 STREAMS AND SIMPLE FILE I/O 458
Introduction to Binary Files 459
Output to Files Using `DataOutputStream` 460
Some Details About `writeUTF` *(Optional)* 468
Gotcha Overwriting a File 469
Reading Input from a File Using `DataInputStream` 469
Gotcha Using `DataInputStream` with a Text File 473
Self-Test Questions 474
Programming Example Reading a File Name from the Keyboard 474
Gotcha Defining a Method to Open a Stream 474
Self-Test Questions 476
9.2 EXCEPTION HANDLING WITH FILE I/O 477
Catching `IOExceptions` 477
The `EOFException` Class 480
Checking for the End of a File 480
Gotcha Forgetting to Check for the End of a File 482
Programming Example Processing a File of Data 483
Programming Tip Objects Should Do Their Own I/O 483
Case Study Writing and Reading a File of Records 486
Self-Test Questions 495
Programming Example A GUI Interface to Files *(Alternative Ordering)* 495
Self-Test Questions (for Alternative Ordering Section) 509
9.3 MORE CLASSES FOR FILE I/O 510
The `File` Class 510
The Classes `FileInputStream` and `FileOutputStream` 513
Self-Test Questions 515
9.4 TEXT FILE I/O 515
Text File Output with `PrintWriter` 517
Gotcha A *try*-Block Is a Block 519
Text File Input with `BufferedReader` 520
The `StringTokenizer` Class *(Optional)* 523
Testing for the End of a Text File 525
Gotcha Checking for the End of a File in the Wrong Way
    (Alternative Ordering) 527
Programming Example The Class `SavitchIn` *(Optional)* 528

Self-Test Questions 529

Chapter Summary 529
Answers to Self-Test Questions 530
Programming Exercises 537

Chapter 10 ARRAYS 539

Prerequisites 540
10.1 ARRAY BASICS 541
Creating and Accessing Arrays 541
Array Details 545
Programming Tip Use Singular Array Names 547
The `length` Instance Variable 547
Gotcha Array Indexes Start with Zero 549
Programming Tip Use a `for`-Loop to Step Through an Array 549
Gotcha Array Index Out of Bounds 549
`ArrayIndexOutOfBoundsException` *(Alternative Ordering)* 551
Initializing Arrays 551
Self-Test Questions 551
10.2 ARRAYS IN CLASSES AND METHODS 552
Case Study Sales Report 552
Self-Test Questions 559
Indexed Variables as Method Arguments 559
Entire Arrays as Method Arguments 561
Gotcha Use of = and == with Arrays 564
Methods That Return Arrays 567
Self-Test Questions 570
10.3 PROGRAMMING WITH ARRAYS AND CLASSES 570
Programming Example A Specialized List Class 570
Partially Filled Arrays 578
Searching an Array 579
Parallel Arrays 579
Gotcha Returning an Array Instance Variable 580
Self-Test Questions 587
10.4 SORTING ARRAYS 587
Selection Sort 588
Programming Tip Correctness versus Efficiency 592
Self-Test Questions 592

Chapter Summary 594
Answers to Self-Test Questions 594
Programming Exercises 599

Chapter 11 MULTIDIMENSIONAL ARRAYS AND VECTORS 603

Prerequisites 604
11.1 MULTIDIMENSIONAL ARRAYS 604
Multidimensional-Array Basics 605
Gotcha Reversing Two-Array Indexes 609
Multidimensional-Array Parameters and Returned Values 609
Implementation of Multidimensional Arrays 610
Ragged Arrays *(Optional)* 613
Programming Example Employee Time Records 615
Self-Test Questions 621
11.2 VECTORS 622
Using Vectors 622
Gotcha Vector Elements Are of Type `Object` 628
Comparing Vectors and Arrays 629
Gotcha Using `capacity` Instead of `size` *629*
Programming Tip Use `trimToSize` to Save Memory 631
Gotcha Using the Method `clone` 631
Self-Test Questions 633

Chapter Summary 634
Answers to Self-Test Questions 634
Programming Exercises 637

Chapter 12 RECURSION 639

Prerequisites 640
12.1 THE BASICS OF RECURSION 640
Case Study Digits to Words 641
How Recursion Works 645
Gotcha Infinite Recursion 647
Self-Test Questions 650
Recursive versus Iterative Definitions 651
Recursive Methods That Return a Value 653
Self-Test Questions 656
12.2 PROGRAMMING WITH RECURSION 657
Handling Exceptions with Recursion *(Alternative Ordering)* 657
Self-Test Questions 658
Case Study Binary Search *(Alternative Ordering)* 658
Self-Test Questions 663

Chapter Summary 665
Answers to Self-Test Questions 665
Programming Exercises 671

Chapter 13 APPLETS AND HTML 673

Prerequisites 674

13.1   HTML 674

HTML Basics 675

Programming Tip A Simple Document Outline 676
Inserting Hyperlinks 680
Self-Test Questions 680

13.2   APPLETS 682

Applet Basics 682
Running an Applet 684
Placing an Applet in an HTML Document 686
Gotcha Using an Old Web Browser 687
Programming Tip Converting an AWT Application to an Applet 690
Self-Test Questions 690

Chapter Summary 691
Answers to Self-Test Questions 691
Programming Exercises 691

Appendix 1   RESERVED WORDS **692**

Appendix 2   SavitchIn **693**

Appendix 3   ASCII CHARACTER SET **706**

Appendix 4   javadoc **707**

Appendix 5   BEYOND PUBLIC AND PRIVATE **710**

Appendix 6   CLONING **711**

Index 714

Chapter 1

INTRODUCTION AND A TASTE OF JAVA

1.1 **COMPUTER BASICS 2**
Hardware and Memory 2
Programs 5
Programming Languages and Compilers 6
Java Byte Code 8
Linking 10

1.2 **DESIGNING PROGRAMS 10**
Algorithms 11
Object-Oriented Programming 12
Reusable Components 13
Testing and Debugging 14
Gotcha Coping with "Gotchas" 15
Gotcha Hidden Errors 15

1.3 **A TASTE OF JAVA 15**
History of the Java Language 16
Applets and the World Wide Web 16
A First Java Program 17
Spelling Rules 22
Compiling a Java Program or Class 23
Running a Java Program 24

Chapter Summary 25
Answers to Self-Test Questions 26
Programming Exercises 27

1

INTRODUCTION AND
A TASTE OF JAVA

• •

> *The computer is no better than its programs.*
> **ELTING ELMORE MORISON,** *Men, Machines and Modern Times* **(1966)**

Introduction

In this chapter, we give you a brief overview of computer hardware and software. Much of this introductory material applies to programming in any language, not just to programming in Java. In Section 1.3, we specialize this introduction to the Java language and explain a simple Java program.

Prerequisites

When reading this book, you can easily make some changes to the ordering of chapters and sections. Each chapter has a section like this one that tells you what parts of the book you should read before reading each section of the chapter.

This first chapter does *not* assume that you have had any previous programming experience, but does assume that you have access to a computer. To get the full value from this chapter, and the rest of this book, you should have a computer that has the Java language installed so that you can try out the things you learn as you learn them. The preface discusses some ways to obtain a free copy of the Java language for your computer.

1.1 Computer Basics

hardware

software

Computer systems consist of **hardware** and **software**. The hardware is the physical computer machine. All the different kinds of programs that are used to give instructions to the computer are referred to as software. In this book, we will be discussing software, but in order to understand the software, it does help to know a few basic things about computer hardware.

Hardware and Memory

Most of the many different kinds of computers that are available today have the same basic components, configured in basically the same way. They all have input devices, such as a keyboard and a mouse. They all have output devices, such as a display screen and a printer to write output on paper. And, they have two or three other basic components that are often housed in some sort of cabinet so that they are not so obvious. These other components are a *processor* and two kinds of *memory*, known as *main memory* and *auxiliary memory.*

The **processor** is the device inside your computer that follows a program's instructions. (The processor is also called the **CPU**, which is an abbreviation of **central processing unit.**) If you buy a PC, you will be told what kind of *chip* it has. The **chip** is the processor. Currently, one of the better known chips is the Pentium processor. One of the reasons it is called a chip is that it is not very large. You can easily hold the chip for a modern PC in your hand. In fact, you could hold several of them. The processor follows the instructions in a program but it can only carry out very simple instructions, such as moving numbers or other items around from one place in memory to another place in memory and performing some simple arithmetic operations like addition and subtraction. The power of a computer comes from its speed and the intricacies of its programs. The basic design of the hardware is relatively simple.

processor

A computer's memory holds data for the computer to process and it holds the result of the computer's intermediate calculations. The way that you program in a language like Java is determined in large part by the nature of a computer's memory, so you need to know something about how a computer's memory is organized. The computer has two basic kinds of memory known as *main memory* and *auxiliary memory.* All of the various kinds of disk drives, diskettes, and compact disks that are used with computers are types of auxiliary memory. They are the (more or less) permanent memory. The working memory that your program uses for intermediate calculations is the main memory. It is the character of the main memory that you most need to be aware of when you are writing programs. Main memory holds the program that is currently being executed, and more importantly from our point of view, it holds much of the data that the program is manipulating.

Main memory consists of a long list of numbered locations, known as **bytes.** These bytes each hold a string of eight digits, each of which is either zero or one. This is often expressed by saying that each byte contains eight bits. A **bit** is a digit that can assume only the two values 0 and 1. (Actually, any two values will do, but the two values are typically written as 0 and 1.) The bytes on this list are numbered and the number of a byte is called its **address**. A piece of data, such as a number or a keyboard character, can be stored in one of these bytes. When the computer later needs to recover the data, the address of the byte is used to find the data item.

main memory
bytes

bit

address

Data of various kinds, such as keyboard characters, numbers, and strings of text, are encoded as strings of zeros and ones and placed in the computer's memory. As it turns out, one byte is just large enough to store a single keyboard character. This is one of the reasons that a computer's memory is divided in these eight-bit bytes, instead of being divided into pieces of some other size. However, in order to store a large number or a string of text, the computer needs more than a single byte. When the computer needs to store a piece of data that cannot be coded so that it fits into a single byte, the computer uses a number of adjacent bytes. These adjacent bytes are then considered to be a single, larger **memory location** and the address of the first byte is used as the address of the entire larger memory location. Display 1.1 shows how a typical computer's main memory might be divided into memory locations. The boundaries between these locations are not fixed by the hardware. The

memory
location

Display 1.1 *Main Memory*

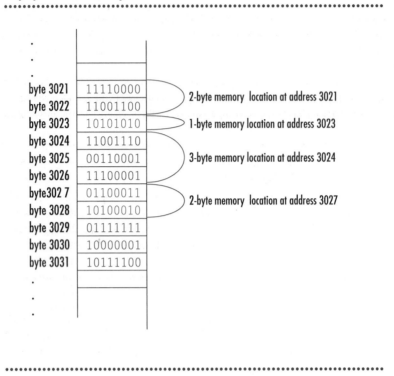

size and location of the boundaries will be different when different programs are run.

Recall that main memory is only used when the computer is running a program. Auxiliary memory is used to hold data in a more or less permanent form. Auxiliary memory is also divided into bytes, but these bytes are then grouped into much larger units known as files. A file may contain (in an encoded form) a program, a letter, a list of numbers, or almost any sort of data. The important characteristics of a file are that it has a name and that it can hold data. When you write a Java program, you will store the program in a file. The file is stored in auxiliary memory, and when you want to run the program, the program is copied from auxiliary memory to main memory. These files are often organized into groups of files known as **directories** or **folders.** Folder and directory are two names for the same thing. Some computer systems use the name *directory* and some use the name *folder,* but they are the same thing. Although we will not need to know about directories (folders) in order to write our Java programs, it would be a good idea to familiarize yourself with how your computer system names and organizes directories (folders). This will help you to organize your own work into coherent groups of files.

directory
folder

Why Just Zeros and Ones

Computers use zeros and ones because it is easy to make a physical device that has only two stable states. However, when you are programming you normally need not be concerned about how data is encoded as zeros and ones. You can program as if the computer directly stored numbers, letters, or strings in memory, and you need not worry about zeros and ones.

There is nothing special about the digits zero and one. We could equally well use any two names, such as *A* and *B* or *true* and *false*, instead of *zero* and *one*. The important thing is that the underlying physical device has two stable states. Calling these two states *zero* and *one* is simply a convention, but a convention that is almost universally followed.

Bytes and Memory Locations

A byte is a memory location that can hold eight digits, each either zero or one. A computer's main memory is divided into numbered **bytes.** The number of a byte is called its **address.** To store a piece of data that is too large to fit in a single byte, the computer uses a number of adjacent bytes. These adjacent bytes are used as larger memory locations and the address of the first of these adjacent bytes is used as the address of this entire larger memory location.

Programs

You undoubtedly have some idea of what a program is. You use programs all the time. If you use a text editor, that is a program. A bank ATM machine is really a computer that is controlled by a program. A **program** is simply a set of instructions for a computer to follow.

program

Display 1.2 is a graphical representation of two ways to view the running of a program. To see the first way, forget the box with the dotted outline. What's left is what really happens when you run a program. Note that, when you run a program, there (normally) are two kinds of input to a computer. The program is one kind of input; it has the instructions that the computer will follow. The other kind of input is

Display 1.2 *Running a Program*

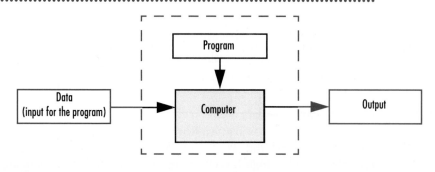

data

often called the **data** for the program. It is the information that the computer will process. For example, if the program is a simple spelling check program, the data would be the text that needs to be checked. As far as the computer is concerned, both these data and the program itself are input. The output is the result (or results) produced when the computer follows the instructions in the program. If the program is a simple spelling check program, then the output might be a list of words that are misspelled. When you give the computer a program and some data and tell the computer to follow the instructions in the program, that is called **running** the program on the data, and the computer is said to **execute** the program on the data.

running or executing

That first view of running a program is what really happens when you run a program on some data, but that is not always the way we think about running a program. The data are often thought of as the input to the program and in this view the computer and the program are considered to be one unit that takes the data as input and produces the output. If you take this view, then the combined program/computer unit is indicated by the box with the dotted outline. When we take this view, we think of the data as input to the program and the output as output from the program, and although the computer is understood to be there, it is presumed to just be something that assists the program.

There are more programs on your computer than you might think when first using your computer. Much of what you think of as "the computer" is actually a program rather than hardware. When you first turn on a computer, you are already running and interacting with a program. That program is called the **operating system**. The operating system is a kind of supervisory program that oversees the entire operation of the computer. If you want to run a program, you tell the operating system that you want to run the program and the operating system retrieves the program and starts it running. The program you run might be an editor, or a program to surf the World Wide Web, or some program that you wrote using the Java language. The way that you tell the operating system to run the program might be by clicking an icon with your mouse or by choosing a menu item or by typing in some simple command. What you probably think of as "the computer" is really the operating system and the operating system is a program that normally is run automatically when you turn on the computer. (Can you run a computer without an operating system? Yes, but you do not want to do so.) Some common operating systems are *DOS, Microsoft Windows,* Apple's *(Macintosh) MacOS,* and *UNIX.*

operating system

Software

The word **software** simply means programs. Thus, a software company is a company that produces programs. The software on your computer is just the collection of programs on your computer. ∎

Programming Languages and Compilers

high-level language

Most modern programming languages are designed to be (relatively) easy for people to write and for people to understand. These kinds of programming languages that are designed for people are called **high-level languages.** Java is a high-level language. Most of the programming languages you are likely to have heard of, such as Pascal, FORTRAN, C, C++, BASIC, COBOL, Lisp, and Ada are also high-level languages.Unfortunately, computer hardware does not understand these high-level languages. So, a program written in a high-level language must be translated into a language that the computer can understand. The languages that the computer can (more or less directly) understand are called **low-level languages**. The translation of a program from a high-level language, like Java, to a language that the computer can understand is done by another program known as a **compiler.**

low-level language

compiler

These low-level languages that the computer can directly understand are usually referred to as **machine languages** or **assembly languages**. The language that the computer can directly understand is called machine language. Assembly language is almost the same thing as machine language, but it does need an additional, very simple translation before the computer can understand it. If a compiler translates your high-level language program to some low-level language program that is not exactly machine language, then it will need some small additional translation before it is run on the computer, but normally this is done automatically for you and need not concern you. In practice, it will look like you are running the program produced by the compiler.

machine language

When you run a high-level language program, such as a Java program, you are actually running a translation of that program into a low-level language. Thus, before you run a high-level language program, you must first run the compiler on the program. When you run a compiler on your program, you are said to **compile** the program.

compile

One disadvantage of the translation process we just described for high-level languages is that you need a different compiler for each make of computer and each operating system. If you want to run your high-level language program on three different makes of computers, then you need to use three different compilers and must compile your program three different times. Moreover, if a manufacturer comes out with a new make of computer, the manufacturer must hire somebody to write a new compiler for that computer. This is a problem because compilers are very large programs that are expensive and time-consuming to produce. Despite this cost, this is the way most high-level language compilers work. Java, however, uses a slightly different and much more versatile approach to compiling. We discuss the Java approach to compiling in the next subsection.

When you use a compiler, the terminology can get a bit confusing, because with a compiler, both the input to the compiler program and the output from the compiler program are also programs. Everything in sight is a program of some kind or other. To help avoid confusion, the input program, which in our case will be a Java program, is called the **source program,** or **source code.** The translated low-level language program that is produced by the compiler is often called the **object program,** or **object code.** The word **code** just means a program or a part of a program.

source code
object code

code

Compiler

A **compiler** is a program that translates a high-level language program, such as a Java program, into a program in a simpler language that the computer can more or less directly understand. ◻

Java Byte Code

byte code

Java Virtual
Machine

interpreter

The Java compiler does not translate your program into the machine language for your particular computer. Instead, the Java compiler translates your Java program into a language called **byte code**. Byte code is not the machine language for any particular computer. Byte code is the machine language for a hypothetical computer that is something like the average of all computers. This hypothetical computer is called the **Java Virtual Machine.** The Java Virtual Machine is not exactly like any particular computer, but it is very similar to all typical computers. Thus, it is very easy to translate from a program written in byte code to a program in the machine language for any particular computer. The program that does this translation is called an **interpreter**. The interpreter works by translating each instruction of byte code into instructions expressed in your computer's machine language and then executes those instructions on your computer. Thus, an interpreter translates and executes the instructions in the byte code one after the other, rather than translating the entire byte-code program all at once. However, the only detail that we really need to know is that the interpreter somehow allows your computer to run Java byte code.[1]

In order to run your Java program on your particular computer, you would proceed as follows. First, you use the compiler to translate your Java program into byte code. Then you use the byte-code interpreter for your computer in order to translate and run each byte-code instruction. The whole process is diagrammed in Display 1.3.

Byte Code

The Java compiler translates your Java program into a language called **byte code**. This byte code is not the machine language for any particular computer, but is a language that is very similar to the machine language of most common computers and that is very easy to translate into the machine language of any particular computer. Each computer will have its own translator (called an *interpreter*) that translates from byte-code instructions to machine-language instructions for that particular computer.

It sounds like Java byte code just adds an extra step in the process. Why not write compilers that translate directly from Java to the machine language for your particular computer? That could be done. That is what is done for most other languages. Moreover, that would produce machine-language programs that typically run faster. However, Java byte code does give Java one important advantage, namely, portability. After you compile your Java program into byte code, you can use that byte code on any computer. When you go to another computer, you do not need to recompile your program. When a manufacturer comes out with a new computer, the manufacturer does not have to design a new Java compiler. One Java compiler works on every computer. Of course, every computer must have its own byte-code interpreter in order to translate byte-code instructions into machine-lan-

---

1. Sometimes people use the term *Java Virtual Machine* to refer to the Java byte-code interpreter (as well as using the term to refer to the underlying hypothetical machine that the interpreter is based on).

Display 1.3 *Compiling and Running a Java Program*

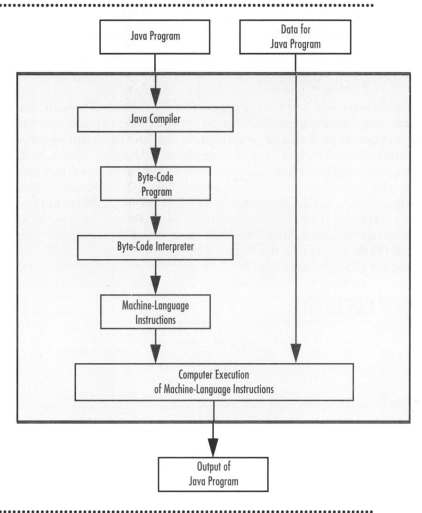

guage instructions for that particular computer, but these interpreters are simple programs when compared to a compiler.

It is important to know about Java byte code, but in the day-to-day business of programming, you are not even aware of the fact that there is byte code for your program. You normally give two commands, one to compile your program (into byte code) and one to *run* your program. The **run command** executes the Java byte-code interpreter on the byte code. This run command might be called "run" or something else, but is unlikely to be called "interpreter." You will come to think of the run command as running whatever the compiler produces and not even think about whether or not that is byte code.

run command

Why Is It Called "Byte Code"?

Low-level languages, such as byte code and machine-language code, consist of instructions, each of which can be stored in a few bytes of memory. This is presumably why byte code was given its name. To the designers of Java, byte code must have looked like "a bunch of bytes."

Linking

As if compilers, byte code, and interpreters were not complicated enough, there is still one other complication to contend with. A Java program is very seldom written as one piece all in one file. A Java program typically consists of different pieces, often written by different people, and each of these pieces is compiled separately. Thus, each piece is translated into a different piece of byte code. In order to run your program, these pieces need to be connected together. The process of connecting these pieces is called **linking** and the program that does this linking is called a **linker**. This problem is unavoidable. Even the simplest of Java programs will use some standard pieces of byte code written by somebody else. These standard pieces come with the Java system. On the bright side, this linking is typically done automatically, so you usually need not be concerned with it.

linking

? SELF-TEST QUESTIONS

Every chapter has answers to these Self-Test Questions at the end of the chapter.

1. What are the two kinds of memory in a computer?
2. What is software?
3. What would be the data for a program that computes the average of all the quizzes you have taken in a course?
4. What is the difference between a machine-language program, a high-level language program, and a program expressed in Java byte code?
5. What is a compiler?
6. What is a source program?
7. What do you call a program that translates Java byte instructions into machine-language instructions?

1.2 Designing Programs

> 'The time has come.' the Walrus said,
> 'To talk of many things:
>   Of shoes–and ships–and sealing wax–
> Of cabbages–and–kings...'
> **LEWIS CARROLL**, *Through the Looking Glass*

Programming is a creative process. We cannot tell you exactly how to write a program to solve whatever task you may want your program to solve. However, we can give you some techniques that experienced programmers have found to be extremely helpful for designing programs. In this section, we discuss some of these techniques. The techniques are applicable to programming in any programming language and are not particular to the Java programming language.

Algorithms

The hardest part of designing a program in the Java language is not figuring out how to express your solution in Java. The hardest part is coming up with a method for solving the problem. For example, if you could come up with a method to predict the direction of the stock market on a daily basis, then you could sell this method for a huge amount of money. On the other hand, the programmer who writes the program to implement this method, while well paid, would not get nearly the same amount of money as you got for designing the basic method. Of course, money paid is not necessarily an indication of difficulty, but in this case it does pretty much indicate the difference in difficulty. In less dramatic settings, such as completing a basic programming assignment or designing a program for balancing your check book, the same rule applies. The hard part is coming up with the method of solution. This method of solution is often expressed as something called an *algorithm.*

An **algorithm** is a set of instructions for solving a problem. To qualify as an algorithm, the instructions must be expressed so completely and so precisely that somebody could follow the instructions without having to fill in any details or make any decisions that are not fully specified in the instructions. An algorithm can be expressed in English or in a programming language, such as Java. However, when we use the word *algorithm,* we usually mean that the instructions are expressed in English or something like English. In practice, programmers do not express their algorithms in ordinary English, but in a mixture of English and a programming language, which in our case will be Java. This mixture of English and a programming language (like Java) is called **pseudocode**. When using pseudocode, you simply write each piece of the algorithm in whatever language is easiest for that part. If the part is easier to express in English, you use English. If another part is easier to express in Java, you use Java for that part.

algorithm

pseudocode

An example may help to clarify the notion of an algorithm. Our first sample algorithm determines the total cost for a list of items. For example, the list of items might be a shopping list that includes the price of each item. The algorithm would then determine the total cost of all the items on the list. The algorithm is as follows:

Algorithm that determines the total cost of a list of items:

1. Write the number 0 on the blackboard.
2. Do the following for each item on the list:
   Add the cost of the item to the number on the blackboard.
   Replace the old number on the blackboard by the result of this addition.
3. Announce that the answer is the number written on the blackboard.

This algorithm uses a blackboard to store intermediate results. Most algorithms need to store some intermediate results. If the algorithm is written in the Java language and run on a computer, then these intermediate results are stored in the computer's main memory.

Algorithm

An **algorithm** is a set of instructions for solving a problem. To qualify as an algorithm, the instructions must be expressed so completely and precisely that somebody could follow the instructions without having to fill in any details or make any decisions that are not fully specified in the instructions. ◻

Pseudocode

Pseudocode is a mixture of English and a programming language (in our case Java). Algorithms are usually written in pseudocode and later translated into a programming language, such as Java. ◻

Object-Oriented Programming

OOP

Java was designed to do **object-oriented programming**, abbreviated **OOP**. What is OOP? What are *objects*? The world around us consists of objects, such as people, automobiles, buildings, trees, shoes, ships, sealing wax, cabbages, kings, and so forth. Each of these objects has the ability to perform certain actions and each of these actions has some effect on some of the other objects in the world. Object-oriented programming is a programming methodology that views a program as this sort of world consisting of objects that interact with each other by means of actions. This is easiest to understand if the program simulates something in the real world. For example consider a program that simulates a highway interchange in order to see how it handles traffic flow. The program would have an object to simulate each of the automobiles that enter the interchange, perhaps other objects to simulate each lane of the highway, and so forth.

object

method
class

Object-oriented programming comes with its own terminology. The objects are called, appropriately enough, **objects.** The actions that an object can take are called **methods**. Objects of the same kind are said to have the same *type* or more often said to be in the same **class**. For example, in a simulation program, all the simulated automobiles might belong to the same class, probably called the `Automobile` class. All objects within a class have the same methods. Thus, in a simulation program, all automobiles have the same methods (or possible actions) such as moving forward, moving backwards, accelerating, and so forth. This does not mean that all simulated automobiles are identical. They can have different characteristics, which are indicated in the program by associating some data (i.e., some information) with each particular automobile object. For example, the data associated with an automobile object might be a word telling the make of the automobile and a number indicating its current speed. All this will become clearer when you start to define classes yourself using the Java programming language.

As we will see, this same object-oriented methodology can be applied to any sort of computer program and is not limited to simulation programs. Object-oriented programming is not a new methodology, but its use in applications outside of simulation programs did not become popular until relatively recently. Although one cannot place a precise date on object-oriented programming's rise to popularity, placing it in the early 1990s is probably as reasonable as any other date.

If Java is your first programming language, then you should skip this paragraph. If you know some other programming language, then this paragraph will try to explain objects in terms of things you may already know about. If you are already familiar with some other object-oriented programming languages such as C++, Smalltalk, or Borland's Turbo Pascal or Delphi, then you already have a good idea of what objects, methods, and classes are. They are basically the same in all object-oriented programming languages, although some other languages use the word *function* or *procedure* to mean the same thing as *method*. If you are familiar with an older form of programming language that does not have anything called objects or classes, then objects can be described in terms of other, older programming constructs. If you have heard of variables and functions, then you can think of an object as a variable that has multiple pieces of data and that has its own functions. Methods are really the same thing as what are called *procedures* or *functions* in older programming languages.

Objects, Methods, and Classes

An **object** is a program construction that has data (i.e., information) associated with it and that can perform certain actions. When the program is run, the objects interact with one another in order to accomplish whatever the program is designed to do. The actions performed by objects are called **method**s. A **class** is a type or kind of object. All objects in the same class have the same kinds of data and the same methods.

? SELF-TEST QUESTIONS

8. What is an algorithm?
9. What is pseudocode?
10. What is a method?
11. What is the relationship between classes and objects?
12. Do all objects of the same class have the same methods?

Reusable Components

When you first start to write programs, you can easily get the impression that each program that is produced is a completely separate project that is designed from scratch. That is not the way good software is produced. Most programs are created by combining already existing components. For example, a highway simulation program might include a new highway object to model a new highway design but would probably model automobiles by using an automobile class that was already designed for some other program. In order to ensure that the classes you use in your programs are easily reusable, you must design them to be reusable. You must specify exactly how objects of that class interact with other objects. You must design your class so that the objects are general and not designed in an ad hoc way for one particular program. For example, if your program requires that all simulated automobiles only move forward, you should still include a reverse in your automobile class. Some other simulation may require automobiles to back up. We will return to the topic of reusability after we learn some details about the Java language and have some examples to work with.

Testing and Debugging

The way to write a correct program is to carefully design the objects your program needs, to carefully design the algorithms for the methods the objects will use, and finally to carefully translate all this into Java code (or code in whatever programming language you are using). Unless you proceed carefully, you will probably never get all of the errors out of your program. However, even a very carefully designed program can contain some errors. When you finish writing a program, you should test the program to see whether or not it performs correctly, and if it does not perform correctly fix any errors in the program.

bug
debugging

A mistake in a program is called a **bug**. For this reason, eliminating mistakes in your program is called **debugging.** There are three commonly recognized types of bugs or errors, and they are known as *syntax errors, run-time errors,* and *logic errors.* Let's consider them in order.

syntax error

A **syntax error** is a grammatical mistake in your program. There are very strict grammar rules for how you write a program. If you violate one of these rules, for example, by omitting a required punctuation, that is a syntax error. The compiler will catch syntax errors and output an error message telling you that it has found the error and what it thinks the error is. If the compiler says you have a syntax error, it is virtually certain that you do have an error. However, the compiler is only guessing at what the error is and so it could be incorrect in what it says the error is.

Syntax

The rules for the correct way to write a program or part of a program (i.e., the grammar rules for a programming language) are called the **syntax** of the language.

◻

---

run-time error

An error that is detected when your program is run is called a **run-time error.** If your program contains a run-time error, then the computer will output an error message when your program is run. The error message may or may not be easy to understand, but at least it lets you know that something is wrong and sometimes can tell you exactly what is wrong.

logic error

If there is some mistake in the underlying algorithm for your program or if you write something in Java that is incorrect but still legal, then your program will compile and run without any error message. You have written a valid Java program, but you have not written the program you want. The program runs and gives output, but gives incorrect output. In this case, your program contains a **logic error.** For example, if you were to mistakenly use the addition sign in place of the subtraction sign, that would be a logic error. You could compile and run your program with no error messages, but the program would give the wrong output. Logic errors are the hardest kind of error to locate, because the computer does not give you any error messages.

⚠ GOTCHA Coping with "Gotchas"

Any programming language has details that can trip you up in ways that are surprising or that are hard to deal with. These sorts of problems are often called *pitfalls*, but a more colorful and more commonly used term is *gotchas*. The term stems from the fact that these problems, or pitfalls, or *gotchas* are like traps waiting to catch you. When you get caught in the trap, the trap has "got you," or as it is more commonly pronounced "gotcha."

gotcha

In this book, we have sections, with headings like this section, that warn you about many of the most common *gotchas* and tell you how to avoid them or how to cope with them.

⚠ GOTCHA Hidden Errors

Just because your program compiles and runs without any errors and even gives "reasonable looking" output, that does not mean your program is correct. You should always run your program with some test data for which you know what the output is supposed to be. To do this, choose some data for which you can compute the correct output with pencil and paper, or by looking up the answer, or by some other means. Even this testing does not guarantee that your program is correct, but the more testing you do, the more confidence you can have in your program.

? SELF-TEST QUESTIONS
....

   13. What is a syntax error?

   14. What kinds of errors are likely to produce error messages that will alert you to the fact that your program contains an error?

   15. Suppose you write a program that is supposed to compute which day of the week (Sunday, Monday, etc.) a given date (like December 1, 2001) will fall on. Now, suppose you forget to account for leap years. Your program will then contain an error. What kind of program error is it?

1.3 A Taste of Java

> Java. An Island of Indonesia, 48,842 square miles in area, lying between the Indian Ocean and the Java Sea.
> java **n.** Informal. Brewed coffee. [From Java.]
> **The American Heritage Dictionary of the English Language, First Edition**

In this section, we describe some of the characteristics of the Java language and explain a simple Java program.

History of the Java Language

Java is widely viewed as a programming language to design applications for the World Wide Web. However, this book, and many other books and people, view Java as a general-purpose programming language that can be used without any reference to the World Wide Web. At its birth, Java was neither of these things, but it did eventually evolve into both of these things.

The history of Java goes back to 1991 when James Gosling and his team at Sun Microsystems Incorporated began designing the first version of Java (which was not yet called *Java*). The first version of Java was intended to be a programming language for programming home appliances, like toasters and TVs. That sounds like a humble engineering task, but in fact, it's a very challenging one. Home appliances are controlled by a wide variety of computer processors (chips). The language that Gosling and his team were designing needed to work on all these different processors. Moreover, a home appliance is typically an inexpensive item, so the manufacturer will not be willing to invest large amounts of time and money into developing complicated compilers. In this appliance language that the team was designing, and now in the Java language that it evolved into, programs are first translated into an **intermediate language** that is the same for all appliances (or all computers), then a small, easy-to-write, and hence inexpensive, program translates this intermediate language into the machine language for a particular appliance or computer. This intermediate language is called **Java byte code** or simply **byte code**.

intermediate language

byte code

In 1994, Gosling realized that his language would be ideal for developing a web browser (a program for finding and viewing sites on the World Wide Web.) The web browser was produced by Patrick Naughton and Jonathan Payne at Sun Microsystems and has evolved into the browser that is today known as HotJava. This was the start of Java's connection to the World Wide Web. In the fall of 1995, Netscape Incorporated decided to make the next release of its Netscape (World Wide Web) browser capable of running Java programs. Other companies associated with the World Wide Web have followed suit and have software that accommodates Java programs.

Why Is the Language Named "Java"?

This question does not have a very interesting answer. The current custom is to name programming languages pretty much the same way that parents name their children. The creator of the programming language simply chooses any name that sounds good to her or him. In the case of the Java language, one hears conflicting explanations of the name. One traditional, and perhaps believable, story is that the name was thought of when, after a fruitless meeting trying to come up with a name for the language, the development team went out for coffee, and the rest is, as they say, history. ∎

Applets and the World Wide Web

applet

application

There are two kinds of Java programs, **applets** and **applications** (i.e., applets and regular programs). An *applet* sounds like a little apple, but the name is meant to convey the idea of a *little application*, not a little apple. Applets and applications are almost identical. The difference is that applications are meant to be run on your computer like any other program, whereas an applet is meant to be sent to another location on the

World Wide Web and run there. Once you know how to design and write one of either applets or applications, it is trivial to learn to write the other of these two kinds of programs. This book emphasizes applications rather than applets. The reason for this is that you need to know a number of things about the World Wide Web and web sites in order to use the applets, and we do not want to stop to discuss that whole other topic.

A First Java Program

Our first Java program is shown in Display 1.4. Below the program we show two screen displays that might be produced when a *user* runs and interacts with this program. The person who interacts with a program is called the **user.** The text typed in by the user is shown in boldface. If you run this program (and you should do so), then both texts would look alike on your computer screen. The user may or may not be the person who wrote the program. In a programming class, they very often are the same person, but in a real world application, they are usually different people. The person who writes the program is called the **programmer.** This book is teaching you to be the programmer and one of the first things you need to learn is that the user of your program cannot be expected to know what you want her or him to do, and so your program must give the user understandable instructions, as we have done in the sample screen dialogues.

user

programmer

In this chapter, we just want to give you a feel for the Java language by giving you a brief, informal description of the program in Display 1.4. In Chapters 2 and 3, we will explain the details of the Java features used in Display 1.4.

For now, ignore the following few lines that come at the start of the program. They set up a context for the program, but we need not worry about them yet.

```
public class FirstProgram
{

    public static void main(String[] args)
    {
```

You can think of these opening lines as being a hard-to-spell way of writing "Begin the program."

The next three lines, shown in what follows, are the first things the program does. Let's discuss these three lines first.

output

```
System.out.println("Hello out there.");
System.out.println("Want to talk some more?");
System.out.println("Answer y for yes or n for no.");
```

Each of these lines begin with `System.out.println`. Each one causes the quoted string given within the parentheses to be output to the screen. For example, consider

```
System.out.println("Hello out there.");
```

This causes the line

```
Hello out there.
```

to be written to the screen.

Display 1.4 A Sample Java Program

```
public class FirstProgram
{
    public static void main(String[] args)
    {
        System.out.println("Hello out there.");
        System.out.println("Want to talk some more?");
        System.out.println("Answer y for yes or n for no.");

        char answerLetter;
        answerLetter = SavitchIn.readLineNonwhiteChar();
        if (answerLetter == 'y')
                System.out.println("Nice weather we are having.");

        System.out.println("Good-bye.");

        System.out.println("Press enter key to end program.");
        String junk;
        junk = SavitchIn.readLine();
    }
}
```

Sample Screen Dialogue 1

```
Hello out there.
Want to talk some more?
Answer y for yes or n for no.
y
Nice weather we are having.
Good-bye.
Press enter key to end program.
```

Sample Screen Dialogue 2

```
Hello out there.
Want to talk some more?
Answer y for yes or n for no.
n
Good-bye.
Press enter key to end program.
```

For now, you can consider these lines that begin with `System.out.println` to be a funny way of saying "output what is shown in parentheses". However, we can tell you a little about what is going on here.

`System.out` is an object used for sending output to the screen; `println` is the method (i.e., the action) that this object carries out in order to send what is in parentheses to the screen. Whenever an object performs an action using a method, that is called **invoking** the method. In a Java program you write such a method invocation by writing the object followed by a period (called a **dot** in computer jargon), followed by the method name, and some parentheses that may or may not have something inside them. The thing (or things) inside of the parentheses is called an **argument** and provides the information needed by the method in order to carry out its action. In each of these first three lines, the method is `println`. The method `println` writes something to the screen and the argument (a string in quotes) tells it what it should write.

The next line of the program, shown in what follows, says that `answerLetter` is the name of a variable.

```
char answerLetter;
```

A **variable** is something that can store a piece of data. The `char` says that the data must be a single character; `char` is an abbreviation for *character*.

The next line reads a character that is typed in at the keyboard and stores this character in the variable `answerLetter`:

```
answerLetter = SavitchIn.readLineNonwhiteChar();
```

`SavitchIn` is a class used for obtaining input from the keyboard and `readLineNonwhiteChar` is a method that reads a single nonblank character from the keyboard. If the user types in some input on a single line and presses the enter key (also called the return key), then this method will read the first nonblank character on that line and discard everything else on that line of keyboard input. The expression

```
SavitchIn.readLineNonwhiteChar();
```

is another kind of method invocation. This method invocation simply reads the first nonblank character, which in the first dialogue is 'y', and dumps the character at the location of the invocation. The rest of that line tells what is to happen to this character 'y'. The rest of the line, highlighted in what follows, says to make this character the value of the variable `answerLetter`.

```
answerLetter = SavitchIn.readLineNonwhiteChar();
```

The equal sign is used differently in Java than it is in everyday mathematics. In the preceding program line, the equal sign does not mean that `answerLetter` *is equal to* `SavitchIn.readLineNonwhiteChar()`. Instead, it is an instruction to the computer to make `answerLetter` equal to `SavitchIn.readLineNonwhite-Char()`; that is, to store the character read from the keyboard in the variable `answerLetter`.

As it turns out, `SavitchIn` is not really an object, but is a class. However, in this context, we are using the class `SavitchIn` as if it were an object. For some special

Margin notes: System.out.println · invoking · dot · argument · variable · SavitchIn

methods, you can use the name of a class rather than the name of an object when you invoke the method. In Chapter 5, we explain the significance of this distinction, but those details need not concern us until we get to Chapter 5.

Java uses the double equal sign for what you might think of as ordinary equals. The following two program lines first check to see if the character stored in the variable `answerLetter` is equal to the character `'y'`. If it is, then `"Nice weather we are having."` is written to the screen.

```
if (answerLetter == 'y')
        System.out.println("Nice weather we are having.");
```

If the character stored in `answerLetter` is anything other than `'y'`, then these two lines cause no output to the screen.

Notice that one sample dialogue outputs the string `"Nice weather we are having."` and one does not. That is because, in the first run of the program, the character `'y'` is stored in the variable `answerLetter`, and in the second run of the program, the character `'n'` is stored in `answerLetter`.

The following three lines at the end of the program are there to stop the screen output from going away before you can read it. Some systems will erase the screen as soon as the program ends. These three lines make the program, and the screen, wait for you to press the enter key (also called the return key):

```
System.out.println("Press enter key to end program.");
String junk;
junk = SavitchIn.readLine();
```

If pressing the enter key one time does not end the program, just press it a second time. This detail can vary a little from one system to another. Although you can use these three lines without understanding them, we can explain a bit more about these three lines.

The line

```
String junk;
```

declares a variable named `junk`. The type `String` means that `junk` can hold an entire string of characters. If the user enters a line of text and ends the line with the enter (return) key, then the following will read the entire line of text and make it the value of `junk`:

```
junk = SavitchIn.readLine();
```

If the user simply presses the enter (return) key, then this will still read the blank line of input, so all that the user needs to do is press the return key. The variable is named `junk`, because the value stored in the variable is not used for anything.

The method `readLine` is similar to the method `readLineNonwhiteChar`, except that `readLine` reads in an entire line of input rather than a single character. You could end the program in Display 1.4 by typing in the words

```
So long for now.
```

Method Invocation

A **method** is an action that an object is capable of performing. When you ask an object to perform the action of a method, that is called **invoking** the method. (Another term used to mean the same thing as *invoking a method* is **calling a method.**) In a Java program, a method invocation is specified by writing the object name, followed by a period (called a **dot**), followed by the method name, and followed by the *arguments* enclosed in parentheses. The **argument**s are information given to the method. (Another term that is often used to mean the same thing as arguments is *parameters*.)

Syntax:

Object_Name .Method_Name (Arguments)

Examples:

```
System.out.println("Hello out there.");
answerLetter = SavitchIn.readLineNonwhiteChar();
```

In the first example, `System.out` is the object and `"Hello out there"` is the argument. If there is more than one argument, the arguments are separated by commas.

In the second example, `SavitchIn` serves the same role as an object and there are no arguments. In some cases, such as the methods of the class `SavitchIn`, you can use a class name in place of an object name when you write a method invocation.

In a program, these method invocations are typically followed by a semicolon.

---

all on one line and ended by pressing the enter key. The entire line of text would be stored in the variable `junk`. However, all we really need the user to do is to press the enter key.

The only things left to explain in this first program are the final semicolons on each line and the curly bracket } at the end of the program. The semicolon acts as ending punctuation like a period in an English sentence. A semicolon ends an instruction to the computer. These instructions are called **statements.** The curly bracket } at the end simply says, "This is the end of the program."

statements

Of course, there are very precise rules for how you write each part of a Java program. These rules form the grammar for the Java language, just like there are rules for the grammar of the English language, but the Java rules are more precise. The grammar rules for a programming language are called the **syntax** of the language.

syntax

OOP Terminology: Messages

When a program contains an invocation of an object's method, such as the following, some programmers say that the object is **sent a message**.

```
System.out.println("Hello out there.");
```

In this case, the object `System.out` is sent the message `println("Hello out there.")`. When you take this view, you think of objects as performing actions in response to messages. In this case, the action taken by the object `System.out` in response to the message `println("Hello out there.")` is to output the string `"Hello out there."` to the screen. In this book, we will, however, use the terms *method invocation* and *method call* rather than phrases like *send a message to the object*.

Spelling Rules

identifier

The technical term for a name in a programming language is an **identifier**. The Java language has precise rules for what is allowed as an identifier (i.e., as the name of something in a Java program), such as a class or a variable. An identifier (i.e., a name) must consist entirely of letters, digits (0 through 9), and the underscore character _, but the first character in a name cannot be a digit.[1] In particular, no name can contain a space or any other character such as a period or an *. There is no limit to the length of a name. (Well, in practice, there is always a limit, but there is no official limit and Java will accept even absurdly long names.) Java is **case-sensitive**. That means that uppercase and lowercase letters are considered to be different characters. For example, `mystuff`, `myStuff`, and `MyStuff` are considered to be three different names and you could have three variables (or other items) with these three names. Of course, it is very poor programming practice to have two names that differ only in that one has uppercase where the other has the same letters in lowercase, but the Java compiler would be happy with them. Java uses a character set, called *Unicode*, that also includes characters that are used in other languages, but that do not exist in English. Java does allow you to use these extra letters in names. (However, most keyboards you are likely to use do not have them, and many people would not recognize them if you did use them). Within these spelling rules, you can use any name you want for a variable or for a class that you define or for an object of that class. But, we will give you some style guidelines for choosing names, so that your programs will be easier to read.

upper- and lowercase

The peculiar use of uppercase and lowercase letters, such as `answerLetter`, that we have used in our sample program deserves some explanation. It would be perfectly legal to use `AnswerLetter` or `answer_letter` instead of `answerLetter`, but there are some well-established conventions about how you should use uppercase and lowercase letters. By convention, we write names using only letters and digits. We punctuate multiword names using uppercase letters (since we cannot use spaces). So, the following are all legal names that also follow this well-established convention:

```
inputStream YourClass CarWash hotCar theTimeOfDay
```

The following are all illegal names in Java, and the compiler will complain if you use any of them:

```
My.Class netscape.com go-team 7eleven
```

The first three contain illegal characters, either a dot or the dash symbol. The last name is illegal because it starts with a digit.

Notice that some of the legal names start with an uppercase letter and others, such as `hotCar`, start with a lowercase letter, which may look a little strange at first. We will always follow the convention that the names of classes start with an upper-

1. Java does allow the dollar sign symbol $ to appear in an identifier, but these identifiers have a special meaning and you should not use the $ symbol in your identifiers.

case letter, and the names of variables, objects, and methods start with a lowercase letter.

Of course, there are words in a Java program, such as the word if, that name neither a variable, nor a class, nor an object. Some words, such as if, are called **reserved words** or **keywords**. These reserved words have a special predefined meaning in the Java language and cannot be used as the names of classes or objects or anything else other than their intended meaning. A full list of reserved words for Java is given in Appendix 1, but it is easier to learn them by usage. From now on, we will show reserved words in italic, like so *if*. Some other words, such as String, have a predefined meaning but are not reserved words. That means you can change their meaning, but it is a bad idea to do so, since it could easily confuse you or somebody else reading your program.

reserved word

Names (Identifiers)

The name of something in a Java program, such as a variable, a class, a method, or an object name, must not start with a digit and must consist entirely of letters, digits (0 through 9), and the underscore character _. Uppercase and lowercase letters are considered to be different characters. (The symbol $ is also allowed, but it is reserved for special purposes, and so you should not use $ in a Java name.)

Names in a program are often called **identifiers**.

Although it is not required by the Java language, the common practice, and the one followed in this book, is to start the names of classes with uppercase letters and to start the names of variables, objects, and methods with lowercase letters. These names are usually spelled using only letters and digits.

Compiling a Java Program or Class

A Java program can consist of any number of class definitions. The program we just discussed (Display 1.4/page 18) consists of two classes. The first is the class named First-Program in Display 1.4. Every program in Java is a class as well as a program. The other class used in this first program is the class SavitchIn, which has already been defined for you. At this point, you would not understand the definition of the class SavitchIn, but you can still obtain a copy of the class SavitchIn, compile it, and use it. A copy of the class SavitchIn is provided on the CD that accompanies this book along with the other classes defined in this book.

Before you can compile a Java program, each class definition used in the program should be in a separate file. Moreover, the name of the file should be the same as the name of the class, except that the file name has .java added to the end. The program we just discussed (Display 1.4/page 18) is a class called FirstProgram and so it should be in a file named FirstProgram.java. That program uses the class SavitchIn. The class definition of SavitchIn should be in a file named SavitchIn.java. Before you can run this program, you must compile both of the classes SavitchIn and FirstProgram. (If you are in a course, then your instructor may have configured the system so that SavitchIn is already compiled for you, but later on when you define your own classes, you will need to compile them.)

.java files

If you are on a system that has a special environment for Java, you will have a menu command that can be used to compile a Java class or Java program. You will have to check your local documentation to see exactly what this command is, but it is bound to be very simple. If your operating system expects you to type in a one-line command, that is easy to do. We will describe the commands for the Java system distributed by Sun Microsystems (usually called "the JDK"). If you have some other version of Java, these commands might be different. Suppose you want to compile a class named `MyClass`. It will be in a file named `MyClass.java`. To compile it, you simply give the following command to the operating system:

```
javac MyClass.java
```

To compile a Java class, the command is `javac` followed by the name of the file containing the class.

Thus, to compile all the classes needed to run the program in Display 1.4, you would give the following two commands (on two separate lines):

```
javac SavitchIn.java
javac FirstProgram.java
```

Remember, if you have an environment that lets you compile with a menu command, you will find it easier to use the menu command rather than the preceding commands.

.class **files**

When you compile a Java class, the resulting byte code for that class is placed in a file of the same name, except that the ending is changed from `.java` to `.class`, so the preceding two compilations will create two files named `SavitchIn.class` and `FirstProgram.class`.

running a Java
program

Running a Java Program

A Java program can involve any number of classes, but when you run a Java program, you only run the class that you think of as the program. You can recognize this class because it will contain words identical to or similar to

```
public static void main(String[] args)
```

These words will probably be someplace near the beginning of the file. The critical word to look for is `main`.

If you are on a system that has a special environment for Java, you will have a menu command that can be used to run a Java program. You will have to check your local documentation to see exactly what this command is. If your operating system expects you to type in a one-line command, then (on most systems) you can run a Java program by giving the command `java` followed by the name of the class you think of as the program. For example, for the program in Display 1.4, you would give the following one-line command:

```
java FirstProgram
```

Note that when you run a program, you use the class name, such as `FirstProgram`. You do not use a full file name like `FirstProgram.java` or `FirstProgram.class`. And remember that if you have a menu command for running a Java program, then that is an easier way to run your Java program.

When you run a Java program, you are actually running the Java byte-code interpreter on the compiled version of your program. The system will automatically link in any classes you need and run the byte-code interpreter on these classes as well.

In the preceding discussion, we were assuming that the Java compiler and other system software was already set up for you. We were also assuming that all the files were in one directory. (Directories are also called *folders*.) If you need to set up the Java compiler and system software, consult the manuals that came with the software. If you wish to spread your class definitions across multiple directories, that is possible and not difficult, but we will not concern ourselves with that detail now.

? SELF-TEST QUESTIONS

16. If the following statement were used in a Java program, it would cause something to be written on the screen. What would it cause to be written on the screen?

```
System.out.println("Java is great!");
```

17. Give a statement or statements that can be used in a Java program to write the following on the screen:

```
Java Java
jig jig jig.
```

18. Suppose `mary` is an object of a class named `Person` and suppose `increaseAge` is a method for the class `Person` that uses one argument that is an integer. How do you write an invocation of the method `increaseAge` for the object `mary` using the argument 5? The method `increaseAge` will change the data in `mary` so that it simulates `mary` aging by 5 years.

19. What is the meaning of the following line, which appears in the program in Display 1.4/page 18:

```
answerLetter = SavitchIn.readLineNonwhiteChar();
```

Chapter Summary

□ A computer's **main memory** holds the program that is currently being executed, and more importantly from our point of view, it holds much of the data that the program is manipulating. A computer's main memory is divided into a series of numbered locations called **bytes.**

□ A computer's **auxiliary memory** is used to hold data in a more or less permanent state.

□ A **compiler** is a program that translates a program written in a high-level language like Java into a program written in a low-level language. The Java compiler translates your Java program into a program in the byte-code language. When you give the command to run your Java program, this byte-code program is translated into machine-language instructions and the machine-language instructions are carried out by the computer.

□ An **algorithm** is a set of instructions for solving a problem. To qualify as an algorithm, the instructions must be expressed so completely and precisely that somebody could follow the instructions without having to fill in any details or make any decisions that are not fully specified in the instructions.

☐ An **object** is something that has data associated with it and that can perform certain actions. The actions performed by objects are called **methods**. A **class** defines a type of object. All objects in the same class have the same methods.

☐ In a Java program, a method invocation is specified by writing the object name (or class name), followed by a period (called a dot), followed by the method name, and followed by the arguments given in parentheses.

? ANSWERS to Self-Test Questions

1. Main memory and auxiliary memory.

2. Software is just another name for programs.

3. All the grades on all the quizzes that you have taken in the course.

4. A machine-language program is written in a form the computer can execute directly. A high-level language program is written in a form that is easy for a human being to write and read. A high-level language program must be translated into a machine-language program before the computer can execute it. Java byte code is a low-level language that is very similar to the machine language of most common computers. It is relatively easy to translate a program expressed in Java byte code into the machine language of almost any computer.

5. A compiler translates a high-level language program into a low-level language program such as a machine-language program or a Java byte-code program. When you compile a Java program, the compiler translates your Java program into a program expressed in Java byte code.

6. The high-level language program that is input to a compiler is called the source program.

7. A program that translates Java byte-code instructions to machine-language instructions is called an *interpreter*.

8. An algorithm is a set of instructions for solving a problem. To qualify as an algorithm, the instructions must be expressed so completely and precisely that somebody could follow the instructions without having to fill in any details or make any decisions that are not fully specified in the instructions.

9. Pseudocode is a mixture of English and a programming language (in our case, Java). Algorithms are usually written in pseudocode and later translated into a programming language, such as Java.

10. A method is an action that an object is capable of taking. (In some other programming languages, methods are called *functions* or *procedures*.)

11. A class is a category of objects. All objects in the same class have the same kind of data and the same methods.

12. Yes, all objects of the same class have the same methods.

13. A syntax error is a grammatical mistake in your program. There are very strict grammar rules for how you write a program. If you violate one of these rules, for example, by omitting a required punctuation, that is a syntax error.

14. Syntax errors and run-time errors.

15. A logic error.

16. `Java is great!`

17.

```
System.out.println("Java Java");
System.out.println("jig jig jig.");
```

18. `mary.increaseAge(5);`

19. This statement skips over blank spaces until it reaches the first nonblank character, and then it reads that nonblank character (in the sample dialogue 'y' or 'n') and stores that character in the variable `answerLetter`.

? PROGRAMMING EXERCISES

1. Obtain a copy of the class `SavitchIn.java` that contains the definition of the class `SavitchIn`. (It is on the CD provided with this book. In a course, your instructor may provide you with a copy. It is also in Appendix 2, but it would be a pain to copy the whole thing from there.) Compile the class `SavitchIn` so that you get no compiler errors. Next, obtain a copy of the Java program shown in Display 1.4/page 18. (That program is also on the CD that comes with this book.) Name the file `FirstProgram.java`. Compile the program so that you receive no compiler error messages. Finally, run the program. If you are in a class and your instructor has already compiled the class `SavitchIn` for you, then you can skip that part.

2. Modify the Java program that you entered in Programming Exercise 1 so that if the user types in the letter n in response to the question

`Want to talk some more?.`

then the program will output the phrase

`Too bad. You seem like such a nice person.`

The program should behave the same as in Display 1.4/page 18 if the user enters y instead of n. Compile and run the modified program. *Hint:* Include a second statement that begins with `if` and that tests whether `answerLetter` is equal to 'n'.

3. Write a complete Java program that outputs the following to the screen when run:

```
Hello World!
```

Your program does nothing else, except that, if the output goes away before you get a chance to read it, then you should add the following to the end of your program:

```
System.out.println("Press the enter key to end the program.");
String junk;
junk = SavitchIn.readLine();
```

Chapter 2

PRIMITIVE TYPES AND STRINGS

2.1 PRIMITIVE TYPES, ASSIGNMENT, AND EXPRESSIONS 30
Variables and Variable Declarations 30
Primitive Types 34
Assignment Statements 35
Specialized Assignment Operators (*Optional*) 37
Simple Input and Output 38
Number Constants 39
Assignment Compatibilities 40
Type Casting 41
Gotcha Type Casting a Character to an Integer 43
Programming Tip Initialize Variables 43
Gotcha Imprecision in Floating-Point Numbers 44
Arithmetic Operators 46
Case Study Vending Machine Change 49
Increment and Decrement Operators 53
More About Increment and Decrement Operators (*Optional*) 54

2.2 THE CLASS STRING 55
String Constants and Variables 55
String Methods 55
String Processing 59
Escape Characters 60
The Unicode Character Set 62

2.3 DOCUMENTATION AND STYLE 63
Programming Tip Use Meaningful Names for Variables 63
Documentation and Comments 64
Indenting 65
Named Constants 67

2.4 KEYBOARD AND SCREEN I/O 71
Screen Output 71
Input Using `SavitchIn` 74
More Input Methods 75
Gotcha `readInt` and `readDouble` 77
Programming Tip Echo Input 78

Chapter Summary 79
Answers to Self-Test Questions 79
Programming Exercises 81

2

PRIMITIVE TYPES AND STRINGS

primitive **adj. 1.** *Not derived from something else; primary or basic.*
string **n. 1.** *A cord usually made of fiber, used for fastening, tying or lacing. ...*
   6. *Computer Science. A set of consecutive characters treated by a*
   computer as a single item.
   The American Heritage Dictionary of the English Language, Third Edition

Introduction

In this chapter, we explain enough about the Java language to allow you to write simple Java programs. You do not need to have done any programming to understand this chapter. On the other hand, if you are already familiar with some other programming language, such as C, C++, Pascal, BASIC, FORTRAN, or Ada, then much of what is in Section 2.1 will already be familiar to you. However, even if the concepts are already familiar to you, you should familiarize yourself with the Java way of expressing these concepts.

Prerequisites

If you have not read Chapter 1, you should at least familiarize yourself with Display 1.4 on page 18.

2.1 Primitive Types, Assignment, and Expressions

Memory is necessary
   for all the operations of reason.
   BLAISE PASCAL

In this section, we explain how simple variables and arithmetic expressions are used in Java programs.

Variables and Variable Declarations

variables

value of a
variable

Variables in a program are used to store data such as numbers and letters. Variables can be thought of as containers of sort, but containers that hold things like numbers and letters. The number or letter or other data item in a variable is called its **value.** This value can be changed so that at one time the variable contains, say 5, and at another time after the program has run for some time, the variable contains a different value, such as 12. In the program in Display 2.1, `numberOfBaskets`, `eggsPerBasket`, and `totalEggs` are variables. For example, when this program is run with the

Display 2.1 A Simple Java Program
••

```java
public class EggBasket
{
    public static void main(String[] args)
    {
        int numberOfBaskets, eggsPerBasket, totalEggs;

        System.out.println("Enter the number of eggs in each basket:");
        eggsPerBasket = SavitchIn.readLineInt();
        System.out.println("Enter the number of baskets:");
        numberOfBaskets = SavitchIn.readLineInt();

        totalEggs = numberOfBaskets * eggsPerBasket;

        System.out.println(eggsPerBasket + " eggs per basket.");
        System.out.println(numberOfBaskets + " baskets.");
        System.out.println("Total number of eggs is " + totalEggs);

        eggsPerBasket = eggsPerBasket - 2;
        totalEggs = numberOfBaskets * eggsPerBasket;

        System.out.println("Now we take two eggs out of each basket.");
        System.out.println(eggsPerBasket + " eggs per basket.");
        System.out.println(numberOfBaskets + " baskets.");
        System.out.println("Total number of eggs is " + totalEggs);

        System.out.println("Press enter key to end program.");
        String junk;
        junk = SavitchIn.readLine();
    }
}
```

Sample Screen Dialogue

```
Enter the number of eggs in each basket:
6
Enter the number of baskets:
10
6 eggs per basket.
10 baskets.
Total number of eggs is 60
Now we take two eggs out of each basket.
4 eggs per basket.
10 baskets.
Total number of eggs is 40
Press enter key to end program.
```

••

input shown in the sample dialogue, `eggsPerBasket` has its value set equal to the number 6 with the following statement, which reads a number from the keyboard.

```
eggsPerBasket = SavitchIn.readLineInt();
```

Later, the value of the variable `eggsPerBasket` is changed to 4 when the program executes the following statement.

```
eggsPerBasket = eggsPerBasket – 2;
```

We will explain these two statements in more detail shortly. For now, simply note that the first one reads in a number that is typed at the keyboard and makes that the value of the variable `eggsPerBasket`, and that the second one changes the value of this variable by subtracting 2 from its value.

variables in memory

In Java, variables are implemented as memory locations. In Chapter 1, we discussed memory locations. Each variable is assigned one such memory location. When the variable is given a value, this value (encoded as a string of zeros and ones) is placed in the memory location assignment to that variable.

The rules for naming variables are given in the box entitled **Variable Names**. However, you should choose variable names so that the names are not simply legal, but are also helpful. Variable names should suggest their use or suggest the kind of data they will hold. For example, if a variable is used to count something, you might name the variable `count`. If the variable is used to hold the speed of an automobile, you might call the variable `speed`. You should almost never use single-letter variable names like `x` and `y`. Somebody reading the following would have no idea of what the program is really adding:

```
x = y + z;
```

Variable Names (Identifiers)

Variable names (and all other names) must satisfy the spelling rules for names that we gave in Chapter 1. The name of a variable, like any other name in a Java program, must *not* start with a digit and must consist entirely of letters, digits (0 through 9), and the underscore character _. Uppercase and lowercase letter are considered to be different characters. (The symbol $ is also allowed, but it is reserved for special purposes, and so you should not use $ in a Java name.)

Although it is not required by the Java language, the common practice, and the one followed in this book, is to start the name of a variable with a lowercase letter.

---

variable declarations

In order to run your program, the computer must be given some basic information about each variable in your program. It needs to know the name of the variable, how much computer memory to reserve for the variable, and how the data item in the variable is to be coded as strings of zeros and ones. All this information can be obtained provided the compiler (and so ultimately the computer) is told the name of the variable and what type of data are stored in the variable. You give this information by **declaring** the variable. Every variable in a Java program must be **declared** before it is used. For example, the following line from Display 2.1 declares

declare

the three variables `numberOfBaskets`, `eggsPerBasket,` and `totalEggs` to be variables of type *int:*

```
int numberOfBaskets, eggsPerBasket, totalEggs;
```

A variable declaration consists of a type name, followed by a list of variable names separated by commas, and then all that is ended with a semicolon. All the variables named in the list are declared to have the type given at the start of the declaration.

The type *int* is the most commonly used type for variables that hold whole numbers, such as 42, −99, 0, and 2001. The word *int* is an abbreviation of *integer*. The reserved word *int* is the word Java uses instead of the longer word *integer*.

int

A variable's **type** determines what kind of value the variable can hold. If the type is *int*, the variable can hold whole numbers. If the type is *double,* the variable can hold numbers with a decimal point and a fractional part after the decimal point. If the type is *char*, the variables can hold any one character from the computer keyboard.

type

A variable declaration tells the computer what type of data the variable will hold. Different types of data are stored in the computer's memory in different ways and so the computer must know the type of a variable in order to know how to store and retrieve the value of the variable from the computer's memory.

Variable Declarations

In a Java program, a variable must be declared before it can be used. Variables are declared as follows:

Syntax Template:

```
Type Variable_1, Variable_2, . . .;
```

Examples:

```
int styleNumber, numberOfChecks, numberOfDeposits;
char answer;
double amount, interestRate;
```

There are two main kinds of types in Java, *class types* and *primitive types*. As the name implies, a **class type** is a type for a class, that is, a type for objects with both data and methods. A primitive type is a simpler type. Values of a **primitive type** are not complex items but simple, indecomposable values, such as a single number or a single letter. The type `SavitchIn` is a class type. `String` is another class type. The types *int*, *double*, and *char* are primitive types. Although variable names for class and primitive types are declared in the same way, there is a different mechanism for storing values in the variables of class types and in variables of primitive types. In this chapter, we will mostly confine our attention to primitive types. In this chapter, we will occasionally use variables of a class type, but only in contexts where they behave pretty much the same as variables of a primitive type. In Chapters 3 and 4, we will explain what is different about variables of a class type.

class type
primitive type

Every variable in a Java program must be declared before the variable can be used. Normally, a variable is declared either just before it is used or at the start of a

location of
declarations

method definition. In the simple programs we have seen so far, there is only one method, which is called `main`, so variables are declared either just before they are used or at the start of the program. However, as we will see, it is possible for a class to have many methods and to declare variables inside of any or all of these methods.

Primitive Types

All the Java primitive types are given in Display 2.2. Notice that there are four types for integers, namely, *byte*, *short*, *int*, and *long*. The only difference between the various integer types is the range of integers they can store and the amount of computer memory they use. If you cannot decide which integer type to use, use the type *int*. It has a large enough range for most purposes and does not use as much memory as the type *long*.

integer
floating-point
number

A whole number such as 0, 1, –1, 2, –2, and so forth is called an **integer**. A number with a fractional part, such as 9.99, 3.14159, –5.63, or 5.0 is called a **floating-point number**. Notice that 5.0 is a floating-point number, not an integer. If we ask the computer to include a fractional part and that fractional part happens to be zero, that does not change the type of the number. If it has a fractional part, even if it is zero, then it is a floating-point number. As shown in Display 2.2, Java has two types for floating-point numbers, namely, *float* and *double*. For example, the following declares two variables, one of type *float* and one of type *double*:

```
float cost;
double capacity;
```

If you cannot decide between the types *float* and *double*, use the type *double*. It allows a wider range of values and is used as a default type for floating-point numbers.

The primitive type *char* is used for single characters, such as letters or the percent sign. For example, the following declares the variable `symbol` to be of type *char*, stores the character for uppercase A in `symbol`, and then writes out that value to the screen so that an A would appear on the screen:

```
char symbol;
symbol = 'A';
System.out.println(symbol);
```

single quotes

Notice that when we give a character in a Java program, like 'A', we enclose the character in single quotes. Also note that there is only one single-quote symbol. The same quote symbol is used on both sides of the character. That one symbol serves as both the left and the right quote symbol. Finally, note that uppercase and lowercase letters are different characters; so, for example, 'a' and 'A' are two different characters.

The last primitive type we have to discuss is the type *boolean*. There are two values of type *boolean*, namely, *true* and *false*. This means we can use a variable of type *boolean* to store the answer to a true/false question such as "Is `myTime` less than `yourTime`?" We will have more to say about the type *boolean* in the next chapter.

Display 2.2 Primitive Types

Type Name	Kind of Value	Memory Used	Size Range
byte	integer	1 byte	−128 to 127
short	integer	2 bytes	−32768 to 32767
int	integer	4 bytes	−2147483648 to 2147483647
long	integer	8 bytes	−9223372036854775808 to 9223372036854775807
float	floating-point number	4 bytes	$\pm 3.40282347 \times 10^{+38}$ to $\pm 1.40239846 \times 10^{-45}$
double	floating-point number	8 bytes	$\pm 1.76769313486231570 \times 10^{+308}$ to $\pm 4.94065645841246544 \times 10^{-324}$
char	single character (Unicode)	2 bytes	all Unicode characters
boolean	true or false	1 bit	not applicable

Assignment Statements

If you know what value you want to give to a variable, you can use an assignment statement to give the variable that value. For example, if answer is a variable of type int and you want to give it the value 42, you would use the following **assignment statement:**

        answer = 42;

The equal sign, =, is called the **assignment operator** when it is used in an assignment statement such as the preceding statement. It does not mean what the equal sign means in other contexts. The assignment statement is an order to the computer telling it to change the value stored in the variable on the left-hand side of the assignment operator, i.e., on the left-hand side of the =. An assignment statement always consists of a single variable on the left-hand side of an assignment operator (equal sign) and an expression on the right-hand side. The assignment statement has a semicolon at the end. So, assignment statements take the form:

        Variable = *Expression*;

assignment statement

assignment operator

The expression can be another variable, a number, or a more complicated expression made up by using arithmetic operators, such as + and *, to combine variables and numbers.

For example, the following are all examples of assignment statements:

```
amount = 3.99;
firstInitial = 'B';
score = numberOfCards + handicap;
eggsPerBasket = eggsPerBasket - 2;
```

(All the names, such as amount, score, and numberOfCards are variables. We are assuming that the variable amount is of type *double*, firstInitial is of type *char*, and the rest of the variables are of type *int*.)

When the assignment statement is executed, the computer first evaluates the expression on the right-hand side of the expression to obtain the value of the expression. Then it uses that value to set the value of the variable on the left-hand side of the assignment operator (equal sign). You can think of the assignment operator (=) as saying, "make the value of the variable equal to what follows."

For example, if the variable numberOfCards has the value 7 and handicap has the value 2, then the following makes 9 the value of the variable score:

```
score = numberOfCards + handicap;
```

The following line from the program in Display 2.1/page 31 is another example of an assignment statement:

```
totalEggs = numberOfBaskets * eggsPerBasket;
```

This assignment statement tells the computer to set the value of totalEggs equal to the number in the variable numberOfBaskets multiplied by the number in the variable eggsPerBasket. The asterisk character '*' is the symbol used for multiplication in Java.

* is multiply

same variable both sides of =

Note that a variable can meaningfully occur on both sides of the assignment operator, =, and can do so in ways that may at first seem a little strange. For example, consider

```
count = count + 10;
```

This does not mean that the value of count is equal to the value of count plus 10, which of course could not be true. This tells the computer to add 10 to the old value of count and then make that the new value of count, which means that this statement will increase the value of count by 10. When an assignment statement is executed, the computer first evaluates the expression on the right-hand side of the assignment operator (i.e., the right-hand side of the equal sign), and then it makes that value the new value of the variable on the left-hand side of the assignment operator. As another example, consider the following assignment statement from Display 2.1:

```
eggsPerBasket = eggsPerBasket - 2;
```

This assignment statement will decrease the value of eggsPerBasket by 2.

The number 2 in the preceding assignment statement is called a **constant.** It is called a *constant* because, unlike a variable such as `eggsPerBasket`, the value of 2 cannot change. (Constants are sometimes also called **literals**.) Constants need not be numbers. For example, `'A'`, `'B'`, and `'$'` are three constants of type *char*. They cannot change their own value, but they can be used in an assignment statement to change the value of a variables of type *char*. For example, the following changes the value of the variable `firstInitial` to `'B'`:

constant

```
firstInitial = 'B';
```

In the preceding assignment statement, the variable `firstInitial` would normally be of type *char*.

Similarly, the following changes the value of the variable `price` to `9.99`:

```
price = 9.99;
```

In the preceding assignment statement, the variable `price` would normally be of type *double*. It cannot be of type *int* or *char*. As the saying goes, "You can't put a square peg in a round hole, and you can't put a *double* value in a variable of type *int*."

Assignment Statements with Primitive Types

An assignment statement with a variable of a primitive type on the left-hand side of the equal sign causes the following action: First, the expression on the right-hand side of the equal sign is evaluated, and then the variable on the left-hand side of the equal sign is set equal to this value.

Syntax Template:

Variable = *Expression*;

Example:

```
score = goals – errors;
interest = rate * balance;
number = number + 5;
```

Specialized Assignment Operators *(Optional)*

You can combine the simple assignment operator (=) with an arithmetic operator, such as +, to produce a kind of special-purpose assignment operator. For example, the following will increase the value of the variable `amount` by 5:

```
amount += 5;
```

This is really just a shorthand for

```
amount = amount + 5;
```

This is hardly a big deal, but it can sometimes be handy.

You can do the same thing with any of the other arithmetic operators –, *, /, and %. For example, consider the following line:

```
amount = amount*25;
```

This line could be replaced by the following equivalent line:

```
amount *= 25;
```

Simple Input and Output

The program in Display 2.1/page 31 uses the same kind of simple input and output as we used in the program we discussed in Chapter 1 (Display 1.4/page 18). In this subsection, we will give you a brief overview of input and output, so you can write and understand programs like the one in Display 2.1. In Section 2.4, we will continue the discussion of input and output that we start here.

As we noted in Chapter 1, `System.out` is an object and `println` is a method of this object that sends output to the screen. So,

```
System.out.println(eggsPerBasket + " eggs per basket.");
```

outputs the value of the variable `eggsPerBasket` (to the screen) followed by the phrase `" eggs per basket."` Be sure to notice that the + sign is not being used for arithmetic here. It is a kind of "and." You can read the preceding output statement as saying output the value of the variable `eggsPerBasket` *and* then output the string `" eggs per basket."`

readLineInt
Next, we consider input. In particular, consider the following line from Display 2.1:

```
numberOfBaskets = SavitchIn.readLineInt();
```

This is an assignment statement that sets the value of the variables `numberOfBaskets` equal to the value returned by the expression

```
SavitchIn.readLineInt()
```

This is an invocation of the method `readLineInt()` of the class `SavitchIn`. As we said in Chapter 1, a method is an action and an invocation of a method causes that action to take place. The action performed by the method `readLineInt` is to read a single integer from a line of input and deliver that value to the program. In this case, the value becomes the new value of the variable `numberOfBaskets`.

There are a few technical details to note about invocations of the method `readLineInt`. First, note that there should be a pair of empty parentheses after the name `readLineInt`. Second, note that the user must input the integer on a line by itself with nothing, except possibly blank space, before or after the number. The value produced by an invocation of the method `readLineInt` (or any similar
value returned
method) is usually referred to as the **value returned** by the method invocation.

The following line from Display 1.4 in Chapter 1 is similar to the invocation of `readLineInt` that we just discussed:

```
answerLetter = SavitchIn.readLineNonwhiteChar();
```

readLine-
NonwhiteChar
The class `SavitchIn` has a number of different methods for reading different kinds of data. The method `readLineNonwhiteChar` reads a single nonblank keyboard character, whereas the method `readLineInt` reads a single integer. Otherwise, the two methods `readLineInt` and `readLineNonwhiteChar` are very similar. There is also a method named `readLineDouble` that can be used to read a value of type *double*, that is, to read a number that contains a decimal point.

We will say more about this kind of input and output in Section 2.4 of this chapter.

Returned Value

An expression like `numberOfBaskets * eggsPerBasket` produces a value. If `numberOfBaskets` has the value 2 and `eggsPerBasket` has the value 10, then the number produced is 20. In computer parlance, this is called the **value returned**. So, we would not say the "the number produced is 20." We would instead say, "the value returned is 20."

The same terminology is used with method invocations. If a method produces a value, we say that the method *returns* the value. For example, in the last of the following program statements, the method invocation `SavitchIn.readLineInt()` produces a value, namely, the value read from the keyboard. This value is called the value *returned* by the method invocation `SavitchIn.readLineInt()`.

```java
int myNumber;
System.out.println("Enter an integer:");
myNumber = SavitchIn.readLineInt();
```

If the Screen Display Goes Away Too Quickly

Some systems make your program output go away as soon as the program ends. Since computers are fast, this means that the screen dialogue can disappear before you get a chance to study it. If this happens on your system, you can add the following (or something very similar) to your programs, and then the screen display will remain visible until the user presses the enter key (also known as the return key):

```java
System.out.println("Press enter key to end program.");
String junk;
junk = SavitchIn.readLine();
```

You insert these three lines at the end of your program. This is what we did in Display Display 1.4/page 18 and in Display 2.1/page 31. However, we will not add these three lines to programs in the rest of this book. Your program may, or may not, need these lines, depending on your particular Java environment.

Number Constants

A variable can have its value changed. That is why it is called a *variable*. Its value *varies*. A literal number like 2 cannot change. It is always 2. It is never 3. Literal values like 2 or 3.7 are called **constants**, because their values do not change. Literal expressions of type other than number types are also called *constant*. So, for example, `'Z'` is a constant of type `char`. There is essentially only one way to write constants of type `char`, namely, placing the character in single quotes. On the other hand, some of the rules for writing number constants are more complicated.

constant

Constants of integer types are written the way you would expect them to be written, like 2, 3, 0, −3, 752, and so forth. An integer constant can be prefaced with a plus or minus sign, as in +12 and −72. Number constants may not contain commas. The expression 1,000 is *not* correct in Java. Integer constants may not contain a decimal point. Numbers with a decimal point are floating-point numbers.

integer
constant

Floating-point constant numbers may be written in either of two forms. The simple form is like the everyday way of writing numbers with digits after the decimal point. The other, slightly more complicated, form is similar to a kind of notation commonly used in the physical sciences.

floating-point
constant

The more complicated notation for floating-point constants is frequently called **e notation, scientific notation,** or **floating-point notation.** For instance, consider the number 865000000.0, which can be expressed more clearly in the following form that is used in mathematics and physics but is not Java notation:

$$8.65 \times 10^8$$

Java has a similar notation, but since keyboards have no way of writing exponents, the 10 is omitted and both the multiplication sign and the 10 are replaced by the letter e. So, in Java 8.65×10^8 is written as 8.65e8 (or in the less convenient form 865000000.0). The two forms 8.65e8 and 865000000.0 are equivalent in a Java program.

Similarly, the number 4.83×10^{-4}, which is equal to 0.000483, could be written as 4.83e-4 in Java The e stands for *exponent*, since it is followed by a number that is thought of as an exponent of 10.

Since multiplying by 10 is the same as moving the decimal point in a number, you can think of the number after the e as telling you to move the decimal point that many digits to the right. If the number after the e is negative, you move the decimal point that many digits to the left. For example, 2.48e4 is the same number as 24800.0 and 2.48e-2 is the same number as 0.0248.

The number before the e may be a number with a decimal point or a number without a decimal point. The number after the e cannot contain a decimal point

In Java, no integer or floating-point number constant may contain a comma. For example, 5,000 is expressed as 5000 without any comma.

What Is "Floating" in a Floating-Point Number?

Floating-point numbers got their name because, with the e notation we described in this subsection, the decimal point can be made to "float" to a new location by adjusting the exponent. The decimal point in 0.000483 can be made to float to after the 4 by expressing this number as the equivalent expression 4.83e-4. Computer language implementers use this trick to store each floating-point number as a number with exactly one digit before the decimal point (and some suitable exponent). Since the implementation always floats the decimal point in these numbers, they are called *floating-point numbers*. (The numbers are actually stored in base 2, rather than as the base 10 numerals we used in our example, but the principle is the same.) □

Assignment Compatibilities

You cannot put a square peg in a round hole, and similarly you cannot put a value of one type in a variable of another type. You cannot put an *int* value like 42 in a variable of type *char*. You cannot put a *double* value like 3.5 in a variable of type *int*. You cannot even put the *double* value 3.0 in a variable of type *int*. You cannot store a value of one type in a variable of another type unless the value is somehow converted to match the type of the variable. However, when dealing with numbers, this conversion will sometimes (but not always) be performed automatically for you. You can always assign a value of an integer type to a variable of a floating-point type, such as

```
double doubleVariable;
doubleVariable = 7;
```

Slightly more subtle assignments such as the following are also allowed:

```
int intVariable;
intVariable = 7;
double doubleVariable;
doubleVariable = intVariable;
```

More generally, you can assign a value of any type on the following list to a variable of any type that appears further down on the list:

```
byte-->short-->int-->long-->float-->double
```

For example, you can assign a value of type *byte* to a variable of any of the other types listed. (Note that this is not an arbitrary ordering of the types. As you move down the list from left to right, the types become more complex, either because they allow larger values or because they allow decimal points in the numbers.)

If you want to assign a value of type *double* to a variable of type *int*, then you must change the type of the value using a *type cast*, as explained in the next subsection.

Assignment Compatibilities

You can assign a value of any type on the following list to a variable of any type that appears further down on the list:

```
byte-->short-->int-->long-->float-->double
```

In particular, note that you can assign a value of any integer type to a variable of any floating-point type.

Type Casting

The title of this subsection has nothing to do with the Hollywood notion of *type casting*. In fact, it has to do with something that is almost the opposite. In Java (and most programming languages), a **type cast** is the changing of the type of a value from its normal type to some other type, such as changing the type of 2.0 from *double* to *int*. In the previous subsection, we described when you could assign a value of one type to a variable of another type. In all other cases, if you want to assign a value of one type to a variable of another type, you must perform a type cast. So, let's discuss how this is done in Java.

type cast

For example, suppose we have the following:

```
double distance;
distance = 9.0;
int points;
points = distance;
```

This is an illegal assignment.

As the note indicates, the last statement is illegal in Java. You cannot assign a value of type *double* to a variable of type *int*, even if the value of type *double* happens to have all zeros after the decimal point and so is conceptually a "whole number."

In order to change a value of type *double* to a value of type *int*, you must place (*int*) in front of the value or the variable holding the value. For example, the preceding illegal assignment can be replaced by the following and you will get a legal assignment:

```
points = (int)distance;
```

This is a legal assignment.

The expression (*int*)distance is called a type cast. This does not change the value stored in the variable distance, but it does change the value returned by the expression. Thus, in the assignment

```
points = (int)distance;
```

neither distance nor the value stored in distance is changed in any way. But, the value stored in points is the "*int* version" of the value stored in distance. If the value of distance is 9.0, then the value of distance remains 9.0, but 9 is used to set the value of points.

In cases where the *double* value is not conceptually a whole number, the effect of a type cast can be even greater. For example, consider the following:

```
double dinnerBill;
dinnerBill = 26.99;
int numberOfDollars;
numberOfDollars = (int)dinnerBill;
```

This does not set numberOfDollars to 27. It sets numberofDollars to 26. In the case of a floating-point value, like 26.99, when you convert the value to an integer value with a type cast, the result is the whole number obtained by discarding the part after the decimal point. So, 26.99 yields the *int* value 26 as a result of the type cast, not the value 27. The result is *not rounded*.

When you assign an integer value to a variable of a floating-point type (such as a variable of type *double*), the integer is type cast to the type of the variable, but in this case the type cast is done automatically for you. For example, consider

```
double point;
point = 7;
```

the preceding assignment statement is equivalent to

```
point = (double)7;
```

The type cast (*double*) is really there in both versions of the assignment, but if you omit the (*double*), then Java acts as if the (*double*) were there.

Type Casting

In many situations, you are not allowed to store a value of one type in a variable of another type. In these situations, you must use a **type cast** that converts the value to an "equivalent" value of the target type.

Syntax Template:

> (*Type_Name*) *Expression*

Example:

```
double guess;
guess = 7.8;
int answer;
answer = (int) guess;
```

The value stored in `answer` will be 7. Note that the value is truncated, *not rounded*. Also note that the variable `guess` is not changed in any way. This only effects the value stored in `answer`.

⚠ GOTCHA Type Casting a Character to an Integer

Java sometimes treats values of type `char` as integers, but the assignment of integers to characters has no connection to the meaning of the characters. For example, the following type cast will output the `int` value corresponding to the character '7':

```
char symbol;
symbol = '7';
System.out.println((int)symbol);
```

You might expect the preceding to output 7 to the screen, but it does not. It outputs the number 55. The `int` value corresponding to '7' is 55. The reason for this is that the `int` values corresponding to `char` values are used for all characters and not just for digits. So, there is nothing special about digits, and so no effort was made to have digits correspond to their intuitive values.

◑ PROGRAMMING TIP Initialize Variables

A variable that has been declared but that has not yet been given a value by some means, such as an assignment statement or being given a value from the keyboard, is said to be **uninitialized.** If the variable is a class variable, it literally has no value. If the variable is a variable of a primitive type, then it may have some default value. However, it makes your program clearer to explicitly give a variable a value, even if you are simply reassigning it the default value. (The exact details on default values is something that can change and should not be counted on.)

uninitialized variable

One easy way to ensure that you do not have an uninitialized variable is to initialize it within the declaration. Simply combine the declaration and an assignment statement as in the following examples:

```
int count = 0;
double taxRate = 0.075;
char grade = 'A';
int balance = 1000, newBalance;
```

Note that you can initialize some variables and not initialize other variables in a declaration.

Sometimes the compiler may complain saying that you have failed to initialize a variable. In most cases, you will indeed have failed to initialize the variable. Occasionally, the compiler is mistaken in giving this advice. However, the compiler will not compile your program until you convince it that the variable in question is initialized. To make the compiler happy, initialize the variable when it is declared, even if the variable will be given a different value before the variable is used for anything. In such cases, you cannot argue with the compiler.

Combining a Variable Declaration and an Assignment

You can combine the declaration of a variable with an assignment statement that gives the variable a value.

Syntax Template:

```
Type Variable_1 = Expression__1,
     Variable_2 = Expresssion__2, . . .;
```

Example:

```
int numberSeen = 0, increment = 5;
double height = 12.34, prize = 7.3 + increment;
char answer = 'y';
```

▲ GOTCHA Imprecision in Floating-Point Numbers

Floating-point numbers are stored with a limited amount of accuracy and so are, for all practical purposes, only approximate quantities. For example, the floating-point number 1.0/3.0 is equal to

```
0.3333333...
```

where the three dots indicate that the 3's go on forever. The computer stores numbers something like the decimal representation on the previously displayed line, but the computer only has room for a limited number of digits. If that number is 10 digits after the decimal, then 1.0/3.0 is stored as

```
0.3333333333  (and no more 3's)
```

So, 1.0/3.0 is stored as a number slightly smaller than one-third. In other words, the value stored as 1.0/3.0 is only approximately equal to one-third. In reality, the computer stores numbers in binary notation, rather than as numbers in base 10, but the principles are the same and the same sort of things happen. Some numbers lose accuracy when they are stored in the computer.

Floating-point numbers (like numbers of type *double*) and integers (like numbers of type *int*) are stored differently. As we indicated in the previous paragraph, floating-point numbers are, in effect, stored as approximate quantities. Integers, on the other hand, are stored as exact quantities. This difference sometimes can be subtle. For example, the numbers 5 and 5.0 are conceptually the same number. But Java considers them to be different. The whole number 5 is of type *int* and is an exact quantity. The number 5.0 is of type *double*, because it contains a fraction part (even though the fraction is 0), and so 5.0 is stored with only a limited amount of accuracy.

? SELF-TEST QUESTIONS

1. Give the declaration for a variable called count of type *int*. The variable should be initialized to zero in the declaration.

2. Give the declaration for two variables of type *double*. The variables are to be named rate and time. Both variables should be initialized to zero in the declaration.

3. Give the declaration for two variables called miles and flowRate. Declare the variable miles to be of type *int* and initialize it to zero in the declaration. Declare the variable flowRate to be of type *double* and initialize it to 50.56 in the declaration.

4. Give a Java assignment statement that will set the value of the variable interest to the value of the variable balance multiplied by 0.05. The variables are of type *double*.

5. Give a Java assignment statement that will set the value of the variable interest to the value of the variable balance multiplied by the value of the variable rate. The variables are of type *double*.

6. Give a Java assignment statement that will increase the value of the variable count by 3. The variable is of type *int*.

7. What is the output produced by the following lines of program code?
```
char a, b;
a = 'b';
System.out.println(a);
b = 'c';
System.out.println(b);
a = b;
System.out.println(a);
```

8. In the section entitled **GOTCHA Type Casting a Character to an Integer,** we saw that the following does not output the integer 7:
```
char symbol;
symbol = '7';
System.out.println((int)symbol);
```

Thus, (*int*)symbol does not produce the number corresponding to the digit in symbol. Can you give an expression that will work to produce the integer that intuitively corresponds to the digit in symbol (assuming that symbol contains one of the 10 digits '0', '1', ..., '9')? *Hint*: The digits do correspond to consecutive integers, so if (*int*)'7' is 55, then (*int*)'8' is 56.

Arithmetic Operators

In Java you can form arithmetic expression involving addition (+), subtraction (−), multiplication (*), and division (/) in basically the same way that you would form them in ordinary arithmetic or algebra. You can combine variables and/or numbers using the arithmetic operators +, −, *, and /. The meaning of such an expression is basically what you expect it to be, but there are some subtleties about the type of the result and occasionally even about the value of the result. All of the arithmetic operators can be used with numbers of any of the integer types, any of the floating-point types, and even with numbers of differing types. The type of the value produced depends on the types of the numbers being combined.

mixing types

Let's start our discussion with simple expressions that only combine two variables and/or numbers. If both operands (i.e., both numbers and/or variables) are of the same type, then the result is of that type. If one of the operands is of a floating-point type and the other is of an integer type, then the result is of the floating-point type. For example, consider the expression

```
amount - adjustment
```

If the variables amount and adjustment are both of type *int*, then the result (the value returned) is of type *int*. If either amount or adjustment, or both, are of type *double*, then the result is of type *double*. If you replace the operator − with any of the operators +, *, or /, then the type of the result is determined in the same way.

Larger expressions using more than two operands can always be viewed as a series of steps each of which involve only two operands. For example, to evaluate the expressions

```
balance + (balance*rate)
```

you (or the computer) evaluate balance*rate and obtain a number, and then you combine that number with balance using addition. This means that the same rule that we used to determine the type of an expression with two operands can also be used for more complicated expressions: If all the items being combined are of the same type, then the result is of that type. If some of the items being combined are of integer type and some are of floating-point type, then the result is of a floating-point type.

Knowing whether the value produced is of an integer type or a floating-point type is typically all that you need to know. However, if you need to know the exact type of the value produced by an arithmetic expression, it can be determined as follows: The type of the value produced is one of the types used in the expression, and of all the types used in the expression, it is the last type (reading left to right) on the following list:

```
byte-->short-->int-->long-->float-->double
```

The division operator / deserves special attention, because the type of the result can affect the value produced in a dramatic way. When you combine two numbers with the division operator / and at least one of the numbers is of type *double* (or of some other floating-point type), then the result is what you would normally expect of a division. For example, 9.0/2 has one operand of type *double*, namely, 9.0. Hence, the result is the type *double* number 4.5. However, when both operands are of an integer type, the result can be surprising. For example 9/2 has two operands of type *int,* and so it yields the type *int* result 4, not 4.5. The fraction after the decimal point is simply lost. Be sure to notice that when you divide two integers, the result *is not rounded*; the part after the decimal point is discarded no matter how large it is. So, 11/3 is 3 (not 3.6666...). If there is nothing but a zero after the decimal point, then that decimal point and zero after the decimal point are still lost, and even this seemingly trivial difference can be of some significance. For example, 8.0/2 evaluates to the type *double* value 4.0, which is only an approximate quantity. However, 8/2 evaluates to the *int* value 4, which is an exact quantity. The approximate nature of 4.0 can affect the accuracy of any further calculation that is performed with this result.

division

integer division

The % **operator** can be used with operands of integer types to recover something equivalent to the fraction after the decimal point. When you divide one integer by another, you get a result (which some call a quotient) and a remainder. For example, 14 divided by 4 yields 3 with a remainder of 2. To rephrase it, 14 divided by 4 is 3 with 2 left over. The % operation gives the remainder, i.e., the amount left over, after doing the division. So, 14/4 evaluates to 3 and 14%4 evaluates to 2, because 14 divided by 4 is 3 with 2 left over.

the % operator

The % operator has more applications than you might at first suspect. It allows your program to count in 2's, 3's, or any other number. For example, if you want to do something to every other integer, you need to know if the integer is even or odd. Then, you can do it to every even integer (or alternatively every odd integer). An integer n is even if n%2 is equal to 0 and the integer is odd if n%2 is equal to 1. Similarly, if you want your program to do something to every third integer, then your program can step through all the integers using an *int* variable n to store the integer and can test n%3. In this case, your program might only do the action when n%3 is equal to 0.

Parentheses can be used to group things in an arithmetic expression in the same way as you use parentheses in algebra and arithmetic. With the aid of parentheses, you can tell the computer which operations are performed first, second, and so forth. For example, consider the following two expressions that differ only in the positioning of their parentheses:

parentheses

```
(cost + tax) * discount
cost + (tax * discount)
```

To evaluate the first expression, the computer first adds cost and tax and then multiplies the result by discount. To evaluate the second expression, it multiplies tax and `discount` and then adds the result to `cost`. If you use some numbers for the values of the variables and carry out the two evaluations, you will see that they produce different results.

If you omit parentheses, the computer will still evaluate the expression. For example, consider the following assignment statement:

```
total = cost + tax * discount;
```

This is equivalent to

```
total = cost + (tax * discount);
```

precedence rules

When parentheses are omitted, the computer performs multiplication before addition. When the order of operations are not determined by parentheses the computer follows rules known as **precedence rules.** These precedence rules are similar to rules used in algebra classes. However, except for some very standard cases, it is best to include the parentheses, even if the intended order of operations is the one indicated by the precedence rules. The parentheses make the expression clearer to a person reading the program code. One standard case where it is normal to omit parentheses is a multiplication within an addition. So,

```
balance = balance + (interestRate*balance);
```

would usually be written

```
balance = balance + interestRate*balance;
```

Both forms are acceptable and the two forms have the same meaning. We will discuss precedence rules in more detail in Chapter 3.

spacing

When writing arithmetic expressions, you can insert spaces before and after operations or you can omit them. Similarly, you can insert or omit spaces around parentheses.

Display 2.3 shows some examples of how you write arithmetic expression in Java and indicates some of the parentheses that would normally be omitted.

Display 2.3 Arithmetic Expression

Ordinary Mathematical Expression	Java Expression (preferred form)	Equivalent Fully Parenthesized Java Expression
$rate^2 + delta$	`rate*rate + delta`	`(rate*rate) + delta`
$2(salary + bonus)$	`2*(salary + bonus)`	`2*(salary + bonus)`
$\dfrac{1}{time + 3mass}$	`1/(time + 3*mass)`	`1/(time + (3*mass))`
$\dfrac{a - 7}{t + 9v}$	`(a - 7)/(t + 9*v)`	`(a - 7)/(t + (9*v))`

Case Study UVending Machine Change

task
specification

Vending machines do sometimes have small computers to control their operation. In this case study, you will write a program that performs one of the tasks that such a computer would need to do. In this case study, the input and output will be performed via the keyboard and screen. To integrate this into a vending machine computer, you would have to embed the code from this program into a larger program that takes its data from someplace other than the keyboard and send its results to someplace other than the screen, but that's another story. In this case study, the user enters an amount of change from 1 to 99 cents. The program responds by telling the user one combination of coins that equals that amount of change. For example, if the user enters 55 for 55 cents, then the program tells the user that 55 cents can be given as two quarters and one nickel. You decide that the dialogue should read as in the following example, which you write out to see how it looks before coding the program:

```
Enter a whole number from 1 to 99.
I will output a combination of coins
that equal that amount of change.
87
87 cents in coins:
3 quarters
1 dime
0 nickels and
2 pennies
```

The program will need variables to store the amount of change and the number of each type of coin. So, it will need at least the following variables:

int amount, quarters, dimes, nickels, pennies;

That takes care of some routine matters, and now you are ready to tackle the heart of the problem. You need an algorithm to compute the number of each kind of coin. You come up with the following pseudocode:

Algorithm to determine the number of coins in amount **cents:**

Read the amount into the variable amount.
Set the variable quarters **equal to the maximum number of quarters in** amount.
Reset amount **to the change left after giving out that many quarters.**
Set the variable dimes **equal to the maximum number of dimes in** amount.
Reset amount **to the change left after giving out that many dimes.**
Set the variable nickels **equal to the maximum number of nickels in** amount.
Reset amount **to the change left after giving out that many nickels.**
pennies = amount;
Output the original amount and the numbers of each coin.

When you look at your pseudocode, you realize that the algorithm changes the value of amount, but at the end, you want the original amount, so you can output the original amount. So, you use one more variable, called originalAmount, to save the original amount. So, you modified the pseudocode as follows:

pseudocode
revised

Algorithm to determine the number of coins in `amount` cents:

Read the amount into the variable `amount`.
`originalAmount = amount;`
Set the variable `quarters` equal to the maximum number of quarters in `amount`.
Reset `amount` to the change left after giving out that many quarters.
Set the variable `dimes` equal to the maximum number of dimes in `amount`.
Reset `amount` to the change left after giving out that many dimes.
Set the variable `nickels` equal to the maximum number of nickels in `amount`.
Reset `amount` to the change left after giving out that many nickels.
`pennies = amount;`
Output `originalAmount` and the numbers of each coin.

coding

You now need to produce Java code that does the same thing as your pseudocode. Much of it is routine. The first line of your pseudocode is a routine example of prompting the user and then reading input from the keyboard. You produce the following Java code for the first line of pseudocode:

```
System.out.println("Enter a whole number from 1 to 99.");
System.out.println("I will output a combination of coins");
System.out.println("that equals that amount of change.");

amount = SavitchIn.readLineInt();
```

The next line of pseudocode, which sets the value of `originalAmount`, is already Java code. So, you need not do any translating.

Thus far, the main part of your program reads as follows:

```
public static void main(String[] args)
{
    int amount, originalAmount,
        quarters, dimes, nickels, pennies;

    System.out.println("Enter a whole number from 1 to 99.");
    System.out.println("I will output a combination of coins");
    System.out.println("that equals that amount of change.");

    amount = SavitchIn.readLineInt();
    originalAmount = amount;
```

Next, you need to translate the following to Java code:

Set the variable `quarters` equal to the maximum number of quarters in `amount`.
Reset `amount` to the change left after giving out that many quarters.

integer division
/ and %

You give this some thought and decide to try an example. For 55 cents, there are 2 quarters, because 55 divided by 25 is 2 with a remainder of 5. Ah ha! You realize that the operators / and % can be used for this kind of division. For example:

```
55/25  is  2  (the maximum number of 25's in 55)
55%25  is  5  (the remainder)
```

Replacing 55 with `amount` and changing to Java syntax, you produce the following:

```
quarters = amount/25;
amount = amount%25;
```

You realize that dimes and nickels are treated in a similar way, so you next produce the code:

```
dimes = amount/10;
amount = amount%10;
nickels = amount/5;
amount = amount%5;
```

The rest of the program coding is routine. You produce the program shown in
Display 2.4 as your final program.

After producing your program, you need to test it on a number of different
kinds of data. You decide to test it on each of the following inputs: 0 cents, 4 cents,
5 cents, 6 cents, 10 cents, 11 cents, 25 cents, 26 cents, 35 cents, 55 cents, 65 cents, and
a number of other cases. This sounds like a lot of different inputs, but you want to
try cases that give zero values for all possible coin values and want to test values
near change points, like 25 and 26 cents, which changes from all quarters to quarters and another coin. All your tests are successful, but the grammar for the output
is not exactly correct. For 26 cents, you get the output:

testing

```
26 cents in coins:
1 quarters
0 dimes
0 nickels and
1 pennies
```

The output is correct but would read a lot nicer if it said 1 quarter instead of 1
quarters and 1 penny instead of 1 pennies. The techniques you need to produce
this nicer looking output will be presented in the next chapter. So, we will let you end
this project here. The output is correct and understandable.

? SELF-TEST QUESTIONS

9. What is the output produced by the following lines of program code?

```
int quotient, remainder;
quotient = 7/3;
remainder = 7%3;
System.out.println("quotient =  " + quotient);
System.out.println("remainder =  " + remainder);
```

10. What is the output produced by the following lines of program code?

```
double result;
result = (1/2) * 2;
System.out.println("(1/2) * 2 equals " + result);
```

11. Consider the following statement from the program in Display 2.4/page
52:

```
System.out.println(originalAmount + " cents in coins:");
```

Display 2.4 Change Program
••

```
public class ChangeMaker
{
    public static void main(String[] args)
    {
        int amount, originalAmount,
            quarters, dimes, nickels, pennies;

        System.out.println("Enter a whole number from 1 to 99.");
        System.out.println("I will output a combination of coins");
        System.out.println("that equals that amount of change.");

        amount = SavitchIn.readLineInt();
        originalAmount = amount;

        quarters = amount/25;
        amount = amount%25;
        dimes = amount/10;
        amount = amount%10;
        nickels = amount/5;
        amount = amount%5;
        pennies = amount;

        System.out.println(originalAmount + " cents in coins:");
        System.out.println(quarters + " quarters");
        System.out.println(dimes + " dimes");
        System.out.println(nickels + " nickels and");
        System.out.println(pennies + " pennies");
    }
}
```

> 25 goes into 87 three times with 12 left over.
> 87/25 is 3
> 87%25 is 12
> 87 cents is three quarters with 12 cents left over.

Sample Screen Dialogue

```
Enter a whole number from 1 to 99.
I will output a combination of coins
that equals that amount of change.
87
87 cents in coins:
3 quarters
1 dimes
0 nickels and
2 pennies
```

Suppose that in that program, you change the preceding line to the following:

```
System.out.println(amount + " cents in coins:");
```

How will this change the sample dialogue in Display 2.4/page 52?

Increment and Decrement Operators

The increment and decrement operators can be used to increase or decrease the value of a variable by one. They are a very specialized operators and you (and Java) could easily get along without them. But, they are sometimes handy and they are of cultural significance. Programmers use them. So, to be "in the club," you should learn how to use them. Even if you do not want to use them, you need to learn about them so you can understand them when you see them in other programmer's code.

The **increment operator** is written as two plus signs ++. For example, the following will increase the value of the variable count by one:

++ and --

```
count++;
```

This is a Java statement. If the variable count had the value 5 before this statement is executed, then count will have the value 6 after this statement is executed. You can use the increment operator with variables of any numeric type, but they are used most often with variables of integer type (such as the type *int.*)

The **decrement operator** is similar, except that it subtracts one rather than add one to the value of the variable. The decrement operator is written as two minus signs --. For example, the following will decrease the value of the variable count by one:

```
count--;
```

If the variable count had the value 5 before this statement is executed, then count will have the value 4 after this statement is executed.

Note that

```
count++;
```

is equivalent to

```
count = count + 1;
```

and

```
count--;
```

is equivalent to

```
count = count - 1;
```

So, the increment and decrement operators are really very specialized operators.

Why does Java have such very specialized operators? It inherited them from C++. In fact, as you might guess, this increment operator is where the ++ came from in the name of the C++ programming language. Why was it added to the C++ language? Because adding or subtracting one is a very common thing to do when programming.

More About Increment and Decrement Operators *(Optional)*

The increment and decrement operators can be used in expressions. When used in an expression, the increment operator both changes the value of the variable it is applied to and it returns a value. Although we do not recommend using the increment and decrement operators in expressions, you should be familiar with them used in this way, because you are likely to see this use in other people's code.

In expressions, you can place the ++ or −− either before or after the variables, but the meaning is different depending on whether it is before or after the variable. For example, consider the code

```
int n = 3;
int m = 4;
int result;
result = n * (++m);
```

After this code is executed, the value of n is unchanged at 3, the value of m is 5, and the value of result is 15. Thus, ++m both changes the value of m and returns that changed value to be used in the arithmetic expression.

In the previous example, we placed the increment operator in front of the variables. If we place it after the variable m, then something slightly different happens. Consider the code

```
int n = 3;
int m = 4;
int result;
result = n * (m++);
```

In this case, after the code is executed, the value of n is 3 and the value of m is 5, just as in the previous case, but the value of result is 12, not 15. What is the story?

The two expressions n * (++m) and n * (m++) both increase the value of m by 1, but the first expression increases the value of m *before* it does the multiplication, whereas the second expression increases the value of m *after* it does the multiplication. Both ++m and m++ have the same effect on the final value of m, but when you use them as part of an arithmetic expression, they give a different value to the expression. If the ++ is *before* the m, then the value of m is increased *before* its value is used in the expression. If the ++ is *after* the m, then the value of m is increased *after* its value is used in the expression.

The −− operator works the same when it is used in an arithmetic expression. Both −−m and m−− have the same effect on the final value of m, but when you use them as part of an arithmetic expression, they give a different value to the expression. If the −− is *before* the m, then the value of m is decreased *before* its value is used in the expression. If the −− is *after* the m, then the value of m is decreased *after* its value is used in the expression.

The increment and decrement operators can be applied only to variables. They cannot be applied to constants or to entire, more complicated arithmetic expressions.

2.2 The Class String

Strings of characters, such as `"Enter the amount:"`, are treated slightly differently from values of the primitive types. There is no primitive type for strings in Java. However, there is a class, called `String`, that can be used to store and process strings of characters. In this section we discuss this class `String`.   `String`

String Constants and Variables

You have already been using constants of type `String`. The quoted string

```
"Enter the number of eggs in each basket:"
```

which appears in the following statement from the program in Display 2.1/page 31, is a string constant:

```
System.out.println("Enter the number of eggs in each basket:");
```

A value of type `String` is one of these quoted strings. That is, a value of type `String` is a sequence of characters treated as a single item. A variable of type `String` can name one of these string values.

The following declares `greeting` to be the name for a `String` variable:

```
String greeting;
```

The following sets the value of `greeting` to the `String` value `"Hello!"`:

```
greeting = "Hello!";
```

These two statements are often combined into one, as follows:

```
String greeting = "Hello!";
```

Once a `String` variable, such as `greeting`, has been given a value, you can write it out to the screen as follows:

```
System.out.println(greeting);
```

If the value of `greeting` has been set as in the preceding line, then this will cause

```
Hello!
```

to be written on the screen.

String Methods

A `String` variable is not just a simple variable, like a variable of type *int* is. A `String` variable is a variable of a class type. Something of a class type is an object with methods as well as a value. Thus, a `String` variable is an object,[1] and as an ob-

---

1. When you declare a name, like `greeting`, to be of type `String`, `greeting` is not really an object of type `String`; `greeting` is merely a name for an object of type `String`. This sounds like so much double talk, and for what we are doing in this chapter is not a very important distinction. This distinction will turn out to be much more important when we study classes other than `String`, and we will discuss this distinction at that time.

ject, it has methods. These `String` methods can be used to manipulate string values. A few of these `String` methods are described in Display 2.5. As with any method, the method is called (invoked) by writing a dot and the name of the method after the object name. In this section, the object name will always be a variable of type `String`. Any arguments to the method are given in parentheses. Let's look at some examples.

length

The method `length` can be used to get the number of characters in a string. For example, suppose we declare `String` variables as follows:

```
String command = "Sit Fido!";
String answer = "bow-wow";
```

Then `command.length()` returns 9 and `answer.length()` returns 7. Notice that you must include a pair of parentheses, even though there are no arguments to the method `length`. Also notice that spaces, special symbols, and repeated characters are all counted in computing the length of a string. All characters are counted.

You can use a call to the method `length` anywhere that you can use a value of type *int*. For example, all of the following are legal Java statements:

```
int count = command.length();
System.out.println("Length is " + command.length());
count = answer.length() + 3;
```

position

index

Many of the methods for the class `String` depend on counting **positions** in the string. Positions are counted starting with 0 not with 1. So, in the string `"Hi Mom"`, `'H'` is in position 0, `'i'` is in position 1, the blank character is in position 2, and so forth. A position is usually referred to as an **index** in computer parlance. So it would be more normal to say: `'H'` is at index 0, `'i'` is at index 1, the blank character is at index 2, and so forth. Display 2.6 illustrates how index positions are numbered in a string.

The method `indexOf` will return the index of the substring given as its one argument. If the substring occurs more than once, `indexOf` returns the index of the first occurrence of its substring argument. For example, consider

```
String phrase = "Time flies like an arrow.";
```

After this declaration, the invocation `phrase.indexOf("flies")` will return 5 because the `'f'` of `"flies"` is at index 5. (Remember, the first index is 0, not 1.)

+ operator
concatenation

You can connect two strings using the + operator. Connecting ("pasting") two strings together to obtain a larger string is called **concatenation**. So, when it is used with strings, the + is sometimes called the **concatenation operator**. For example, consider the following:

```
String greeting = "Hello";
String sentence;
sentence = greeting + "my friend.";
System.out.println(sentence);
```

This will set the variable `sentence` to `"Hellomy friend."` and will write the following on the screen:

```
Hellomy friend.
```

Display 2.5 Methods in the Class `String`

....

Method	Description	Example
`length()`	Returns the length of the string object.	`String greeting = "Hello!";` `greeting.length()` **returns** 6.

`toLowerCase()`	Returns a string with the same characters as the string object, but with all characters converted to lowercase.	`String greeting = "Hi Mary!";`
		`greeting.toLowerCase()` **returns**
		`"hi mary!"`

`toUpperCase()`	Returns a string with the same characters as the string object, but with all characters converted to uppercase.	`String greeting = "Hi Mary!";`
		`greeting.toUpperCase()` **returns**
		`"HI MARY!"`

`trim()`	Returns a string with the same characters as the string object, but with leading and trailing white space removed.	`String pause = "   Hmm   ";` `pause.trim()` **returns** `"Hmm"`
`charAt(`*Position*`)`	Returns the character in the string at the *Position*. Positions are counted 0, 1, 2, etc.	`String greeting = "Hello!";` `greeting.charAt(0)` **returns** `'H'`. `greeting.charAt(1)` **returns** `'e'`.
`substring(`*Start*`)`	Returns the substring of the string object starting from *Start* through to the end of the string object. Positions are counted 0, 1, 2, etc.	`String sample = "AbcdefG";` `sample.substring(2)` **returns** `"cdefG"`.
`substring(`*Start, End*`)`	Returns the substring of the string object starting from position *Start* through, but not including, position *End* of the string object. Positions are counted 0, 1, 2, etc.	`String sample = "AbcdefG";` `sample.substring(2, 5)` **returns** `"cde"`.

Display 2.5 Methods in the Class `String` **(continued)**

`indexOf(A_String)`	Returns the position of the first occurrence of the string *A_String* in the string object. Positions are counted 0, 1, 2, etc. Returns −1 if *A_String* is not found.	```String greeting = "Hi Mary!";``` `greeting.indexOf("Mary")` returns 3. `greeting.indexOf("Sally")` returns −1.
`indexOf(A_String, Start)`	Returns the position of the first occurrence of the string *A_String* in the string object that occurs at or after position *Start*. Positions are counted 0, 1, 2, etc. Returns −1 if *A_String* is not found.	```String name = "Mary, Mary quite contrary";``` `name.indexOf("Mary", 1)` returns 6. The same value is returned if 1 is replaced by any number up to and including 6. `name.indexOf("Mary", 0)` returns 0. `name.indexOf("Mary", 8)` returns −1.
`lastIndexOf(A_String)`	Returns the position of the last occurrence of the string *A_String* in the string object. Positions are counted 0, 1, 2, etc. Returns −1, if *A_String* is not found.	```String name = "Mary, Mary, Mary quite so";``` `name.lastIndexOf("Mary")` returns 12.
`compareTo(A_String)`	Compares the calling string object and the string argument to see which comes first in the lexicographic ordering. Lexicographic ordering is the same as alphabetical ordering when both strings are either all uppercase or all lowercase. If the calling string is first, it returns a negative value. If the two strings are equal, it returns zero. If the argument is first, it returns a positive number.	```String entry = "adventure";``` `entry.compareTo("zoo")` **returns a negative number.** `entry.compareTo("adventure")` returns zero. `entry.compareTo("above")` returns a positive number.

Notice that no spaces are added when you concatenate two strings using the + operator. If you wanted `sentence` set to `"Hello my friend."`, then you should change the assignment statement to the following (or something that accomplishes the same thing):

```
sentence = greeting + " my friend.";
```

Notice the space before the word `"my"`.

You can concatenate any number of `String` objects using the + operator. You can even connect a `String` object to any other type of object using the + operator. The result is always a `String` object. Java will figure out some way to express any

Display 2.6 String Indexes

The twelve characters in the string "Java is fun." have indexes 0 through 11. The index of each character is given below.

0	1	2	3	4	5	6	7	8	9	10	11
J	a	v	a		i	s		f	u	n	.

Note that the blanks and the period count as characters in the string.

object as a string when you connect it to a string with the + operator. For simple things like numbers, it does the obvious thing. For example:

```
String solution = "The answer is " + 42;
```

will set the String variable solution to "The answer is 42". This is so natural that it may seem like nothing special is happening, but this does require a real conversion from one type to another. The constant 42 is a number, whereas "42" is a string consisting of the two characters '4' followed by '2'. Java converts the number constant 42 to the string constant "42" and then concatenates the two strings "The answer is " and "42".

Using the + Sign with Strings

You can concatenate two strings by connecting them with the + sign.

Example:
```
String name = "Neelix";
String greeting = "Hi " + name;
System.out.println(greeting);
```

This sets greeting to the string "Hi Neelix". So, it outputs the following to the screen:

```
Hi Neelix
```

Note that we needed to add a space at the end of "Hi ".

String Processing

Many references on the Java language say objects of type String cannot be changed. There is a sense in which that is true, but it is a misleading statement. Notice that none of the methods in Display 2.5/page 57 changes the value of the `String` object. There are more `String` methods than those shown in Display 2.5, but none of them lets you write statements that say things like "Change the fifth character in the string object to `'z'`". This is not an accident. This was done intentionally in order to make the implementation of the `String` class more efficient; that is, in order to make the methods execute faster and use less computer memory. There is another string class that has methods for altering the string object. It is called `StringBuffer`, but we will not discuss it here because we do not need it. Although there is no method that allows you to change the value of a `String` object, you can still write programs that change the value of a `String` variable. To perform the change, you simply use an assignment statement, as in the following example:

```
String name = "Mulder";
name = "Fox " + name;
```

The assignment statement in the second line changes the value of the `name` variable so that the string it names changes from `"Mulder"` to `"Fox Mulder"`. Display 2.7 shows a sample program that demonstrates how to do some simple string processing that changes the value of a `String` variable. Part of that program is explained in the next subsection.

Escape Characters

quotes in quotes

Suppose you want to output a string with quotes inside of it. For example, suppose you want to output the following to the screen:

```
The word "hard" starts at index 19
```

The following will not work:

```
System.out.println("The word "hard" starts at index " + 19);
```

This will produce a compiler error message. The problem is that the compiler sees

```
"The word "
```

as a perfectly valid quoted string. Then the compiler sees `hard"`, which is not anything valid in the Java language (although the compiler might guess that it is a quoted string with one missing quote or guess that you forgot a + sign). The compiler has no way to know that you mean to include the `'"'` symbol as part of the quoted string, unless you tell it that you mean to do so. You tell the compiler that you mean to include the quote in the string by placing a **backslash ** before the troublesome character, like so.

backslash \

```
System.out.println("The word \"hard\" starts at index " + 19);
```

This is exactly what we did in the program in Display 2.7 (except that we used a variable, rather than the constant number 19).

escape sequence

Some other special characters that are spelled using a backslash are listed in Display 2.8. These are often called **escape characters** because they escape from the usual meaning of a character such as the usual meaning of the double quote.

Display 2.7 Using the String **Class**

••

```
public class StringDemo
{
    public static void main(String[] args)
    {
        String sentence = "Text processing is hard!";
        int position;

        position = sentence.indexOf("hard");
        System.out.println(sentence);
        System.out.println("01234567890123456789  0123");
        System.out.println("The word \"hard\" starts at index "
                                + position);

        sentence = sentence.substring(0, position) + "easy!";
        System.out.println("The changed string is:");
        System.out.println(sentence);
    }
}
```

Sample Screen Dialogue

```
Text processing is hard!
01234567890123456789  0123
The word "hard" starts at index 19
The changed string is:
Text processing is easy!
```

••

   Including a backslash in a quoted string is a little tricky. For example, the string
"abc\def" is likely to produce the error message "Invalid escape character." To
include a backslash in a string, you need to use two backslashes. The string
"abc\\def", if output to the screen, would produce

    abc\def

Display 2.8 **Escape Characters**

••

\ " Double quote.
\ ' Single quote.
\ \ Backslash.
\ n New line. Go to the beginning of the next line.
\ r Carriage return. Go to the beginning of the current line.
\ t Tab. White space up to the next tab stop.

••

The escape sequence \n indicates that the string starts a new line at the \n. For example, the statement

```
System.out.println("The motto is\nGo for it!");
```

will write the following to the screen

```
The motto is
Go for it!
```

It is important to note that each escape sequence is a single character, even though it is spelled with two symbols. For example, suppose you declare request as follows:

```
String request = "Say \"Hi\"!";
```

then, request.length() returns the value 9, not 11. The 9 characters are

'S' 'a' 'y' the blank '\"' 'H' 'i' '\"' and '!'

It may seem that there is no need for the escape sequence \', since it is perfectly valid to include a single quote inside a quoted string, such as "How's this?". But, you do need \' if you want to indicate the constant for the single-quote character, as in

```
char singleQuote = '\'';
```

The Unicode Character Set

ASCII

Unicode

Most other programming languages use the **ASCII** character set, which is given in Appendix 3. The ASCII character set is simply a list of all the characters normally used on an English-language keyboard together with a standard number assigned to each character. Java uses the **Unicode** character set instead. The Unicode character set includes all the ASCII character set plus many of the characters used in languages that have an alphabet different from English. As it turns out, this is not likely to be a big issue if you are using an English-language keyboard. Normally, you can just program as if Java were using the ASCII character set. The advantage of the Unicode character set is that it makes it possible to easily handle languages other than English. The disadvantage of the Unicode character set is that it sometimes requires more computer memory to store each character than it would if Java used the ASCII character set.

? SELF-TEST QUESTIONS

....

12. What is the output produced by the following?

```
String test = "abcdefg";
System.out.println(test.length());
System.out.println(test.charAt(1));
```

13. What is the output produced by the following?

```
String greeting = "How do you do";
System.out.println(greeting + "Seven of Nine.");
```

14. What is the output produced by the following?

```
String test = "abcdefg";
System.out.println(test.substring(3));
```

2.3 Documentation and Style

> *"Don't stand there chattering to yourself like that,"* Humpty Dumpty said,
> *looking at her for the first time, "but tell me your name and your*
> *business."*
> *"My* name *is Alice, but—"*
> *"It's a stupid name enough!"* Humpty Dumpty interrupted impatiently.
> *"What does it mean?"*
> *"Must a name mean something?"* Alice asked doubtfully.
> *"Of course it must,"* Humpty Dumpty said with a short laugh: *"my* name
> *means the shape I am—and a good handsome shape it is too. With a name*
> *like yours, you might be any shape, almost."*
> **LEWIS CARROLL,** *Through the Looking Glass*

A program that gives the correct output is not necessarily a good program. Obviously, you want your program to give the correct output, but that is not the whole story. Most programs are used many times and are changed to either fix bugs or to accommodate new demands by the user. If the program is not easy to read and understand, it will not be easy to change or might even be impossible to change with any realistic effort. Even if the program is going to be used only once, you should pay some attention to readability. After all, you will have to read the program in order to debug the program.

In this section, we discuss four techniques that can help make your program more readable: meaningful names, indenting, documentation, and defined constants.

◑ PROGRAMMING TIP *Use Meaningful Names for Variables*

The names x and y are almost never good variable names. The name you give to a variable should be suggestive of what the variable is used for. If the variable holds a count of something, you might name it `count`. If the variable holds a tax rate, you might name it `taxRate`.

In addition to giving variables meaningful names and giving them names that the compiler will accept, you should also choose the names that follow the normal practice of programmers. That way it will be easier for others to read your code and to combine your code with their code, should you work on a project with more than one programmer. By convention, variable names are made up entirely of letters and digits. If the name consists of more than one word, punctuate it by using capital letters at the word boundaries, as in `taxRate`, `numberOfTries`, and `timeLeft`. Also, start each variable with a lowercase letter as in the examples we just gave. This convention of starting with a lowercase letter may look strange at first, but it is a convention that is commonly used and you quickly get used to it. The reason we do not start variable names with an uppercase letter is because we use names that start with an uppercase letter for something else (namely, for class names like `String` and `SavitchIn`).

Self-Documenting Code

A **self-documenting** program (or other piece of code) is one that uses well-chosen variable names (and other names) and has a style so clear that what the program does and how it does it is obvious to any programmer who reads the program, even if the program has no comments. To the extent that it is possible, you should strive to make your programs self-documenting. ◻

Documentation and Comments

self-documenting

The documentation for program tells what the program does and how it does it. The best programs are **self-documenting.** That means that, thanks to a very clean style and very well-chosen variable names (and other names), what the program does and how it does it is obvious to any programmer who reads the program. You should strive for such self-documenting programs, but sometimes your programs will need a bit of explanation to make them completely clear. This explanation can be given in the form of what are called *comments.*

`//` comments

Comments are things written into your program that help a person understand the program, but that are ignored by the compiler. In Java, there are two ways of forming comments. Everything after the two symbols `//` through to the end of the line is a comment and is ignored by the compiler. These sorts of comments are handy for short comments, such as

```
String sentence; //Spanish version;
```

If you want a comment of this form to span several lines, then each line must contain the symbols `//`.

`/* */` comments

The second form of comments can more easily span multiple lines. Anything written between the matching symbol pairs `/*` and `*/` is a comment and is ignored by the compiler. For example,

```
/*This program should only
  be used on alternate Thursdays,
  except during leap years when it should
  only be used on alternate Tuesdays.*/
```

This is not a very likely comment, but it does illustrate the use of /* and */ to form comments. These sorts of comments are often formed into boxes by adding extra asterisks as follows:

```
/***************************************
 *This program should only
 *be used on alternate Thursdays,
 *except during leap years when it should
 *only be used on alternate Tuesdays.
 ***************************************/
```

In this book, we will write comments in italic, as illustrated just above. Many text editors automatically highlight comments in some way, such as showing them in a second color.

It is difficult to explain just when you should and when you should not put in a comment. Too many comments can be as bad as too few comments. With too many comments, the really important comments can be lost in a sea of comments that just state the obvious. As we show you more Java features, we will mention likely places for comments. For now, you should normally only need two kinds of comments.

First, every program file should have an explanatory comment at the beginning of the file. This comment should give all the important information about the file, what the program does, the name of the author, how to contact the author, the date that the file was last changed, and in a course, what the assignment is. This comment should be similar to the one shown at the top of Display 2.9.

The second kind of comment you need is a comment to explain any nonobvious details. For example, look at the program in Display 2.9. Note that there are two variables named radius and area. It is obvious that these two variables will hold the values for the radius and area of a circle, respectively. It would be a *mistake* to include comments like the following:

```
double radius; //holds the radius of a circle.
```

However, there is something that is not obvious. What units are used for the radius? Inches? Feet? Meters? Centimeters? So, you should add a comment that explains the units used, as follows:

```
double radius; //in inches
double area; //in square inches
```

These two comments are also shown in Display 2.9. In a well-written program, there should seldom be a need to explain such nonobvious detail, but occasionally such comments are needed.

Indenting

A program has a lot of structure. There are smaller parts within larger parts. For example, there is the part that starts with

Display 2.9 Comments and Indenting

```
/*********************************************
 *Program to determine area of a circle.
 *Author: Jane Q. Programmer.
 *Email Address: janeq@somemachine.etc.etc.
 *Programming Assignment 2.
 *Last Changed: October 7, 1999.
 *********************************************/
public class CircleCalculation
{
    public static void main(String[] args)
    {
        double radius; //in inches
        double area; //in square inches

        System.out.println("Enter the radius of a circle in inches:");
        radius = SavitchIn.readLineDouble();

        area = 3.14159 * radius * radius;

        System.out.println("A circle of radius " + radius + " inches");
        System.out.println("has an area of " + area + " square inches.");
    }
}
```

The vertical lines indicate the indenting pattern

Later in this chapter, we will give an improved version of this program.

Sample Screen Dialogue

```
Enter the radius of a circle in inches:
2.5
A circle of radius 2.5 inches
has an area of 19.6349 square inches.
```

```
public static void main(String[] args)
{
```

This part is ended with a closing curly bracket }. Within this part, there are state- indenting
ments, like assignment statements and `System.out.println` statements. In a simple program of the kinds we have seen thus far, there are basically three levels of
nested structure as indicated by the vertical lines in Display 2.9. Each level of nesting
should be indented to show the nesting more clearly. The outermost structure is not
indented at all. The next level of nested structure is indented. The nested structure
within that is double indented. This is illustrated in Display 2.9.

These levels of nesting are frequently indicated by **curly brackets** { }, but
whether or not there are any curly brackets, you should still indent each level of
nesting.

We prefer to indent by four spaces for each level of indenting. Indenting more
than that results in too little room left on the line. Indenting much less than that just
does not show. Indenting two or three spaces would not be unreasonable, but we
find four spaces to be the clearest. If you are in a class, follow the rules on indenting
given by your instructor. On a programming project, there is likely to be a style
sheet that dictates the number of spaces you should indent. In any event, you
should indent consistently within any one program.

Java Comments

There are two ways to add comments to a Java program (or piece of Java code).
1. Everything after the two symbols // through to the end of the line is a comment and is ignored by the
   compiler.
2. Anything written between the matching symbols pairs /* and */ is a comment and is ignored by
   the compiler.

□

Named Constants

Look again at the program in Display 2.9. You probably recognize the number
`3.14159` as the approximate value of *pi,* the number that is used in many circle calculations and that is often written as π. However, you might not be sure that `3.14159`
is *pi* and not some other number, and somebody other than you might have no idea
of where the number `3.14159` came from. To avoid such confusions, you should always give a name to constants, such as `3.14159`, and use the name instead of writing
out the number. For example, you might give the number `3.14159` the name `PI`.
Then the assignment statement:

```
area = 3.14159 * radius * radius;
```

could be written more clearly as

```
area = PI * radius * radius;
```

How do you give a number, or other constant, a name like `PI`? You could use a
variable named `PI` and initialize it to the desired value, like `3.14159`. But, you
might then inadvertently change the value of this variable. Java provides a mecha-

---

Naming Constants

To define a name for a constant, such as a number, place the reserved words *public static final* in front of a variable declaration that includes the constant as the initializing value. Place this declaration within the class definition, but outside of the *main* method and outside of any other method definitions. (See Display 2.10/ page 69 for a complete example.)

Syntax Template:

```
public static final Type Variable = Constant;
```

Example:

```
public static final int MAX_STRIKES = 3;
public static final double MORTGAGE_INTEREST_RATE = 6.99;
public static final String MOTTO = "The customer is right!";
public static final char SCALE = 'K';
```

Although it is not required, it is the normal practice of programmers to spell named constants using all uppercase letters.

---

nism that allows you to define and initialize a variable and moreover fix the variable's value so it cannot have its value changed. The syntax is

```
public static final Type Variable = Constant;
```

For example, the name PI can be given to the constant 3.14159 as follows:

```
public static final double PI = 3.14159;
```

You can simply take this as a long, peculiarly spelled way of giving a name (like PI) to a constant (like 3.14159), but we can explain most of what is on this line. The part

```
double PI = 3.14159;
```

simply declares PI as a variable and initializes it to 3.14159. The words that precede this modify the variable PI in various ways. The word *public* says there are no restrictions on where you can use the name PI. The word *static* will have to wait until Chapter 5 for an explanation, but be sure to include it. The word *final* means the value 3.14159 is the *final* value assignment to PI, or to phrase it another way, it means that the program is not allowed to change the value of PI.

In Display 2.10, we have rewritten the program from Display 2.9/page 66 so that it uses the name PI as a defined name for the constant 3.14159. Note that the definition of PI is placed outside of the *main* part of the program. As indicated there, defined names for constants need not be near the beginning of a file, but it is good practice to place them near the beginning of the file. This is handy in case you need to change the definition of a named constant. You are not likely to want to change the definition of the named constant PI, but you may want to change the definition of some other named constant in some other program. For example, suppose you have a banking program that contains the defined constant

```
public static final double MORTGAGE_INTEREST_RATE = 6.99;
```

Display 2.10 Naming a Constant

```
/*********************************************
*Program to determine area of a circle.
*Author: Jane Q. Programmer.
*Email Address: janeq@somemachine.etc.etc.
*Assignment Number: 2.
*Last Changed: October 7, 1999.
*********************************************/
public class CircleCalculation
{
    public static final double PI = 3.14159;

    public static void main(String[] args)
    {
        double radius; //in inches
        double area; //in square inches

        System.out.println("Enter the radius of a circle in inches:");
        radius = SavitchIn.readLineDouble();

        area = PI * radius * radius;

        System.out.println("A circle of radius " + radius + " inches");
        System.out.println("has an area of " + area + " square inches.");
    }

}
```

Although it would not be as clear, it is legal to place the definition of PI here instead.

Sample Screen Dialogue

```
Enter the radius of a circle in inches:
2.5
A circle of radius 2.5 inches
has an area of 19.6349 square inches.
```

and suppose the interest rate changes to 8.5%. You can simply change the defined constants to

```
public static final double MORTGAGE_INTEREST_RATE = 8.5;
```

You would then need to recompile your program, but you need not change anything else in your program.

Note that a defined constant, like MORTGAGE_INTEREST_RATE, can save you a lot of work if the constant ever needs to be changed. In order to change the mortgage interest rate from 6.99% to 8.5%, you only needed to change one number. If the program did not use a defined constant, then you would have to look for every occurrence of 6.99 and change it to 8.5. Moreover, even this might not be right. If some of the numbers 6.99 represented the mortgage interest rate and some of the numbers 6.99 represented some other kind of interest, then you would have to decide just what each 6.99 means and that would surely produce confusion and probably introduce errors.

Notice that we have always spelled named constants using all uppercase letters (with the underscore symbol _ used for punctuation), as in the named constants PI and MORTGAGE_INTEREST_RATE. This is not required by the definition of the Java language. However, this is a custom that is almost universally followed and one that it would pay you to adopt. It helps when reading a program if you can easily tell what is a variable, what is a constant, and so forth.

? SELF-TEST QUESTIONS

15. What are the two kinds of comments in Java?

16. What is the output produced by the following Java code:

```
/********************
*Code for Exercise.
********************/
System.out.println("One");
//System.out.println("Two");
System.out.println("And hit it!");
```

17. Although it is kind of silly, state legislatures have been known to pass laws "changing" the value of *pi*. Suppose you live in a state where by law the value of *pi* is exactly 3.14. How must you change the program in Display 2.10/page 69 so as to make the program comply with the law on the value of *pi*?

2.4 Keyboard and Screen I/O

Garbage in, garbage out.
PROGRAMMER'S SAYING

I/O

Input and output of program data are usually referred to as **I/O**. There are many different ways that a Java program can perform I/O (input and output). In this section, we present some very simple ways to handle simple text input typed in at the keyboard and simple text output sent to the screen. In future chapters, we will discuss more elaborate ways to do I/O, including windowing systems for input/output. In order to do I/O in Java, you almost always need to add some classes to the language. Sometimes these are classes that, although not part of the language proper, are nonetheless provided in all implementations of Java. Other times, these classes are not provided along with the language and you must obtain them from whoever wrote the class definitions. In this section, we will do output using a class provided automatically along with the Java language. However, you cannot do simple keyboard input unless you add some class that is not automatically provided along with the Java language. So, we will do input using the class SavitchIn, which is not provided with the Java language but that was written expressly for readers of this text.

Screen Output

We have been using simple output statements since the beginning of this book. This section will simply summarize and explain what we have already been doing. In Display 2.1/page 31, we used statements like the following to send output to the display screen:

```
System.out.println("Enter the number of eggs in each basket:");
     . . .
System.out.println(eggsPerBasket + " eggs per basket.");
```

System.out.
println

System.out is an object that is part of the Java language. It may seem strange to spell an object name with a dot in it, but that need not concern us at this point.

This object, System.out, has println as one of its methods. So the preceding output statements are calls to the method println of the object System.out. Of course, you need not be aware of these details in order to use these output statements. You can consider System.out.println as one rather peculiarly spelled statement. However, you may as well get used to this dot notation and the notion of methods and objects.

In order to use output statements of this form, simply follow the expression System.out.println by what you want to output enclosed in parentheses and then follow that with a semicolon. The things you can output are strings of text in double quotes, like " eggs per basket.", variables like eggsPerBasket, numbers like 5 or 7.3, and almost any other object or value. If you want to output more than one thing, simply place an addition sign between the things you want to output. For example,

```
System.out.println("Lucky number = " + 13
                          + "Secret number = " + number);
```

If the value of number is 7, the output will be

```
Lucky number = 13Secret number = 7
```

Notice that no spaces are added. If you want a space between the 13 and the word Secret in the preceding output (and you probably do), then you should add a space to the string

```
"Secret number = "
```

so that it becomes

```
" Secret number = "
```

Notice that you use double quotes not single quotes and that the left and right quotes are the same symbol. Finally, notice that it is OK to place the statement on two lines if it is too long. However, you should indent the second line and you should break the line before or after a + sign, not in the middle of a quoted string or a variable name.

You can also use the println method to output the value of a String variable, as was done by the following line from Display 2.7/page 61:

```
System.out.println(sentence);
```

Every invocation of println ends a line of output. For example, consider the following statements:

```
System.out.println("One, two, buckle my shoe.");
System.out.println("Three, four, shut the door.");
```

These two statements will cause the following output to appear on the screen:

```
One, two, buckle my shoe.
Three, four, shut the door.
```

print **versus** println

If you want the output from two or more output statements to place all their output on a single line, then use print instead of println. For example:

```
System.out.print("One, two,");
System.out.print(" buckle my shoe.");
System.out.println(" Three, four,");
System.out.println(" shut the door.");
```

will produce the following output:

```
One, two, buckle my shoe. Three, four,
 shut the door.
```

Notice that a new line is not started until you use a println, rather than a print. Also notice that the new line starts *after* outputting the items specified in the println. This is the only difference between print and println.

If there is more than one nonwhitespace character on the line, then readLineNon-whiteChar will read the first such character and discard the rest of the input line. **Whitespace** characters are all characters that print as white space if you output them to paper (or the screen). The only whitespace character you are likely to be concerned with at first is the blank space character. (The start of a new line is also a whitespace character, but that fact is not likely to concern you yet.)

There is a slight difference between readLineNonwhiteChar and the methods that read a single number. For the methods readLineInt and readLineDouble the input number must be on a line with nothing before or after the number except possibly whitespace. The method readLineNonwhiteChar allows anything to be on the line after the first nonwhite character, but ignores the rest of the line. This way, when the user enters a word like yes, readLineNonwhiteChar can read the first letter, like 'y', and ignore the rest of the word yes.

If you want to read in an entire line, you would use the method readLine (without any Int or Double or such at the end). For example,

```
String sentence;
sentence = SavitchIn.readLine();
```

reads in one line of input and places that string in the variable sentence.

The class SavitchIn also has other methods, some of which are discussed in the next subsection.

SavitchIn **Is Not Part of the Java Language**

The class SavitchIn is not part of the Java language and does not come with the Java language. You must add the class yourself. This class was defined by the author for readers of this book. That is why it is named SavitchIn. That way you will know that it was written by Savitch and not think it is part of the Java language. The class SavitchIn is given in Appendix 2 and a copy is provided on the CD that accompanies this book. So, it is easy to obtain.

Why do we use the class SavitchIn? Why don't we simply use the classes provided with the Java language? Unfortunately, the Java language does not provide any classes for simple input. If you want to do simple input from the keyboard, you must add some class or classes.

More Input Methods

All the methods in the class SavitchIn that begin with readLine, such as readLine and readLineInt, always read an entire line of text. That is why their names start with "read line." But, sometimes you do not want to read a whole line. For example, given the input

```
2 4 6
```

you might want to read these three numbers with three statements that put the numbers in three different variables. You can do this with the method readInt. For example, the following might appear in some program:

Input Using `SavitchIn`

You use methods in the class `SavitchIn` to read values from the keyboard. When you invoke one of these methods, you use the class name `SavitchIn` as if it were the calling object. In other words, a typical method invocation has the form

   Variable = `SavitchIn.`*Method_Name*`();`

Although there are other methods in `SavitchIn`, you should normally use the methods that include the word `Line`. These methods each read a single value, such as a number, on a line by itself. The value may have whitespace before and/or after it, but should not have other characters on the line. (The method `readLineNonwhiteChar` is an exception and does allow nonwhitespace to follow the character that it reads.) There is a different method for each type of value you want to read from the keyboard. You need to use the method that matches the type of the value read, such as *int* for a whole number or *char* for a single character.

Syntax Template:
```
Int_Variable = SavitchIn.readLineInt();
Long_Variable = SavitchIn.readLineLong();
Float_Variable = SavitchIn.readLineFloat();
Double_Variable = SavitchIn.readLineDouble();
Char_Variable = SavitchIn.readLineNonwhiteChar();
String_Variable = SavitchIn.readLine();
```

Example:
```
int count;
count = SavitchIn.readLineInt();
long bigOne;
bigOne = SavitchIn.readLineLong();
float increment;
increment = SavitchIn.readLineFloat();
double distance;
distance = SavitchIn.readLineDouble();
char letter;
letter = SavitchIn.readLineNonwhiteChar();
String wholeLine;
wholeLine = SavitchIn.readLine();
```

```
System.out.println("Enter 3 numbers on one line:");
int n1 = SavitchIn.readInt();
int n2 = SavitchIn.readInt();
int n3 = SavitchIn.readInt();
```

The user will be given the prompt:
```
Enter 3 numbers on one line:
```

Suppose that, in response to the prompt, the user enters the following, all on one line, and then presses the enter key:
```
2 4 6
```

Then n1 will be given the value 2, n2 will be given the value 4, and n3 will be given the value 6.

After an integer is read with readInt, the input continues on the same line (unless it just happens to have reached the end of the line). For example, if the user enters

    10 20 30

then the following code

```
int n = SavitchIn.readInt();
String theRest = SavitchIn.readLine();
```

will set n equal to 10 and will set theRest equal to the string "20 30".

Two other similar methods in SavitchIn that read less than a whole line are readDouble and readNonwhiteChar. The only difference between these and readInt is that with readDouble, a value of type *double* is read, and with read-NonwhiteChar, a nonwhitespace character is read. **Whitespace** characters are blanks, tabs, and new lines. For the sort of simple things we will do, the only whitespace that will be relevant are blanks.

whitespace

The methods readInt, readDouble, and readNonwhiteChar each require that the input items be separated by one or more blank spaces. Moreover, these methods do not prompt the user if the input format is incorrect. When using these methods, you need to be certain the input will be entered correctly the first time.

The last method from the class SavitchIn that we will consider here is read-Char. The method readChar reads whatever single character is next in the input stream. For example, consider

```
char c1 = SavitchIn.readChar();
char c2 = SavitchIn.readChar();
char c3 = SavitchIn.readChar();
```

If the user enters

    a b c d e f g h i

where 'a' is the first thing on the line. In this case, c1 will be set to the value 'a', c2 will have its value set to the blank symbol, and c3 will have its value set to 'b'. Any further reading would begin with the blank after the letter 'b'.

As indicated in the next Gotcha section, it is safer to use the methods that begin with readLine and that read a whole line and to only use the other methods sparingly and with caution.

⚠ *GOTCHA* readInt *and* readDouble

The methods readLineInt and readLineDouble in the class SavitchIn will prompt the user to reenter the input if the user enters it in an incorrect format. The methods readInt and readDouble, on the other hand, have no such recovery mechanisms. If the user enters the input in an incorrect format, the program will be aborted. For this reason, you should try to use the methods readLineInt and readLineDouble and avoid using the methods readInt and readDouble. The methods readInt and readDouble should be reserved for when you are certain that the input will be in the correct format, and for most of our applications, you cannot count on the user entering the input in the correct format.

The methods `readChar` and `readNonwhiteChar` also do no checking for the format of the input, but they are less dangerous since they will process almost any kind of input the user enters. After all, all input consists of characters of some sort. Even the input 178, which might be considered to be an integer, can be processed as the three-character input '1', followed by '7', followed by '8'.

Why Aren't `readInt` and `readDouble` Better?

Why don't `readInt` and `readDouble` prompt the user to correctly reenter input that is incorrect? They could easily be written that way, but they would confuse the user. The reason is that such prompts are likely to be in confusing places. The operating system always reads an entire line and then gives the entire line to Java. If the user enters four things on a line, and there is a format mistake in the second thing, then the operating system will read the whole line before Java notices anything wrong. So, the prompt to reenter would come after the fourth thing on the line, not after the second thing on the line where it applies. It would be possible to design `readInt` and `readDouble` so that they prompted for correctly reentering input and did so in an understandable way, but it would not be either simple to write or simple to understand. Moreover, many input methods in many languages behave like `readInt` and `readDouble`, so you should be made aware of such problems. ◻

◉ *PROGRAMMING TIP* Echo Input

echoing input

You should always write out all input so that the user can check that the input was entered correctly. This is called **echoing the input.** For example, the following two statements from the program in Display 2.1/page 31 are echoing the two input values that were read into the variables `eggsPerBasket` and `numberOfBaskets`:

```
System.out.println(eggsPerBasket + " eggs per basket.");
System.out.println(numberOfBaskets + " baskets.");
```

It may seem that echoing input is not needed. After all, when the user enters input, it appears on the screen as it is entered. Why bother to write it to the screen a second time? There are several reasons for this. First of all, the input might be incorrect even though it looks correct. For example, the user might use a comma instead of a decimal point, or the letter "Oh" in place of a zero. Echoing the input will reveal such problems. Also, the echoed input gets the user's attention. Some users do not look at the screen as they type in input. In an ideal program, the user should even be given the opportunity to reenter the input if it is incorrect, but we do not yet have enough tools to do that. However, when something is wrong with the input, we do want the user to at least be aware that there is a problem.

? SELF-TEST QUESTIONS

18. Write Java statements that will cause the following to be written to the screen:

```
Once upon a time,
there were three little programmers.
```

19. What is the difference between `System.out.println` and `System.out.print`?

20. Write a Java statement that will set the value of the variable `amount` equal to the number typed in at the keyboard. Assume that `amount` is of type *double* and that the input is entered on a line by itself.

21. Write a Java statement that will set the value of the variable `answer` equal to the first nonwhitespace character typed in at the keyboard. The rest of the line of input is discarded. The variable `answer` is of type *char*.

22. What are the whitespace characters?

Chapter Summary

☐ A variable can be used to hold values, like numbers. The type of the variable must match the type of the value stored in the variable.

☐ Variables (and all other items in a program) should be given names that indicate how the variable is used.

☐ All variables should be initialized before the program uses their value.

☐ Parentheses in arithmetic expressions indicate the order in which the operations are performed.

☐ You should define names for number constants in a program and use these names rather than writing out the numbers within your program.

☐ Programs should be self-documenting to the extent possible. Occasionally, however, you will need to insert comments to explain some unclear points.

☐ The methods in the class `SavitchIn` can be used to read keyboard input. The class `SavitchIn` is not part of the Java language, and so you must have a copy of `SavitchIn` in order to use it.

☐ Your program should output a prompt line when the user is expected to enter data from the keyboard.

☐ All input from the keyboard should be written out (echoed) at some point before the program ends.

? ANSWERS to Self-Test Questions

1. *int* count = 0;
2. *double* rate = 0.0, time = 0.0;

    The following is also correct, since Java will automatically convert the *int* value 0 to the *double* value 0.0:

    double rate = 0, time = 0;

3.
    int miles = 0;

```
double flowRate = 50.56;
```

4. `interest = 0.05 * balance;`

The following is also correct:

```
interest = balance * 0.05;
```

5. `interest = balance * rate;`

6. `count = count + 3;`

7.
```
b
c
c
```

The last output is c because the last assignment (shown in what follows) has no quotes:

```
a = b;
```

This last assignment sets the variable a equal to the value of the variable b, which is `'c'`.

8.

```
(int)symbol - (int)'0'
```

To see that this works, note that it works for `'0'`, then see that it works for `'1'`, then `'2'`, and so forth. You can use an actual number in place of `(int)'0'`, but this way, using `(int)'0'`, is a bit easier to understand.

9.
```
quotient = 2;
remainder = 1;
```

10. `(1/2) * 2 is equal to 0.0`
This is because `1/2` is integer division, which discards the part after the decimal point and produces `0`, instead of `0.5`.

11. The dialogue would change to the following. (The only change is shown in color.)

```
Enter a whole number from 1 to 99
I will output a combination of coins
that equals that amount of change.
87
2 cents in coins:
3 quarters
1 dimes
0 nickels and
2 pennies
```

12.
```
7
b
```

13. `How do you doSeven of Nine.`
Note that there is no space in `doSeven`.

14. `defg`

15. The two kinds of comments are `//` comments and `/* */` comments. Everything following a `//` on the same line is a comment. Everything between a `/*` and a matching `*/` is a comment.

16.
```
One
And hit it!
```

17. Change the line

public static final double `PI = 3.14159;`

to

public static final double `PI = 3.14;`

Since values of type *double* are only stored with a limited amount of accuracy, you could argue that this is not "exactly" 3.14, but any legislator who is stupid enough to legislate the value of *pi* is unlikely to be aware of this subtlety.

18.
```
System.out.println("Once upon a time,");
System.out.println("there were three little programmers.");
```

Since we did not specify where the next output goes, the following is also correct:

```
System.out.println("Once upon a time,");
System.out.print("there were three little programmers.");
```

19. With `System.out.println`, the next output goes on the next line. (By the next output, we mean the output that is produced by the first output statement after the `System.out.println` under discussion.) With `System.out.print`, the next output goes on the same line.

20. `amount = SavitchIn.readLineDouble();`

21. `answer = SavitchIn.readLineNonwhiteChar();`

22. The whitespace characters are the blank symbol, the tab symbol, and the new-line symbol `'\n'`. At this point you are likely to be concerned mostly with the blank symbol when discussing nonwhitespace characters.

? PROGRAMMING EXERCISES

1. Write a program that reads in three whole numbers and outputs the average of the three numbers.

2. Write a program that reads in the amount of a mortgage payment, the outstanding balance (i.e., the amount still owed), and that outputs the amount of the payment that goes to interest and the amount that goes to principal (i.e., the amount that goes to reducing the debt). Assume the annual interest rate is 6.79%. Use a defined constant for the interest rate. Note that payments are made monthly, so the interest is only one-twelfth of the annual interest of 6.79%.

3. Write a program that reads in a four digit number (like 1998) and that outputs the number one digit per line, like so:

```
1
9
9
8
```

Your prompt should tell the user to enter a four-digit number and can then assume that the user follows directions. Your program will not read the number as a value of type *int*, but as four characters of type *char*.

4. Write a program that reads in a line of text and then outputs that line of text with the first occurrence of "hate" changed to "love". For example, a possible sample dialogue might be

```
Enter a line of text.
I hate you.
I have rephrased that line to read:
I love you.
```

You can assume that the word "hate" occurs in the input. If the word "hate" occurs more than once in the line, then your program will only replace the first occurrence of "hate".

5. Write a program that will read a line of text as input and then output the line with the first word moved to the end of the line. For example, a possible sample dialogue might be'

```
Enter a line of text. No punctuation please.
Java is the language
I have rephrased that line to read:
is the language Java
```

Assume that there is no space before the first word and that the end of the first word is indicated by a blank (not by a comma or other punctuation).

Chapter 3

FLOW OF CONTROL

3.1 BRANCHING STATEMENTS 84
The *if-else*-Statement 84
Introduction to Boolean
    Expressions 88
Gotcha Using == with Strings 91
Nested Statements and Compound
    Statements 94
Gotcha Matching *else*'s and *if*'s 95
Multibranch *if-else*-
    Statements 97
Programming Example Assigning Letter
    Grades 98
The *switch*-Statement 101
Gotcha Omitting a *break*-
    Statement 104

3.2 JAVA LOOP STATEMENTS 107
while-Statements 108
Programming Tip A *while*-Loop Can
    Perform Zero Iterations 110
The *do-while*-Statement 111
Programming Example
    Bug Infestation 113
Gotcha Infinite Loops 116
The *for*-Statement 118
The Comma in *for*-Statements
    (Optional) 121
Gotcha Extra Semicolon in a Loop
    Statement 121

Choosing a Loop Statement 124
The *break*-Statement in
    Loops 124
Gotcha Misuse of *break*-
    Statements 124
The *exit* Method 126

3.3 PROGRAMMING WITH LOOPS 128
The Loop Body 128
Initializing Statements 129
Ending a Loop 130
Programming Example
    Nested Loops 132
Programming Tip Do Not Declare
    Variables in a Loop Body 132
Loop Bugs 135
Tracing Variables 137

3.4 THE TYPE *boolean* 138
Boolean Expressions and Boolean
    Variables 139
Precedence Rules 140
Input and Output of Boolean
    Values 144
Case Study Using a Boolean Variable
    to End a Loop 144

Chapter Summary 146
Answers to Self-Test Questions 148
Programming Exercises 152

3

FLOW OF CONTROL

. . . .

> *"Would you tell me, please, which*
> *way I ought to go from here?"*
> *"That depends a good deal on where*
> *you want to get to," said the Cat.*
> **LEWIS CARROLL,** *Alice in Wonderland*

Introduction

flow of control

Flow of control refers to the order in which actions are performed by your program. Until this chapter, that order has been very simple. The actions were taken in the order in which they were written down. In this chapter, we show you how to write programs with more complicated flow of control. Java, and most other programming languages, uses two kinds of statements to produce this more complicated flow of control: A **branching statement** chooses one action from a list of two or more possible actions. A **loop statement** repeats some action again and again until some stopping condition is met

branching
statement

loop statement

Prerequisites

You need to be familiar with the material in Chapter 2 before reading this chapter.

3.1 Branching Statements

> *When you come to a fork in the road, take it.*
> **ATTRIBUTED TO YOGI BERRA**

The most basic branching statement in Java chooses between two possible alternative actions. We begin our discussion with this basic kind of Java statement.

The *if-else*-Statement

In programs, as in everyday life, things can sometimes go in one of two different ways. If you have money in your checking account, the bank will pay you a little interest. On the other hand, if you have overdrawn your checking account so your account balance is negative, then you will be charged a penalty that will make your balance more negative. This might be reflected in the bank's accounting program by the following Java statement, known as an *if-else*-statement:

if-else

```
if (balance >= 0)
    balance = balance + (INTEREST_RATE * balance)/12;
else
    balance = balance - OVER_DRAWN_PENALTY;
```

The two symbols >= are used for greater-than-or-equal-to in Java, because the symbol ≥ is not on the keyboard.

The meaning of an *if-else*-statement is really just the meaning it would have if read as an English sentence. When your program executes an *if-else*-statement, it first checks the expression in parentheses after the *if*. This expression must be something that is either true or false. If it is true, then the statement before the *else* is executed. If the expression is false, then the statement after the *else* is executed. In the preceding example, if balance is positive (or zero), then the following action is taken. (The division by 12 is because this is for only one of twelve months.)

```
balance = balance + (INTEREST_RATE * balance)/12;
```

On the other hand, if the value of balance is negative, the following is done instead:

```
balance = balance - OVER_DRAWN_PENALTY;
```

Display 3.1 shows this *if-else*-statement in a complete program.

If you want to include more than one statement in each branch, then simply enclose the statements in curly brackets, as in the following example:

```
if (balance >= 0)
{
    System.out.println("Good for you. You earned interest.");
    balance = balance + (INTEREST_RATE * balance)/12;
}
else
{
    System.out.println("You will be charged a penalty.");
    balance = balance - OVER_DRAWN_PENALTY;
}
```

If you omit the *else* part, then when the expression after the *if* is false, nothing happens. For example, if your bank does not charge any overdraft penalty, then the statement in their program would be the following, instead of the preceding one:

else is optional

```
if (balance >= 0)
{
    System.out.println("Good for you. You earned interest.");
    balance = balance + (INTEREST_RATE * balance)/12;
}
```

To see how this statement works, let's give it a little more context by adding some additional statements, as shown in what follows:

<Text continues on page 88.>

Display 3.1 A Program Using *if-else*

● ●

```java
public class BankBalance
{
    public static final double OVER_DRAWN_PENALTY = 8.00;
    public static final double INTEREST_RATE = 0.02;//2% annually

    public static void main(String[] args)
    {
        double balance;

        System.out.print("Enter your checking account balance: $");
        balance = SavitchIn.readLineDouble();
        System.out.println("Original balance $" + balance);

        if (balance >= 0)
            balance = balance + (INTEREST_RATE * balance)/12;
        else
            balance = balance - OVER_DRAWN_PENALTY;

        System.out.println("After adjusting for one month");
        System.out.println("of interest and penalties,");
        System.out.println("your new balance is $" + balance);
    }
}
```

Sample Screen Dialogue 1

```
Enter your checking account balance: $505.67
Original balance $505.67
After adjusting for one month
of interest and penalties,
your new balance is $506.51278
```

Sample Screen Dialogue 2

```
Enter your checking account balance: $-15.53
Original balance $-15.53
After adjusting for one month
of interest and penalties,
your new balance is $-23.53
```

● ●

if-else-**Statements**

The *Boolean_Expression* referred to in the following is an expression that is either true or false, such as `balance <= 0`.

Syntax Template (Basic Form):

```
if (Boolean_Expression)
    Statement_1
else
    Statement_2
```

If the *Boolean_Expression* is true, then *Statement_1* is executed; otherwise, *Statement_2* is executed.

Example:

```
if (time < limit)
    System.out.println("You made it");
else
    System.out.println("You missed the deadline.");
```

Syntax Template (Omitting the *else*-Part):

```
if (Boolean_Expression)
    Action_Statement
```

If the *Boolean_Expression* is true, then the *Action_Statement* is executed; otherwise, nothing happens and the program goes on to the next statement.

Example:

```
if (weight > ideal)
    calorieAllotment = calorieAllotment - 500;
```

Multistatement Alternatives:

If you want to include several statements as an alternative, then group the statements using curly brackets as in the following example:

```
if (balance >= 0)
{
    System.out.println("Good for you. You earned interest.");
    balance = balance + (INTEREST_RATE * balance)/12;
}
else
{
    System.out.println("You will be charged a penalty.");
    balance = balance - OVER_DRAWN_PENALTY;
}
```

```
System.out.print("Enter your balance $");
balance = SavitchIn.readLineDouble();
if (balance >= 0)
{
    System.out.println("Good for you. You earned interest.");
    balance = balance + (INTEREST_RATE * balance)/12;
}
System.out.println("Your new balance is $" + balance);
```

Now, suppose your checking account balance is $100.00. Then, the dialogue would be

```
Enter your balance $100.00
Good for you. You earned interest.
Your new balance is $100.16
```

The expression after the *if* is true, so you earn a little interest. (We are using an interest rate of 2% per year as in Display 3.1, but all you need to note is that some interest was added. The exact amount is irrelevant to this example.)

Next, suppose your balance is $–50.00 (i.e., minus 50 dollars). The dialogue would then be as follows:

```
Enter your balance $–50.00
Your new balance is $–50.00
```

In this case, the expression after the *if* is false and there is no *else* part, so nothing happens, the balance is not changed, and the program simply goes on to the next statement, which is an output statement.

Introduction to Boolean Expressions

boolean expression

A **boolean expression** is simply an expression that is either true or false. The name *boolean* is derived from the name of George Boole, a nineteenth-century English logician and mathematician whose work was related to these kinds of expressions.

We have already been using simple boolean expressions in *if-else*-statements. The simplest boolean expressions are comparisons of two things, such as numbers, variables, or other expressions, such as

```
time < limit
```

and

```
balance <= 0
```

Note that a boolean expression need not be enclosed in parentheses to qualify as a boolean expression. However, within an *if-else*-statement, and with most other Java statements, a boolean expression does need to be enclosed in parentheses.

Display 3.2 shows the various Java comparison operators you can use to compare two expressions.

Often, when you are writing an *if-else*-statement, you will want to use some boolean expression that is more complicated than a simple comparison. You can form more complicated boolean expressions from simpler ones, by joining the expression with the Java version of "and." The Java version of "and" is spelled &&.

&& for "and"

For example, consider the following:

Display 3.2 Java Comparison Operators

Math Notation	Name	Java Notation	Java Examples
=	equal to	==	`balance == 0` `answer == 'y'`
≠	not equal to	!=	`income != tax` `answer != 'y'`
>	greater than	>	`expenses > income`
≥	greater than or equal to	>=	`points >= 60`
<	less than	<	`pressure < max`
≤	less than or equal to	<=	`expenses <= income`

```
if ((pressure > min) && (pressure < max))
    System.out.println("Pressure is OK.");
else
    System.out.println("Warning: Pressure is out of range.");
```

If the value of `pressure` is greater than `min` *and* the value of `pressure` is less than `max`, then the output will be

```
Pressure is OK.
```

Otherwise, the output is

```
Warning: Pressure is out of range.
```

Note that you *cannot* use a string of inequalities in Java, like the following

```
min < pressure < max
```

You must express each inequality separately and connect them with &&, as follows:

```
(pressure > min) && (pressure < max)
```

When you form a larger boolean expression by connecting two smaller expression with &&, the entire larger expression is true provided that both of the smaller expressions are true. If at least one of the smaller expressions is false, then the larger expression is false. For example,

```
(pressure > min) && (pressure < max)
```

is true provided that both `(pressure > min)` and `(pressure < max)` are true; otherwise, the expression is false.

Use && for "and"

The symbol pair && is the way that you spell "and" in Java. Using &&, you can form a larger boolean expression out of two smaller boolean expressions.

Syntax Template:

(*Sub_Expression_1*) && (*Sub_Expression_2*)

Example:

```
if ((pressure > min) && (pressure < max))
    System.out.println("Pressure is OK.");
else
    System.out.println("Warning: Pressure is out of range.");
```

|| for "or"

The Java way of spelling "or" is ||. The symbolism || is two vertical lines. (The symbol | prints with a break in the line on some systems.) You can form a larger boolean expression from smaller ones using || in the same way that you do using &&, but the meaning of the expression is different when you use ||. The meaning is essentially the same as the English word "or." For example, consider

```
if ((salary > expenses) || (savings > expenses))
    System.out.println("Solvent");
else
    System.out.println("Bankrupt");
```

If the value of salary is greater than the value of expenses or the value of savings is greater than the value of expenses (or both), then the output will be Solvent; otherwise, the output will be Bankrupt.

The boolean expression in an *if-else*-statement must be enclosed in parentheses. An *if-else*-statement that uses the && operator is normally parenthesized as follows:

```
if ((pressure > min) && (pressure < max))
    System.out.println("Pressure is OK.");
else
    System.out.println("Warning: Pressure is out of range.");
```

The parentheses in (pressure > min) and the parentheses in (pressure < max) are not required, but we will normally include them.

Parentheses are used in expressions using || in the same way as they are used with &&.

In Java, you can negate a boolean expression with !. For example,

---

Use || for "or"

The symbol pair || is the way that you spell "or" in Java. Using ||, you can form a larger boolean expression out of two smaller boolean expressions.

Syntax Template::

   (*Sub_Expression_1*) || (*Sub_Expression_2*)

Example:

```
if ((salary > expenses) || (savings > expenses))
    System.out.println("Solvent");
else
    System.out.println("Bankrupt");
```

```
if (!(number >= min))
    System.out.println("Too small");
else
    System.out.println("OK");
```

This will output `Too Small` if `number` is not greater than or equal to `min`, and `OK` otherwise.

You normally can, and should, avoid using `!`. For example, the previous *if-else*-statement is equivalent to

```
if (number < min)
    System.out.println("Too small");
else
    System.out.println("OK");
```

If you avoid using `!`, your programs will be easier to understand.

⚠ GOTCHA *Using == with Strings*

Although `==` does correctly test two values of a primitive type, such as two numbers, to see if they are equal, it has a different meaning when applied to objects.[1] Recall that an object is something that is a member of a class, such as a string. All strings are in the class `String`, and so `==` applied to two strings does not test to see whether the strings are equal. To test two strings (or any two objects) to see if they have equal values, you should use the method `equals` rather than `==`.

The program in Display 3.3 illustrates the use of the method `equals` as well as the `String` method `equalsIgnoreCase`. The notation may seem a bit awkward at first, since it is not symmetric between the two things being tested for equality. The two expressions

---

1. When applied to two strings (or any two objects), `==` tests to see if they are stored in the same memory location, but we will not discuss that until Chapter 4. For now, we need only note that `==` does something other than test for the equality of two strings.

Display 3.3 Testing Strings for Equality

```java
public class StringEqualityDemo
{
    public static void main(String[] args)
    {
        String s1, s2;

        System.out.println("Enter two lines of text:");
        s1 = SavitchIn.readLine();
        s2 = SavitchIn.readLine();

        if (s1.equals(s2))
            System.out.println("The two lines are equal.");
        else
            System.out.println("The two lines are not equal.");

        if (s2.equals(s1))
            System.out.println("The two lines are equal.");
        else
            System.out.println("The two lines are not equal.");

        if (s1.equalsIgnoreCase(s2))
            System.out.println("But, the lines are equal ignoring case.");
        else
            System.out.println("Lines are not equal even ignoring case.");
    }
}
```

These two invocations of the method equals are equivalent.

Sample Screen Dialogue

```
Enter two lines of text:
The truth is out there.
The TRUTH is out THERE.
The two lines are not equal.
The two lines are not equal.
But, the lines are equal ignoring case.
```

```
s1.equals(s2)
s2.equals(s1)
```

are equivalent.

The method `equalsIgnoreCase` behaves similarly to `equals`, except that with `equalsIgnoreCase` the upper- and lowercase versions of the same letter are considered the same. For example, `"Hello"` and `"hello"` are not equal because their first characters, `'H'` and `'h'`, are different characters. But they would be considered equal by the method `equalsIgnoreCase`. For example, the following will output `Equal`:

```
if ("Hello".equalsIgnoreCase("hello"))
    System.out.println("Equal");
```

Notice that it is perfectly legal to use a quoted string with a `String` method, such as the preceding use of `equalsIgnoreCase`. A quoted string is an object of type `String` and has all the methods that any other object of type `String` has.

For the kinds of applications we are looking at in this chapter, you could use `==` to test for equality of objects of type `String`, and it would deliver the correct answer. However, there are situations in which `==` does not correctly test strings for equality and so you should get in the habit of using `equals` rather than `==` to test strings to see if they are equal.

The Methods `equals` **and** `equalsIgnoreCase`

When testing strings for equality, do not use `==`. Instead, use either `equals` or `equalsIgnoreCase`.

Syntax Template:

String.`equals`(*Other_String*)

String.`equalsIgnoreCase`(*Other_String*)

Example:

```
String s1;
s1 = SavitchIn.readLine();
if ( s1.equals("Hello") )
    System.out.println("The string is Hello.");
else
    System.out.println("The string is not Hello.");
```

? SELF-TEST QUESTIONS

1. Suppose `goals` is a variable of type *int*. Write an *if-else*-statement that outputs the word `Wow` if the value of the variable `goals` is greater than 10 and the words `Oh Well` if the value of `goals` is at most 10.

2. Suppose `goals` and `errors` are variables of type *int*. Write an *if-else*-statement that outputs the word `Wow` if the value of the variable `goals` is greater than 10 and the value of `errors` is zero. Otherwise, the *if-else*-statement outputs the words `Oh Well`.

3. Suppose `salary` and `deductions` are variables of type *double* that have been given values. Write an *if-else*-statement that outputs OK and sets the variable `net` equal to `salary` minus `deductions`, provided that `salary` is at least as large as `deductions`. If, however, `salary` is less than `deductions`, the *if-else*-statement simply outputs the word Crazy, and does not change the value of any variables.

4. Suppose `speed` and `visibility` are variables of type *int*. Write an *if-else*-statement that sets the variable speed equal to 25 and outputs the word Caution, provided the value of `speed` is greater than 25 and the value of `visibility` is under 20. There is no *else* part.

5. Suppose `salary` and `bonus` are variables of type *double*. Write an *if-else*-statement that outputs the word OK provided `salary` is greater than or equal to MIN_SALARY or `bonus` is greater than or equal to MIN_BONUS and outputs Too low otherwise. MIN_SALARY and MIN_BONUS are named constants.

Nested Statements and Compound Statements

Notice that an *if-else*-statement contains two smaller statements within it. For example, consider the statement

```
if (balance >= 0)
    balance = balance + (INTEREST_RATE * balance)/12;
else
    balance = balance - OVER_DRAWN_PENALTY;
```

This statement contains within it the following two smaller statements:

```
balance = balance + (INTEREST_RATE * balance)/12;
balance = balance - OVER_DRAWN_PENALTY;
```

indenting   Note that these smaller statements are indented one more level than the *if* and the *else*.

An *if-else*-statement can contain any sort of statements within it. In particular, you can use an *if-else*-statement within an *if-else*-statement, as illustrated by the following:

```
if (balance >= 0)
    if (INTEREST_RATE >= 0)
        balance = balance + (INTEREST_RATE * balance)/12;
    else
        System.out.println("Cannot have a negative interest.");
else
    balance = balance - OVER_DRAWN_PENALTY;
```

If the value of `balance` is greater than or equal to 0, then the entire following *if-else*-statement is executed:

```
if (INTEREST_RATE >= 0)
    balance = balance + (INTEREST_RATE * balance)/12;
else
    System.out.println("Cannot have a negative interest.");
```

Later in this chapter, we will discuss the most common way of using *if-else*-statements nested within an *if-else*-statement.

Another very simple, but very useful, way of nesting smaller statements within a larger statement is to place a list of statements in curly brackets { }. When you enclose a list of statements within curly brackets, they are considered to be one larger statement. So, the following is one large statement that has two smaller statements inside of it:

```
{
    System.out.println("Good for you. You earned interest.");
    balance = balance + (INTEREST_RATE * balance)/12;
}
```

These statements formed by enclosing a list of statements within curly brackets are called **compound statements.** They are seldom used by themselves, but are often used as substatements of larger statements such as *if-else*-statements. The preceding compound statement might occur in *if-else*-statements such as the following:

compound statement

```
if (balance >= 0)
{
    System.out.println("Good for you. You earned interest.");
    balance = balance + (INTEREST_RATE * balance)/12;
}
else
{
    System.out.println("You will be charged a penalty.");
    balance = balance - OVER_DRAWN_PENALTY;
}
```

Notice that compound statements can simplify our description of an *if-else*-statement. Once you know about compound statements, we can say that every *if-else*-statement is of the form

```
if (Boolean_Expression)
    Statement_1
else
    Statement_2
```

If you want one branch to contain several statements instead of just one statement, you just use a compound statement, as shown in the preceding example of an *if-else*-statement that deals with a bank balance That compound statement is technically speaking just one statement, so each branch of the *if-else*-statement is technically speaking a single statement. This turns out to be a big help to compiler writers and others working with programming languages, because it simplifies the definition of the language.

⚠ **GOTCHA** Matching *else*'s and *if*'s

When writing nested *if-else*-statements, you may sometimes become confused about which *if* goes with which *else*. To eliminate this confusion, you can use curly brackets like parentheses to group things. For example, consider the following nested statement that we used earlier in this chapter:

```
if (balance >= 0)
    if (INTEREST_RATE >= 0)
        balance = balance + (INTEREST_RATE * balance)/12;
    else
        System.out.println("Cannot have a negative interest.");
else
    balance = balance - OVER_DRAWN_PENALTY;
```

This statement can be made clearer with the addition of curly brackets as follows:

```
if (balance >= 0)
{
    if (INTEREST_RATE >= 0)
        balance = balance + (INTEREST_RATE * balance)/12;
    else
        System.out.println("Cannot have a negative interest.");
}
else
    balance = balance - OVER_DRAWN_PENALTY;
```

In the previous case, the curly brackets were an aid to clarity but were not strictly speaking needed. In other cases, they are needed. If we omit one of the *else*'s, then things get a bit trickier. The following two statements differ only in that one has a pair of curly brackets, but they do not have the same meaning:

```
//First Version
if (balance >= 0)
{
    if (INTEREST_RATE >= 0)
        balance = balance + (INTEREST_RATE * balance)/12;
}
else
    balance = balance - OVER_DRAWN_PENALTY;
```

and

```
//Second Version
if (balance >= 0)
    if (INTEREST_RATE >= 0)
        balance = balance + (INTEREST_RATE * balance)/12;
else
    balance = balance - OVER_DRAWN_PENALTY;
```

In an *if-else*-statement each *else* is paired with the nearest unmatched *if*. Thus, in the *Second Version* (the one without curly brackets), the *else* is paired with the second *if*, so the meaning is

```
//Equivalent to Second Version
if (balance >= 0)
{
    if (INTEREST_RATE >= 0)
        balance = balance + (INTEREST_RATE * balance)/12;
    else
        balance = balance - OVER_DRAWN_PENALTY;
}
```

To clarify the difference a bit more, consider what happens when balance is greater than or equal to zero. In the *First Version*, this causes the following action:

```
if (INTEREST_RATE >= 0)
    balance = balance + (INTEREST_RATE * balance)/12;
```

If balance is not greater than or equal to zero in the *First Version*, then the following action is taken instead:

```
balance = balance - OVER_DRAWN_PENALTY;
```

In the *Second Version*, if balance is greater than or equal to zero, then the following entire *if-else*-statement is executed:

```
if (INTEREST_RATE >= 0)
    balance = balance + (INTEREST_RATE * balance)/12;
else
    balance = balance - OVER_DRAWN_PENALTY;
```

If balance is not greater than or equal to zero in the *Second Version*, then no action is taken.

Multibranch *if-else*-Statements

If you have the ability to branch two ways, then you have the ability to branch four ways. Just branch two ways and have each of those two outcomes branch two ways. Using this trick, you can use nested *if-else*-statements to produce multiway branches that branch into any number of possibilities. There is a standard way of doing this. In fact, it has become so standard that it is treated as if it were a new kind of branching statement rather than just a nested statement made up of a lot of nested *if-else*'s. Let's start with an example.

Suppose balance is a variable that holds your checking account balance and you want to know whether your balance is positive, negative (overdrawn), or zero. (To avoid any questions about accuracy, let's assume that balance is of type *int*. To be specific, let's say balance is the number of dollars in your account with the cents ignored.) To find out if your balance is positive, negative, or zero, you could use the following nested *if-else*-statement:

```
if (balance > 0)
    System.out.println("Positive balance");
else if (balance < 0)
    System.out.println("Negative balance");
else if (balance == 0)
    System.out.println("Zero balance");
```

indenting

First, note the way we have indented this statement. This is the preferred way of indenting a multibranch *if-else*-statement. This is really an ordinary nested *if-else*-statement, but the way we have indented it reflects the way we think about these multibranch *if-else*-statements.

When a multibranch *if-else*-statement is executed, the boolean expressions are tested one after the other starting from the top. When the first true boolean expression is found, the statement following that true boolean expression is executed. For example, if balance is greater than zero, then the preceding will output "Positive balance". If balance is less than zero, then "Negative balance" will be output. If balance is equal to zero, then "Zero balance" will be output. Exactly one of the three possible outputs will be produced depending on the value of the variable balance.

In this first example, we had three possibilities, but you can have any number of possibilities; just add more *else-if* parts if there are more possibilities.

In this first example, the possibilities were mutually exclusive. However, you can use any boolean expressions, even if they are not mutually exclusive. If more than one boolean expression is true, then only the action associated with the first boolean expression is executed. A multibranch *if-else*-statement never performs more than one action.

default case

If none of the boolean expressions is true, then nothing happens. However, it is a good practice to add an *else* clause (without any *if*) at the end, so that the *else* clause will be executed in case none of the boolean expressions is true. In fact, we can rewrite our original example (about a checking account balance) in this way. We know that if balance is neither positive nor negative, then it must be zero. So we do not need the test

```
if (balance == 0)
```

Our preceding multibranch *if-else*-statement is equivalent to the following:

```
if (balance > 0)
    System.out.println("Positive balance");
else if (balance < 0)
    System.out.println("Negative balance");
else
    System.out.println("Zero balance");
```

▼ *PROGRAMMING EXAMPLE* Assigning Letter Grades

Display 3.4 contains a program that assigns letter grades according to the traditional rule that 90 or above is an A, 80 or above (up to 90) is a B, and so forth.

Display 3.4 Multibranch *if-else*-**Statement**

```
public class Grader
{
    public static void main(String[] args)
    {
        int score;
        char grade;

        System.out.println("Enter your score: ");
        score = SavitchIn.readLineInt();


        if (score >= 90)
            grade = 'A';
        else if (score >= 80)
            grade = 'B';
        else if (score >= 70)
            grade = 'C';
        else if (score >= 60)
            grade = 'D';
        else
            grade = 'F';


        System.out.println("Score = " + score);
        System.out.println("Grade = " + grade);
    }
}
```

Sample Screen Dialogue

```
Enter your score:
85
Score = 85
Grade = B
```

Note that, as with any multibranch *if-else*-statement, the boolean expressions are checked in order, and so the second boolean expression is not checked unless the first boolean expression is false. Thus, when and if the second boolean expression is checked, we know that the first boolean expression is false and so we know that `score < 90`. Thus, the multibranch *if-else*-statement would have the same meaning if we replaced

```
(score >= 80)
```

with

```
((score >= 80) && (score < 90))
```

Using the same sort of reasoning on each boolean expression, we see that the multibranch *if-else*-statement in Display 3.4 is equivalent to the following:

```
if (score >= 90)
    grade = 'A';
else if ((score >= 80) && (score < 90))
    grade = 'B';
else if ((score >= 70) && (score < 80))
    grade = 'C';
else if ((score >= 60) && (score < 70))
    grade = 'D';
else
    grade = 'F';
```

Most programmers would use the version in Display 3.4 since it is a bit more efficient, but either version is acceptable.

? SELF-TEST QUESTIONS

6. What output will be produced by the following code?

```
int time = 2, tide = 3;
if (time + tide > 6)
    System.out.println("Time and tide wait for no one.");
else
    System.out.println("Time and tide wait for me.");
```

7. What output will be produced by the following code?

```
int time = 4, tide = 3;
if (time + tide > 6)
    System.out.println("Time and tide wait for no one.");
else
    System.out.println("Time and tide wait for me.");
```

Multibranch *if-else*-Statement

Syntax Template:

```
if (Boolean_Expression_1)
    Action_1
else if (Boolean_Expression_2)
    Action_2
        .
        .
        .
else if (Boolean_Expression_n)
    Action_n
else
    Default_Action
```

Example:

```
if (number < 10)
    System.out.println("number < 10");
else if (number < 50)
    System.out.println("number >= 10 and number < 50");
else if (number < 100)
    System.out.println("number >= 50 and number < 100");
else
    System.out.println("number >= 100.");
```

The *Action*s are Java statements. The boolean expressions are tested one after the other starting from the top one. When the first true boolean expression is found, the action following that true boolean expression is executed. The *Default_Action* is executed if none of the boolean expressions is true.

---

8. What output will be produced by the following code?

```
int time = 2, tide = 3;
if (time + tide > 6)
    System.out.println("Time and tide wait for no one.");
else if (time + tide > 5)
    System.out.println("Time and tide wait for some one.");
else if (time + tide > 4)
    System.out.println("Time and tide wait for every one.");
else
    System.out.println("Time and tide wait for me.");
```

9. Suppose number is a variable of type *int* that has been given a value. Write a multibranch *if-else*-statement that outputs the word high if number is greater than 10, outputs low if number is less than 5, and outputs so-so if number is anything else.

The *switch*-Statement

The *switch*-**statement** is a multiway branch that makes its decision on which way to branch based on the value of an integer or character expression. Display 3.5 shows a sample *switch*-statement. The *switch*-statement begins with the word *switch* followed by an expression in parentheses; in Display 3.5 the expression is

Display 3.5 A *switch*-**Statement** *(Part 1 of 2)*

```
public class MultipleBirths
{
    public static void main(String[] args)
    {
        int numberOfBabies;
        System.out.print("Enter number of babies: ");
        numberOfBabies = SavitchIn.readLineInt();

        switch (numberOfBabies)
        {
            case 1:
                System.out.println("Congratulations.");
                break;
            case 2:
                System.out.println("Wow. Twins.");
                break;
            case 3:
                System.out.println("Wow. Triplets.");
                break;
            case 4:
            case 5:
                System.out.println("Unbelieveable.");
                System.out.println(numberOfBabies + " babies");
                break;
            default:
                System.out.println("I don't believe you.");
                break;
        }
    }
}
```

Sample Screen Dialogue 1

```
Enter number of babies: 1
Congratulations.
```

Sample Screen Dialogue 2

```
Enter number of babies: 3
Wow. Triplets.
```

Display 3.5 A *switch*-**Statement** *(Part 2 of 2)*

••

Sample Screen Dialogue 3

```
Enter number of babies: 4
Unbelievable.
4 babies
```

Sample Screen Dialogue 4

```
Enter number of babies: 6
I don't believe you.
```

••

the variable numberOfBabies. This expression is called the **controlling expression.** *controlling expression*
Below this is a list of cases, each case consisting of the reserved word *case* followed
by a constant and a colon and then a list of statements, which are the actions for
that case. The constant that is placed after the word *case* is called a **case label**.
When the *switch*-statement is executed the controlling expression, in this example, numberOfBabies, is evaluated. The list of alternatives is searched until a case
label that matches the controlling expression (numberOfBabies in the example) is
found and the action associated with that action is executed. You are not allowed
to have repeated case labels. That would produce an ambiguous situation. If no
match is found, then the case labeled *default* is executed. *default*

The *default* case is optional. If there is no *default* case and no match is found
to any of the cases, then no action takes place. Although the *default* case is
optional, you are encouraged to always use it. If you think your cases cover all the
possibilities without a *default* case, then you can insert an error message as the
default case. You never know when you might have missed some obscure case.

Notice that the action for each case in Display 3.5 ends with the word *break*.
This is a *break*-**statement** and it ends the case. The *break*-statement consists of *break*
the word *break* followed by a semicolon. If there is no *break*-statement, then the
action just continues on into the next case until either a *break*-statement is encountered or the end of the *switch*-statement is reached.

Sometimes you do want a case without a *break*-statement. You cannot have
multiple labels in one case, but you can list cases one after the other so that they all
apply to the same action. For example, in Display 3.5, both the 4 and the 5 produce
the same case action, since the 4 case has no *break*-statement (and, in fact, the 4
case has no action statements at all).

As another example, consider the following *switch*-statement:

```
switch (eggGrade)
{
    case 'A':
    case 'a':
        System.out.println("Grade A");
        break;
    case 'C':
    case 'c':
        System.out.println("Grade C");
        break;
    default:
        System.out.println("We only buy grade A and grade C.");
        break;
}
```

In this example, the variable eggGrade would be of type *char*.

Note that the cases need not form any sort of range; you can have 'A' and 'C' and no 'B', as in the preceding example. Similarly, in a *switch*-statement with integer case labels, you could have integers 1 and 3, but no 2.

The controlling expression in a *switch*-statement need not be a single variable. It can be a more complicated expression involving +, *, and/or other things, but the expression must evaluate to something of type *int* or of type *char*. (The types *byte* and *short* are also allowed, but the controlling expression cannot be of type *long*.)

The box labeled **switch-Statement** gives the syntax details for the *switch*-statement. Be sure to notice the colons after the case labels.

▲ *GOTCHA* **Omitting a** *break***-Statement**

If you test a program that contains a *switch*-statement and it executes two cases when you expect it to execute only one case, then you have probably forgotten to include a *break*-statement where one is needed.

switch-**Statement**

Syntax Template:

```
switch (Controlling_Expression)
{
    case Case_Label:
        Statement;
        Statement;
            . . .
        Statement;
        break;
    case Case_Label:
        Statement;
        Statement;
            . . .
        Statement;
        break;
```

Each Case_Label is a constant of the same type as the Controlling_Expression. Each case must have a different Case_Label. The Controlling_Expression must be of type char, int, short, or byte.

A break may be omitted. In that case execution just continues to the next case.

<There can be any number of cases like the above. The following default case is optional:>

```
    default:
        Statement;
        Statement;
            . . .
        Statement;
        break;
}
```

Example:

```
int seatLocationCode;
    . . .
switch (seatLocationCode)
{
    case 1:
        System.out.println("Orchestra.");
        price = 40.00;
        break;
    case 2:
        System.out.println("Mezzanine.");
        price = 30.00;
        break;
    case 3:
        System.out.println("Balcony.");
        price = 15.00;
        break;
    default:
        System.out.println("Unknown ticket code.");
        break;
}
```

? SELF-TEST QUESTIONS

10. What is the output produced by the following code?

```
int code = 2;
switch (code)
{
    case 1:
        System.out.println("Hello.");
    case 3:
        System.out.println("Good-bye.");
        break;
    default:
        System.out.println("Till we meet again.");
        break;

}
```

11. Suppose you change the code in Question 10 so that the first line is the following:

```
int code = 1;
```

What output would be produced?

12. What is the output produced by the following code?

```
char letter = 'B';
switch (letter)
{
    case 'A':
    case 'a':
        System.out.println("Some kind of A.");
    case 'B':
    case 'b':
        System.out.println("Some kind of B.");
        break;
    default:
        System.out.println("Something else.");
        break;
}
```

13. What output will be produced by the following code?

```java
int key = 1;
switch (key + 1)
{
    case 1:
        System.out.println("Cake");
        break;
    case 2:
        System.out.println("Pie");
        break;
    case 3:
        System.out.println("Ice cream");
    case 4:
        System.out.println("Cookies");
        break;
    default:
        System.out.println("Diet time");
}
```

14. Suppose you change the code in Question 13 so that the first line is the following:

```java
int key = 3;
```

What output would be produced?

15. Suppose you change the code in Question 13 so that the first line is the following:

```java
int key = 5;
```

What output would be produced?

3.2 Java Loop Statements

One more time.
COUNT BASIE, RECORDING OF *April in Paris*

Play it again, Sam.
REPUTED (INCORRECTLY) TO BE IN THE MOVIE *Casablanca*, WHICH CONTAINS SIMILAR
PHRASES SUCH AS *Play it, Sam.*

Programs often need to repeat some action. For example, a grading program would contain some code to assign a letter grade to a student based on the student's scores on assignments and exams. To assign grades to the entire class, the program would repeat this action for each student in the class. A portion of a program that repeats a statement or group of statements is called a **loop.** The statement (or group of statements) to be repeated in a loop is called the **body** of the loop. Each repetition of the loop body is called an **iteration** of the loop. When you design a loop, you need

body

iteration

to determine what action the body of the loop will take and you need to determine a mechanism for deciding when the loop should stop repeating the loop body.

while-**Statements**

while- loop

One way to construct a loop in Java is with a *while*-**statement**, which is also known as a *while*-**loop.** A *while*-statement repeats its action again and again until a controlling boolean expression becomes false. That is why it is called a *while* loop; the loop is repeated *while* the controlling boolean expression is true. For example, Display 3.6 contains a toy example of a *while*-statement. The statement starts with the reserved word *while* followed by a boolean expression in parentheses. That is the controlling boolean expression. The loop body (the part repeated) is repeated while that controlling boolean expression is true. The loop body is a statement, typically a compound statement enclosed in curly brackets { }. The loop body normally contains some action that can change the controlling boolean expression from true to false and so end the loop. Let's step through this sample *while*-loop.

Consider the first sample dialogue for the *while*-statement in Display 3.6. The user enters a 2 and this 2 becomes the value of the variable number. The controlling boolean expression is

```
(count <= number)
```

Since count is 1 and number is 2, this boolean expression is true, so the loop body, shown in what follows, is executed:

```
{
    System.out.println(count);
    count++;
}
```

The loop body writes out the value of count to the screen and then increase the value of count by one, so 1 is written to the screen and the value of count becomes 2.

After iterating the loop body one time, the controlling boolean expression is checked again. Since count is 2 and number is 2, the boolean expression is still true. So, the loop body is executed one more time. The loop body again writes out the value of count to the screen and again increases the value of count by one, so 2 is written to the screen and the value of count becomes 3.

After iterating the loop body the second time, the controlling boolean expression is checked again. The value of count is now 3 and the value of number is still 2, and so, the controlling boolean expression, repeated in what follows, is now false.

```
(count <= number)
```

Since the controlling boolean expression is false, the *while*-loop ends and the program goes on to execute the two System.out.println-statements that follow the *while*-statement. The first System.out.println-statement ends the line of numbers output in the *while*-loop, and the second System.out.println-statement outputs "Buckle my shoe."

All *while*-statements are formed in a way similar to the sample shown in Display 3.6. The statement has the general form

Display 3.6 A *while*-**Loop**

```
public class WhileDemo
{
    public static void main(String[] args)
    {
        int count, number;

        System.out.println("Enter a number");
        number = SavitchIn.readLineInt();

        count = 1;
        while (count <= number)
        {
            System.out.print(count + ", ");
            count++;
        }
        System.out.println();
        System.out.println("Buckle my shoe.");
    }
}
```

Sample Screen Dialogue 1

```
Enter a number:
2
1, 2,
Buckle my shoe.
```

Sample Screen Dialogue 2

```
Enter a number:
3
1, 2, 3,
Buckle my shoe.
```

Sample Screen Dialogue 3

```
Enter a number:
0

Buckle my shoe.
```

The loop body is iterated zero times.

```
while(Boolean_Expression)
    Body_Statement
```

The *Body_Statement* can be a simple statement, as in the following example:

```
while(next > 0)
    next = SavitchIn.readLineInt();
```

But it is much more likely that the *Body_Statement* is a compound statement, as in Display 3.6, so the most common form of a *while*-loop is

```
while(Boolean_Expression)
{
    First_Statement
    Second_Statement
        .  .  .
    Last_Statement
}
```

The *while*-**Statement**

Syntax Template:

```
while (Boolean_Expression)
    Body
```

The *Body* may be either a simple statement, or more likely, a compound statement consisting of a list of statements enclosed in curly brackets { }.

Example:

```
while (next > 0)
{
    next = SavitchIn.readLineInt();
    total = total + next;
}
```

◐ *PROGRAMMING TIP* A *while*-Loop Can Perform Zero Iterations

zero loop
iterations

The body of a *while*-loop can be executed zero times. The first thing that happens when a *while*-loop is executed is that the controlling boolean expression is checked. If that boolean expression is false, then the loop body is not executed even one time. This may seem strange. After all, why write a loop if the body is never executed? The answer is that you may want a loop whose body is executed zero times or more than zero times depending on input from the user. Perhaps the loop adds up the sum of all your bills for the day. If you did not go shopping one day, then you want the loop to be iterated zero times. Sample Screen Dialogue 3 of Display 3.6 shows a toy example of a *while*-loop that iterates its loop body zero times.

The *do-while*-Statement

The *do-while*-**statement** (also called a *do-while*-loop) is very similar to the *while*-statement. The main difference in how they behave is that, with a *do-while*-statement, the loop body is always executed at least once. As you will recall, with a *while*-loop, the loop body might be executed zero times. Display 3.7 contains a sample *do-while*-loop that is similar to (but not identical to) the *while*-loop in Display 3.6/page 109. Note that with the *do-while*-loop, the loop body is always executed at least once even if the boolean expression starts out false, as in Sample Dialogue 3.

do-while-statement

The syntax for a *do-while*-statement is as follows:

```
do
      Body_Statement
while(Boolean_Expression);
```

The *Body_Statement* can be a simple statement, as in the following example:

```
do
      next = SavitchIn.readLineInt();
while(next > 0);
```

However, it is much more likely that the *Body_Statement* is a compound statement, as in Display 3.7, so the most common form of a *do-while*-loop is

```
do
{
      First_Statement
      Second_Statement
            . . .
      Last_Statement
}
while(Boolean_Expression);
```

Be sure to notice the semicolon after the *Boolean_Expression* in parentheses.

When a *do-while*-loop is executed, the first thing that happens is that the loop body is executed. *After that,* a *do-while*-loop behaves exactly the same as a *while*-loop. The boolean expression is checked. If the boolean expression is true, then the loop body is executed one more time. If the boolean expression is false, the loop ends. This is done again and again as long as the boolean expression is true.

Although we do not recommend rewriting your *do-while*-loops this way, it may help you to understand a *do-while*-loop if you see the following rewriting done one time. The *do-while*-loop in Display 3.7 can be written as the following equivalent code that includes a *while*-loop:

Display 3.7 A *do-while*-**Loop**

•••

```
public class DoWhileDemo
{
    public static void main(String[] args)
    {
        int count, number;

        System.out.println("Enter a number");
        number = SavitchIn.readLineInt();

        count = 1;
        do
        {
            System.out.print(count + ", ");
            count++;
        }while (count <= number);
        System.out.println();
        System.out.println("Buckle my shoe.");
    }
}
```

Sample Screen Dialogue 1

```
Enter a number:
2
1, 2,
Buckle my shoe.
```

Sample Screen Dialogue 2

```
Enter a number:
3
1, 2, 3,
Buckle my shoe.
```

Sample Screen Dialogue 3

```
Enter a number:
0
1,
Buckle my shoe.
```

The loop body is always iterated at least one time.

•••

```
    {
        System.out.print(count + ", ");
        count++;
    }
    while (count <= number)
    {
        System.out.print(count + ", ");
        count++;
    }
```

When viewed in this way, it is obvious that a *do-while*-loop differs from a *while*-loop in only one detail. With a *do-while*-loop, the loop body is always executed at least once. (Recall that, with a *while*-loop, the loop body may be executed zero times.)

The *do-while*-Statement

With a *do-while*-statement, the loop body is always executed at least one time.

Syntax Template:

```
do
    Body
while (Boolean_Expression);
```

The *Body* may be either a simple statement, or more likely, a compound statement consisting of a list of statements enclosed in curly brackets { }. Be sure to notice the semicolon after the *Boolean_Expression* in parentheses.

Example:

```
do
{
    next = SavitchIn.readLineInt();
    total = total + next;
}while (next > 0);
```

▼ *PROGRAMMING EXAMPLE* Bug Infestation

Your hometown has been hit with an infestation of roaches. This is not the most pleasant topic, but fortunately a local company called Debugging Experts Inc. has a treatment that can eliminate roaches from a house. As the saying goes, "It's a dirty job, but somebody has to do it." The only problem is that the population is too complacent and may not exterminate the roaches before they get out of hand. So, the company has installed a computer at the local shopping mall in order to let people know how bad the problem is at their particular house. The program that is run on this computer is shown in Display 3.8.

Display 3.8 Roach Population Program *(Part 1 of 2)*

```
/*************************************************************
 *Program to calculate how long it will take a population of
 *roaches to completely fill a house from floor to ceiling.
 *************************************************************/
public class BugTrouble
{
    public static final double GROWTH_RATE = 0.95;//95% per week
    public static final double ONE_BUG_VOLUME = 0.002;//cubic feet

    public static void main(String[] args)
    {
      System.out.println("Enter the total volume of your house");
        System.out.print("in cubic feet: ");
        double houseVolume = SavitchIn.readLineDouble();

        System.out.println("Enter the estimated number of");
        System.out.print("roaches in your house:");
        int startPopulation = SavitchIn.readLineInt();
        int countWeeks = 0;
        double population = startPopulation;
        double totalBugVolume = population*ONE_BUG_VOLUME;

        while (totalBugVolume < houseVolume)
        {
            population = population + (GROWTH_RATE*population);
            totalBugVolume = population*ONE_BUG_VOLUME;
            countWeeks++;
        }

        System.out.println("Starting with a roach population of "
                                           + startPopulation);
        System.out.println("and a house with a volume of "
                              + houseVolume + " cubic feet,");
        System.out.println("after " + countWeeks + " weeks,");
        System.out.println("the house will be filled");
        System.out.println("floor to ceiling with roaches.");
        System.out.println("There will be " + (int)population
                                            + " roaches.");
        System.out.println("They will fill a volume of "
                      + (int)totalBugVolume + " cubic feet");
        System.out.println("Better call Debugging Experts Inc.");
    }
}
```

(*int*) is a type cast as discussed in Chapter 2.

Display 3.8 Roach Population Program *(Part 2 of 2)*

•••

Screen Output

```
Enter the total volume of your house
in cubic feet: 20000
Enter the estimated number of
roaches in your house: 100
Starting with a roach population of 100
and a house with a volume of 20000 cubic feet,
after 18 weeks,
the house will be filled
floor to ceiling with roaches.
There will be 16619693 roaches.
They will fill a volume of 33239 cubic feet
Better call Debugging Experts Inc.
```

•••

The defined constants give the basic facts about this species of roaches. The population grows relatively slowly for roaches, but that is still pretty bad. Left unchecked, the population of roaches will almost double every week. If the population doubled every week, the growth rate would be 100% per week, but fortunately it is only 95% per week. These roaches are also pretty big. Expressed in cubic feet their average size is 0.002 cubic feet (which is just a bit smaller that 0.3 cubic inches). The program does make some simplifying assumptions. It assumes there is no furniture in the house and it assumes that the roaches would fill the house with no space between them. The real situation would be even worse than that portrayed by this program with its simplifying assumptions.

In the following we reproduce the *while*-loop from the program in Display 3.8:

```
while (totalBugVolume < houseVolume)
{
    population = population + (GROWTH_RATE*population);
    totalBugVolume = population*ONE_BUG_VOLUME;
    countWeeks++;
}
```

This program simply updates the population of the roaches and the volume of roaches by the following statements, which show how the population and volume will change in one week:

```
population = population + (GROWTH_RATE*population);
totalBugVolume = population*ONE_BUG_VOLUME;
```

Since the growth rate and the volume of one bug are both positive, we know that the value of `population` and hence the value of `totalBugVolume` will increase on each loop iteration. So, eventually, the value of `totalBugVolume` will exceed the value of `houseVolume` and the controlling boolean expression, reproduced in what follows, will become false and end the *while*-loop:

```
(totalBugVolume < houseVolume)
```

The variable `countWeeks` starts out as zero and is increased by one on each loop iteration, and so, when the loop ends, the value of `countWeeks` is the total numbers of weeks it takes to make the volume of roaches exceed the volume of the house.

⚠ GOTCHA *Infinite Loops*

A common program bug is a loop that does not end, but that simply repeats its loop body again and again forever. (Well, conceptually forever.) A loop that iterates its body repeatedly without ever ending is called an **infinite loop.** Normally, some statement in the body of a *while*-loop or *do-while*-loop will change some variables so that the controlling boolean expression becomes false. If you do not get this variable change to happen in the right way, you can get an infinite loop. In order to see an example of an infinite loop, we need only make a slight change to a loop you have already seen.

infinite loop

Let's consider a slight variation of the program in Display 3.8. Suppose your town is hit by an infestation of roach-eating frogs. These frogs are eating roaches so quickly that the roach population is actually decreasing, so that the roaches have a negative growth rate. To reflect this fact you could change the definition of one defined constant to the following and recompile the program in Display 3.8:

```
public static final double GROWTH_RATE = -0.05;//-5% per week
```

If you make this change and run the program, the *while*-loop will be an infinite loop (provided the house starts out with a relatively small number of roaches). This is because the total number of roaches and so the volume of roaches is continually *decreasing* and hence the controlling boolean expression, shown again in what follows, is always true:

```
(totalBugVolume < houseVolume)
```

and so the loop never ends.

Some infinite loops will not really run forever, but will instead end your program in some abnormal state when some system resource is exhausted. However, some infinite loops will run forever if left alone. In order to end such a program with an infinite loop, you should learn how to force a program to stop running. The way to do this is different for different operating systems. On many systems (but not all), you can stop a program by typing control-C, which you type by holding down the control key while pressing the C key.

There are situations where a programmer might intentionally write an infinite loop. For example, an airline reservation system would typically have an infinite loop that asks for and makes more reservations forever. However, at this point in your programming, an infinite loop is likely to be an error.

? SELF-TEST QUESTIONS

16. What screen output will be produced by the following code?

```java
int count = 0;
while (count < 5)
{
    System.out.println(count);
    count++;
}
System.out.println("count after loop = " + count);
```

17. Can a *while*-loop execute the body of the loop zero times? Can a *do-while*-loop execute the body of the loop zero times?

18. What screen output will be produced by the following code?

```java
int count = 0;
do
{
    System.out.println(count);
    count++;
}while (count < 0);
System.out.println("count after loop = " + count);
```

19. Rewrite the following *do-while*-loop to obtain some equivalent code that does not contain a *do-while*-loop.

```java
int number;
do
{
    System.out.println("Enter a whole number:");
    number = SavitchIn.readLineInt();
    System.out.println("You entered " + number);
}while (number > 0);
System.out.println("number after loop = " + number);
```

20. What screen output will be produced by the following code?

```java
int count = 0;
while (count < 5)
{
    System.out.println(count);
    count--;
}
System.out.println("count after loop = " + count);
```

The *for*-Statement

for-loop

The *for*-statement is a specialized loop statement that allows you to easily convert pseudocode such as the following into a Java loop:

Do the following for each value of `count` from 1 to 3:
```
    System.out.println(count);
System.out.println("Go");
```

This particular pseudocode can be expressed in Java as the following *for*-statement (followed by an output statement):

```
for (count = 1; count <= 3; count++)
    System.out.println(count);
System.out.println("Go");
```

The first two of the preceding lines are a *for*-statement that causes the output

```
1
2
3
```

After the *for*-statement ends, the last line outputs the word "Go".

In this first example of a *for*-statement, the loop body is the statement

```
System.out.println(count);
```

The iteration of the loop body is controlled by the line

```
for (count = 1; count <= 3; count++)
```

The first of the three expressions in parentheses, `count = 1`, tells what happens before the loop body is executed for the first time. The third expression, `count++`, is executed after each iteration of the loop body. The middle expression, `count <= 3`, is a boolean expression that determines when the loop will end and that does so in the same way as the controlling boolean expression in a *while*-loop. Thus, the loop body is executed while `count <= 3` is true. To rephrase what we just said, the *for*-statement

```
for (count = 1; count <= 3; count++)
    for-loop body
```

is equivalent to

```
count = 1;
while (count <= 3)
{
    for-loop body
    count++;
}
```

The syntax for a *for*-statement is as follows:

```
for (Initializing_Action; Boolean_Expression; Action_After_Each_Iteration)
    Body_Statement
```

The *for*-Statement

Syntax Template:

> for (*Initializing_Action*; *Boolean_Expression*; *Action_After_Each_Iteration*)
> *Body*

The *Body* may be either a simple statement, or more likely, a compound statement consisting of a list of statements enclosed in curly brackets { }. Notice that the three things in parentheses are separated by two, not three, semicolons.

Our *for*-loops will always use only one variable in the three expressions in parentheses after the word *for*. However, you are allowed to use any Java expression and so can use more, or fewer than, one variable in the expressions.

Example:

```
for (next = 0; next <= 10; next = next + 2)
{
    sum = sum + next;
    System.out.println("sum now is " + sum);
}
```

The *Body_Statement* can be a simple statement, as in the following example:

```
for (count = 1; count <= 3; count++)
    System.out.println(count);
```

However, it is more likely that the *Body_Statement* is a compound statement, as in Display 3.9, so the more common form of a *for*-loop can be described as follows:

> for (*Initializing_Action*; *Boolean_Expression*; *Action_After_Each_Iteration*)
> {
>   *First_Statement*
>   *Second_Statement*
>   .
>   .
>   .
>   *Last_Statement*
> }

When it is executed, a *for*-statement of the preceding form is equivalent to the following:

> *Initializing_Action*;
> while(*Boolean_Expression*)
> {
>   *First_Statement*
>   *Second_Statement*
>   .
>   .
>   .
>   *Last_Statement*
>   *Action_After_Each_Iteration*;
> }

Display 3.9 A *for* **-Statement**

```
public class ForDemo
{
    public static void main(String[] args)
    {

        int countDown;

        for (countDown = 3; countDown >= 0; countDown--)
        {
            System.out.println(countDown);
            System.out.println("and counting.");
        }

        System.out.println("Blast off!");
    }
}
```

Screen Output

```
3
and counting.
2
and counting.
1
and counting.
0
and counting.
Blast off!.
```

Notice that a *for*-statement is basically another notation for a kind of *while*-loop. Thus, just like a *while*-loop, a *for*-statement might repeat its loop body zero times.

The Comma in *for*-Statements *(Optional)*

A *for*-loop can have multiple initialization actions. To use a list of actions, simply separate the actions with commas, as in the following example:

comma operator

```
for (n = 1, sum = 0; n <= 10; n++)
    sum = sum + n;
```

This *for*-loop will initialize n to 1 and will also initialize sum to 0. Note that we use a comma, not a semicolon, to separate the initialization actions.

You cannot have multiple boolean expressions to test for ending a *for*-loop. However, you can string together multiple tests using the && operator to form one larger boolean expression.

You can have multiple update actions by stringing them together with commas. This can sometimes lead to a situation where the *for*-statement has an empty body and still does something useful. For example, the previous *for*-statement can be rewritten to the following equivalent version:

```
for (n = 1, sum = 0; n <= 10; sum = sum + n, n++);
```

In effect, we have made the loop body part of the update action. It is a more readable style to use the update action only for variables that control the loop, as in the previous version of this *for*-loop. We do not advocate these *for*-loops with no body, but many programmers consider them "clever" or even "cool." As indicated in the section **GOTCHA Extra Semicolon in a Loop Statement**, these *for*-loops with no body can also often occur as the result of a programer error.

(If you have programmed in other programming languages that have a general-purpose comma operator, you need to be warned that, in Java, the comma operator can only be used in *for*-statements.)

⚠ *GOTCHA* Extra Semicolon in a Loop Statement

The following code looks quite ordinary. Moreover, it will compile and run with no error messages. It does, however, contain a mistake. See if you can find the mistake before reading on.

```
int sum = 0, number;
for (number = 1; number <= 10; number++);
    sum = sum + number;
System.out.println("Sum of the numbers 1 through 10 is " + sum);
```

If you include this code in a program and run the program, the output will be

```
Sum of the numbers 1 through 10 is 11
```

Now do you know what is wrong? Try to explain the problem before reading on.

If you were testing the program that produced this puzzling output, it could leave you bewildered. Clearly, something is wrong with the *for*-loop, but what? The *for*-loop is suppose to set the value of sum equal to

```
1 + 2 + 3 + 4 + 5 + 6 + 7 + 8 + 9 + 10
```

but, instead it sets the value of sum equal to 11. It seems to have missed all the numbers from 2 through 9. How could that happen? Well, that is not what happened. The 11 comes from a slightly different problem.

The problem is typographically very small. The *for*-statement has an extra semicolon at the end of the first line:

```
for (number = 1; number <= 10; number++;)
    sum = sum + number;
```

empty
statement

What does this *for*-statement do? The semicolon at the end means that the body of the *for*-statement is empty. A semicolon by itself is considered a statement that does nothing. (This statement that does nothing is called the **empty statement** or the **null statement.**) This *for*-statement with the extra semicolon is equivalent to

```
for (number = 1; number <= 10; number++)
{
    //Do nothing.
}
```

Thus, the body of the *for*-statement is in fact executed 10 times, but each time it does nothing, except that it does increment the variable number by one on each of the 10 loop iterations. That leaves number equal to 11 when the program reaches the statement

```
sum = sum + number;
```

(Remember number starts out equal to 1 and is increased by one ten times which adds 10 more to the initial 1 so the value becomes 11.)

Now let's look again at the entire piece of troublesome code:

```
int sum = 0, number;
for (number = 1; number <= 10; number++);
    sum = sum + number;
System.out.println("Sum of the numbers 1 through 10 is " + sum);
```

After executing the line that starts with *for*, the value of sum is 0 and, as we have just seen, the value of number is 11. Then the following assignment statement is executed:

```
sum = sum + number;
```

This sets the value of sum to 0 + 11 and so sum ends up with the value 11, which is what the output says.

The same sort of problem can occur with a *while*-loop. The following *while*-loop has the same sort of problem as our troublesome *for*-loop, but the results are even worse:

```
int sum = 0, number = 1;
while (number <= 10 ; )
{
    sum = sum + number;
    number++;
}
System.out.println("Sum of the numbers 1 through 10 is " +
sum);
```

The extra semicolon ends the *while*-loop so that the body of the *while*-loop is the empty statement. Since the body of the loop is the empty statement, nothing happens on each loop iteration. So, the value of number never changes and the condition

```
number <= 10
```

is always *true*. So the loop is an infinite loop that does nothing and does it forever!

? SELF-TEST QUESTIONS

21. What output is produced by the following Java code?

    ```
    int n;
    for (n = 1; n <= 4; n++)
        System.out.println(n);
    ```

22. What output is produced by the following Java code?

    ```
    int n;
    for (n = 1; n > 4; n++)
        System.out.println(n);
    ```

23. What output is produced by the following Java code?

    ```
    int n;
    for (n = 4; n > 0; n--)
        System.out.println(n);
    ```

24. What output is produced by the following Java code?

    ```
    double test;
    for (test = 0; test < 3; test = test + 0.5)
        System.out.println(test);
    ```

25. Write a *for*-statement that writes out the even numbers, 2, 4, 6, 8, and 10. The output should put each number on a separate line. Declare all the variables you use.

Choosing a Loop Statement

Suppose you decide that your program needs a loop. How do you decide whether to use a *while*-statement, a *do-while*-statement, or a *for*-statement? There are some general guidelines we can give you: You *cannot* use a *do-while*-statement unless you are certain that for all possible inputs to your program, you know the loop should be iterated at least one time. If you do know that your loop will always be iterated at least one time, then a *do-while*-statement is likely to be a good choice. However, more often than you might think, a loop requires the possibility of iterating the body zero times. In those cases, you must use either a *while*-statement or a *for*-statement. If it is a computation that changes some numeric quantity by some equal amount on each iteration, then consider a *for*-statement. If the *for*-statement does not work well, use a *while*-statement. The *while*-statement is always the safest choice. You can easily realize any sort of loop as a *while*-statement, but sometimes one of the other alternatives is nicer.

The *break*-Statement in Loops

break

As we have presented them so far, the *while*-statement, the *do-while*-statement, and the *for*-statement always complete their entire loop body on each iteration. Sometimes, you may want to end a loop in the middle of the loop body. You can do this using the *break*-statement. For example, the program in Display 3.10 reads a list of purchase amounts and totals them to see how much the user has spent. However, the user has a limit of $100, so as soon as the total reaches (or exceeds) $100, the program uses a *break*-statement to end the loop immediately. When a *break*-statement is executed, the immediately enclosing loop ends, and the remainder of the loop body is not executed. The *break*-statement can be used with a *while*-loop, a *do-while*-loop, or a *for*-loop.

This is the same *break*-statement that we used in *switch*-statements. If the loop is contained within a larger loop (or if the loop is inside of a *switch*-statement), then the *break*-statement ends only the innermost loop. Similarly, if the *break*-statement is within a *switch*-statement that is inside of a loop, then the *break*-statement ends the *switch*-statement but not the loop. The *break*-statement ends only the innermost loop or *switch*-statement that contains the *break*-statement.

⚠ GOTCHA   Misuse of *break*-Statements

A loop *without* a *break*-statement has a simple, easy-to-understand structure. There is a test for ending the loop at the top (or bottom) of the loop and every iteration will go to the end of the loop body. When you add a *break*-statement, it can make it more difficult to understand the loop. The loop might end because of the condition given at the start (or bottom) of the loop or because of the *break*-statement. Some loop iterations may go to the end of the loop body, but one loop iteration may end prematurely. Because of the complications they introduce, *break*-statements in loops should be avoided. Some authorities contend that a *break*-statement should never be used to end a loop, but virtually all programming authorities agree that they should be used at most sparingly.

Display 3.10 Ending a Loop with a *break*-**Statement**

••

```
public class BreakDemo
{
    public static void main(String[] args)
    {
        int itemNumber;
        double amount, total;

        System.out.println("You may buy ten items, but");
        System.out.println("the total price must not exceed $100.");

        total = 0;
        for (itemNumber = 1; itemNumber <= 10; itemNumber++)
        {
            System.out.print("Enter cost of item #"
                                        + itemNumber + ": $");
            amount = SavitchIn.readLineDouble();
            total = total + amount;
            if (total >= 100)
            {
                System.out.println("You spent all your money.");
                break;
            }
            System.out.println("Your total so far is $" + total);
            System.out.println("You may purchase up to "
                            + (10 - itemNumber) + " more items.");
        }
        System.out.println("You spent $" + total);
    }
}
```

Sample Screen Dialogue

```
You may buy ten items, but
the total price must not exceed $100.
Enter cost of item #1: $90.93
Your total so far is $90.93
You may purchase up to 9 more items.
Enter cost of item #2: $10.50
You spent all your money.
You spent $101.43
```

••

The *break*-**Statement**

The *break*-statement can be used in a *switch*-statement or in any kind of loop statements. When the *break*-statement is executed, the immediately enclosing loop (or *switch*-statement) ends, and the remainder of the loop body is not executed.

The exit **Method**

Sometimes your program can encounter a situation that makes continuing with the program pointless. In these cases, you can end your program with a call to the exit method, as follows:

```
System.exit(0);
```

The preceding statement will end a Java program as soon as it is executed.

For example:

```
if (numberOfWinners == 0)
{
    System.out.println("Error: Dividing by zero.");
    System.exit(0);
}
else
{
    oneShare = payoff/numberOfWinners;
    System.out.println("Each winner will receive $" + oneShare);
}
```

This statement will normally output the share that each winner should receive. However, if the number of winners is zero, then that would produce a division by zero, which is an illegal operation. To avoid this division by zero, the program checks to see if the number of winners is zero, and if it is zero, it ends the program with a call to the exit method.

The number 0 given as the argument to System.exit is returned to the operating system. In many situations, you can use any number and the program will behave the same. But, most operating systems use 0 to indicate a normal termination of the program and 1 to indicate an abnormal termination of the program (just the opposite of what most people would guess). Thus, if your System.exit statement ends your program normally, the argument should be 0. In this case, *normal* means the program did not violate any system or other important constraints. It does not mean that the program did what you wanted it to do. So, you would almost always use a 0 as the argument.

The exit **Method**

An invocation of the exit method ends the program. The normal form for an exit method invocation is

```
System.exit(0);
```

? SELF-TEST QUESTIONS

26. What output is produced by the following Java code?

```
int n;
for (n = 1; n <= 5; n++)
{
    if (n == 3)
        break;
    System.out.println("Hello");
}
System.out.println("After the Loop.");
```

27. What output is produced by the following Java code?

```
int n;
for (n = 1; n <= 5; n++)
{
    if (n == 3)
        System.exit(0);
    System.out.println("Hello");
}
System.out.println("After the Loop.");
```

28. What output is produced by the following Java code?

```
int n;
for (n = 1; n <= 3; n++)
{
    switch (n)
    {
        case 1:
            System.out.println("One.");
            break;
        case 2:
            System.out.println("Two.");
            break;
        case 3:
            System.out.println("Three.");
            break;
        default:
            System.out.println("Default case.");
            break;
    }
}
System.out.println("After the Loop.");
```

3.3 Programming with Loops

The cautious seldom err.
CONFUCIUS

In this section we give you some techniques to help you design loops. A loop is often broken into three parts: the initializing statements that must precede the loop, the loop body, and the mechanism for ending the loop. In this section we give you techniques for designing each of these loop constituents. Although the initializing statements come before the loop body, the loop body is naturally designed first, so we will start our discussion with the loop body.

The Loop Body

One way to design a loop body is to write out the sequence of actions that you want your code to accomplish. For example, you might want your loop to perform the following actions:

```
Output instructions to the user.
Initialize variables.
Read a number into the variable next.
sum = sum + next;
Output the number and the sum so far.
Read another number into the variable next.
sum = sum + next;
Output the number and the sum so far.
Read another number into the variable next.
sum = sum + next;
Output the number and the sum so far.
Read another number into the variable next.
        and so forth.
```

Then, look for a repeated pattern in the list of actions. In this case, a repeated pattern is

```
Read another number into the variable next.
sum = sum + next;
Output the number and the sum so far.
```

So, the body of the loop, expressed in pseudocode, can be the preceding three actions and the entire pseudocode can be

```
Output instructions to the user.
Initialize variables.
Do the following for the appropriate number of times:
{
        Read a number into the variable next.
        sum = sum + next;
        Output the number and the sum so far.
}
```

Note that the pattern need not start with the first action. There may be some actions that need to be done before or after the loop is executed.

Pseudocode

In Chapter 1, we said that algorithms are usually written in pseudocode. **Pseudocode** is a mixture of English and Java. When using pseudocode, you simply write each piece of the algorithm in whatever language is easiest for that part. If the part is easier to express in English, you use English. If another part is easier to express in Java, you use Java for that part. The following simple algorithm (from the section entitled **The Loop Body**) is an example of pseudocode:

Read another number into the variable `next`.
```
sum = sum + next;
```
Output the number and the sum so far.

Initializing Statements

Consider the pseudocode we designed in the previous subsection. Notice that the variable `sum` is expected to have a value every time the following loop body statement is executed:

```
sum = sum + next;
```

In particular, this is true the first time the loop is iterated. So, `sum` must be initialized to some value before the loop starts. When trying to decide on the correct initializing value for `sum`, it helps to consider what you want to happen after one loop iteration. After one loop iteration, the value of `sum` should be set to the first value of `next`. The only way that `sum + next` can evaluate to `next` is if `sum` is 0. That means the value of `sum` must be initialized to 0. Thus, one of the variable initializations must be

```
sum = 0;
```

The only other variable used in the loop is `next`. The first statement performed with `next` is

Read a number into the variable `next`

This statement gives `next` a value, so `next` does not need to have a value before the loop is started. Thus, the only variable that needs to be initialized is `sum`, and we can rewrite the pseudocode to the following:

Output instructions to the user.
```
sum = 0;
```
Do the following the appropriate number of times:
{
       Read a number into the variable `next`
```
        sum = sum + next;
```
       Output the number and the sum so far.
}

Variables are not always initialized to zero. To see this, consider another example. Suppose your loop was computing the product of n numbers as follows:

```
for (count = 1; count <= n; count++)
{
    Read a number into the variable next
    product = product * next;
}
```

In this case, let's say that all variables are of type *int*.

If you initialize the variable product to zero, then no matter how many numbers are read in and multiplied, the value of product will still be zero. So, zero clearly is not the correct initialization value for product. The correct initializing value for product is 1. To see that 1 is the correct initial value, notice that the first time through the loop, you want product to be set equal to the first number read in. Initializing product to 1 will make this happen. Thus, the loop, with a correct initialization statement, is

```
product = 1;
for (count = 1; count <= n; count++)
{
    Read a number into the variable next
    product = product * next;
}
```

Ending a Loop

In this subsection, we discuss some standard techniques you can use to end a loop. Most loops can be ended by one of these techniques or some variant on one of these techniques.

count-controlled loops

If you are lucky, your program may know exactly how many times the loop body must be repeated before the loops starts. In this simple case, you can use a *for*-loop to count the number of loop body iterations. For example, suppose numberOfStudents contains the number of students in a class and you want to know the average score on an exam in the course. The following will do nicely:

```
double next, average, sum = 0;
int count;
for (count = 1; count <= numberOfStudents; count++)
{
    next = SavitchIn.readLineDouble();
    sum = sum + next;
}
if (numberOfStudents > 0)
    average = sum/numberOfStudents;
else
    System.out.println("No scores to average.");
```

Be sure to notice that the variable count is not used in the loop body. The *for*-loop mechanism is simply being used to count from 1 to numberOfStudents and repeat the loop body that many times. Loops, such as this one, that know the number of loop iterations before the loop starts are called **count-controlled loops.** Count-controlled loops do not need to be implemented as *for*-loops, but that is the easiest way to implement a count-controlled loop. (Also note that we have allowed for the possibility of no students being in the class. In that case, the loop body is iterated zero times and the *if-else*-statement prevents division by zero.)

The most straightforward way of ending a loop is to simply ask the user if it is time to end the loop. This works very well in situations where the total number of loop body iterations is expected to be fairly small. For example, the following would work nicely if each customer makes only a few purchases:

asking the user

```
do
{
    System.out.println("Enter price $");
    price = SavitchIn.readLineDouble();
    System.out.print("Enter number purchased: ");
    number = SavitchIn.readLineInt();
    System.out.println(number + " items at $" + price);
    System.out.println("Total cost $" + price*number);
    System.out.println("Want to make another purchase?");
    System.out.println("Enter y for yes or n for no.");
    answer = SavitchIn.readLineNonwhiteChar();
}while ((answer == 'y') || (answer == 'Y'));
```

In some situations, this is best done with a *while*-loop. But, if you know that each user will want at least one loop iteration, then a *do-while*-loop works fine.

For long input lists, you can sometimes use a **sentinel value**. A sentinel value is used for signaling the end of the input. It must be a value that is different from all possible real input values. For example, suppose you want some code to compute the highest and lowest scores on an exam, and suppose you know that there will be at least one exam score. If you know that nobody is ever given a negative score on the exam, then you can ask the user to mark the end of the lists of scores with a negative number. The negative number is the sentinel value. It is not one of the exam scores. It is just an end marker. The code for computing the highest and lowest scores could be as follows:

sentinel value

```
System.out.println("Enter scores for all students");
System.out.println("Enter a negative number after");
System.out.println("you have entered all the scores.");
double max = SavitchIn.readLineDouble();
double min = max;//The max and min so far are the first score.
double next = SavitchIn.readLineDouble();
while (next >= 0)
{
    if (next > max)
        max = next;
    if (next < min)
        min = next;
    next = SavitchIn.readLineDouble();
}
System.out.println("The highest scores is " + max);
System.out.println("The lowest scores is " + min);
```

Be sure to notice that the last number is not used to determine the lowest score (or to determine the highest score). Suppose the user enters the scores as follows:

```
100
90
10
−1
```

then the output will be

```
The highest scores is 100
The lowest scores is 10
```

Be sure to note that the lowest score is 10, not −1. The −1 is just an end marker.

In Section 3.4 we will discuss another method for ending a loop, but these three methods cover most situations you are likely to encounter

---

▽ *PROGRAMMING EXAMPLE* Nested Loops

The body of a loop can contain any sort of statements. In particular, you can have a loop statement within the body of a larger loop statement. For example, the program in Display 3.11 computes the average of a list of scores using a `while`-loop. The program asks the user to enter a list of nonnegative scores with a negative sentinel value to mark the end of the list. The code for this `while`-loop is almost identical to the code we produced in the preceding subsection. This `while`-loop is then placed inside a `do-while`-loop so that the user can repeat the entire process for another exam, and another, until the user wishes to end the program.

◐ *PROGRAMMING TIP* Do Not Declare Variables in a Loop Body

Note that the `while`-loop in Display 3.11 is almost identical to a `while`-loop we designed in the subsection entitled **Ending a Loop**. However, there is one difference. We have moved the declaration of all the variables to the beginning of the program so that they are outside of the body of the outer `do-while`-loop. If we had left the declarations inside the `do-while`-loop, then the declarations would be repeated on each execution of the body of the `do-while`-loop. Depending on how the compiler is written, this can be inefficient, since it may be recreating the variables on each loop iteration. There are times when it makes sense to declare a variable in a loop body, but if the variable declaration can easily be moved outside the loop, it is usually a good idea to do so.

? SELF-TEST QUESTIONS

29. Give a Java loop statement that will output the phrase `"One more time."` to the screen four times. Also, give any declarations or initializing statements that are needed.

30. Give a Java loop statement that will set the variable `result` equal to 2^5. Do this with a loop that starts out with the value of `result` equal to 1 and multiplies the value of `result` by 2 for each of 5 loop iterations. Also, give any declarations or initializing statements that are needed.

<More questions on page 135.>

Display 3.11 Nested Loops (Part 1 of 2)

```java
/***********************************************************************
*Determines the average of a list of (nonnegative) exam scores.
*Repeats for more exams, until the user says she/he is finished.
***********************************************************************/
public class ExamAverager
{
    public static void main(String[] args)
    {
        System.out.println("This program computes the average of");
        System.out.println("a list of (nonnegative) exam scores.");

        double sum;
        int numberOfStudents;
        double next;
        char answer;

        do
        {
            System.out.println();
            System.out.println("Enter all the scores to be averaged.");
            System.out.println("Enter a negative number after");
            System.out.println("you have entered all the scores.");
            sum = 0;
            numberOfStudents = 0;
            next = SavitchIn.readLineDouble();
            while (next >= 0)
            {
                sum = sum + next;
                numberOfStudents++;
                next = SavitchIn.readLineDouble();
            }
            if (numberOfStudents > 0)
                System.out.println("The average is "
                                    + (sum/numberOfStudents));
            else
                System.out.println("No scores to average.");

            System.out.println("Want to average another exam?");
            System.out.println("Enter y for yes or n for no.");
            answer = SavitchIn.readLineNonwhiteChar();
        }while ((answer == 'y') || (answer == 'Y'));
    }
}
```

Display 3.11 Nested Loops *(Part 2 of 2)*

Sample Screen Dialogue

```
This program computes the average of
a list of (nonnegative) exam scores.

Enter all the scores to be averaged.
Enter a negative number after
you have entered all the scores.
100
90
100
90
-1
The average is 95
Want to average another exam?
Enter y for yes or n for no.
y

Enter all the scores to be averaged.
Enter a negative number after
you have entered all the scores.
90
70
80
-1
The average is 80
Want to average another exam?
Enter y for yes or n for no.
n
```

31. What output is produced by the following Java code:

```java
int count, innerCount;
for (count = 0; count <= 3; count++)
    for (innerCount = 0; innerCount < count; innerCount++)
        System.out.println(innerCount);
```

32. Give a Java loop statement that will read in a list of numbers of type *double* and then output their average. The numbers are all greater than or equal to 1.0. The list is ended with a sentinel value. You must specify the sentinel value. Also, give any declarations or initializing statements that are needed.

Loop Bugs

Programs that contain loops are significantly more likely to contain mistakes than the programs you saw before you started using loops. Fortunately, there is a pattern to the kinds of mistakes you are most likely to make in designing a loop, so we can tell you what to look for. Moreover, there are some standard techniques you can use to locate and fix any bugs in your loops

The two most common kinds of loop errors are unintended infinite loops and *off-by-one errors.* Let's consider them in order.

We have already discussed infinite loops. There is, however, one subtlety about   *infinite loops*
infinite loops that we need to emphasize. A loop might terminate for some input value but be an infinite loop for other values. Just because you tested your loop for some program input values and found that the loop ended, that does not mean that it will not be an infinite loop for some other input values. Let's consider an example.

You have a friend whose checking account balance is overdrawn. The bank charges a penalty each month that the balance is negative. Your friend wants a program that will tell her or him how long it will take to get the account balance to be nonnegative by making a fixed size deposit each month. You design the following code:

```java
count = 0;
while (balance < 0)
{
    balance = balance - penalty;
    balance = balance + deposit;
    count = count++;
}
System.out.println("You will have a nonnegative balance in "
                        + count + " months.");
```

You place this code in a complete program and test the code with some reasonable values, like $15 for the penalty and $50 for the size of the deposit. The program runs fine. So you give it to your friend who runs it and it then turns out to have an infinite loop. What happened? Your friend obviously does not have a head for numbers and decided to make her or his deposits small. Your friend decided to deposit $10 per month. But, the bank charges a penalty of $15 a month when an account goes negative. So, the account simply gets a larger negative balance every month, even though your friend makes deposits.

It may seem that this could not happen. Your friend would not be so stupid. Don't count on it! It can happen even if your friend is not stupid. People are careless. One way to fix this bug is to add code that will test to see if the loop is infinite or not. For example, you might change the code to the following:

```
if (payment <= penalty)
    System.out.println("payment is too small.");
else
{
    count = 0;
    while (balance < 0)
    {
        balance = balance − penalty;
        balance = balance + payment;
        count++;
    }
    System.out.println("You will have a nonnegative balance in "
                                        + count + " months.");
}
```

off-by-one
error

The other very common kind of loop bug is an **off-by-one error**. This means that your loop repeats the loop body one too many or one too few times. These sort of errors can result from carelessness in designing a controlling boolean expression. For example, if you use less-than when you should use less-than-or-equal, this can easily make your loop iterate the body the wrong number of times.

Another common problem with the controlling boolean expression of a loop has to do with the use of == to test for equality. This sort of equality testing works satisfactorily for integers and characters, but is not reliable for floating point numbers. This is because the floating point numbers are approximate quantities and == test for exact equality. The result of such a test is unpredictable. When comparing floating point numbers, always use something involving less-than or greater-than, such as <=; do not use == or !=. Using a == or != to test floating point numbers can produce an off-by-one error or an unintended infinite loop or even some other type of error.

One big danger with off-by-one errors is that they can easily go unnoticed. If a loop is iterated one too many times or one too few times, then the results might still look reasonable, but be off by enough to cause trouble later on. Always make a specific check for off-by-one errors by comparing your loop results to results you know to be true by some other means, such as a pencil-and-paper calculation of a simple case.

Always Retest

Whenever you find a bug in a program and "fix it," always retest the program. There may be yet another bug, or your "fix" may have introduced a new bug. ◻

Tracing Variables

tracing
variables

If your program misbehaves but you cannot see what is wrong, then your best bet is to *trace* some key variables. **Tracing variables** means watching the variables change

? SELF-TEST QUESTIONS

33. Add some suitable output statements to the following code, so that all variables are traced.

```
int n, sum = 0;
for (n = 1; n < 10; n++)
    sum = sum + n;
System.out.println("1 + 2 + ...+ 9 + 10 == " + sum);
```

34. What is the bug in the following code? What do you call this kind of loop bug?

```
int n, sum = 0;
for (n = 1; n < 10; n++)
    sum = sum + n;
System.out.println("1 + 2 + ...+ 9 + 10 == " + sum);
```

3.4 The Type *boolean*

> *The truth is out there.*
> INCLUDED IN THE CREDITS FOR THE TELEVISION PROGRAM *The X Files.*

> *He who would distinguish the true from the false must have an adequate idea of what is true and false.*
> BENEDICT SPINOZA, *Ethics*

The type *boolean* is a primitive type, just like the types *int*, *double*, and *char*. Just like these other types, you can have expressions of type *boolean*, values of type *boolean*, constants of type *boolean*, and variables of type *boolean*. However, there are only two values of type *boolean*: *true* and *false*. The two values *true* and *false* can be used in a program, just like numeric constants such as 2, 3.45, and the character constant 'A'.

Boolean variables can be used, among other things, to make your program easier to read. For example, a program might contain the following statement, where systemsAreOK is a boolean variable that is *true* if in fact the launch systems are ready to go:

```
if (systemsAreOK)
    System.out.println("Initiate launch sequence.");
else
    System.out.println("Abort launching sequence.");
```

If you do not use something like a boolean variable, then the preceding code is likely to read something like the following:

```
if ((temperature <= 100) && (thrust >= 12000) && (cabinPressure > 30))
    System.out.println("Initiate launch sequence.");
else
    System.out.println("Abort launching sequence.");
```

value while the program is running. A program typically does not output a variable's value every time it changes the value of the variable, but it can help you to debug your program if you can see all these variable changes.

Many systems have a built-in utility that lets you easily trace variables without making any changes to your program. These debugging systems vary from one installation to another. If you have such a debugging facility, it is worth learning how to use it. If you do not have such a debugging facility, you can trace variables by simply inserting some extra temporary output statements in your program. For example, suppose you want to trace the variables in the following code (which does contain an error):

```
count = 0;
while (balance < 0)
{
    balance = balance + penalty;
    balance = balance - deposit;
    count = count++;
}
System.out.println("You will have a positive balance in "
                                + count + " months.");
```

You can trace the variables by adding the following output statements:

```
count = 0;
System.out.println("count == " + count);//trace
System.out.println("balance == " + balance);//trace
System.out.println("penalty == " + penalty);//trace
System.out.println("deposit == " + deposit);//trace
while (balance < 0)
{
    balance = balance + penalty;
    System.out.println("balance + penalty == " + balance);//trace
    balance = balance - deposit;
    System.out.println("balance - deposit == " + balance);//trace
    count = count++;
    System.out.println("count == " + count);//trace
}
System.out.println("You will have a positive balance in "
                                + count + " months.");
```

After you have discovered the error and fixed the bugs in the code, you can remove the trace statements.

It may seem like a lot of bother to insert all the trace statements in the preceding example, but it is not so very much work. If you wish, you can first try tracing only some of the variables to see if that gives you enough information to find the problem, However, it is usually fastest to just trace all, or almost all, the variables right from the start.

Clearly, the first version with the boolean variable is easier for a human being to understand.

Of course, your program does need to set the value of the boolean variable `systemsAreOK` in some way but, as we will see, that is easy to do.

Boolean Expressions and Boolean Variables

A **boolean expression** evaluates to one of the two values *true* or *false*. For example, the expression `number > 0` in the following is a boolean expression:

boolean expression

```
if (number > 0)
    System.out.println("The number is positive.");
else
    System.out.println("The number is negative or zero.");
```

If `number > 0` evaluates to *true*, then the output is "The number is positive." If, on the other hand, `number > 0` evaluates to *false*, then the output is "The number is negative or zero." The meaning of a a boolean expression like `number > 0` is a bit easier to understand within a context, such as an *if-else*-statement. However, when programming with boolean variables you need to think about a boolean expression more or less without a context. A boolean expression can be evaluated and can produce a value of *true* or *false* without reference to any *if-else*-statement or *while*-loop or other context that you have seen before this section.

A boolean variable can be assigned the value of a boolean expression by using an assignment statement in the same way that you use an assignment statement to set the value of an *int* variable, or any other type of variable. For example, the following sets the value of the boolean variable `positive` to *false*.

boolean variables in assignments

```
int number = -5;
boolean isPositive;
isPositive = (number > 0);
```

If you prefer, you can combine the last two lines as follows:

```
boolean isPositive = (number > 0);
```

The parentheses are not needed, but they do make it a bit easier to read.

Once a boolean variable has a value, you can use a boolean variable just like any other boolean expression. For example,

```
boolean isPositive = (number > 0);
if (isPositive)
    System.out.println("The number is positive.");
else
    System.out.println("The number is negative or zero.");
```

is equivalent to

```
if (number > 0)
    System.out.println("The number is positive.");
else
    System.out.println("The number is negative or zero.");
```

Of course, this is just a toy example. It is unlikely that anybody would use the first of the preceding two examples, but you might use something like this if the value of number, and so the value of the boolean expression, might change, as in the following, which might be part of a program to evaluate lottery tickets (by some stretch of the imagination):

```
System.out.println("Enter your number:");
number = SavitchIn.readLineInt();
boolean isPositive = (number > 0);
while (number > 0);
{
    System.out.println("Wow!");
    number = number - 1000;
}
if (isPositive)
    System.out.println("Your number is positive.");
else
    System.out.println("Sorry, your number is not positive.");
System.out.println("Only positive numbers can win.");
```

More complicated boolean expressions can be used in the same way. For example, if systemsAreOK is a variable of type *boolean*, it can be given a value as follows:

```
systemsAreOK =
  (temperature <= 100) && (thrust >= 12000) && (cabinPressure > 30);
```

Precedence Rules

Java evaluates boolean expressions using the same strategy that it uses to evaluate arithmetic expressions. Let's consider an example:

```
(score >= 80) && (score < 90)
```

and suppose the value of score is 95. The first subexpression (score >= 80) evaluates to *true*. The second subexpression (score < 90) evaluates to *false*. So the entire expression is reduced to

```
true && false
```

The computer combines the values of *true* and/or *false* according rules called **truth tables** that are given in Display 3.12. So, the preceding expression evaluates to *false*.

When writing boolean expressions or arithmetic expressions, it is usually best to indicate the order of operations with parentheses. However, if parentheses are omitted, then the computer will perform the operations in an order determined by the **precedence rules** shown in Display 3.13. Operators that are listed higher on the list are said to have **higher precedence.** When the computer is deciding which of two operators to perform first and the order is not dictated by parentheses, then it does the operator of higher precedence before the operator of lower precedence. Some operators have equal precedence, in which the order of operations is determined by the left-to-right order of the operators. Binary operators of equal precedence are

precedence
rules

Display 3.12 Truth Tables for Boolean Operators

&& *(and)*

value of A	value of B	resulting value of A && B
true	true	true
true	false	false
false	true	false
false	false	false

|| *(or)*

value of A	value of B	resulting value of A || B
true	true	true
true	false	true
false	true	true
false	false	false

! *(not)*

value of A	resulting value of $!(A)$
true	false
false	true

Display 3.13 **Precedence Rules**

....

Highest Precedence

First: the unary operators: +, −, ++, −−, and !

Second: the binary arithmetic operators: *, /, %

Third: the binary arithmetic operators: +, −

Fourth: the boolean operators: <, >, <=, >=

Fifth: the boolean operators: ==, !=

Sixth: the boolean operator &

Seventh: the boolean operator |

Eighth: the boolean operator &&

Ninth: the boolean operator ||

Lowest Precedence

....

performed in left-to-right order. Unary operators of equal precedence are performed in right-to-left order. Let's consider an example.

The following is rather poor style, but the computer has no problem with it and
it will be a good exercise to evaluate it using the precedence rules:

```
score < min/2 - 10 || score > 90
```

Of all the operators in the expression, the division operator has the highest precedence and so is done first:

```
score < (min/2) - 10 || score > 90
```

Of the remaining operators in the expression, the subtraction operator has the highest precedence and so is done next:

```
score < ((min/2) - 10) || score > 90
```

Of the remaining operators in the expression the > and < operators have the highest
precedence and so they are done next. Since the > and < operators have equal precedence, they are done in left-to-right order:

```
(score < ((min/2) - 10)) || (score > 90)
```

Thus, we have produced a fully parenthesized version of the expression by using the
precedence rules. To the computer, the two expressions are equivalent.

You should include most parentheses in order to make your arithmetic and
boolean expressions easier to understand. However, one place where parentheses
can be safely omitted is a simple string of &&'s or ||'s (but not a mixture of the

two). For example, the following is good style even though a few parentheses are omitted:

```
(temperature > 95) || (rainFall > 20) || (humidity >= 60)
```

The way that Java handles || and && is just a bit more complicated than what we have said so far. Consider the following boolean expression:

short-circuit evaluation

```
(score > 90) || (assignmentsDone > 8)
```

Now, suppose that the value of score is 95. In this case we know that the boolean expression evaluates to *true*, no matter what the value of assignmentsDone is. This is because *true* || *true* and *true* || *false* both evaluate to *true*. So, it does not matter whether assignmentsDone > 8 evaluates to *true* or *false*. The value of the whole expression is bound to be *true*. Java evaluates an expression connected with || or && in just this way. It evaluates the first subexpression and if that is enough information to determine the value of the whole expression, then it does not evaluate the second subexpression. So, in this example, Java never bothers to evaluate the expression assignmentsDone > 8. This way of evaluating only as much of an expression as it needs is called **short-circuit evaluation** and is the kind of evaluation that is done by Java with && and ||. (Short-circuit evaluation is also sometimes called **lazy evaluation**.)

Now, let's look at an example using && and let's give the boolean expression some context by placing it in an *if-else*-statement:

```
if ((assignmentsDone > 0) && ((totalScore/assignmentsDone) > 60))
    System.out.println("Good work.");
else
        System.out.println("Work harder.");
```

Suppose AssignmentsDone has a value of 0. Then the first subexpression is *false*. Now, both *false* && *true* and *false* && *false* evaluate to *false*. So, no matter whether the second expression is *true* or *false*, the entire boolean expression is *false*. So, Java does not bother to evaluate the second subexpression

```
(totalScore/assignmentsDone) > 60
```

In this case, not evaluating the second subexpression does make a big difference, because the second subexpression includes a division by zero. If Java had tried to evaluate the second subexpression, that would have produced a run-time error. By using short-circuit evaluation Java has prevented a run-time error.

Java also allows you to ask for **complete evaluation.** In complete evaluation, when two expressions are joined by an "and" or an "or," *both* subexpressions are *always evaluated* and then the truth tables are used to obtain the value of the final expression. To obtain complete evaluation in Java, you use & rather than && for "and" and use | in place of || for "or."

complete evaluation

In most situations, short-circuit evaluation and complete evaluation give the same result, but as we have seen, there are some cases in which short-circuit evaluation can avoid a run-time error. There are some situations where complete evaluation is preferred, but we will not use those techniques in this book, and so we will always use && and || so as to obtain short-circuit evaluation.

Input and Output of Boolean Values

The values *true* and *false* of the type *boolean* can be input and output in the same way as values of the other primitive types, such as *int* and *double*. For example, consider the following fragment from a Java program:

```
boolean booleanVar = false;
System.out.println(booleanVar);
System.out.println("Enter a boolean value:");
booleanVar = SavitchIn.readLineBoolean();
System.out.println("You entered " + booleanVar);
```

This code could produce the following dialogue:

```
false
Enter a boolean value:
true
You entered true
```

As you can see from this example, the class SavitchIn has a method named readLineBoolean that will read a single *boolean* value on a line by itself. For this method, you may spell *true*, and *false*, with either upper- or lowercase letters; you also may use a single letter t or f (upper- or lowercase) for *true* and *false*. These spelling variations of *true* and *false* apply only to input and only when using the method readLineBoolean. In a Java program, the spelling must always be either *true* or *false*, spelled out and in all lowercase.

T and F

task specification

Case Study Using a Boolean Variable to End a Loop

In this case study, you will not solve a complete problem, but you will design a loop for a commonly occurring subtask and place it in a demonstration program. This will allow you to get used to one of the most common uses of boolean variables. In this case study, you want to design a loop to read in a list of numbers and compute the sum of all the numbers on the list. You know that the numbers are all nonnegative. For example, the numbers might be a list of the number of hours worked for each person on a programming team. Since nobody works a negative number of hours, you know the numbers are all nonnegative and so you can use a negative number as a sentinel value to mark the end of the list of numbers. For this task, you know the numbers will all be integers, but the same technique would work for other kinds of numbers and even for reading in nonnumeric data.

You will get a better grasp of the problem and possible solutions if you first design the loop in pseudocode. So, you design the following pseudocode:

```
int sum = 0;
Do the following for each number on the list:
        if (the number is negative)
                Make this the last loop iteration.
        else
                sum = sum + the number;
```

Since you know that there is a negative number marking the end of the list, you refine the pseudocode to the following:

```
int next, sum = 0;
while (There are numbers left to read.)
{
    next = SavitchIn.readLineInt();
    if (next < 0)
        Make this the last loop iteration.
    else
        sum = sum + next;
}
```

There are a number of different ways to finish converting this pseudocode to Java code. Since you have just learned about boolean variables, you decide to try them (and that will turn out to be a good decision). One nice thing about a boolean variable is that it can read just like an English sentence. So you decide to try a boolean variable named `thereAreNumbersLeftToRead`. Simply declaring this boolean variable and substituting it for the phrase "There are numbers left to read." yields the following:

```
int next, sum = 0;
boolean thereAreNumbersLeftToRead;
Initialize the variable ThereAreNumbersLeftToRead.
while (thereAreNumbersLeftToRead)
{
    next = SavitchIn.readLineInt();
    if (next < 0)
        Make this the last loop iteration.
    else
        sum = sum + next;
}
```

Now it is straightforward to complete this loop to produce working Java code. The phrase "Make this the last loop iteration." can be translated in one obvious way. The loop ends when the boolean variable `thereAreNumbersLeftToRead` has a value of *false*. So, the way to end the loop is to set `thereAreNumbersLeftToRead` equal to *false*. So, "Make this the last loop iteration." will translate into

```
thereAreNumbersLeftToRead = false;
```

All that is left to do is to determine the initial value for the boolean variable `thereAreNumbersLeftToRead`. You know that even if the list of numbers is empty, there will at least be the sentinel value to read, so you know the loop body must be iterated at least once. So, in order for the loop to get started, `thereAreNumbersLeftToRead` must be *true*. So, you know that `thereAreNumbersLeftToRead` must be initialized to *true*. Thus, you come up with the following code:

```
int next, sum = 0;
boolean thereAreNumbersLeftToRead = true;
while (thereAreNumbersLeftToRead)
{
    next = SavitchIn.readLineInt();
    if (next < 0)
        thereAreNumbersLeftToRead = false;
    else
        sum = sum + next;
}
```

When the loop ends, the variable `sum` contains the sum of the numbers on the input list (not including the sentinel value).

All that is left is to put the loop into a program. You decide that the variable name `thereAreNumbersLeftToRead` is a bit too long and so you shorten it to `numbersLeft` and produce the program shown in Display 3.14.

? SELF-TEST QUESTIONS

35. What is the output produced by the following statements?

```
int number = 7;
boolean isPositive = (number > 0);
if (number > 0);
    number = -100;
if (isPositive)
    System.out.println("Positive.");
else
    System.out.println("Not positive.");
```

36. What is the output produced by the following statements?

```
System.out.println(false);
System.out.println(7 < 0);
System.out.println(7 > 0);
int n = 7;
System.out.println(n > 0);
```

Chapter Summary

- A statement that chooses one of a number of actions to perform is called a **branch**. `if-else`-statements and `switch`-statements are branch statements.

- Java has two forms of multiway branches: the `switch`-statement and the multibranch `if-else`-statement.

- A **loop** is a programming construct that repeats an action some number of times. The part that is repeated is called the **body** of the loop. Every repetition of the loop body is called a loop **iteration**.

- Java has three kinds of loop statements: `while`-statements, `do-while`-

Display 3.14 Use of a Boolean Variable to End a Loop

```java
//Illustrates the use of a boolean variable to control loop ending.
public class BooleanDemo
{
    public static void main(String[] args)
    {
        System.out.println("Enter nonnegative numbers, one per line.");
        System.out.println("Place a negative number at the end");
        System.out.println("to serve as an end marker.");

        int next, sum = 0;
        boolean numbersLeft = true;
        while (numbersLeft)
        {
            next = SavitchIn.readLineInt();
            if (next < 0)
                numbersLeft = false;
            else
                sum = sum + next;
        }

        System.out.println("The sum of the numbers is " + sum);
    }
}
```

Sample Screen Dialogue

```
Enter nonnegative numbers, one per line.
Place a negative number at the end
to serve as an end marker.
1
2
3
-1
The sum of the numbers is 6
```

statements, and *for*-statements.

□ One way to end an input loop is to place a sentinel value at the end of the input list and have your loop check for the sentinel value.

□ The most common kinds of loop bugs are unintended infinite loops and off-by-one errors.

□ Tracing a variable means that the value of the variable is output every time the variable is changed. This can be done with special debugging utilities or by inserting temporary output statements. (Sometimes you do not output every change but just selected changes.)

□ The value of a boolean expression can be stored in a variable of type *boolean*. The variable of type *boolean* can then be used to control an *if-else*-statement, a *while*-statement, or anyplace else that a boolean expression is allowed.

? ANSWERS to Self-Test Questions

1.
```java
if (goals > 10)
    System.out.println("Wow");
else
    System.out.println("Oh Well");
```

2.
```java
if ((goals > 10) && (errors == 0))
    System.out.println("Wow");
else
    System.out.println("Oh Well");
```

3.
```java
if (salary >= deductions)
{
    System.out.println("OK");
    net = salary - deductions;
}
else
    System.out.println("Crazy.");
```

4.
```java
if ((speed > 25) && (visibility < 20))
{
    speed = 25;
    System.out.println("Caution");
}
```

5.
```java
if ((salary >= MIN_SALARY) || (bonus >= MIN_BONUS))
    System.out.println("OK");
else
    System.out.println("Too low");
```

6. Time and tide wait for me.

7. Time and tide wait for no one.

8. Time and tide wait for every one.

9.

```
if (number > 10)
    System.out.println("high");
else if (number < 5)
    System.out.println("low");
else
    System.out.println("so-so");
```

10. Till we meet again.

11.

```
Hello
Good-bye
```

12. Some kind of B.

13. Pie

14. Cookies

15. Diet time:

16.

```
0
1
2
3
4
count after loop = 5
```

17. Yes, a `while`-loop can execute the body of the loop zero times. No, a `do-while`-loop cannot execute the body of the loop zero times.

18.

```
0
count after loop = 1
```

19.

```
int number;
{
    System.out.println("Enter a whole number:");
    number = SavitchIn.readLineInt();
    System.out.println("You entered " + number);
}
while (number > 0)
{
    System.out.println("Enter a whole number:");
    number = SavitchIn.readLineInt();
    System.out.println("You entered " + number);
}
System.out.println("number after loop = " + number);
```

20. This is an infinite loop. The `println`-statement after the loop will never be executed. The output begins

    ```
    0
    -1
    -2
    -3
     .
     .
     .
    ```

21.
    ```
    1
    2
    3
    4
    ```

22. This loop causes no output. The boolean expression n > 4 is not satisfied the first time through the loop, so the loop ends without iterating its body.

23.
    ```
    4
    3
    2
    1
    ```

24.
    ```
    0.0
    0.5
    1.0
    1.5
    2.0
    2.5
    ```

25.
    ```
    int n;
    for (n = 1; n <= 5; n++)
        System.out.println(2*n);
    ```

26.
    ```
    Hello
    Hello
    After the Loop.
    ```

27.
    ```
    Hello
    Hello
    ```

    Note that it does not output "After the Loop.", because the program ends.

28.

```
One
Two
Three
After the Loop.
```

Note that the *break*-statement ends the *switch*-statement but does not end the *for*-loop.

29.

```
int time;
for (time = 1; time <= 4; time++)
    System.out.println("One more time.");
```

30.

```
int result = 1;
int count;
for (count = 1; count <= 5; count++)
    result = 2*result;
```

31.

```
0
0
1
0
1
2
```

32. You can use any number less than 1.0 as a sentinel value, but to avoid any problems with the approximate nature of *double* values, it should be significantly less than 1.0.

```
double sum = 0, next;
System.out.println("Enter a list of numbers. All the");
System.out.println("numbers must be 1.0 or larger");
System.out.println("Place a zero at the end");
System.out.println("to mark the end of the list.");
next = SavitchIn.readLineDouble();
int count = 0;
while (next > 0.9)//next >=1.0 runs a risk of being inaccurate.
{
    sum = sum + next;
    count++;
    next = SavitchIn.readLineDouble();
}
if (count > 0)
    System.out.println("Average is " + (sum/count));
else
    System.out.println("No numbers to average.");
```

33.

```
int n, sum = 0;
System.out.println("sum == " + sum);
for (n = 1; n < 10; n++)
{
    sum = sum + n;
    System.out.println("n == " + n);
    System.out.println("sum == " + sum);
}
System.out.println("1 + 2 + ...+ 9 + 10 == " + sum);
```

34. The boolean expression should be n <= 10 not n < 10. This is an off-by-one error.

35. `Positive`

36. The output produced is

```
false
false
true
true
```

? PROGRAMMING EXERCISES

1. Write a program that takes a one-line sentence as input and then outputs the following response: If the sentence ends with the question mark '?' and the input contains an even number of characters, then output the word "Yes". If the sentence ends with the question mark '?' and the input contains an odd number of characters, then output the word "No". If the sentence ends with an exclamation mark '!', then output the word "Wow". In all other cases, your program will output the string "You always say " followed by the input string enclosed in quotes. Your output should all be on one line. Be sure to note that in the last case, your output must include quotation marks around the echoed input string. In all other cases, there are no quotes in the output. Your program should have a loop that allows the user to repeat this until the user indicates that she/he wants to end the program. Your program does not have to check the input to see that the user entered a legitimate sentence.

2. Write a program to read in a list of nonnegative integers and output: the largest integer, the smallest integer, and the average of all the integers. The end of the input is indicated by the user entering a negative sentinel value. Note that the sentinel value is not used in finding the largest, smallest, or average. It is only an end marker. The average should be a value of type *double* so that the average is computed with a fractional part.

3. Write a program that takes as input a bank account balance and an interest rate and that outputs the value of the account in 10 years. The output should show the value of the account for three different methods of compounding interest: annually, monthly, and daily. When compounded annu-

ally, the interest is added once per year at the end of the year. When compounded monthly the interest is added in 12 times per year. When computed daily, the interest is added 365 times per year. You do not have to worry about leap years. Assume all years have 365 days. On annual interest, you can assume that the interest is posted exactly one year from the date of deposit. In other words, you do not have to worry about interest being posted on a specific day of the year, like December 31. Similarly, you can assume monthly interest is posted exactly one month after it in entered. Since the account earns interest on the interest, the account should have a higher balance when interest is posted more frequently. Be sure to adjust the interest rate for the time period of the interest. If the rate is 5%, then when posting monthly interest, you use (5/12)%. When posting daily interest, you use (5/365)%. Do your calculation using a loop that adds in the interest for each time period. (Do not use some sort of algebraic formula.) Your program should have an outer loop that allows the user to repeat this calculation for a new balance and interest rate. The calculation is repeated until the user indicates that she/he wants to end the program.

Chapter 4

CLASSES, OBJECTS, AND METHODS

4.1 **CLASS AND METHOD DEFINITIONS 156**
Class Files and Separate
  Compilation 156
Instance Variables 157
Using Methods 161
void-Method Definitions 163
Methods that Return a Value 165
Programming Tip Use of *return* in
  void-Methods 168
The *this* Parameter 169
Local Variables 172
Blocks 173
Gotcha Variables Declared in a
  Block 175
Declaring Variables in a *for*-
  Statement *(Optional)* 175
Parameters of a Primitive Type 176
Gotcha Use of the Terms "Parame-
  ter" and "Argument" 182
Summary of Class and Method
  Definition Syntax 182

4.2 **INFORMATION HIDING AND
        ENCAPSULATION 184**
Information Hiding 185
Programming Tip Formal Parameter
  Names Are Local to the
  Method 185
Precondition and Postcondition
  Comments 187

The Public and Private
  Modifiers 188
Programming Tip Instance Variables
  Should Be Private 191
Programming Example
  Purchase Class 194
Abstract Data Types (ADTs) 198
Case Study Changing the
  Implementation of an ADT 202

4.3 **OBJECTS AND REFERENCE 206**
Variables of a Class Type and
  Objects 207
Gotcha Use of = and == with
  Variables of A Class Type 209
Programming Tip Define an *equals*
  Method for Your Classes 210
Programming Example
  A Species Class 213
Boolean-Valued Methods 213
Class Parameters 217
Comparing Class Parameters and
  Primitive-Type Parameters 220
Programming Tip Make the Compiler
  Happy 223

Chapter Summary 225
Answers to Self-Test Questions 225
Programming Exercises 230

4

CLASSES, OBJECTS, AND METHODS

. . . .

> *class* n. *1.a.* A set, collection, group, or configuration containing members
> having or thought to have at least one attribute in common; kind; sort. ...
> **The American Heritage Dictionary of the English Language, Third Edition**

Introduction

Recall that an object is named by a variable of a class. Like variables of the primitive types (such as *int*), objects have data, but they also can take actions. The actions are called *methods*. You have already been using some objects. The type String is a class and values of type String are objects. For example, if name is an object of type String, then the method named length can be used to determine the length of the string. The length of the string is the value returned by the expression name.length() (i.e., the value produced by the method invocation name.length()). In this chapter, we will show you how to define and use your own simple classes and how to use objects of those classes.

Prerequisites

You need to be familiar with the material in Chapters 2 and 3 before reading this chapter.

4.1 Class and Method Definitions

A Java program consists of objects from various classes interacting with one another. You are now ready to define some simple classes.

Class Files and Separate Compilation

We are about to tell you how to define classes in Java. If you want to follow this discussion by running the programs, all the classes and programs in this book are available on the CD provided with this book. Whether you use a class we write in this book or a class that you yourself write, you need to know a few basic details about how a Java class definition is stored in a file. Each Java class definition should be in a file by itself.[1] Not only should each Java class definition be in a separate file, but the name of the file should be the same as the name of the class, and the file name should end in .java. So, if you write a class called MyClass, then it should be in a file named MyClass.java.

---

1. There are exceptions to this rule, but we will seldom encounter these exceptions and we need not be concerned about them now.

You can compile a Java class before you have any program in which to use it. The compiled byte code for the class will be stored in a file of the same name but ending in .class rather than .java. So, if you compile the file MyClass.java, you will create a file called MyClass.class. Later, you can compile a program file with a main part that uses the class MyClass, and you will not need to recompile the class definition for MyClass. This naming requirement applies to full programs as well as classes. Notice that every program with a main has a class name at the start of the file; this is the name you need to use for the file that holds the program. For example, the program in Display 4.2/page 159 should be in a file named SpeciesFirstTryDemo.java. As long as all the classes you use in a program are in the same directory as the program file, you need not worry about directories. In Chapter 5, we will discuss how you can place files in more than one directory.

Instance Variables

Display 4.1 contains a simple class definition. We have simplified this class to make this first example easier to explain. Later in this chapter, we will give this same example in a better style. But, this example has all the essentials of a class definition. It will take several subsections to fully explain this class definition. So, let's get started.

The class name is SpeciesFirstTry and is designed to hold records of endangered species. (It's called FirstTry because we will later give an improved version of this class.) Each object of this class has three pieces of data: a name, a population size, and a growth rate. The objects have three methods: readInput, writeOutput, and populationIn10. Both the data items and the methods are sometimes called **members** of the object, because they belong to the object; they are also sometimes called **fields**. However, we will use different names. We will call the data items *instance variables* and we will call the methods *methods*. Let's discuss the data items (i.e., the instance variables) first.

The following three lines from the end of the class definition define three **instance variables** (three data members):

```java
public String name;
public int population;
public double growthRate;
```

The word public simply means that there are no restrictions on how these instance variables are used. Each of these lines declares one instance variable. You can think of an object of the class as a complex item with instance variables inside of it. So, you can think of an instance variable as a smaller variable inside of each object of the class. In this case, the instance variables are called name, population, and growth-Rate. Display 4.2 contains a program that demonstrates the use of this class definitions. Let's see how it handles these instance variables.

The following line from Display 4.2 creates an object of type Species-FirstTry and attaches the name speciesOfTheMonth to this object:

```java
SpeciesFirstTry speciesOfTheMonth = new SpeciesFirstTry();
```

Like all objects of type SpeciesFirstTry, the object speciesOfTheMonth has three instance variables called name, population, and growthRate. You can refer to one

member

field

instance variable

Display 4.1 A Class Definition

```java
public class SpeciesFirstTry
{
    public void readInput()
    {
        System.out.println("What is the species' name?");
        name = SavitchIn.readLine();
        System.out.println("What is the population of the species?");
        population = SavitchIn.readLineInt();
        System.out.println("Enter growth rate (percent increase per year):")
        growthRate = SavitchIn.readLineDouble();
    }

    public void writeOutput()
    {
        System.out.println("Name = " + name);
        System.out.println("Population = " + population);
        System.out.println("Growth rate = " + growthRate + "%");
    }

    public int populationIn10()
    {
        double populationAmount = population;
        int count = 10;
        while ((count > 0) && (populationAmount > 0))
        {
            populationAmount = (populationAmount +
                             (growthRate/100) * populationAmount);
            count--;
        }
        if (populationAmount > 0)
            return (int)populationAmount;
        else
            return 0;
    }

    public String name;
    public int population;
    public double growthRate;
}
```

We will give a better version of this class later in this chapter.

(int) is a type cast, as discussed in Chapter 2 starting on page 41.

Later in this chapter we will see that the modifier public should be replaced with private.

Display 4.2 Using Classes and Methods *(Part 1 of 2)*

● ●

```java
public class SpeciesFirstTryDemo
{
    public static void main(String[] args)
    {
        SpeciesFirstTry speciesOfTheMonth = new SpeciesFirstTry();
        int futurePopulation;

        System.out.println("Enter data on the Species of the Month:");
        speciesOfTheMonth.readInput();
        speciesOfTheMonth.writeOutput();

        futurePopulation = speciesOfTheMonth.populationIn10();
        System.out.println("In ten years the population will be " +
                                                futurePopulation);

        speciesOfTheMonth.name = "Klingon ox";
        speciesOfTheMonth.population = 10;
        speciesOfTheMonth.growthRate = 15;
        System.out.println("The new Species of the Month:");
        speciesOfTheMonth.writeOutput();
        System.out.println("In ten years the population will be " +
                                speciesOfTheMonth.populationIn10());
    }
}
```

● ●

of these instance variables by writing the object name followed by a dot and then the instance variables name. For example,

```java
spciesOfTheMonth.name
```

denotes the `name` instance variable for the object `speciesOfTheMonth`. Look again at the three lines that define the instance variables (repeated in what follows).

```java
public String name;
public int population;
public double growthRate;
```

Notice that each instance variable has a type. For example, the instance variable `name` is of type `String`, so the instance variable `speciesOfTheMonth.name` is a variable of type `String` and it can be used anyplace that you can use a variable of type `String`. For example, all of the following are legal Java expressions:

Display 4.2 Using Classes and Methods *(Part 2 of 2)*

Sample Screen Dialogue

```
Enter data on the Species of the Month:
What is the species' name?
Ferengie fur ball
What is the population of the species?
1000
Enter growth rate (percent increase per year):
-20.5
Name = Ferengie fur ball
Population = 1000
Growth rate = -20.5%
In ten years the population will be 100
The new Species of the Month:
Name = Klingon ox
Population = 10
Growth rate = 15.0%
In ten years the population will be 40
```

```
speciesOfTheMonth.name = "Klingon ox.";
System.out.println("Save the " + speciesOfTheMonth.name);
String niceName = speciesOfTheMonth.name;
```

Each object of type `SpeciesFirstTry` has its own three instance variables. For example, suppose your program were to also contain

```
SpeciesFirstTry speciesOfLastMonth = new SpeciesFirstTry();
```

Then `speciesOfTheMonth.name` and `speciesOfLastMonth.name` are two different instance variables that might have different string values.

Why Do You Need *new*?

When used in an expression such as the following, you can think of the *new* as creating the instance variables of the object.

```
SpeciesFirstTry speciesOfLastMonth = new SpeciesFirstTry();
```

A variable of a primitive type, such as a variable of type `int` or `double`, is a simple variable. A variable of a class type, such as `speciesOfLastMonth`, is a more complex variable that can, in some sense, have smaller variables inside of it, namely, the instance variables of the object. The *new* places these instance variables inside of the object. We will explain this use of *new* more completely in Section 4.3.

Using Methods

Methods are actions that can be taken by an object of a class. A method **invocation** invocation
is an order to the method to perform its action and to do it with the object mentioned. Some other terms that are used to mean the same thing as invoke a method
are to *call a method* and to *pass a message to the object*. You have already used method invocations. For example, you have used the method `readLineInt()` of the class
`SavitchIn`. You have also used the method `println` with the object `System.out`,
as in the following statement:

```
System.out.println("Enter data on the Species of the Month:");
```

There are two kinds of methods: those that return a single value and those that
perform some action other than returning a single value. The method `readLineInt`
is an example of a method that returns a single value. The method `readLineInt`
returns a value of type *int*. The method `println` is an example of a method that
performs some action other than returning a single value. These two different kinds
of methods are used in slightly different ways.

Two Kinds of Methods

There are two kinds of methods: those that return a single value and those that perform some action other than
return a value. Methods that perform some action other than returning a single value are called *void*-**methods.**

□

Let's first discuss how you invoke a method that returns a single value, using
the method `readLineInt` as an example that should be familiar to you. Suppose
you have the following declarations in a program:

```
int next;
```

The following is an example of an invocation of the method `readLineInt` for the
class `SavitchIn`:

```
next = SavitchIn.readLineInt();
```

(If you want to see this in the context of a full program, see Display 3.14/page 147.)
Let's look at this method invocation in more detail.

A method defined in a class is usually invoked using an object of that class. This
object is known as the **calling object** and it is the first item that you give when writ- calling object
ing a method invocation. For certain special methods, you can use the name of the
class instead of using an object of the class, and our first example will use the class
name `SavitchIn` rather than an object of that class. The way that you invoke a
method is to write the calling object name or the class name (such as `SavitchIn`),
followed by a dot, then the name of the method (such as `readLineInt`), and finally
a set of parentheses that may (or may not) have information for the method. If the value returned
method is one that returns a single value, such as the method `readLineInt`, then
you can use this method invocation anyplace that it is legal to use a value of the
type returned by the method. The method `readLineInt` returns a value of type *int*
and so you can use the method invocation

```
SavitchIn.readLineInt()
```

anyplace that it is legal to use a value of type *int*; that is, anyplace you can use a value such as the value 6 or 937. A value of type *int*, such as 6, can be used in an assignment statement, like this:

```
next = 6;
```

and so the method invocation `SavitchIn.readLineInt()` can be used in the same way, like so:

```
next = SavitchIn.readLineInt();
```

When a method that returns a single value is invoked, it is as if the method invocation were replaced by the value returned. So, if `SavitchIn.readLineInt()` returns the value 3, then the assignment statement

```
next = SavitchIn.readLineInt();
```

produces the same effect as

```
next = 3;
```

not returning a value

Methods that perform some action other than returning a single value are similar, except that they are used to produce Java statements rather than Java values. For example, the following statement from the program in Display 4.2/page 159 includes an invocation of the method `println` with the calling object `System.out`:

```
System.out.println("Enter data on the Species of the Month:");
```

This method call causes the string `"Enter data on the Species of the Month:"` to be written to the screen. The method `writeOutput` for the class `Species-FirstTry` (used in Display 4.2) is similar, except that you do not have to tell `writeOutput` what to output by putting something inside the parentheses. (The method `writeOutput` gets the information to send to the screen from its calling object.)

For example, the program in Display 4.2 (after doing some other things) sets the values of the instance variables of the object `speciesOfTheMonth` with the following three assignment statements:

```
speciesOfTheMonth.name = "Klingon ox";
speciesOfTheMonth.population = 10;
speciesOfTheMonth.growthRate = 15;
```

The program then uses the following statements to output these values:

```
System.out.println("The new Species of the Month:");
speciesOfTheMonth.writeOutput();
```

The second line is an *invocation* of the method `writeOutput` with the calling object `speciesOfTheMonth`. This invocation produces the output

```
Name = Klingon ox
Population = 10
Growth rate = 15.0%
```

A method invocation is an order to the method to perform its action and to do it with the calling object. In this sample case, the method is `writeOutput` and the action is to write something on the screen, specifically to write the values of the instance variables of the object `speciesOfTheMonth`.

Method Invocation (Calling a Method)

You **invoke** a method by writing down the calling object followed by a dot, then the name of the method, and finally a set of parentheses that may (or may not) have information for the method.

If the method invocation returns a value, then you can use the method invocation anyplace that you are allowed to write a value of the type returned by the method. For example, the following includes an invocation of the method `populationIn10` by the calling object `speciesOfTheMonth`:

```
futurePopulation = speciesOfTheMonth.populationIn10();
```

If the method invocation is one that performs some action other than returning a single value, then you place a semicolon after the method invocation, and that produces a Java statement. (These methods that perform actions are called *void*-methods.) For example, the following is an invocation of the method `readInput` with the calling object `speciesOfTheMonth`:

```
speciesOfTheMonth.readInput();
```

This method invocation causes the method to perform whatever action is specified in the method definition.

For certain special methods (like the methods in the class `SavitchIn`), you can use the class name rather than a calling object. These kinds of methods are discussed more fully in Chapter 5.

Recall that the way that you **invoke** a method for an object is to write the calling object name (such as `speciesOfTheMonth`), followed by a dot, then the name of the method (such as `writeOutput`), and finally a set of parentheses that may have information for the method. If, as is true in this case, the method invocation is one that produces some action other than returning a single value, then you make it into a Java statement by placing a semicolon after the method invocation. So the following is an invocation of the method `writeOutput` for the object `speciesOfThe-Month` used as a statement:

invoke

```
speciesOfTheMonth.writeOutput();
```

This causes the method to perform whatever action is specified in the method definition, so let's look at method definitions.

void-Method Definitions

The following is a method invocation from Display 4.2/page 159:

```
speciesOfTheMonth.writeOutput();
```

Let's look at the definition of this method `writeOutput` in order to see how method definitions are written. The definition is given in Display 4.1/page 158 and is repeated here:

```
public void writeOutput()          ◄──── heading
{
    System.out.println("Name = " + name);
    System.out.println("Population = " + population);      ⟩ body
    System.out.println("Growth rate = " + growthRate + "%");
}
```

All method definitions belong to some class and all method definitions are given inside the definition of the class to which they belong. If you look at Display 4.1, you will see that this method definition is inside the definition of the class `Species-FirstTry`. This means that this method can only be used with objects of the class `SpeciesFirstTry`.

void-
method

The definition of a method that does not return a value starts with the reserved words *public* *void* followed by the name of the method and a pair of parentheses. The word *public* indicates that there are no special restrictions on the use of the method. Later in this chapter, we will see that the word *public* can sometimes be replaced with other modifiers to restrict the use of the method. The word *void* is a rather poor choice for use here, but it is what is used in Java and in other languages. The word *void* indicates that the method takes some action other than returning a single value. The word *void* is used to indicate that no value is returned. The parentheses enclose a description of any extra information that the method will need. In this case, no extra information is needed, and so there is nothing inside the parentheses. Later in this chapter, we will see examples of the sorts of things that might appear inside these parentheses (for other method definitions). This first part

heading

of the method definition is called the **heading** for the method and it is normally written on a single line; but if it is too long for one line, it can be broken into two (or more) lines. Because of the use of the word *void* in the method heading, these methods (that do not return a value) are called *void*-**methods**.

body

After the heading comes the **body** of the method definition, and that completes the method definition. The body of the method definition is enclosed between a pair of curly brackets { }. Between the curly brackets, you can place any statement or declaration that you can place in the `main` part of a program. Any variable used in a method definition (other than an instance variable) should be declared within that method definition.

When a *void*-method is invoked, it is as if the method invocation were replaced by the body of the method invocation and the statements (and declarations) within the body are executed. There are some subtleties about this replacement process, but for the simple examples we will look at now, it is like a literal replacement of the method invocation by the method definition body. Eventually, you want to think of the method definition as defining an action to be taken, rather than thinking of it as a list of statements to substitute for the method invocation, but this substitution idea is correct and is a good way to start thinking about method invocations.

For example, the following method invocation occurs in the program in Display 4.2/page 159:

```
speciesOfTheMonth.writeOutput();
```

When this method invocation is executed, it is as if the line with the method invocation were replaced by the body of the method definition for the method `writeOutput`. In this case, it is as if the preceding method invocation were replaced with the following:

```
{
    System.out.println("Name = " + name);
    System.out.println("Population = " + population);
    System.out.println("Growth rate = " + growthRate + "%");
}
```

These lines of code are the body of the method definition for the method `writeOut-put`, and we just copied them from Display 4.1/page 158. The instance variable names, `name`, `population`, and `growthRate`, refer to the instance variables of the calling object; so in this example, they refer to the instance variables of the object `speciesOfTheMonth`. To be more precise, the invocation is equivalent to the following:

```
{
    System.out.println("Name = " + speciesOfTheMonth.name);
    System.out.println("Population = "+speciesOfTheMonth.population);
    System.out.println("Growth rate= "+speciesOfTheMonth.growthRate +"%");
}
```

To be very concrete, if `speciesOfTheMonth.name` has the value "Klingon ox", `speciesOfTheMonth.population` has the value 10, and `speciesOfThe-Month.growthRate` has the value 15, then the method invocation

```
speciesOfTheMonth.writeOutput();
```

will cause the following to be written to the computer screen:

```
Name = Klingon ox
Population = 10
Growth rate = 15.0%
```

which is why the sample dialogue contains these three lines near the end of the dialogue.

If you look at the program in Display 4.2/page 159, you will see that the program looks like a class definition that has no instance variables and only a single method that is named `main`. It is in fact true that `main` is a method. A program is nothing other than a class that has a method named `main`. All the programs that we have written so far have no instance variables and no methods other than the method `main`, but a program can have other methods and can have instance variables. When you run a program, you are simply invoking the *void*-method that is named `main`. Of course, this is a special kind of method invocation, but it is a method invocation. For now, those extra words like *static* and `String[] args` will remain a bit of a mystery. Just put them in and eventually we will explain them all.

main **method**

Methods that Return a Value

A method that returns a single value is defined in basically the same way that a *void*-method is defined, except that there is one added complication, namely, specifying the value returned. Let's consider the method `populationIn10` from the class `speciesFirstTry`. The method is used in the following line of the program in Display 4.2/page 159:

methods that return a value

```
futurePopulation = speciesOfTheMonth.populationIn10();
```

This sets the value of the *int* variable `futurePopulation` equal to the value returned by the method invocation

```
speciesOfTheMonth.populationIn10()
```

The definition of the method `populationIn10` tells the computer how to compute this value returned. Let's look at that method definition.

In what follows, we have reproduced the definition of the method `populationIn10()` from Display 4.1/page 158:

```
public int populationIn10()
{
    double populationAmount = population;
    int count = 10;
    while ((count > 0) && (populationAmount > 0))
    {
        populationAmount = (populationAmount +
                        (growthRate/100) * populationAmount);
        count--;
    }
    if (populationAmount > 0)
        return (int)populationAmount;
    else
        return 0;
}
```

(int) is a type cast, as discussed in Chapter 2.

As was true of a `void`-method definition, the definition of a method that returned a value can be divided into two parts: the *method heading* and the *method body*. The following is the method heading for the method `populationIn10`.

```
public int populationIn10()
```

The description of a method heading for a method that returns a value is almost the same as that for the heading of a `void`-method. The only difference is that for a method that returns a value, there is a type name instead of the reserved word `void`. The heading for a method that returns a value begins with the reserved word `public`, followed by a type name (rather than the word `void`), followed by the name of the method, and a pair of parentheses. The parentheses enclose a description of any extra information that the method will need. In this case, no extra information is needed, and so there is nothing inside the parentheses. Later in this chapter, we will see examples of the sort of things that might appear inside these parentheses. The reserved word `public` indicates that there are no special restrictions on the use of the method. Later in this chapter, we will see that the word `public` can be replaced with other modifiers to restrict the use of the method. The important new element is the use of a type name, in this example `int`, in the method heading. Let's consider that type name.

type returned
The heading of a method that returns a value includes a type name. The type name is the type of the value returned. Each method can return values of only one type. In different situations, a method may return different values, but they must all be values of the type specified in the method heading.

***return-*
statement**
The body of a method definition that returns a value is just like the body of a `void`-method definition, except that it must contain the following in one or more places:

```
return Expression;
```

This is called a *return*-**statement**. The *Expression* can be any expression that produces a value of the type specified in the heading of the method definition. This statement says that the value returned by the method is the value of this expression. For example, in the definition of the method `populationIn10`, there are two *return*-statements:

```
return (int)populationAmount;
```

and

```
return 0;
```

When a method that returns a value is invoked, the statements in the body of the method definition are executed. For example, consider the following method invocation from Display 4.2/page 159:

```
futurePopulation = speciesOfTheMonth.populationIn10();
```

When this assignment statement is executed, the body of the method definition for `populationIn10` is executed. That body follows:

```
{
    double populationAmount = population;
    int count = 10;
    while ((count > 0) && (populationAmount > 0))
    {
        populationAmount = (populationAmount +
                        (growthRate/100) * populationAmount);
        count––;
    }
    if (populationAmount > 0)
        return (int)populationAmount;
    else
        return 0;
}
```

> (*int*) is a type cast, as discussed in Chapter 2.

The instance variable `population` refers to the instance variable of the calling object `speciesOfTheMonth`. The value of `population` is copied into the variable `populationAmount`, and then the *while*-loop is executed. Each iteration of the loop increase the value of `populationAmount` by the amount that the population will change in one year, and the loop is iterated 10 times. So, when the *while*-loop ends, the value of `populationAmount` is the projected size of the population in 10 years. At that point `populationAmount` has the value that we want the method to return. For now, let's assume that that number is positive (i.e., that the species is not extinct). In that case, the following *return*-statement is executed, and it says that the value of (*int*)`populationAmount` is the value computed by (returned by) the method invocation:

```
return (int)populationAmount;
```

The (*int*) is a type cast that changes the *double* value to an *int* value so you do not have a fraction of an animal (Ugh!). It is as if the method invocation were replaced by (`int`)`populationAmount`. In this case, the method invocation `speciesOfThe-Month.populationIn10()` is in the following assignment statement

```
futurePopulation = speciesOfTheMonth.populationIn10();
```

so the variable `futurePopulation` is set to the value of (`int`)`populationAmount`.

If the `populationAmount` happens to be zero or negative, the following *return*-statement is executed instead:

```
return 0;
```

This is a minor detail that ensures that the project population will not yield a negative population value. After all, in the real world, once a population reaches zero individuals, the population just stays at zero; it does not go negative.

When a *return*-statement is executed, the value returned by the method is determined by that *return*-statement. When a *return*-statement is executed, that also ends the method invocation. If there are more statements after the *return*-statement, they are not executed.

A method that returns a value may perform some acton, such as reading a value from the keyboard, as well as returning a value, but it definitely must return a value, and the most important thing about a method that returns a value is that it returns a value.

Naming Methods

Java will let you use any legal identifier as the name for a method. But, if you choose clear, meaningful names, your code will be easier to read. A good rule to follow when naming methods is to (usually) use verbs to name *void*-methods and to (usually) use nouns to name methods that return a value. This is because, like a verb, a *void*-method names an action. On the other hand, a method that returns a value can be used like a value, and a value is a thing, and nouns are used to denote things.

The normal convention when naming classes and methods is to start all method names with a lowercase letter and to start all class names with an uppercase letter.

◑ PROGRAMMING TIP Use of *return* in *void*-Methods

A *void*-method returns no value and so it is not required to have any *return*-statement. However, there is a kind of *return*-statement that you may sometimes want to use in a *void*-method. A *return*-statement within a *void*-method has the form

```
return;
```

It is just like the other *return*-statements we have seen, except that you do not include any expression for the value returned (since there is no value returned). When this *return*-statement is executed, the invocation of the *void*-method ends. This can be used to end a method invocation early, such as when the method discovers some sort of problem. For example, you might add the following method to the definition of the class `SpeciesFirstTry`:

```
public void showLandPortion()
{
    if (population == 0)
    {
        System.out.println("Population is zero.");
        return;//Ends here to avoid division by zero.
    }
    int subgroup;
    double fraction;
    fraction = 6.0/population;
    System.out.println("If the population were spread");
    System.out.println("over 6 continents, then each");
    System.out.println("individual would have a fraction of");
    System.out.println("its continent equal to " + fraction);
}
```

The method ends with a *return* if the rest of the method would involve a division by zero. (OK, it's not a very likely method, but it does illustrate the point.)

The *this* Parameter

Look back at the class definition of the class SpeciesFirstTry in Display 4.1/page 158 and look at the program in Display 4.2/page 159 that uses this class. Notice that instance variables are written differently depending on whether you are within the class definition or someplace outside the class definition, such as in a program that uses the class. Outside of the class definition, we give the name of an object of the class, followed by a dot and the name of the instance variable, as in the following reference to the instance variable name that appears in Display 4.2/page 159:

```
speciesOfTheMonth.name = "Klingon ox";
```

However, inside the definition of a method of that same class, you can simply use the instance variable name without any object name or dot. For example, the following line occurs inside the definition of the method readInput of the class Species-FirstTry in Display 4.1/page 158:

```
name = SavitchIn.readLine();
```

Now, every instance variable is an instance variable of some object. So, this instance variable name must be the instance variable of some object. The instance variable name is an instance variable of an object that is understood to be there, but that usually is not written. However, you can write in this understood object if you want. This understood object has the somewhat unusual name of *this*. For example, the preceding assignment of the instance variable name, which we copied from the definition of the method readInput in Display 4.1, is equivalent to the following:

this

```
this.name = SavitchIn.readLine();
```

As another example, the following is a rewrite of the method definition for the method writeOutput from Display 4.1. This one is equivalent to the version used in Display 4.1.

Method Definitions

Every method belongs to some class. The definition of a method is given in the definition of the class to which it belongs. The two most common forms for a method definition follow.

void-Method Definition:

```
public void Method_Name(Parameters)
{
    Statement_1
    Statement 2
       . . .
    Statement_Last

}
```

(So far we have not discussed *Parameters*, but we will do so shortly. If there are no *Parameters*, then the parentheses are empty.)

Example:

```
public void writeOutput()
{
    System.out.println("Name = " + name);
    System.out.println("Population = " + population);
    System.out.println("Growth rate = " + growthRate + "%");
}
```

Definition of a Method That Returns a Value:

```
public Type_Returned Method_Name(Parameters)
{
    <List of statements, at least one of which
        must contain a return-statement.>
}
```

(So far, we have not discussed *Parameters*, but we will do so shortly. If there are no *Parameters*, then the parentheses are empty.)

Example (this could be added to the class in Display 4.1/page 158):

```
public int halfThePopulation()
{
    return (population/2);
}
```

```
public void writeOutput()
{
    System.out.println("Name = " + this.name);
    System.out.println("Population = " + this.population);
    System.out.println("Growth rate = " + this.growthRate + "%");
}
```

The reserved word *this* stands for the name of the calling object. Since we do not know the name of the calling object when we write the method definition, we use *this* as a stand-in for that name. For example, consider the following method invocation from Display 4.2:

```
speciesOfTheMonth.writeOutput();
```

This invocation of the method writeOutput is equivalent to

```
{
    System.out.println("Name = " + speciesOfTheMonth.name);
    System.out.println("Population = " + speciesOfTheMonth.population);
    System.out.println("Growth rate = " + speciesOfTheMonth.growthRate + "%");
}
```

which we got by replacing *this* with speciesOfTheMonth.

The reserved word *this* is like a blank waiting to be filled in by the object that invokes the method. Since you would be using *this* so often if it were required, Java lets you omit the *this* and the dot as an abbreviation, but the *this* and the dot are understood to be there implicitly. This is an abbreviation that is almost always used. Programmers seldom use the *this* parameter, but there are some situations where it is needed.

? SELF-TEST QUESTIONS

••

1. Consider the program in Display 4.2/page 159. Suppose you wanted to add another species object called `speciesOfTheYear` and suppose you wanted the user to give it data, specifically a name, population, and growth rate. What code do you need to add to the program? (*Hint:* It only requires three or four lines of code.)

2. Suppose `Employee` is a class with a *void*-method named `readInput` and `dilbert` is an object of the class `Employee`. So, `dilbert` was named and created by the following:

   ```
   Employee dilbert = new Employee();
   ```

   Write an invocation of the method `readInput` with `dilbert` as the calling object. The method `readInput` needs no information in parentheses.

3. Suppose you want to assign a number as well as a name to each species in the world, perhaps to make it easier to catalog them. Modify the definition of the class `SpeciesFirstTry` in Display 4.1/page 158 so that it allows for a number. The number is to be of type *int*. (*Hint:* You mostly have to just add stuff. Note, part of what you need to do is to change some methods by adding stuff.)

4. Suppose you live in an idealized world where every species has exactly the same number of male and female members in its population (or as close to that as is logically possible). Give the definition of a method, called `femalePopulation`, that you could add to the definition of the class `SpeciesFirstTry` in Display 4.1/page 158. The method `female-Population` returns the number of females in the population. If the population is an odd number, then you have one species member left over after pairing; assume that member is a female. For example, if the population is 6, there are 3 males and 3 females. If the population is 7, there are 3 males and 4 females. Also give the definition of a method called `male-Population` that similarly returns the number of males in the population. (*Hint:* The definitions are very short. The bodies of the two definitions are a little bit different.)

5. Rewrite the definition of the method `writeOutput` in Display 4.1/page 158 using the *this* parameter. Note that the meaning of the definition will not change at all. You will just write it slightly differently. (*Hint:* All that you need to do is add *this* and dots in certain places.)

6. Rewrite the definition of the method `readInput` in Display 4.1/page 158 using the *this* parameter.

Local Variables

Notice the definition of the method `populationIn10` given in Display 4.1/page 158. That method definition includes the declaration of variables called `populationA-mount` and `count`. A variable declared within a method is called a **local variable**. It is called *local* because its meaning is local to, that is, confined to, the method defini-

local variable

tion. If you have two methods and each of them declares a variable of the same name, for example, both named `populationAmount`, then these are two different variables that just happen to have the same name. Any change that is made to the variable named `populationAmount` within one method will have no effect upon the variable named `populationAmount` that is in the other method. It is as if the two methods were executed on different computers. Alternatively, it is as if the computer changed the name of the variable named `populationAmount` in one of the two methods to `populationAmount2`.

Since the `main` part of a program is itself a method, all variables declared in `main` are local variables for the method `main`. If they happen to have the same name as some variable declared in some other method, then these are two different variables that just happen to have the same name. For example, look at the program in Display 4.3. The method `main` includes the declaration of a variable named `number`. The method `showOff` also declares a variable named `number`. These are two different variables, both of which are named `number`. That variable `number` in `main` is set equal to 10. After that, there is the following method invocation:

```
anObject.showOff();
```

If you look at the definition of the method `showOff`, you will see that within that method, another variable named `number` is set equal to 99.9. Yet, this has no effect on the other variable named `number` that is in `main`. After that method invocation, the variable named `number` in `main` is written out and its value is still 10. Changing the value of the variable `number` in the method `showOff` had no effect on the variable named `number` in `main`. In this case, the two variables with the same name are of different types, but the story is the same whether they are of the same type or not. In that same program, we have two methods each with a variable named `letter` that is of type *char*. These are two different variables named `letter`.

Local Variable

A variable declared within a method definition is called a **local variable**. If two methods each have a local variable of the same name, then these are two different variables, even though they have the same name.

Global Variables

Thus far, we have discussed two kinds of variables: instance variables, whose meaning is confined to an object of a class, and local variables, whose meaning is confined to a method definition. Some programming languages have another kind of variable, called **global variables**, whose meaning is only confined to the program, which means it's not confined at all. Java does not have these global variables.

Blocks

The terms *block* and *compound statement* really mean the same thing, namely, a set of Java statements enclosed in curly brackets {}. However, the two terms tend to be used in different contexts. When you declare a variable within a compound state-

compound
statement

Display 4.3 Local Variables

```
/******************************************************************
 *This is just a toy program to illustrate how local variables behave.
 ******************************************************************/
public class LocalVariablesDemo
{
    public static void main(String[] args)
    {
        LocalVariablesDemo anObject = new LocalVariablesDemo();
        int number = 10;
        char letter = 'A';

        anObject.showOff();

        System.out.println("In main number is still " + number);
        System.out.println("In main letter is still " + letter);
    }

    public void showOff()
    {
        double number = 99.9;
        char letter = 'Z';
        System.out.println("In showOff number = " + number);
        System.out.println("In showOff letter = " + letter);
    }
}
```

Two different variables named number *and two different variables named* letter.

Screen Output

```
In showOff number = 99.9
In showOff letter = Z
In main number is still 10
In main letter is still A
```

ment, the compound statement is usually called a **block** (although it would not be incorrect to call it a *compound statement.*)

If you declare a variable within a block (i.e., within a compound statement), that variable is local to the block (i.e., local to the compound statement). That means that when the compound statement ends, all variables declared within the compound statement disappear. In many programming languages, you can even use that variable's name to name some other variable outside of the block. However, *in Java, you cannot have two variables with the same name inside of a single method definition.*

Local variables within blocks can sometimes be a little troublesome in Java. In Java, you cannot reuse the local variable name outside the block for another variable. As a result, it is sometimes easier to declare the variable outside the block. If you declare a variable outside of a block, then you can use it in the block and it will have the same meaning whether it is in the block or outside the block (but all within the same method definition).

Blocks

A **block** is a compound statement, i.e., a list of statements enclosed in curly brackets. Although a block and compound statement are the same thing, we tend to use the term *block* when there is a variable declaration contained within the curly brackets. The variables declared in a block are local to the block and so these variables disappear when the execution of the block is completed. However, even though the variables are local to the block, their names cannot be used for anything else within the same method definition.

◻

▲ *GOTCHA* Variables Declared in a Block

When you declare a variable within a block, i.e., within a pair of curly brackets { }, that variable becomes a local variable for the block. This means that you cannot use the variable outside of the block. If you want to use a variable outside of a block, then you must declare it outside of the block. Declaring the variable outside of the block will let you use the variable both outside the block and inside the block.

Declaring Variables in a *for*-Statement *(Optional)*
You can declare a variable within the initialization part of a *for*-statement as in the following example:

```
int sum = 0;
for (int n = 1; n <= 10; n++)
    sum = sum + n;
```

If you do this, then the variable, in this case n, will be **local to the** *for*-**loop**, and cannot be used outside of the *for*-loop. For example, the following use of n in the System.out.println-statement is not allowed.

```
for (int n = 1; n <= 10; n++)
    sum = sum + n;
System.out.println(n);
```

This can sometimes be more of a nuisance than a helpful feature. Moreover, these variables declared in the initialization part of a *for*-loop are treated differently in different programming languages and even in different versions of Java. For these reasons, we prefer to not use this feature, and to instead declare our variables outside of the *for*-loop. However, you should be aware of this feature, since you will see it in other programmer's code.

Parameters of a Primitive Type

Consider the method `populationIn10` for the class `SpeciesFirstTry` defined in Display 4.1/page 158. It returns the projected population of a species 10 years in the future. But what if you want the projection for 5 years in the future or 50 years in the future? It would be much more useful to have a method that starts with an integer for some number of years and returns the projected population for that many years into the future. In order to do this, we need some way of having something like a blank in a method so that each call of the method can have the blank filled in with a different value. For a method that computes projected population, the blank would be filled in with some number of years. The things that serve as kinds of blanks for methods are called **parameters**. They are a bit more complicated than simple blanks, but you will not go too far wrong if you think of them as blanks or placeholders to be filled in with some value when the method is called.

parameter

The class definition in Display 4.4 includes a method called `projectedPopulation` that has one formal parameter called `years`. When the method is called, you give the value that you want substituted in for the parameter `years`. For example, in the program in Display 4.2/page 159, we had the following method call:

```
futurePopulation = speciesOfTheMonth.populationIn10();
```

This sets the variable `futurePopulation` equal to the projected population of the species in 10 years. The class `SpeciesSecondTry` (Display 4.4) does not have a method named `populationIn10`, but we could instead use the method `projected-Population` as follows:

```
futurePopulation = speciesOfTheMonth.projectedPopulation(10);
```

In Display 4.5, we have rewritten the program from Display 4.2/page 159 so that it uses the class `SpeciesSecondTry` that has the method `projectedPopulation`. With this version of the class, we could project any number of years into the future by replacing the 10 by some other number. We could even use a variable for the number of years, as follows:

```
int projectedYears, futurePopulation;
System.out.println("Enter the projected number of years:");
projectedYears = SavitchIn.readLineInt();
futurePopulation =
        speciesOfTheMonth.projectedPopulation(projectedYears);
System.out.println("In " + projectedYears + " years, the");
System.out.println("population will be " + futurePopulation);
```

Display 4.4 A Method with A Parameter

```
public class SpeciesSecondTry
{
    public void readInput()
    {
        <The definition of the method readInput is the same as in Display 4.1/page 158.>
    }

    public void writeOutput()
    {
        <The definition of the method writeOutput is the same as in Display 4.1.>
    }

    /*************************************************************
     *Returns the projected population of the calling object
     *after the specified number of years.
     *************************************************************/
    public int projectedPopulation(int years)
    {
        double populationAmount = population;
        int count = years;
        while ((count > 0) && (populationAmount > 0))
        {
            populationAmount = (populationAmount +
                        (growthRate/100) * populationAmount);
            count—;
        }
        if (populationAmount > 0)
            return (int)populationAmount;
        else
            return 0;
    }

    public String name;
    public int population;
    public double growthRate;
}
```

> We will give an even better version of the class later in this chapter.

> Later in this chapter, we will see that the modifier *public* should be replaced with *private*.

Display 4.5 Using a Method with a Parameter

```
/*************************************************************
 *Demonstrates the use of a parameter with the method projectedPopulation.
 *************************************************************/
public class SpeciesSecondTryDemo
{
    public static void main(String[] args)
    {
        SpeciesSecondTry speciesOfTheMonth = new SpeciesSecondTry();
        int futurePopulation;

        System.out.println("Enter data on the Species of the Month:");
        speciesOfTheMonth.readInput();
        speciesOfTheMonth.writeOutput();

        futurePopulation = speciesOfTheMonth.projectedPopulation(10);
        System.out.println("In ten years the population will be " +
                                                futurePopulation);

        speciesOfTheMonth.name = "Klingon ox";
        speciesOfTheMonth.population = 10;
        speciesOfTheMonth.growthRate = 15;
        System.out.println("The new Species of the Month:");
        speciesOfTheMonth.writeOutput();
        System.out.println("In ten years the population will be " +
                        speciesOfTheMonth.projectedPopulation(10));
    }
}
```

Sample Screen Dialogue

The dialogue is exactly the same as in Display 4.2 on page 159

Let's look at the definition of the method `projectedPopulation` in some more detail. The heading, reproduced in what follows, has something new.

```
public int projectedPopulation(int years)
```

formal parameter

argument

The word `years` is called a **formal parameter**. A formal parameter is used in the method definition as a stand-in for a value that will be plugged in when the method is called. The thing that is plugged in is called an **argument** or **actual parameter**. For example, in the following call, the value 10 is an argument:

```
futurePopulation = speciesOfTheMonth.projectedPopulation(10);
```

When you have a method invocation, like the preceding, the argument, in this case 10, is, in a sense to be made precise shortly, plugged in for the formal parameter *every place that the formal parameter occurs in the method definition.* In this case, the argument 10 would be plugged in for the formal parameters `years` in the definition of the method `projectedPopulation` in Display 4.4. After that, the method invocation proceeds as in all previous cases. The statements in the body of the method definition are executed until they reach a *return*-statement. At that point, the value specified by the expression in the *return*-statement is returned as the value returned by the method call.

It is important to note that only the value of the argument is used in this substitution process. If the argument in a method invocation is a variable, then it is the value of the variable that is plugged in, not the variable name. For example, consider the following, which might occur in some program that uses the class `SpeciesSecondTry` defined in Display 4.4:

```
SpeciesSecondTry mySpecies = new SpeciesSecondTry();
int yearCount = 12;
int futurePopulation;
futurePopulation =
        mySpecies.projectedPopulation(yearCount);
```

call-by-value

In this case, it is the value 12 that is plugged in for the formal parameter `years` in the definition of the method `projectedPopulation` (in Display 4.4). It is *not* the variable `yearCount` that is plugged in for `years`. Since it is only the value of the argument that is used, this method of plugging in arguments for parameter is known as the **call-by-value** mechanism of parameter substitution. In Java, this is the only method of substitution that is used with parameters of a primitive type, such as `int`, `double`, and `char`. However, we will eventually see that parameters of a class type use a somewhat different substitution mechanism, but for now, we are only concerned with parameters and arguments of primitive types, such as `int`, `double`, and `char`.

parameters as local variables

The exact details of this parameter substitution method are a bit more complicated than what we have said so far. Usually, you need not be concerned with this extra detail, but occasionally, you need to know all the details of the substitution. So, here are the exact technical details: *The formal parameter that occurs in the method definition is a local variable that is initialized to the value of the argument.* The argument is given in parentheses in the method invocation. For example, for the method call:

```
futurePopulation =
    mySpecies.projectedPopulation(yearCount);
```

The formal parameter `years` of the method `projectedPopulation` in Display 4.4 is a local variable of the method `projectedPopulation`, and in this method invocation, the local variable `years` is set equal to the value of the argument `yearCount`, so the effect is the same as if the body of the method definition were changed to the following:

This is the effect of plugging in the argument, `yearCount`.

```
{
    years = yearCount;
    double populationAmount = population;
    int count = years;
    while ((count > 0) && (populationAmount > 0))
    {
        populationAmount = (populationAmount +
                           (growthRate/100) * populationAmount);
        count--;
    }

    if (populationAmount > 0)
        return (int)populationAmount;
    else
        return 0;
}
```

parameters have a type

Finally, notice that the formal parameter in a method heading has a type, such as the type `int` before the formal parameter `years`, shown in what follows:

```
public int projectedPopulation(int years)
```

Every formal parameter has a type and the argument that is plugged in for the formal parameter in a method invocation must match the type of the formal parameter. Thus, for the method `projectedPopulation`, the argument given in parentheses in a method invocation must be of type `int`. This rule is not as strict in practice as what we have just said. In many cases, Java will perform an automatic type conversion (type cast) if you use an argument in a method call that does not match the type of the formal parameter. For example, if the type of the argument in a method call is *int* and the type of the formal parameter is *double*, then Java will convert the value of type *int* to the corresponding value of type *double*. The following list shows the type conversions that will be performed for you automatically. An argument in a method invocation that is of any of these types will be automatically converted to any of the types that appear to its right if that is needed to match a formal parameter:[1]

```
byte --> short --> int --> long --> float --> double
```

(Note that this is exactly the same sort of automatic type casting that we discussed in Chapter 2 for storing values of one type in a variable of another type. You can store a value of any of the listed types in a variable of any type that occurs further down on the list. Thus, we can express both the automatic type casting for arguments and the automatic type casting for variables as one more general rule: You can use a value of any of the listed types anywhere that Java expects a value of a type further down on the list. For example, you can use an *int* value anywhere that Java expects a *double* value.)

Parameters of a Primitive Type

Formal parameters are given in parentheses after the method name at the beginning of a method definition. A formal parameter of a primitive type, such as *int*, *double*, or *char*, is a local variable. When there is an invocation of the method, the parameter is initialized to the value of the corresponding argument in the method invocation. This mechanism is known as the **call-by-value** parameter mechanism. The argument in a method invocation can be a literal constant, like 2 or 'A', a variable, or any expression that yields a value of the appropriate type.

Note that if you use a variable of a primitive type as an argument in a method invocation, then the method invocation cannot change the value of this argument variable.

All of our examples so far have been methods that return a value, but everything we said about formal parameters and arguments applies equally well to *void*-methods; *void*-methods may have parameters and they are handled in exactly the same way as what we just described for methods that return a value.

It is possible, even common, to have more than one formal parameter in a method definition. In that case, each formal parameter is listed in the method heading and each formal parameter is preceded by a type. For example, the following might be the heading of a method definition:

more than one parameter

```
public void doStuff(int n1, int n2, double cost, char code)
```

Note that even if there is more than one formal parameter of the same type, then each of the formal parameters must be preceded by the type name.

When you have a method invocation, there must be exactly the same number of arguments in parentheses as there are formal parameters in the method definition heading. For example, the following might be an invocation of our hypothetical method doStuff:

```
anObject.doStuff(42, 100, 9.99, 'Z');
```

As suggested by this example, the correspondence is one of order. The first argument in the method call is plugged in for the first formal parameter in the method definition heading, the second argument in the method call is plugged in for the second formal parameter in the heading of the method definition, and so forth. The argument must match its corresponding parameter in type, except for the automatic type conversion that we discuss earlier.

---

1. An argument of type *char* will also be converted to a value of a suitable number type, if the formal parameter is of a number type. However, we do not advocate using this feature.

class
parameters

One word of warning: Parameters of a class type behave differently from parameters of a primitive type. We will discuss parameters of a class type later in this chapter.

Correspondence between Formal Parameters and Arguments

Formal parameters are given in parentheses after the method name at the beginning of a method definition. In a method invocation, arguments are given in parentheses after the method name. There must be exactly the same number of arguments in a method invocation as there are formal parameters in the corresponding method definition. The arguments are plugged in (in a sense made precise in the text) for the formal parameters according to their position in the lists in parentheses. The first argument in the method invocation is plugged in for the first formal parameter in the method definition, the second argument in the method invocation is plugged in for the second formal parameter in the method definition, and so forth. Arguments should be of the same types as their corresponding formal parameter, although in some cases, Java will perform an automatic type conversion when the types do not match.

⚠ GOTCHA Use of the Terms "Parameter" and "Argument"

The use of the terms *formal parameter* and *argument* that we follow in this book is consistent with common usage, but people also often use the terms *parameter* and *argument* interchangeably. When you see the terms *parameter* and *argument,* you must determine their exact meaning from context. Many people use the term *parameter* for both what we called *formal parameters* and what we called *arguments.* Other people use the term *argument* both for what we called *formal parameters* and what we called *arguments.* Do not expect any consistency in how people use these two terms.

Summary of Class and Method Definition Syntax
In basic outline, a class definition has the following form:

```
public class Class_Name
{
    Method_Definition_1
    Method_Definition_2
         . . .
    Method_Definition_Last
    Instance_Variable_Declaration_1
    Instance_Variable_Declaration_2
         . . .
    Instance_Variable_Declaration_Last
}
```

This is the form we will use most often, but you are allowed to intermix the method definitions and the instance variable declarations.

The instance variable declarations that we have seen thus far are of the form

```
public Type_Name Instance_Variable_Name;
```

such as

```
public String name;
public int population;
public double growthRate;
```

As we will see in the next section, it is preferable to use the modifier *private* in place of the modifier *public* when declaring instance variables, but the other details are typical.

A method definition consist of two parts, in the following order:

Method_Heading
Method_Body

The method headings we have seen thus far are all of the form

public **Type_Name_Or_**void **Method_Name(** *Parameter_List* **)**

The *Parameter_List* consists of a list of formal parameter names, each preceded by a type. If the list has more than one entry, the entries are separated by commas. There may be no parameters at all, in which case there is nothing inside the parentheses.

Here are some sample method headings:

```
public double Total(double price, double tax)
public void setValue(int count, char rating)
public void readInput()
public int projectedPopulation(int years)
```

The *Method_Body* consists of a list of Java statements enclosed in curly brackets {}. If the method returns a value, then the method definition must include one or more *return*-statements. Here is a sample method, which you have seen before. The first line is the method heading and the rest is the method body.

```
public int projectedPopulation(int years)
{
    double populationAmount = population;
    int count = years;
    while ((count > 0) && (populationAmount > 0))
    {
        populationAmount = (populationAmount +
                        (growthRate/100) * populationAmount);
        count--;
    }
    if (populationAmount > 0)
        return (int)populationAmount;
    else
        return 0;
}
```

To see complete examples of class definitions, see Display 4.1/page 158 and Display 4.4/page 177.

? SELF-TEST QUESTIONS

7. Define a method called `density` that could be added to the definition of the class `SpeciesSecondTry` in Display 4.4/page 177. The method `density` has one parameter of type *double* that is named `area`. The parameter `area` gives the area occupied by the species expressed in square miles. The method `density` returns a value of type *double* that is equal to the number of individuals per square mile of the species. You can assume that the area is always greater than zero. (*Hint:* The definition is very short.)

8. Define a method called `fixPopulation` that could be added to the definition of the class `SpeciesSecondTry` in Display 4.4/page 177. The method `fixPopulation` has one parameter of type *double* that is named `area`, which gives the area occupied by the species in square miles. The method `fixPopulation` changes the value of the instance variable `population` so that there will be one pair of individuals per square mile.

9. Define a method called `changePopulation` that could be added to the definition of the class `SpeciesSecondTry` in Display 4.4/page 177. The method `changePopulation` has two parameters. One parameter is of type *double*, is named `area`, and gives the area occupied by the species in square miles. The other parameter is of type *int*, is named `numberPerMile`, and gives the desired number of individuals per square mile. The method `changePopulation` changes the value of the instance variable `population` so that the number of individuals per square mile is (approximately) equal to `numberPerMile`.

4.2 Information Hiding and Encapsulation

The cause is hidden, but the result is well known.
OVID, *Metamorphoses*

Information hiding sounds like it could be a bad thing to do. What advantage could there be to hiding information (except for nefarious schemes)? As it turns out the term *information hiding* as it is used in Computer Science does indeed refer to a kind of genuine hiding of information, and it is considered a good programming technique. The basic idea is that when certain kinds of information are hidden, the programmer's job becomes simpler and the programmer's code becomes easier to understand. It is basically a way to avoid "information overload." A programmer who is using a method that you have defined does not need to know the details of the code in the body of the method definition in order to use the method. The programmer only needs to know what task the method accomplishes. For example, you can use the method `SavitchIn.readlineInt` without even looking at the definition of that method. It is not that code contains some secret that is forbidden to you. If you really want to see the definition, it is in Appendix 2. The point is that viewing the code will not help you use the method, but will give you more things to keep track of, and that could distract you from your programming tasks. If a method (or other piece of software) is well written, then a programmer who uses the method need only know *what* the method accomplishes and need not worry about *how* the method accomplishes its task. This section is concerned with various kinds of information hiding.

If the word *information hiding* sounds too negative to you, you might use the term *abstraction*. The terms *information hiding* and *abstraction* mean the same thing in this context. This should not be a surprising use of the term *abstraction*. When you *abstract* something, you lose some information. For example, an abstract of a paper or a book is a brief description of the paper or book, as opposed to the entire book or paper.

abstraction

Information Hiding

If a method is well-designed, the programmer can use the method without knowing the details of how the method body is coded. All the programmer needs to know is that if she or he provides the method with appropriate arguments, then the method will somehow perform the appropriate action. Designing a method so that it can be used without any need to understand the fine detail of the code is called **information hiding** in order to emphasize the fact that the programmer acts as if the body of the method were hidden from view.

information hiding

Display 4.6 contains two definitions of the method `projectedPopulation`. Either definition could be used in the definition of the class `SpeciesSecondTry` in Display 4.4/page 177. The class definition can only contain one of these two definitions of `projectedPopulation`, but the point we are making is that it does not matter which definition is used. The method will return the same number no matter which of the two definitions is used. In order to use the method `projectedPopulation`, all the programmer needs to know is that it returns the projected population of the species for the number of years into the future that is given as the argument.

☉ *PROGRAMMING TIP Formal Parameter Names Are Local to the Method*

Methods should be self-contained units that are designed separately from the incidental details of other methods of the class and separately from any program that uses the class. One incidental detail is the name of the formal parameters. Fortunately, in Java (and most all programming languages) the formal parameter names can be chosen without any concern that the name of a formal parameter will be the same as some other identifier used in some other method. This is because the formal parameters are really local variables and so their meanings are confined to their respective method definitions. Among other things, this means that on programming projects, one programmer can be assigned the job of writing a method definition while another programmer writes another part of the program that uses that method, and the two programmers need not agree on what names are used for formal parameters. They can choose their identifier names completely independently without any concern that some, all, or none of their identifiers may be the same.

Display 4.6 Equivalent Method Definitions

```
/***********************************************************
*Returns the projected population of the calling object
*after the specified number of years.
***********************************************************/
public int projectedPopulation(int years)
{
    double populationAmount = population;
    int count = years;
    while ((count > 0) && (populationAmount > 0))
    {
        populationAmount = (populationAmount +
                      (growthRate/100) * populationAmount);
        count--;
    }
    if (populationAmount > 0)
        return (int)populationAmount;
    else
        return 0;
}
```

> The class `SpeciesSecondTry` will only have one of these two definitions of the method `projectedPopulation`, but the programmer who uses the class does not care which one it has.

```
/***********************************************************
*Returns the projected population of the calling object
*after the specified number of years.
***********************************************************/
public int projectedPopulation(int years)
{
    double populationAmount = population;
    double growthFraction = growthRate/100.0;
    int count = years;
    while ((count > 0) && (populationAmount > 0))
    {
        populationAmount = (populationAmount +
                      growthFraction * populationAmount);
        count--;
    }
    if (populationAmount < 0)
        populationAmount = 0;
    return (int)populationAmount;
}
```

Precondition and Postcondition Comments

The programmer who uses a method should not need to look at the method definition. The method heading and a description of what the method does (as opposed to how it does it) should be all that the programmer needs to know. An efficient and standard way to describe what a method does is by means of specific kinds of comments known as *preconditions* and a *postconditions*. The **precondition** for a method states the conditions that must be true before the method is invoked. The method should not be used and cannot be expected to perform correctly unless the precondition is satisfied. The **postcondition** describes the effect of the method call. The postcondition tells what will be true after the method is executed in a situation in which the precondition holds. For a method that returns a value, the postcondition will describe the value returned by the method. For a `void`-method, the postcondition will, among other things, describe any changes to the calling object. In general, the postcondition describes all the effects produced by a method invocation.

precondition

postcondition

For example, the following shows some suitable precondition and postcondition comments for the method `writeOutput` shown in Display 4.1/page 158:

```
/************************************************************
*Precondition: The instance variables of the calling
*object have values.
*Postcondition: The data stored in (the instance variables
*of) the calling object have been written to the screen.
************************************************************/
public void writeOutput()
```

The comment for the method `projectedPopulation` in Display 4.6 (either version) can be expressed as follows:

```
/************************************************************
*Precondition: years is a nonnegative number.
*Postcondition: Returns the projected population of the
*calling object after the specified number of years.
************************************************************/
public int projectedPopulation(int years)
```

If the only postcondition is a description of the value returned, programmers omit the word *Postcondition* (although it would not be incorrect to include the word *Postcondition*). The previous comments would typically be written in the following alternative way:

```
/************************************************************
*Precondition: years is a nonnegative number.
*Returns the projected population of the calling object
*after the specified number of years.
************************************************************/
public int projectedPopulation(int years)
```

Some design specifications may require preconditions and postconditions for all methods. Others omit explicit preconditions and postconditions from certain methods whose names make their action obvious. Names such as `readInput`, `writeOutput`, and `set` are often considered self-explanatory. However, the sound rule to follow is to adhere to whatever guidelines your instructor or supervisor give, and when in doubt, add preconditions and postconditions.

The Public and Private Modifiers

It is *not* considered good programming practice to make the instance variables of a class *public*. Normally, all instance variables are given the modifier *private*. In this subsection, we explain the differences between the modifiers *public* and *private*.

public

The modifier *public* means, as we already said, that any other class or program can directly access the instance variable and can directly change the instance variable. For example, the program in Display 4.5/page 178 contains the following three lines, which set the values of the *public* instance variables for the object speciesOfTheMonth:

```
speciesOfTheMonth.name = "Klingon ox";
speciesOfTheMonth.population = 10;
speciesOfTheMonth.growthRate = 15;
```

The object speciesOfTheMonth is an object of the class SpeciesSecondTry and the definition for that class is given in Display 4.4/page 177. As you can see by looking at that class definition, the instance variables name, population, and growthRate all have the modifier *public*, and so the preceding three statements are perfectly legal.

private

Now suppose that the modifier *public* before the instance variable name in the definition of the class SpeciesSecondTry in Display 4.4 were changed to *private* so that the class definition ends as follows:

```
    private String name;
    public int population;
    public double growthRate;
}
```

With this change, it is illegal to have the following statement in the program in Display 4.5:

```
speciesOfTheMonth.name = "Klingon ox"; //Illegal when private.
```

The following two statements remain legal, because we left the modifiers of population and growthRate as *public*:

```
speciesOfTheMonth.population = 10;
speciesOfTheMonth.growthRate = 15;
```

It is considered good programming practice to make all instance variables *private*, as illustrated in Display 4.7. Whenever you place the modifier *private* before an instance variable, then that instance variable *name* is not accessible outside of the class definition. Within any method of the class definition, you can use the instance variable name in any way you wish. In particular, you can directly change the value of the instance variable. However, outside of the class definition, you cannot make any direct reference to the instance variable name.

For example, consider the class SpeciesThirdTry shown in Display 4.7. Since the instance variables are all marked *private*, the last three of the following lines would all be illegal in any program (or any class method definition other than methods of the class SpeciesThirdTry):

Display 4.7 A Class with Private Instance Variables

```
public class SpeciesThirdTry
{
    public void readInput()
    {
        System.out.println("What is the species' name?");
        name = SavitchIn.readLine();
        System.out.println("What is the population of the species?");
        population = SavitchIn.readLineInt();
        System.out.println("Enter growth rate (percent increase per
                year");
        growthRate = SavitchIn.readLineDouble();
    }


    public void writeOutput()
```

> We will give an even better version of the class later in this chapter.

<The definition of the method `writeOutput` is the same as in Display 4.1/page 158.>

```
    /***********************************************************
     *Precondition: years is a nonnegative number.
     *Returns the projected population of the calling object
     *after the specified number of years.
     ***********************************************************/
    public int projectedPopulation(int years)
```

<The definition of the method `projectedPopulation` can
be either of the definitions in Display 4.6/page 186.>

```
    private String name;
    private int population;
    private double growthRate;
}
```

```
SpeciesThirdTry secretSpecies = new SpeciesThirdTry();//Legal
secretSpecies.readInput();//Legal
secretSpecies.name = "Aardvark";//Illegal. name is private.
System.out.println(secretSpecies.population);//Illegal
                    //population is private.
System.out.println(secretSpecies.growthRate);//Illegal.
                    //growthRate is private.
```

Notice that the invocation of the method readInput is legal. So, there is still a way to set the instance variables of an object, even though those instance variable are *private*. Making an instance variable *private* does not mean that there is no way to change it; it only means that you cannot use the *instance variable name* to directly refer to the variable (except within the class definition that includes the instance variable).

Within the definition of methods in the same class, you can access private instance variables in any way that you want. Notice the definition of the method readInput, which is shown in Display 4.7. It sets the value of instance variables with assignment statements such as the following:

```
name = SavitchIn.readLine();
```

and

```
population = SavitchIn.readLineInt();
```

Within any class method, you can access all the instance variables of that class in any way you want, even if the instance variables are marked *private*.

private methods

Class methods can also be *private*. If a method is marked *private*, then it cannot be used outside of the class definition, but it can still be invoked within the definition of any other method in that same class. Most methods are marked *public*, but if you have a method whose only purpose is to be used within the definition of other methods of that class, then it makes sense to mark this *helping* method *private*.

The *public* and *private* Qualifiers

Within a class definition, each instance variable declaration and each method definition can be preceded with either *public* or *private*. If an instance variable is preceded with *private*, then it cannot be referred to by name anyplace except within the definitions of methods of the same class. If it is preceded by *public*, there are no restrictions on the use of the instance variable name. If a method definition is preceded with *private*, then the method cannot be used outside of the class definition. If the method is preceded by *public*, there are no restrictions on the method's use.

Normally, all instance variables are marked *private* and most or all methods are marked *public*.

◑ PROGRAMMING TIP *Instance Variables Should Be Private*

You should make all the instance variables in a class *private*. The reason for this is that it forces the programmer who uses the class (whether that is you or somebody else) to only access the instance variables via methods. This allows the class to control how a programmer accesses the instance variables.

Making all instance variables *private* does control access to them, but what if you have a legitimate reason to access an instance variable? For these cases, you should provide *accessor methods*. An **accessor method** is simply a method that allows you to read or to set one or more instance variables. In Display 4.8, we have rewritten the class for a species yet another time. This version has accessor methods for reading each instance variable. They are the methods that start with the word species, as in speciesName. We also have an accessor method, called set, for setting the instance variables to new values. The program in Display 4.9 illustrates the use of the assessor method set. That program is similar to the one in Display 4.5/page 178, but since this version of our species class has *private* instance variables, we must use the method set to reset the values of the instance variables.

accessor method

It may seem that accessor methods defeat the purpose of making instance variables *private*, but there is a method to this madness. (No pun intended, I think.) When you use accessor methods, the accessor method can check that any change is appropriate and warn the user if there is a problem. For example, the accessor method set checks to see if the program inadvertently sets the population equal to a negative number.

? SELF-TEST QUESTIONS

10. In Display 4.9/page 193, we set the data for the object speciesOfThe-Month as follows:

    ```
    speciesOfTheMonth.set("Klingon ox", 10, 15);
    ```

    Could we have used the following code instead?

    ```
    speciesOfTheMonth.name = "Klingon ox";
    speciesOfTheMonth.population = 10;
    speciesOfTheMonth.growthRate = 15;
    ```

    If we could have used this alternative code, why didn't we? If we could not use this alternative code, explain why we cannot use it.

11. Give preconditions and postconditions for the following method, which is intended to be added to the class SpeciesFourthTry in Display 4.8/page 192.

    ```
    public void updatePopulation()
    {
        population = (int)(population
                          + (growthRate/100)*population);
    }
    ```

12. Give the complete definition of a class called Person that has two instance variables, one for the person's name and the other for the person's age. Include accessor methods following the model in Display 4.8/page 192. Also include methods for input and output. There are no other methods.

Display 4.8 A Class with Accessor Methods

Yes, we will define an even better version of this class later.

```java
public class SpeciesFourthTry
{
    <The definition of the methods readInput, writeOutput, and projectedPopulation
     go here. They are the same as in Display 4.1/page 158 and Display 4.4/page 177.>

    public void set(String newName,
                              int newPopulation, double
            newGrowthRate)
    {
        name = newName;
        if (newPopulation >= 0)
            population = newPopulation;
        else
            System.out.println("ERROR: using a negative
                population.");
        growthRate = newGrowthRate;
    }

    public String speciesName()
    {
        return name;
    }

    public int speciesPopulation()
    {
        return population;
    }

    public double speciesGrowthRate()
    {
        return growthRate;
    }


    private String name;
    private int population;
    private double growthRate;
}
```

Display 4.9 Using an Accessor Method *(Part 1 of 2)*

```
/***********************************************
 *Demonstrates the use of accessor method set.
 ***********************************************/
public class SpeciesFourthTryDemo
{
    public static void main(String[] args)
    {
        SpeciesFourthTry speciesOfTheMonth = new SpeciesFourthTry();
        int numberOfYears, futurePopulation;

        System.out.println("Enter number of years to project:");
        numberOfYears = SavitchIn.readLineInt();


        System.out.println("Enter data on the Species of the Month:");
        speciesOfTheMonth.readInput();
        speciesOfTheMonth.writeOutput();


        futurePopulation =
                speciesOfTheMonth.projectedPopulation(numberOfYears);
        System.out.println("In " + numberOfYears
                + " years the population will be " + futurePopulation);


        speciesOfTheMonth.set("Klingon ox", 10, 15);
        System.out.println("The new Species of the Month:");
        speciesOfTheMonth.writeOutput();
        System.out.println("In " + numberOfYears
                + " years the population will be "
                + speciesOfTheMonth.projectedPopulation(numberOfYears));
    }
}
```

Display 4.9 Using an Accessor Method *(Part 2 of 2)*

Sample Screen Dialogue

```
Enter number of years to project:
10
Enter data on the Species of the Month:
What is the species' name?
Ferengie fur ball
What is the population of the species?
1000
Enter growth rate (percent increase per year):
-20.5
Name = Ferengie fur ball
Population = 1000
Growth rate = -20.5%
In 10 years the population will be 100
The new Species of the Month:
Name = Klingon ox
Population = 10
Growth rate = 15.0%
In 10 years the population will be 40
```

▼ PROGRAMMING EXAMPLE Purchase Class

Display 4.10 contains a class for a single purchase, such as 12 apples or 2 quarts of milk. It is designed to be part of a program to be used at the checkout stand of a supermarket. Recall that supermarkets give prices not in unit costs, that is, not as the price for one, but as the price for some number, such as 5 for $1.25 or 3 for a $1.00. They hope that if they price apples at 5 for $1.25, then you will buy 5 apples instead of two apples. But, 5 for $1.25 is really $0.25 each and if you buy two apples, they still only charge you $0.50.

The instance variables are reproduced in what follows:

```
private String name;
private int groupCount;//Part of price, like the 2 in 2 for $1.99.
private double groupPrice;//Part of price,like the $1.99 in 2 for $1.99.
private int numberBought;//Total number being purchased.
```

It is easiest to explain the meaning of these instance variables with an example. If you buy 12 apples at 5 for $1.25, then name has the value "apples", groupCount has the value 5, groupPrice has the value 1.25, and numberBought has the value 12.

Display 4.10 Purchase Class *(Part 1 of 3)*

```
/****************************************************************
 *Class for the purchase of one kind of item, such as 3 oranges.
 *Prices are set supermarket style, such as 5 for $1.25.
 ****************************************************************/
public class Purchase
{
    public void setName(String theName)
    {
        name = theName;
    }

    /****************************************************************
     *Sets price to count pieces for $costForCount. E.g., 2 for $1.99.

     ****************************************************************/
    public void setPrice(int count, double costForCount)
    {
        if ((count <= 0) || (costForCount <= 0))
        {
            System.out.println("Error: Bad parameter in setPrice.");
            System.exit(0);
        }
        else
        {
            groupCount = count;
            groupPrice = costForCount;
        }
    }

    /**************************************************************
     *Sets the total number of items purchased to number.
     **************************************************************/
    public void setNumber(int number)
    {
        numberBought = number;
    }

    public String nameOfItem()
    {
        return name;
    }
```

Display 4.10 Purchase Class *(Part 2 of 3)*

```java
public double totalCost()
{
    return ((groupPrice/groupCount)*numberBought);
}

public double unitCost()
{
    return (groupPrice/groupCount);
}

/*********************************************
*Returns the total number of items purchased.
*********************************************/
public int number()
{
    return numberBought;
}

/***************************************************
 *Gets price and number being purchased from keyboard.
 ***************************************************/
public void readInput()
{
    String itemName;
    int count;//Part of price, like the 2 in 2 for $1.99.
    double cost;//Part of price, like the $1.99 in 2 for $1.99.
    int totalNumber; //Total number being purchased.
    System.out.println("Enter name of item you are purchasing:");
    itemName = SavitchIn.readLine();
    System.out.println("Enter price of item on two lines");
    System.out.println("For example, 3 for $2.99 is entered as");
    System.out.println("3");
    System.out.println("2.99");
    System.out.println("Enter price of item on two lines, now:");
    count = SavitchIn.readLineInt();
    cost = SavitchIn.readLineDouble();
    System.out.println("Enter number of items purchased");
    totalNumber = SavitchIn.readLineInt();
```

Display 4.10 Purchase Class *(Part 3 of 3)*

```
        System.out.println(totalNumber + " " + itemName);
        System.out.println("at " + count + " for $" + cost);
        System.out.println("Is that correct?(y/n)");
        char ans = SavitchIn.readLineNonwhiteChar();
        while ((ans != 'y') && (ans != 'Y'))
        {//Try again:
            System.out.println("Enter name of item you are purchasing:");
            itemName = SavitchIn.readLine();
            System.out.println("Enter price of item on two lines");
            System.out.println("For example, 3 for $2.99 is entered as");
            System.out.println("3");
            System.out.println("2.99");
            System.out.println("Enter price of item on two lines, now:");
            count = SavitchIn.readLineInt();
            cost = SavitchIn.readLineDouble();
            System.out.println("Enter number of items purchased");
            totalNumber = SavitchIn.readLineInt();
            System.out.println(totalNumber + " " + itemName);
            System.out.println("at " + count + " for $" + cost);
            System.out.println("Is that correct?(y/n)");
            ans = SavitchIn.readLineNonwhiteChar();
        }

        name = itemName;
        groupCount = count;
        groupPrice = cost;
        numberBought = totalNumber;
    }

    /*****************************************************
     *Outputs price and number being purchased to screen.
     *****************************************************/
    public void writeOutput()
    {
        System.out.println(numberBought + " " + name);
        System.out.println("at " + groupCount + " for $" + groupPrice);
    }

    private String name;
    private int groupCount;//Part of price, like the 2 in 2 for $1.99.
    private double groupPrice;//Part of price, like the $1.99 in 2 for $1.99.
    private int numberBought;//Total number being purchased.

}
```

Display 4.11 Use of Purchase Class *(Part 1 of 2)*

```
public class PurchaseDemo
{
    public static void main(String[] args)
    {
        Purchase oneSale = new Purchase();

        oneSale.readInput();
        oneSale.writeOutput();
        System.out.println("Cost each $" + oneSale.unitCost());
        System.out.println("Total cost $" + oneSale.totalCost());
    }
}
```

Note that the price of 5 for $1.25 is stored in the two instance variables `groupCount` (for the 5) and `groupPrice` (for the $1.25).

Thus, for example, consider the method `totalCost`. The total cost of the purchase is calculated as

```
(groupPrice/groupCount)*numberBought
```

Or to be very specific: if this is 12 apples at 5 for $1.25, the total cost is

```
(1.25 / 5) * 12
```

Also notice the method `readInput`. Note that it echoes the input and asks the user if the input is OK. If the user is not happy with the input, she or he is given a chance to reenter the input. A simple demonstration program that uses this class is given in Display 4.11.

Abstract Data Types (ADTs)

data type

As the name suggests, a **data type** is a kind of data, like *int* or *double* or String or the class Purchase in Display 4.10. When you think of a data type, the first thing that comes to mind is the set of data values. For example, the data values for the type *int* are all the whole numbers, like 1, 2, 3, 0, −1, −2, etc., and people often think the type *int* is just these values. However, a data type is not just a set of values. It is a set of values together with some operations on those values. For the type *int*, the operations are things like addition, subtraction, the % operator, and so forth. For a class the operations are the methods of the class. A **data type** is a collection of values *and* a collection of operations for manipulating these values.

Display 4.11 Use of Purchase Class *(Part 2 of 2)*

Sample Screen Dialogue

```
Enter name of item you are purchasing:
apples
Enter price of item on two lines
For example, 3 for $2.99 is entered as
3
2.99
Enter price of item on two lines, now:
5
125
Enter number of items purchased:
12
12 apples
at 5 for $125.0
Is that correct?(y/n)
n
Enter name of item you are purchasing:
apples
Enter price of item on two lines
For example, 3 for $2.99 is entered as
3
2.99
Enter price of item on two lines, now:
5
1.25
Enter number of items purchased:
12
12 apples
at 5 for $1.25
Is that correct?(y/n)
y
12 apples
at 5 for $1.25
Cost each = $0.25
Total cost = $3.0
```

ADT

An **abstract data type** is a data type that is defined following modern principles of information bidding. An **abstract data type** (abbreviated **ADT**) is a data type defined so that the programmers who use the type do not have access to the details of how the values and operations are implemented. The predefined types, such as `int`, `double`, `char`, and `String`, are abstract data types (ADTs). You do not know and probably do not care about how the operations, such as + and %, are implemented for the type `int`. The classes that you define are also data types, but they will not be ADTs unless you follow the information hiding principles we have been discussing. We have already described some of the principles you use in order to make a class definition an ADT, such as making all instance variables private. In this subsection, we will summarize those principles and say a bit more about ADTs. Be sure to note that ADT terminology is not part of the Java language. It is a style rule for how to define classes and can be used with any programming language.

user interface

implementation

An ADT can be divided into two parts, which we will call the *user interface*[1] and the *implementation*. The **user interface** of an ADT tells a programmer all that she or he needs to know in order to use the class. When you define an ADT as a Java class, the user interface consists of the headings for the public methods of the class along with the comments that tell you how to use these public methods. The user interface of the ADT should be all you need to know in order to use the ADT in your program. The **implementation** of the ADT tells how this user interface is realized as Java code. The implementation of the ADT consists of the private instance variables of the class and the definitions of both the public and private methods. The user interface and implementation of an ADT are not separated in your Java code. They are mixed together. For example, for the class `Purchase` in Display 4.10, the user interface is shown in color and the implementation is shown in black text. Although you need the implementation in order to run a program that uses the ADT, you should not need to know anything about the implementation in order to write the code that uses the class ADT. Some of the most important guidelines for making your class definitions into ADTs are the following:

1. Place a comment before the class definition that describes how the programmer should think about the class data and methods. (Note that this need not be a list of instance variables. If the class describes an amount of money, the programmer should think in terms of dollars and cents and not in terms of an instance variable of type `double`, if that is what is used to record the amount of money, nor should the programmer think in terms of two instance variables of type `int` for dollars and cents, if that is what is used to record the amount of money. In fact, the programmer using the class should not care whether the money is represented as an instance variable of type `double` or two instance variables of type `int` or represented in some other way.)

---

1. The word *interface* also has a technical meaning in the Java language. We are using the word slightly differently when we say *user interface*, although in spirit, the two uses of the word *interface* are the same.

2. All the instance variables in the class should be marked `private`.

3. Provide `public` accessor methods to read and change the data in an object. Also, provide `public` methods for any other basic methods that a programmer needs in order to manipulate the data in the class; for example, you should provide input and output methods.

4. Fully specify how to use each public method with a comment placed before the method heading.

5. Make any helping methods `private`.

When you comment a class definition, some of the comments are part of the user interface telling the user of the class how to use the class. These comments are usually placed before the class definition to describe general properties and before particular method definitions to explain how to use that particular method. Other comments are only needed to understand the implementation. A good rule to follow is to use the `/**/` types of comments for user-interface comments and the `//` types of comments for implementation comments. In Display 4.10, the user-interface comments are shown in color and the implementation comments are shown in black text.

If you define a class so that it is an ADT, then you can go back and change the implementation details of the class definition and any program that uses the class will not need to be changed. This is a good way to test to see if you have written an ADT. Moreover, there are often very good reasons for changing the implementation details of some class definition. For example, you may come up with a more efficient way to implement some method so that the method invocations run faster. You may even decide to change some details of what the implementation does without changing the way the methods are invoked and the basic things they do. For example, if you have a class for bank account objects, you might change the amount of the penalty charged to an account when the account is overdrawn (i.e., goes negative).

Encapsulation

Encapsulation is a term often heard when describing modern programming techniques. **Encapsulation** means that the data and the actions are combined into a single item (in our case, a class object) and that the details of the implementation are hidden. Thus, *information hiding, ADTs,* and *encapsulation* all refer to basically the same general idea: In very operational terms, the idea is to spare the programmer who uses your class from needing to read the details of how your class is implemented.

◻

Case Study U*Changing the Implementation of an ADT*

One sure test to see if you have defined a class as an ADT is to see if you can change the implementation and not have to change any code that uses the class. One reason you might want to change the implementation is to make it more efficient, that is, to make it work faster and/or use less storage. For example, after you have used the class `Purchase` (Display 4.10/page 195) for a while, you might discover that you can

---

Automatic Documentation with `javadoc`

If your copy of Java came from Sun Microsystems (or even from certain other places), it will come with a program named `javadoc` that will automatically generate documentation for the user interface to your classes. This documentation tells somebody who uses your program or class what she or he needs to know in order to use it. To get a more useful `javadoc` document, you must give your comments in a particular way. All the classes in this book have been commented for use with `javadoc`. (Although because of space constraints in the book, the comments are a little sparser than would be ideal.) If you comment your class definition correctly, such as the way the class in Display 4.10/page 195 is commented, then the program `javadoc` will take your class definition as input and produce a nicely formatted display of the user interface for your class as the output of the program `javadoc`. For example, if `javadoc` is run on the class definition in Display 4.10, then the output will look like the class with all the black text removed and only the colored text left. (It will also adjust spacing and line breaks and such.)

You do not need to use `javadoc` in order to understand this book. You do not need to use `javadoc` in order to write Java programs. Moreover, in order to read the documents produced by `javadoc`, you must use a web browser (or other HTML viewer). However, if you are already using a web browser, such as Netscape Navigator or Microsoft's Internet Explorer, then you are likely to find `javadoc` both easy to use and very useful. Appendix 4 covers `javadoc`.

---

improve the code in a number of ways. Display 4.12 shows a rewritten definition of the class `Purchase` that you might write so as to get an improved implementation of the class `Purchase`. Note that this definition of `Purchase` has the same user interface, but an implementation that is different from the old definition of `Purchase` given in Display 4.10. In both definitions, the user interface is shown in color and those parts of the definitions are identical. The program in Display 4.11/page 198 (or any other program that uses the class `Purchase`) could be run using either definition of the class `Purchase` and the program would produce identical input/output dialogues. This shows that your definition of the class `Purchase` is an ADT. To complete our discussion of this class, let's look at how these two implementation differ.

The revised definition of the class `Purchase` (Display 4.12) has one additional instance variable, named `priceForOne`, that holds the price for one item. This way, when an object of the class needs to know the unit cost or compute the price for a number of items (as in the methods `unitPrice` and `totalCost`), the revised version of the `Purchase` class can simply use the value of `priceForOne`, whereas the old version of `Purchase` (Display 4.10) needs to recompute the price of one item as

```
groupPrice/groupCount
```

and it must recompute this quantity every time it invokes the method `unitPrice` or the method `totalCost`. The second definition computes this quantity only once and stores it in the instance variable `priceForOne`.

The new version of `Purchase` (Display 4.12) has an easier-to-understand definition of the method `readInput`. In this version, the method `readInput` uses two helping methods: the method `writeOutput` and a new private method named `getData`. Since `getData` is a private method, it cannot be used anyplace except in the implementation of `Purchase`. So, this does not affect any program (or other code) that uses the class `Purchase`. As far as programs that use the class `Purchase` are concerned, the two definitions are interchangeable.

Display 4.12 Purchase Class Alternative Implementation (Part 1 of 3)

```
/***************************************************************
 *Class for the purchase of one kind of item, such as 3 oranges.
 *Prices are set supermarket style, such as 5 for $1.25.
 ***************************************************************/
public class Purchase
{
    public void setName(String theName)
    {
        name = theName;
    }

    /***************************************************************
     *Sets price to count pieces for $costForCount. E.g., 2 for
     *     $1.99.
     ***************************************************************/
    public void setPrice(int count, double costForCount)
    {
        if ((count <= 0) || (costForCount <= 0))
        {
            System.out.println("Error: Bad parameter in setPrice.");
            System.exit(0);
        }
        else
        {
            groupCount = count;
            groupPrice = costForCount;
            priceForOne = costForCount/groupCount;
        }
    }

    /***********************************************************
     *Sets the total number of items purchased to number.
     ***********************************************************/
    public void setNumber(int number)
    {
        numberBought = number;
    }

    public String nameOfItem()
    {
        return name;
    }
```

Programs will do the same thing whether you use this definition of Purchase or the one in Display 4.10/page 195.

Display 4.12 Purchase Class Alternative Implementation *(Part 2 of 3)*

```java
public double totalCost()
{
    return (priceForOne*numberBought);
}

public double unitCost()
{
    return priceForOne;
}


/*********************************************
*Returns the total number of items purchased.
*********************************************/
public int number()
{
    return numberBought;
}



/*****************************************************
 *Gets price and number being purchased from keyboard.
 *****************************************************/
public void readInput()
{
    getData();

    writeOutput();
    System.out.println("Is that correct?(y/n)");
    char ans = SavitchIn.readLineNonwhiteChar();
    while ((ans != 'y') && (ans != 'Y'))
    {//Try again:
        getData();
        writeOutput();
        System.out.println("Is that correct?(y/n)");
        ans = SavitchIn.readLineNonwhiteChar();
    }
}
```

Display 4.12 Purchase Class Alternative Implementation *(Part 3 of 3)*

```java
//Helping method for readInput method.
private void getData()
{
    System.out.println("Enter name of item you are purchasing:");
    name = SavitchIn.readLine();
    System.out.println("Enter price of item on two lines");
    System.out.println("For example, 3 for $2.99 is entered as");
    System.out.println("3");
    System.out.println("2.99");
    System.out.println("Enter price of item on two lines, now:");
    groupCount = SavitchIn.readLineInt();
    groupPrice = SavitchIn.readLineDouble();
    if (groupCount <= 0)
    {
        System.out.println("Error: illegal group size.");
        System.exit(0);
    }
    else
        priceForOne = groupPrice/groupCount;
    System.out.println("Enter number of items purchased");
    numberBought = SavitchIn.readLineInt();
}

/*****************************************************
 *Outputs price and number being purchased to screen.
 *****************************************************/
public void writeOutput()
{
    System.out.println(numberBought + " " + name);
    System.out.println("at " + groupCount + " for $" + groupPrice);
}


    private String name;
    private int groupCount;//Part of price, like the 2 in 2 for $1.99.
    private double groupPrice;//Part of price, like the $1.99 in 2 for $1.99.
    private int numberBought;//Total number being purchased.
    private double priceForOne;
}
```

Private methods are part of the implementation, not part of the user interface.

Most programmers would say that the definition of the class `Purchase` given in Display 4.12 is preferable to the definition in Display 4.10, but that is a secondary point. The point we want to emphasize is that you can separate the user interface and the implementation of this class definition.

? SELF-TEST QUESTIONS

13. Why is the method `getData` in Display 4.12/page 203 labeled *private* instead of *public*?

14. In a class definition, is anything labeled *private* ever part of the user interface.

15. In a class definition, is the body of any method definition ever part of the user interface?

4.3 Objects and Reference

"You are sad," the Knight said in anxious tone: "let me sing you a song to comfort you.

"Is it very long?" Alice asked, for she had heard a good deal of poetry that day.

"It's long," said the Knight, "but it's very, very beautiful. Everybody that hears me sing it—either it brings the tears into their eyes, or else—"

"Or else what?" said Alice, for the Knight had made a sudden pause.

"Or else it doesn't, you know. The name of the song is called 'Haddocks' Eyes.'"

"Oh, that's the name of the song, is it?" Alice asked, trying to feel interested.

"No, you don't understand," the Knight said, looking a little vexed. "That's what the name is called. The name really is 'The Aged Aged Man.'"

"Then I ought to have said 'That's what the song is called'?" Alice corrected herself.

"No, you oughtn't: that's quite another thing! The song is called 'Ways and Means': but that's only what it's called, you know!"

"Well, what is the song, then?" said Alice, who was by this time completely bewildered.

"I was coming to that," the Knight said. "The song really is 'A-sitting On A Gate': and the tune's my own invention."

LEWIS CARROLL, *Through The Looking-Glass*

Variables of a class type, such as the variable `oneSale` in Display 4.11/page 198, behave very differently from variables of the primitive types, such a *int*, *double*, and *char*. Variables of a class type are names for objects of their class, but the objects are not the values of the variables in the same way as, say, the number 6 can be the value of a variable of type *int*. A variable of a class type can name object, but the naming process is a bit subtle. In this section, we discuss how a variable of a class type names objects and we also discuss the related topic of how method parameters of a class type behave in Java.

Variables of a Class Type and Objects

The following line from Display 4.9/page 193 creates an object of type `Species-FourthTry` and attaches the name `speciesOfTheMonth` to this object:

```
SpeciesFourthTry speciesOfTheMonth = new SpeciesFourthTry();
```

This is really an abbreviation for the following two lines, which we could have used instead in that program:

```
SpeciesFourthTry speciesOfTheMonth;
speciesOfTheMonth = new SpeciesFourthTry();
```

The first line declares a variable named `speciesOfTheMonth` and says that it is a suitable name for an object of the class `SpeciesFourthTry`. This line does not create the object itself. After this line is executed, you merely have a name. It is the second line, the one with the *new*, that actually creates an object of type `SpeciesFourthTry` and associates it with the name `speciesOfTheMonth`. You can think of the *new* as creating the instance variables of the object.

new

   This may not seem like a big distinction, but it truly is. Variables of a class type behave very differently from variables of a primitive type. Consider the following lines of code that might begin the `main` part of a program:

```
SpeciesFourthTry klingonSpecies, earthSpecies;
klingonSpecies = new SpeciesFourthTry();
earthSpecies = new SpeciesFourthTry();
int n, m;
n = 42;
m = n;
```

As you would expect, there are two variables of type *int*: n and m. Both have a value of 42, but if you change one, the other still has a value of 42. For example, if the program continues with

```
n = 99;
System.out.println(n + " and " + m);
```

then the output produced will be

```
99 and 42
```

   No surprises so far, but let's suppose the program continues as follows:

assignment with variables of a class type

```
klingonSpecies.set("Klingon ox", 10, 15);
earthSpecies = klingonSpecies;
earthSpecies.set("Naked mole rat", 100, 12);
System.out.println("earthSpecies:");
earthSpecies.writeOutput();
System.out.println("klingonSpecies:");
klingonSpecies.writeOutput();
```

You might think that the `klingonSpecies` is the Klingon ox and the `earthSpecies` is the naked mole rat, but the output produced may surprise you. It is the following:

```
earthSpecies:
Name = Naked mole rat
Population = 100
Growth rate = 12%
klingonSpecies:
Name = Naked mole rat
Population = 100
Growth rate = 12%
```

What has happened? You have two names, klingonSpecies and earthSpecies, but you only have one object. Both names refer to the same object. When you change klingonSpecies, you also change earthSpecies, and vice versa; when you change earthSpecies, you also change klingonSpecies, because they are the same object. To make sense of this, consider an everyday situation that is similar. Perhaps you know somebody named *Robert,* and perhaps his family calls him *Robert,* but his friends call him *Bob.* If you take Bob out for coffee, you also take Robert out for coffee. If your sister marries Robert, she will discover that she is married to Bob, and that will not surprise her. The situation with names for objects is no different than the situation with names for people. Now let's look at some of the details about how Java handles object names.

Let's consider the assignment statement when it is used with classes. Consider

```
earthSpecies = klingonSpecies;
```

This makes earthSpecies an alternative name for whatever object is named by klingonSpecies. Now, that is a little hard to keep track of, so let's think of it another way. Let's think of it the way the computer thinks of it.

memory
addresses

Each object is stored in the computer's memory in some location and that location has an address. (If this does not make sense, reread Chapter 1.) The variables earthSpecies and klingonSpecies are really just ordinary variables (like the kind we use for *int* variables), but they store memory addresses for objects of the class SpeciesFourthTry. *When we say that a variable of a class type names an object, that means that the variable contains the memory address of that object.* When we have an assignment statement like

```
earthSpecies = klingonSpecies;
```

this just copies the memory address in klingonSpecies into the variable earthSpecies, and now they both have the same memory address and so they both name the same object.

One word of warning about memory addresses: A memory address is a number, but it is not the same kind of number as an *int* value. So, do not try to treat it as an ordinary integer.

▲ *GOTCHA* Use of = and == with Variables of A Class Type

==

with variables
of a class type

In the previous subsection, we saw some of the surprises you can get when using the assignment operator with variables of a class type. The test for equality also behaves in what may seem like a peculiar way. Suppose the class SpeciesFourthTry is defined as in Display 4.8/page 192 and suppose you have the following in a program:

Variables of a Class Type Store Memory Addresses

A variable of a primitive type stores a value of that type. Variables of a class type behave differently. *A variable of a class type does not store an object of that class.* A variable of a class type stores the memory address of where the object is located in the computer's memory. This does allow a variable of a class type to be used as a name for an object of that class. However, some operations, such as = and ==, behave quite differently for variables of a class type than they do for variables of a primitive type.

Memory Addresses Are and Are Not Numbers

A variable of a class type stores a memory address. A memory address is a number. But, a variable of class type cannot be used like a variable that stores a number. This is not crazy. This is abstraction. The important property of a memory address is that it identifies a memory location. The fact that the implementors used numbers, rather than letters or colors or something else, to identify memory locations is just an accidental property. Java prevents you from using this accidental property. This prevents you from doing things you should not do, such as obtain access to restricted memory or otherwise screw up the computer. It also makes your code easier to understand.

What's *new*?

Variables of a class type work differently than variables of a primitive type. A variable of a primitive type holds a value of that type. A variable of a class type does not actually hold an object of that class. A variable of a class type only holds the address of where that object is stored in memory. The declaration

```
SpeciesFirstTry s;
```

creates a variable s that can hold a memory address. At this point, your program has a place to store a memory address, but no place to store the data in the instance variables of an object of type SpeciesFirstTry. To get a memory location to store the values of instance variables, your program needs to use *new*. The following assigns a memory location to an object of type SpeciesFirstTry and places the address of that memory location in the variable s. In a very informal sense, you can think of the *new* as creating the instance variables of the object.

```
s = new SpeciesFirstTry();
```

```
SpeciesFourthTry klingonSpecies = new SpeciesFourthTry();
SpeciesFourthTry earthSpecies = new SpeciesFourthTry();
klingonSpecies.set("Klingon ox", 10, 15);
earthSpecies.set("Klingon ox", 10, 15);
if (klingonSpecies == earthSpecies)
    System.out.println("They are EQUAL.");
else
    System.out.println("They are NOT equal.");
```

This will produce the output

```
They are NOT equal.
```

But, the two species are equal in an intuitive sense. The problem is that a variable of a class type really contains only a memory address. There are two objects of type SpeciesFourthTry in memory. Both of them represent the same species in

Display 4.13 Defining an `equals` **Method**

```
public class Species
{
      <The definition of the methods readInput, writeOutput, and
                  projectedPopulation
            go here. They are the same as in Display 4.1/page 158 and Display 4.4/page 177.>

      <The definition of the methods set, speciesName, speciesPopulation,
            and speciesGrowthRate go here. They are the same as in Display 4.8/page 192.>

      public boolean equals(Species otherObject)
      {
          return ((this.name.equalsIgnoreCase(otherObject.name))
                  && (this.population == otherObject.population)
                  && (this.growthRate == otherObject.growthRate));
      }

      private String name;
      private int population;
      private double growthRate;
}
```

the real world, but they have different memory addresses and the == operator only checks to see if the memory addresses are equal. The == operator tests for a kind of equality, but not the kind of equality that you usually want. When defining a class, you should normally define a method for the class that is called `equals` and that tests objects to see if they are equal.

◑ PROGRAMMING TIP *Define an* `equals` *Method for Your Classes*

When you compare two objects using the == operator, you are checking to see if the two objects have the same address in memory. You are not testing for what you would intuitively call "being equal." To test for your intuitive notion of two species being equal, you should define a method called `equals` to test two species to see if they satisfy your idea of "being equal." In Display 4.13, we have redefined our definition of a class for species one last time. This time we have added a method called `equals`. This method `equals` is used with objects of the class `Species` in exactly the same way as we used the `String` method `equals` with objects of type `String`. For example, the program in Display 4.14 demonstrates use of the method `equals`.

returning a
boolean
value

Notice that the method `equals` always returns either *true* or *false*, and so the type for the value returned is *boolean*. The *return*-statement may seen a bit strange, but is nothing other than a boolean expression of the kind you might use in

Display 4.14 Demonstrating an equals **Method**

• •

```java
public class SpeciesEqualsDemo
{
    public static void main(String[] args)
    {
        Species s1 = new Species(), s2 = new Species();

        s1.set("Klingon Ox", 10, 15);
        s2.set("Klingon Ox", 10, 15);

        if (s1 == s2)
            System.out.println("Match with ==.");
        else
            System.out.println("Do Not match with ==.");

        if (s1.equals(s2))
            System.out.println("Match with the method equals.");
        else
            System.out.println("Do Not match with the method equals.");

        System.out.println("Now we change one Klingon Ox to all
                lowercase.");
        s2.set("klingon ox", 10, 15);
        if (s1.equals(s2))
            System.out.println("Still match with the method equals.");
        else
            System.out.println("Do Not match with the method equals.");
    }
}
```

Sample Screen Dialogue

```
Do Not match with ==.
Match with the method equals.
Now we change one Klingon Ox to all lowercase.
Still match with the method equals.
```

• •

an *if-else*-statement. It may help you to understand things if you note that the definition of equals in Display 4.13 can be expressed by the following pseudocode:

```
if ((this.name.equalsIgnoreCase(otherObject.name))
            && (this.population == otherObject.population)
            && (this.growthRate == otherObject.growthRate))
    then return true
    otherwise return false.
```

So, the following (from the program in Display 4.14):

```
if (s1.equals(s2))
   System.out.println("Match with the method equals.");
else
   System.out.println("Do Not match with the method equals.");
```

is equivalent to the following pseudocode:

```
if "it is true that
        (s1.name.equalsIgnoreCase(s2.name))
        && (s1.population == s2.population)
        && (s1.growthRate == s2.growthRate), then"
    System.out.println("Match with the method equals.");
else
    System.out.println("Do Not match with the method equals.");
```

use of *this* is optional

We did not need to use the *this* parameter in the definition of equals in Display 4.13. The definition given there is equivalent to the following:

```
public boolean equals(Species otherObject)
{
    return ((name.equalsIgnoreCase(otherObject.name))
            && (population == otherObject.population)
            && (growthRate == otherObject.growthRate))
}
```

The instance variable population by itself always means the same as *this*.population. Similarly, any other instance variable by itself means the same as if it were preceded by a *this* and a dot.

We will say more about methods that return a value of type *boolean* in the subsection **Boolean-Valued Methods** a little later in this chapter.

There is not a unique definition of equals that has been handed down by the gods for all time. The definition of equals that you give will depend on how you intend to use the class. The definition we gave in Display 4.13 says that two objects of the class Species are equal if they represent the same records, that is, the same species name, the same population size, and the same growth rate. In some other context, you might want to define equals to mean that two objects are equal if they have the same species name, but possibly different populations, and/or different growth rates. This would correspond to considering two objects to be equal if they are records for the same species, even if they are records for the same species at different times.

If you do not define an `equals` method for your class, then Java will automatically create a default definition of `equals`, but it is unlikely to behave the way you want it to behave. So, it is best to define your own `equals` method.

▼ *PROGRAMMING EXAMPLE* *A Species Class*

The final version of our class for a species objects is given in Display 4.15. It is the same definition as the one in Display 4.13/page 210, but this time, we have included all of the details so that you can see a complete example. We have also written the definition of the method `equals` without using the *this* parameter, since that is the form most programmers use. The definition of `equals` in Display 4.15 is completely equivalent to the definition in Display 4.13. It is only expressed using the abbreviation of leaving out the explicit writing of *this*.

Class Types and Reference Types

A variable of a class type does not actually hold an object of that class. A variable of a class type only holds the address of where that object is stored in memory. This memory address is often called a **reference** to the object in memory. For this reason, class types are often called *reference types*. A **reference type** is just a type whose variables hold references (i.e., hold memory addresses), as opposed to actual values of objects. However, there are reference types other than class types, so we will use the term *class type* when referring to the name of a class. All class types are reference types, but as we will see in Chapter 10, there are reference types that are not class types.

Boolean-Valued Methods

Methods can return a value of type *boolean*. There is really nothing new about these methods: You just specify a return type of *boolean* and use a boolean expression in the *return*-statement. We have already seen one such method when we defined the `equals` method for the class `Species` from Display 4.15. In what follows, we reproduce the definition of the boolean-valued method `equals` from Display 4.15:

```
public boolean equals(Species otherObject)
{
    return ((name.equalsIgnoreCase(otherObject.name))
            && (population == otherObject.population)
            && (growthRate == otherObject.growthRate));
}
```

The method simply evaluates the boolean expression, shown in color. That produces a value of *true* or *false*. That value of *true* or *false* is the value returned by the method `equals`.

As we have already been doing, you can use an invocation of the method `equals` in an *if-else*-statement, *while*-statement, or other statement that requires a boolean expression. You can also store the value returned by the method `equals`, or any other boolean-valued method, in a variable of type *boolean*. For example:

Display 4.15 A Complete Species Class *(Part 1 of 2)*

```
/***************************************
 *Class for data on endangered species.
 ***************************************/
public class Species
{
    public void readInput()
    {
        System.out.println("What is the species' name?");
        name = SavitchIn.readLine();
        System.out.println("What is the population of the species?");
        population = SavitchIn.readLineInt();
        System.out.println("Enter growth rate (percent increase per year):");
        growthRate = SavitchIn.readLineDouble();
    }

    public void writeOutput()
    {
        System.out.println("Name = " + name);
        System.out.println("Population = " + population);
        System.out.println("Growth rate = " + growthRate + "%");
    }

    /**********************************************************
     *Precondition: years is a nonnegative number.
     *Returns the projected population of the calling object
     *after the specified number of years.
     **********************************************************/
    public int projectedPopulation(int years)
    {
        double populationAmount = population;
        int count = years;
        while ((count > 0) && (populationAmount > 0))
        {
            populationAmount = (populationAmount +
                        (growthRate/100) * populationAmount);
            count--;
        }
```

This is the same class definition as in Display 4.13/page 210, but with all the details shown.

<Definition of projectedPopulation continued on next page.>

Display 4.15 A Complete Species Class *(Part 2 of 2)*

```
            if (populationAmount > 0)
                return (int)populationAmount;
            else
                return 0;
        }

    public void set(String newName, int newPopulation,
                                    double newGrowthRate)
    {
        name = newName;
        if (newPopulation >= 0)
            population = newPopulation;
        else
            System.out.println("ERROR: using a negative population.");
        growthRate = newGrowthRate;
    }

    public String speciesName()
    {
        return name;
    }

    public int speciesPopulation()
    {
        return population;
    }

    public double speciesGrowthRate()
    {
        return growthRate;
    }

    public boolean equals(Species otherObject)
    {
        return ((name.equalsIgnoreCase(otherObject.name))
                && (population == otherObject.population)
                && (growthRate == otherObject.growthRate));
    }

    private String name;
    private int population;
    private double growthRate;
}
```

This version of `equals` is equivalent to the version in Display 4.13/page 210. In Display 4.13, we explicitly used the `this` parameter. In this version, the `this` parameter is omitted but understood to be there implicitly.

```
Species s1 = new Species(), s2 = new Species();
<Some code to set the values of s1 and s2.>
boolean areEqual;
areEqual = s1.equals(s2);
<Some more code.>
if (areEqual)
    System.out.println("They are equal.");
else
    System.out.println("They are not equal.");
```

examples

As another example, you might add the following method to the definition of the class Species from Display 4.15:

```
/*************************************************************
 *Precondition: The calling object and the argument otherSpecies
 *both have values for their population.
 *Returns true if the population of the calling object is greater
 *than the population of otherSpecies; otherwise, returns false.
 *************************************************************/
public boolean largerPopulationThan(Species otherSpecies)
{
    return (population > otherSpecies.population);
}
```

You can then use the method largerPopulationThan in the same sorts of ways as you do the method equals. For example, the following might appear in some program:

```
Species s1 = new Species(), s2 = new Species();
<Some code to set the values of s1 and s2.>
if (s1.largerPopulationThan(s2))
    System.out.println(s1.speciesName()
                                    + " has the larger population.");
else
    System.out.println(s2.speciesName()
                                    + " has the larger population.");
```

As an additional example, you might also add the following method to the definition of the class Species from Display 4.15:

```
/*************************************************************
 *Precondition: The calling object has a value for its population.
 *Returns true if the population of the calling object is
 *zero; otherwise, returns false.
 *************************************************************/
public boolean isExtinct()
{
    return (population == 0);
}
```

The following sample code might then appear in some program:

```
Species s1 = new Species();
<Some code to set the values of s1.>
if (s1.isExtinct())
    System.out.println(s1.speciesName() + " is extinct.");
else
    System.out.println(s1.speciesName() + " is still with us.");
```

? SELF-TEST QUESTIONS

16. Write a method definition for a method called `largerGrowthRateThan` that could be added to the class `Species` from Display 4.15/page 214. The method `largerGrowthRateThan` has one argument of type `Species`. The method returns *true* if the calling object has a larger growth rate than the growth rate of the one argument; otherwise, it returns *false*.

17. Write a method definition for a method called `largerGrowthRateThan` that could be added to the class `Species` from Display 4.15/page 214. The method `largerGrowthRateThan` has one argument of type *double*. The method returns *true* if the calling object has a larger growth rate than the one argument; otherwise, it returns *false*. Note that this is not the same method as the one in Question 16.

Class Parameters

Parameters of a class type are treated differently from parameters of a primitive type. In a sense, we have already discussed this difference when we discussed using the assignment operator with objects of a class type. Recall the following two points, which will help us describe how class parameters work:

1. First, recall how the assignment operator works with classes:

    When you use an assignment operator with objects of a class type, you are actually copying a memory address. Suppose `Species` is the class defined in Display 4.15/page 214 and consider the following code:

    ```
    Species species1 = new Species(), species2 = new Species();
    species2.readInput();
    species1 = species2;
    ```

    As we discussed in the previous section, `species1` and `species2` are now two names for the same object.

2. Now consider how parameters *of a primitive type* work. For example, consider the following call to the method `projectedPopulation` that we used in Display 4.9/page 193:

    ```
    futurePopulation =
        speciesOfTheMonth.projectedPopulation(numberOfYears);
    ```

    The method definition for `projectedPopulation` is in Display 4.15. The definition begins as follows:

```
public int projectedPopulation(int years)
{
    double populationAmount = population;
    int count = years;
    while ((count > 0) && (populationAmount > 0))
    {
             . . .
```

Recall that the formal parameter `years` is actually a local variable, and when the method `projectedPopulation` is invoked, this local variable `years` is initialized to the value of the argument `numberOfYears`. So when the method is called, it is as if the following assignment statement were temporarily inserted into the method definition:

```
years = numberOfYears;
```

So, it is as if the definition of the method `projectedPopulation` was, for the duration of this method invocation, changed as follows:

```
public int projectedPopulation(int years)
{
    years = numberOfYears;
    double populationAmount = population;
    int count = years;
    while ((count > 0) && (populationAmount > 0))
    {
             . . .
```

Wow, that's a long preamble; but if you understand those two points, it will be very easy to explain how parameters of a class type work. Parameters of a class type work the same as described in the preceding point 2 for parameters of a primitive type, *but since the assignment operator means something different for variables of a class type, the effect is very different!* [1]

Let's go through that explanation again with slightly different words (but the same message). Here is a rephrasing of how parameters of a class type are handled in Java: Consider the following call to the method `equals` that was used in Display 4.14/page 211:

---

1. Some programmers refer to the parameter mechanism for class parameters as **call-by-reference** parameter passing. Others say that is incorrect terminology. The problem is that there is more than one commonly used definition of *call-by-reference*. One point is clear, class parameters in Java behave a bit differently from what is known as *call-by-reference* parameters in other languages. So, we will not use the term *call-by-reference*. In any event, the important thing is to understand how class parameters work, no matter what you call them.

```
if (s1.equals(s2))
    System.out.println("Match with the method equals.");
else
    System.out.println("Do Not match with the method equals.");
```

s2 is an argument of the class type Species defined in Display 4.13/page 210. In what follows, we reproduce the definition for the method equals:

```
public boolean equals(Species otherObject)
{
    return ((this.name.equalsIgnoreCase(otherObject.name))
            && (this.population == otherObject.population)
            && (this.growthRate == otherObject.growthRate))
}
```

When the method equals is called in s1.equals(s2), it is as if the following assignment statement was temporarily inserted at the start of the method definition

```
otherObject = s2;
```

so that the method definition, for the duration of this call to equals, is equivalent to

```
public boolean equals(Species otherObject)
{
    otherObject = s2;//You cannot do this, but
                     //Java acts as if you could and did do this.
    return ((this.name.equalsIgnoreCase(otherObject.name))
            && (this.population == otherObject.population)
            && (this.growthRate == otherObject.growthRate))
}
```

But, recall that this assignment statement merely copies the memory address of s2 into the variable otherObject, so otherObject just becomes another name for the object named by s2. Thus, anything done with the object named otherObject will in fact be done with the object named s2. Thus, it is as if the method performed the following action:

```
    return ((this.name.equalsIgnoreCase(s2.name))
            && (this.population == s2.population)
            && (this.growthRate == s2.growthRate))
```

Notice that, with a parameter of a class type, whatever action is taken with the formal parameter (in this example, otherObject) is actually taken with the argument used in the method call (in this case, s2). So the argument used in the method call is actually acted upon and can be changed by the method call.

In the case of the method equals, the effect of this parameter-passing mechanism for parameters of a class type is not so different from what happens with parameters of a primitive type, but with some other methods, the difference is more dramatic. The next subsection gives a more dramatic example of how parameters of a class type differ from parameters of a primitive type.

Display 4.16 Just a Demonstration Class

```
/***************************************************************
 *This is a version of the class Species, but is only a toy example
 *designed to demonstrate the difference between parameters of
 * a class type and parameters of a primitive type.
 ***************************************************************/
public class DemoSpecies
{
    /*********************************************************
     *Precondition: Calling object has been given values.
     *Postcondition: otherObject has the same data as the
     *calling object. The calling object is unchanged.
     *********************************************************/
    public void makeEqual(DemoSpecies otherObject)
    {
        otherObject.name = this.name;
        otherObject.population = this.population;
        otherObject.growthRate = this.growthRate;
    }


    /*********************************************************
     *Tries to set intVariable equal to the population of
     *the calling object. But it cannot succeed, because
     *arguments of a primitive type cannot be changed.
     *********************************************************/
    public void tryToMakeEqual(int intVariable)
    {
        intVariable = this.population;
    }


    public boolean equals(DemoSpecies otherObject)
```

<The rest of the class definition of the method equals is same as in Display 4.15/page 214.>

<The rest of the class definition is the same as that of the class Species in Display 4.15.>

```
    private String name;
    private int population;
    private double growthRate;
}
```

Parameters of a Class Type

Formal parameters are given in parentheses after the method name at the beginning of a method definition. A formal parameter of a class type is a local variable that holds the memory address of an object of that class type. When there is an invocation of the method, the parameter is initialized to the address of the corresponding argument in the method invocation. In less technical terms, this means that the formal parameter will serve as an alternative name for the object given as the corresponding argument in a method invocation.

Note that this means that if you use an argument of a class type in a method invocation, then the method invocation can change the argument.

Comparing Class Parameters and Primitive-Type Parameters

Suppose we add a method named `makeEqual` to the class `Species` to form a new class called `DemoSpecies`, as shown in Display 4.16. This class is only for our demonstration, so do not worry about the rest of the class definition. Notice that the method `makeEqual` has formal parameters of type `DemoSpecies` and that `makeEqual` changes the formal parameter. Now, let's play with this toy class.

Look at the demonstration program in Display 4.17 and look at the call to this method `makeEqual`, which has an argument `s2` of type `DemoSpecies`. Note that the change performed in the method body is actually performed on the argument named by `s2`. A method can actually change the value of an argument of a class type.

But, now look at the method named `tryToMakeEqual` also in Display 4.16. Notice that the method `tryToMakeEqual` has a formal parameter of the primitive type *int* and that `tryToMakeEqual` changes the formal parameter. Now, look again at the demonstrating program in Display 4.17 and look at the call to this method `tryToMakeEqual`, which has an argument `aPopulation` of type *int*. Note that the change performed in the method body has no effect on the argument `aPopulation`. This is because, with arguments of a primitive type, Java uses the call-by-value parameter mechanism, which means the parameter is a local variable that holds the value of the argument, and so any changes are made to this local variable and not to the argument.

Parameters of a class type are more versatile than parameters of a primitive type. Parameters of a primitive type can be used to give values to a method, but a method cannot change the value of any primitive-type variable that is given to it as an argument. On the other hand, parameters of a class type not only can be used to give information to a method, but the method can also change the object named by an argument of a class type.

Differences between Primitive and Class-Type Parameters

A method cannot change the value of a variable of a primitive type that is an argument to the method. On the other hand, a method can change the values of the instance variables of an argument of a class type.

◑ PROGRAMMING TIP *Make the Compiler Happy*

The compiler will try to check to make sure you do certain necessary things, such as initializing variables and including a *return*-statement in the definition of a method

Display 4.17 Comparing Parameters of a Class and a Primitive Type

```java
public class ParametersDemo
{
    public static void main(String[] args)
    {
        DemoSpecies s1 = new DemoSpecies(),
                    s2 = new DemoSpecies();

        s1.set("Klingon Ox", 10, 15);
        s2.set("Ferengie Fur Ball", 90, 56);
        System.out.println("Value of s2 before call to method:");
        s2.writeOutput();
        s1.makeEqual(s2);
        System.out.println("Value of s2 after call to method:");
        s2.writeOutput();

        int aPopulation = 42;
        System.out.println("Value of aPopulation before call to method: "
                                                       + aPopulation);
        s1.tryToMakeEqual(aPopulation);
        System.out.println("Value of aPopulation after call to method: "
                                                       + aPopulation);
    }
}
```

Screen Output

```
Value of s2 before call to method:
Name = Ferengie Fur Ball
Population = 90
Growth Rate = 56.0%
Value of s2 after call to method:
Name = Klingon Ox
Population = 10
Growth Rate = 15.0%
Value of aPopulation before call to method: 42
Value of aPopulation after call to method: 42
```

An argument of a class type can change.

An argument of a primitive type cannot change.

that returns a value. Sometimes, you may find yourself in a situation where the compiler is asking you do one of these things and you are certain that either you have done it or you do not need to do it. In such cases, it does no good to argue with the compiler. You should just change something to make the compiler stop complaining. First of all, check to make sure the compiler is not correct; it usually is. If you cannot find a true error in your code, then change your code so that it is more obvious that you have done what the compiler is asking for.

For example, if you declare a variable `line` as follows

```
String line;
```

and the compiler insists that you initialize the variable `line,` then change the declaration to

```
String line = null;
```

The constant value *null* is a special constant that can be used to give a value to any variable of any class type.

As another example, suppose you have a method that returns a value of type *int* and the method definition ends with the following:

```
if (something > somethingElse)
    return something;
else
    return somethingElse;
```

In this case, every computation probably does end with a *return*-statement. If the compiler nonetheless complains saying you need a *return*-statement, change that last *if-else*-statement to the following

```
int answer;
if (something > somethingElse)
    answer = something;
else
    answer = somethingElse;
return answer;
```

This assumes the method returns a value of type *int*. For other types, just make the obvious adjustments.

---

null

null is a special constant that can be used to give a value to any variable of any class type. The constant *null* is not an object, but a sort of place holder for an object address. Since it is like an address, you use == and != rather than the method `equals` when you test to see if a variable is equal to *null*. ∎

? SELF-TEST QUESTIONS

18. What's wrong with a program that starts as follows? The class `Species` is defined in Display 4.15/page 214.

```java
public class SpeciesEqualsDemo
{
    public static void main(String[] args)
    {
        Species s1, s2;

        s1.set("Klingon Ox", 10, 15);
        s2.set("Klingon Ox", 10, 15);

        if (s1 == s2)
            System.out.println("Match with ==.");
        else
            System.out.println("Do Not match with ==.");
```

19. What is the biggest difference between a parameter of a primitive type and a parameter of a class type?

20. What is the output produced by the following program? The class `Species` is defined in Display 4.15/page 214.

```java
public class ExerciseClass
{
    public static void main(String[] args)
    {
        Species s1 = new Species();
        ExerciseClass mysteryMaker = new ExerciseClass();
        int n = 0;
        s1.set("Hobbit", 100, 2);
        mysteryMaker.mystery(s1, n);
        s1.writeOutput();
        System.out.println("n = " + n);
    }
    public void mystery(Species s, int m)
    {
        s.set("Klingon Ox", 10, 15);
        m = 42;
    }
}
```

(If the fact that the `main` is in the class definition bothers you, you can assume the `main` is in some other class in some other file. The answer will be the same.)

21. Redefine the class `Person` from Self-Test Question 12 so that it includes an `equals` method.

Chapter Summary

- ☐ Classes have instance variables to store data and methods to perform actions.

- ☐ All instance variables in a class should be declared to be *private*. When they are declared *private*, they cannot be accessed except within the definition of a method of the same class.

□ There are two kinds of methods: methods that return a value and *void*-methods.

□ Methods can have parameters of a primitive type and/or parameters of a class type, but they behave differently.

□ A parameter of a primitive type is a local variable that is initialized to the value of the corresponding argument when the method is called. This mechanism of substituting arguments for formal parameters is known as the **call-by-value** mechanism.

□ A parameter of a class type becomes another name for the corresponding argument in a method invocation. Thus, any change that is made to the parameter will be made to the corresponding argument.

□ The operators = and ==, when used on objects of a class, do not behave the same as they do on primitive types.

□ You usually want to define an `equals` method for the classes you define.

? ANSWERS to Self-Test Questions

....

1.
```
SpeciesFirstTry speciesOfTheYear = new SpeciesFirstTry();
System.out.println("Enter data for Species of the Year:");
speciesOfTheYear.readInput();
```

2. `dilbert.readInput();`

3.

```java
public class SpeciesFirstTry
{
    public void readInput()
    {
        System.out.println("What is the species' name?");
        name = SavitchIn.readLine();
        System.out.println("What is the species' number?");
        number = SavitchIn.readLineInt();
        System.out.println("What is the population of the species?");
        population = SavitchIn.readLineInt();
        System.out.println(
                "Enter growth rate (percent increase per year):");
        growthRate = SavitchIn.readLineDouble();
    }

    public void writeOutput()
    {
        System.out.println("Name = " + name);
        System.out.println("Number = " + number);
        System.out.println("Population = " + population);
        System.out.println("Growth rate = " + growthRate + "%");
    }

    public int populationIn10()
    <This method does not change.>

    public String name;
     public int number;
    public int population;
    public double growthRate;
}
```

4.

```java
    public int femalePopulation()
    {
        return (population/2 + population%2);
    }

    public int malePopulation()
    {
        return population/2;
    }
```

5.

```java
    public void writeOutput()
    {
        System.out.println("Name = " + this.name);
        System.out.println("Population = " + this.population);
        System.out.println("Growth rate = " + this.growthRate + "%");
    }
```

6.
```
public void readInput()
{
    System.out.println("What is the species' name?");
    this.name = SavitchIn.readLine();
    System.out.println("What is the population of the species?");
    this.population = SavitchIn.readLineInt();
    System.out.println(
            "Enter growth rate (percent increase per year):");
    this.growthRate = SavitchIn.readLineDouble();
}
```

7.
```
public double density(double area)
{
    return population/area;
}
```

8.
```
public void fixPopulation(double area)
{
    population = (int)(2*area);
}
```

9.
```
public void changePopulation(double area, int numberPerMile)
{
    population = (int)(numberPerMile*area);
}
```

10. We cannot use the alternative code because the instance variables are labeled `private` in the class definition and so cannot be accessed directly except within a method definition of the class `SpeciesFourthTry`.

11.
```
/************************************************************
*Precondition: Calling object's population and growth rate
*have been given values.
*Postcondition: Calling object's population was updated to
*reflect one year's change. Other data values are unchanged.
************************************************************/
```

12.

```java
public class Person
{
    public void readInput()
    {
        System.out.println("What is the person's name?");
        name = SavitchIn.readLine();

        System.out.println("What is the person's age?");
        age = SavitchIn.readLineInt();
    }

    public void writeOutput()
    {
        System.out.println("Name = " + name);
        System.out.println("Age = " + age);
    }

    public void set(String newName, int newAge)
    {
        name = newName;
        if (newAge >= 0)
            age = newAge;
        else
            System.out.println("ERROR: Used a negative age.");
    }

    public String personName()
    {
        return name;
    }

    public int personAge()
    {
        return age;
    }

    private String name;
    private int age;
}
```

13. It is labeled *private* because it is only a helping method and so is not part of the public user interface, but is part of the private implementation.

14. No, it is part of the implementation.

15. No, it is part of the implementation.

16.
```
/****************************************************************
*Precondition: The calling object and the argument otherSpecies
*both have values for their growth rates.
*Returns true if the growth rate of the calling object is greater
*than the growth rate of otherSpecies; otherwise, returns false.
****************************************************************/
public boolean largerGrowthRateThan(Species otherSpecies)
{
    return (growthRate > otherSpecies.growthRate);
}
```

17.
```
/****************************************************************
*Precondition: Calling object has a value for its growth rate.
*Returns true if the growth rate of the calling object is greater
*than otherGrowthRate; otherwise, returns false.
****************************************************************/
public boolean largerGrowthRateThan(double otherGrowthRate)
{
    return (growthRate > otherGrowthRate);
}
```

18. The variables s1 and s2 are names for object of type Species, but this program does not create any objects for them to name. They are just names, not yet objects. The program should begin as

```
public class SpeciesEqualsDemo
{
    public static void main(String[] args)
    {
        Species s1 = new Species(), s2 = new Species();
        <The rest of the code is OK.>
```

19. The biggest difference is how a method handles arguments that correspond to the different kinds of parameters. A method cannot change the value of a variable of a primitive type that is an argument to the method. On the other hand, a method can change the values of the instance variables of an object of a class type whose name is an argument to the method.

20.
```
Name = Klingon ox
Population = 10
Growth rate = 15.0%
n = 0
```

21. The class definition is the same as before except for the addition of the method equals. In what follows are two possible definitions of equal. The first corresponds to saying a person at one age is equal to the same person at another, later age. The second one corresponds to saying that a person at one age is not equal to what she or he will be at another age.

```
public boolean equals(Person otherObject)
{
    return (this.name.equalsIgnoreCase(otherObject.name));
}

public boolean equals(Person otherObject)
{
    return ((this.name.equalsIgnoreCase(otherObject.name))
            && (this.age == otherObject.age) );
}
```

They are also correct if you omit all the occurrences of *this* and the following dot.

? PROGRAMMING EXERCISES

1. Write a program to answer questions like the following: Suppose the species Klingon ox has a population of 100 and a growth rate of 15%, and the species naked mole rat has a population of 10 and a growth rate of 35%. How many years will it take for the naked mole rat population to exceed the Klingon ox population? Use the class Species in Display 4.15/ page 214. Your program will ask for the data on both species and will respond by telling how many years it will take for the species with the lower population to get a population that exceeds that of the species that starts with the higher population. The two species may be entered in any order. Note that it is possible that the species with the smaller population will never exceed that of the other species. In this case, your program should output a suitable message stating this fact.

2. Define a class called Counter. An object of this class is used to count things, so it records a count that is a nonnegative whole number. Include methods to set the counter to zero, to increase the count by 1, and to decrease the count by 1. Be sure that no method allows the value of the counter to become negative. Also, include an accessor method that returns the current count value. Also, include a method that outputs the count to the screen. There will be no input method. The only method that can set the counter is the one that sets it to zero. Also, write a program to test your class definition. *Hint:* You only need one instance variable.

3. Write a grading program for a class with the following grading policies:

   (a) There are two quizzes, each graded on the basis of 10 points.

   (b) There is one midterm exam and one final exam, each graded on the basis of 100 points.

   (c) The final exam counts for 50% of the grade, the midterm counts for 25%, and the two quizzes together count for a total of 25%. (Do not forget to normalize the quiz scores. They should be converted to a percent before they are averaged in.)

Any grade of 90 or more is an A, any grade of 80 or more (but less than 90) is a B, any grade of 70 or more (but less than 80) is a C, any grade of 60 or more (but less than 70) is a D, and any grade below 60 is an F. The program will read in the student's scores and output the student's record, which consists of two quiz and two exam scores as well as the student's overall numeric score for the entire course and final letter grade.

Define and use a class for the student record. The class should have instance variables for the quizzes, midterm, final, course overall numeric score, and course final letter grade. The overall numeric score is a number in the range 0 to 100, which represents the weighted average of the student's work. The class should have input and output methods. The input method should not ask for the final numeric grade nor should it ask for the final letter grade. The class should have methods to compute the overall numeric grade and the final letter grade. These last two methods will be *void*-methods that set the appropriate instance variables. Remember, one method can call another method. If you prefer, you can define a single method that sets both the overall numeric score and the final letter grade, but if you do this, use a helping method. Your program should use all the methods we discussed. Your class should have a reasonable set of accessor methods, whether or not your program uses them. You may add other methods if you wish.

Chapter 5

PROGRAMMING WITH
CLASSES AND METHODS

5.1   **PROGRAMMING WITH METHODS 234**
Methods Calling Methods 235
Programming Tip Write Toy
    Programs 239
Programming Tip Make Helping
    Methods Private 239
Programming Tip You Can Put a `main`
    in Any Class 239
Static Methods 240
The `Math` Class 243
Case Study Formatting Output 246
Top–Down Design 252
Testing Methods 252
Integer, Double, and Other
    Wrapper Classes 255
Gotcha Assigning a Primitive Value
    to a Wrapper Class 257

5.2   **POLYMORPHISM 258**
Overloading 259
Programming Example A Pet Class 261
Gotcha Overloading and Automatic
    Type Conversion 264
Gotcha You Cannot Overload Based
    on the Returned Type 265

5.3   **CONSTRUCTORS 267**
Defining Constructors 268
Gotcha Omitting the Default
    Constructor 274

5.4   **INFORMATION HIDING REVISITED 275**
Gotcha Instance Variables of a Class
    Type 275

5.5   **PACKAGES *(Optional)* 279**
Packages and Importing 279
Package Names and Directories 280

Chapter Summary 282
Answers to Self-Test Questions 283
Programming Exercises 286

5

PROGRAMMING WITH CLASSES AND METHODS

*A tourist stopped an elderly gentleman on the streets of New York
    City and asked him,*
"Please sir, could you tell me how I can get to Carnegie Hall?"
"Practice, practice, practice," the old gentleman replied.
A VERY OLD JOKE

Introduction

In this chapter, we continue our discussion of how to define classes and their methods. Our discussion will cover one of the main concepts of object-oriented programming, which is known as *polymorphism*. As you will see, *polymorphism* is a way of having the same name mean different things in different contexts, rather like what happens in English. We also introduce *constructors*, which are methods used to automatically initialize a new object. Our last topic is packages, which are a way of grouping classes for convenient use later on. Along the way, we also cover a number of techniques that will help you to write better method definitions.

Prerequisites

Chapters 4, 5, and 6 are three parts of one long story. You must know the material in Chapter 4 before doing much in this chapter.

Section 5.4 discusses some subtle points about using instance variables of a class type. Strictly speaking, it is not required for the rest of the material in this book and so can be postponed. However, Section 5.4 does discuss fundamental issues that you should read at some point.

The material on packages in Section 5.5 requires a knowledge of directories (folders) and PATH variables. This material on packages is not required for any other material in this book, so you need not cover Section 5.5 until you are ready to do so, and you can read the rest of this book without reading Section 5.5.

5.1 Programming with Methods

*The greatest invention of the nineteenth century was the invention of the
    method of invention.*
ALFRED NORTH WHITEHEAD, *Science and the Modern World*

In this section, we describe a number of basic techniques to use for designing and testing methods.

Methods Calling Methods

A method body may contain a call to (i.e., an invocation of) another method. The situation for these sorts of method calls is exactly the same as it would be if the method call had occurred in the `main` part of a program. However, if all the methods are in the same class, then there is an abbreviated notation that is usually used. Display 5.1 contains the definition of a class called `Oracle`. The method `answer` of this class conducts a dialogue with the user that answers any one-line question that the user asks. (Of course, this is just a simple program, so the answer is actually obtained from the user herself/himself.) Notice that within the definition of the method `answer`, there are calls to the two other methods `seekAdvice` and `update`, both of which are also in the same class `Oracle`. Note that the methods named `seekAdvice` and `update` are not preceded by an object and a dot. If you had an object, `delphi`, of the class `Oracle`, and you performed a call to `answer` with this object, the method call would be

omitting `this`

```
delphi.answer();
```

Within the definition of `answer`, the call to `seekAdvice` is written as just

```
seekAdvice();
```

but if the calling object to `answer` is `delphi`, then it is understood that the preceding call to `seekAdvice` means

```
delphi.seekAdvice();
```

When you write the definition of a method like `answer`, you do not know what the name of the calling object will be. It could be different names at different times, such as

```
delphi.answer();
```

in one program and

```
myObject.answer();
```

in another program. Since you do not, in fact cannot, know the name of the calling object, you omit it. So, in the definition of the class `Oracle` in Display 5.1, when you write

```
seekAdvice();
```

within the definition of the method `answer`, this means

```
The_Calling_Object.seekAdvice();
```

Since the *this* parameter just means *The_Calling_Object*, you can use the *this* parameter to name the calling object, so the following two calls to `seekAdvice` are equivalent:

```
seekAdvice();
```

Display 5.1 Method Calling Another Method *(Part 1 of 2)*

●●

```java
public class Oracle
{
    public static void main(String[] args)
    {
        Oracle delphi = new Oracle();
        char ans;

        do
        {
            delphi.answer();
            System.out.println("Do you wish to ask another question? (y/n)");
            ans = SavitchIn.readLineNonwhiteChar();
        } while ((ans != 'n') && (ans != 'N'));

        System.out.println("The oracle will now rest.");
    }

    public void answer()
    {
        System.out.println("I am the oracle.");
        System.out.println("I will answer any one-line question.");
        System.out.println("What is your question?");
        question = SavitchIn.readLine();
        seekAdvice();
        System.out.println("You asked the question:");
        System.out.println(question);
        System.out.println("Now, here is my answer:");
        System.out.println(oldAnswer);
        update();
    }

    private void seekAdvice()
    {
        System.out.println("Hmm, I need some help on that.");
        System.out.println("Please give me one line of advice.");
        newAnswer = SavitchIn.readLine();
        System.out.println("Thank you. That helped a lot.");
    }
```

●●

Display 5.1 Method Calling Another Method *(Part 2 of 2)*

●●●

```
    private void update()
    {
        oldAnswer = newAnswer;
    }

    private String oldAnswer =
        "The answer can be found at a secret place in the woods.";
    private String newAnswer;
    private String question;
}
```

Sample Screen Dialogue

```
I am the oracle.
I will answer any one-line question.
What is your question?
What time is it?
Hmm, I need some help on that.
Please give me one line of advice.
Seek and ye shall find the answer.
Thank you. That helped a lot.
You asked the question:
What time is it?
Now, here is my answer:
The answer can be found at a secret place in the woods.
Do you wish to ask another question? (y/n)
yes
I am the oracle.
I will answer any one-line question.
What is your question?
What is the meaning of life?
Hmm, I need some help on that.
Please give me one line of advice.
Ask the car guys.
Thank you. That helped a lot.
You asked the question:
What is the meaning of life?
Now, here is my answer:
Seek and ye shall find the answer.
Do you wish to ask another question? (y/n)
no
The oracle will now rest.
```

●●●

and the equivalent

```
this.seekAdvice();
```

This omitting of the *this* and a dot when you refer to method in the same class is not really new. We have already been doing the exact same thing with instance variables.

This omitting of the calling object and dot only works for the calling object of the method being defined. If you call a method of one class within the definition of a method of another class, you must include the name of the calling object followed by a dot.

Also, this omitting of the calling object only applies if the calling object can be expressed with the *this* parameter. If the calling object is some object declared and created with *new* within a method definition, then within that method definition, you must include the object name and dot. That is why you almost always have to include a calling object and dot in a method invocation within the method `main`, even if the method being called belongs to the same class as the method `main`. As a simple and sure test, remember that omitting the calling object and dot is only allowed if the call object is the *this* parameter

---

Omitting the Calling Object

When the calling object in a method invocation is the *this* parameter, you can omit the *this* and the dot.

Example:

The following are equivalent:

```
public void answer()
{
        . . .
    this.seekAdvice();
        . . .
    this.update();
}
```

and

```
public void answer()
{
        . . .
    seekAdvice();
        . . .
    update();
}
```

◐ PROGRAMMING TIP *Write Toy Programs*

The program in Display 5.1 is just a toy program. It is just a game. It does not do any engineering or business calculation. Moreover, it is not a very sophisticated game. No user is likely to be fooled, but is certain to notice that she or he is providing her or his own answers. So why bother with such a useless program? The answer is practice, practice, practice. The way to learn how to program is to practice each new technique and new program feature. Moreover, the first time you use a new feature, it pays to use it in a very simple context so you are not distracted by having to design and debug a lot of things that are not directly relevant to what you are learning. If you look through more advanced programming books, you will see that the experts typically introduce a new feature with an example of just a few lines that may not do anything particularly useful and may not even be a complete program. This gives an uncluttered view of the feature being introduced.

◐ PROGRAMMING TIP *Make Helping Methods Private*

Look again at Display 5.1/page 236. The two methods `seekAdvice` and `update` are labeled *private*, rather than *public*. Recall that if a method is labeled *private*, then it can only be used in the definitions of other methods of the same class. Thus, in some other class or program, the following invocation of the private method `seekAdvice` would be illegal and would produce a compiler error message:

```
Oracle myOracle = new Oracle();
myOracle.seekAdvice(); //Illegal: seekAdvice is private.
```

whereas the following call to the public method `answer` would be perfectly legal:

```
myOracle.answer(); //Legal.
```

The reason for making `seekAdvice` and `update` private is that they are just helping methods. A user of the class `Oracle` is not expected to use these methods. The methods `seekAdvice` and `update` are only used in the definition of the method `answer`. That means that the methods `seekAdvice` and `update` are part of the class implementation and not part of the user interface for the class. As we discussed in the subsection **Abstract Data Types (ADTs)** of Chapter 4, it is good programming practice to keep the implementation portion of a class private. Thus, we labeled some methods *private* because they are not intended to be seen by the outside world. They are part of the implementation (the inner workings) of the class, just like the private instance variables.

◐ PROGRAMMING TIP *You Can Put a* `main` *in Any Class*

The definition of our class `Oracle` (Display 5.1/page 236) has the `main` part of a program inside the class definition. We did not place that test program in a separate class. You can add a `main` to any class definition and then run that class definition as a program. This does not prevent you from also using the class in some other program. When you use the class in some other program, the `main` in the class definition is simply ignored. One handy trick is to place a a small diagnostic program in a `main`

that is inside of your class definition. That way you can always test the class definition if you suspect something is wrong.

Look at the `main` for the class `Oracle`, shown in Display 5.1, and note that
within the `main` method, you must create an object of the class before you can call
any of the methods. To call the method `answer` within `main`, you need to create an
object of type `Oracle` in the usual way, namely,

```
Oracle delphi = new Oracle();
```

Then, you call a method of this object in the usual way, namely,

```
delphi.answer();
```

This is true even though both `main` and `answer` are methods in the same class.

When you write the code for the `main` method in a class, you (usually) cannot
invoke another method, within the same class, without using an object. Why is the
`main` method different from other methods in this regard? The easiest way to think
of this is to note that when you write a `main` within the class definition, you handle
objects and methods of that class the same as you do within a `main` that is in some
other file. The technical reason for this is that `main` is a *static* method. We discuss
static methods in the next subsection.

Every Class Can Have a `main`.

Every class can have a `main` method added to it. It can then be run as a program. If the class is not intended as
a program, you still might want to include a `main` that is a test program for the class.

Static Methods

Sometimes you need a method that does not require an object of any kind. For example, you might need a method to compute the maximum of two integers, or a
method to compute the square root of a number, or a method to convert a letter
character from lowercase to uppercase. None of these methods has any obvious object to which they should belong. In these cases, you can define the method to be *static*. When you define a method to be **static**, you still define the method in a class, so it
is still a member of a class, but the method can be invoked without using any object.
Instead of using an object name, you usually use the class name when invoking a static method. (Static methods are also sometimes called **class methods**.)

static method

For example, Display 5.2 has the definition of a class named `CircleFirstTry`,
which has two static method definitions. The methods may be called as in the following example:

```
double areaOfCircle = CircleFirstTry.area(12.7);
double circumOfCircle = CircleFirstTry.circumference(12.7);
```

Note that a static method is called by giving the name of the class, `CircleFirstTry`
in this case, followed by a dot, and then the method name and parameters. So, the
class name serves the same purpose as a calling object. (It would be legal to create
an object of the class `CircleFirstTry` and use it to invoke the method `area` or the
method `circumference`, but that is confusing style, so we usually use the class name

Display 5.2 Static Methods

```
/*************************************************************
 *Class with static methods to perform calculations on circles.
 *************************************************************/
public class CircleFirstTry
{
    public static final double PI = 3.14159;

    public static double area(double radius)
    {
        return (PI*radius*radius);
    }

    public static double circumference(double radius)
    {
        return (PI*(radius + radius));
    }
}
```

Later in this chapter, we will give an alternate version of this class.

Static Methods

If you place the reserved word `static` in the heading of the definition of a method, then the method can be invoked using the class name in place of a calling object. Since it does not need a calling object, a static method cannot refer to a (nonstatic) instance variable of the class, nor can it invoke a nonstatic method of the class (unless it creates a new object of the class and uses this object as the calling object).

Example (of invoking a static method):

```
int result = Math.max(n1, n2);
```

`Math` is a predefined class.

---

when invoking a static method.) Another sample use of these static methods is given in Display 5.3.

Note that when you define a static method, you define it exactly the same as you would define any other method, but you add the reserved word `static` to the heading, as shown in the examples in Display 5.2.

In the example of the class `CircleFirstTry` in Display 5.2, the class had no instance variables, but it is perfectly legal for a class to have both instance variable and static methods (and regular, nonstatic methods). However, if the class does have instance variables, then they cannot be referenced in the definition of any

Display 5.3 Using Static Methods

```
public class CircleDemo
{
    public static void main(String[] args)
    {
        double radius;

        System.out.println("Enter the radius of a circle in inches:");
        radius = SavitchIn.readLineDouble();

        System.out.println("A circle of radius " + radius + " inches");
        System.out.println("has an area of " +
                CircleFirstTry.area(radius) + " square inches,");
        System.out.println("and a circumference of " +
                CircleFirstTry.circumference(radius) + " inches.");
    }
}
```

Sample Screen Dialogue

```
Enter the radius of a circle in inches:
2.3
A circle of radius 2.3 inches
has an area of 16.61901 square inches,
and a circumference of 14.45131 inches.
```

Static Variables

Although we will not be covering them (except for one case mentioned in the next paragraph), it is possible for a class to have variables that are static as well as methods that are static.

We actually do use static variables in one special case, namely, the definition of constant values such as

```
public static final double PI = 3.14159;
```

There are also static variables that can change value. However, static variables that can change are seldom needed and will not be covered in this text

Static variables are also called **class variables**. Do not confuse the term *class variable* (which simply means a static variable within a class) with the notion of a variable of a class type (which means a variable whose type is a class, i.e., a variable that is used to name objects). .

static method. Moreover, within the definition of any static method, you cannot invoke a nonstatic method of the class (unless you create a new object of the class and use this object as the calling object for the nonstatic method). This makes perfectly good sense, since a static method can be invoked without using any calling object and so can be invoked when there are no instance variables or calling object to refer to.[1]

The Methods in Savitch In **Are Static**

The method readLineInt and all of the other input methods in the class SavitchIn are static methods, so they can be used with the class name in place of a calling object, as we have been doing all along. For example:

```
int n = SavitchIn.readLineInt();
```

□

The Math **Class**

The predefined class Math provides you with a number of the standard mathematical methods. The class Math is automatically provided when you use the Java language. Some of the methods in the class Math are described in Display 5.4. All of these methods are static, which means that you do not need (and in fact have no real use for) an object of the class Math. You call these methods by using the class name, Math, in place of a calling object. For example, the following outputs the maximum of the two numbers 2 and 3.

Math methods

```
int ans;
ans = Math.max(2, 3);
System.out.println(ans);
```

It would also be legal to omit the variables ans and simply write

```
System.out.println("The maximum of 2 and 3 = " + Math.max(2, 3));
```

The class Math also has the two predefined constants E and PI. The constant PI (often written π in mathematical formulas) is used in calculations involving circles, spheres, and other geometric figures based on circles. PI is approximately 3.14159. The constant E is the base of the natural logarithm system (often written e in mathematical formulas) and is approximately 2.72. (We do not use the predefined constant E in this text.) The constants PI and E are defined constants as described in Chapter 2. For example, the following computes the area of a circle, given its radius:

Math constants

```
area = Math.PI * radius * radius;
```

Be sure to note that since the constants PI and E are defined in the class Math, they must have the class name Math and dot before them. For example, you could use these constants in the definition of the class CircleFirstTry in Display 5.2/

---

1. A static method can create a new object of its own class using *new* and can then reference the instance variables, even private instance variables, of this object within the definition of the static method. This is, in fact, often done in the main method.

Display 5.4 **Static Methods in the Class Math**

Name	Description	Type of Argument	Type of Value Returned	Example	Value Returned
pow	powers	*double*	*double*	Math.pow(2.0,3.0)	8.0
abs	absolute value	*int*, *long*, *float*, or *double*	same as the type of the argument	Math.abs(−7) Math.abs(7) Math.abs(−3.5)	7 7 3.5
max	maximum	*int*, *long*, *float*, or *double*	same as the type of the arguments	Math.max(5, 6) Math.max(5.5, 5.3)	6 5.5
min	minimum	*int*, *long*, *float*, or *double*	same as the type of the arguments	Math.min(5, 6) Math.min(5.5, 5.3)	5 5.3
round	rounding	*float* or *double*, respectively	*int* or *long*, respectively	Math.round(6.2) Math.round(6.8)	6 7
ceil	ceiling	*double*	*double*	Math.ceil(3.2) Math.ceil(3.9)	4.0 4.0
floor	floor	*double*	*double*	Math.floor(3.2) Math.floor(3.9)	3.0 3.0
sqrt	square root	*double*	*double*	sqrt(4.0)	2.0

page 241. In Display 5.5, we have rewritten the class in Display 5.2 so that it uses Math.PI.

If you look at the methods in the table in Display 5.4, you will find three similar, but not identical, methods named round, floor, and ceil. Some of these return a value of type *double*, but they all return a value that is intuitively a whole number that is close to the value of their arguments. The method round rounds a number to the nearest whole number and (if the argument is a *double*) returns that whole number as a value of type *long*. If you want that whole number as a value of type *int* you must use a type cast as in the following:[1]

```
double start = 3.56;
int answer = (int)Math.round(start);
```

1. You cannot store a *long* value in a variable of type *int*, even if it is a value like 4 which could just as well have been an *int*. The value 4, for example, can be of type either *int* or *long* depending on how it was created.

Display 5.5 Predefined Constants

```
/**************************************************************
 *Class with static methods to perform calculations on circles.
 **************************************************************/
public class Circle
{
    public static double area(double radius)
    {
        return (Math.PI*radius*radius);
    }

    public static double circumference(double radius)
    {
        return (Math.PI*(radius + radius));
    }
}
```

This class behaves the same as the class CircleFirstTry *in Display 5.2/page 241. This version differs only in that it uses the predefined constant* Math.PI, *rather than defining* PI *within the class.*

The methods floor and ceil are similar to round, but are just a bit different. floor and ceil Neither one really rounds, although they both yield a whole number that is close to their argument. They both return a whole number as a value of type *double* (not of type *int* or *long*). The method floor returns the nearest whole number that is less than or equal to its argument. So, Math.floor(3.9) returns 3.0, not 4.0. Math.floor(3.3) also returns 3.0.

The method ceil returns the nearest whole number that is greater than or equal to its argument. So, Math.ceil(3.1) returns 4.0, not 3.0. Of course, Math.ceil(3.9) also returns 4.0.

If you want to store the value returned by either floor or ceil in a variable of type *int*, you must use a type cast as in the following example:

```
double start = 3.56;
int lowAnswer = (int)Math.floor(start);
int highAnswer = (int)Math.ceil(start);
```

In this example, Math.floor(start) returns the *double* value 3.0, and the variable lowAnswer received the *int* value 3. Math.ceil(start) returns the *double* value 4.0, and the variable highAnswer received the *int* value 4.

Case Study Formatting Output

If you have a variable of type *double* that stores some amount of money, you would like your programs to output the amount in some nice format. However, if you just use `System.out.println`, you are likely to get output that looks like the following:

```
Your cost, including tax, is $19.98123576432
```

You would like the output to show only two digits for cents. You would like the output to look like the following:

```
Your cost, including tax, is $19.98
```

task
specification

In this case study, you will define a class called `Dollars` with two static methods named `write` and `writeln` that can be used to produce this kind of nicely formatted output. For example, if the amount of money is in a variable of type *double* that is named `amount`, then (after you finish with this case study) the output can be produced as follows:

```
System.out.print("Your cost, including tax, is ");
Dollars.writeln(amount);
```

Note that the method should add the dollar sign for you and that the method should always output exactly two digits after the decimal point. So, it would output $2.10, not $2.1.

truncate or
round?

When the amount being written out has more than two digits after the decimal point, your method must either truncate the digits, that is, discard all digits after the first two, or it must round. So, if the value to be output is 9.128, you would get an output of $9.12 if you decide to truncate and $9.13 if you decide to round. After consulting with users for this class, you decide that your output methods will always truncate, so 9.128 will be output as $9.12.

The difference between `write` and `writeln` will be the same as the difference between `print` and `println`. With `write`, the *next* output will go on the same line. With `writeln`, the *next* output will go on the next line.

In order to output an amount like 9.98, you have little choice but to break it into the pieces 9 and 98, and then output each piece separately.[1] So, you come up with the following pseudocode as an outline for the method `write`:

1.Java has classes that allow you to output numbers in any format that you wish. However, using these classes can get quite involved. It will be instructive, and perhaps even easier to program the details ourselves. If you want to know more about these formatting classes, look up the classes `Format` and `DecimalFormat` in a more advanced reference.

Algorithm to Output a *double* **Amount as Dollars and Cents**

(The Amount is in a variable named `amount`)

Determine the number of whole dollars in `amount` and store it in an *int* variable called `dollars`.
Determine the number of cents in `amount` and store it in an *int* variable `cents`. Truncate if there are more than two digits after the decimal point.

```
System.out.print('$');
System.out.print(dollars);
System.out.print('.');
```
Output `cents` in the usual dollars and cents format.

You now need to convert each of these pseudocode instructions to Java code. Let's take them in order.

To obtain the number of whole dollars and the number of cents as two *int* values, you need to somehow get rid of the decimal point. One way to get rid of the decimal point is to convert the amount of money to all cents. To convert 10.95 dollars and cents to all cents, multiply by 100 to obtain $10.95*100$, which is 1095.0. If there is a fraction of a penny, such as converting 10.9567 to 1095.67 (pennies), you can use the `floor` method:

```
Math.floor(1095.67) returns 1095.0
```

Then, all you need to do is convert this *double* value to an *int* value with a type cast:

```
(int)(Math.floor(1095.67)) returns 1095
```

Thus, your code will begin with something like

```
int allCents = (int)(Math.floor(amount*100));
```

(Since the type cast (*int*) discards all digits after the decimal point, you could eliminate the invocation of `Math.floor`. However, the use of `Math.floor` does make the code clearer.)

Now, you need to convert `allCents` to a dollar amount and a cents amount. There are 100 cents in a dollar, so you use integer division to obtain the number of dollars:

```
int dollars = allCents/100;
```

The number of cents is just the amount left over when you divide `allCents` by 100, so you can use the % operator to obtain the amount of cents:

```
int cents = allCents%100;
```

Thus, you have translated the first two steps in your pseudocode to the following Java code:

```
int allCents = (int)(Math.floor(amount*100));
int dollars = allCents/100;
int cents = allCents%100;
```

The next three instructions in your pseudocode are already expressed in Java, so all that is left to do is to translate the last instruction into Java code. That last instruction is

Output `cents` in the usual dollars and cents format.

This looks pretty easy. So, you try

```
System.out.println(cents);
```

early testing

You then go test your code and see output that looks like the following:

```
$10.15
```

which looks pretty good. So, you try some more examples and run into a problem with amounts less than 10. For example, one output you get is

```
$7.5
```

when you were expecting:

```
$7.05
```

This quick test makes you realize that you need to output a 0 before the amount of cents whenever the amount of cents is less than 10. So, you change your code for outputting the number of cents to

```
if (cents < 10)
{
    System.out.print('0');
    System.out.print(cents);
}
else
    System.out.print(cents);
```

The full definition of the class you derived is shown in Display 5.6.

more testing

Now that you have a complete definition of the class, it is time for some serious testing. Display 5.7 shows the program you use to test the method `write`. These

driver program

sorts of programs are often called **driver programs** because they do nothing but exercise the method ("drive the method"). Any method can be tested in a program like this.

The testing goes quite well until you decide to try a negative number. After all, there is such a thing as a negative amount of money. It's called a *debt*. But, the amount −1.20 is output as $−1.0−20. Something is wrong with the way your method handles negative amounts.

It is easy to see what is wrong with negative amounts like −1.20. After outputting $−1., you want to output 20 not −20. There are a number of ways to fix this, but you hit on one clean and simple way. Since you have code that correctly outputs nonnegative numbers, you can convert any negative number to a positive number and then output the positive number and insert the minus sign. The revised version of the class is shown in Display 5.8. Notice that the new method `writePositive` (Display 5.8) has a body that is almost the same as the old method `write` (Display 5.6/page 249). The only difference is that `writePositive` does not output the dollar sign. The dollar sign is output in the new version of the method `write`.

Display 5.6 DollarsFirstTry

....

```
public class DollarsFirstTry
{
    /*****************************************************************
     *Outputs amount in dollars and cents notation.  Truncates after two
     *decimal points. Does not advance to the next line after output.
     *****************************************************************/
    public static void write(double amount)
    {
        int allCents = (int)(Math.floor(amount*100));
        int dollars = allCents/100;
        int cents = allCents%100;

        System.out.print('$');
        System.out.print(dollars);
        System.out.print('.');
        if (cents < 10)
        {
            System.out.print('0');
            System.out.print(cents);
        }
        else
            System.out.print(cents);
    }


    /*****************************************************************
     *Outputs amount in dollars and cents notation. Truncates after
     *two decimal points. Advances to the next line after output.
     *****************************************************************/
    public static void writeln(double amount)
    {
        write(amount);
        System.out.println();
    }
}
```

....

Display 5.7 Testing a Method

```
public class DollarsFirstTryDemo
{
    public static void main(String[] args)
    {
        double amount;
        char ans;

        System.out.println("Testing DollarsFirstTry.write:");
        do
        {
            System.out.println("Enter a value of type double:");
            amount = SavitchIn.readLineDouble();
            DollarsFirstTry.write(amount);
            System.out.println();
            System.out.println("Test again?(y/n)");
            ans = SavitchIn.readLineNonwhiteChar();
        }while ((ans == 'y') || (ans == 'Y'));
        System.out.println("End of test.");
    }
}
```

This kind of testing program is often called a **driver program.**

Sample Screen Dialogue

```
Testing DollarsFirstTry.write:
Enter a value of type double:
1.2345
$1.23
Test again?(y/n)
y
Enter a value of type double:
9.02
$9.02
Test again?(y/n)
y
Enter a value of type double:
-1.20
$-1.0-20      ◄——— OOPS. A problem here.
Test again?(y/n)
n
```

Display 5.8 Corrected Class Dollars *(Part 1 of 2)*

```java
public class Dollars
{
    /****************************************************************
     *Outputs amount in dollars and cents notation.  Truncates after two
     *decimal points. Does not advance to the next line after output.
     ****************************************************************/
    public static void write(double amount)
    {
        if (amount >= 0)
        {
            System.out.print('$');
            writePositive(amount);
        }
        else
        {
            double positiveAmount = -amount;
            System.out.print('$');
            System.out.print('-');
            writePositive(positiveAmount);
        }
    }

    //Precondition: amount >= 0;
    //Outputs amount in dollars and cents notation. Truncates
    //after two decimal points. Omits the dollar sign.
    private static void writePositive(double amount)
    {
        int allCents = (int)(Math.floor(amount*100));
        int dollars = allCents/100;
        int cents = allCents%100;

        System.out.print(dollars);
        System.out.print('.');
        if (cents < 10)
        {
            System.out.print('0');
            System.out.print(cents);
        }
        else
            System.out.print(cents);
    }
```

Display 5.8 Corrected Class Dollars *(Part 2 of 2)*

```
/*************************************************************
 *Outputs amount in dollars and cents notation. Truncates after
 *two decimal points. Advances to the next line after output.
 *************************************************************/
public static void writeln(double amount)
{
    write(amount);
    System.out.println();
}
}
```

retest

Every time you change the definition of a class or method, you should test it. So, you retest the class Dollars with a program similar to the one you used to test DollarsFirstTry. In this case, the test is successful.

Top–Down Design

In the last case study, we used the following pseudocode for our first attempt to design the method write of the class Dollars (Display 5.8/page 251):

Determine the number of whole dollars in amount and store it in an *int* variable called dollars.
Determine the number of cents in amount and store it in an *int* variable cents. Truncate if there
        are more than two digits after the decimal point.
```
System.out.print('$');
System.out.print(dollars);
System.out.print('.');
```
Output cents in the usual dollars and cents format.

What we have done with this pseudocode is to decompose the task for outputting an amount of money into a number of subtasks, such as

Determine the number of whole dollars in amount and store it in an *int* variable called dollars.

We then solved each of these subtasks separately and produced code for each subtask. After that, all we had to do to produce the final definition of the method was to combine the code for the subtasks.

As it turned out, we ended up using the code derived from the preceding pseudocode for the method writePositive, rather than the method write. But this was just a further illustration of using subtasks. The method writePositive solved a subtask that we used in the final definition of the method write.

Often, though not always, the solutions to subtasks are implemented as private helping methods. If the task is large, then to design these helping methods, you use the same technique: Divide the subtask into smaller subsubtasks and solve the subsubtasks separately. These subsubtasks may be further decomposed into smaller tasks, but eventually the tasks become small enough to be easy to design and code.

This technique of dividing the task to be performed by a method into subtasks is called **top–down design**. (Other terms that are used to mean the same thing as top–down design are **stepwise refinement** and **divide and conquer**.) This top–down design technique, although very simple in concept, is extremely powerful and can sometimes be the only way you can manage to write code for a method whose task is very large, or even only moderately large.

Testing Methods

One way to test a method is to use a driver program like the one in Display 5.7/page 250. Programs like that one are often called **driver programs** because they do nothing but exercise the method. These driver programs are just for your use and so they can be quite simple. They need not have any fancy output or anything else very fancy. All they have to do is to give the method some arguments and invoke the method. Any method can be tested in a similar driver program.

driver program

Every method you write for a class should be tested. Moreover, it should be tested in a program in which it is the only method that has not yet been fully tested. In that way, if you discover that something is wrong, you know which method contains the mistake. If you test more than one method in the same program, you can easily be fooled into thinking that the mistake is in one method, when in fact it is in some other method.

Test Methods Separately

Every method should be tested in a program in which it is the only untested method.

One way to test every method in a program in which it is the only untested program is a technique called **bottom–up testing**. With bottom–up testing, if method A uses method B, then method B is fully tested before you test method A.

bottom–up testing

Bottom–up testing is a good and safe method of testing, but sometimes it can become tedious, and there are other methods that can sometimes find bugs quicker and less painfully. Sometimes you want to test a method before all the methods it uses are tested. However, you should still test the method in a program in which it is the only untested method. For example, you might want to test your general approach to the problem before even writing all the methods. Sometimes, you will find yourself in the situation where method A uses method B, and you want to test method A before you test method B (maybe even before you write method B). This presents a problem. If method A uses method B and method B is not yet tested, how can you test method A in a program in which it is the only untested method? The answer is to use a *stub* for method B.

A **stub** is a simplified version of a method that is not good enough for the final class definition, but that is good enough for testing and that is simple enough to be sure it is correct (or as sure as one can be about correctness). For example, suppose you are testing the class `Dollars` in Display 5.8/page 251 and you want to test the method `writeln` before you test the method `write`. You can use a stub for the method `write`. The following is a stub for the method `write`:

stub

```
public static void write(double amount)
{
    System.out.println("99.12");
}
```

Now this is certainly not a correct definition of the class `write`. It always outputs `99.12`, no matter what it gets as an argument. However, it is good enough to use in testing the method `writeln`. If you test the method `writeln` using this stub for the method `write`, and `writeln` outputs `99.12` in the correct way, then `writeln` is almost certain to be correct. Note that using this stub for `write` will let you test the method `writeln` before you even write either of the methods `write` or `writePositive`.

? SELF-TEST QUESTIONS

1. Is the following legal? The class `Circle` is defined in Display 5.5/page 245.

```
Circle c = new Circle();
double areaOfCircle = c.area(2.5);
```

2. Can a class contain both static and nonstatic (i.e., regular) methods? Can it contain both instance variables and static methods?

3. In this question, you will design a class to output values of type *double* (not necessarily for money amounts). The class will be called `Format` and it will have two static methods `write` and `writeln`, each of which take two arguments. The first argument gives a *double* value to be written to the screen. The second argument is an *int* value telling how many digits to show after the decimal point. Have your methods truncate any extra digits. This is very similar to the methods `write` and `writeln` in the class `Dollars`, and you can use the class `Dollars` as a model, but there are some differences between the methods in the two classes. As you would expect, output after `write` goes on the same line and output after `writeln` goes on the following line; otherwise, `write` and `writeln` do the same thing. The following is some sample output:

```
Format.writeln(9.1234567, 4);
Format.writeln(9.9999, 2);
Format.writeln(7.00123, 4);
```

It should produce the following output:

```
9.1234
9.99
7.0012
```

Do not forget to test your methods on numbers with zeros after the decimal point, like `1.023` and `1.0023`. *Hint:* You may find the static method `Math.pow` (Display 5.4/page 244) helpful as part of an expression to move a decimal point. This is a fairly difficult exercise, so allow yourself some time to complete it. If you do not succeed in writing this class, be sure that you at least understand the answer given at the end of this chapter. This is a very useful class.

4. (You should do Self-Test Question 3 before doing this question.) In your definition of the class `Format` in Self-Test Question 3, would it be legal to use the names `print` and `println`, rather than `write` and `writeln`, or would this produce a name conflict with `System.out.println`?

Integer, Double, and Other Wrapper Classes

Java makes a distinction between the primitive types, such as *int*, *double*, and *char*, and the class types, such as the class `String` and the programmer-defined classes. As we have seen, Java sometimes treats primitive and class types differently. For example, we saw in Chapter 4 that an argument to a method is treated differently depending on whether the argument is of a primitive type or of a class type. In Chapter 4, we also saw that the assignment operator = behaves differently for primitive types and class types. To make things uniform, it would be handy sometimes to be able to convert a value of a primitive type, such as the *int* value 42, to an object of some class type that corresponds to the primitive type *int*.

Integer class

In order to convert a value of a primitive type to an "equivalent" value of a class type, Java provides **wrapper classes** for each of the primitive classes. For example, the wrapper class for the primitive type *int* is the predefined class `Integer`. If you want to convert an *int* value, such as 42, to an object of type `Integer`, you can do so as follows:

```
Integer n = new Integer(42);
```

After the preceding, n names an object of the class `Integer` that corresponds to the *int* value 42. (The object n does in fact have the *int* value 42 stored in an instance variable of the object n.) To convert in the reverse direction, from an object of type `Integer` to an *int* value, you can do the following:

```
int i = n.intValue();//n names an object of the class Integer.
```

The method `intValue()` recovers the equivalent *int* value from an object of type `Integer`.

other wrapper classes

The wrapper classes for the primitive types *long*, *float*, *double*, and *char* are `Long`, `Float`, `Double`, and `Character`, respectively. And, of course, rather than the method `intValue`, the classes `Long`, `Float`, `Double`, and `Character` use the methods `longValue`, `floatValue`, `doubleValue`, and `charValue`, respectively.

Wrapper Classes

Every primitive type has a wrapper class. Wrapper classes allow you to have something like a primitive type that is of a class type. Wrapper classes also contain a number of useful predefined constants and static methods.

This brief introduction to wrapper classes explains why they were created and explains why they are called *wrapper classes*, but for us, the main importance of these wrapper classes is not contained in this introduction. For our purposes, the importance of wrapper classes is that they contain a number of very useful constants and static methods.

largest and smallest values

You can use the associated wrapper class to find the value of the largest and smallest values of any of the primitive number types. For example, the largest and smallest values of type *int* are

```
Integer.MAX_VALUE and Integer.MIN_VALUE
```

The largest and smallest values of type *double* are

```
Double.MAX_VALUE and Double.MIN_VALUE
```

strings to numbers

For our purposes, perhaps the most important property of wrapper classes is that they contain a number of useful static methods. Among other things, there are static methods that can be used to convert a string to the corresponding number of type *int*, *double*, *long*, or *float*. For example, suppose your program needs to convert the string "199.98" to a *double* value (which will turn out to be 199.98, of course). The static method valueOf of the wrapper class Double will convert a string to an object of type Double. So,

```
Double.valueOf("199.98")
```

returns an object of type Double that corresponds to the *double* value 199.98. To get the actual *double* value, you must go one step further and use the method dou- ble- Value. So, the following returns the *double* value 199.98:

```
Double.valueOf("199.98").doubleValue()
```

Of course, you knew that the number value is 199.98 and so it hardly seems worth all this effort. But, the same technique can be used to change the value of a string variable. For example, suppose theString is a variable of type String whose value is the string representation of a number of type *double*. Then, the following returns the *double* value corresponding to the string value of theString:

```
Double.valueOf(theString).doubleValue()
```

This conversion of a string to a number can be done with any of the wrapper classes Integer, Long, and Float, as well as the wrapper class Double.

numbers to strings

Each of the numeric wrapper classes also has a static method called toString that will convert in the other direction, that is, convert from a numeric value to a string representation of the numeric value. For example,

```
Integer.toString(42)
```

returns the string value "42". And

```
Double.toString(199.98)
```

returns the string value "199.98".

Character

Character is the wrapper class for the primitive type *char*. The following piece of code illustrates some of the basic methods for this class:

```
Character c1 = new Character('a');
Character c2 = new Character('A');
if (c1.equals(c2))
    System.out.println(c1.charValue() +
                          " is the same as " + c2.charValue());
else
    System.out.println(c1.charValue() +
                          " is not the same as " + c2.charValue());
```

This outputs

```
a is not the same as A
```

The `equals` method checks for equality as characters, so uppercase and lowercase letters are considered different.

Some of the static methods in the class `Character` are give in Display 5.9.

▲ *GOTCHA* *Assigning a Primitive Value to a Wrapper Class*

The wrapper class `Integer` was designed to be something like a class version of the primitive type *int*. This may make it seem reasonable to think of assigning a value of type *int* to a variable of type `Integer`. However, this is not allowed in Java. The second of the following two assignment statements will produce a compiler error message:

```
Integer n = new Integer(42); //OK. You can assign an initial value.
n = 99; //ILLEGAL! You cannot change the corresponding
                //primitive value in this way.
```

Similarly, you cannot assign a primitive value to a variable of any of the other wrapper classes.

The way to get the effect you are trying to get with the preceding illegal assignment of 99 to the `Integer` object n is

```
n = new Integer(99);
```

? SELF-TEST QUESTIONS

5. Which of the following are legal? If any are illegal, tell how to write a legal Java statement that does what the illegal statement "says" to do.

```
Integer n = new Integer(77);
int m = 77;
n = m;
m = n;
```

Display 5.9 Static Methods in the Class Character

Name	Description	Type of Arguments	Type of Value Returned	Example	Value Returned
toUpperCase	**convert to uppercase**	*char*	*char*	Character.toUpperCase('a') Character.toUpperCase('A')	**Both return** 'A'
toLowerCase	**convert to lowercase**	*char*	*char*	Character.toLowerCase('a') Character.toLowerCase('A')	**Both return** 'a'
isUpperCase	**test for uppercase**	*char*	*boolean*	Character.isUpperCase('A') Character.isUpperCase('a')	*true* *false*
isLowerCase	**test for lowercase**	*char*	*boolean*	Character.isLowerCase('A') Character.isLowerCase('a')	*false* *true*
isWhitespace	**test for whitespace**	*char*	*boolean*	Character.isWhitespace(' ') Character.isWhitespace('A')	*true* *false*

Whitespace characters are those that print as white space, such as the blank, the tab character ('\t'), and the line break symbol ('\n').

6. Write a Java expression to convert the number in the *double* variable x to a string. The expression returns a string that is the normal way of writing the value in x.

7. Write a Java expression to convert the string in the variable s to the corresponding value of type *int*. The variable s is of type String. Assume that s contains a string that is the normal way of writing some integer, such as "123".

5.2 Polymorphism

In Display 4.15/page 214 of Chapter 4, we defined a method called equals for the class Species. We also have a method called equals for the class String. How does Java know which method named equals applies when it sees a method invocation such as

```
firstOne.equals(secondOne);
```

The way that Java knows which version of equals to use is by checking the type of the object firstOne. If firstOne is of type String, it uses the definition of equals that applies to objects of the class String. If firstOne is of type Species, it uses the definition of equals that applies to objects of the class Species. Giving multiple definitions for the same word, such as equals, is called **polymorphism.** *Polymorphism* is a Greek word meaning many forms and is one of the important features of object-oriented programming

---

Polymorphism

Giving multiple definitions to the same word is called **polymorphism**. Polymorphism is one of the key features of a type of programming known as *object-oriented programming*. There are many forms of polymorphism in Java. For example, two different classes can have methods with the same name. Because of something known as *overloading*, two different methods can sometimes have the same name even if they are in the same class.

Overloading

Using the same name, like equals, for methods of two different classes is one form of polymorphism. Another, more dramatic form of polymorphism is *overloading* a method name. When you **overload** a method name, you give the same method name two different definitions *within the same class.* For example, in Display 5.10, we have written a very simple example of overloading.

overloading

The class Statistician (Display 5.10) has three different methods all named average. When there is an invocation of Statistician.average how does Java know which definition of average to use? First, let's assume the arguments are all of type *double*. In that case, Java can tell which definition of average to use by the number of arguments. If there are two arguments of type *double*, then it uses the first definition of average. If there are three arguments, it uses the second definition of average.

Now, suppose there is an invocation of the method average that has two arguments of type *char*. Java knows that it should use the third definition of average because of the types of the arguments. There is only one definition that has two arguments of type *char*. (For now, don't worry about how this method averages two letters. That's a side issue that we will come back to shortly.)

Suppose you give more than one definition to the same method name within the same class definition. When there is an invocation of that method name for that class, Java determines which definition to use according to the number of arguments and the types of the arguments. If there is a definition of that method name that has the same number of parameters as there are arguments in the invocation and if the types also match, i.e., the first argument has the same type as the first parameter, the second argument has the same type as the second parameter, and so forth, then that is the definition of the method name that is used. If there is no such match, Java will try some simple type conversions of the kinds we discussed before, such as casting an *int* to a *double*, to see if that produces a match. If that fails, you will get an error message.

OK, now let's take a short side trip to explain how we average two characters. For this toy example, it does not matter if we use a crazy way of averaging two characters, but, in fact, the way we average characters in Display 5.10 is a very sensible

averaging
characters

Display 5.10 Overloading

```
/****************************************************
 *This is just a toy class to illustrate overloading.
 ****************************************************/
public class Statistician
{
    public static void main(String[] args)
    {
        double average1 = Statistician.average(40.0, 50.0);
        double average2 = Statistician.average(1.0, 2.0, 3.0);
        char average3 = Statistician.average('a', 'c');

        System.out.println("average1 = " + average1);
        System.out.println("average2 = " + average2);
        System.out.println("average3 = " + average3);
    }

    public static double average(double first, double second)
    {
        return ((first + second)/2.0);
    }

    public static double average(double first,
                                      double second, double third)
    {
        return ((first + second + third)/3.0);
    }

    public static char average(char first, char second)
    {
        return (char)(((int)first + (int)second)/2);
    }
}
```

Sample Screen Dialogue

```
average1 = 45.0
average2 = 2.0
average3 = b
```

way of averaging characters, or at least of averaging two letters. If the two letters are both lowercase, then the average computed will be the lowercase letter half way between them in alphabetical order. (If there is no letter exactly half way, it chooses one of the two that is as close to half way as possible.) Similarly, if the two letters are both uppercase, then the average computed will be the uppercase letter half way between them in alphabetical order. This works because the letters are assigned numbers in order. The number assigned to 'b' is one more than the number assigned to 'a', the number assigned to 'c' is one more than the number assigned to 'b', and so forth. So if you convert two letters to numbers, average the numbers, and then convert back to letters, you get the letter half way in between.

As we will see, most class definitions have some overloading of method names. We have not seen any overloading until now because we carefully avoided it until we could explain it. Overloading can be applied to any kind of method. It can be applied to *void*-methods, to methods that return a value, to static methods, to non-static methods, or to any combination of these.

Note that you have already been using overloading, even though you may not have known the term before. In the previous section, many of the methods of the class Math use overloading. For example, the max method uses overloading based on the type of its arguments. If its two arguments are of type *int*, it returns a value of type *int*. If its two arguments are of type *double*, it returns a value of type *double*. Of course, this is not a very dramatic use of overloading, since the different definitions of max would be identical except for some type names. A more dramatic example is the division operator /, which we discussed in Chapter 2. If its arguments are of type *double,* it is defined to do floating-point division; so 5.0/2.0 returns 2.5. But, if both arguments are of type *int*, it is defined to perform integer division; so, 5/2 is 2.

Overloading

Within one class, you can have two (or more) definitions of a single method name. This is called **overloading** the method name. When you overload a method name, any two definitions of the same method name must either have different numbers of parameters or some parameter position must be of differing types in the two definitions. ◻

▼ *PROGRAMMING EXAMPLE* *A Pet Class*

Display 5.11 shows another simple class with overloading. In this case, we have overloaded the method name set. This is a class for a pet and the various set methods set different instance variables. There are four methods named set. One sets all three of name, age, and weight. The other three set only one each of these. There is a main method with a simple demonstration program. Notice that each invocation of the method set has either a different number of arguments or an argument whose type is different from the other invocations of set. Thus, each invocation of set uses a different definition of set.

Display 5.11 Pet Class (Part 1 of 3)

```
/***************************************************
 *Class for basic pet records: name, age, and weight.
 ***************************************************/
public class Pet
{
    /*********************************************
     *This main is just a demonstration program.
     *********************************************/
    public static void main(String[] args)
    {
        Pet myDog = new Pet();
        myDog.set("Fido", 2, 5.5);
        myDog.writeOutput();
        System.out.println("Changing name.");
        myDog.set("Rex");
        myDog.writeOutput();
        System.out.println("Changing weight.");
        myDog.set(6.5);
        myDog.writeOutput();
        System.out.println("Changing age.");
        myDog.set(3);
        myDog.writeOutput();
    }

    public void writeOutput()
    {
        System.out.println("Name: " + name);
        System.out.println("Age: " + age + " years");
        System.out.println("Weight: " + weight + " pounds");
    }

    public void set(String newName, int newAge, double newWeight)
    {
        name = newName;
        age = newAge;
        weight = newWeight;
    }
```

Display 5.11 Pet Class *(Part 2 of 3)*

```java
public void set(String newName)
{
    name = newName;
    //age and weight are unchanged.
}

public void set(int newAge)
{
    age = newAge;
    //name and weight are unchanged.
}

public void set(double newWeight)
{
    weight = newWeight;
    //name and age are unchanged.
}

public String nameValue()
{
    return name;
}

public int ageValue()
{
    return age;
}

public double weightValue()
{
    return weight;
}


    private String name;
    private int age;//in years
    private double weight;//in pounds
}
```

Display 5.11 Pet Class *(Part 3 of 3)*

Sample Screen Dialogue

```
Name: Fido
Age: 2 years
Weight: 5.5 pounds
Changing name.
Name: Rex
Age: 2 years
Weight: 5.5 pounds
Changing weight.
Name: Rex
Age: 2 years
Weight: 6.5 pounds
Changing age.
Name: Rex
Age: 3 years
Weight: 6.5 pounds
```

⚠ GOTCHA *Overloading and Automatic Type Conversion*

In some situations, two friends are not better than one. In some situations, two good things interact in a bad way. Overloading is a friend, or at least a helpful feature of the Java language. Automatic type conversion of arguments is also a helpful feature of the Java language (such as converting an *int* like 2 to a *double* like 2.0 when a method wants a *double* as argument). But these two nice features can sometimes get in the way of each other.

automatic type conversion

For example, look at the main method in Display 5.11 and consider the following lines:

```
System.out.println("Changing weight.");
myDog.set(6.5);
```

This changes the weight of myDog to 6.5 pounds. But now suppose my dog does not weigh 6.5 pounds, but instead weighs only 6 pounds. In that case, I should change those two lines to

```
System.out.println("Changing weight.");
myDog.set(6.0);
```

This will change myDog's weight to 6 pounds. But, suppose that I forget the decimal point and the zero and write the following:

```
System.out.println("Changing weight.");
myDog.set(6);
```

I want this to change myDog's weight to 6, but instead it will change myDog's age to 6. This is because 6 is of type *int* and the definition of set that has one parameter of type *int* will change the instance variable age, not the instance variable weight. If Java can find a definition of set that matches the number and types of arguments, it will not do any type conversion of *int*s to *double*s, or any other type conversions for that matter.

In the case we just went through, we needed a type conversion, but we did not get one. There are also cases where you do not want a type conversion and you do get one. For example, suppose I want to set myDog's name to "Cha Cha", weight to 2, and age to 3. I might try the following:

```
myDog.set("Cha Cha", 2, 3);
```

This will set myDog's age to 2, not 3, and myDog's weight to 3.0, not 2.0. The real problem, of course, is that I have reversed arguments 2 and 3, but let's look at it as Java does. Given the preceding invocation, Java looks for a definition of set with a heading of the following form:

```
public void set(String Name_1, int Name_2, int Name_3)
```

There is no such definition of set. So, there is no exact match to the invocation. So, Java tries to convert an *int* to a *double* to get a match. It notices that if it converts the 3 to 3.0, it will have a match to

```
public void set(String newName, int newAge, double newWeight)
```

and so it does the type conversion.

What went wrong (besides reversing two arguments)? I should have given the weight as 2.0, not 2. If I had used 2.0, or if Java had not done any automatic type conversions for me, then I would have received an error message. In this case, Java tried to help, but the help just got in the way.

Overloading and Automatic Type Conversion

Java always tries to use overloading before it tries to use automatic type conversion. If Java can find a definition of a method that matches the types of the arguments, then Java will use that definition. Java will not do an automatic type conversion of a method's argument until after it has tried and failed to find a definition of the method name with parameter types that exactly match the arguments in the method invocation.

◻

⚠ GOTCHA *You Cannot Overload Based on the Returned Type*

You cannot overload a method name by giving two definitions with headings that differ only in the type of the value returned. For example, consider the class Pet in Display 5.11/page 262. You might have wanted to add a method called weightValue, which returns a character telling if the pet is overweight or underweight; say, '+'

for overweight, '−' for underweight, and '*' for just right. This would return a value of type *char*. If you did add this method weightValue, you would then have two methods with the following headings:

```
/*****************************
 *Returns the weight of the pet.
 *****************************/
public double weightValue()


/********************************
 *Returns '+' if overweight, '−' is
 *underweight and '*' if weight OK.
 ********************************/
public char weightValue()
```

You CANNOT have both of these methods within a single class.

Unfortunately this is illegal. In any class definition, any two definitions of the same method name must have different numbers of parameters or one or more parameters of differing types. You cannot overload based on the type returned.

If you think about it, it is not even possible to write the compiler so it overloads on the basis of the type returned. For example, suppose you have

```
Pet myFriend = new Pet();
    . . .
double value = myFriend.weightValue();
```

Now suppose that, contrary to actual fact, we allowed methods with both of the above headings and consider the job of the poor compiler. Although we have not made an issue of it, it is true that you can store a value of type *char* in a variable of type *double*. Java will perform an automatic type cast to change the *char* to a *double*. Thus, in this hypothetical scenario, the above variable value is happy with either a *double* or a *char*. So, there is no way to tell if the programmer who wrote this code meant weightValue to return a *char* or a *double*. The compiler would have to ask the programmer what she/he meant, and compilers are not allowed to ask the programmer questions.

? SELF-TEST QUESTIONS

8. Would the following be a legal method invocation to include in the program in Display 5.11/page 262?

   ```
   myDog.set("Fido", 2, 7);
   ```

9. Can a class possibly contain both of the following method definitions?

```
/******************************************
 *Postcondition: Returns the number of people
 *in numberOfCouples couples.
 ******************************************/
public static int howMany(int numberOfCouples)
{
    return 2*numberOfCouples;
}
```

```
/**********************************************
 *Postcondition: Returns the number of children
 *assuming that each couple has 2.3 children.
 **********************************************/
public static double howMany(int numberOfCouples)
{
     return 2.3*numberOfCouples;
}
```

10. Can a class possibly contain both of the following method definitions?

```
/*************************************************************
 *Postcondition: Returns an int value approximately equivalent
 *to number. But, converts all negative numbers to zero.
 *************************************************************/
public static int convertedValue(double number)
{
    if (number > 0.0)
        return (int) number;
    return 0;
}


/*************************************************************
 *Postcondition: Returns a double value approximately equivalent
 *to number. But, converts all negative numbers to zero.
 *************************************************************/
public static double convertedValue(int number)
{
    if (number > 0)
        return (double) number;
    return 0.0;
}
```

11. Consider the class Species in Display 4.15/page 214 of Chapter 4. It has a method called set that sets the name, population, and growth rate of a species. Could this class have another method that is also named set, that only has one parameter for the name of the species, and that sets both the population and growth rate to zero? If so, give the definition of this other method named set.

5.3 Constructors

First things first.
COMMON SAYING

When you create an object of a class, you often want certain initializing actions performed, such as giving values to the instance variables. A *constructor* is a special kind of method that is designed to perform such initializations. In this section, we tell you how to define and use constructors.

Defining Constructors

Until now, we created new objects as in the following example:

```
Pet goodScout = new Pet();
```

(The definition of the class `Pet` is in Display 5.11/page 262, but the point is independent of the details of this particular class.) For the classes we've seen thus far, this creates an object whose instance variables have no initial values (or have some default
initial value that may not be what you want as the default). You may wish to have
some or all instance variables automatically initialize to your specifications when an
object is created. You can do this with a special kind of method called a *constructor*.

constructor

A **constructor** is a method that is called when a new object is created. A constructor can perform any action you write into its definition, but constructors were
designed to perform initializing actions, such as initializing the values of instance
variables. Constructors serve very much the same purpose as the methods named
`set` in our definition of the class `Pet` in Display 5.11/page 262. But unlike the `set`
methods, the constructors are called almost automatically whenever you create an
object using the *new* operator.

One property of constructors that may seem strange at first is that constructors
have the same name as the class. So, if the class is named `Pet`, then the constructors
will be named `Pet`. If the class is named `Species`, then the constructors will be
named `Species`. Although this may seem peculiar when you first hear this rule, it
works out very well in practice.

As an example, in Display 5.12, we have rewritten our definition of the class for
pet records so that it has constructor methods. As was true of our methods named
`set`, constructors are normally overloaded so that there are multiple definitions of
the constructor, each with different numbers or types of parameters. Display 5.12
and Display 5.11/page 262 are very similar, but most of the differences between them
are important. Let's look at those differences.

1. There are some mundane changes to review before going on to the interesting changes. In Display 5.12, the class name is changed from `Pet` to `Pet-
   Record`, since each class must have a different name. Also, in Display 5.12,
   we have deleted the method `main`, since it was just a toy demonstration program that we no longer need. Now, on to the important differences.

2. We have added methods named `PetRecord`. These methods named `Pet-
   Record` are constructors. Note that the headings of these constructors do
   not have the word *void* as the `set` methods do. When you define a constructor, you do not specify any return type. You do not even write *void*
   in place of a return type. These constructors are very much like the `set`
   methods. However, unlike some of the methods named `set`, the constructors give values to all the instance variables, even though there may not
   be an argument for each instance variable. The constructors would compile even if some of the instance variables were not given values, but it is
   normal practice to give values to all the instance variables when defining
   a constructor. As we will see, constructors and the `set` methods are used
   in related but different ways. <List continued on page 271.>

Display 5.12 Pet Class with Constructors *(Part 1 of 3)*

```java
/***************************************************
 *Class for basic pet records: name, age, and weight.
 ***************************************************/
public class PetRecord
{
    public void writeOutput()
    {
        System.out.println("Name: " + name);
        System.out.println("Age: " + age + " years");
        System.out.println("Weight: " + weight + " pounds");
    }

    public PetRecord(String theName, int theAge, double theWeight)
    {
        name = theName;
        age = theAge;
        weight = theWeight;
    }

    public void set(String newName, int newAge, double newWeight)
    {
        name = newName;
        age = newAge;
        weight = newWeight;
    }

    public PetRecord(String theName)
    {
        name = theName;
        age = 0;
        weight = 0;
    }

    public void set(String newName)
    {
        name = newName; //age and weight are unchanged.
    }
```

Constructors are only called when you create an object with *new*. To change an already existing object, you need one or more methods like these `set` methods.

Display 5.12 Pet Class with Constructors *(Part 2 of 3)*
••

```java
public PetRecord(int theAge)
{
    name = "No name yet.";
    age = theAge;
    weight = 0;
}

public void set(int newAge)
{
    age = newAge;
    //name and weight are unchanged.
}

public PetRecord(double theWeight)
{
    name = "No name yet";
    age = 0;
    weight = theWeight;
}

public void set(double newWeight)
{
    weight = newWeight;
    //name and age are unchanged.
}

public PetRecord()                    ◄———— Default constructor
{
    name = "No name yet.";
    age = 0;
    weight = 0;
}

public String nameValue()
{
    return name;
}
```

••

Display 5.12 Pet Class with Constructors *(Part 3 of 3)*

```
    public int ageValue()
    {
        return age;
    }

    public double weightValue()
    {
        return weight;
    }

    private String name;
    private int age;//in years
    private double weight;//in pounds
}
```

3. We have added a constructor, named `PetRecord`, that has no parameters. Whenever you define at least one constructor, you should be sure to include a constructor with zero parameters. A constructor with no parameters is called a **default constructor**.

default constructor

Constructors are called at the time that you use *new* to create an object. We have already been using constructors in statements such as the following, from the program in Display 5.11/page 262:

new calls a constructor

```
    Pet myDog = new Pet();
```

This line defines `myDog` to be a name for an object of the class `Pet` and then creates a new object of the class `Pet`. The part that creates the new object is

```
    new Pet()
```

The part `Pet()` is a call to a constructor for the class `Pet`. The parentheses are empty because this constructor takes no arguments.

If you look at the definition of the class `Pet` (Display 5.11), you might object that the class definition includes no constructor definitions at all. However, whenever a class definition does not have a constructor definition, Java automatically creates one with zero parameters. This automatically created constructor does essentially nothing, but it does allow you to create objects of the class. However, once you add at least one constructor definition to a class, then you are in charge of constructors. *Once you add at least one constructor to a class, then no constructors are created automatically.* Thus, in Display 5.12, where we defined a class called `PetRecord` with constructors, we were careful to include a constructor with no parameters. A constructor with no parameters is called a **default constructor**. A

automatically defined constructor

complete program illustrating the use of constructors with the class `PetRecord` is given in Display 5.13.

constructor
arguments

When you create a new object with the operator *new*, you must always include a call to a constructor after the operator *new*. As with any method invocation, you list any arguments in parentheses after the constructor name (which is the same as the class name). For example, suppose you want to use *new* to create a new object of the class `PetRecord` defined in Display 5.12/page 269. You might do so as follows:

```
PetRecord fish = new PetRecord("Wanda", 2, 0.25);
```

The part `PetRecord("Wanda", 2, 0.25)` is a call to the constructor for the class `PetRecord` that takes three arguments: one of type `String`, one of type `int`, and the last of type *double*. This creates a new object to represent a pet named Wanda who is 2 years old and weighs 0.25 pound. Let's look at another example.

Consider the following:

```
PetRecord newBorn = new PetRecord();
```

This creates a new object of the class `PetRecord` and calls the default constructor (i.e., the constructor with zero parameters). If you look at the definition of the class `PetRecord` in Display 5.12, you will see that the constructor with zero parameters gives the object the name `"No name yet"` and sets both the `age` and `weight` instance variables to zero. (A newborn pet does not weigh zero, of course. The value of `0` is just being used as a placeholder until the real weight can be determined; but anyway, that's biology not computer science.)

resetting object
values

A constructor can only be called when you create a new object with the operator *new*. Calls such as the following to objects of the class `PetRecord` are illegal:

```
newBorn.PetRecord("Fang", 1, 50.0); //Illegal!
```

Since you cannot call a constructor for an object after it is created, you need some other way to change the values of the instance variables of an object. That is the purpose of the `set` methods in Display 5.12. The way to accomplish what we tried with the preceding illegal invocations of the constructor `PetRecord` is to call `set` as follows:

```
newBorn.set("Fang", 1, 50.0);
```

You need not name these methods `set`; you can use any method name that is convenient. For example, you might prefer to call these methods `reset` or `giveNewValues`.[1]

---

1. Other authors use the term **mutator method** for methods that change the data in an object, like the methods named `set`. These authors reserve the term *accessor method* for methods that only read data from an object, such as the methods `nameValue`, `ageValue`, and `weightValue` in Display 5.12/page 269. In this book, we use the term *accessor method* for both of these kinds of methods, i.e., for any method that either reads or changes data in a method. We do not use the term *mutator method*.

Display 5.13 Using Constructors and Reset Methods
••

```
public class PetRecordDemo
{
    public static void main(String[] args)
    {
        PetRecord usersPet = new PetRecord("Jane Doe");
        System.out.println("My records on your pet are inaccurate.");
        System.out.println("Here is what they currently say:");
        usersPet.writeOutput();

        System.out.println("Please enter the correct pet name:");
        String correctName = SavitchIn.readLine();
        System.out.println("Please enter the correct pet age:");
        int correctAge = SavitchIn.readLineInt();
        System.out.println("Please enter the correct pet weight:");
        double correctWeight = SavitchIn.readLineDouble();
        usersPet.set(correctName, correctAge, correctWeight);
        System.out.println("My updated records now say:");
        usersPet.writeOutput();
    }
}
```

Sample Screen Dialogue

```
My records on your pet are inaccurate.
Here is what they currently say:
Name: Jane Doe
Age: 0
Weight: 0.0 pounds
Please enter the correct pet name:
Moon Child
Please enter the correct pet age:
5
Please enter the correct pet weight:
10.5
My updated records now say:
Name: Moon Child
Age: 5
Weight: 10.5 pounds
```

Constructor

A **constructor** is a method that is called when an object of the class is created using *new*. Constructors are used to initialize objects. A constructor must have the same name as the class to which it belongs. Arguments for a constructor are given in parentheses after the class name as in the following examples:

Examples:
```
PetRecord myDog = new PetRecord("Fido", 2, 4.5),
            yourDog = new PetRecord("Cha Cha", 3, 2.3);
```

A constructor is defined like any other method except that it does not have a type returned and does not even include a *void* in the method heading. See Display 5.12/page 269 for examples of constructor definitions. ◻

▲ *GOTCHA* Omitting the Default Constructor

Suppose we were to omit the constructor with zero parameters from the definition of the class `PetRecord` in Display 5.12/page 269; that is, suppose we *omitted* the following constructor definition:

```
public PetRecord()
{
    name = "No name yet";
    age = 0;
    weight = 0;
}
```

With this constructor omitted, the following would be illegal and would produce an error message:

```
PetRecord heinz57 = new PetRecord();
```

You might object that Java automatically provides a default constructor if none is defined and so this should be legal. However, the situation is slightly more complicated than that. If your class definition includes no constructors whatsoever, then Java will automatically provide a default constructor. However, if your class definition contains at least one constructor definition, then Java does not provide any constructors for you. *Once you start defining constructors, you are completely in charge of constructors and no constructors are generated other than the ones that you define.*

Since classes are often reused again and again and since sooner or later you will probably want to create a new object without specifying parameters, as in

```
PetRecord heinz57 = new PetRecord();
```

you will avoid a lot of problems if you follow a policy of including a default constructor definition in every class you define.

Default Constructor

A constructor with no parameters is called the **default constructor.** Most of the classes you define should include a default constructor. ◻

? SELF-TEST QUESTIONS

12. If a class is named `Student`, what name can you use for a constructor for this class?

13. When defining a constructor, what do you specify for the type of the value returned? A primitive type? A class type? *void*?

14. What is a default constructor?

15. Does every class in Java automatically have a default constructor? If not, when is a default constructor provided automatically by Java and when is it not provided?

5.4 Information Hiding Revisited

The material in this section is not needed to understand most of the rest of this book, but it is very important material. You can safely postpone reading this material until you are more comfortable with classes, but do not postpone reading it indefinitely. When you start to write more complicated class definitions, you will need the material in this section in order to avoid certain kinds of subtle problems.

▲ *GOTCHA* *Instance Variables of a Class Type*

A class can have instance variables of any type, including any class type. This can sometimes be a natural and handy thing to do. However, using instance variables of a class type takes special care and we do not have the tools to handle them in the correct way. In this Gotcha section, we explain the problem and the general approach to the solution, but the full details of the solution are beyond the scope of this book. Some of the details are covered briefly in Appendix 6. After you become comfortable with using classes in simple cases, you may wish to read Appendix 6. If you do not wish to read this Gotcha section now but still want to avoid the problem, just note that the problem discussed here does not apply to any class you define provided that the class only has instance variables that are each either of a primitive type (such as *int*, *double*, *char*, and *boolean*) or of the type `String`. So, you can define lots of classes without being concerned with this problem.

The problem results from the fact that variables of a class type contain the memory address of where an object is stored in memory. For example, suppose `goodGuy` and `badGuy` are both variables of type `PetRecord`, a class we defined in Display 5.12. Now, suppose `goodGuy` names some object, and your program executes the following assignment statement:

```
badGuy = goodGuy;
```

After this assignment statement is executed, `badGuy` and `goodGuy` are two names for the same object. So, if you change `badGuy`, you will also change `goodGuy`. (There must be a moral lesson there someplace.) Let's give this assignment statement a bit more context to see the implications of this:

Display 5.14 An Insecure Class

```
/*********************************************
 *Example of a class that does NOT correctly
 *hide its private instance variable.
 *********************************************/
public class CadetClass
{
    public CadetClass()
    {
        pet =
            new PetRecord("Faithful Guard Dog", 5, 75);
    }

    public void writeOutput()
    {
        System.out.println("Here's the pet:");
        pet.writeOutput();
    }

    public PetRecord thePet()
    {
        return pet;
    }

    private PetRecord pet;
}
```

> A realistic class would have more methods, but these are all we need for our demonstration.

```
PetRecord goodGuy = new PetRecord();
goodGuy.set("Faithful Guard Dog", 5, 75);
PetRecord badGuy;
badGuy = goodGuy;
badGuy.set("Dominion Spy", 1200, 500);
goodGuy.writeOutput();
```

Because badGuy and goodGuy name the same object, this code will produce the following output:

```
Name: Dominion Spy
Age: 1200 years
Weight 500.0 pounds
```

The same thing can happen with instance variables and can cause some subtle problems. Let's look at an example.

Display 5.14 contains the definition of a class called CadetClass, which was written by a cadet programmer as a homework exercise. It does not have very many methods, but that is not the problem. (This is, after all, just an exercise.) The problem is that our cadet programmer mistakenly thinks that the data named by the instance variable `pet` cannot be changed by any program using the class `PetRecord`. An easy mistake for a cadet programmer to make. After all, our cadet made the instance variable `pet` private so it cannot be accessed by name. And just to be super safe, the cadet did not include any accessor methods that change the private instance variable `pet`. Our cadet will let anybody see the value of the object `pet` by using the public accessor method `thePet`, but our naive cadet thinks that no programmer can change the `"Faithful Guard Dog"`. Our cadet is in for a rude awakening.

Look at the program in Display 5.15. That program has changed the values of the instance variables in the object named by the private instance variable `pet`! How could that be? The problem is that a variable of a class type stores a memory address, and as we saw at the beginning of this section, this means you can use the assignment operator to produce two names for the same object. That is what our hacker programmer who wrote the program in Display 5.15 did. Our hacker programmer had the accessor method `thePet` return "the value" of the private instance variable `pet`. But, that value was a memory address that was stored in the variable `badGuy`. So, `badGuy` is another name for `pet`. Our hacker cannot use the private name `pet`, but our hacker can use the equivalent name `badGuy`. All that our hacker needs to do is to use the name `badGuy` to invoke the method `set` of the class `PetRecord`, and since `badGuy` is another name for the object named by `pet`, our hacker has changed the object named by the private instance variable `pet`.

How do you write your class definitions so that you avoid this problem? It seems like it is impossible to have a private instance variable of a class type that is truly secure. A hacker can always get at it some other way, or so it seems. There are at least two ways around this problem: an easy way and a harder but better way.

The easy way around this problem is to only use instance variables that are of a primitive type or of the type `String`. The type `String` has no accessor methods that can change the `String` object's data, and so our hacker's trick will not work on them. Primitive types are not class types and so the hackers method will not work on them either. This easy solution is the one we will take in this book. (You can also have private instance variables of class types other than `String`, provided these class types do not have methods that can change an object. However, the only class of this kind that we will encounter is the class `String`.)

The harder solution is the better solution, but it is beyond the scope of this book, although we can give you a hint of it. There are methods that can produce an exact copy of an object. These exact copies are called **clones**. The harder solution is to never return an object named by a private instance variable of a class type that could be insecure, but to instead return a clone of the object. That way the hacker can do whatever she/he wants with the clone and the private data will not be affected. There is a brief introduction to cloning in Appendix 6. After you become comfortable with classes, you may wish to look at that appendix.

clone

Do not get the impression that instance variables of a class type are a bad idea. They are very natural and very useful. However, it does require more skill and care to deal with them effectively. Think of them the way you think of brain

Display 5.15 Changing Private Data in a Poorly Defined Class
••

```
/************************************************************
 *Toy program to demonstrate how a programmer can access
 *and change private data in an object of the class CadetClass.
 ************************************************************/
public class Hacker
{
    public static void main(String[] args)
    {
        CadetClass starFleetOfficer = new CadetClass();
        System.out.println("starFleetOfficer contains:");
        starFleetOfficer.writeOutput();
        PetRecord badGuy;
        badGuy = starFleetOfficer.thePet();
        badGuy.set("Dominion Spy", 1200, 500);
        System.out.println("Looks like a security breach:");
        System.out.println("starFleetOfficer now contains:");
        starFleetOfficer.writeOutput();
        System.out.println("The pet wasn't so private!");
    }
}
```

Screen Output

```
starFleetOfficer contains:
Here's the pet:
Name: Faithful Guard Dog
Age: 5 years
Weight: 75.0 pounds
Looks like a security breach:
starFleetOfficer now contains:
Here's the pet:
Name: Dominion Spy
Age: 1200 years
Weight: 500.0 pounds
The pet wasn't so private!
```

This program has changed an object named by a private instance variable of the object starFleetOfficer.

surgery: if you need it, it is very very good, but don't try it unless you know what you are doing.

? SELF-TEST QUESTIONS

●●●

16. Give the definition of three accessor methods that you can use instead of the single access method `thePet`. These new accessor methods will not produce the problem described in the section **GOTCHA Instance Variables of a Class Type**. These three methods will return all the data in an object of the class `CadetClass` but will not return any object with accessor methods that can change anything. In the previous section, we gave two ways to avoid the problem in the Gotcha section. This question suggests a third way to avoid the problem.

5.5 Packages *(Optional)*

> *From mine own library with volumes that*
> *I prize above my dukedom.*
> **WILLIAM SHAKESPEARE,** *The Tempest*

Packages are a way of grouping and naming a collection of related classes so that they can serve as a library of classes that you can use in any program without having to place all those classes in the same directory as your program. Although this is an important and useful topic, it is nevertheless true that the rest of the material in this book does not use the material on packages presented here. So, you may cover this section at any time during your reading of this book. In order to understand this material, you need to know about directories (which are called *folders* in some operating systems) and you need to know how your operating system uses a `PATH` variable. If you do not know about directories (folders) or `PATH` variables, you may wish to skip this section until you have had some experience with these two topics. Directories (folders) and `PATH` variables are not Java topics. They are part of your operating system and the details depend on your particular operating system.

We will describe one typical way of using packages. There are other ways to set up the details of using packages, but that is beyond the scope of this book.

Packages and Importing

A **package** is nothing other than a collection of classes that have been grouped together and given a package name. The classes in the package are each placed in a separate file and the file is named the same as the class, just as we have been doing all along. The only difference is that each file has the following as the *first line* in the file:

```
package Package_Name;
```

The *Package_Name* typically consists of all lowercase letters often punctuated with the dot (period) symbol. For example, if you name the package `mystuff.utilities`, then each of the files in the package would have the following as its first line:

```
package mystuff.utilities;
```

The classes in the package are stored in a directory (folder[1]) and the package is named in a way we will describe shortly. Any program or class definition can then use all the classes in the package by placing a suitable *import* statement at the start of the file containing the program or class definition, and this is true even if the program or class definition is not in the same directory as the classes in the package. For example, if you want to use the classes in the package `mystuff.utilities`, you would place the following at the start of the file you are writing:

import
```
import mystuff.utilities.*;
```

This use of packages allows you to define libraries (packages) of classes that you frequently use and store them away in a single directory. After that, you can use the classes in the package in any program or class you write no matter what directory the program or class is in. In effect, this lets you add classes to the Java language and so customize Java to your needs. Packages should, of course, consist of groups of related classes so that you can easily keep track of which classes are in which packages.

Package

A **package** is a collection of classes that have been grouped together and given a package name. The classes in the package are each placed in a separate file and the file is named the same as the class, just as we have been doing all along. The only difference is that each file has the following as the first line in the file:

Syntax:
```
package Package_Name;
```

Examples:
```
package mystuff.utilities;
package java.io;
```

Package Names and Directories

A package name is not an arbitrary identifier. A package name tells the compiler where to find the classes in the package. In effect, the package name tells the compiler the path name for the directory containing the classes in the package. For example, suppose your classes were in the directory

directory
```
\myjavastuff\lib\math\stat
```

---

1. Some operating systems used the word *folder* to mean the same thing as *directory*. We will use the word *directory*. If your operating system has things called *folders*, they are the same things as directories. Just read *folder* wherever you see *directory*.

---

import **Statement**

You can use all the classes in a package in any program or class definition by placing an *import* statement that names the package at the start of the file containing the program or class definition. The program or class need not be in the same directory as the classes in the package.

Syntax:

> *import* *Package_Name*;

Examples:

> *import* mystuff.utilities.*;
> *import* java.io.*;

The dot and the * at the end mean that you are importing all the classes in this package. You can also import just a single class from a package, but that is seldom done and is seldom needed.

◻

---

then, provided your system is set up correctly for this, the package name can be

    myjavastuff.lib.math.stat

(Your operating system may use / instead of \, but it means the same thing.) A package name must be a path name for the directory that contains the classes in the package, but the package name uses dots in place of \ or / (whichever one of \ or / that your operating system uses) and a package name has no dot at the start of the name.

The path name for a package need not be a full path name, and almost never is a full path name. In fact, you may not even be able to get a full path name to work unless your system is set up for that.[1] However, you can use a relative path name that starts from any directory named in the setting of the CLASSPATH environment variable. The CLASSPATH environment variable is used just like the PATH environment variable, but it is used to locate classes in packages. For example, if the directory \myjavastuff\lib is named in your CLASSPATH variable setting, then you can use the simpler name math.stat as the package name instead of myjava-stuff.lib.math.stat.

To find the directories in your CLASSPATH, look for some initializing file that includes something like *one* of the following lines:

    CLASSPATH=c:\jdk\lib;c:\somename
    SET CLASSPATH=c:\jdk\lib;c:\somename
    CLASSPATH /usr/jdk/lib:/usr/somename

or

    setenv CLASSPATH /usr/jdk/lib:/usr/somename

You are likely to find this in the same file that has your PATH variable setting. The exact things listed and the punctuation will depend on your particular operating system, but you should find the name CLASSPATH followed by a list of directories. These directories are the ones in your CLASSPATH. You can place a package in a subdirectory of

---

1.In order to use a full path name, the root directory must be listed in the setting of your CLASSPATH variable.

any of these directories and name the package using a relative path name that starts at a directory in your CLASSPATH settings. You can also add a directory to the class path so that all (or some of) your packages are subdirectories of some directory that you set up.

Package Names

A package name must be a path name for the directory that contains the classes in the package, but the package name uses dots in place of \ or / (whichever one of \ or / that your operating system uses). When naming the package, you use a relative path name that starts from any directory named in the setting of the CLASSPATH environment variable.

Examples:
```
mystuff.utilities
java.io
```

? SELF-TEST QUESTIONS

17. Suppose you want to use classes in the package mypackages.library1 in a program you write. What do you need to put near the start of the file containing your program?

18. Suppose you want to make a class a member of the package named mypackages.library1. What do you need to put in the file containing the class definition? Where does this statement go in the file?

19. Can a package have any name you might want or are there restrictions on what you can use for a class name? Explain any restrictions.

Chapter Summary

- A method definition can include a call to another method of the same class.
- If a method definition is labeled *static*, then that method can be invoked using the class name, rather than an object name. (It can also be invoked using an object name.)
- The top–down design method helps you to write method definitions by breaking the task to be accomplished by the method into subtasks.
- Every method should be tested in a program in which it is the only untested method.
- Each primitive type has a wrapper class that serves as a class version of that primitive type.
- A method name can have two different definitions within the same class, provided the two definitions have different numbers of parameters or some parameters of differing types. This is called **overloading** the method name.
- Giving multiple definitions to the same word is called **polymorphism.**

Overloading is one form of polymorphism.

- ☐ A constructor is a class method that is called when you create an object of the class using *new*. A constructor must have the same name as the class.
- ☐ A constructor with no parameters is called a **default constructor.** Class definitions typically include a default constructor.

? ANSWERS to Self-Test Questions

1. It is legal, but a more normal way of doing the same thing is

```
double areaOfCircle = Circle.area(2.5);
```

2. Yes, you can have all these kinds of things together in one class.

3. The class Format is in the file Format.java included with the software that goes with this text.

```
public class Format
{
    /**********************************************************
    *Writes out number with digitsAfterPoint digits after
    *the decimal point. Truncates any extra digits.
    *Does not advance to the next line after output.
    **********************************************************/
    private static void write(double number,
                                          int digitsAfterPoint)
    {
        if (number >= 0)
            writePositive(number, digitsAfterPoint);
        else
        {
            double positiveNumber = -number;
            System.out.print('-');
            writePositive(positiveNumber, digitsAfterPoint);
        }
    }

    //Precondition: number >= 0
    //Writes out number with digitsAfterPoint digits after the
    //decimal point. Truncates any extra digits.
    private static void writePositive(double number,
                                          int digitsAfterPoint)
    {
```

```
        int mover = (int)(Math.pow(10, digitsAfterPoint));
                //1 followed by digitsAfterPoint zeros
        int allWhole;//number with the decimal point
                    //moved digitsAfterPoint places
        allWhole = (int)(Math.floor(number*mover));
        int beforePoint = allWhole/mover;
        int afterPoint = allWhole%mover;

        System.out.print(beforePoint);
        System.out.print('.');
        writeFraction(afterPoint, digitsAfterPoint);
    }

    //Outputs the integer afterPoint with enough 0s
    //in front to make it digitsAfterPoint digits long.
    private static void writeFraction(int afterPoint,
                                       int digitsAfterPoint)
    {
        int n = 1;
        while (n < digitsAfterPoint)
        {
            if (afterPoint < Math.pow(10, n))
                System.out.print('0');
            n = n + 1;
        }
        System.out.print(afterPoint);
    }

    /*****************************************************
     *Writes out number with digitsAfterPoint digits after
     *the decimal point. Truncates any extra digits.
     *Advances to the next line after output.
     *****************************************************/
    public static void writeln(double number, int digitsAfterPoint)
    {
        write(number, digitsAfterPoint);
        System.out.println();
    }
}
```

4. Yes, you could use the names `print` and `println`, rather than `write` and `writeln`, in the class `Format`. This would produce no name confusion with `System.out.println`, since when you invoke the method in `Format`, you specify the class name before the dot. (If you invoke the method with an object, instead of the class name, Java still knows the class name because it knows the type of the object.) However, the methods in `Format` behave a little differently from the method `System.out.println`, so it seems that a different name would be clearer.

5.
```
Integer n = new Integer(77); //Legal
int m = 77; //Legal
n = m; //Illegal, should be:
n = new Integer(m);
m = n;//Illegal, should be
m = n.intValue();
```

6. `Double.toString(x)`

7. `Integer.valueOf(s).intValue()`

8. Yes, the 7 would be converted to 7.0 by Java so that the types match the heading of one of the definitions of `set`.

9. No, you cannot overload a method name on the basis of the type returned.

10. Yes, they differ in the type of their parameter, so this is a legal overloading of the method name `convertValue`. (Note that the fact that they return values of different types does not affect whether or not both definitions can be used. It is only the types of the parameters that count in making overloading legal.)

11. Yes, it would be legal because no other method named `set` has the same number and types of parameters. The definition follows:
```
public void set(String newName)
{
    name = newName;
    population = 0;
    growthRate = 0;
}
```

12. If a class is named `Student`, then every constructor for this class must also be named `Student`.

13. You specify no type returned for a constructor, not even *void*.

14. A default constructor is a constructor with no parameters.

15. No. Here are the details: If you give no constructor definition for a class, then Java will automatically provide a default constructor. If you provide one or more constructors of any sort, then Java does not provide any constructors beyond what you define. So, if you define one or more constructors and none of them is a default constructor, then the class has no default constructor.

16.
```
public String petName()
{
    return pet.nameValue();
}
```

```
public int petAge()
{
    return pet.ageValue();
}

public double petWeight()
{
    return pet.weightValue();
}
```

17. `import mypackages.library1.*;`

18. You must make the following the first line in the file:

    `package mypackages.library1;`

19. A package name must be a path name for the directory that contains the classes in the package, but the package name uses dots in place of \ or / (whichever one of \ or / that your operating system uses). When naming the package, you use a relative path name that starts from any directory named in the setting of the CLASSPATH environment variable.

? PROGRAMMING EXERCISES

1. Define a utility class for outputting values of type *double*. Call the class DoubleOut. Include all the methods from the class Dollars in Display 5.8/page 251, all the methods from the class Format of Self-Test Question 3/page 254 (answer on page 283), and a method called scienceWrite that outputs a value of type *double* in the e notation, such as 2.13e–12. (This e notation is also called *scientific notation*, which explains the method name.) When output in e notation, the number should always show exactly one digit before the decimal point. The method scienceWrite will not advance to the next line. Also add a method called science-Writeln that is the same as scienceWrite except that all future output goes on the next line. All but the last two method definitions can be simply copied from the text (or more easily from the files in the software that comes with this text). Note that you will be overloading the method names write and writeln. Write a driver program to test your method scienceWriteln. This driver program should use a stub for the method scienceWrite. (Note that this means you can write and test science-Writeln before you even write scienceWrite.) Then, write a driver program for the method scienceWrite. Then, write a program that is a sort of super driver program that takes a *double* value as input and then outputs it using the two writeln methods and the scienceWriteln method. Use the number 5 for the number of digits after the decimal point when you need to specify such a number. This super driver program should allow the user to repeat this testing with additional *double* numbers until the user is ready to end the program.

2. Modify the definition of the class Species in Display 4.15/page 214 by removing the method set and adding the following methods: (1) five constructors, one for each instance variable, one with three parameters for the three instance variables, and a default constructor; (2) four methods named set, which can reset values; one is the same as the method set in Display 4.15/page 214; the other three each reset one of the instance variables. Be sure that each constructor sets all of the instance variables. Then, write a test program to test all the methods you have added. Then, redo (or do for the first time) Programming Exercise 1/page 230 from Chapter 4. Be sure to use some constructor other than the default constructor when you define new objects in the class Species.

3. Redo (or do for the first time) Programming Exercise 3/page 230 of Chapter 4. This time, be sure your class definition contains suitable constructors and reset methods. Use at least one of the methods from the class Format of Self-Test Exercise 3/page 254.

Chapter 6

INHERITANCE

6.1 **INHERITANCE BASICS 290**
Programming Example
   A Person Class 291
Derived Classes 293
Programming Tip Overriding Method
   Definitions 295
Gotcha Use of Private Instance Vari-
   ables from the Base Class 298
Gotcha Private Methods Are Not
   Inherited 299

6.2 **PROGRAMMING WITH INHERITANCE 300**
Constructors in Derived Classes 300
The *this* Method *(Optional)* 301
Call to an Overridden Method
   (Optional) 302
Programming Tip An Object of a
   Derived Class Has More than
   One Type 302
Case Study Character Graphics 304
Dynamic Binding 313

Chapter Summary 317
Answers to Self-Test Questions 317
Programming Exercises 321

6

INHERITANCE

· ·

Like mother, like daughter.
COMMON SAYING

Introduction

In this chapter, we cover one of the key concepts in object-oriented programming and one that is needed in order to use many of the libraries that come with Java. For example, in order to understand the next chapter, which shows you how to build windowing interfaces for your programs, you will need the material in this chapter. As the title of this chapter indicates, this key concept is known as *inheritance*. Inheritance will allow you to use an exiting class to help you define new classes. This is a key concept in allowing you to reuse software.

Prerequisites

You need the material in previous chapters before you can understand this chapter. (Of course, you do not need those sections that state that they are not used later in the book.) Chapters 1 through 6 are the introductory material that you need no matter what you wish to do with Java. After this chapter, you will have a good deal more freedom in deciding what order you read the remaining chapters in this book.

6.1 Inheritance Basics

All men are mortal
Socrates is a man.
Therefore Socrates is mortal.
TYPICAL SYLLOGISM

Inheritance is a major component of a powerful and popular programming technique known as *object-oriented programming*. Inheritance is a technique that will allow you to define a very general class and then later define more specialized classes by simply adding some new details to the older more general class definitions. This saves work because the more specialized class *inherits* all the properties of the general class and you, the programmer, need only program the new features.

For example, you might define a class for vehicles that has instance variables to record the vehicle's speed and number of occupants. You might then define a class for automobiles and let the automobile class *inherit* all the instance variables and methods of the class for vehicles. The class for automobiles would have added instance variables for such things as the name of the manufacturer and the number of cylinders and would also have some added methods. You would have to describe the added instance variables and added methods, but if you use Java's inheritance mechanism, you would get the instance variables and methods from the vehicle class automatically.

Before we construct an example of inheritance within Java, we first need to set the stage by giving the following Programming Example.

▼ PROGRAMMING EXAMPLE *A Person Class*

Display 6.1 contains a simple class called `Person`. This class is so simple that the only property it gives a person is a name. We will not have a lot of direct uses for the class `Person` by itself, but we will use the class `Person` in defining other classes. So, it is important to understand this class.

Most of the methods for the class `Person` are straightforward. Notice that the method `changeName` and the constructor with one `String` parameter do the same thing. We need these two methods, even though they do the same thing, because only the constructor can be used after *new* when we create a new object of the class `Person`, but we need a different method, such as `changeName`, to make changes to an object after the object is created.

The method `sameName` is similar to the `equals` methods we've seen, but since it uses a few techniques that you may not have completely digested yet, let's go over that definition, which we reproduce in what follows:

```
public boolean sameName(Person otherPerson)
{
    return ((this.name.equalsIgnoreCase(otherPerson.name));
}
```

`sameName`

Recall that when this method `sameName` is used, there will be a calling object of the class `Person` and an argument of the class `Person`. The `sameName` method will tell whether the two objects have the same name. For example, here is some sample code that might appear in a program:

```
Person p1 = new Person("Sam");
System.out.println("Enter the name of a person:");
String name = SavitchIn.readLine();
Person p2 = new Person(name);
if (p1.sameName(p2))
    System.out.println("They have the same name.");
else
    System.out.println("They have different names.");
```

Consider the call `p1.sameName(p2)`. When the method `sameName` is called, the *this* parameter is replaced with p1 and the formal parameter `otherPerson` is replaced with p2, so that the value of *true* or *false* that is returned is

```
p1.name.equalsIgnoreCase(p2.name)
```

Thus, the two objects are considered to have the same name (i.e., `sameName` returns *true*) provided the two objects have the same value for their `name` instance variables (ignoring any differences between uppercase and lowercase letters).

Display 6.1 A Base Class

```java
public class Person
{
    public Person()
    {
        name = "No name yet.";
    }

    public Person(String aName)
    {
        name = aName;
    }

    public void changeName(String newName)
    {
        name = newName;
    }

    public String theName()
    {
        return name;
    }

    public void writeOutput()
    {
        System.out.println("Name: " + name);
    }

    public boolean sameName(Person otherPerson)
    {
        return (this.name.equalsIgnoreCase(otherPerson.name));
    }


    private String name;
}
```

To be very concrete, if the user enters `Sam` in response to the prompt

```
Enter the name of a person:
```

then the output will be

```
They have the same name.
```

If instead of `Sam`, the user enters `Mary`, then the output will be

```
They have different names.
```

Derived Classes

Suppose we are designing a college record-keeping program that has records for students, faculty, and (nonteaching) staff. There is a natural hierarchy for grouping these record types. They are all records of people. Students are one subclass of people. Another subclass is employees, which includes both faculty and staff. Display 6.2 diagrams this hierarchical arrangement. Although your program may not need any class corresponding to people or employees, thinking in terms of such types can be useful. For example, all people have names, and the methods of initializing, reading, and changing names will be the same for student, staff, and faculty records. In Java, you can define a class called `Person` that includes instance variables for the properties that belong to all subclasses of people, such as students, faculty, and staff. The class definition can also contain all the methods that manipulate the instance variables for the class `Person`. In fact, we have already defined such a `Person` class in Display 6.1.

Display 6.3 contains the definition of a class for students. A student is a person, so we define the class `Student` to be a *derived* class of the class `Person`. A **derived class** is a class defined by adding instance variables and methods to an existing class. The existing class that the derived is built upon is called the **base class**. In our example, the class `Person` is the base class and the class `Student` is the derived class. The derived class has all the instance variables and methods of the base class, plus what-

derived class

base class

Display 6.2 A Class Hierarchy

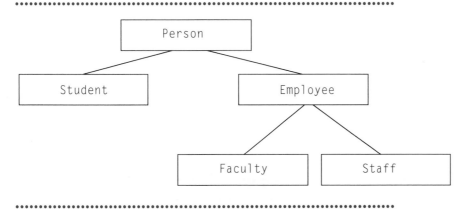

Display 6.3 A Derived Class

```
public class Student extends Person
{
    public Student()
    {
        super();
        classYear = 1;
    }

    public Student(String aName, int aYear)
    {
        super(aName);
        classYear = aYear;
    }

    public void reset(String newName, int newYear)
    {
        changeName(newName);
        classYear = newYear;
    }

    public int theClassYear()
    {
        return classYear;
    }
    public void changeYear(int newYear)
    {
        classYear = newYear;
    }

    public void writeOutput()
    {
        System.out.println("Name: " + theName());
        System.out.println("Year: " + classYear);
    }

    public boolean equals(Student otherStudent)
    {
        return (this.sameName(otherStudent)
                    && (this.classYear == otherStudent.classYear));
    }

    private int classYear;//1, for freshman, 2 for sophomore, etc.
}
```

super is explained in a later section. Do not worry about it until you reach the discussion of it in the text.

ever added instance variables and methods you wish to add. If you look in Display 6.3, you will see that the way we indicate that Student is a derived class of the class Person is by including the phrase *extends* Person on the first line of the class def- inition, so that the class definition of Student begins

extends

```
public class Student extends Person
```

When you define a derived class, you give only the added instance variables and the added methods. For example, the class Student has all the instance variables and all the methods of the class Person, but you do not have to mention them in the definition of the class Student. Every object of the class Student has an instance variable called name, but you do not specify the instance variable name in the definition of the class Student. The class Student (or any other derived class) is said to **inherit** the instance variables and methods of the base class that it extends. For example, suppose you create a new object of the class Student as follows:

inheritance

```
Student s = new Student();
```

There is an instance variable s.name. Since name is a private instance variable, there are very few places that it is legal to write s.name, but the instance variable is there and it can be accessed and changed. Similarly, you can have the following method invocation:

```
s.changeName("Warren Peace");
```

The class Student inherits the method changeName (and all the other methods of the class Person) from the base class Person.

A derived class, like Student, can also add some instance variables and/or methods to those it inherits from its base class. For example, the class Student adds the instance variable classYear and the methods writeOutput, changeYear, theClassYear, reset, and equals, as well as some constructors. (But we will post- pone the discussion of constructors until we finish explaining the other parts of these class definitions.)

Display 6.4 contains a very small demonstration program to illustrate inherit- ance. Notice that the object s can invoke the method changeName, even though this is a method of its base class Person. The class Student inherits changeName from the class Person. The class Student also adds new methods. In the sample pro- gram, the object s of the class Student invokes the method changeYear. The method changeYear was not in the class Person.

◑ *PROGRAMMING TIP* Overriding Method Definitions

In the definition of the class Student, we added a method called writeOutput that has no parameters (Display 6.3). But, the class Person also has a method called writeOutput that has no parameters. If the class Student were to inherit the meth- od writeOutput from the base class Person, then the class Student would contain two methods with the name writeOutput, both of which have no parameters. Java has a rule to avoid this problem. If a derived class defines a method with the same name as a method in the base class and that also has *the same number and types of*

overriding a method

Display 6.4 Demonstrating Inheritance
••

```java
public class InheritanceDemo
{
    public static void main(String[] args)
    {
        Student s = new Student();

        s.changeName("Warren Peace");
        s.changeYear(4);//for senior
        s.writeOutput();
    }
}
```

> changeName is inherited from the class Person.

Screen Output

```
Name: Warren Peace
Year: 4
```

••

Derived Class

You define a **derived class** by starting with another already defined class and adding (and/or changing) methods and instance variables. The class you start with is called the **base class**. The derived class inherits all of the methods and instance variables from the base class and adds more instance variables and/or methods.

Syntax:

```java
public class Derived_Class_Name extends Base_Class_Name
{
        Definitions_of_Added_Methods
        Declarations_of_Added_Instance_Variables
}
```

Example:

See Display 6.3/page 294.

Parent and Child Classes

When discussing derived classes, it is very common to use terminology derived from family relationships. A base class is often called a **parent class**. A derived class is then called a **child class**. This makes the language of inheritance very smooth. For example, we can say that a child class inherits instance variables and methods from its parent class. This analogy is often carried one step further. A class that is a parent of a parent of a parent of another class (or some other number of "parent of" iterations) is often called an **ancestor class**. If class A is an ancestor of class B, then class B is often called a **descendent** of class A.

parent and child

ancestor and descendent

parameters as in the base class, then the definition in the derived class is said to **override** the definition in the base class and the definition in the derived class is the one that is used for objects of the derived class. For example, in Display 6.4, the following invocation of the method writeOutput for the object s of the class Student will use the definition of writeOutput in the class Student, not the definition of the method writeOutput in the class Person:

```
s.writeOutput();
```

Do not confuse method overriding with method overloading. When you override a method definition, the new method definition given in the derived class has the exact same number and types of parameters. On the other hand, if the method in the derived class were to have a different number of parameters or a parameter of a different type from the method in the base class, then the derived class would have both methods. That would be overloading. For example, suppose we added the following method to the definition of the class Student:

overriding vs. overloading

```
public void theName(String namePlate)
{
    namePlate = theName();
}
```

In this case, the class Student would have two methods named theName: It would still inherit the method theName from the base class Person (Display 6.1/page 292), and it would also have the method named theName that we just defined. This is because these two methods called theName have different numbers of parameters.

If you get overloading and overriding confused, you do have one small consolation. They are both legal. So, it is more important to learn to use them than it is to learn to distinguish them. Nonetheless, you should learn the difference between them.

Overriding Method Definitions

If in a derived class you include a method definition that has the same name and the *exact* same number and types of parameters as a method already exiting in the base class, then *for the derived class,* this new definition replaces the old definition of the method.

⚠ *GOTCHA* *Use of Private Instance Variables from the Base Class*

An object of the class Student (Display 6.3/page 294) inherits an instance variable called name from the class Person (Display 6.1/page 292). For example, the following would set the value of the instance variable name of the object joe to "Josephine": (This also sets the instance variable classYear to 1.)

```
Student joe = new Student("Josephine", 1);
```

If you want to change joe.name (and joe.classYear), you can do so as follows:

```
joe.reset("Joesy", 4);
```

But, you must be a bit careful about how you manipulate inherited instance variables such as name. The instance variable name of the class Student was inherited from the class Person, but the instance variable name is a private instance variable in the definition of the class Person. That means that name can only be directly accessed in the definition of a method for the class Person. An instance variable (or method) that is private in a base class is not accessible *by name* in the definition of a method for *any other class, not even in a method definition of a derived class.* Thus, although the class Student does have an instance variable named name, it is illegal to directly access the instance variable name in the definition of any method in the class definition of Student!

For example, the following is the definition of the method reset from the definition of the class Student:

```
public void reset(String newName, int newYear)
{
    changeName(newName);        Legal definition
    classYear = newYear;
}
```

You might have wondered why we needed to use the method changeName to set the value of the name instance variable. You might be tempted to rewrite the method definition as follows:

```
public void reset(String newName, int newYear)
{
    name = theName;//ILLEGAL!    Illegal definition
    classYear = newYear;
}
```

As the comment indicates, this will not work. The instance variable name is a private instance variable in the class Person, and although a derived class like Student inherits the variable name, it cannot access it directly. It must use some public accessor method to access the instance variable name. The correct way to accomplish the definition of reset in the class Student is the way we did it in Display 6.3 (which we reproduced as the first of the preceding two possible definitions of reset).

The fact that a private instance variable of a base class cannot be accessed in the definition of a method of a derived class often seems wrong to people. After all, if you are a student and you want to change your name, nobody says, "Sorry name is a private instance variable of the class Person." After all, if you are a student, you are also a person. In Java, this is also true; an object of the class Student is also an object of the class Person. However, the laws on the use of private instance variables and methods must be as we described, or else they would be pointless. If private instance variables of a class were accessible in method definitions of a derived class, then anytime you wanted to access a private instance variable, you could simply create a derived class and access it in a method of that class, and that would mean that all private instance variables would be accessible to everybody who wants to put in a little extra effort.

⚠ GOTCHA *Private Methods Are Not Inherited*

As we noted in the previous Gotcha section: An instance variable (or method) that is private in a base class is not directly accessible in the definition of a method for *any other class, not even in a method definition for a derived class.* Note that private methods are just like private variables in terms of not being directly available. But, in the case of methods, the restriction is more dramatic. A private variable can be accessed indirectly via an accessor method. A private method is simply not available. It is just as if the private method were not inherited.

This should not be a problem. Private methods should just be used as helping functions, and so their use should be limited to the class in which they are defined. If you want a method to be used as a helping method in a number of inherited classes, then it is not *just* a helping method, and you should make the method public.

? SELF-TEST QUESTIONS

1. Suppose the class named SportsCar is a derived class of a class called Automobile and suppose the class Automobile has instance variables named speed, manufacturer, and numberOfCylinders. Will an object of the class SportsCar have instance variables named speed, manufacturer, and numberOfCylinders?

2. Suppose the class named SportsCar is a derived class of a class called Automobile and suppose the class Automobile has public methods named accelerate and addGas. Will an object of the class SportsCar have methods named accelerate and addGas? Do these methods have to perform the exact same action in the class SportsCar as they do in the class Automobile?

3. If you are defining a derived class, can you directly access a private instance variable of the base class?

4. If you are defining a derived class, can you use a private method of the base class?

6.2 Programming with Inheritance

You do not have to die in order to pass along your inheritance.
AD FOR AN ESTATE PLANNING SEMINAR

Inheritance via derived classes is a powerful tool. It does, however, require that you learn some new techniques in order to use it productively. In this section, we discuss some of these techniques.

Constructors in Derived Classes

A derived class, such as the class `Student` in Display 6.3/page 294, has its own constructors. The base class from which it was derived, such as `Person`, also has its own constructors. When defining a constructor for the base class, the typical first action is to call a constructor of the base class. For example, consider defining a constructor for the class `Student`. One of the things that need to be initialized is the student's name. This name initializing is normally done by the constructors for the base class `Person` (since the instance variable `name` was introduced in the definition of `Person`). Thus, a natural first action for a constructor for the class `Student` is a call to a constructor for its base class `Person`. For example, consider the following definition of a constructor for the derived class `Student` (from Display 6.3):

```
public Student(String aName, int aYear)
{
    super(aName);
    classYear = aYear;
}
```

The line

```
super(aName);
```

super

is a call to a constructor for the base class, in this case, a call to a constructor for the class `Person`. Notice that you use the reserved word *super* to call the constructor of the base class. You do not use the name of the constructor; you do *not* use `Person(aName)`.

There are some details to worry about with the use of *super*: It must always be the first action taken in a constructor definition. You cannot use it later in the definition of a constructor. In fact, if you do not include a call to the base-class constructor, then Java will automatically include a call to the default constructor of the base class as the first action of any constructor for a derived class. Consider the following definition of constructor for the class `Student` (Display 6.3):

```
public Student()
{
    super();
    classYear = 1;
}
```

This definition is completely equivalent to the following:

```
public Student()
{
    classYear = 1;
}
```

If there is no call to a constructor of the base class, then Java will automatically insert a call to the default constructor of the base class; that is, Java will automatically insert a call to *super*(). We prefer to explicitly write in such calls to a base-class default constructor, whether or not Java would call it automatically. That makes the code a bit clearer, since all actions are explicitly shown.

Call to a Base-Class Constructor

When defining a constructor for a derived class, you can use *super* as a name for the constructor of the base class. Any call to *super* must be the first action taken by the constructor.

Example:
```
public Student(String aName, int aYear)
{
    super(aName);
    classYear = aYear;
}
```

The *this* Method *(Optional)*

When defining a constructor another common action is a call to one of the other constructors. You can use the reserved word *this* in a way similar to how you use *super*, but with *this*, the call is to a constructor of the same class and not a call to a constructor for the base class. For example, consider the following definition of a constructor that you might want to add to the class Student (from Display 6.3/page 294):

this as a method

```
public Student(String aName)
{
    this(aName, 1);
}
```

The one statement in the body of this constructor definition is a call to the constructor whose definition begins

```
public Student(String aName, int aYear)
```

As with *super*, any use of *this* must be the first action in a constructor definition. Thus, a constructor definition cannot contain both a call using *super*, and a call using *this*. What if you want a call with *super* and a call with *this*? In that case, use a call with *this* and have the constructor that is called with *this* have *super* as its first action.

Call to Another Constructor in the Same Class *(Optional)*

When defining a constructor for a class, you can use *this* as a name for another constructor in the same class. Any call to *this* must be the first action taken by the constructor.

Example:

```
public Student(String aName)
{
    this(aName, 1);
}
```

Call to an Overridden Method *(Optional)*

When you are defining a constructor for a derived class, you can use *super* as a name for the constructor of the base class. You can also use *super* to call a method of the base class that is overridden (redefined) in the derived class, but the way you do this is a bit different.

For example, consider the method writeOutput for the class Student in Display 6.3/page 294. It uses the following to output the name of the Student:

```
System.out.println("Name: " + theName());
```

Alternatively, you could output the name by calling the method writeOutput *of the class* Person (Display 6.1/page 292), since the writeOutput method for the class Person will output the person's name. The only problem is that if you use the name writeOutput for a method in the class Student, it will mean the method named writeOutput in the class Student. What you need is a way to say "writeOutput() as it is defined in the base class." The way you say that is *super*.writeOutput(). So, an alternative definition of the writeOutput method for the class Student is the following:

```
public void writeOutput()
{
    super.writeOutput();
    System.out.println("Year: " + classYear);
}
```

If you replace the definition of writeOutput in the definition of Student (Display 6.3/page 294) with the preceding, then the class Student will behave exactly the same as it did before.

Within the definition of a method of a derived class, you can call an overridden method of the base class by prefacing the method name with *super* and a dot.

◐ *PROGRAMMING TIP* An Object of a Derived Class Has More than One Type

Consider the class Student in Display 6.3/page 294. It is a derived class of the class Person. In the real world, every student is also a person. This relationship holds in Java as well. Every object of the class Student is also an object of the class Person. Thus, if you have a method that has a formal parameter of type Person, then the argument in an invocation of this method can be an object of type Student. In this case, the method could only use those instance variables and methods that belong to the class Person, but every object of the class Student has all these instance variables and methods so there are still lots of meaningful things that the method can do with an object of type Student.

For example, suppose that the classes Person and Student are defined as in Display 6.1/page 292 and Display 6.3/page 294 and consider the following code, which might occur in a program:

```
Person joe = new Person("Josephine");
String newName = SavitchIn.readLineWord();
Student student1 = new Student(newName, 1);
if (joe.sameName(student1))
    System.out.println("Wow, same names!");
```

If you look at the heading for the method sameName in Display 6.1, you will see that it has one parameter and that parameter is of type Person. However, the call

```
joe.sameName(student1)
```

which is used in the preceding if-statement is perfectly legal, even though the argument student1 is an object of the class Student (i.e., is of type Student) and the argument is supposed to be of type Person. This is because every object of the class Student is also an object of the class Person. The object student1 is of type Student, and it is also of type Person. This is one of the nice features of inheritance. Everything that works for objects of a base class also works for objects of a derived class.

Incidentally, the following is also legal

```
if (student1.sameName(joe))
    System.out.println("Wow, same names!");
```

Since sameName is a method of the class Person, it is also a method of the derived class Student so we can use sameName with a calling object from the class Student, in this case the object student1 of the class Student.

An Object of a Derived Class Has More than One Type

An object of a derived class has the type of the derived class and it also has the type of the base class.

An object can actually have more than two types as a result of inheritance. If A is a derived class of class B, and B is a derived class of class C, then an object of the class A is of type A, it is also of type B, and it is also of type C. This works for any chain of derived classes no matter how long the chain is. Java has an "Eve" class, that is, a class that is an ancestor of every class. In Java, every class is a derived class of a derived class of ... (for some number of iterations of "a derived class of") of the class Object. So, every object of every class is of type Object, as well as being of the type of its class and maybe also of the type of other ancestor classes as well. Even classes that you yourself define are descendent classes of the class Object. If you do not make your class a derived class of some class, then Java acts as if you made it a derived class of the class `Object`.

The Class `Object`

In Java, every class is a descendent of the predefined class `Object`. So, every object of every class is of type `Object`, as well as being of the type of its class (and probably also of the type of other ancestor classes as well).

Case Study *Character Graphics*

Java has classes to draw graphics on your terminal screen. In Chapter 7, we will discuss one set of such classes that is used to draw windows and menu interfaces on your screen. However, there are situations in which you have no graphics capability available on your screen or other output device. For example, some older terminals only allow for text output. In this case study, you will design three simple classes to be used to produce simple graphics on a screen using only text output. These classes will produce their graphic figures by placing ordinary keyboard characters at certain places on each line, and will do this in such a way as to produce some simple pictures.

The origin of this case study is a request for graphics to be included in Email messages. The only thing you can be certain that you can include in an Email message so that the message can be handled by any mailer program, and so, understood by any person who receives the message, is plain text. So, this sort of character graphics is the only kind of graphics that will work for all people to whom you might send Email. In this case study, you will do this character graphics using the screen in order to have a demonstration prototype. The prototype will be used to demonstrate the graphics in the hope of obtaining a contract to create graphics that can be output to a file that can then be sent via Email. Although we have not yet covered output to files, it will turn out to be easy to modify these classes to send their output to a file rather than to the screen.

task specification The exact details of what you will do in this demonstration project is as follows: You will create two classes, one for a box and one for a triangle. You will then write a simple demonstration program that draws a pine tree using the triangle and box classes. If this prototype is successful with customers, you will then write more classes for figures, but these two are all you will do in this case study.

Each of the figures, the box and the triangle, will have an offset telling how far they are indented from the edge of the screen. Each of these figures will also have a size, although the size will be determined differently for a box and a triangle.

For a box, the size is given as the width and the height, *expressed in the number of characters*. Because characters are taller than they are wide, a box will look taller than you might expect when it is written on the screen. For example, a 5-by-5 box will not look square on the screen, but will look like what is shown in Display 6.5.

For a triangle, the size will be given by its base. The triangle will point up and the base will be at the bottom. The slope of a side of the triangle is limited to what you get by indenting one character per line (if you want it to be smooth). So, once

Display 6.5 Sample Boxes and Triangles

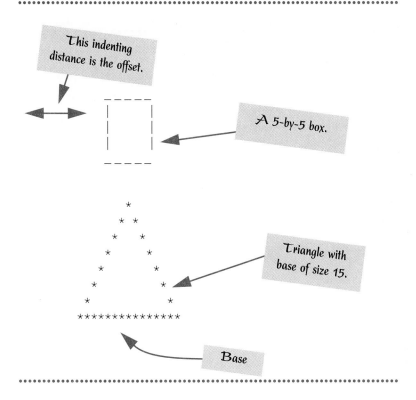

the base is chosen, you have no choice in what the sides of the triangle will be. Display 6.5 shows a sample of both a box and a triangle.

Since both a box and a triangle are figures with many properties in common, you decide to design a base class named Figure. The classes Box and Triangle will then be derived classes of the class Figure. The class Figure will have instance variables for any properties that all figures have in common and will have methods for the actions that all figures have. Your analysis produces the following list of properties and actions:

Properties. All figures can have an offset, which is the number of spaces it is indented, so you decide to store the offset in an instance variable of type *int*. All figures will have a size, but the size of some figures is described by one number and the size of other figures is determined by two or more numbers. For example, the size of the kind of triangle we will be using in this case study is given by one number, but the size of a box is given as two numbers, the height and the width. So, you

base class

Figure

Display 6.6 The Figure **Base Class** *(Part 1 of 2)*

```
/****************************************************************
 *Class for simple character graphics figures to send to screen.
 *This class can draw an asterisk on the screen as a test. But,
 *it is not intended to be a figure used in graphics.
 *It is intended to be used as a base class for the kinds
 *of figures that will be used in graphics applications.
 ****************************************************************/
public class Figure
{
    public Figure()
    {
        offset = 0;
    }

    public Figure(int theOffset)
    {
        offset = theOffset;
    }

    public void resetOffset(int newOffset)
    {
        offset = newOffset;
    }

    public int offsetValue()
    {
        return offset;
    }


    /*****************************************
     *Draws the figure at lineNumber lines down
     *from the current line.
     *****************************************/
    public void drawAt(int lineNumber)
    {
        int count;
        for (count = 0; count < lineNumber; count++)
            System.out.println();
        drawHere();
    }
```

Display 6.6 The F i g u r e **Base Class** *(Part 2 of 2)*

```
/*********************************************
*Draws the figure at the current line.
*********************************************/
public void drawHere()
{
    int count;
    for (count = 0; count < offset; count++)
        System.out.print(' ');
    System.out.println('*');
}

    private int offset;
}
```

decide not to specify size as part of the class Figure. Thus, you decide that the class Figure will have only the following one instance variable:

```
    private int offset;
```

Actions. The only actions you need for all figures are to set the parameters for the figures and to draw the figures. Setting the parameters will be taken care of by constructors and reset methods. Display 6.6 contains the definition for the class Figure that you produce. The method drawHere will simply indent a number of spaces on the screen equal to the offset and then write an asterisk on the screen. This is just so you can have something to test. You do not intend to use this version of drawHere in any application. You will override the definition of drawHere when you define classes for boxes and triangles. The method drawAt has one parameter of type int. The method drawAt inserts a number of blank lines equal to this parameter and then draws the figure by calling drawHere. Of course, in this case, that does not produce very much, but when we override drawHere, then drawAt will also produce more interesting figures.

Next you turn your attention to the class for drawing a box. The class, called Box, will be a derived class of the class Figure. You need to decide on the instance variables and methods that will be added to those in the class Figure. You also need to decide which if any method definitions in Figure will be overridden with a changed definition.

Box class

Properties. The class Box inherits the offset instance variables, but you need to add instance variables for the height and the width of the box, Thus, the class definition looks like the following:

```
public class Box extends Figure
{
```
        <Still needs method definitions.>
```
    private int height;
    private int width;
}
```

Note that you do not list the instance variable `offset`, which `Box` inherits from the base class `Figure`.

Actions. The class `Box` has the usual constructors, reset method, and accessor methods, It inherits both the method `drawAt` and the method `drawHere` from the class `Figure`. However, you need to override the definition of the method `drawHere` so that it does indeed draw a box. So, you put `drawHere` on your list of methods to define.

Next, you consider the method `drawAt`. Does it need to be overridden? When you look at the method `drawAt` (Display 6.6/page 306), you will see that, as long as `drawHere` is correctly defined, the method `drawAt` will work fine for a box or any other figure. Thus, you need not redefine the method `drawAt`. You only need to redefine the method `drawHere`.

Let's look first at a sample constructor. You will design one of the constructors so that it sets all instance variables to values given as arguments to the constructor. But, one instance variable, namely, `offset`, is a private instance variable of the base class `Figure`. Thus, you cannot access it directly, but must use a call to the base class constructor, *super*. Thus, the definition of this constructor is

```
public Box(int theOffset, int theHeight, int theWidth)
{
    super(theOffset);
    height = theHeight;
    width = theWidth;
}
```

The default constructor and `reset` method that you define are shown in Display 6.7. Note that the `reset` method needs to use an accessor method to reset the private instance variable `offset` that is inherited from the base class `Figure`.

In your definition of the default constructor for the class `Box`, you could omit the call to the base-class constructor *super( )*, and it would be called automatically anyway, but you decide to leave it in for clarity.

Most of these definitions of constructors and accessor methods are similar to what they would be in any class definition. The definition of the method `drawHere`, however, depends heavily on the particulars of what figure it is drawing. You decide to define the method `drawHere` using the technique known as *top–down design*. The basic technique in top–down design is to break down the task to be done by the method into subtasks. You decide on the following subtasks:

drawHere

subtasks

```
To Draw a Box:
```
1. Draw the top line.
2. Draw the side lines.
3. Draw the bottom line.

Display 6.7 The Box **Class (Part 1 of 2)**

```
/**********************************************************
 *Class for a rectangular box to be drawn on the screen.
 *Because each character is higher than it is wide,
 *these boxes will look higher than you might expect.
 *Inherits offsetValue, resetOffset, and drawAt from Figure.
 **********************************************************/
public class Box extends Figure
{
    public Box()
    {
        super();
        height = 0;
        width = 0;
    }

    public Box(int theOffset, int theHeight, int theWidth)
    {
        super(theOffset);
        height = theHeight;
        width = theWidth;
    }

    public void reset(int newOffset, int newHeight, int newWidth)
    {
        resetOffset(newOffset);
        height = newHeight;
        width = newWidth;
    }

    /*******************************************
     *Draws the figure at the current line.
     *******************************************/
    public void drawHere()
    {
        drawHorizontalLine();
        drawSides();
        drawHorizontalLine();
    }
```

Display 6.7 The Box **Class** *(Part 2 of 2)*

```java
    private void drawHorizontalLine()
    {
        spaces(offsetValue());
        int count;
        for (count = 0; count < width; count++)
            System.out.print('-');
        System.out.println();
    }

    private void drawSides()
    {
        int count;
        for (count = 0; count < (height - 2); count++)
            drawOneLineOfSides();
    }

    private void drawOneLineOfSides()
    {
        spaces(offsetValue());
        System.out.print('|');
        spaces(width - 2);
        System.out.println('|');
    }

    //Writes the indicated number of spaces.
    private static void spaces(int number)
    {
        int count;
        for (count = 0; count < number; count++)
            System.out.print(' ');
    }

    private int height;
    private int width;
}
```

The method `spaces` was made `static` because it does not need a calling object. The class would work fine, if `spaces` were not made `static`, but it is clearer if you make `spaces` `static`.

Note that not every way of choosing subtasks will work. You might at first be tempted to have two subtasks, one for each side of the box. However, output must be produced one line after the other and you are not allowed to back up, so you must draw the two sides together (if you want them to be side by side as they should be).

Thus, the definition of the method drawHere is easy:

```java
public void drawHere()
{
    drawHorizontalLine();
    drawSides();
    drawHorizontalLine();
}
```

Although that was easy, it does postpone most of the work. You still need to define the methods drawHorizontalLine and drawSides. Since these are helping methods, they will be private methods.

You come up with the following pseudocode for drawHorizontalLine:

> **Output** offset **blank spaces.**
> **Output** width **copies of the character** '-'.
> System.out.println();

drawHorizontalLine

The final code for the method drawHorizontalLine is given in Display 6.7. Note that the task of writing a specified number of blanks is broken out as another helping method called spaces.

Next, you turn your attention to the method drawSides. This task is to draw a figure like the following:

drawSides

Noticing that each line is identical, you decide to break out the writing of one of these lines as a subtask. So, the definition of the method drawSides is

```java
private void drawSides()
{
    int count;
    for (count = 0; count < (height - 2); count++)
        drawOneLineOfSides();
}
```

Note that you output two fewer lines than the height. The top and bottom horizontal lines account for those extra two units of height.

Just about all that there is left to do is to define the helping method drawOneLineOfSides. You design the following pseudocode for drawOneLineOfSides:

```
    spaces(offsetValue());
    System.out.print('|');
    spaces(width - 2);
    System.out.println('|');
```

testing

Since you already have a method for the subtask of writing spaces, the pseudocode turns out to be Java code, so the definition of drawOneLineOfSides is done. The complete class definition of Box is given in Display 6.7.

Although we will not stop to describe the testing process in this case study, all the methods in the class Figure, the class Box, and the class Triangle (which we have not yet discussed) need to be tested, and remember, each method should be tested in a program in which it is the only untested method.

Triangle class

Display 6.8/page 314 contains the definition of the class Triangle. You can design that class using the same techniques you used to design the class Box. We will only discuss one part of the method drawHere for which the technical details may not be clear at first reading. The method drawHere divides its task into two subtasks, draw the inverted V for the top of the triangle, and draw the horizontal line for the bottom of the triangle. We will only discuss the method drawTop that draws the inverted V.

The method drawTop draws a figure like the following:

Note that there is an offset for the entire figure. The indenting for the wide bottom of the figure is exactly this offset. But going up from bottom to top, each line has a greater indentation. Alternatively, going down (as the computer must go), each line has a slightly smaller indentation. The indentation is smaller by one character each line. So if the indentation is given by the value of the *int* variable startOfLine, then the indentation can be performed by

```
    spaces(startOfLine);
```

This can be made one line of a loop, and then the value of startOfLine will be decreased by one on each loop iteration. The size of the gap between the two asterisks on the same line increases by two as you go down one line. If this gap is given by the value of the *int* variable insideWidth, then the loop for drawing all of the inverted V except for the top asterisk can be

```
for (count = 0; count < lineCount; count++)
{
    spaces(startOfLine);
    System.out.print('*');
    spaces(insideWidth);
    System.out.println('*');
    insideWidth = insideWidth + 2;
    startOfLine--;//THIS LINE WILL MOVE.
}
```

The complete method definition of `drawTop` is given in Display 6.8. The preceding loop is given in color. Also, in order to accommodate the code that comes before the loop, the line

```
startOfLine--;
```

becomes the first line of the loop instead of the last, but it is still decremented once on each loop iteration.

To complete this project you produce the sample application program shown in Display 6.9/page 316.

application program

Dynamic Binding

Look at the definition of the method `drawAt` in the class `Figure` (Display 6.6/page 306). It makes a call to the method `drawHere`. If the only class around were `Figure`, this would not be anything exciting. But, we derived the classes `Box` from the base class `Figure`. The class `Box` inherits the method `drawAt` from the class `Figure`, but the method `Box` overrides the definition of the method `drawHere`. "So what?" you may say. So plenty! Look at the poor compiler's job.

Consider the following:

```
Box b = new Box(1, 4, 4);
b.drawAt(2);
```

The method `drawAt` was defined in the class `Figure`, but it calls the method `drawHere` that was redefined in the method `Box`. The code for `drawAt` was compiled with the class `Figure`, and that class was compiled before the class `Box` was even written. So, this compiled code is using a definition of the method `drawHere` that was not even written at the time that `drawAt` was compiled. How can that be? When the code for `drawAt` is compiled, nothing is inserted for the call to `drawHere` except for an annotation that says, "use the currently applicable definition of `drawHere`." Then, when you invoke `b.drawAt(2)`, the compiled code for `drawAt` reaches the annotation equivalent to "use the currently applicable definition of `drawHere`." This annotation is replaced by an invocation of the version of `drawHere` that goes with `b`. Since, in this case, `b` is of type `Box`, the version of `drawHere` will be the definition in the class `Box`.

This way of handling an invocation of a method that may be overridden later is called **late binding** or **dynamic binding,** because the meaning of the method invocation is not bound to the location of the method invocation until you run the program. If Java did not use dynamic binding, then when you ran the preceding code, you would not see a triangle on the screen, but would only see what was drawn by the method `drawHere` of the class `Figure` (which happens to be a single asterisk).

(Java is so good at figuring out which definition of a method to use that even a type cast will not fool it. Because of late binding, the meaning of `b.drawAt(2)` will always have the meaning defined in the method `Box`, even if you use a type cast to change the type of `b` to the type `Figure` such as the following:

```
Box b = new Box(1, 4, 4);
Figure f = (Figure)b;
f.drawAt(2);
```

Display 6.8 The Triangle **Class** *(Part 1 of 2)*

```
/******************************************************************************
*Class for triangles to be drawn on screen. For this class, a triangle
*points up and is completely determined by the size of its base. (Screen
*character spacing determines the length of the sides, given the base.)
*Inherits offsetValue, resetOffset, and drawAt from Figure.
******************************************************************************/
public class Triangle extends Figure
{
    public Triangle()
    {
        super();
        base = 0;
    }


    public Triangle(int theOffset, int theBase)
    {
        super(theOffset);
        base = theBase;
    }


    public void reset(int newOffset, int newBase)
    {
        resetOffset(newOffset);
        base = newBase;
    }


    /*******************************************
    *Draws the figure at current line.
    *******************************************/
    public void drawHere()
    {
        drawTop();
        drawBase();
    }
```

```
    private void drawBase()
    {
        spaces(offsetValue());
        int count;
        for (count = 0; count < base; count++)
            System.out.print('*');
        System.out.println();
    }

    private void drawTop()
    {
        //startOfLine will be the number of spaces to the first '*' on a
        //line. Initially set to the number of spaces before the top '*'.
        int startOfLine = offsetValue() + (base/2);
        spaces(startOfLine);
        System.out.println('*');//top '*'
        int count;
        int lineCount = (base/2) - 1;//height above base
        //insideWidth == number of spaces between the two '*'s on a line.
        int insideWidth = 1;
        for (count = 0; count < lineCount, count++)
        {
            //Down one line so the first '*' is one more space to the left.
            startOfLine--;
            spaces(startOfLine);
            System.out.print('*');
            spaces(insideWidth);
            System.out.println('*');
            //Down one line so the inside is 2 spaces wider.
            insideWidth = insideWidth + 2;
        }
    }

    private static void spaces(int number)
    {
        int count;
        for (count = 0; count < number; count++)
            System.out.print(' ');
    }

    private int base;
}
```

Display 6.9 Character Graphics Application

```java
public class GraphicsDemo
{
    public static final int indent = 5;
    public static final int topWidth = 21;
    public static final int bottomWidth = 4;
    public static final int bottomHeight = 4;

    public static void main(String[] args)
    {
        System.out.println("          Save The Redwoods!");

        Triangle top = new Triangle(indent, topWidth);
        Box base = new Box(indent + (topWidth/2) - (bottomWidth/2),
                                        bottomHeight, bottomWidth);

        top.drawAt(1);
        base.drawAt(0);
    }
}
```

Screen Output

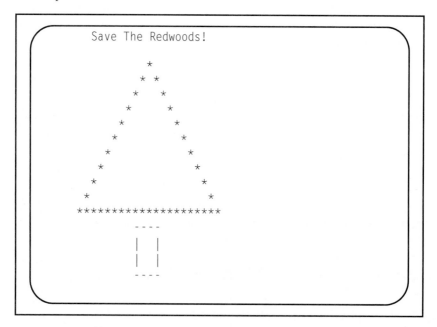

In this case, `f.drawAt(2)` will use the definition of `drawAt` given in `Box`, not the definition of `drawAt` given in `Figure`.)

Other languages do not automatically do late binding as Java does. In many other languages, you must specify in advance what methods may need late binding. This makes Java less efficient but easier to program and less prone to errors.

? SELF-TEST QUESTIONS

5. What is the difference between *this* and *super* when these words are used as the names of methods that are called in a constructor definition?

6. Give the complete definition of a class called `TitledPerson`. `TitledPerson` is to be a derived class of the class `Person` in Display 6.1/page 292. The class `TitledPerson` has one additional `String` instance variable for a title, such as `"Ms"` or `"Mr."` or `"The Honorable"`. The class `TitledPerson` has two constructors, a default constructor and one that sets both the name and the title. It has an `writeOutput` method, a `reset` method, an `equals` method, an accessor method that returns the title, and a `changeTitle` method. For two titled people to be equal, they must have the same name and the same title. You may want to use the class `Student` in Display 6.3/page 294 as a model.

7. Define a class called `Diamond` that is a derived class of the class `Figure`. The class `Diamond` is similar to the class `Triangle`. However, when a `Diamond` is drawn, it has the same sort of top half as a `Triangle`, but it has a bottom half that is an inverted version of its top half.

Chapter Summary

- ◻ A derived class is obtained from a base class by adding addition instance variables and/or additional methods. The derived class inherits all the instance variables and methods that are in the base class.

- ◻ When defining a constructor for a derived class, normally, the first thing that happens is a call to the constructor for the base class.

- ◻ You can redefine a method from a base class so that it has a different definition in the derived class. This is called *overriding* the method definition.

- ◻ Private instance variables and private methods of a base class cannot be accessed directly in a derived class.

- ◻ If A is a derived class of class B, then an object of class A is a member of class A (of course), but it is also a member of class B.

? ANSWERS to Self-Test Questions

1. Yes, a derived class has all the instance variables that the base class has, and can add more instance variables besides.

2. Yes, it will have the methods. Yes, a derived class has all the public methods that the base class has, and also can add more methods. If the derived class does not redefine (override) a method definition, then it does exactly the same action in the derived class as in the base class. However, the base class can contain a new definition (an overriding definition) of the method and the new definition will replace the old definition (provided it has the same number and types of parameters).

3. No.

4. No.

5. *this* names a constructor in the same class as the one being defined. *super* names a constructor for the base class when you are defining a constructor for a derived class.

6.

```
public class TitledPerson extends Person
{
    public TitledPerson()
    {
        super();
        title = "no title yet";
    }

    public TitledPerson(String theName, String theTitle)
    {
        super(theName);
        title = theTitle;
    }

    public void reset(String theName, String theTitle)
    {
        changeName(theName);
        title = theTitle;
    }

    public String theTitle()
    {
        return title;
    }
    public void changeTitle(String newTitle)
    {
        title = newTitle;
    }

    public void writeOutput()
    {
        System.out.println("Name: " + theName());
        System.out.println("Title: " + title);
    }
```

```java
    public boolean equals(TitledPerson otherPerson)
    {
        return (this.sameName(otherPerson)) &&
                (this.title.equalsIgnoreCase(otherPerson.title));
    }

    private String title;
}
```

7.
```java
/************************************************************
 *Class for diamonds to be drawn on screen. For this class, a
 *diamond is completely determined by its diameter.
 *(Screen character spacing determines the rest of the figure.)
 *Inherits offsetValue, resetOffset, and drawAt from Figure.
 ************************************************************/
public class Diamond extends Figure
{
    public Diamond()
    {
        super();
        diameter = 0;
    }

    public Diamond(int theOffset, int theDiameter)
    {
        super(theOffset);
        diameter = theDiameter;
    }

    public void reset(int newOffset, int newDiameter)
    {
        resetOffset(newOffset);
        diameter = newDiameter;
    }

    /*******************************************
     *Draws the figure at the current line.
     *******************************************/
    public void drawHere()
    {
        drawTop();
        drawBottom();
    }
```

```java
public void drawTop()
{
    int startOfLine = offsetValue() + (diameter/2);
    spaces(startOfLine);
    System.out.println('*');
    int count;
    int lineCount = (diameter/2) - 1;
    int insideWidth = 1;
    for (count = 0; count < lineCount; count++)
    {
        startOfLine--;
        spaces(startOfLine);
        System.out.print('*');
        spaces(insideWidth);
        System.out.println('*');
        insideWidth = insideWidth + 2;
    }
}

public void drawBottom()
{
    int startOfLine = offsetValue();
    int count;
    int lineCount = (diameter/2);
    int insideWidth = 2*lineCount - 1;
    for (count = 0; count < lineCount; count++)
    {

        spaces(startOfLine);
        System.out.print('*');
        spaces(insideWidth);
        System.out.println('*');
        insideWidth = insideWidth - 2;
        startOfLine++;
    }
    spaces(startOfLine);
    System.out.println('*');
}

private static void spaces(int number)
{
    <This definition is identical to  that of the method named
         spaces in the class Triangle (Display 6.8/page 314).>
}

private int diameter;
}
```

This question points out that an alternative, and good, way to do these
character graphics classes is to have a utility class with public static meth-

ods, like the method `spaces` and other methods that do things like draw horizontal lines, draw big V's, and inverted big V's.

? PROGRAMMING EXERCISES

1. Give the definition of a class named `Employee` whose objects are records for an employee. This class will be a derived class of the class `Person` given in Display 6.1/page 292. An employee record has an employee's name (inherited from the class `Person`), an annual salary represented as a single value of type *double*, a hired date that gives the year hired as a single value of type *int*, and a social security number, which is a value of type `String`. The social security number could be stored as an integer, but it might be too large an integer. So, use a string. (After all, a social security number is just an arbitrary identifier that does not use any numeric properties. Have you ever had to add two social security numbers? What could the result possible mean?) Be sure your class has a reasonable complement of constructors and accessor methods. Be sure your class has an `equals` method as well. Write a program to fully test your class definitions.

2. In this exercise, you will define two derived classes of the class `Figure` in Display 6.6/page 306. Your two classes will be called `RightArrow` and `LeftArrow`. These classes will be like the classes `Triangle` and `Box`, but they will draw left- and right-pointing arrows that look like the following, which is a right-pointing array:

The size of the arrow is determined by two numbers, one for the size of the "tail," which is 12 in the preceding example, and one for the base of the arrow head, which is 7 in the preceding example. (If the size of the base is an even number, then the tail will not be exactly in the middle of the arrow head. That is OK.) Write a test program for each class that tests all the methods in the class.

Chapter 7

EVENT-DRIVEN PROGRAMMING USING THE AWT

7.1 SOME BACKGROUND 325
GUIs—Graphical User
  Interfaces 325
Event-Driven Programming 325

7.2 SIMPLE WINDOW INTERFACES 327
Gotcha Save All Your Work Before
  Running an AWT Program 327
Programming Example A Simple
  Window 328
Programming Tip Ending an AWT
  Program 332
More About Window Listeners 333
Gotcha Confusing the Classes Frame
  and Window 333
Size Units for Screen Objects 334
Coordinate System for Screen
  Objects 335
More on `paint` and
  `setVisible` 336
Programming Example Another Simple
  Window 340
Some Methods of the Class
  `Frame` 343

**7.3 COMPONENTS, CONTAINERS, AND LAYOUT
  MANAGERS 345**
Programming Example
  Adding Buttons 346
Adding Components to a Container
  Class 349
More Layout Managers 351
The `Button` Class 353

Action Events and Action
  Listeners 354
Programming Tip Copy Other
  Programmer's Code 356
Programming Tip Guide for Creating
  Simple Window Interfaces 357
The `WindowListener` Interface
  (Optional) 362

7.4 PANELS AND TEXT COMPONENTS 365
The `Panel` Class 365
Text Areas and Text Fields 368
Labels for Text Fields and Other
  Components 372
Inputting and Outputting
  Numbers 376
Case Study
  A GUI Adding Machine 379

7.5 ADDING MENUS 385
Programming Example A GUI with a
  Menu 385
Menu Bars, Menus, and Menu
  Items 389
Nested Menus 390
Gotcha Different Events with the
  Same Labels 392
Additional Examples of Using the
  AWT 392

7.6 INNER CLASSES *(Optional)* 393
Helping Classes *(Optional)* 393
Chapter Summary 396
Answers to Self-Test Questions 397
Programming Exercises 401

7

Event-Driven Programming Using the AWT

....

One picture is worth more than a thousand words.
CHINESE PROVERB

Introduction

So far, your programs have used the simplest form of input. The user enters simple text at the keyboard and simple, unadorned text is sent to the screen as output. Modern programs do not work this way. Modern programs have a host of graphical interfaces for the user, such as menus that allow the user to make choices with a mouse. In this chapter, you will learn how to write Java programs that create such modern windowing environments for input and output. We will do this using a special library of classes called the **Abstract Window Toolkit**, or **AWT** for short. It's called a *toolkit* because it includes classes that are designed to be the tools or building blocks of a windowing system. The AWT is a standard library that comes with all versions of Java. The AWT is not the world's fanciest windowing toolkit, but it is quite adequate for our purposes, and at the present time, it is the only really portable windowing toolkit that is available for Java.

Even though the AWT is not the world's fanciest windowing toolkit, it is still a complex collection of software. This chapter will introduce you to enough of the AWT to write simple windowing interfaces, but we will not be able to cover every aspect of the AWT.

Prerequisites

Except for those sections that state that they are not used later in the book, you need to have read Chapters 1 through 6 for this or almost any of the following chapters. However, this is the first major choice point in reading this book. You need not read this chapter next. If you prefer, you may read some or all of Chapter 8 on exception handling before you read this chapter. Alternatively, you could read much of Chapter 9 on files and/or much of Chapter 10 on arrays before reading either this chapter or Chapter 8. In fact, most of the rest of this book can be read without reading this chapter, but to write modern programs with nice user interfaces, you will want the material in this chapter at some point.

7.1 Some Background

> *event* **n. 1.** *An occurrence, incident, or experience, especially one of some*
> *significance.*
> **The American Heritage Dictionary of the English Language, First Edition**

We begin with some general background about the elements in any windowing interface and about a method of programming known as *event-driven programming.*

GUIs — Graphical User Interfaces

Windowing systems that interact with the user are often called *GUIs*. **GUI** is pronounced "gooey" and stands for **graphical user interface**. The words are pretty much
self-explanatory. It's called *graphical* because it uses graphical elements such as windows, buttons, and menus. It's called a *user interface* because it is the part of a program that interfaces with the user. A GUI obtains information from the user and
gives it to the program for processing, and when the program is finished processing
the information, the GUI gives the results to the user, usually in some sort of window.

GUI

     Let's just briefly list the terms used for some basic elements that make up a
GUI. Although you have undoubtedly used all these elements before, you may not
have given them the same names that we will use. A **window** is a portion of the
user's screen that serves as a smaller screen within the screen. A window usually
has a border defining its outside edges and a title of some sort giving the window a
name. Inside of a window you may have smaller windowlike objects. Some of these
smaller windowlike objects are *menus*. A **menu** is a list of alternatives offered to the
user, usually by offering a list of names. The user chooses one of these alternatives,
usually by clicking it with a mouse. A **button** is very similar to an entry in a menu. A
button is simply something that looks like a button to be pushed and that typically
has a label. The user can click the mouse on the button to do the equivalent of
pushing the button.These elements will have more precise definitions within the
AWT, but these are the basic properties they have within any windowing system.

window

menu

button

GUI

Windowing systems that interact with the user are often called **GUI**s. *GUI* is pronounced "gooey" and stands for
graphical user interface.

    ◻

Event-Driven Programming

AWT programs and virtually all other graphical user interface (GUI) programs use
events and *event handlers*. An **event** in a graphical user interface is an object that represents some action such as clicking a mouse, dragging the mouse, pressing a key on
the keyboard, choosing a close-window command on a menu, or any other action
that is expected to elicit a response. Events are more general than just the events of
a graphical user interface. For example, a message from a printer to the operating

event

system saying that the printer is ready to print another document can be considered an event. However, in this chapter, the only events that we will be concerned with are those generated within a graphical user interface.

firing an event

listener

event handler

When an object generates an event, that is called **firing** the event. In the AWT, every object that can fire events, such as a button that might be clicked, can have one or more **listener objects**. You the programmer specify what objects are the listener objects for any given object that might fire an event. For example, if you click a button, that fires an event, and if the button has a listener object associated with it, then the event is automatically sent to this listener object. A listener object has methods that specify what will happen when events of various kinds are sent to the listener. These methods that handle events are called **event handlers**. You the programmer will define (or redefine) these event-handler methods.

Notice that event-driven programming is very different from the sort of programming we've seen before now. All our previous programs consisted of a list of statements executed in some order. There were some variations on this theme of performing a list of statements: Loops repeat statements, branches choose one of a list of statements to do next, and a method invocation brings in a different list of statements to be executed. However, at some level, all the programs we have seen so far were designed to be performed by one agent (the computer) following a simple set of instructions of the form "first do this, then do that, then do something else, and so forth." Event-driven programming is a very different game. In event-driven programming, you create objects that can fire events and you create listener objects to react to the events. For the most part, your program does not determine the order in which things happen. The events determine the order in which things happen. When an event-driven program is running, the next thing that happens depends on the next event. Listener objects are almost like people sitting around a room waiting for phone calls. Each person has her or his own phone. When the phone rings, the person with that phone answers and does whatever the phone call says to do. Maybe the message says, "Joe this is your mother calling, I want you to close the window in your room." Then, Joe goes home and closes the window in her or his room. In a graphical user interface, the message is something like "close the window" or "The 'A' key has been pressed" or "The mouse was dragged" from someplace to someplace else. When an event is fired, it is automatically sent to the listener object(s) for the particular object that fired the event. The listener object then calls the appropriate event-handling method to handle the event.

If you have never done event-driven programming before, one aspect of event-driven programming may seem strange to you: *You will be writing definitions for methods that you will never invoke in any program.* This may seem strange because a method is of no value unless it is invoked. So somebody or something other than you the programmer must be invoking these methods. That is exactly what does happen. The AWT system automatically calls certain methods when an event signals that the method needs to be called. For example, objects that are drawn on the screen have a method called `paint` that draws the object. For example, the inside of a window is drawn on your monitor screen by a suitable `paint` method. The AWT system knows when to call the method `paint`, but sometimes you must define (or redefine) the method `paint`, because only you the programmer know what is supposed to be drawn on the screen.

The event-driven programming that we will be doing with the AWT library makes extensive use of inheritance. The classes that you define will be derived classes of some basic predefined classes that are in the AWT library. When you define these classes, they will inherit methods from their parent class, such as the `paint` method (which displays objects on the screen). Some of these inherited methods will work fine just as they were written for the parent class (i.e., the base class). However, very often it will be necessary to override a method definition to provide a new definition that is appropriate to the derived class. For example, suppose you create a window that displays some text, perhaps a help window that explains something to the user. This window will inherit a `paint` method. However, the inherited `paint` method does not know anything about what text is to be displayed. So you must redefine the `paint` method for this class so that it displays the appropriate text. In Section 7.2, we illustrated all this with some actual Java programs.

? SELF-TEST QUESTIONS

1. How does event-driven programming differ from the sort of programming we did in previous chapters?

2. How is *GUI* pronounced and what do the letters stand for?

7.2 Simple Window Interfaces

You can observe a lot just by watching.
ATTRIBUTED TO YOGI BERRA

A **window** is a portion of the user's screen that serves as a smaller screen within the screen. A window has a border defining its outside edges and a title, usually given within the top border. In this section, we will tell you how to create simple windows using the AWT. There are lots of things you can put in a window when designing a GUI interface. We will start with some simple, but very useful, elements and show you how to build windows with these elements. The window elements we will introduce in this section are a way to close (i.e., end) the window, a way to put text in the window, a way to color the window, and way to put a title on the window. This may not seem like much to do with a window, but this will introduce you to the basic methods for doing all kinds of programming with the AWT. In future sections, we will use the techniques you learn here to introduce menus, buttons, and more versatile text areas to your windows.

⚠ GOTCHA Save All Your Work Before Running an AWT Program

Programs that use the AWT can take control of your computer screen, mouse, and keyboard. If they go awry, and they often do, then the usual ways of communication with the computer may be shut down. On a PC, this may require that you reboot your computer. On any system, this may require that you, in some sense, "restart the whole thing." If you are editing some file, or performing some other task, do not simply stop doing the editing but actually close the file before running any AWT program that you have not yet fully debugged. If the AWT causes you to restart your computer, any open files may be damaged.

▼ *PROGRAMMING EXAMPLE* A Simple Window

Display 7.1 contains a Java program that produces a simple window using the AWT. Below it is a rendering of what the screen will look like when you run this program. This window does not do very much. It simply appears on the screen and contains
close-window
button
the text "Please, don't click that button!" Just about the only other thing it can do is disappear. If you click the close-window button, the program will end and the window will disappear. The picture shown is a typical example of the kind of window produced. The window may look slightly different on your system, but should look similar to other windows on your system. On many systems, the close-window button is in the upper right-hand corner, as it is in Display 7.1. On other systems, the close-window button is in the upper left-hand corner. Also, you may need to double click the close-window button to get the window to close. The close-window button on an AWT window will probably behave the same as on any other window on your system. Now, let's look at the code for this first GUI program.

The first two lines, repeated in what follows, says that the program uses the AWT library and that it uses the event model in the AWT library. Any program using the AWT library should contain these two lines at the beginning of the file containing the program (possibly along with other *import* statements).

java.awt.*
```
import java.awt.*;
import java.awt.event.*;
```

After these *import* statements, we have the first line of the class definition, which we repeat:

```
public class FirstWindow extends Frame
```

Frame
This says that our window is a Frame (i.e., it is a derived class with base class Frame). A Frame in the AWT is what you probably think of as a window. There is an AWT class called Window, but it is so simple that it is seldom used when you are writing GUI applications with the AWT. (The class Window is actually the parent class of the class Frame. Objects of the class Window are little more than an area of the screen with nothing on them.) A Frame is a very simple window, but it does have a border, a place for a title, and the close-window button that you expect to find on any window. Think of Frame as a basic window class that is defined in the AWT. When you define a class, like FirstWindow that extends Frame, you are adding properties to the Frame. So, an object of the class FirstWindow is a slightly more complicated window than a Frame.

The class FirstWindow only has two methods, a paint method and a main method. The method paint is not called by our code, but is called by the AWT system. The code for paint is

Display 7.1 A Simple Window Constructed with the AWT
••

```java
import java.awt.*;
import java.awt.event.*;

public class FirstWindow extends Frame
{
    public static final int WIDTH = 300;
    public static final int HEIGHT = 200;

    /**********************************************************
     *A simple demonstration of a window constructed with AWT.
     **********************************************************/
    public static void main(String[] args)
    {
        FirstWindow myWindow = new FirstWindow();
        myWindow.setSize(WIDTH, HEIGHT);

        WindowDestroyer listener = new WindowDestroyer();
        myWindow.addWindowListener(listener);

        myWindow.setVisible(true);
    }

    public void paint(Graphics g)
    {
        g.drawString("Please, don't click that button!", 75, 100);
    }
}
```

Resulting GUI

Close-window button. It might be in a different place on your system.

Untitled			$\times$

```
    Please, don't click that button!
```

••

```
public void paint(Graphics g)
{
    g.drawString("Please, don't click that button!", 75, 100);
}
```

Graphics

drawString

This method is called automatically by the AWT system and is passed one argument of type Graphics. You can think of the parameter g of type Graphics as a portion of the screen in which the "painting" is to take place. In this case, the AWT will pass paint a Graphics object g such that g determines the portion of the screen that is inside our window, and that is where the text in our first window is written. Every Graphics object, such as g, has a (predefined) method called drawString and our paint method calls this method g.drawString. The effect in this case is to write the string "Please don't click that button!" in the window starting at the coordinates specified by the next two arguments, 75 and 100. The units for the numbers 75 and 100 are dependent on your particular programming environment, so you may have to fiddle with these numbers to get things to look good on your screen. The AWT coordinate system is discussed in a later subsection of this chapter. Notice that the AWT takes care of creating the Graphics object g and passing it to the paint method. This is all done automatically. You do not normally write an explicit call to the paint method.

OK, now let's run the program. When we run the program, the method main, shown in what follows, is called:

```
public static void main(String[] args)
{
    FirstWindow myWindow = new FirstWindow();
    myWindow.setSize(WIDTH, HEIGHT);

    WindowDestroyer listener = new WindowDestroyer();
    myWindow.addWindowListener(listener);

    myWindow.setVisible(true);
}
```

This code creates a new object called myWindow that is a member of the class FirstWindow. It then calls the predefined method setSize, which is inherited from the class Frame, and this gives the window a size of 300 by 200, since the defined constants WIDTH and HEIGHT were defined to be 300 and 200. The units of size are implementation-dependent and so the size will actually vary from one system to another. Since we made the window dimensions defined constants, it is easy to change the constant values if you need to do so in order to make the window look better on your particular system.

You close this window by clicking the close-window button. When you click that button, the window fires an event and sends it to a listener object. The listener object closes the window. In this program, the listener object is an object named listener, which is a member of the class WindowDestroyer. The following line (from the preceding main) creates a new object of the class WindowDestroyer and names it listener:

Window-
Destroyer

```
WindowDestroyer listener = new WindowDestroyer();
```

The next line, shown in what follows, associates the object `listener` with the object (the window) `myWindow` so that `listener` will receive any event fired by the object `myWindow`:

```
myWindow.addWindowListener(listener);
```

An object, like `listener`, that receives events from an object is called a **listener**. Associating the listener with the object it is listening to is called **registering the listener**.

registering a listener

An object of the class `WindowDestroyer` will close the window `myWindow` when `myWindow` fires an appropriate event. We need to define the class `WindowDestroyer`, but let's postpone that for a bit, and for now, just assume that the class `WindowDestroyer` has been defined so that, when the user clicks the close-window button of `myWindow`, the object `listener` will close `myWindow` and end the program.

The last statement in `main` is a call to the method `setVisible`:

```
myWindow.setVisible(true);
```

This call to `setVisible` makes the window named `myWindow` visible on the screen. The method `setVisible` is another predefined, inherited method. With the argument *true*, as in Display 7.1/page 329, the object is displayed. If the argument *false* were to be used instead, then the object would not be shown.

That's the end of the code for `main`, but not the end of the program. The window just sits on the screen looking pretty until the user clicks the close-window button. At that point, an event `e` is fired by the object `myWindow`; the event `e` is sent to the listener object called `listener`. The object `listener` recognizes `e` as an event signaling that the object `myWindow` should be closed and `listener` then closes the window and ends the program.

The object `listener` is a member of the class `WindowDestroyer`. We have been assuming that the class `WindowDestroyer` has already been defined, but we need to define it and compile it before we can really run the program in Display 7.1. So, let's define the class `WindowDestroyer`.

The listener class `WindowDestroyer` is defined in Display 7.2. A listener class for a GUI that involves windows (more precisely, that involves a descendent class of the class `Frame`) will often be a derived class of the class `WindowAdapter`. This is indicated by the phrase *extends* `WindowAdapter` on the first line of the class definition. A derived class of the class `WindowAdapter`, such as our class `WindowDestroyer`, inherits all its methods from `WindowAdapter`. Each of these methods automatically respond to a different kind of event. Normally, no new methods are added, since there already is a method for each kind of event. However, the way the event is handled is up to you and should depend on the window you are defining. So, normally, you would redefine (override) one or more of the method definitions that your class inherits from `WindowAdapter`.

WindowAdapter

The class `WindowAdapter` has a number of different methods, each of which processes a different kind of event. All these methods are inherited by the class `WindowDestroyer`. These inherited methods determine the names of the methods, but you need to determine what the methods do by redefining the methods. However, you only need to define (actually redefine) those methods that your window will use. For this application, the only kind of event that we need our listener class to respond to is an event that signals the closing of the window. The method that

Display 7.2 A Listener Class for Window Events

```java
import java.awt.*;
import java.awt.event.*;

/***********************************************************************
 *If you register an object of this class as a listener to any object
 *of the class Frame, then if the user clicks the close-window button
 *in the Frame, the object of this class will end the program and
 *close the Frame. (It will also respond to other "closing-window"
 *events, but you need not worry about that now.)
 ***********************************************************************/
public class WindowDestroyer extends WindowAdapter
{
    public void windowClosing(WindowEvent e)
    {
        System.exit(0);
    }
}
```

handles those events is named `windowClosing`. So, we have only redefined the method `windowClosing`. The method definition is very simple, it simply executes the one command

```java
System.exit(0);
```

and as we explain in the following programming tip, this ends the program and so closes the window.

In order to run the program in Display 7.1, you must define and compile both the class `FirstWindow` in Display 7.1 and the class `WindowDestroyer` in Display 7.2.

◑ PROGRAMMING TIP *Ending an AWT Program*

A GUI program is normally based on an infinite loop of sorts. There may or may not be a Java loop statement in the program, but, normally, the GUI program still need not ever end. The windowing system normally stays on the screen until the user indicates that it should go away (e.g., by clicking a close-window button). If the user never asked the system to go away, it would never go away. When you write a GUI program (using the AWT), you need some way to say "End the program now." The following statement will end a Java program as soon as this statement is executed:

System.exit

```java
System.exit(0);
```

This will end any Java program. A Java program that uses System.exit does not have to use the AWT, but we will often use this statement in AWT programs.

The number 0 given as the argument to System.exit is returned to the operating system. In many situations, you can use any number and the program will behave the same. But, most operating systems use 0 to indicate a normal termination of the program and 1 to indicate an abnormal termination of the program (just the opposite of what most people would guess). Thus, if your System.exit statement ends your program normally, the argument should be 0. An example of using this System.exit statement can be found in the definition of the method window-Closing in Display 7.2.

More About Window Listeners

As with our window listener class named WindowDestroyer in Display 7.2, any window listener class is normally a derived class of the class WindowAdapter. The class WindowAdapter has a number of different methods, each of which is automatically invoked when the listener object is sent an event that matches that method. The methods and corresponding events are given in the table in Display 7.3. When you define a derived class of the class WindowAdapter, you only define those methods that you need. The class WindowDestroyer is only needed to close windows, and so when we defined WindowDestroyer, we only defined the method windowClosing. We will not need any of these methods except windowClosing, but Display 7.3 lists all the methods for completeness.

    In discussing our definition of the class WindowDestroyer in Display 7.2, it would be more proper for us to say that we *redefined* the method windowClosing rather than saying we *defined* it. This is because we are changing the definition of windowClosing. If in the definition of a derived class of the class WindowAdapter we give no definition for a method, then the class inherits the definition from the class WindowAdapter. But, that is not as big an issue as it seems. All of the methods in the class windowAdapter do absolutely nothing. The methods are only useful if they are overridden in some derived class, such as the class WindowDestroyer. The class WindowAdapter is a special kind of class known as an **abstract class**, which means that you cannot use it directly. You can only use it as a base class when defining other classes.

WindowAdapter

abstract class

⚠ **GOTCHA** *Confusing the Classes Frame and Window*

The basic AWT class for a window in a GUI is the Frame class. When you construct a class for a *windowing interface*, you normally do so by defining a derived class of the class Frame. There is also a class called Window in the AWT. However, the class Window corresponds to a much simpler screen object than what we usually think of as a *window*. Thus, when people speak loosely of *windows*, then, in terms of the AWT, they are speaking of the class Frame. They are not talking about the class Window. Remember, that the word *window*, with a lowercase *w*, is a general term and

Display 7.3 Methods in the Class `WindowAdapter`
••

`public void windowOpened(WindowEvent e)`
Invoked when a window has been opened.

`public void windowClosing(WindowEvent e)`
Invoked when a window is in the process of being closed. The close operation can be overridden at this point. Clicking the close-window button causes an invocation of this method.

`public void windowClosed(WindowEvent e)`
Invoked when a window has been closed.

`public void windowIconified(WindowEvent e)`
Invoked when a window is iconified.

`public void windowDeiconified(WindowEvent e)`
Invoked when a window is deiconified.

`public void windowActivated(WindowEvent e)`
Invoked when a window is activated.

`public void windowDeactivated(WindowEvent e)`
Invoked when a window is deactivated.

not a technical term in the AWT. When you see or hear *window*, think `Frame` if you are writing an AWT program.

(To confuse things even more, the class `Frame` is a derived class of the class `Window`. So, every `Frame` is also a `Window`. However, you would normally refer to a `Frame` as a `Frame`, since `Frame` is the more specific term.)

Size Units for Screen Objects

pixel

When using the AWT, the size of an object on the screen is measured in *pixels*. A **pixel** is the smallest unit of space on which your screen can write. Think of a pixel as a small rectangle that can have one of a small fixed number of colors and think of your screen as being paved with these little pixels. (It may help to think in terms of a simple black-and-white screen where a pixel is either black or white, even though most screens now offer more colors than just black and white.) The more pixels you have on your screen, the greater the resolution on your screen. That is, the more pixels you have, the more fine detail you can see. The size of a pixel depends on the size of your screen and the resolution of your screen. Although the AWT uses pixels as if they were units of length, they do not represent any fixed length. The length of a pixel will vary from one screen to another. On a screen with high resolution (lots of pixels), an object of size 300 by 200 will look very small. On a screen with low resolution (not many pixels), an object of size 300 by 200 will look very large. For example, consider the following statement from Display 7.1/page 329:

```
myWindow.setSize(WIDTH, HEIGHT);
```

which is equivalent to

```
myWindow.setSize(300, 200);
```

This says that the object myWindow (which happens to be a kind of window) will be 300 pixels wide and 200 pixels high, but the actual size will depend on the resolution of the screen you are using when you run the program.

Notice that, although Java and the AWT are portable and the code you write with the AWT will run on any system that supports Java, the exact size of what you produce on the screen will vary from one screen to another. This is one feature of Java that is not as portable as would be ideal. To get the desired size for a window created with the AWT, you may need to change the dimensions to suit your particular screen size and screen resolution. However, it is only the absolute size that will vary. At least the relative size of things will be the same no matter where you run your AWT application. Moreover, for most windowlike objects on most systems, after the window is displayed, the user can resize the window using the mouse.

Pixels

A **pixel** is the smallest unit of space on which your screen can write. The more pixels you have on a screen, the greater the screen resolution. With the AWT, both size and position of objects on the screen are measured in pixels. Thus, a screen object will look smaller on a screen with high resolution and larger on a screen with low resolution.

Resolution versus Size

The relationship of resolution and size can seem confusing at first. A high-resolution screen is a screen of better quality than a low-resolution screen, so why does an object look smaller on a high-resolution screen? Isn't bigger better? It's not quite that simple. You have to think of counting pixels if you want a complete explanation, but here's one way to make it seem more sensible: If a screen has low resolution, you cannot see smaller things. Thus, when a screen has low resolution, the only way it can display a small object is to make it larger.

Coordinate System for Screen Objects

A Graphics object, such as the parameter g for the paint method in Display 7.1/page 329 can be thought of as an area of the screen. Within this area of the screen, you use coordinates to refer to a particular spot. The Graphics object has a coordinate system that is illustrated in Display 7.4. The origin point (0, 0) is the upper left-hand corner of the Graphics object. The x-coordinate, or horizontal coordinate, is positive and increasing to the right. The y-coordinate, or vertical coordinate, is positive and increasing in the downward direction. Thus, a Graphics object has all positive coordinates for the locations within its screen area. For example, consider the following:

```
g.drawString("Please, don't click that button!", 75, 100);
```

This statement (taken from Display 7.1) will write the string "Please, don't click that button!" starting at a point with x-coordinate 75 and y-coordinate

Display 7.4 Screen Coordinate System

(width, height)

(0, 0)

Increasing x direction

X (75, 100)

Increasing y direction

100. To see where that point is, you start in the upper left-hand corner of the window and count 75 pixels to the right and 100 pixels down.

More on `paint` and `setVisible`

Every window and in fact every object of any kind that you display on the screen will

paint

normally have a method called `paint` that draws the object on the screen. Often, you the programmer will need to give the definition of the method `paint`. In some cases, the method `paint` will be simply inherited by the object, but for the objects we are looking at now, the programmer must define the method `paint`.

The method `paint` is called for you automatically. You do not have to worry about when it should be called or by whom or how it is called, but you do have to worry about what `paint` needs to do. Notice the screen display in Display 7.1/page 329. That entire window display needs to be "painted" on the screen, but our definition of the method `paint` only says to paint the text `"Please don't click that button!"` Another portion of the AWT takes care of "painting" the window borders, the title bar (which is untitled in this example), and the close-window button. This is all fine. The more that is done for you, the easier it is for you. But how do you decide what you must do and what is done for you? Here are some guidelines for what to put in the definition of `paint`: The method `paint` only repaints the things you, the programmer, put inside an object. Those things that are a standard part of your local windowing system are taken care of automatically. When deciding what needs to go in the definition of the method `paint`, ask yourself if it is something that is on every window in your windowing system, such as a border or a close-window button? If so, then do not try to put it in the method paint. Then ask yourself, is it something that you have added to this particular window and that is not in every window, like some text in the window? If so, then you probably need to put it in paint.

Now that you know what kinds of things the method paint needs to do, you next need to know the details of how to express these instructions. To start with, let's explain the parameter g in the following definition of the method paint, which we have copied from Display 7.1 and displayed in what follows:

Graphics

```
public void paint(Graphics g)
{
    g.drawString("Please, don't click that button!", 75, 100);
}
```

The parameter g is an object of type Graphics. The method paint will normally have a parameter of type Graphics. You can think of this Graphics object g as a portion of the screen. When the method paint is invoked, it is given an argument that is an object g of type Graphics. Among other things, this object g tells the method paint where on the screen it should do its "painting." But, an object g of type Graphics is not just a portion of the screen. An object of type Graphics does define a portion of the screen, but it also is an object with methods of its own, such as the method drawString. The method drawString writes the string given as its first argument starting at the coordinates specified by the last two arguments.

drawString

The drawString **Method**

Every object of type Graphics has a method called drawString that can write text starting at specified coordinates.

Syntax:

Graphics_Object.drawString(*String*, *x_Coordinate*, *y_Coordinate*);

The *String* is written starting at position (*x_Coordinate, y_Coordinate*) of the *Graphics_Object*.

Example (used within a paint **method):**

```
public void paint(Graphics g)
{
    g.drawString("Please, don't click that button!", 75, 100);
}
```

Next let's consider the method setVisible, which is called in the main part of the program in Display 7.1/page 329. The particular line from Display 7.1 is the following:

setVisible

```
myWindow.setVisible(true);
```

Every AWT object that can be displayed on the screen has a setVisible method. If you the programmer do not define a method setVisible for a GUI class, then the method setVisible will be inherited. In practice, you can just assume that the method setVisible will be there when you need it.

The paint **Method**

Every window and in fact every object of any kind that you display on the screen will normally have a paint method. You do not normally need to write any invocations of the method paint. The method paint is normally called for you automatically, but you will often need to give the definition of the method paint.

Syntax:

```
public void paint(Graphics g)
{
        <Instructions for displaying all but the very standard
             features of the window (or other object) go here.>
}
```

The parameter g can be thought of as an area of the screen that will contain the window (or other object).

Example:

```
public void paint(Graphics g)
{
    g.drawString("Please, don't click that button!", 75, 100);
}
```

The method setVisible takes one argument of type *boolean*. In other words, the argument to setVisible is either *true* or *false*. If w is an object, such as a window, that can be displayed on the screen, then the call

```
w.setVisible(true);
```

will make w visible and the call

```
w.setVisible(false);
```

will make w invisible.

You might think that displaying an object on the screen should happen automatically. After all, why would you define a window display unless you want it to be displayed on the screen? The answer is that you may not want it to be displayed at all times. You have undoubtedly worked with windowing systems where some windows come and go, either because they are no longer needed (like a pull-down menu after you make a choice) or because the window is covered by other windows. The AWT cannot read the programmer's mind to determine when the window (or other GUI object) should be displayed and so the programmer must tell the system when to display the window. The programmer tells the system when to display the window by inserting a call to the method setVisible. If you rerun the program from Display 7.1 but omit the invocation of setVisible, then you will see nothing on the screen. The window will be constructed, but will not be displayed. (But be warned, if you eliminate the call to setVisible and then run the program in Display 7.1, you will then have no close-window button and so no way to end the program!)

The setVisible **Method**

Every AWT object that can be displayed on the screen will have a setVisible method. Normally, you the programmer do not define the method setVisible. Normally, the method setVisible is simply inherited.

The method setVisible takes one argument of type *boolean*. If w is an object, such as a window, that can be displayed on the screen, then the call

```
w.setVisible(true);
```

will make w visible and the call

```
w.setVisible(false);
```

will hide w, that is, will make w invisible.

Syntax (for an invocation of the setVisible **method):**

Object_For_Screen.setVisible(*true_or_false*);

Example (from Display 7.1/page 329):

```
public static void main(String[] args)
{
    FirstWindow myWindow = new FirstWindow();
    myWindow.setSize(WIDTH, HEIGHT);


    WindowDestroyer listener = new WindowDestroyer();
    myWindow.addWindowListener(listener);

    myWindow.setVisible(true);
}
```

You know that you need an invocation of setVisible in order to display a window, but why do you need both setVisible and paint? Aren't they doing the same thing? Well, yes and no. The method paint is a tool that gives instructions for displaying some elements of a GUI object. The method setVisible is the command to display (or hide) the entire object on the screen. An invocation of setVisible(*true*), among other things will lead to an invocation of paint. The method paint is a tool. The method setVisible is one of your commands and setVisible may use the tool paint. (In fact, the process is a bit more involved. The method setVisible(*true*) typically produces a call to the method repaint and the method repaint then produces a call to the method paint. Moreover, some of this may pass through calls to your local windowing system. But, since most of this is automatic, you need not worry about the exact details.)

? SELF-TEST QUESTIONS

....

3. How would you change the program in Display 7.1/page 329 so that the text in the window reads "I love you!" instead of "Please, don't click that button!"?

4. What units of measure are used in the following call to setSize that appeared in the main method of the program in Display 7.1/page 329? In other words, 300 of what? Inches? Feet? Centimeters? And similarly 200 of what?

```
myWindow.setSize(WIDTH, HEIGHT);
```

which is equivalent to

```
myWindow.setSize(300, 200);
```

5. What predefined class from the AWT do you normally use to define a window? Any window class that you define would be normally a derived class of this class.

6. Give a Java statement that, when executed, will immediately end the program.

▼ PROGRAMMING EXAMPLE Another Simple Window

Display 7.5 contains a slight variant on the class shown in Display 7.1/page 329. This version has three new elements, a title, namely, "Second Window", a background color, namely, blue, and a new way of invoking the method addWindowListener. Moreover, we have placed most of the initializing for the window in a constructor (so that the initializations are essentially part of the class definition and not simply actions performed by objects of the class).

We have given the window a title with the following method invocation

setTitle

```
setTitle("Second Window");
```

The method setTitle is inherited from the class Frame. (Recall that the class for our window is a derived class of the class Frame.) The method setTitle takes one string argument and writes that string in the title bar of the window. There is no calling object for this invocation because it is in a constructor and the calling object is an implicit *this*. The preceding invocation is equivalent to

```
this.setTitle("Second Window");
```

Other method invocations in the constructor also have an implicit *this*.

In Display 7.5, we have also given the window a background color with the method call

set-
Background

```
setBackground(Color.blue);
```

The method setBackground is another method that is inherited from the class Frame. The method setBackground takes one argument, which is a color. The AWT has a

Display 7.5 Another Simple Window Constructed with the AWT

```java
import java.awt.*;
import java.awt.event.*;

public class SecondWindow extends Frame
{
    public static final int WIDTH = 550;
    public static final int HEIGHT = 400;

    /************************************************************
    *Creates and displays a window of the class SecondWindow.
    *************************************************************/
    public static void main(String[] args)
    {
        SecondWindow myWindow = new SecondWindow();
        myWindow.setVisible(true);
    }

    public SecondWindow()
    {
        super();
        addWindowListener(new WindowDestroyer());
        setTitle("Second Window");
        setSize(WIDTH, HEIGHT);
        setBackground(Color.blue);
    }

    public void paint(Graphics g)
    {
        g.drawString("Coming to you in living color!", 10, 100);
    }
}
```

Resulting GUI

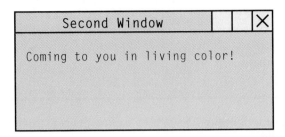

class, named `Color`, that defines many of the common colors. `Color.blue` is a predefined constant that stands for the color blue. Other color constants are listed in Display 7.6. To see what each of these colors looks like, replace the constant `Color.blue` in Display 7.6 with the color you want to see, compile, and then run the modified program. You can also define your own colors with the class `Color`, but we will not go into that topic in this text.

We added a listener for our window with the following invocation of the method `addWindowListener`:

new in
arguments

```
addWindowListener(new WindowDestroyer());
```

Certain methods, such as `addWindowListener`, need objects as arguments, but once the object is given as an argument to the method, you never need to refer to it again in your programming. That means that you do not need a name for the argument. An argument such as *new* `Windowdestroyer()` in the preceding invocation of the method `addWindowListener` is a way to create an object and pass it as an argument to the method `addWindowListener`, and yet not have to give the argument a name. The invocation

```
addWindowListener(new WindowDestroyer());
```

is equivalent to the following:

```
WindowDestroyer listener = new WindowDestroyer();
addWindowListener(listener):
```

The only difference between the preceding two ways of adding a window listener is that in the first form, we do not bother to create a name for the object of type `WindowDestroyer`, and in the second, two-line version, we give the listener object the name `listener`.

Using *new* as Part of a Method Argument

You can create an object and pass it as an argument to a method without bothering to give the object a name. You do this by using *new* and the class name as the argument. In these cases, the class name is being used as the name of the constructor for the class.

Syntax:

Method_Name(*new Class_Name_As_Constructor*(*Arguments*));

Example (within a constructor or other method definition for the class):

```
addWindowListener(new WindowDestroyer());
```

Example (with a calling object named `myWindow`**):**

```
myWindow.addWindowListener(new WindowDestroyer());
```

Note that the constructor in Display 7.5 starts by calling the constructor for the parent class `Frame` with the line

```
super();
```

This ensures that any initialization that is normally done for all objects of type `Frame` in fact will be done. When defining classes by inheritance from AWT classes, this is

Display 7.6 Some AWT Colors

```
Color.white          Color.yellow
Color.gray           Color.green
Color.black          Color.magenta
Color.red            Color.cyan
Color.pink           Color.blue
Color.orange
```

always safe and sometimes absolutely necessary. (Actually, *if the base-class construc-tor you call has no arguments,* then it will be called automatically whether or not you put in `super()`; however, it is clearer to explicitly include a call to the base-class constructor in all cases.)

You may wonder why we left the call to `setVisible` in the method `main` instead of putting in the constructor along with the other initializing actions in Dis-play 7.5/page 341. It would be legal to put the call to `setVisible` in the constructor, but showing a window is normally something that is done by some program compo-nent that uses the window and not by the window itself. In this way, an application can make the window appear and disappear.

Finally, you may wonder why we do not need to say anything about the title `"Second Window"` in the `paint` method. The reason we do not need to say anything about the title is that every object of the class `Frame` has a title and so your local windowing system will take care of painting in the title. On the other hand, not every window has text, such as `"Coming to you in living color!"` written inside the window. So, you must tell `paint` about this text. Now, you may object that the window in Display 7.1/page 329 has no title, but in fact it does. The title of the window in Display 7.1 is `"Untitled"`. If you do not specify a title for an object of the class `Frame` (or of one of its derived classes), then the title will be the string `"Untitled"`.

Some Methods of the Class `Frame`

Display 7.7 contains some of the methods for the class `Frame`. You will recall that `Frame` is the basic class out of which you normally build windows.

? SELF-TEST QUESTIONS

7. How would you modify the program in Display 7.5/page 341 so that the window is pink instead of blue.

8. How do you set the title of a window you create with the AWT?

9. What is the command to display a window on the screen?

10. Rewrite the following without using a name for the object `listener`:

```
WindowDestroyer listener = new WindowDestroyer();
addWindowListener(listener);
```

Display 7.7 Some Methods in the Class `Frame`

Method	Description
`void addWindowListener(` `        WindowListener ear)`	Registers `ear` as a listener for events fired by the `Frame`.
`void setSize(int width, int height)`	Resizes the window to the specified width and height.
`void setVisible(boolean b)`	Makes the window visible if the argument is `true`. Makes it invisible if the argument is `false`.
`void show()`	Similar to `setVisible(true)`, but it does more. If there are multiple windows on the screen, then `show` will not only make it visible, but will also bring it to the front. WARNING: `show` should not be used for objects that are *not* descendents of the class `Frame` or the class `Window`, even though that might work on some older systems.
`void setTitle(String title)`	Writes the title on the title bar of the window.
`void setForeground(Color c)`	Sets the foreground color to `c`.
`void setBackground(Color c)`	Sets the background color to `c`.
`void repaint()`	Repaints the window. This will result in a call to `paint`. If you think you need to write an explicit invocation of `paint`, it is probably preferable instead to write an invocation of `repaint`.
`void paint(Graphics g)`	Paints the window using `g` to specify where the painting is done.

7.3 Components, Containers, and Layout Managers

An empty bag cannot stand upright.
BENJAMIN FRANKLIN, *Poor Richard's Almanac* **(1740)**

When you use the AWT to make a GUI, you build new classes for the windows out of already existing classes. There are two principal ways that you build new classes out of old classes. First, as you have already seen in our introductory examples, you use inheritance. For example, to build a window interface, you normally use the AWT class `Frame` and make your window a derived class of the class `Frame`. The second way to make new classes out of old classes is to use one of the AWT classes as a *container* and to place items in the *container*.[1] For example, a window might be a container and you might place various subwindows, menus, and buttons in the window. There is a predefined AWT class called `Container`. Any descendent class of the class `Container` can have components added to it. The class `Frame` is a descendent class of the class `Container`, so any descendent class of the class `Frame` can serve as a container to hold buttons, subwindows, and other components. That means that windows of the kind we have already built (Display 7.1/page 329 and Display 7.5/page 341) can serve as containers. Let's explore the idea of a container class a bit more.

container

When you are dealing with a container class, you have three kinds of objects to deal with: the container class itself (probably some sort of window), the components you add to the container (like buttons, menus, and text fields), and a **layout manager,** which is an object that positions the components inside the container. The layout manager has some general strategy for laying out objects in the container and within the bounds of this strategy tries to make the layout as neat and attractive as it can. Almost every GUI interface you build will be made up of these three kinds of objects. Let's start with an example.

layout
manager

Container Classes

A **container class** is any descendent class of the class `Container`. In particular, this means that any descendent class of the class `Frame` is a container class. Every container class has a method called `add`. You can use the method `add` to add almost any AWT objects, such as buttons and text fields, to the container class. ■

---

1. Technically speaking, adding components to a container class does not necessarily make it a new class. However, the way that we will eventually advocate adding components will be in the class constructor; so, for all practical purposes, it will produce a new class. In any event, this is a technical detail that need not concern you when first learning about the AWT. For our purposes, we will think of adding components as producing a new class.

▼ *PROGRAMMING EXAMPLE* *Adding Buttons*

Display 7.8 contains a program that creates a window with two buttons, labeled "Red" and "Green". When the program is run, the window shown in Display 7.8 is displayed. If you click the button marked "Red" with your mouse, then the color of the window changes from blue (or whatever color it is) to red and the text "Watch me!" (or whatever text is in the screen) changes to "Stop". If you click the button labeled "Green," the color of the window changes to green and the text in the window changes to "Go". That is all the program does (but as you can see, you are slowly learning to build more complicated windows). To end the program and make the window disappear, you click the close-window button.

Much of what appears in Display 7.8 is already familiar to you. The class ButtonDemo is a derived class of the class Frame and so it is a window interface similar to the ones we have already seen in this chapter. There is text in the window that is placed there with a call to the method drawString, just as in our previous GUI programs. However, in this case, the method drawString uses an instance variable named theText as its argument. To change the text in the window, the class need only change the value of the instance variable theText and repaint the screen with a call to the method repaint.

repaint

The method repaint is used for repainting the screen. It takes care of some overhead details and calls the method paint, which you already know about. If the method paint is defined correctly, then the method repaint will work correctly. Note that we need only define the method paint; we do *not* need to define the method repaint. Normally, you define the paint method but do *not* call the paint method. On the other hand, normally you do *not* define the repaint method, but you do sometimes call the repaint method. Although this may seem strange at first, it makes perfectly good sense. The duties of repaint almost never change. The method repaint does a few standard things and calls the method paint. So you normally do not need to define repaint. The duties of the paint method depend on what you want the window to look like. So you do need to define paint.

The repaint **and** paint **Methods**

When you change the contents in a window and want to *repaint* the window so that the new contents show on the screen, you do not call the paint method; you call the repaint method. The repaint method takes care of some overhead and then calls the paint method. Normally, you do not define the repaint method. As long as you define the paint method correctly, the repaint method should work correctly. Note that you normally define the paint method but do not call the paint method. On the other hand, normally, you do not define the repaint method, but you do sometimes call the repaint method.

So far our description of the window in Display 7.8 has been mostly old stuff. What is new in this GUI is the use of buttons and a new kind of listener class. We will discuss buttons and the new listener class in the next few subsections.

Display 7.8 A GUI with Buttons Added *(Part 1 of 2)*
• •

```java
import java.awt.*;
import java.awt.event.*;

/****************************************************************
 *Simple demonstration of putting buttons in a container class.
 ****************************************************************/
public class ButtonDemo extends Frame implements ActionListener
{
    public static final int WIDTH = 300;
    public static final int HEIGHT = 200;

    /*************************************************************
     *Creates and displays a window of the class ButtonDemo.
     *************************************************************/
    public static void main(String[] args)
    {
        ButtonDemo buttonGui = new ButtonDemo();
        buttonGui.setVisible(true);
    }

    public ButtonDemo()
    {
        setSize(WIDTH, HEIGHT);

        addWindowListener(new WindowDestroyer());
        setTitle("Button Demonstration");
        setBackground(Color.blue);

        setLayout(new FlowLayout());

        Button stopButton = new Button("Red");
        stopButton.addActionListener(this);
        add(stopButton);

        Button goButton = new Button("Green");
        goButton.addActionListener(this);
        add(goButton);
    }

    public void paint(Graphics g)
    {
        g.drawString(theText, 75, 100);
    }
```

*It will take several subsections to fully explain this program. The explanation does not end until the end of the subsection entitled **Action Events and Action Listeners.***

• •

Display 7.8 A GUI with Buttons Added *(Part 2 of 2)*

```
public void actionPerformed(ActionEvent e)
{
    if (e.getActionCommand().equals("Red"))
    {
        setBackground(Color.red);
        theText = "STOP";
    }
    else if (e.getActionCommand().equals("Green"))
    {
        setBackground(Color.green);
        theText = "GO";
    }
    else
        theText = "Error in button interface.";

    repaint(); //force color and text change
}


    private String theText = "Watch me!";
}
```

Resulting GUI

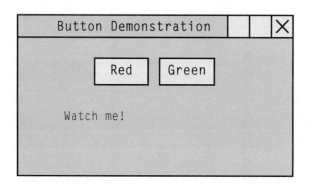

Adding Components to a Container Class

Display 7.9 contains a portion of the AWT class hierarchy. The predefined class Object is not in the AWT. Object is the *Eve class* in Java. Every class in Java is a descendent of the class Object. All the other classes in Display 7.9 are in the AWT. Any class that is a descendent of the class Container is called a **container class**. Every container class has a method called add. A container class can have things added to it with invocations of the add method. For example, the class ButtonDemo in Display 7.8/page 347 adds two buttons to the GUI display with the following:

container class
<code>add</code> method

```
Button stopButton = new Button("Red");
    . . .
add(stopButton);

Button goButton = new Button("Green");
    . . .
add(goButton);.
```

As is typical, these invocations of add are in a constructor for the class. You use the method add to build a custom window (or other GUI object) and the natural place to do the building is in a constructor. What kind of things can you add to a container class? You can add any of the things that you are likely to want, such as buttons, menus, text fields, and so forth. The things that you add to a container class are called *components*. If you look again at the AWT class hierarchy in Display 7.9, you will see that there is a class called Component. Any descendent of the class Component can be added to a container class using the add method. Also, any descendent of the class MenuComponent can be added to a container using a form of the add method.

component

The Close-Window Button is Not in the Class Button

The buttons that you add to a GUI are all objects of the class Button. The close-window button (which you get automatically in any derived class of the class Frame) is not an object of the class Button. That close-window button is part of the Frame object

---

Abstract Classes

If you look at Display 7.9/page 350, you will see that some of the classes are *abstract classes*. An **abstract class** is a kind of class that is used solely to simplify your thinking. You do not, in fact you cannot, create objects of an abstract class. So, what do you do with an abstract class? You derive new classes using the abstract class as the base class. The abstract class is a way of grouping together all the classes that are derived from the abstract class. For example, Component is an abstract class. You can have lots of Components. You can have Buttons, you can have Labels, and you can have TextComponents. These are all derived classes of the class Component. However, you cannot have an object that is just a Component. Any object must be a specific kind of Component. An analogy in everyday life is the class of all automobiles. It is an abstract class. You can have Fords, Toyotas, Hondas, BMWs, and so forth. But, you cannot have just a plain old automobile. It must be some specific kind of automobile. Similarly, you cannot have just a plain old Component. It must be some specific kind of Component, such as a Button or a Label.

It is possible to define your own abstract classes, but we will not cover that topic in this book.

Display 7.9 Hierarchy of AWT Classes

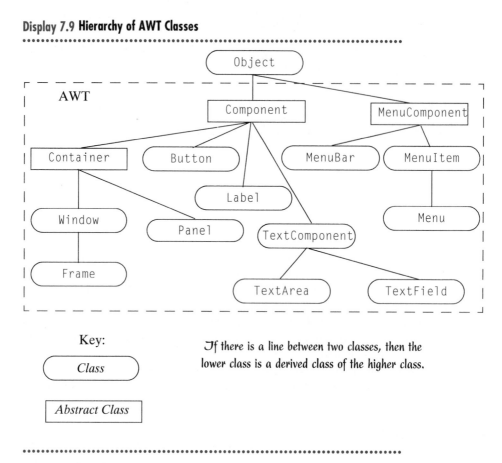

Key:

Class

Abstract Class

If there is a line between two classes, then the lower class is a derived class of the higher class.

This means that you can add just about any object in the AWT to your container classes. There are more components that can be added than those few that are shown in Display 7.9, but those will do for now.

We still need to describe how the objects added to a class are arranged, and we need to describe what kind of listeners listen for button-clicking events. Let's first consider how the added items are arranged.

layout manager

The method add simply throws objects into a container. Another object called a **layout manager** determines how they are arranged. The following call from the constructor definition in Display 7.8/page 347 creates a new object of type Flow-Layout and sets this FlowLayout object to work as the layout manager for the class.

setLayout

```
setLayout(new FlowLayout());
```

This invocation of setLayout is equivalent to

```
FlowLayout manager = new FlowLayout();
setLayout(manager);
```

The add **Method**

Every container class has a method called add. You can use the method add to add almost any AWT object, whether predefined or defined by you, to the container class.

Syntax (inside of a constructor):

```
add(Component_Object);
```

Example (within a constructor for a class called ButtonDemo):

```
public ButtonDemo()
{
    . . .
    setLayout(new FlowLayout());
    Button stopButton = new Button("Red");
    . . .
    add(stopButton);
    . . .
}
```

An object of the class FlowLayout is a layout manager that arranges the components you add to a class in the most obvious way. The components are arranged one after the other along the top of the window (or other object). When the top line is full, a second line is started, then a third, and so forth until all the components are laid out. The components are laid out in the order in which you add them to the class using the method add. We discuss other layout managers in the next subsection.

FlowLayout

More Layout Managers

Display 7.10 lists three basic layout managers that are provided with the AWT. There are other layout managers provided with the AWT, but we will only discuss

Display 7.10 Some Layout Managers

Layout Manager	Description
FlowLayout	Displays components left to right and top to bottom, in the same fashion that you normally write things on a piece of paper.
BorderLayout	Displays the components in five areas, north, south, east, west, and center. You specify which area a component goes into in a second argument of the add method.
GridLayout	Lays components out in a grid with each component stretched to fill its grid.

Layout Managers

The objects that you add to a container class are arranged by an object known as a **layout manager**. You add a layout manager with the method `setLayout`, which is a method of every container class. If you do not add a layout manager, then some default layout manager will be provided for you by the AWT.

Syntax (inside of a constructor):

```
setLayout(new Layout_Manager_Class());
```

Example (within a constructor for a class called `ButtonDemo`):

```
public ButtonDemo()
{
       . . .
    setLayout(new FlowLayout());
    Button stopButton = new Button("Red");
       . . .
    add(stopButton);

    Button goButton = new Button("Green");
       . . .
    add(goButton);
}
```

---

these three. We have already seen the `FlowLayout` manager. Let's discuss the other two layout managers described in Display 7.10.

BorderLayout   A `BorderLayout` manager places components into the five regions `"North"`, `"South"`, `"East"`, `"West"`, and `"Center"`. For example, the following adds five buttons, as shown in the display that follows. (`f` is some container object such as a `Frame`. We only show the buttons.)

```
f.setLayout(new BorderLayout()):
f.add(new Button("Up"), "North");
f.add(new Button("Down"), "South");
f.add(new Button("Right"), "East");
f.add(new Button("Left"), "West");
f.add(new Button("Straight ahead"), "Center");
```

(If this were in a constructor for `f`, then the `f` and dot would be omitted.)

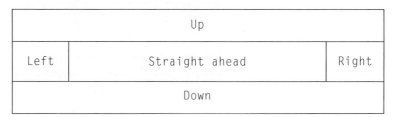

You do not have to use all five positions when using a `BorderLayout` manager.

Any extra space will be given to the position "Center". As we will see later in this chapter, you can group things together to put a collection of items at each position.

A GridLayout manager arranges components in rows and columns with each entry being the same size. For example, the following says to use the a GridLayout manager with f (which can be a Frame or other container). *GridLayout*

```
f.setlayout(new GridLayout(2, 3));
```

The two numbers given as arguments to the constructor GridLayout specify the number of rows and columns. This would produce the following sort of layout.

The Button **Class**

Consider the following code from Display 7.8/page 347 that adds two buttons to a window: *adding buttons*

```
setLayout(new FlowLayout());

Button stopButton = new Button("Red");
stopButton.addActionListener(this);
add(stopButton);

Button goButton = new Button("Green");
goButton.addActionListener(this);
add(goButton);
```

The first statement adds a layout manager to the window class so that the buttons added will be added using the FlowLayout layout manager.

The following statement is similar to other statements we've seen for creating new objects using *new* and a constructor:

```
Button stopButton = new Button("Red");
```

The string argument to the constructor, in this example "Red", specifies the label that will appear on the button when it is displayed on the screen. If you look at the GUI in Display 7.8, you will see that the two buttons are labeled "Red" and "Green".

The line

```
stopButton.addActionListener(this);
```

registers a listener to receive events from the button. We will discuss this line in the subsection **Action Events and Action Listeners**, which follows this subsection.

Buttons are added to a container class using the add method with an invocation, such as

```
add(stopButton);
```

The `Button` **Class**

An object of the class `Button` is displayed in a GUI as a button with a label. You click the button with your mouse instead of actually pushing it. You can add objects of the class `Button` to any container class using the method `add`. When creating a button using *new*, you can give a string argument to the constructor and the string will be displayed as a label on the button.

Example (within a constructor for a class called `ButtonDemo`**):**

```
public ButtonDemo()
{
    . . .
    setLayout(new FlowLayout());
    Button stopButton = new Button("Red");
    stopButton.addActionListener(this);
    add(stopButton);
    . . .
}
```

Action Events and Action Listeners

Different kinds of components require different kinds of listener classes to handle the events they fire. A button fires events known as **action events,** which are handled by listeners known as **action listeners**. In this section, we describe these action listeners. Among other things, we will explain the following line, and the related method `actionPerformed`, from Display 7.8/page 347:

```
stopButton.addActionListener(this);
```

This will complete our description of the program in Display 7.8.

ActionListener Buttons fire action events and action events are handled by `ActionListener`s. `ActionListener` is not a class, but is a property that you can give to any class you define. (These properties, such as `ActionListener`, are known as **interfaces.**) To make a class into an `ActionListener`, you need to do two things:

1. You add the phrase *implements* `ActionListener` to the beginning of the class definition, normally at the end of the first line.

actionPerform 2. You define a method named `actionPerformed`.

In Display 7.8, we made the class `ButtonDemo` into an `ActionListener` in just this way. In what follows, we reproduce the relevant parts of the definition of the class `ButtonDemo` (with the omitted sections indicated by three dots).

```
public class ButtonDemo extends Frame implements ActionListener
{
       . . .
    public void actionPerformed(ActionEvent e)
    {
          . . .
    }
          . . .
}
```

We could have defined a separate class that did nothing but handle button events, but it's more convenient to make the window class ButtonDemo into the Action-Listener that will handle button events. This is convenient because the button events are supposed to change what is in the window and the easiest way to change a window is by a method within the window itself.

The class ButtonDemo is itself the listener class for the buttons inside of ButtonDemo. To accomplish this, we use the *this* parameter. Recall that within the definition of a class, an object of that class is called *this*. Thus, in Display 7.8/page 347, we made *this* a listener for the button stopButton and then added the button stopButton as follows:

```
public ButtonDemo()
{
       . . .
    Button stopButton = new Button("Red");
    stopButton.addActionListener(this);
    add(stopButton);
       . . .
}
```

As shown, this normally takes place inside of a constructor. (We have omitted some of the constructor and used three dots to indicate the omitted sections.)

Now, suppose we create an object, w, of the class ButtonDemo as follows:

```
ButtonDemo w = new ButtonDemo();
```

Then the *this* parameter in the definition of the class ButtonDemo refers to w, so w is the action listener for the two buttons inside of w.

All that is left to explain is how the method actionPerformed works. Let's continue with our object w of the class ButtonDemo. If you click one of the buttons inside of w with your mouse, that sends an action event to the action listener for that button. But, w is the action listener for the buttons in w, so the action event goes to w. When an action listener receives an action event, the event is automatically passed to the method actionPerformed. The method actionPerformed is typically a branching statement that determines what kind of action event was fired and then performs some appropriate action. Let's look at the code for the

action-
Performed

method `actionPerformed` in the class `ButtonDemo` in Display 7.8. For convenience, we reproduce the definition in what follows:

```java
public void actionPerformed(ActionEvent e)
{
    if (e.getActionCommand().equals("Red"))
    {
        setBackground(Color.red);
        theText = "STOP";
    }
    else if (e.getActionCommand().equals("Green"))
    {
        setBackground(Color.green);
        theText = "GO";
    }
    else
        theText = "Error in button interface.";

    repaint(); //force color and text change
}
```

getAction-
Command

In this case, the method `actionPerformed` needs to know whether the action event came from the button labeled `"Red"` or the button labeled `"Green"`. If e is an action event that was fired by clicking a button, then `e.getActionCommand()` returns the string label on the button. So, all that the method `actionPerformed` needs to do is to see if `e.getActionCommand()` is `"Red"` or `"Green"` and perform the appropriate action for that button. The appropriate action is to change the color of the window with a call to `setBackground` and to change the text in the window. To change the text, `actionPerformed` changes the value of the instance variable `theText`. Finally, the method `actionPerformed` calls the method `repaint` so that the window is repainted and these changes become visible.

◑ *PROGRAMMING TIP* Copy Other Programmer's Code

Before I get in trouble with any instructors, let me clarify what the title of this section does not mean. It does not mean that you should have somebody else do your assignments. What this means is that one very good way to learn how to program and to produce good programs in a hurry is to start out with a program that does something similar to what you want and then change it to do exactly what you want. For example, if you want to write a program for a window that has something written in it and some buttons in it, you can start with the program in Display 7.8/page 347 and change the details. Code for AWT interfaces can be pretty complicated, and it is not easy to learn all the details of all the various predefined classes and methods. Sometimes, the best way to learn these details is to copy and change code until the details become routine.

Action Events and Action Listeners

Buttons, and certain other components, fire events in the class `ActionEvent`. These action events must be handled by an action listener. Any class can be an action listener class. The details in outline form are as follows:

1. Make some class (maybe a window class) into an `ActionListener` by adding the phrase *implements* `ActionListener` to the heading of the class definition and adding a definition for a method named `actionPerformed`. The `ActionListener` can be any class. In particular, the class may serve some other function besides being an `ActionListener`.

2. Register the `ActionListener` object with the button (or other component that will fire the action event). To do this, you use the method `addActionListener`. A button or other component may register more than one listener.

Example (the complete details are in Display 7.8/page 347):

```
public class ButtonDemo extends Frame implements ActionListener
{
    public ButtonDemo()
    {
        . . .
        Button stopButton = new Button("Red");
        stopButton.addActionListener(this);
        add(stopButton);
        . . .
    }
    . . .
    public void actionPerformed(ActionEvent e)
    {
        . . .
    }
    . . .
}
```

◉ *PROGRAMMING TIP* *Guide for Creating Simple Window Interfaces*

Most simple windowing GUIs follow a pattern that is easy to learn and that will get you started with the AWT. Here is an outline of some of the main points we've seen so far:

1. A typical GUI consists of some windowing object that is derived from the class `Frame` and that contains a number of components, such as buttons or text fields.

2. When the user clicks the close-window button, the window should close, but this will not happen unless your program registers a window listener to

The `actionPerformed` **Method**

In order to be an `ActionListener`, a class must, among other things, have a method named `action-Performed` that has one parameter of type `ActionEvent`. This is the only method required by the `ActionListener` interface.

Syntax:

```
public void actionPerformed(ActionEvent e)
{
    Code_for_Actions_Performed
}
```

The *Code_for_Actions_Performed* is typically a branching statement depending on some property of e. Often the branching depends on e.getActionCommand(). If e is an event fired by clicking a button, then e.getActionCommand() is the string written on the button.

Example:

```
public void actionPerformed(ActionEvent e)
{
    if (e.getActionCommand().equals("Red"))
    {
        setBackground(Color.red);
        theText = "STOP";
    }
    else if (e.getActionCommand().equals("Green"))
    {
        setBackground(Color.green);
        theText = "GO";
    }
    else
        theText = "Error in button interface.";

    repaint(); //force color and text change
}
```

Interfaces

Look again at Display 7.8/page 347. We want the class `ButtonDemo` to be both a `Frame` and an `ActionListener`. But, `ButtonDemo` can only be a derived class of one base class, so we made it a derived class of the class `Frame`. That means that `ActionListener` must serve a similar but different function from that of the base class `Frame`. This `ActionListener` thing is not a class but is an *interface*. An **interface** is a property of a class that says what methods it must have. A class such as `ButtonDemo` that satisfies an interface is said to **implement the interface**. In order to implement an interface, a class must include the phrase *implements* `ActionListener` (or whatever the name of the interface is) and it must define all the methods specified in the interface. (The particular interface `ActionListener` specifies only the one method `actionPerformed`.)

An interface is similar to an abstract class. However, you do not have classes that are derived classes of an interface. You have classes that are defined in some other way but also satisfy the interface specifications.

close the window. One way to accomplish this is to add the following to the GUI class definition within a constructor definition:

```
addWindowListener(new WindowDestroyer());
```

You can use the definition of `WindowDestroyer` given in Display 7.2/page 332.

3. If any of the components, such as a button, generate action events, then you need to make the GUI (or some other class) an action listener. Every component that generates an action event should have an action listener registered with it. You register an action listener with the method `addActionListener`.

4. In order to make your windowing GUI (or other class) into an action listener, you need to add the following to the beginning of the class definition:

```
implements ActionListener
```

You also need to add a definition of the method `actionPerformed` to the class.

This is not the only way to create a GUI window class, but it shows a simple and common way to do it, and it is basically the only way we know of so far. Display 7.11 gives an outline for GUI window displays of the kinds we've seen so far. You can use it as a guide for writing your own GUIs.

? SELF-TEST QUESTIONS

11. The following occurs in the definition of the constructor in Display 7.8/page 347. What is the meaning of the *new*? What kind of argument is being used?

```
setLayout(new FlowLayout());
```

12. Suppose you want the `paint` method to write the following text in a window:

```
Live long and prosper.
```

Give a definition of the `paint` method that will do this.

13. Suppose you declared and created a window object of the class `MyWindowClass` with the following code:

```
MyWindowClass gui = new MyWindowClass();
```

The window `gui` is not yet visible on the screen. Give a program statement that will make it visible.

14. What kind of listener do you need for a button component? How do you create such a listener?

<Additional questions on page 361.>

Display 7.11 Outline for a Simple GUI Class *(Part 1 of 2)*
••

```
import java.awt.*;
import java.awt.event.*;

/***********************************************
 *A simple outline that will work for the types
 *of window GUIs you've seen so far.
 ***********************************************/
public class GUI_Class_Name extends Frame
                            implements ActionListener
{
    public static final int WIDTH = Width_In_Pixels;
    public static final int HEIGHT = Height_In_Pixels;


    public static void main(String[] args)
    {
        <Whatever you want, possibly intermixed with the statements below.>
        Gui_Class_Name GUI_Object_Name = new Gui_Class_Name();
        GUI_Object_Name.setVisible(true);
    }



    public GUI_Class_Name()
    {
        setSize(WIDTH, HEIGHT);



        addWindowListener(new WindowDestroyer());
        setTitle(Some_String);
        setBackground(Color.Some_Color);//Optional

        setLayout(new FlowLayout());//You can use another layout
                                    //manager if you prefer.


        <Add buttons or other components. Below is a sample of adding one button:>
        Button b = new Button(Some_String_As_Label);
        b.addActionListener(this);
        add(b);
    }
```

> This `main` could be in another class instead of here.

> You can use the definition of `WindowDestroyer` in Display 7.2/page 332.

••

Display 7.11 Outline for a Simple GUI Class *(Part 2 of 2)*
••

```
    public void actionPerformed(ActionEvent e)
    {
        if (e.getActionCommand().equals(Some_String_Maybe_A_Label))
        {
            <action for this case.>
        }
        else if (e.getActionCommand().equals(Some_String_Maybe_A_Label))
        {
            <action for this case.>
        }
            <Repeat for any number of else-if-clauses.>
        else
            <Output an error message. This case normally does not happen.>

        repaint(); //force color and text change
    }

    public void paint(Graphics g)
    {
        g.drawString(Some_Text, x_Coordinate, y_Coordinate);
    }
}
```

You may or may not need paint.

••

15. Consider the following code from Display 7.8/page 347:

```
Button stopButton = new Button("Red");
stopButton.addActionListener(this);
add(stopButton);

Button goButton = new Button("Green");
goButton.addActionListener(this);
add(goButton);
```

Can you replace this code with the following and have it mean the same thing?

```
Button b;
b = new Button("Red");
b.addActionListener(this);
add(b);

b = new Button("Green");
b.addActionListener(this);
add(b);
```

In other words, can you use only the one named b, even though there are two buttons?

The WindowListener **Interface** *(Optional)*

When we placed buttons in a window, we made the window itself the button listener class. On the other hand, when we wanted a window listener to respond to window-closing events, we made the window listener a separate class, named WindowDe-stroyer. We could have made the window itself the window listener, but that is just a bit more involved. We made the window itself a button listener by making it implement the interface named ActionListener. There is also an interface named WindowListener that is used in a similar way. For example, in Display 7.8/page 347, we made the window class ButtonDemo an ActionListener by adding *implements* ActionListener as follows:

```
public class ButtonDemo extends Frame implements ActionListener
```

If we wanted to make ButtonDemo a WindowListener instead of an ActionListener, the definition would begin

```
public class ButtonDemo extends Frame implements WindowListener
```

If, as is more likely, we wanted to make ButtonDemo both an ActionListener and a WindowListener, it would begin

```
public class ButtonDemo extends Frame
             implements ActionListener, WindowListener
```

The reason we tend to avoid making a window its own window listener is that when a class implements an interface, such as the ActionListener or the WindowListener interfaces, it must include definitions for *all* of the methods specified for the interface. The interface ActionListener has only the single method ActionPerformed, so this is not an onerous requirement. The method WindowListener, however, has the same seven methods as the class WindowAdapter. The methods are given in Display 7.3/page 334. If a class implements the class WindowListener, it must have definitions for all seven of these methods. If you do not need all of these methods, then you can define the ones you do not need to have empty bodies, like this:

```
public void windowDeiconified(WindowEvent e)
{}
```

If you only need one or two methods in the WindowListener interface, this is a nuisance, although it is not difficult to do.

Display 7.12 A WindowListener *(Part 1 of 2) (Optional)*

```java
import java.awt.*;
import java.awt.event.*;

public class SecondWindowRedone extends Frame implements WindowListener
{
    public static final int WIDTH = 550;
    public static final int HEIGHT = 400;

    public static void main(String[] args)
    {
        SecondWindowRedone myWindow = new SecondWindowRedone();
        myWindow.setVisible(true);
    }

    public SecondWindowRedone()
    {
        super();
        addWindowListener(this);
        setTitle("Second Window");
        setSize(WIDTH, HEIGHT);
        setBackground(Color.blue);
    }

    public void paint(Graphics g)
    {
        g.drawString("Coming to you in living color!", 10, 100);
    }

    public void windowOpened(WindowEvent e)
    {}

    public void windowClosing(WindowEvent e)
    {
        this.dispose();
        System.exit(0);
    }

    public void windowClosed(WindowEvent e)
    {}

    public void windowIconified(WindowEvent e)
    {}
```

This version does not need the class WindowDestroyer from Display 7.2/page 332.

Display 7.12 A `WindowListener` *(Part 2 of 2) (Optional)*

```
        public void windowDeiconified(WindowEvent e)
        {}

        public void windowActivated(WindowEvent e)
        {}

        public void windowDeactivated(WindowEvent e)
        {}
    }
```

The GUI produced is the same as in Display 7.5/page 341.

There are advantages to using the `WindowListener` interface. If you make the window class a derived class of the class `Frame` and have it implement the `WindowListener` interface, then it is easy to call a method in the class `Frame` within the window listener.

For example, the program in Display 7.12 is a variant of the program in Display 7.5/page 341. In Display 7.12, the GUI class is its own window listener. That allows it to have the following invocation in the method `windowClosing`:

```
        this.dispose();
```

The method `dispose` is a method in the class `Frame` and the class `SecondWindowRedone` is a derived class of the class `Frame`, so this makes sense. The method `dispose` releases any resources used by the window. In a program this simple, the call to `dispose` is not really needed because the resources are automatically released when the program ends, but if the program had several windows and was going to run longer and only eliminate this one window, then the call to `dispose` might make the program more efficient. We only used `dispose` to have a simple example. (Actually, `dispose` is always called automatically, but there is no guarantee that it will be called quickly. So, an explicit call to `dispose` can help efficiency.)

Why bother to have both `WindowListener` and `WindowAdapter`? The reason is that `WindowAdapter` is a variant of `WindowListener` that is provided solely for the convenience of the programmer. `WindowAdapter` is a class that implements the interface `WindowListener` by giving every method an empty body. That way when you define a derived class of `WindowAdapter`, you do not have to put in those empty definitions. So, why not use `WindowAdapter` all the time? Often times, you want a listener class to be a derived class of some class, such as `Frame`, and to also be a window listener. A class cannot be a derived class of two classes, such as `Frame` and `WindowAdapter`. So, in this situation, you cannot use `WindowAdapter`. In this situation, you make the class a derived class of the class `Frame` and you make it implement `WindowListener`. A class can be a derived class of only one class, but it can also implement one or more interfaces.

7.4 Panels and Text Components

> *Polonius: What do you read my lord?*
> *Hamlet: Words, words, words.*
> **WILLIAM SHAKESPEARE,** *Hamlet*

A GUI is often organized in a hierarchical fashion, with windowlike containers inside of other window containers. In this section, we introduce two new kinds of classes that facilitate this organization: The class `Panel` is a very simple container class that does little more than group objects. We also introduce classes for text components that allow a GUI to collect text input and display text output.

The `Panel` Class

`Panel` is one of the simplest of container classes, but one you will use frequently. A `Panel` object is little more than an area of the screen into which you put other objects, such as buttons and text areas. The `Panel` object is then, typically, put in a `Frame`. Thus, one of the main functions of `Panel` objects is to subdivide a `Frame` into different areas. The judicious use of panels can affect the arrangement of components in a window as much as the choice of a layout manager. For example, suppose you use a `BorderLayout` manager, then you can place components in each of the five locations: `"North"`, `"South"`, `"East"`, `"West"`, and `"Center"`. But, what if you want to put two components at the bottom of the screen, in the `"South"` position? To get two components in the `"South"` position, you put the two components in a panel and then place the panel in the `"South"` position.

Display 7.13 contains a slight variation of the program in Display 7.8/page 347. In Display 7.13, we have placed the buttons in a `Panel`, called `buttonPanel`, so that the portion of the window with the buttons does not change color when the rest of the window changes color. As was true for the program in Display 7.8, when you click the `"Red"` button in the GUI in Display 7.13, the blue color changes to red and the text changes, and, similarly, the appropriate color and text appear when you click the `"Green"` button. But, in Display 7.13, the buttons are in a separate panel that is white and that does not change color. As you can see, you use a layout manager and the method `add` with a `Panel` in exactly the same way that you do for a `Frame`. The buttons are placed in the `Panel` with `add` as in the following example:

```
buttonPanel.add(stopButton);
```

and then the `Panel` is placed in the `Frame` with `add` as follows:

```
add(buttonPanel, "South");
```

The extra argument `"South"` is there because we are using a layout manager from the class `BorderLayout`.

Display 7.13 Putting the Buttons in a Panel *(Part 1 of 2)*

```
import java.awt.*;
import java.awt.event.*;

/*****************************************************************
 *Simple demonstration of putting buttons in a panel. If you do
 *not see the colored part of the window with text in it, use your
 *mouse to increase the size of the window and it will appear.
 *****************************************************************/
public class PanelDemo extends Frame implements ActionListener
{
    public static final int WIDTH = 300;
    public static final int HEIGHT = 200;

    public static void main(String[] args)
    {
        PanelDemo guiWithPanel = new PanelDemo();
        guiWithPanel.setVisible(true);
    }

    public PanelDemo()
    {
        setTitle("Panel Demonstration");
        setSize(WIDTH, HEIGHT);
        setBackground(Color.blue);
        addWindowListener(new WindowDestroyer());

        Panel buttonPanel = new Panel();
        buttonPanel.setBackground(Color.white);

        buttonPanel.setLayout(new FlowLayout());

        Button stopButton = new Button("Red");
        stopButton.addActionListener(this);
        buttonPanel.add(stopButton);

        Button goButton = new Button("Green");
        goButton.addActionListener(this);
        buttonPanel.add(goButton);

        setLayout(new BorderLayout());
        add(buttonPanel, "South");
    }
```

Display 7.13 Putting the Buttons in a Panel *(Part 2 of 2)*

```
    public void paint(Graphics g)
    {
        g.drawString(theText, 75, 100);
    }


    public void actionPerformed(ActionEvent e)
    <The method actionPerformed is the same as in Display 7.8/page 347.>

    private String theText = "Watch me!";
}
```

Resulting GUI

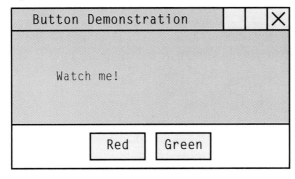

Notice how the action listeners are set up. Before a button is placed in the Panel, the button registers the *this* parameter as a listener, with the following line:

```
    stopButton.addActionListener(this);
```

Since this line appears inside of the constructor for the class PanelDemo, the *this* parameter refers to PanelDemo, which is the entire window interface. Thus, the entire window container is the listener, not the Panel. (Remember PanelDemo is the window with the Panel. It is not itself the Panel.) So, when you click the button labeled "Red", it is the background of the bigger window that turns red. The Panel with the buttons always stays white.

Note that since it is the PanelDemo that is the listener for the button click events, it is PanelDemo that implements ActionListener and has the method actionPerformed.

The Panel **Class**

The class Panel is a container class defined in the AWT. A Panel object is little more than an area of the screen into which you can add other objects, such as buttons and text areas. The Panel object is then, typically, added to a Frame. Thus, one of the main functions of Panel objects is to subdivide a Frame into different areas.

Text Areas and Text Fields

The GUI in Display 7.13 has some text in the window but it is text-generated by the program itself. If we are going to have text input from the user as part of a GUI, then we need some way for the user to enter text into the GUI. Display 7.14 contains a program that produces a GUI with a text area in which the user can write any text she or he wishes. That text is then saved as a memo that can be recalled later. In this simple example, the user is only allowed two memos, but that is good enough to illustrate how a text area is created and used. The area in the center, colored white, is an object of the class `TextArea`. The user can type any sort of text into this `TextArea`. If the user clicks the `"Save Memo 1"` button, the text is saved as memo 1. If the user clicks the `"Save Memo 2"` button, the text is saved as memo 2. Either memo can be called back up to the `TextArea` by clicking one of the buttons `"Get Memo 1"` or `"Get Memo 2"`. The `TextArea` can be cleared by clicking the `"Clear"` button. Now, let's look at how the program does this.

TextArea

The buttons in Display 7.14 are put in a `Panel` and then that `Panel` is put in the `Frame` just as they were in Display 7.13. The `TextArea` is set up with the following code, which appears in the constructor definition in Display 7.14:

```
textPanel = new Panel();
textPanel.setBackground(Color.blue);
theText = new TextArea(10, 40);
theText.setBackground(Color.white);
textPanel.add(theText);
add(textPanel, "Center");
```

The object `theText` is a member of the class `TextArea`. The arguments 10 and 40 to the constructor for `TextArea` say that the text area will be 10 lines from top to bottom and will allow 40 characters per line. You can actually type in as much text as you wish, but only 10 lines of 40 characters per line will be visible at any one time. The text area will have scroll bars that let the user scroll through the text in cases where the text is too large for the text area. The text area `theText` is given a background color and added to the `Panel` called `textPanel` in the usual ways.

We are using a `BorderLayout` manager. The `textPanel` is added to the `Frame` in the `"Center"` position. The `"Center"` position always takes up all the `Frame` room that is left. This much of our program sets up the look of the GUI, but we still need to discuss how writing in the text area is handled by the GUI.

getText

The two memos are stored in the two instance variables `memo1` and `memo2`, both of type `String`. When the user clicks the `"Save Memo 1"` button, the text in the text area is saved as the value of the instance variable `memo1`. This is done by the following code, which is the first three lines in the definition of the `actionPerformed` method:

```
String actionCommand = e.getActionCommand();
if (actionCommand.equals("Save Memo 1"))
    memo1 = theText.getText();
```

Recall that the `getActionCommand` method returns the label of the button that is clicked. So, this says that when the button with label `"Save Memo 1"` is clicked, the following happens:

```
memo1 = theText.getText();
```

Display 7.14 Panels and Text Area *(Part 1 of 2)*

```
import java.awt.*;
import java.awt.event.*;
public class TextAreaDemo extends Frame implements ActionListener
{
    public static final int WIDTH = 400;
    public static final int HEIGHT = 300;

    public TextAreaDemo()
    {
        setTitle("Memo Saver");
        setLayout(new BorderLayout());
        setSize(WIDTH, HEIGHT);
        addWindowListener(new WindowDestroyer());

        Panel buttonPanel = new Panel();
        buttonPanel.setBackground(Color.white);
        buttonPanel.setLayout(new FlowLayout());

        Button memo1Button = new Button("Save Memo 1");
        memo1Button.addActionListener(this);
        buttonPanel.add(memo1Button);
        Button memo2Button = new Button("Save Memo 2");
        memo2Button.addActionListener(this);
        buttonPanel.add(memo2Button);
        Button clearButton = new Button("Clear");
        clearButton.addActionListener(this);
        buttonPanel.add(clearButton);
        Button get1Button = new Button("Get Memo 1");
        get1Button.addActionListener(this);
        buttonPanel.add(get1Button);
        Button get2Button = new Button("Get Memo 2");
        get2Button.addActionListener(this);
        buttonPanel.add(get2Button);

        add(buttonPanel, "South");

        textPanel = new Panel();
        textPanel.setBackground(Color.blue);
        theText = new TextArea(10, 40);
        theText.setBackground(Color.white);
        textPanel.add(theText);
        add(textPanel, "Center");
    }
```

> There is a demonstration main in part 2 of this display.

> textPanel and theText are instance variables.

Display 7.14 Panels and Text Area *(Part 2 of 2)*

```
public void actionPerformed(ActionEvent e)
{
    String actionCommand = e.getActionCommand();
    if (actionCommand.equals("Save Memo 1"))
        memo1 = theText.getText();
    else if (actionCommand.equals("Save Memo 2"))
        memo2 = theText.getText();
    else if (actionCommand.equals("Clear"))
        theText.setText("");
    else if (actionCommand.equals("Get Memo 1"))
        theText.setText(memo1);
    else if (actionCommand.equals("Get Memo 2"))
        theText.setText(memo2);
    else
        theText.setText("Error in memo interface");

    textPanel.repaint();//Shows changes in textPanel
}

public static void main(String[] args)
{
    TextAreaDemo guiMemo = new TextAreaDemo();
    guiMemo.setVisible(true);
}


private Panel textPanel;
private TextArea theText;
private String memo1 = "No Memo 1.";
private String memo2 = "No Memo 2.";
}
```

We need names for `textPanel` *and* `theText` *because we need to refer to them in our code.*

If you `Get Memo 1` *before you set* `memo1`*, you get the message* `"No Memo 1"`.

Resulting GUI

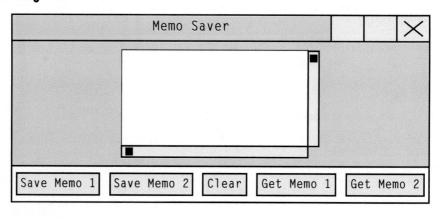

The method `getText()` returns the text that is written in the object `theText` of the class `TextArea`. In other words, it returns what the user typed into the text area. If you read further in the definition of the method `actionPerformed`, you see that the second memo is stored in a similar way.

The memos are displayed in the text area and the text area is cleared with the following clauses from the definition of the method `actionPerformed`:

```
else if (actionCommand.equals("Save Memo 2"))
    memo2 = theText.getText();
else if (actionCommand.equals("Clear"))
    theText.setText("");
else if (actionCommand.equals("Get Memo 1"))
    theText.setText(memo1);
else if (actionCommand.equals("Get Memo 2"))
    theText.setText(memo2);
```

setText

The method `setText` of the class `TextArea` changes the text in the text area into what is given as the argument to `setText`. Two quotes with nothing in between are given as the argument to `setText` in the second line of the preceding code. These two quotes denote the empty string and so produce a blank text area.

empty string

---

getText **and** setText

The classes `TextArea` and `TextField` both contain methods called `getText` and `setText`. The method `getText` can be used to retrieve the text written in the text area or text field. The method `setText` can be used to change the text written in the text area or text field.

Example (`theText` **can be an object of the class** `TextArea`
                    or an object of the class `TextField`**):**

```
memo1 = theText.getText();
theText.setText("Hi Mom!");
```

◻

The Classes `TextArea` **and** `TextField`

The classes `TextArea` and `TextField` can be used to add areas for text to a GUI. An object of the class `TextArea` has a size consisting of a specified number of lines and a specified number of characters per line. An object of the class `TextField` has only one line that contains some specified number of characters. More text can be typed into a `TextArea` or `TextField` than is specified in its size, but you need to scroll to see the text that is not visible.

Example (using `TextArea`**):**

```
Panel aPanel = new Panel();
TextArea someText = new TextArea(10, 30);//10 lines of 30 chars
aPanel.add(someText);
```

Example (using `TextField`**):**

```
Panel anotherPanel = new Panel();
TextField name = new TextField(30);//30 characters.
anotherPanel.add(name);
```

◻

TextField

The class TextField (which is not used in Display 7.14) is very similar to the class TextArea except that it displays only one line of text. It is useful for interfaces where the user gives only a few characters of text, like a single number, the name of a file, or the name of a person. The constructor for TextField takes one argument, which is the number of characters visible in the text field. You can enter more characters than this in a text field, but you will need to scroll in order to see the text, and it may not be easy to do the scrolling. So, be sure to make the text field one or two characters longer than the longest string you expect to have entered into the text field. In practice, the size of the text field may not even be what you specify in the constructor. Fortunately, it is more likely to be longer rather than shorter than what you specify.

initializing text

Both the classes TextArea and TextField can have some initial text contents specified when you create an object using *new*. The initial text is a string given as the first argument to the constructor. For example,

```
TextField inputOutputField = new TextField("Hello User.", 20);
```

The text field inputOutputField will have room for 20 visible characters and will start out containing the text "Hello User."

Both the classes TextArea and TextField have a constructor with no argument that sets the various parameters to some default values.

? SELF-TEST QUESTIONS

16. What is the difference between a text area and a text field?

17. How would you change the program in Display 7.14/page 369 so that the buttons appear above the text area instead of below the text area?

18. Write a statement that will create a text field called name that has room for 30 visible characters and that starts out with text "Your name here."

19. Change the definition of the method actionPerformed in Display 7.14/ page 369 so that when the user saves the text as memo 1, the text area changes so that it says "Memo 1 saved." and so that when memo 2 is saved, it changes to "Memo 2 saved."

Labels for Text Fields and Other Components

Sometimes you want a label for a text field. For example, suppose the GUI asks for a name and an identification number and expects the user to enter these in two text fields. In this case, the GUI needs to label the two text fields so that the user knows in which field to write the name and in which field to write the number. You can use an object of the class Label to label a text field or any other component in an AWT GUI.

An object of the class Label is little more than a single line of text that can be added to any container. For example, the following creates a Label with the text "This is a label." and adds the Label to the container c:

```
Label tag = new Label("This is a label.");
c.add(tag);
```

If c is a window, then this has an effect very similar to using drawString to write the string "This is a label." in the window. In practice, it is more likely that c is a Panel that will contain both the label tag and some component that it labels.

Display 7.15 contains a program that demonstrates the use of a Label. Except for the part in color, the details are all things that you have seen before. The part in color, reproduced in what follows, shows how you can label a text field with the instruction "Enter your name here:".

```
Panel namePanel = new Panel();
namePanel.setLayout(new BorderLayout());

name = new TextField(20);
namePanel.add(name, "South");
Label nameLabel = new Label("Enter your name here:");
namePanel.add(nameLabel, "Center");
```

Note that the way we attach a label to a text field (or any other component) is to put both the text field and the label in a panel. You can then add the entire panel to a container as follows:

```
add(namePanel);
```

The program in Display 7.15 is just a demonstration program and does not do very much. If the user enters a name in the text field and clicks the "Test" button, then the GUI gives an evaluation of the name. However, all names receive the same evaluation, namely, "A very good name!" So, if the user enters a name and then clicks the "Test" button, the display will look like the GUI shown in Display 7.15.

The Label **Class**

An object of the class Label is little more than one line of text that can be added to a container. You can label a text field or other component by placing both the component and a label object into a panel. The panel can then be added to the desired container.

Example (within a constructor for a class called LabelDemo**):**

```
public LabelDemo()
{
    . . .
    Panel namePanel = new Panel();
    namePanel.setLayout(new BorderLayout());

    name = new TextField(20);
    namePanel.add(name, "South");
    Label nameLabel = new Label("Enter your name here:");
    namePanel.add(nameLabel, "Center");

    add(namePanel);
    . . .
}
```

Display 7.15 Labeling a Text Field (Part 1 of 2)

```java
import java.awt.*;
import java.awt.event.*;

/**********************************************************
*Class to demonstrate placing a label on a text field.
**********************************************************/
public class LabelDemo extends Frame implements ActionListener
{
    public static final int WIDTH = 300;
    public static final int HEIGHT = 200;

    public LabelDemo()
    {
        setTitle("Name Tester");
        setLayout(new GridLayout(2, 1));
        setSize(WIDTH, HEIGHT);
        addWindowListener(new WindowDestroyer());

        Panel namePanel = new Panel();
        namePanel.setLayout(new BorderLayout());

        name = new TextField(20);
        namePanel.add(name, "South");
        Label nameLabel = new Label("Enter your name here:");
        namePanel.add(nameLabel, "Center");

        add(namePanel);

        Panel buttonPanel = new Panel();
        buttonPanel.setBackground(Color.gray);
        Button b = new Button("Test");
        b.addActionListener(this);
        buttonPanel.add(b);
        b = new Button("Clear");
        b.addActionListener(this);
        buttonPanel.add(b);

        add(buttonPanel);
    }
```

Display 7.15 Labeling a Text Field *(Part 2 of 2)*

```
    public void actionPerformed(ActionEvent e)
    {
        if (e.getActionCommand().equals("Test"))
            name.setText("A very good name!");
        else if (e.getActionCommand().equals("Clear"))
            name.setText("");
        else
            name.setText("Error in window interface.");

        repaint();
    }


    public static void main(String[] args)
    {
        LabelDemo w = new LabelDemo();
        w.setVisible(true);
    }


    private TextField name;
}
```

Resulting GUI

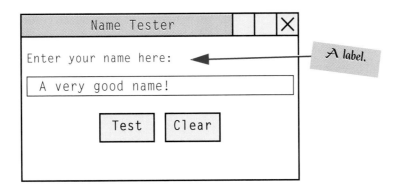

A label.

Inputting and Outputting Numbers

inputting
numbers

When you want to input numbers using a GUI, your GUI must convert input text to numbers. For example, when you input the number 42 in a `TextArea` or `TextField`, your program will receive the string `"42"`, not the number 42. Your program must convert the input string value `"42"` to the integer value 42. When you want to output numbers using a GUI constructed with the AWT, you must convert numbers to a string and then output that string. For example, if you want to output the number 43, your program would convert the integer value 43 to the string value `"43"`. With the AWT, all input is string input and all output is string output.

Let's consider inputting numbers. Your program will need to convert a string, such as `"42"`, to a number. The static method `valueOf` of the predefined class `Integer` will convert a string to a kind of integer. For example,

```
Integer.valueOf("42")
```

returns something like the integer 42, but unfortunately it does not return exactly what you want. Recall that the method `valueOf` returns an object of the wrapper class `Integer`, rather than a value of the primitive type *int*. Since you want a value of type *int*, you need to do one more conversion. The method `intValue` will convert an `Integer` value to an *int* value. So, the following expression, will return the simple *int* value 42:

```
Integer.valueOf("42").intValue()
```

If these details do not make sense to you, you should review the section **Integer, Double, and Other Wrapper Classes** in Chapter 5.

If the number were written in a `TextField` named `inputOutputField`, then you can recover the input string with the method `getText`. So `inputOutputField.getText()` would produce the input string. To change the input string to a number, you can use the following expression:

```
Integer.valueOf(inputOutputField.getText()).intValue()
```

trim

If there is any chance that the user might add extra white space before or after the input, you can add an invocation of the method `trim` to the string object `inputOutputField.getText()`. Thus, a more robust way to obtain the number that was input would be the following (which adds an invocation of the method `trim`):

```
Integer.valueOf(inputOutputField.getText().trim()).intValue()
```

Once your program has this number, it can use it just like any other number. For example, to store this number in an *int* variable named n, the following assignment statement will work fine:

```
int n =
  Integer.valueOf(inputOutputField.getText().trim()).intValue();
```

If you want to input numbers of type *double*, just use the class `Double` in place of the class `Integer` and the method `doubleValue` in place of the method `intValue`.

For example, to store this number in a *double* variable named x, the following assignment statement will work fine:

```
double x =
    Double.valueOf(inputOutputField.getText().trim()).doubleValue();
```

You can also do the analogous thing with the classes Long and Float.

You should be able to understand and even write long expressions like

```
Integer.valueOf(stringObject.trim()).intValue()
```

However, your code will be easier to read and easier to write if you define a method to express this as a simple method invocation. Here is one such method:

stringToInt
method

```
private static int stringToInt(String stringObject)
{
    return Integer.valueOf(stringObject.trim()).intValue();
}
```

Then an expression like

```
n =
    Integer.valueOf(inputOutputField.getText().trim()).intValue();
```

can be expressed more clearly as

```
n = stringToInt(inputOutputField.getText());
```

If the method is to be merely a tool in some GUI class, then it should be declared as private, since it has no use outside of the class. Alternatively, it could be part of a utility class with a number of different useful functions. In that case, it would make more sense to make it public.

To send an output number to a TextField or TextArea of a GUI, you use the static method toString. For example, suppose you have the number 43 stored in the *int* variable sum. You can convert this 43 to the string "43" as follows:

outputting
numbers

```
Integer.toString(sum)
```

We used the class Integer when invoking toString because we were dealing with integers. If on the other hand, you have a variable total of type *double* and you want to convert the number in total to a string, you would use

```
Double.toString(total)
```

If you want the number in the *int* variable sum to appear in the TextField named inputOutputField, then you use setText as follows:

```
inputOutputField.setText(Integer.toString(sum));
```

This produces the string for the integer. If you wanted a string for the value in the variable total of type *double*, you would instead use

```
inputOutputField.setText(Double.toString(total));
```

These techniques for inputting and outputting numbers are illustrated in the next case study.

Inputting Numbers within a GUI

You can design a GUI using the AWT so that input can consist of a number typed into a text field (or text area). The following will return the number of type *int* that is typed into the text field. This assumes that nothing other than the number and white space are typed into the text fields.

Syntax:

```
Integer.valueOf(Name_Of_Text_Field.getText().trim()).intValue()
```

Example (that stores an *int* value in a variable n**):**

```
int n =
    Integer.valueOf(inputOutputField.getText().trim()).intValue();
```

You can do the same things for numbers of the types *double*, *float*, and *long*. Just use the class Double, Float, or Long in place of the class Integer, and use the method doubleValue, floatValue, or longValue in place of the method intValue.

Example (that stores a *double* value in a variable x**):**

```
double x =
    Double.valueOf(inputOutputField.getText().trim()).doubleValue();
```

Example:

You can also package these sorts of long formulas into methods such as

```
private static double stringToDouble(String stringObject)
{
    return Double.valueOf(stringObject.trim()).doubleValue();
}
```

(Depending on where this method is defined and used, it might be either *public* or *private*.) You can use this method to shorten the above example to:

```
double x =
    stringToDouble(inputOutputField.getText());
```

Outputting Numbers within a GUI

You can design a GUI using the AWT so that output consisting of a number (or numbers) is displayed in a text field (or text area). The following will take a number in a variable and display the number in the text field. (The details are the same if you are working with a TextArea rather than a TextField.)

Syntax:

```
Name_Of_Text_Field.setText(Wrapper_Class.toString(Variable));
```

Examples:

```
inputOutputField.setText(Integer.toString(sum));
inputOutputField.setText(Double.toString(area));
```

You can do the same things for numbers of the types *float* and *long*. Just use the class Float or Long in place of the class Integer or Double.

? SELF-TEST QUESTIONS

....

20. Write an expression to convert the *double* value 7.77 to the string "7.77". Include it in an assignment statement that stores that string in the variable s of type String. (Use the techniques in the preceding subsection.)

21. Write an expression to convert the string "3.14159" to the *double* value 3.14159. Include it in an assignment statement that stores that value in the variable x of type *double*. (Use the techniques in the preceding subsection.)

22. Suppose the String object s has the value "   3.14159   ". Write an expression that starts with the String object s and returns the *double* value 3.14159. Include it in an assignment statement that stores that value in the variable x of type *double*. (Use the techniques in the preceding subsection.)

Case Study A GUI Adding Machine

In this case study, you will design a program that uses the AWT to produce an adding machine program. The required interface is illustrated in Display 7.16. The white text field initially contains the text "Numbers go here." The user can enter a number by dragging the mouse over the text in the white text field and then typing in the number so that the number typed in becomes the contents of the text field. When the user clicks the "Add In" button, the number is added to a running total and the new total is displayed in the text field. The user can continue to add in more numbers for as long as she or he wants. To start over, the user clicks the "Reset" button, which makes the running sum equal to zero.

task specification

You decide that the adding machine will be an object of a class named Adder. You begin by making a list of the data needed to accomplish the adding machine

Adder class

Display 7.16 GUI Interface for an Adding Machine
....

computation and the AWT objects you will need to construct your class `Adder`. The user will enter a number in a text field, so you will need one instance variable of type `TextField`. You also need a number to keep a running sum of the numbers entered so far. Since these numbers might contain a decimal point, you make this an instance variable of type *double*. Thus, you come up with the following instance variables for your class:

data

```
private TextField inputOutputField;
private double sum = 0;
```

You next make the following list of additional objects needed to construct an object of the class `Adder`:

objects

As always, you need to be able to close the window and end your program. So, you decide to use an object of the class `WindowDestroyer` in the usual way.

`textPanel`: A panel to hold the text field `inputOutputField`.

`addButton` and `resetButton`: The two buttons.

`buttonPanel`: A panel to hold the two buttons.

A layout manager to arrange the buttons in their panel. You decide that this should be a `FlowLayout` manager.

A layout manager to place the text field in its panel. Since there is just one item in this panel, it does not matter what layout manager you use, so you decide to just accept the default layout manager.

A layout manager to arrange the panels in the window. You decide that this should be a `BorderLayout` manager

You need listeners to listen to the buttons. You decide to use the window itself as the only listener and have it respond to button events.

The class `Adder` itself will be a window class and so will be a derived class of the class `Frame`. So, you know the class definition begins like the following:

base class

Frame

```
public class Adder extends Frame
```

When listing the objects you need, you decided that the window itself would be the listener for the button events. Button events are action events, so you need to make the window (i.e., any object of the class `Adder`) an action listener. You do that as follows:

Action-
Listener

```
public class Adder extends Frame implements ActionListener
```

The building of the interface by placing components in containers and initializing the components, colors, and such is done in the constructor. So, you begin by doing the default constructor, which will be the only constructor. First, there are the routine details, namely, setting up the mechanisms for closing the window and placing a title in the title bar and setting the initial size of the window. So, you know the constructor starts something like

```
setTitle("Adding Machine");
addWindowListener(new WindowDestroyer());
myWindow.setSize(WIDTH, HEIGHT);
```

You add the buttons to a button panel in the usual way:

components in
containers

```
Panel buttonPanel = new Panel();
buttonPanel.setBackground(Color.gray);
buttonPanel.setLayout(new FlowLayout());
Button addButton = new Button("Add In");
addButton.addActionListener(this);
buttonPanel.add(addButton);
Button resetButton = new Button("Reset");
resetButton.addActionListener(this);
buttonPanel.add(resetButton);
```

The window
itself is the
listener.

In your outline of objects, you said that the window containing this panel would use the BorderLayout manager, and the specifications for the GUI say the buttons go on the bottom of the window, so you add the button panel as follows:

adding a panel

```
add(buttonPanel, "South");
```

In order to add a panel in this way, you need to give the window a BorderLayout manager as follows:

```
setLayout(new BorderLayout());
```

This should be executed before any components are added. So, you decide to place this line near the start of the constructor definition along with the other actions that set things like the initial size of the window.

The text field is inserted into its panel in a manner similar to the way you added buttons to the button panel, and then the panel with the text field is inserted in the window. The only differences from the button case are that the text panel goes in the "Center" and you need to decide how many characters you will allow in the text field. Thirty characters seem plenty long enough for a number and some extra white space. So, you produce the following code:

adding a
text field

```
Panel textPanel = new Panel();
textPanel.setBackground(Color.blue);
inputOutputField = new TextField("Numbers go here.", 30);
inputOutputField.setBackground(Color.white);
textPanel.add(inputOutputField);
add(textPanel, "Center");
```

Display 7.17 An Addition GUI *(Part 1 of 2)*

```java
import java.awt.*;
import java.awt.event.*;

/***************************************
 *GUI for totaling a series of numbers.
 ***************************************/
public class Adder extends Frame implements ActionListener
{
    public static final int WIDTH = 300;
    public static final int HEIGHT = 100;

    public static void main(String[] args)
    {
        Adder guiAdder = new Adder();
        guiAdder.setVisible(true);
    }

    public Adder()
    {
        setTitle("Adding Machine");
        addWindowListener(new WindowDestroyer());
        setSize(WIDTH, HEIGHT);

        setLayout(new BorderLayout());

        Panel buttonPanel = new Panel();
        buttonPanel.setBackground(Color.gray);
        buttonPanel.setLayout(new FlowLayout());
        Button addButton = new Button("Add In");
        addButton.addActionListener(this);
        buttonPanel.add(addButton);
        Button resetButton = new Button("Reset");
        resetButton.addActionListener(this);
        buttonPanel.add(resetButton);
        add(buttonPanel, "South");

        Panel textPanel = new Panel();
        textPanel.setBackground(Color.blue);
        inputOutputField = new TextField("Numbers go here.", 30);
        inputOutputField.setBackground(Color.white);
        textPanel.add(inputOutputField);
        add(textPanel, "Center");
    }
```

The GUI display produced by this program is shown in Display 7.16/page 379.

Display 7.17 An Addition GUI *(Part 2 of 2)*

```java
    public void actionPerformed(ActionEvent e)
    {
        if (e.getActionCommand().equals("Add In"))
        {
            sum = sum +
                stringToDouble(inputOutputField.getText());
            inputOutputField.setText(Double.toString(sum));
        }
        else if (e.getActionCommand().equals("Reset"))
        {
            sum = 0;
            inputOutputField.setText("0.0");
        }
        else
            inputOutputField.setText("Error in adder code.");

        repaint();
    }

    private static double stringToDouble(String stringObject)
    {
        return Double.valueOf(stringObject.trim()).doubleValue();
    }

    private TextField inputOutputField;
    private double sum = 0;
}
```

This completes your definition of the default constructor. The full definition is given in Display 7.17.

As you can see from your work on the constructor, placing components in containers is fairly routine. If you start with a picture like the one in Display 7.16, you can almost read the code from the picture. The only subtle part is deciding what will be the listener objects. Often, the best choice is the window itself, which is what you decided to do this time.

Handling events is not as routine as adding components to containers, but it does follow from a careful analysis of the problem specification (and perhaps a bit of inspiration). For this GUI, there are four basic things that can happen:

handling
events

1. The user can click the close-window button to end the program.
2. The user can write a number in the text field.
3. The user can push the add button.
4. The user can push the clear button.

Closing the window by clicking the close-window button is handled by an object of the class `WindowDestroyer`, as in all our examples. That is routine.

When the user types some number in the text field, that does not require any action. In fact, you do not want any action as a result of just writing a number. After all, the user may decide the input was entered incorrectly and change it. You do not want any action until one of the two buttons is pushed. So, the two button-pushing events are the only events that still need to be handled.

Pushing a button is an action event and an action event is handled by the method `actionPerformed` of the `ActionListener`. The window itself is the `ActionListener`, so the method `actionPerformed` is a method of the class `Adder`.

action-Performed

The header of the method `actionPerformed` is determined for you:

```
public void actionPerformed(ActionEvent e)
```

pseudocode

You have no choice on the header, but you must decide what the method does. You produce the following pseudocode for the method `actionPerformed`:

```
if (e.getActionCommand().equals("Add In"))
{
    sum = sum + the number written in inputOutputField.
    Display the value of sum in inputOutputField.
}
else if (e.getActionCommand().equals("Reset"))
{
    sum = 0;
    Display "0.0" in inputOutputField.
}
Repaint the screen.
```

stringTo-Double

You decide to use a private method to convert strings to numbers. You use the method `stringToDouble` given in the box entitled **Inputting Numbers within a GUI** on page 378. That means the method `stringToDouble` will be a private helping method, and the pseudocode for the method `actionPerformed` can be refined to the following:

```
if (e.getActionCommand().equals("Add In"))
{
    sum = sum +
            stringToDouble(inputOutputField.getText());
    Display the value of sum in inputOutputField.
}
```

```
else if (e.getActionCommand().equals("Reset"))
{
    sum = 0;
    Display "0.0" in inputOutputField.
}
```
Repaint the screen.

The rest of the translation from pseudocode to Java is straightforward. You decide to add a final *else*-clause to the nested *if-else*-statement, just in case of an unexpected error. The final code you produce and the final definition of the class Adder is given in Display 7.17.

This is only a very simple adding machine, but it has the elements you need to create a GUI for a display equivalent to a complete hand-held calculator. Programming Exercise 2 asks you to produce just such a calculator GUI. The program for that Programming Exercise will be longer than the one in Display 7.17, but each of the GUI features that you need to add are only slight variants of features that already appear in Display 7.17.

? SELF-TEST QUESTIONS

23. What would happen if the user running the GUI in Display 7.17/page 382 were to type the number 10 into the text field and then click the "Add In" button three times? Explain your answer.

24. In the GUI in Display 7.17/page 382, how come we made the text field inputOutputField an instance variable, but we did not make either of the buttons (addButton and resetButton) instance variables?

7.5 Adding Menus

You pays your money and you takes your choice.
Punch (1846)

In the AWT, menus are not a component, but are added to a GUI in ways very similar to how you add components. We will present one very simply way to add a menu (or menus) to a windowing system. Early versions of the AWT include little more than what we will present for adding menus. Later versions of the AWT provide much richer resources for designing menus, but the simple tools we present here will get you started.

▼ *PROGRAMMING EXAMPLE* A GUI with a Menu

Display 7.18 contains a program that constructs a GUI with a menu. This GUI has the exact same functionality as the GUI in Display 7.14/page 369, except that the GUI in Display 7.18 uses a pull-down menu and the GUI in Display 7.14 uses buttons to specify the actions. The user writes memos in the text area just as in Display 7.14. When memos are recalled, they appear in the text area just as in Display 7.14.

Display 7.18 A GUI with a Menu *(Part 1 of 3)*

```java
import java.awt.*;
import java.awt.event.*;
/****************************************************
 *GUI for saving and retrieving memos using a menu.
 ****************************************************/
public class MenuDemo extends Frame implements ActionListener
{
    public static final int WIDTH = 500;
    public static final int HEIGHT = 500;

    public MenuDemo()
    {
        setTitle("Memo Saver");
        setSize(WIDTH, HEIGHT);
        setBackground(Color.blue);
        addWindowListener(new WindowDestroyer());

        Menu memoMenu = new Menu("Memos");
        MenuItem m;
        m = new MenuItem("Save Memo 1");
        m.addActionListener(this);
        memoMenu.add(m);

        m = new MenuItem("Save Memo 2");
        m.addActionListener(this);
        memoMenu.add(m);

        m = new MenuItem("Get Memo 1");
        m.addActionListener(this);
        memoMenu.add(m);

        m = new MenuItem("Get Memo 2");
        m.addActionListener(this);
        memoMenu.add(m);

        m = new MenuItem("Clear");
        m.addActionListener(this);
        memoMenu.add(m);

        m = new MenuItem("Exit");
        m.addActionListener(this);
        memoMenu.add(m);
```

<Constructor `MenuDem` continued in next part of display.>

Display 7.18 A GUI with a Menu *(Part 2 of 3)*

<*public* MenuDemo() **continued.**>

```java
        MenuBar mBar = new MenuBar();
        mBar.add(memoMenu);
        setMenuBar(mBar);

        Panel textPanel = new Panel();
        textPanel.setBackground(Color.blue);
        theText = new TextArea(20, 50);
        theText.setBackground(Color.white);
        textPanel.add(theText);
        setLayout(new FlowLayout());
        add(textPanel);
    }

    public void actionPerformed(ActionEvent e)
    {
        String actionCommand = e.getActionCommand();
        if (actionCommand.equals("Save Memo 1"))
            memo1 = theText.getText();
        else if (actionCommand.equals("Save Memo 2"))
            memo2 = theText.getText();
        else if (actionCommand.equals("Clear"))
            theText.setText("");
        else if (actionCommand.equals("Get Memo 1"))
            theText.setText(memo1);
        else if (actionCommand.equals("Get Memo 2"))
            theText.setText(memo2);
        else if (actionCommand.equals("Exit"))
            System.exit(0);
        else
            theText.setText("Error in memo interface.");

        repaint();
    }

    public static void main(String[] args)
    {
        MenuDemo menuGUI = new MenuDemo();
        menuGUI.setVisible(true);
    }

    private TextArea theText;
    private String memo1 = "No Memo 1.";
    private String memo2 = "No Memo 2.";
}
```

Display 7.18 A GUI with a Menu *(Part 3 of 3)*

Resulting GUI

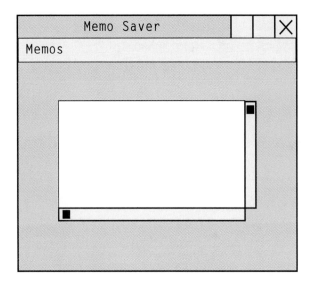

Resulting GUI (after clicking Memos in the menu bar)

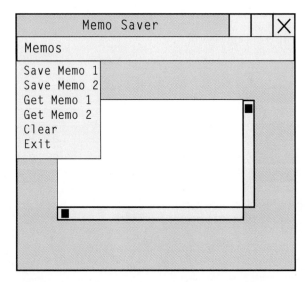

But the GUI in Display 7.18 does not have any buttons. Instead, it has a menu bar at the top of the window. The menu bar lists the names of all the pulldown menus. This GUI has only one pulldown menu, which is named "Memos". However, there could be more pulldown menus and they would be listed in the same menu bar.

The user can pull down a menu by clicking the menu name in the menu bar. Display 7.18 contains two pictures of the GUI. The first is what you see when the GUI first appears. In that picture, the menu name "Memos" can be seen in the menu bar, but you cannot see the menu. If you click the word "Memos" with your mouse, the menu pulls down, as shown in the second picture of the GUI. If you click "Save Memo 1", the text in the text area is saved. The other menu choices similarly behave the same as the buttons in Display 7.14.

There is one new choice on this menu, namely, Exit. When the user clicks on the entry Exit, the program ends and the window disappears. The exact same thing happens if the user clicks her or his mouse in the close-window button. So, there are two ways that a user can end this GUI.

In the next few sections, we go over the details of the program in Display 7.18.

Menu Bars, Menus, and Menu Items
When adding menus in the way we did in Display 7.18, you use the three AWT classes MenuBar, Menu, and MenuItem. MenuItems are placed in Menus, and then the Menus are placed in a MenuBar. Let's look at the details.

An object of the class MenuItem is one of the choices on a menu. It is identified by the string that labels it, such as "Save Memo 1". An object of the class Menu is a menu such as the one shown in the GUI in Display 7.18. You can add as many MenuItems as you wish to a menu. The menu lists the items in the order in which they are added. The following code, taken from the constructor in Display 7.18, creates a new Menu object named memoMenu and then adds a MenuItem labeled "Save Memo 1". Other menu items are added in a similar way.

MenuItem
Menu

```
Menu memoMenu = new Menu("Memos");
MenuItem m;
m = new MenuItem("Save Memo 1");
m.addActionListener(this);
memoMenu.add(m);
```

Note that, just as we did for buttons, we have registered the *this* parameter as an ActionListener. Defining ActionListeners and registering listeners for menu items are done in the exact same way as they are done for buttons. In fact, the syntax is even exactly the same. If you compare Display 7.14/page 369 and Display 7.18, you will see that the method actionPerformed is defined in the exact same way in both cases. The only difference is that in Display 7.18, the method has one additional case for the new entry labeled "Exit".

The class Menu is not a descendent of the class Container and the class MenuItem is not a descendent of the class Component. However, they act pretty much as if they were. You add a MenuItem to an object of the class Menu using the method add in exactly the same way that you add a component, such as a button, to a container object. Moreover, if you look at the preceding code, you will see that you specify a string for a `MenuItem` in exactly the same way that you specify a string label for a button. So, the syntax for adding menu items to a menu is really nothing new.

You add a menu to a menu bar using the method `add` in exactly the same way as you just saw for adding menu items to a menu. The following code from the constructor in Display 7.18 creates a new menu bar named `mBar` and then adds the menu named `memoMenu` to this menu bar:

MenuBar

```
MenuBar mBar = new MenuBar();
mBar.add(memoMenu);
```

Thus, adding menu items to menus and adding menus to a menu bar is done with the method `add` in the same way as you saw for adding buttons and other items to a `Frame`. However, adding a menu bar to a `Frame` is done in a different way. *You do **not** add a menu bar to a `Frame` with the method* `add`. A `Frame` has only one menu bar. Every `Frame` (and every descendent of the class `Frame`) has one instance variable of type `MenuBar`. To add the menu bar `mBar` to our `Frame`, we use the method `setMenuBar` as shown by the following code from Display 7.18:

```
setMenuBar(mBar);
```

This sets the one instance variable of type `MenuBar` so that it names the menu bar `mBar`. Saying it less formally, this adds the menu bar `mBar` to the `Frame`.

Menus and the Menu Bar

A menu item is an object of the class `MenuItem`. A menu is an object of the class `Menu`, and a menu bar is an object of the class `MenuBar`. None of these is a member of the classes `Container` or `Component`, but in some cases, they use the method `add` as if they were containers and components. A menu item is added to a menu using the method `add`. A menu is added to a menu bar using the method `add`. However, a menu bar is *not* added to a `Frame` using the method `add`. A menu bar is added to a `Frame` using the method `setMenuBar`. Events and listeners for menu items are handled exactly the same as they are for buttons. ◻

Why Only One Menu Bar?

There are ways to get more than one menu bar in a `Frame`, but to do so, you must put the second menu bar inside another `Frame` or inside of some other component of the `Frame`. A `Frame` can have only one menu bar that goes directly into the `Frame`. The reason for this is that a menu bar is not a component that is added to a `Frame` the way a button or a text area is added. Instead, menu bars are done in a totally different way. Each `Frame` has an instance variable of type `MenuBar`. The way you add a menu bar is to set the value of this instance variable (which you do with the method `setMenuBar`). Since there is only one instance variable of type `MenuBar`, there can only be one menu bar. ◻

Nested Menus

If you look at the class hierarchy in Display 7.9/page 350, you will see that the `Menu` class is a descendent of the `MenuItem` class. That means that a `Menu` can be a menu item in another menu. Thus, you can nest menus. For example, the outer menu might give you a list of menus. You can choose one of the menus on that list by clicking the name of the desired menu. You then choose from that menu list using your mouse

Adding Menus to a `Frame`

To see the following examples put together to produce a complete GUI, see the constructor in Display 7.18/page 386. In outline form, the details are as follows. (In this box, we are assuming that all the additions take place inside a constructor for a [derived class of] `Frame`. Otherwise, most method invocations would require an object name and dot before them.)

Creating Menu Items

A menu item is an object of the class `MenuItem`. You create a new menu item in the usual way, as illustrated by the following example. The string in the argument position is the label of the menu item.

```
MenuItem m;
m = new MenuItem("Save Memo 1");
```

Menu Item Listeners

Events and listeners for menu items are handled in the same way as they are for buttons: Menu items fire action events that are received by objects of the class `ActionListener`.

Syntax:

Menu_Item_Name `.addActionListener(`*Action_Listener*`);`

Example:

```
m.addActionListener(this);
```

Add Menu Items to a Menu

A menu is an object of the class `Menu`. You can use the method `add` to add menu items to a menu.

Syntax:

Menu_Name `.add(`*Menu_Item*`);`

Example (`memoMenu` **is an object of the class** `Menu`**):**

```
memoMenu.add(m);
```

Add the Menu to a Menu Bar

A menu bar is an object of the class `MenuBar`. You can add a menu to a menu bar as follows:

Syntax:

Menu_Bar_Name `.add(`*Menu_Name*`);`

Example (`mBar` **is an object of the class** `MenuBar`**):**

```
mBar.add(memoMenu);
```

Add the Menu Bar to the Frame

You do not use the method `add` to add a menu bar to a `Frame`. Instead, you use the predefined method `setMenuBar` as follows:

Syntax:

```
setMenuBar(Menu_Bar_Name);
```

Example:

```
setMenuBar(mBar);
```

again. There is nothing new you need to know to create these nested menus. You simply add menus to menus just as you add other menu items.

⚠ *GOTCHA* *Different Events with the Same Labels*

Look again at the definitions of the methods `actionPerformed` for the classes defined in Display 7.14/page 369 and Display 7.18/page 386. The version in Display 7.18 has one extra case for the label `"Exit"`, which we do not have in Display 7.14, but, all the other cases are identical. For example, the button event `"Save Memo 1"` in Display 7.14 and the menu item event `"Save Memo 1"` in Display 7.18 are both identified by the label `"Save Memo 1"`, and, as it turns out, are defined to produce the same action. But, what if you had a menu item labeled `"Save Memo 1"` and a button labeled `"Save Memo 1"` both in *the same* `Frame`? If you do things the way we have done them, then both of these events, the button click and the menu choice, *must have the same action* because they have the same label. Thus, you should be sure that every menu item and every button label has a different label. This is a severe restriction if you have nested menus, and so the designers of the AWT did provide a way to give different events with the same label differing actions, but those details are beyond the scope of this book.

Additional Examples of Using the AWT

If you skipped ahead in the book and are now returning to this chapter, then you may have skipped some of the sections on the AWT that follow this chapter. So, we have listed them after this paragraph. It would be good to now go back and read these sections for more examples of building GUIs using the AWT. For sections in chapters that you have not yet read, your best bet is to wait until you read that chapter and then read the AWT section in your normal course of reading the chapter.

Chapter 8: **PROGRAMMING EXAMPLE Catching a** `NumberFormatException` **(Alternative Ordering)** starting on page 431. This is an example of coping with incorrectly entered numeric input in a GUI.

Chapter 9: **PROGRAMMING EXAMPLE A GUI Interface to Files (Alternative Ordering)** starting on page 495. This gives an example of a GUI with multiple windows.

? *SELF-TEST QUESTIONS*

25. Write code to create a new menu item named `mItem` that has the label `"Choose Me!"`

26. Suppose you build a GUI interface using the AWT. If the user clicks a menu item, this fires an event. To what class does the event object belong? What kind of listener receives the event.

27. Suppose you are defining a class called `MenusGalor` that is a derived class of the class `Frame`. Write code to add the menu item `mItem` to the menu `m`

and then add m to the menubar mBar, and then add the menu bar to the Frame menusGalor. Assume this all takes place inside a constructor for MenusGalor. Assume everything has already been constructed with *new* and that all necessary listeners are registered. You just need to do the adding of things.

7.6 Inner Classes *(Optional)*

Inner classes are classes defined within other classes. Their use is not confined to programs and classes using the AWT. However, they are often used when programming using the AWT. A full description of inner classes is beyond the scope of this book. However, some simple use of inner classes can be both easy and helpful. We will describe one of the most useful applications of inner classes, namely, inner classes used as helping classes.

Helping Classes *(Optional)*

All of our AWT windows used the class WidowDestroyer (Display 7.2/page 332) for closing the window. Doing things as we have been doing them, we must always have this class WindowDestroyer around. Inner classes let us move the definition of a helping class, like WindowDestroyer, inside the class definition. For example, the class in Display 7.19 is a button demonstration similar to the one we gave in Display 7.8/page 347, but it has two differences:

1. We have defined a class caller InnerDestroyer inside the definition of our outer class, named InnerDemo. This class InnerDestroyer serves a purpose similar to, but not exactly the same as, the class WindowDestroyer that we used in our previous GUIs.

2. We have added some more code so that the user cannot exit the GUI unless the screen color is set to green. The behavior of this GUI is identical to the one we gave in Display 7.8, except that if the user clicks the close-window button and the window is not green, the screen produces the message shown in the GUI picture in Display 7.19. If the user clicks the "Green" button, then the screen turns green, the message changes to "GO", and after that, the user can then click the close-window button and the GUI will end. (When the GUI first appears, it also shows the message shown in Display 7.19.)

When you define an inner class, the methods in the inner class have access to all the instance variables and methods of the class in which it is defined, even if they are private. Note that the class InnerDestroyer resets the private instance variable theText of the class InnerDemo.

There are two big advantages to inner classes. First, since they are defined within a class, they can be used to make the outer class self-contained or more self-contained than it would otherwise be. Second, they make very useful helping classes because they can do things more easily than a class defined outside of the class they are helping. Notice the class InnerDestroyer. It directly accesses the

Display 7.19 An Inner Class *(Part 1 of 2) (Optional)*

```
import java.awt.*;
import java.awt.event.*;

//This class uses an inner class.
/*********************************************
 *GUI that demonstrates the use of buttons.
 *********************************************/
public class InnerDemo extends Frame implements ActionListener
{
    public static final int WIDTH = 300;
    public static final int HEIGHT = 200;

    /***************************************************************
     *Creates and displays a window of the class InnerDemo.
     ***************************************************************/
    public static void main(String[] args)
    {
        InnerDemo buttonGui = new InnerDemo();
        buttonGui.setVisible(true);
    }

    public InnerDemo()
    {
        setSize(WIDTH, HEIGHT);
        addWindowListener(new InnerDestroyer());
        setTitle("Button Demonstration");
        setBackground(Color.blue);

        setLayout(new FlowLayout());
        Button stopButton = new Button("Red");
        stopButton.addActionListener(this);
        add(stopButton);

        Button goButton = new Button("Green");
        goButton.addActionListener(this);
        add(goButton);
    }

    public void paint(Graphics g)
    {
        g.drawString(theText, 75, 100);
    }
```

Display 7.19 An Inner Class *(Part 2 of 2) (Optional)*

```java
    public void actionPerformed(ActionEvent e)
    {
        if (e.getActionCommand().equals("Red"))
        {
            setBackground(Color.red);
            theText = "STOP";
        }
        else if (e.getActionCommand().equals("Green"))
        {
            setBackground(Color.green);
            theText = "GO";
        }
        else
            theText = "Error in button interface.";
        repaint(); //force color and text change
    }

    private class InnerDestroyer extends WindowAdapter
    {
        public void windowClosing(WindowEvent e)
        {
            if (! (theText.equals("GO")))
            {
                theText = "Color must be green before exiting.";
                repaint();
            }
            else
                System.exit(0);
        }
    }

    private String theText = "Color must be green before exiting.";
}
```

An inner class.

Resulting GUI

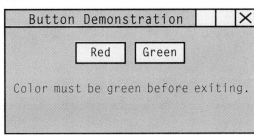

private instance variable `theText` of the outer class. If `InnerDestroyer` were defined in a separate file, then it would be very much more difficult to program it to do its job, since it would not have direct access to the private instance variables of the outer class. (Try it and see.) Because of these convenient features, inner classes are frequently used as listeners to handle events fired from within the outer class or component of the outer class.

There is yet one more advantage to inner classes. The name of the inner class is local to the class in which it is defined. You could have another class named `Inner-Destroyer` that is not an inner class, and the program in Display 7.19 would completely ignore that other class named `InnerDestroyer`.

We have made the inner class `InnerDestroyer` private because it is a helping class. It is possible to have a public inner class, but there are some subtleties involved in using public inner classes and we will not go into that in this book.

? SELF-TEST QUESTIONS (For the Optional Section)

28. Rewrite the class definition in Display 7.19/page 394 so that it has a second inner class that is the action listener instead of making the class `InnerDemo` the action listener.

Chapter Summary

- GUIs (graphical user interfaces) are programmed using *event-driven programming*. In **event-driven programming,** a user action, like a mouse click, generates an event and that event is automatically passed to an event-handling method that performs the appropriate action.

- There are two main ways of building up a GUI using the AWT. You can use inheritance to create a derived class of one of the predefined AWT classes or you can build up a GUI by adding components to a container class or you can do both in defining a single class.

- The class `Frame` is the AWT class that you use to create windows in a GUI. A window is defined as a derived class of the class `Frame`.

- A button is an object of the class `Button`.

- When adding components to an object of a container class, such as adding a button to a window, you use the method `add`. The components in a container are arranged by an object called a layout manager.

- A panel is a container object that is used to group components inside of a larger container.

- Text fields and text areas are used for text input and output in a GUI constructed with the AWT.

- A menu item is an object of the class `MenuItem`. A menu is an object of the class `Menu`, and a menu bar is an object of the class `MenuBar`. None of these is a member of the classes `Container` or `Components`, but in some cases, they use the method `add` as if they were containers and components.

However, a menu bar is added to a `Frame` using the method `setMenuBar`.

☐ Both buttons and menu items fire action events and so should have an `ActionListener` registered with them to respond to the event.

? ANSWERS to Self-Test Questions

1. All the programs we have seen before this chapter were designed to be performed by one agent (the computer) following a simple set of instructions of the form "first do this, then do that, then do something else, and so forth." In event-driven programming, you create a number of objects and let them interact via events. Each object simply waits around for some event to happen and then, if appropriate, it reacts to it. So the next thing that happens depends on the next event.

2. *GUI* is pronounced "gooey" and stands for *graphical user interface*.

3. Change the `paint` method to the following:

```
public void paint(Graphics g)
{
    g.drawString("I love you!", 75, 100);
}
```

4. Sizes and positions in the AWT are measured in pixels.

5. The `Frame` class. Note that you do not use the `Window` class.

6. `System.exit(0);`

7. Change the following line in the constructor in Display 7.5 from

`setBackground(Color.blue);`

to

`setBackground(Color.pink);`

8. You use the `setTitle` method, which is inherited from the class `Frame`. For example, the following line from the constructor in Display 7.5/page 341 sets the window title to `"Second Window"`.

`setTitle("Second Window");`

9. The `setVisible` method, which is inherited from the class `Frame`, will display a window on the screen. For example, if w is the window, the following will display the window

`w.setVisible(true);`

To make the window invisible, you use

`w.setVisible(false);`

10. `addWindowListener(new WindowDestroyer());`

11. The argument *new* `FlowLayout()` creates a new object of the class `FlowLayout` and passes this argument to the method `setLayout`. This use of

new is a way to create an argument without having to give the argument a name.

12.
```
public void paint(Graphics g)
{
    g.drawString("Live long and prosper.", 25, 100);
}
```

The coordinates 25 and 100 tell where the text begins. They could be some other numbers.

13. `gui.setVisible(true);`

14. You need an action listener. You make a class into an action listener by adding *implements* ActionListener at the end of the class heading (after *extends* Frame if it is a window object). You also must add a definition of the method actionPerformed to the class. Every component that generates an action event should have an action listener registered with it. You do this with the method addActionListener.

15. Yes. The two pieces of code are equivalent. Some people think each button must have its own name, but that is not needed in this case. In the alternative piece of code, the name b is used for one button, and then, *after* the button is set up and added to the GUI, the name b is reused for the second button. This second way of writing the code is, in fact, the way most experienced programmers would write it, but we used the first way, with two names, to avoid confusion, and that is also OK.

16. A text field displays only a single line. A text area can display more than one line of text.

17. Change the following line in the constructor

```
add(buttonPanel, "South");
```

to

```
add(buttonPanel, "North");
```

18. `TextField name = new TextField("Your name here.", 30);`

19. The portions in color are changed from Display 7.14.

```
public void actionPerformed(ActionEvent e)
{
    String actionCommand = e.getActionCommand();
    if (actionCommand.equals("Save Memo 1"))
    {
        memo1 = theText.getText();
        theText.setText("Memo 1 saved.");
    }
    else if (actionCommand.equals("Save Memo 2"))
    {
        memo2 = theText.getText();
        theText.setText("Memo 2 saved.");
    }
```

```
        else if (actionCommand.equals("Clear"))
            theText.setText("");
        else if (actionCommand.equals("Get Memo 1"))
            theText.setText(memo1);
        else if (actionCommand.equals("Get Memo 2"))
            theText.setText(memo2);
        else
            theText.setText("Error in memo interface.");

        textPanel.repaint();//Shows changes in textPanel
    }
```

20. s = Double.toString(7.77)

21. x = Double.valueOf("3.14159").doubleValue();

22. x = Double.valueOf(s.trim()).doubleValue();

23. Every time the user clicks the "Add In" button, the following clause from the method actionPerformed applies:

```
if (e.getActionCommand().equals("Add In"))
{
    sum = sum +
            stringToDouble(inputOutputField.getText());
    inputOutputField.setText(Double.toString(sum));
}
```

The assignment to sum takes place every time the "Add In" button event is generated. So, the number in the text field is added in as many times as the user clicks the "Add In" button. Moreover, the last line updates the value in the text field, so that the number that is added in is the updated number. If the user clicks the "Add In" button three times, the number *in the text field* will be added in three times. Let's say the user starts the GUI and types in 10. Now the user clicks the "Add In" button. That adds in the 10, so the value of sum is 10 and 10 is displayed. Now the user clicks the "Add In" button again. That adds in the 10, so the value of sum is 20 and 20 is displayed. Now the user clicks the "Add In" button a third time. This time the 20 is added in, so the value of sum is 40 and 40 is displayed. Note that it is always the number in the text field that is added in.

24. We made the text field an instance variable because we needed to refer to it in the definition of the method actionPerformed, as in the following:

```
sum = sum
        + stringToDouble(inputOutputField.getText());
```

On the other hand, the only reference we had to the buttons was in the constructor. So, we only need names for the buttons in the constructor definition. (An object need not be named by an instance variable to be part of an AWT object, or any kind of object for that matter. Objects do not go away as long as they are being used and the buttons are being used by the object of the class Adder, so they stay around whether or not you have a permanent name for them.)

25. ```MenuItem mItem = new MenuItem("Choose Me!");```

or, equivalently,

```
MenuItem mItem;
mItem = new MenuItem("Choose Me!");
```

26. A menu item fires events of the class `ActionEvent`. Listeners for `ActionEvent` objects are in the class `ActionListener`.

27.
```
m.add(mItem);
mBar.add(m);
setMenuBar(mBar);
```

In case you are wondering why we did not mention the class `MenusGalor`, it is because it is named implicitly. This will all take place inside a constructor named `MenusGalor`.

28.
```
import java.awt.*;
import java.awt.event.*;

public class InnerDemoExercise extends Frame
{
    public static final int WIDTH = 300;
    public static final int HEIGHT = 200;

    public static void main(String[] args)
```
<The definition of `main` is the same as in Display 7.19/page 394.>
```
    public InnerDemoExercise()
    {
        setSize(WIDTH, HEIGHT);

        addWindowListener(new InnerDestroyer());
        setTitle("Button Demonstration");
        setBackground(Color.blue);

        setLayout(new FlowLayout());
        Button stopButton = new Button("Red");
        stopButton.addActionListener(new InnerListener());
        add(stopButton);

        Button goButton = new Button("Green");
        goButton.addActionListener(new InnerListener());
        add(goButton);
    }

    public void paint(Graphics g)
```
<The definition of this method is the same as in Display 7.19/page 394.>

```
private class InnerListener implements ActionListener
{
    public void actionPerformed(ActionEvent e)
    {
```
<The definition of this method is the same as in Display 7.19/page 394.
It is just in a different place.>
```
    }
}

private class InnerDestroyer extends WindowAdapter
```
<The definition of this inner class is the same as in Display 7.19/page 394.>
```
private String theText =
        "Color must be green before exiting.";
}
```

? PROGRAMMING EXERCISES

1. Rewrite the program in Display 7.13/page 366 so that it is the panel with the buttons that changes to red or green instead of the window area with the text that changes color. Note that only the location of the color should be different. The text should appear in the same place and change in the same way.

2. Write a program that produces a GUI with the functionality and look of a hand-held calculator. Your calculator should allow for addition, subtraction, multiplication, and division. It should allow you to save and later recall two different values. Use the program in Display 7.17/page 382 as a model.

Chapter 8

EXCEPTION HANDLING

8.1 **BASIC EXCEPTION HANDLING 404**
Exceptions in Java 405
Predefined Exception Classes 413

8.2 **DEFINING AND USING EXCEPTION CLASSES 415**
Defining Your Own Exception Classes 415
Programming Tip Preserve `getMessage` When You Define Exception Classes 417
Programming Tip When to Define an Exception Class 422
Declaring Exceptions (Passing the Buck) 422
Exceptions that Do Not Need to Be Caught 426

Multiple Throws and Catches 427
Programming Tip Catch the More Specific Exception First 430
Programming Example Catching a `NumberFormatException` (Alternative Ordering) 431
Gotcha Overuse of Exceptions 435
Programming Tip When to Throw An Exception 435
The *finally* Block *(Optional)* 436
Case Study
A Line-Oriented Calculator 437

Chapter Summary 453
Answers to Self-Test Questions 453
Programming Exercises 454

8

EXCEPTION HANDLING

It's the exception that proves the rule.
COMMON MAXIM (possibly a corruption of
something like: *It's the exception that tests the rule.*)

Introduction

Exception handling is the preferred way to handle anomalous conditions in your program. Exception handling allows you to divide a program or method definition into separate sections for the normal case and the exceptional case, thereby dividing one larger programming task into two smaller and more easily doable programming tasks.

Prerequisites

Section	Prerequisite
Section 8.1	Chapters 1–5
Section 8.2 (omitting the following programming example)	Chapters 1–6
PROGRAMMING EXAMPLE Catching a `NumberFormatException` (Alternative Ordering)	Chapters 1–7

Chapter 7 (the AWT chapter) is not required except for one programming example that illustrates the use of exceptions in designing AWT interfaces. If you have not covered Chapter 7, you should skip that programming example.

8.1 Basic Exception Handling

buck **n.** *small object placed before the dealer in poker.*
    (Thus) **pass the buck** *(means) shift responsibility (to).*
The Little Oxford Dictionary of Current English,
    OXFORD UNIVERSITY PRESS, 1986

The buck stops here.
HARRY S. TRUMAN (SIGN ON TRUMAN'S DESK WHILE HE WAS PRESIDENT)

One way to write a program is to first assume that nothing very unusual or incorrect will happen. For example, if the program takes an entry off of a list, you might assume that the list is not empty. Once you have the program working for the core situation where things always go as planned, you can then make your program more robust by adding code to take care of the exceptional cases. In Java, there is a way to reflect this approach in your code. Basically, you write your code as if nothing very unusual happens. After that, you use the Java *exception-handling* facilities to add code for the exceptional cases.

In Java, **exception handling** proceeds as follows: Either the Java language itself or your code provides a mechanism that signals when something unusual happens. This is called **throwing an exception**. At another place in your program, in a separate class or just in another part of the code for your program, you place the code that deals with the exceptional case. This is called **handling the exception**. This method of programming makes for cleaner code. Of course, we still need to explain the details of how you do this in Java.

exception handling

Exceptions in Java

Most short programs do not need very much, if any, exception handling, and what exception handling they do use is often not easy to see in the code. So, in order to get a simple example, we will use a toy program for our first example. First, we will do the program without using Java's exception-handling facilities, and then we will redo it using exception handling.

For this example, suppose that milk is such an important food in our culture that people almost never run out of milk, but still we would like our programs to accommodate the very unlikely situation of running out of milk. The basic code, which assumes we do not run out of milk, might be as follows:

```
System.out.println("Enter number of donuts:");
donutCount = SavitchIn.readLineInt();

System.out.println("Enter number of glasses of milk:");
milkCount = SavitchIn.readLineInt();

donutsPerGlass = donutCount/(double)milkCount;
System.out.println(donutCount + " donuts.");
System.out.println(milkCount + " glasses of milk.");
System.out.println("You have " + donutsPerGlass
                    + " donuts for each glass of milk.");
```

If there is no milk, then this code will include a division by zero, which is an error. To take care of this anomalous situation where we run out of milk, we can add a test for this unusual situation. The complete program with this added test for the anomalous situation is shown in Display 8.1. Now, let's see how this program can be rewritten using Java's exception-handling facilities.

In Display 8.2, we have rewritten the program in Display 8.1 using an exception. This is only a toy example, and you would probably not use an exception in this case. However, it does give us a simple example. Although the program as a whole is not simpler, at least the part between the words *try* and *catch* is cleaner, and this hints at the advantage of using exceptions. Look at the code between the

Display 8.1 One Way to Deal with a Problem Situation

```
public class GotMilk
{
    public static void main(String[] args)
    {
        int donutCount, milkCount;
        double donutsPerGlass;

        System.out.println("Enter number of donuts:");
        donutCount = SavitchIn.readLineInt();

        System.out.println("Enter number of glasses of milk:");
        milkCount = SavitchIn.readLineInt();

        if (milkCount < 1)
        {
            System.out.println("No Milk!");
            System.out.println("Go buy some milk.");
            System.out.println("Program aborted.");
            System.exit(0);
        }

        donutsPerGlass = donutCount/(double)milkCount;
        System.out.println(donutCount + " donuts.");
        System.out.println(milkCount + " glasses of milk.");
        System.out.println("You have " + donutsPerGlass
                        + " donuts for each glass of milk.");
    }
}
```

Sample Screen Dialogue

```
Enter number of donuts:
2
Enter number of glasses of
milk:
0
No Milk!
Go buy some milk.
Program aborted.
```

Display 8.2 An Example of Exception Handling (Part 1 of 2)

```java
public class ExceptionDemo
{
    public static void main(String[] args)
    {
        int donutCount, milkCount;
        double donutsPerGlass;

        try
        {
            System.out.println("Enter number of donuts:");
            donutCount = SavitchIn.readLineInt();

            System.out.println("Enter number of glasses of milk:");
            milkCount = SavitchIn.readLineInt();          throw-statement

            if (milkCount < 1)
                throw new Exception("Exception: No Milk!");

            donutsPerGlass = donutCount/(double)milkCount;
            System.out.println(donutCount + " donuts.");
            System.out.println(milkCount + " glasses of milk.");
            System.out.println("You have " + donutsPerGlass
                            + " donuts for each glass of milk.");
        }

        catch(Exception e)
        {
            System.out.println(e.getMessage());
            System.out.println("Go buy some milk.");
            System.out.println("Program aborted.");
            System.exit(0);
        }

    }
}
```

try-block

catch-block

This is just a toy example to learn the basic syntax for exception handling.

Display 8.2 An Example of Exception Handling *(Part 2 of 2)*

Sample Screen Dialogue 1

```
Enter number of donuts:
3
Enter number of glasses of milk:
2
3 donuts.
2 glasses of milk.
You have 1.5 donuts for each glass of milk.
```

Sample Screen Dialogue 2

```
Enter number of donuts:
2
Enter number of glasses of milk:
0
Exception: No Milk!
Go buy some milk.
Program aborted.
```

words *try* and *catch*. That code is the same as the code in Display 8.1, except that the big *if*-statement (shown in color in Display 8.1) is replaced by the following smaller *if*-statement:

```
if (milkCount < 1)
    throw new Exception("Exception: No Milk!");
```

This *if*-statement says that if there is no milk, then do something exceptional. That something exceptional is given after the word *catch*. The idea is that the normal situation is handled by the code following the word *try* and that the code following the word *catch* is only used in exceptional circumstances. So, we have separated the normal case from the exceptional case. In this toy example, that does not really buy us too much, but in other situations, it will prove to be very helpful, and this short example will at least allow us to learn the basics of Java exception handling. Let's look at the details.

The basic way of handling exceptions in Java consists of the *try-throw-catch* threesome. A *try*-**block** has the syntax

```
try
{
    Code_To_Try
}
```

This *try*-block contains the code for the basic algorithm that tells what the computer does when everything goes smoothly. Of course, it is called a *try-block* because you are not 100% sure that all will go smoothly, but you want to "give it a try."

Now if something does go wrong, you want to throw an exception, which is a way of indicating that something went wrong. So the basic outline, when we add a *throw*, is as follows:

```
try
{
    Code_To_Try
    Possibly_Throw_An_Exception
    More_Code
}
```

In Display 8.2, the *try*-block with a *throw*-statement included is

```
try
{
    System.out.println("Enter number of donuts:");
    donutCount = SavitchIn.readLineInt();

    System.out.println("Enter number of glasses of milk:");
    milkCount = SavitchIn.readLineInt();

    if (milkCount < 1)
        throw new Exception("Exception: No Milk!");

    donutsPerGlass = donutCount/(double)milkCount;
    System.out.println(donutCount + " donuts.");
    System.out.println(milkCount + " glasses of milk.");
    System.out.println("You have " + donutsPerGlass
                       + " donuts for each glass of milk.");
}
```

Exception is a predefined class, and the following is called a *throw*-**statement**. A *throw*-statement creates a new object of the class Exception and *throws it:*

```
throw new Exception("Exception: No Milk!");
```

When an exception is **thrown**, the code in the surrounding *try*-block stops executing and another portion of code, known as a *catch*-**block**, begins execution. This executing of the *catch*-block is called **catching the exception.** When an exception is thrown, it should ultimately be caught by some *catch*-block. In Display 8.2, the appropriate *catch*-block immediately follows the *try*-block. We repeat the *catch*-block in what follows:

```
catch(Exception e)
{
    System.out.println(e.getMessage());
    System.out.println("Go buy some milk.");
    System.out.println("Program aborted.");
    System.exit(0);
}
```

The `catch`-block looks a little like a method definition that has a parameter of a type `Exception`. *It is not a method definition*, but in some ways, it is like a method. It is a separate piece of code that is executed when your program encounters (and executes) the following (within the preceding `try`-block):

> `throw new` Exception(*Possibly_Some_Arguments*);

So, this `throw`-statement is similar to a method call, but instead of calling a method, it calls the `catch`-block and says to execute the code in the `catch`-block.

---

throw-**Statement**

Syntax:

> `throw new` *Exception_Class_Name*(*Possibly_A_String*);

When the `throw`-statement is executed, the program execution is stopped and an exception is *thrown*. If the exception is caught in a `catch`-block, then the code in the `catch`-block is executed next. See the box entitled `try-throw-catch` on page 412 for more details.

Example:

> `throw new` Exception("Unexpected End of Input.");

■

What is that identifier e in the following line from a `catch`-block?

> `catch`(Exception e)

catch-block parameter

That identifier e looks like a parameter, and acts very much like a parameter. So, we will call this e **the** `catch`-**block parameter**. (But remember, this does not mean that the `catch`-block is a method.) The `catch`-block parameter does two things:

> First, the `catch`-block parameter is preceded by a class name that specifies what kind of exception the `catch`-block can catch.
>
> The second function of the `catch`-block parameter is to give you a name for the exception that is caught, so you can write code in the `catch`-block that does things with the exception object that is caught.

We will discuss these two functions of the `catch`-block parameter in reverse order. In this subsection, we will discuss using the `catch`-block parameter as a name for the exception object that is caught. In the subsection entitled **Multiple Throws and Catches** on page 427, we will discuss which exception objects go to which `catch`-block. Our current example has only one `catch`-block, so in this simple example, there is no issue of which `catch`-block to use. The most common name for a `catch`-block parameter is e, but you can use any legal identifier in place of e.

Let's see how the *catch*-block in Display 8.2 works. In order to understand how it works, we need to also look at the *throw*-statement in the *try*-block. That is also in Display 8.2 and is reproduced here:

throw-
statement

```
throw new Exception("Exception: No Milk!");
```

This *throw*-statement is embedded in an *if*-statement, but for our purposes here, we do not need to know how it comes to be executed. We only want to show you what happens when it is executed. When this *throw*-statement is executed, a new object of the class Exception is created by the part

```
new Exception("Exception: No Milk!")
```

The string "Exception: No Milk!" is an argument for the constructor for the class Exception. The Exception object, created with the *new*, stores that string in an instance variable of the object, so that it can be recovered in the *catch*-block. The word *throw* indicates that this object created with the *new* is **thrown**. When an object is thrown, execution of the code in the *try*-block ends and control passes to the *catch*-block (or blocks) that are placed right after the *try*-block. The *catch*-block from Display 8.2 is reproduced here:

throwing

```
catch(Exception e)
{
    System.out.println(e.getMessage());
    System.out.println("Go buy some milk.");
    System.out.println("Program aborted.");
    System.exit(0);
}
```

When an exception is thrown, the exception must be of type Exception in order for this particular *catch*-block to apply; but as we will see, all exceptions are of type Exception, so this *catch*-block will catch any exception. The object thrown is plugged in for the *catch*-block parameter e and the code in the *catch*-block is executed. So in this case, you can think of e as being the exception thrown by the following *throw*-statement:

```
throw new Exception("Exception: No Milk!");
```

Every exception has a method called getMessage, and unless you do something to change things, this method retrieves the string that was given to the exception object by its constructor (when it was thrown). So, in this case, e.getMessage() returns "Exception: No Milk!" Thus, when the *catch*-block in Display 8.2 is executed, it causes the following to be written to the screen:

getMessage

```
Exception: No Milk!
Go buy some milk.
Program aborted.
```

To summarize, a *try*-block contains some code that normally includes a *throw*-statement. The *throw*-statement is normally executed only in exceptional circumstances, but when it is executed, it throws an exception of some exception class. (So far, Exception is the only exception class we know of, but there are others as well.) When an exception is thrown, that is the end of the *try*-block. All the

---

try-throw-catch

This is the basic mechanism for throwing and catching exceptions. The *throw*-**statement** throws the exception. The *catch*-**block** catches the exception. When the exception is thrown, the *try*-block ends and then the code in the *catch*-block is executed. After the *catch*-block is completed, the code after the *catch*-block(s) is executed (provided the *catch*-block has not ended the program or performed some other special action).

If no exception is thrown in the *try*-block, then after the *try*-block is completed, program execution continues with the code after the *catch*-block(s). (In other words, if no exception is thrown, then the *catch*-block(s) are ignored.)

Syntax:

```
try
{
    Some_Statements
    <Either some code with a throw-statement or a method invocation that might throw an exception.>
    Some_More_Statements
}
catch(Exception_Class_Name e)
{
    <Code to be performed if an exception of the named exception class is thrown in the try-block.>
}
```

You may use any legal identifier in place of e. The code in the *catch*-block may refer to e. If there is an explicit *throw*-statement, it is usually embedded in an *if*-statement or *if-else*-statement. There may be any number of *throw*-statements and/or any number of method invocations that may throw exceptions. Each *catch*-block can list only one exception, but there may be more than one *catch*-block.

Example:
See Display 8.2.

---

rest of the code in the *try*-block is ignored and control passes to a suitable *catch*-block. A *catch*-block applies only to an immediately preceding *try*-block. If the exception thrown is an object of the class specified for the exception parameter of the *catch*-block, then the *catch*-block is executed. For example, if you look at the dialogue in Display 8.2, you will see that as soon as the user enters a nonpositive number, the *try*-block stops and the *catch*-block is executed. For now, we will assume that every *try*-block is followed by an appropriate *catch*-block. We will later discuss what happens when there is no appropriate *catch*-block.

Next, we summarize what happens when no exception is thrown in a *try*-block. If no exception is thrown in the *try* block, then after the *try*-block is completed, program execution continues with the code after the *catch*-block. In other words, if no exception is thrown, then the *catch*-block is ignored. Most of the time when the program is executed, the *throw*-statement will not be executed and so in most cases, the code in the *try*-block will run to completion and the code in the *catch*-block will be ignored completely.

The `getMessage` **Method**

Every exception has a `String` instance variable that contains some message, which typically identifies the reason for the exception. For example, if the exception is thrown as follows:

```
throw new Exception(Quoted_String_Argument);
```

then the quoted string given as an argument to the constructor `Exception` is used as the value of this `String` instance variable. If the object is called `e`, then the method call `e.getMessage()` returns this string.

Example:
Suppose the following `throw`-statement is executed in a `try`-block:

```
throw new Exception("Input must be positive.");
```

and suppose the following is a `catch`-block immediately following the `try`-block:

```
catch(Exception e)
{
    System.out.println(e.getMessage());
    System.out.println("Program aborted.");
    System.exit(0);
}
```

In this case, the method call `e.getMessage()` returns the string
`"Input must be positive."`

Predefined Exception Classes

When you learn about the methods of predefined classes, you will sometimes be told that they might throw certain kinds of exceptions. Usually, these are predefined exception classes. If you use one of these methods, you can put the method invocation in a *try*-block and follow it with a *catch*-block to catch the exception. Names of predefined exceptions are designed to be self-explanatory. Some sample predefined exceptions are

```
IOException,
ClassNotFoundException, and
FileNotFoundException.
```

When you catch an exception of one of these predefined exception classes, the string returned by the `getMessage` method will usually provide you with enough information to identify the source of the exception. Thus, if you have a class called `Sample-Class` and it has a method called `doStuff` which throws exceptions of the class `IOException`, you might use the following:

```
SampleClass object = new SampleClass();
try
{
    <Possibly some code>
    object.doStuff();//may throw IOException
    <Possibly some more code>
}
catch(IOException e)
{
    <Code to handle the exception, probably including the following:>
    System.out.println(e.getMessage());
}
```

If you think the exception makes proceeding with the program infeasible, then the *catch*-block can end the program with a call to System.exit, as follows:

```
catch(IOException e)
{
    System.out.println(e.getmessage());
    System.out.println("Program aborted");
    System.exit(0);
}
```

You will hear about more predefined exception classes as you learn more about Java, but for now, the only predefined exception class you are likely to use is the class Exception. The class Exception is the root class of all exceptions. Every exception class is a descendent[1] of the class Exception (i.e., either it is directly derived from the class Exception, or it is derived from a class that is derived from the class Exception, or it arises from some longer chain of derivations ultimately starting with the class Exception). You can use the class Exception itself, just as we did in Display 8.2/page 407, but you are even more likely to use it to define a derived class[1] of the class Exception.

The Class Exception

Every exception class is a descendent class of the class Exception. You can use the class Exception itself in a class or program, but you are even more likely to use it to define a derived class[1] of the class Exception.

◻

? SELF-TEST QUESTIONS

1. What output is produced by the following code?

---

1. If you have not yet read Chapter 6, you can disregard all the references to *descendent classes* and *derived classes*.

```
int waitTime = 46;

try
{
    System.out.println("Try-block entered.");
    if (waitTime > 30)
        throw new Exception("Time Limit Exceeded.");
    System.out.println("Leaving try-block.");
}

catch(Exception e)
{
    System.out.println("Exception: " + e.getMessage());
}
System.out.println("After catch-block");
```

2. What would be the output produced by the code in Self-Test Question 1 if we make the following change? Change the line

```
int waitTime = 46;
```

   to

```
int waitTime = 12;
```

3. Write a statement that will throw an exception if the value of the String variable named status is "bad". This would be inside of a *try*-block, but you need not write the entire *try*-block. The exception is supposed to be a member of the class Exception, and the string recovered by get-Message should be "Exception thrown: Bad Status." You need not write the *catch*-block.

8.2 Defining and Using Exception Classes

I'll make an exception this time.
MY MOTHER

In this section, we show you how to define your own exception classes and give you techniques for when and how to throw and catch exceptions.

Defining Your Own Exception Classes

You can define your own exception classes, but they must be derived classes of some already defined exception class. An exception class can be a derived class of any pre-defined exception class or of any exception class that you have already successfully defined. Our examples will be derived classes of the class Exception, but you can use any existing exception class.

When defining an exception class, the constructors are the most important methods and often are the only methods, other than those inherited from the base class. For example, in Display 8.3, we defined an exception class called DivideBy-ZeroException and the only methods we defined were a default constructor and a constructor with one String parameter. For our purposes, that is all we needed to

constructors

Display 8.3 A Programmer-Defined Exception Class
•••

```
public class DivideByZeroException extends Exception
{
    public DivideByZeroException()
    {
        super("Dividing by Zero!");
    }

    public DivideByZeroException(String message)
    {
        super(message);
    }
}
```

You can do more in an exception constructor, but this form is common.

super is an invocation of the constructor for the base class Exception.

•••

define. However, the class does inherit all the methods of the class `Exception`.[1] In particular, the class `DivideByZeroException` inherits the method `getMessage`, which returns a string message. In the default constructor, this string message is set with the following, which is the first line in the default constructor definition:

```
super("Dividing by Zero!");
```

This is a call to a constructor of the base class `Exception`. As we have already noted, when you pass a string to the constructor for the class `Exception`, it sets the value of a `String` instance variable that can later be recovered with a call to `getMessage`. The class `DivideByZeroException` inherits this `String` instance variable as well as the method `getMessage`. For example, in Display 8.4, we give a sample program that uses this exception class. In Display 8.4, the exception is thrown using the default constructor as follows:

```
throw new DivideByZeroException();
```

---

1. Some programmers would prefer to make the `DivideByZeroException` class a derived class of the `ArithmeticException` class, but that would make it a kind of exception that you are not required to catch in your code and so would lose the help of the compiler in keeping track of uncaught exceptions. For more details, see the topic `RunTimeException` in a more advanced Java manual. If this footnote does not make sense to you, you can safely ignore it. This footnote is primarily for any expert who might be looking over your, or my, shoulder.

This exception is caught in the *catch*-block shown in Display 8.4. Consider the following line from that *catch*-block:

```
System.out.println(e.getMessage());
```

This line produces the following output to the screen in Dialogues 2 and 3:

```
Dividing by Zero!
```

The definition of the class `DivideByZeroException` in Display 8.3 has a second constructor that has one parameter of type `String`. This constructor allows you to choose any message you wish when you throw an exception. If the *throw*-statement in Display 8.4 had instead used the following string argument:

```
throw new DivideByZeroException("Oops. Shouldn't Have Used Zero.");
```

then in Dialogues 2 and 3, the statement

```
System.out.println(e.getMessage());
```

would have produced the following output to the screen:

```
Oops. Shouldn't Have Used Zero.
```

Notice that in Display 8.4, the *try*-block is the normal part of the program. If all goes normally, that is the only code that will be executed and the dialogue will be like the dialogue shown in Sample Screen Dialogue 1. In the exceptional case where the user enters a zero for a denominator, the exception is thrown and then caught in the *catch*-block. The *catch*-block outputs the message of the exception and then calls the method `secondChance`. The method `secondChance` gives the user a second chance to enter the input correctly and then carries out the calculation. (If the user tries a second time to divide by zero, the method ends the program.) The method `secondChance` is there only for this exceptional case. So, we have separated the code for the exceptional case of a division by zero into a separate method where it will not clutter the code for the normal case.

◐ **PROGRAMMING TIP** *Preserve* `getMessage` *When You Define Exception Classes*

For all predefined exception classes, `getMessage` will return the string that is passed as an argument to the constructor, or will return a default string if no argument is used with the constructor. For example, if the exception is thrown as follows:

```
throw new Exception("This is a big exception!");
```

then "`This is a big exception!`" is used as the value of the `String` instance variable. If the object is called e, then the method call `e.getMessage()` returns "`This is a big exception!`"

It is a good idea to preserve this behavior of the method `getMessage` in any exception class you define. For example, suppose you define an exception class called `MySpecialException` and an exception is thrown as follows:

```
throw new MySpecialException("Wow what an exception!");
```

If e is a name for the exception thrown, then `e.getMessage()` should return "`Wow what an exception!`" To ensure that the exception classes that you define behave

Display 8.4 Using a Programmer-Defined Exception *(Part 1 of 3)*

```java
public class DivideByZeroExceptionDemo
{

    public static void main(String[] args)
    {
        DivideByZeroExceptionDemo oneTime =
                          new DivideByZeroExceptionDemo();
        oneTime.doIt();
    }


    public void doIt()
    {
        try
        {
            System.out.println("Enter numerator:");
            numerator = SavitchIn.readLineInt();
            System.out.println("Enter denominator:");
            denominator = SavitchIn.readLineInt();
            if (denominator == 0)
                throw new DivideByZeroException();
            quotient = numerator/(double)denominator;
            System.out.println(numerator + "/"
                              + denominator
                              + " = " + quotient);
        }
        catch(DivideByZeroException e)
        {
            System.out.println(e.getMessage());
            secondChance();
        }

    }
```

We will present an improved version of this program later in this chapter.

Display 8.4 Using a Programmer-Defined Exception *(Part 2 of 3)*
••

```
public void secondChance()
{
    System.out.println("Try Again:");
    System.out.println("Enter numerator:");
    numerator = SavitchIn.readLineInt();
    System.out.println("Enter denominator:");
    System.out.println("Be sure the denominator is not zero.");
    denominator = SavitchIn.readLineInt();

    if (denominator == 0)
    {
        System.out.println("I cannot do division by zero.");
        System.out.println("Since I cannot do what you want,");
        System.out.println("the program will now end.");
        System.exit(0);
    }

    quotient = ((double)numerator)/denominator;
    System.out.println(numerator + "/"
                                + denominator
                                + " = " + quotient);
}


    private int numerator;
    private int denominator;
    private double quotient;
}
```

Sometimes it is better to handle an exceptional case without throwing an exception.

Sample Screen Dialogue 1

```
Enter numerator:
5
Enter denominator:
10
5/10 = 0.5
```

••

Display 8.4 Using a Programmer-Defined Exception *(Part 3 of 3)*

Sample Screen Dialogue 2

```
Enter numerator:
5
Enter denominator:
0
Dividing by Zero!
Try again.
Enter numerator:
5
Enter denominator:
Be sure the denominator is not zero
10
5/10 = 0.5
```

Sample Screen Dialogue 3

```
Enter numerator:
5
Enter denominator:
0
Dividing by Zero!
Try again.
Enter numerator:
5
Enter denominator:
Be sure the denominator is not zero
0
I cannot do division by zero.
Since I cannot do what you want,
the program will now end.
```

Programmer-Defined Exception Classes

You may define your own exception classes, but every such class must be a derived class of an already existing exception class (either predefined or successfully defined by you).

Guidelines:

- If you have no compelling reason to use any particular class as the base class, use the class `Exception` as the base class.

- You should define two (or more) constructors, as described in what follows. Your exception class normally inherits the method `getMessage` unchanged. Normally, you do not need to add any other methods, but it is legal to add other methods.

- You should start each constructor definition with a call to the constructor of the base class, such as the following sample:

      super("MySpecialException thrown.");

- You should include a default constructor, in which case the call to `super` should have a string argument that indicates what kind of exception it is. This string can then be recovered using the `getMessage` method.

- You should also include a constructor that takes a single string argument. In this case, that string should be an argument in the call to `super`. In this way, the string can be recovered with a call to `getMessage`.

Example:

```java
public class TidalWaveException extends Exception
{
    public TidalWaveException()
    {
        super("Tidal Wave Exception thrown!");
    }

    public TidalWaveException(String message)
    {
        super(message);
    }
}
```

> `super` is a call to the constructor for the base class `Exception`.

---

this way, be sure to include a constructor with a string parameter that begins with a call to *super*, as illustrated by the following constructor:

```java
public MySpecialException(String message)
{
    super(message);
    //There can be more code here, but often there is none.
}
```

The call to *super* is a call to the base class. If the base class handles the message correctly, then so will a class defined in this way.

You should also include a default constructor in each exception class, and this default constructor should set up a default value to be retrieved by `getMessage`. This default constructor should begin with a call to *super*, as illustrated by the following constructor:

```
public MySpecialException()
{
    super("MySpecialException thrown.");
    //There can be more code here, but often there is none.
}
```

If getMessage works as we described for the base class, then this sort of default con-structor will work correctly for the new exception class being defined.

◑ PROGRAMMING TIP *When to Define an Exception Class*

As a general rule, if you are going to insert a *throw*-statement in your code, then it is probably best to define your own exception class. In that way, when your code catches an exception, your *catch*-blocks can tell the difference between your excep-tions and exceptions thrown by predefined class methods. For example, in Display 8.4/page 418, we used the exception class DivideByZeroException, which we de-fined in Display 8.3/page 416.

Although it would not be a good idea, you might be tempted to throw the exception using the predefined class Exception, as follows:

```
throw new Exception("Dividing by Zero!");
```

You could then catch this exception with the *catch*-block

```
catch(Exception e)
{
    System.out.println(e.getMessage());
    secondChance();
}
```

Although this will work for the program in Display 8.4, it is not the best technique. This is because the preceding *catch*-block will catch any exception, such as an IOException. But, an IOException might need a different action than second-Chance(). Rather than using the class Exception to catch division by zero, it is bet-ter to use the more specialized programmer-defined class DivideByZeroException, as we did in Display 8.4.

Declaring Exceptions (Passing the Buck)

Sometimes it makes sense to delay handling an exception. For example, you might have a method with code that throws an exception if there is an attempt to divide by zero, but you may not want to catch the exception in that method. Perhaps, some programs that use that method should simply end if the exception is thrown and oth-er programs that use the method should do something else, so you would not know what to do about the exception if you caught it inside the method. In these cases, it makes sense to not catch the exception in the method definition, but instead to have any program (or other code) that uses the method place the method invocation in a *try*-block and catch the exception in a *catch*-block that follows that *try*-block.

However, if a method does not catch an exception, it must at least warn pro-grammers that any invocation of the method might possibly throw an exception. This warning is called a **throws clause**. For example, a method that might possibly throw a `DivideByZer0Exception` and that does not catch the exception would have a heading like the following:

```
public void sampleMethod() throws DivideByZeroException
```

The part *throws* `DivideByZeroException` is a throws clause that says that an invocation of the method `sampleMethod` might throw a `DivideByZeroException`.

Most exceptions that might be thrown when a method is invoked must be accounted for in one of two ways:

1. The possible exception can be caught in a *catch*-block within the method definition.

2. The possible exception can be declared at the start of the method definition by placing the exception class name in a *throws*-clause (and letting whoever uses the method worry about how to handle the exception).

In any one method, you can mix these two alternatives catching some exceptions and declaring other exceptions in a *throws*-clause.

You already know about method 1, handling exceptions in a *catch*-block. Method 2 is a form of "passing the buck." For example, suppose `methodA` has a *throws*-clause as follows:

```
public void methodA() throws DivideByZeroException
```

In this case, `methodA` is absolved of the responsibility to catch any exceptions of type `DivideByZeroException`, which might occur when `methodA` is called. If, however, there is some `methodB` that includes an invocation of `methodA`, then `methodB` must handle the exception. When `methodA` adds the *throws*-clause, it is saying to `methodB`, "If you call me, you must handle any `DivideByZeroException` exceptions that I throw." In effect, `methodA` has passed the responsibility ("passed the buck") for any exceptions of type `DivideByZeroException` from itself to any method that calls it.

Of course, if `methodA` passes the buck to `methodB` by including a *throws*-clause such as

```
throws DivideByZeroException
```

then `methodB` may also pass the buck to whoever calls it by including the same *throws*-clause in its definition. But in a well-written program, every exception that is thrown should eventually be caught by a *catch*-block in some method that does not "pass the buck."

In Display 8.5, we have rewritten the program from Display 8.4/page 418, so that the normal case is in a method called `normal`. The method `main` includes a call to the method `normal` and puts the call in a *try*-block. Since the method `normal` can throw a `DivideByZeroException` that is not caught in the method `normal`, we need to declare this in a *throws*-clause at the start of the definition of `normal`. If we set up our program in this way, the case where nothing goes wrong is completely isolated and easy to read. It is not even cluttered by *try*-blocks and *catch*-blocks.

A *throws*-clause can contain more than one exception type. In such cases, you separate the exception types with commas as follows:

```
public int superMethod() throws IOException, DivideByZeroException
```

Display 8.5 Passing the Buck with a *throws* **-Clause** *(Part 1 of 2)*

```
public class DoDivision
{
    public static void main(String[] args)
    {
        DoDivision doIt = new DoDivision();

        try
        {
            doIt.normal();
        }
        catch(DivideByZeroException e)
        {
            System.out.println(e.getMessage());
            doIt.secondChance();
        }
    }


    public void normal() throws DivideByZeroException
    {
        System.out.println("Enter numerator:");
        numerator = SavitchIn.readLineInt();
        System.out.println("Enter denominator:");
        denominator = SavitchIn.readLineInt();
        if (denominator == 0)
            throw new DivideByZeroException();
        quotient = numerator/(double)denominator;
        System.out.println(numerator + "/"
                                        + denominator
                                        + " = " + quotient);
    }
```

Display 8.5 Passing the Buck with a *throws* **-Clause *(Part 2 of 2)***

```
public void secondChance()
{
    System.out.println("Try Again:");
    System.out.println("Enter numerator:");
    numerator = SavitchIn.readLineInt();
    System.out.println("Enter denominator:");
    System.out.println("Be sure the denominator is not zero.");
    denominator = SavitchIn.readLineInt();
    if (denominator == 0)
    {
        System.out.println("I cannot do division by zero.");
        System.out.println("Since I cannot do what you want,");
        System.out.println("the program will now end.");
        System.exit(0);
    }
    quotient = ((double)numerator)/denominator;
    System.out.println(numerator + "/"
                                  + denominator
                                  + " = " + quotient);
}



    private int numerator;
    private int denominator;
    private double quotient;
}
```

Sample Screen Dialogue

The input/output dialogues are identical to those for the program in Display 8.4/page 418.

Throwing an Exception Can End a Method

If a method throws an exception, and the exception is not caught inside the method, then the method invocation ends immediately after the exception is thrown.

---

throws-Clause

If you define a method that might throw exceptions of some particular class, then normally your method definition must either include a *catch*-block that will catch the exception or else you must declare the exception class with a *throws*-clause, as described in what follows.

Syntax (covers most common cases):

```
public Type_Or_void Method(Parameter_List) throws List_Of_Exceptions
Body_Of_Method
```

Example:

```
public void MyMethod(int n) throws IOException, MyExceptionClass
{
    . . .
}
```

Uncaught Exceptions

If every method up to and including the main method simply includes a *throws*-clause for a particular class of exceptions, then it may turn out that an exception of that class is never caught. In such cases, when an exception is thrown but never caught, either the program ends or else its performance may become unreliable. Here is a rule of thumb for what happens when an exception is thrown but never caught: If the program uses a GUI interface for I/O, as in Chapter 7 (i.e., an interactive window), then when an exception is thrown but never caught, the program will probably not end, but the program's behavior may be unreliable from then on. In most other cases, the program ends when an exception is thrown but never caught.

Exceptions that Do Not Need to Be Caught

As we have presented exceptions so far, we said that, in most cases, an exception must either be caught in a *catch*-block or declared in a *throws*-clause. That is the basic rule, but there are exceptions to this rule. (An exception to a rule about exceptions! Seems reasonable enough.) There are some exceptional exceptions that you do not need to account for in this way. These are basically exceptions that result from errors of some sort. Normally, you do not write a *throw*-statement for these exceptions. Normally, they are thrown by predefined classes that you use.

Exceptions that are descendents of the class Error or of the class RuntimeException do not need to be accounted for in a *catch*-block or *throws*-clause. For example, one such exception is `NoSuchMethodError`. This means your code has used a method but you have provided no definition for that method name. For all these sorts of exceptions, you should repair your code by fixing the bug in your code, not by adding a *catch*-block. Other exceptions that you do not need to catch or declare are exceptions that are more or less beyond your control. One such exception is `OutOfMemoryError`. If this is thrown, then your program has run out of memory, which means you have a very inefficient program or you need to buy more memory for your computer. Adding a *catch*-block will not help in this case and it is not required. [1]

How do you know if an exception is one that you must account for by either catching or else declaring in a *throws*-clause? As a rule of thumb, your code must either catch or declare in a *throws*-clause every exception that is explicitly thrown by your code, as in, for example:

```
if (denominator == 0)
    throw new DivideByZeroException();
```

Also, if a method has a *throws*-clause for a type of exception and your code includes an invocation of that method, then your code must either catch the exception or declare it in a *throws*-clause. However, you need not worry too much about which exceptions you do and do not need to declare. If you should fail to account for some exception that Java requires you to account for, then the compiler will tell you about the exception and you can then either catch it or add it to a *throws*-clause.

Details on *throws*-Clauses in Derived Classes

If you redefine a method in a derived class, then the *throws*-clause for the redefined method cannot contain any exception classes that are not in the *throws*-clause of the same method in the base class. In other words, you cannot add exceptions to the *throws*-clause when you redefine a method. This, of course, means that you cannot throw any exceptions that are not either caught in a *catch*-block or already listed in the *throws*-clause of the same method in the base class. You can, however, declare fewer exceptions in the *throws*-clause of the redefined method.

Multiple Throws and Catches

A *try*-block can potentially throw any number of exceptions and they can be of deferring types. Each *catch*-block can only catch exceptions of one type, but you can catch exceptions of differing types by placing more than one *catch*-block after a *try*-block. For example, the program in Display 8.6 has two *catch*-blocks after its *try*-block. The class `NegativeNumberException` is defined in Display 8.7/page 430.)

---

1. Technically speaking, the class `Error` and its descendent classes are not considered to be exception classes. They are not descendents of the class `Exception`. However, these classes can be thrown and can have *catch*-blocks just like real exceptions. So, to us, they look like exceptions.

Display 8.6 Catching Multiple Exceptions *(Part 1 of 2)*

```java
public class TwoCatchesDemo
{
    public static void main(String[] args)
    {
        try
        {
            int jemHadar, klingons;
            double portion;

            System.out.println("Enter number of Jem Hadar warriors:");
            jemHadar = SavitchIn.readLineInt();
            if (jemHadar < 0)
                throw new NegativeNumberException("Jem Hadar");
            System.out.println("How many Klingon warriors do you have?");
            klingons = SavitchIn.readLineInt();
            if (klingons < 0)
                throw new NegativeNumberException("Klingons");

            portion = exceptionalDivision(jemHadar, klingons);
            System.out.println("Each Klingon must fight "
                                            + portion + " Jem Hadar.");
        }
        catch(DivideByZeroException e)
        {
            System.out.println("Today is a good day to die.");
        }
        catch(NegativeNumberException e)
        {
            System.out.println("Cannot have a negative number of "
                            + e.getMessage());
        }

        System.out.println("End of program.");
    }

    public static double exceptionalDivision(double numerator,
                    double denominator) throws DivideByZeroException
    {
        if (denominator == 0)
                throw new DivideByZeroException();
        return (numerator/denominator);
    }
}
```

This is just a toy example to learn the basic syntax for exception handling.

Display 8.6 Catching Multiple Exceptions *(Part 2 of 2)*

Sample Screen Dialogue 1

```
Enter number of Jem Hadar warriors:
1000
How many Klingon warriors do you have?
500
Each Klingon must fight 2.0 Jem Hadar.
End of program.
```

Sample Screen Dialogue 2

```
Enter number of Jem Hadar warriors:
-10
Cannot have a negative number of Jem Hadar
End of program.
```

Sample Screen Dialogue 3

```
Enter number of Jem Hadar warriors:
1000
How many Klingon warriors do you have?
0
Today is a good day to die.
End of program.
```

Display 8.7 NegativeNumberException

```
public class NegativeNumberException extends Exception
{
    public NegativeNumberException()
    {
        super("Negative Number Exception!");
    }
    public NegativeNumberException(String message)
    {
        super(message);
    }
}
```

Exceptions and the AWT (Alternative Ordering)
(This box only applies if you have already covered Chapter 7 on the AWT.)

When you define an action listener class in the AWT, you cannot declare any exceptions in a *throws*-clause of the method `actionPerformed`. All exceptions thrown in your definition of the method `actionPerformed` must be caught in that method definition. This is because the `ActionListener` interface completely specifies the interface for the method `actionPerformed` and you cannot change that interface. The interface for the method `ActionPerformed` does not specify any *throws*-clause, and so you cannot add a *throws*-clause. Similar remarks apply to other methods, such as `paint`, whose heading is already defined in the AWT.

◑ *PROGRAMMING TIP Catch the More Specific Exception First*

When catching multiple exceptions, the order of the *catch*-blocks can be important. When an exception is thrown in a *try*-block, the *catch*-blocks are tried in order, and the first one that matches the type of the exception thrown is the one that is executed. Thus, the following ordering of *catch*-blocks would not be good:

```
catch (Exception e)
{
    . . .
}
catch(DivideByZeroExecption e)
{
    . . .
}
```

The second catch*-block can never be reached.*

With this ordering, the *catch*-block for DivideByZeroException would never be used, because all exceptions are caught by the first *catch*-block. Fortunately, the compiler will probably warn you about this. The correct ordering is to reverse the *catch*-blocks so the more specific exception comes before its parent exception class, as shown:

```
catch(DivideByZeroException e)
{
    . . .
}
catch(Exception e)
{
    . . .
}
```

▼ **PROGRAMMING EXAMPLE** *Catching a* NumberFormatException
(Alternative Ordering)

This programming example uses material from Chapter 7 on the AWT. If you have not yet covered that material, you should skip this programming example until after you cover Chapter 7. Nothing further in this book requires this programming example. If you have already covered Chapter 7, this section is not especially difficult and there is no need to skip it.

The GUI in Display 7.17/page 382 serves as an adding machine with the user entering numbers and adding them into a total. There is, however, one problem with that GUI. If the user enters a number in an incorrect format, such as placing a comma in a number, then one of the methods throws a NumberFormatException. In an AWT program, throwing an uncaught exception does not end the GUI, but it does leave it in an unpredictable state. On some systems, the user might be able to reenter the number, but you cannot count on that, and even if it is true, the user may not know that she/he should and could reenter the last number. Display 8.8 contains a slight modification of the GUI class given in Display 7.17. When the user tries to add in an incorrectly formatted number, a NumberFormatException is thrown, but in this version the exception is caught and the user is given a message telling her/him to reenter the number (as shown in the GUI display in Display 8.8).

When the user clicks one of the buttons in the GUI in Display 8.8, that fires an action event e. The method actionPerformed is then automatically invoked with this action event e as the argument. The method actionPerformed invokes the method tryingCorrectNumberFormats using the action event e as an argument. The method tryingCorrectNumberFormats then processes the event just as it was processed in the previous version (Display 7.17 of Chapter 7). If the user enters all numbers in the correct format, then everything behaves as in the previous version (Display 7.17). But, if the user tries to add in an incorrectly formatted number, such as 2,000 with a comma instead of 2000 without a comma, then something different happens.

If the user tries to add in a number with an incorrectly formatted number, such as 2,000 instead of 2000, then the method tryingCorrectNumberFormats makes an invocation of the method stringToDouble with the alleged number string "2,000" as an argument. Then, stringToDouble calls Double.valueOf, but Dou-

Display 8.8 A GUI with Exception Handling *(Alternate Ordering) (Part 1 of 2)*

```java
import java.awt.*;
import java.awt.event.*;


/********************************************************
 *GUI for totaling a series of numbers. If the user
 *tries to add in a number in an incorrect format,
 *such as 2,000 with a comma, then an error message is
 *generated and the user can restart the computation.
 ********************************************************/
public class ImprovedAdder extends Frame
                                    implements ActionListener
{
    public static final int WIDTH = 300;
    public static final int HEIGHT = 100;


    public static void main(String[] args)
    {
        ImprovedAdder guiAdder = new ImprovedAdder();
        guiAdder.setVisible(true);
    }


    public ImprovedAdder()
```
<The rest of the definition is the same as the constructor
                Adder in **Display 7.17/page 382 of Chapter 7.**>

```java
    public void actionPerformed(ActionEvent e)
    {
        try
        {
            tryingCorrectNumberFormats(e);
        }
        catch (NumberFormatException e2)
        {
            inputOutputField.setText("Error: Reenter Number.");
        }

        repaint();
    }
```

This class is identical to the classes Adder *in* Display 7.17/page 382, *except that the name of the class is changed and the method* actionPerformed *is changed.*

Display 8.8 A GUI with Exception Handling (Alternate Ordering) (Part 2 of 2)

> `NumberFormatExceptions` do not require a `throws`-clause, but they can be caught like other exceptions.

```
//This method can throw NumberFormatExceptions.
private void tryingCorrectNumberFormats(ActionEvent e)
{
    if (e.getActionCommand().equals("Add In"))
    {
        sum = sum +
            stringToDouble(inputOutputField.getText());
        inputOutputField.setText(Double.toString(sum));
    }
    else if (e.getActionCommand().equals("Reset"))
    {
        sum = 0;
        inputOutputField.setText("0.0");
    }
    else
        inputOutputField.setText("Error in adder code.");
}

//This method can throw NumberFormatExceptions.
private static double stringToDouble(String stringObject)
{
    return Double.valueOf(stringObject.trim()).doubleValue();
}


    private TextField inputOutputField;
    private double sum = 0;
}
```

> As long as the user enters correctly formatted numbers, this GUI behaves exactly the same as the one in Display 7.17/page 382.

Resulting GUI

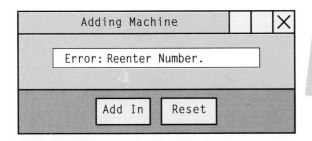

> If the user tries to add in an incorrectly written number, such as a number with a comma, then the GUI looks like this.

ble.valueOf cannot convert "2,000" to a number, because no Java number string can contain a comma. So the method valueOf throws a NumberFormatException. Since this happens within an invocation of stringToDouble, stringToDouble throws a NumberFormatException. The invocation of stringToDouble takes place inside the invocation of tryingCorrectNumberFormats. So, tryingCorrectNumberFormats throws the NumberFormatException that it received from the invocation of stringToDouble. However, the invocation of tryingCorrectNumberFormats is inside of a *try-catch* block (shown in color in Display 8.8). The exception is caught in the *catch*-block. At that point, the TextField (named inputOutputField) is set to the error message "Error: Reenter Number." so that the GUI looks like the picture in Display 8.8.

Whenever you have numeric input in an AWT, interface your code must convert the string input, like "2000", to a number like 2000. If the user enters a string that is not in the correct format for a number of the appropriate type, then a NumberFormatException will be thrown. It is a good idea to catch any such NumberFormatException so that the GUI can do something graceful, such as giving an error message and restarting, instead of entering some unfortunate state.

Notice that if a NumberFormatException is thrown, then the value of the instance variable sum is not changed. NumberFormatException is possibly thrown by an invocation of stringToDouble in the following line of code from the method tryingCorrectNumberFormats:

```
sum = sum +
        stringToDouble(inputOutputField.getText());
```

If an exception is thrown because an incorrectly written number was entered, then the execution of the method ends as soon as the exception is thrown. The exception is thrown by the method stringToDouble and so the exception is thrown before the above addition is performed. Thus, if an exception is thrown, the addition that would change the value of sum is not performed. So, sum is unchanged, and the user can re-enter the last number and proceed with the GUI as if that incorrect number were never entered.

Notice that none of the methods in Display 8.8 has a *throws*-clause of the form

```
throws NumberFormatException
```

That is because NumberFormatException is a descendent of the class RuntimeException and Java does not require a *throws*-clause when a RuntimeException might be thrown. However, you can still catch a NumberFormatException, just like any of the other exceptions we have seen.

? SELF-TEST QUESTIONS

4. Define an exception class that is called CoreBreachException. The class should have a constructor with no parameters. If an exception is thrown with this zero argument constructor, then getMessage should return "Core Breach! Evacuate Ship!" The class should also have a constructor that has a single parameter of type String. If an exception is

thrown with this constructor, then `getMessage` returns the value that was used as an argument to the constructor.

5. Correct the following method definition by adding a suitable *throws*-clause:

```
public void doStuff(int n)
{
    if (n < 0)
        throw new Exception("Negative number.");
}
```

⚠ **GOTCHA** *Overuse of Exceptions*

Exceptions allow you to write programs whose flow of control is so involved that it is almost impossible to understand the program. Moreover, this is not hard to do. Throwing an exception allows you to transfer flow of control from anyplace in your program to almost anyplace else in your program. In the early days of programming, this sort of unrestricted flow of control was allowed via a construct known as a *goto*. It is now almost universally agreed among programming experts that such unrestricted flow of control is very poor programming style. Exceptions allow you to revert to these bad old days of unrestricted flow of control. Exceptions should be used sparingly and only in certain ways. In the next subsection, we discuss where it is good to use an exception. Another good rule of thumb is the following: If you are tempted to include a *throw*-statement, then think about how you might write your program or class definition without this *throw*-statement. If you think of an alternative that produces reasonable code, then you probably do not want to include the *throw*-statement.

◑ **PROGRAMMING TIP** *When to Throw An Exception*

We have given some very simple code in order to illustrate the basic concepts of exception handling. However, our examples were sometimes unrealistically simple. A more complicated but better guideline is to separate throwing an exception and catching the exception into separate methods. In most cases, you should include any *throw*-statement within a method definition, declare the exception in a *throws*-clause in that method, and place the *catch*-clause in *a different method*. Thus, the preferred use of the *try-throw-catch* triple is as illustrated here:

```
public void MethodA(int n) throws MyException
{
        . . .
        throw new MyException("Bla Bla Bla");
        . . .
}
```

Then, in *some other method* (perhaps even some other method in some other class), you have

```
public void MethodB()
{
        . . .
    try
    {
            . . .
        MethodA(42);
            . . .
    }
    catch(MyException e)
    {
        Handle_Exception
    }
        . . .
}
```

Moreover, even this kind of use of a `throw`-statement should be reserved for cases where it is unavoidable. If you can easily handle a problem in some other way, do not throw an exception. Reserve `throw`-statements for situations in which the way the exceptional condition is handled depends on how and where the method is used. If the way that the exceptional condition is handled depends on how and where the method is invoked, then the best thing to do is to let the programmer who invokes the method handle the exception. In all other situations, it is preferable to avoid throwing exceptions. You can see a more complete example of this technique in the case study **A Line-Oriented Calculator**.

The use of exceptions that we discussed in the previous paragraph is very often used in predefined methods. Very often when you learn of a predefined method, you will be told that it throws exceptions of certain kinds. You the programmer who uses the predefined method is then expected to handle any exception thrown by the method.

The `finally` Block (Optional)

You can add a `finally`-block after a `throw`-block and its following `catch`-blocks. The code in the `finally`-block is executed whether or not an exception is thrown. The general syntax is as follows:

```
try-Block
catch-Block(s)
finally
{
    <Code to be executed whether or not an exception is thrown.>
}
```

At this stage of your programming, you may not have much need for a `finally`-block, but we include a description of it for completeness. At some point, you may find it useful.

Case Study *A Line-Oriented Calculator*

You have been asked to write a program that can be used as a calculator, similar to a hand-held calculator. The calculator should do addition, subtraction, multiplication, and division. This program is going to be used with rather old equipment and so it cannot use a windowing interface, but must use simple line-by-line text input and text output (like most of the other programs in this chapter).[1]

task specification

You need to be more specific about what the user interface will be. You propose that the user will be instructed to input operations and numbers as follows. Each operation and number is input on a line by itself as in the following example:

specification refinement

```
+ 3.4
```

It should not matter if there is or is not whitespace before or after either the operation, like +, or the number, like 3.4. As the user enters more operations and numbers, the program keeps track of the results of the operations performed so far, as in the following sample dialogue. (The program assumes that the initial "result" is zero. The user's input is shown in bold. The other text is output from the program.)

```
result = 0
+ 80
result + 80 = 80
updated result = 80
-2
result - 2 = 78
updated result = 78
```

Notice that the input is echoed so that the user can see what the computer is doing. You further suggest that the user indicate the end of a calculation by entering the letter E (in either upper- or lowercase).

Your suggested interface is accepted and you begin the project design. You decide to design a class for a calculator. The class will have a `main` method that is a complete, simple calculator program that follows the specification you have refined. Later on, you might design a more elaborate interface for the calculator. So, the class will be a bit more powerful than what is needed for the method `main`.

The program keeps track of one number that serves the same purpose as the number displayed on a hand-held calculator. On the screen, it is shown as, for example:

data for class

```
updated result = 80
```

---

1. If you have read Chapter 7, you will recall that in the subsection entitled **A GUI Adding Machine**, we showed you how to do something similar to this with a GUI interface. However, this program uses ordinary keyboard and screen text I/O. If you have not read Chapter 7, that is no problem. We do not use any of the material from Chapter 7.

result

The user can, add, subtract, multiply, and divide with instructions such as

+3

The current result is kept in a private instance variable called result. The program always adds, subtracts, multiplies, or divides the current result and the number entered. For instance, if the user enters

−9.5

and the current value of result is 80, then the value of result is changed to 70.5. When the user enters an 'e' or an 'E', that ends the program. If you look ahead to the Sample Screen Dialogue in Display 8.11 (part 5 on page 450), you can get an idea of how this calculator is used.

method actions

You decide that you need the class to have at least the following methods:

A method named reset to reset the value of result to zero.

A method to calculate the result of one operation. You decide to produce the result of one operation as a returned value, rather than immediately updating the instance variable result. This will make your class more versatile. You decide that the method should be approximately as follows

```
/*********************************************************
 *Returns n1 op n2, provided op is one of '+', '−', '*', or '/'.
 *********************************************************/
public double evaluate(char op, double n1, double n2)
```

An accessor method resultValue to recover the value of the instance variable result.

A method called setResult to reset the value of result to any specified value.

A method doCalculation that includes a loop to do one series of operations (with a call to evaluate on each loop iteration) producing a final result.

unexceptional part

You decide to first write the code as if everything went smoothly, perhaps noting exceptions where they might occur, but you defer writing the exception handling until after the heart of the class actions is designed. The definitions of the methods reset, setResult, and resultValue are routine, but the methods evaluate and doCalculation require a bit of thought. Let's consider doCalculation first.

doCalculation

The heart of the calculator's action is performed by the method doCalculation. Until the user enters the letter 'e' or an improper operator, the basic loop sequence should repeat the following again and again:

```
nextOp = SavitchIn.readNonwhiteChar();
nextNumber = SavitchIn.readLineDouble();
result = evaluate(nextOp, result, nextNumber);
```

Here nextOp is a variable of type char, nextNumber is one of type double, and result is the instance variable. When the user enters the letter 'e' (in lowercase or uppercase), the loop ends and the calculation ends. You convert this to the following more complete Java loop:

```
boolean done = false;
while (! done)
{
    nextOp = SavitchIn.readNonwhiteChar();
    if ((nextOp == 'e') || (nextOp == 'E'))
        done = true;
    else
    {
        nextNumber = SavitchIn.readLineDouble();
        result = evaluate(nextOp, result, nextNumber);
        System.out.println("result " + nextOp + " "
                            + nextNumber + " = " + result);
        System.out.println("updated result = " + result);
    }
}
```

Note that `readLineDouble` reads the rest of the line after the method `read-NonWhiteChar` has read a single character. The method `readLineDouble` does not have to start reading at the beginning of a line. If the user enters

+ 8.95

the method `readNonwhiteChar` reads the `'+'` and the `readLineDouble` reads the 8.95.

Next, you need to design the method `evaluate`, which you described as follows: `evaluate`

```
/************************************************************
 *Returns n1 op n2, provided op is one of '+', '-', '*', or '/'.
 ************************************************************/
 public double evaluate(char op, double n1, double n2)
```

The heart of the method `evaluate` can be a large *switch*-statement, something like the following:

```
switch (op)
{
    case '+':
        answer = n1 + n2;
        break;
    case '-':
        answer = n1 - n2;
        break;
    case '*':
        answer = n1 * n2;
        break;
    case '/':
        if (n2 == 0.0)
            throw new DivideByZeroException();
        answer = n1/n2;
        break;
}
return answer;
```

You decided to throw an exception in the case that the user attempts to do a division by zero, and so the preceding case for division includes the following:

```
if (n2 == 0.0)
    throw new DivideByZeroException();
```

precision of
floating-point
numbers

This is conceptually fine, but there is one problem. The numbers involved are of type *double*. Floating-point numbers, such as numbers of type *double*, only represent approximate quantities and so it does not make sense to use == to test them for exact equality. The value of n2 may be so close to zero that it behaves like division by zero and yet the test would say it is not equal to 0.0. You therefore decide to throw a DivideByZeroException whenever the denominator is very close to zero. However, you are not sure of what you should use as a definition of very close to zero. So, you decide that any quantity that is less than one ten-thousandth will be considered zero. However, since you are not sure this is the best choice, you decide to use an instance variable, named precision, that will tell how close a number must be to zero in order to be treated as if it were zero. The definition of precision is thus

```
private double precision = 0.0001;
```

The test for division by zero then becomes

```
if ( (-precision < n2) && (n2 < precision))
    throw new DivideByZeroException();
```

Thus, you rewrite the *switch*-statement to the following:

```
switch (op)
{
    case '+':
        answer = n1 + n2;
        break;
    case '-':
        answer = n1 - n2;
        break;
    case '*':
        answer = n1 * n2;
        break;
    case '/':
        if ( (-precision < n2) && (n2 < precision))
            throw new DivideByZeroException();
        answer = n1/n2;
        break;
}
```

But what if the user enters some character other than '+', '-', '*', or '/' for the op? You decide that that will be handled by throwing an exception. So the *switch*-statement now looks like

```
switch (op)
{
    case '+':
        answer = n1 + n2;
        break;
    case '-':
        answer = n1 - n2;
        break;
    case '*':
        answer = n1 * n2;
        break;
    case '/':
        if ( (-precision < n2) && (n2 < precision))
            throw new DivideByZeroException();
        answer = n1/n2;
        break;
    default:
        throw new UnknownOpException(op);
}
```

The DivideByZeroException class was defined in Display 8.3/page 416. UnknownOpException is a new exception class that you need to define. You also need to write code to catch and handle all exceptions.

The code for the UnknownOpException class is similar to the other exceptions we have written and is given in Display 8.9. Note that when the user enters an

UnknownOp-
Exception

Display 8.9 Unknown Operator Exception

```
public class UnknownOpException extends Exception
{
    public UnknownOpException()
    {
        super("UnknownOpException");
    }

    public UnknownOpException(char op)
    {
        super(op + " is an unknown operator.");
    }

    public UnknownOpException(String message)
    {
        super(message);
    }
}
```

unknown operator, you want to tell the user that that particular operator is unknown and so there is a constructor that takes an argument of type *char* that names the operator.

preliminary
version

At this point, you have all of the program written except for the exception handling. This lets you produce a preliminary version of your program, as shown in Display 8.10. You can use this version to test and debug the unexceptional portion of your program. As long as the user does not enter an unknown operator or perform a division by zero, this version will run fine. This allows you to test and debug the unexceptional portions of your program before you write the exception-handling portion of your program.

exception
handling

After you have debugged the preliminary version of your program that is shown in Display 8.10, you are then ready to add exception handling to your program. The most significant exception is the UnknownOpException and you consider it first. You have already given the definition of the class UnknownOpException, but you have not yet done anything with it other than declare it in a *throws*-clause. To make your program robust, you want to do something more serious and effective when an exception is thrown.

To make your program more robust, you use the *try-throw-catch* technique. The UnknownOpException will be thrown by the method evaluate, The method evaluate is invoked in the method doCalculation and the method doCalculation is invoked in the method main. You have three normal ways of handling the exception:

1. Catch the exception in the method evaluate.

2. Declare the exception UnknownOpException in a *throws*-clause in the method evaluate and then catch the exception in the method doCalculation.

3. Declare the exception UnknownOpException in a *throws*-clause in both the method evaluate and the method doCalculation and then catch the exception in the method main.

Which approach you choose depends on what you want to happen when an exception is thrown. You would use method 1 or 2 if you wanted the user to reenter the operator. You would use method 3 if you wanted to restart the calculation. You decide that the thing to do is to restart the calculation. So you decide to use method 3, which places the *try*- and *catch*-blocks in the method main. This leads you to rewrite the method main, as shown in Display 8.11/page 446. This has introduced two new methods, handleUnknownOpException and handleDivideByZeroException. All that is left to do is to define these two methods for handling exceptions.

handle-
UnknownOp-
Exception

If you look at the *catch*-block in the method main, you will see that when an UnknownOpException is thrown, it is handled by the method handleUnknownOpException. You design the method handleUnknownOpException so that it gives the user a second chance to do the calculation (starting from the beginning). If the user enters an unknown operator during this second chance, then again an UnknownOpException is thrown, but this time it is caught in the method handleUnknownOpException. To see this, look at the *catch*-block in the method

Display 8.10 Unexceptional Cases *(Part 1 of 3)*

```
/*******************************************************
 *PRELIMINARY VERSION without exception handling.
 *Simple line-oriented calculator program. The class
 *can also be used to create other calculator programs.
 *******************************************************/
public class PrelimCalculator
{
    public static void main(String[] args)
                                    throws DivideByZeroException,
                                           UnknownOpException

    {
        PrelimCalculator clerk = new PrelimCalculator();

        System.out.println("Calculator is on.");
        System.out.print("Format of each line: ");
        System.out.println("operator number");
        System.out.println("For example: + 3");
        System.out.println("To end, enter the letter e.");
        clerk.doCalculation();

        System.out.println("The final result is "
                                    + clerk.resultValue());
        System.out.println("Calculator program ending.");
    }

    public PrelimCalculator()
    {
        result = 0;
    }

    public void reset()
    {
        result = 0;
    }

    public void setResult(double newResult)
    {
        result = newResult;
    }
```

The definition of the `main` method will change before this case study ends.

Display 8.10 Unexceptional Cases *(Part 2 of 3)*

```java
public double resultValue()
{
    return result;
}


public void doCalculation() throws DivideByZeroException,
                                    UnknownOpException
{
    char nextOp;
    double nextNumber;
    boolean done = false;
    result = 0;
    System.out.println("result = " + result);

    while (! done)
    {
        nextOp = SavitchIn.readNonwhiteChar();
        if ((nextOp == 'e') || (nextOp == 'E'))
            done = true;
        else
        {
            nextNumber = SavitchIn.readLineDouble();
            result = evaluate(nextOp, result, nextNumber);
            System.out.println("result " + nextOp + " "
                            + nextNumber + " = " + result);
            System.out.println("updated result = " + result);
        }
    }

}
```

This does not do exception handling and so is not yet complete. However, it does run and can be used for debugging.

Display 8.10 Unexceptional Cases *(Part 3 of 3)*

```
    /*********************************************************
    *Returns n1 op n2, provided op is one of '+', '-', '*',or '/'.
    *Any other value of op throws UnknownOpException.
    *********************************************************/
    public double evaluate(char op, double n1, double n2)
                                throws DivideByZeroException,
                                       UnknownOpException
    {
        double answer;
        switch (op)
        {
            case '+':
                answer = n1 + n2;
                break;
            case '-':
                answer = n1 - n2;
                break;
            case '*':
                answer = n1 * n2;
                break;
            case '/':
                if ( (-precision < n2) && (n2 < precision))
                    throw new DivideByZeroException();
                answer = n1/n2;
                break;
            default:
                throw new UnknownOpException(op);
        }

        return answer;
    }


    private double result;
    private double precision = 0.0001;
    //Numbers this close to zero are treated as if equal to zero.
}
```

Display 8.11 Complete Line-Oriented Calculator *(Part 1 of 5)*

```
/*******************************************************
 *Simple line-oriented calculator program. The class
 *can also be used to create other calculator programs.
 *******************************************************/
public class Calculator
{
    public static void main(String[] args)
    {
        Calculator clerk = new Calculator();

        try
        {
            System.out.println("Calculator is on.");
            System.out.print("Format of each line: ");
            System.out.println("operator number");
            System.out.println("For example: + 3");
            System.out.println("To end, enter the letter e.");
            clerk.doCalculation();
        }
        catch(UnknownOpException e)
        {
            clerk.handleUnknownOpException(e);
        }
        catch(DivideByZeroException e)
        {
            clerk.handleDivideByZeroException(e);
        }

        System.out.println("The final result is "
                                + clerk.resultValue());
        System.out.println("Calculator program ending.");
    }

    public Calculator()
    {
        result = 0;
    }
```

Display 8.11 Complete Line-Oriented Calculator *(Part 2 of 5)*

```java
public void reset()
{
    result = 0;
}

public void setResult(double newResult)
{
    result = newResult;
}

public double resultValue()
{
    return result;
}

/***********************************************
 *The heart of a calculator.  This does not give
 *instructions.  Input errors throw exceptions.
 ***********************************************/
public void doCalculation() throws DivideByZeroException,
                                    UnknownOpException
{
    char nextOp;
    double nextNumber;
    boolean done = false;
    result = 0;
    System.out.println("result = " + result);
    while (! done)
    {
        nextOp = SavitchIn.readNonwhiteChar();
        if ((nextOp == 'e') || (nextOp == 'E'))
            done = true;
        else
        {
            nextNumber = SavitchIn.readLineDouble();
            result = evaluate(nextOp, result, nextNumber);
            System.out.println("result " + nextOp + " "
                            + nextNumber + " = " + result);
            System.out.println("updated result = " + result);
        }
    }
}
```

reset, setResult, and resultValue are not used in this program, but might be needed by some other application that uses this class.

Display 8.11 Complete Line-Oriented Calculator *(Part 3 of 5)*

```
/******************************************************
 *Returns n1 op n2, provided op is one of '+', '-', '*',or '/'.
 *Any other value of op throws UnknownOpException.
 ******************************************************/
public double evaluate(char op, double n1, double n2)
            throws DivideByZeroException, UnknownOpException
{
    double answer;
    switch (op)
    {
        case '+':
            answer = n1 + n2;
            break;
        case '-':
            answer = n1 - n2;
            break;
        case '*':
            answer = n1 * n2;
            break;
        case '/':
            if ( (-precision < n2) && (n2 < precision))
                throw new DivideByZeroException();
            answer = n1/n2;
            break;
        default:
            throw new UnknownOpException(op);
    }

    return answer;
}

public void
    handleDivideByZeroException(DivideByZeroException e)
{
    System.out.println("Dividing by zero.");
    System.out.println("Program aborted");
    System.exit(0);
}
```

Display 8.11 Complete Line-Oriented Calculator *(Part 4 of 5)*

```java
public void handleUnknownOpException(UnknownOpException e)
{
    System.out.println(e.getMessage());
    System.out.println("Try again from the beginning:");

    try
    {
        System.out.print("Format of each line: ");
        System.out.println("operator number");
        System.out.println("For example: +3");
        System.out.println("To end, enter the letter e.");
        doCalculation();
    }
    catch(UnknownOpException e2)
    {
        System.out.println(e2.getMessage());
        System.out.println("Try again at some other time.");
        System.out.println("Program ending.");
        System.exit(0);
    }
    catch(DivideByZeroException e3)
    {
        handleDivideByZeroException(e3);
    }
}




    private double result;
    private double precision = 0.0001;
    //Numbers this close to zero are treated as if equal to zero.
}
```

This is done the first time UnknownOpException is thrown.

This catches UnknownOpException if it is thrown a second time.

Display 8.11 Complete Line Oriented Calculator *(Part 5 of 5)*

Sample Screen Dialogue

```
Calculator is on.
Format of each line: operator number
For example: +3
To end, enter the letter e.
result = 0.0
+80
result + 80.0 = 80.0
updated result = 80.0
-2
result - 2.0 = 78.0
updated result = 78.0
%4
% is an unknown operator.
Try again from the beginning:
Format of each line is: operator number
For example: +3
To end, enter the letter e.
result = 0.0
+80
result + 80.0 = 80.0
updated result = 80.0
-2
result - 2.0 = 78.0
updated result = 78.0
* 0.04
result * 0.04 = 3.12
updated result = 3.12
e
The final result is 3.12
Calculator program ending.
```

handleUnknownOpException (Display 8.11, part 4). If there is such a second throwing of an UnknownOpException, then the program ends. (There are other good ways to handle an UnknownOpException, but this is one satisfactory way to handle the exception.)

Notice that in the definition of the method doCalculation (Display 8.11, part 2), you needed to include a *throws*-clause for the exception classes UnknownOpException and DivideByZeroException, even though the body of the method doCalculation does not include any *throw*-statements. This is because the method doCalculation includes a call to the method evaluate, and the method evaluate can throw an UnknownOpException or a DivideByZeroException.

You decide that if the user attempts to do a division by zero, you will simply end the program. (Perhaps you will do something more elaborate in a future version of this program, but this will do for now.) Thus, the method handleDivide-ByZero is very simple.

handling division
by zero

Your program is now complete and is shown in Display 8.11. (The program is adequate, but it would be even nicer if it had a windowing interface. If you have read Chapter 7 on the AWT, you can produce such a windowing interface. Programming Exercise 3/page 456 asks you to produce such a windowing interface.)

? SELF-TEST QUESTIONS

6. What is the output produced by the following program?

```java
public class CatchDemo
{
    public static void main(String[] args)
    {
        CatchDemo object = new CatchDemo();

        try
        {
            System.out.println("Trying");
            object.sampleMethod();
            System.out.println("Trying after call.");
        }
        catch(Exception e)
        {
            System.out.println("Catching");
            System.out.println(e.getMessage());
        }
    }
```

```
    public void sampleMethod() throws Exception
    {
        System.out.println("Starting SampleMethod.");
        throw new
            Exception("From sampleMethod with love.");
    }
}
```

7. This exercise is for those who read the optional section **The** `finally` **Block (Optional).** What is the output produced by the following program? The part in color is code that was added to the program in Self-Test Question 6.

```
public class CatchDemo
{
    public static void main(String[] args)
    {
        CatchDemo object = new CatchDemo();

        try
        {
            System.out.println("Trying");
            object.sampleMethod();
            System.out.println("Trying after call.");
        }
        catch(Exception e)
        {
            System.out.println("Catching");
            System.out.println(e.getMessage());
        }

        finally
        {
            System.out.println("In finally Block.");
        }
    }

    public void sampleMethod() throws Exception
    {
        System.out.println("Starting SampleMethod.");
        throw new
            Exception("From sampleMethod with love.");
    }
}
```

8. Write two accessor methods that can be added to the class `Calculator` in Display 8.11. One method is called `precisionValue` and it returns the value of the instance variable `precision`. The other method is called `setPrecision` and it changes the value of the instance variable `precision`.

Chapter Summary

- An exception is an object of a class that is a descendent of the class `Exception`. (Descendents of the class `Error` are not exceptions, but behave like exception, so we are also considering them to be exceptions.)

- Exception handling allows you to design and code the normal case for your program separately from the code that handles exceptional situations.

- There are predefined exception classes. You can also define your own exception classes.

- Certain Java statements themselves might throw an exception. Methods from class libraries might throw exceptions. You can also explicitly throw an exception in your code by using a `throw`-statement.

- An exception can be thrown in a `try`-block. Alternatively, an exception can be thrown in a method definition that does not include a `try`-block. In this case, an invocation of the method can be placed in a `try`-block.

- When a method might throw an exception and not catch the exception, the exception class usually must be listed in a `throws`-clause for the method.

- An exception is caught in a `catch`-block.

- A `try`-block may be followed by more than one `catch`-block. In this case, always list the `catch`-block for a more specific exception class before the `catch`-block for a more general exception class.

- Every exception has a `getMessage` method that can be used to recover a description of the exception caught.

- Do not overuse exceptions.

? ANSWERS to Self-Test Questions

1.
```
Try-block entered.
Exception: Time Limit Exceeded.
After catch-block.
```

2.
```
Try-block entered.
Leaving try-block.
After catch-block.
```

3.
```
if (status.equals("bad"))
    throw new Exception("Exception thrown: Bad Status.");
```

4.
```java
public class CoreBreachException extends Exception
{
    public CoreBreachException()
    {
        super("Core Breach! Evacuate Ship!");
    }

    public CoreBreachException(String message)
    {
        super(message);
    }
}
```

5.
```java
public void doStuff(int n) throws Exception
{
    if (n < 0)
        throw new Exception("Negative number.");
}
```

6.
```
Trying
Starting SampleMethod.
Catching
From sampleMethod with love.
```

7.
```
Trying
Starting SampleMethod.
Catching
From sampleMethod with love.
In finally Block.
```

8.
```java
public double precisionValue()
{
    return precision;
}
public void setPrecision(double newPrecision)
{
    precision = newPrecision;
}
```

? PROGRAMMING EXERCISES

1. Write a program that converts from 24-hour time to 12-hour time. The following is a sample dialogue:

```
Enter time in 24-hour notation:
13:07
That is the same as
1:07 PM
Again?(y/n)
y
Enter time in 24-hour notation:
10:15
That is the same as
10:15 AM
Again?(y/n)
y
Enter time in 24-hour notation:
10:65
There is no such time as 10:65
Try Again:
Enter time in 24-hour notation:
16:05
That is the same as
4:05 PM        .
Again?(y/n)
n
End of program
```

You will define an exception class called `TimeFormatException`. If the user enters an illegal time, like `10:65` or even gibberish like `8&*68`, then your program will throw and catch a `TimeFormatException`.

2. Write a program that uses the class `Calculator` in Display 8.11 to create a more powerful calculator. This calculator will allow you to save a result in memory and call the result back. Commands are

`e` for end
`c` for clear, sets result to `0`
`m` for save in memory, sets memory equal to `result`
`r` for recall memory, displays the value of memory,
 but does not change `result`

You should define a derived class of the class `Calculator` that has one more instance variable for the memory, a new `main`, a redefinition of the method `handleUnknownOpException`, a `main` method that runs the improved calculator, and anything else new or redefined that you need. What a sample dialogue should look like is shown in what follows. Your program need not produce an identical dialogue, but it should be similar and just as nice or nicer.

```
Calculator on:
result = 0.0
+4
result + 4.0 = 4.0
updated result = 4.0
/2
result / 2.0 = 2.0
updated result = 2.0
m
result saved in memory
c
result = 0.0
+99
result + 99.0 = 99.0
updated result = 99.0
/3
result / 3.0 = 33.0
updated result = 33.0
memory recall
memory value = 2.0
result = 33.0
+2
result + 2.0 = 35.0
updated result = 35.0
```

3. Do a version of Programming Exercise 2 that uses a GUI interface. You need to have covered Chapter 7 before you can do this project. You will have to decide the details of the interface yourself, but it should have at least as much functionality as that given in Programming Exercise 2.

Chapter 9

STREAMS AND FILE I/O

9.1 **STREAMS AND SIMPLE FILE I/O 458**
Introduction to Binary Files 459
Output to Files Using
    DataOutputStream 460
Some Details About writeUTF
    (Optional) 468
Gotcha Overwriting a File 469
Reading Input from a File Using
    DataInputStream 469
Gotcha Using DataInputStream
    with a Text File 473
Programming Example Reading a File
    Name from the Keyboard 474
Gotcha Defining a Method to Open a
    Stream 474

9.2 **EXCEPTION HANDLING WITH FILE I/O 477**
Catching IOExceptions 477
The EOFException Class 480
Checking for the End of a File 480
Gotcha Forgetting to Check for the
    End of a File 482
Programming Example Processing a File of
    Data 483
Programming Tip Objects Should Do
    Their Own I/O 483

Case Study Writing and Reading a File
    of Records 486
Programming Example A GUI Interface to
    Files (Alternative Ordering) 495

9.3 **MORE CLASSES FOR FILE I/O 510**
The File Class 510
The Classes FileInputStream and
    FileOutputStream 513

9.4 **TEXT FILE I/O 515**
Text File Output with
    PrintWriter 517
Gotcha A *try*-Block Is a Block 519
Text File Input with
    BufferedReader 520
The StringTokenizer Class
    (Optional) 523
Testing for the End of a Text File 525
Gotcha Checking for the End of a File
    in the Wrong Way *(Alternative
    Ordering)* 527
Programming Example The Class
    SavitchIn *(Optional)* 528

Chapter Summary 529
Answers to Self-Test Questions 530
Programming Exercises 537

STREAMS AND FILE I/O

> *I'll note you in my book of memory.*
> **WILLIAM SHAKESPEARE**, *Henry VI, Part II*

Introduction

I/O refers to program input and output. Input can be taken from the keyboard or from a file. Similarly, output can be sent to the screen or to a file. In this chapter, we explain how you can write your programs to take input from a file and/or send output to another file. One advantage of files is that they give you a permanent copy of your data that can exist after (and/or before) your program is run.

Since input from a file and input from the keyboard are so similar, we will develop enough general material on input that we can explain the code for the class `SavitchIn` in an optional section at the end of this chapter.

Prerequisites

Section	Prerequisite
Section 9.1	Chapters 1–5
Sections 9.2 and 9.3 (omitting the following programming example)	Chapters 1–6, Sections 8.1 and 8.2 of Chapter 8
PROGRAMMING EXAMPLE A GUI Interface to Files (Alternative Ordering)	Chapters 1–7, Sections 8.1 and 8.2 of Chapter 8
Section 9.4 on text files (omitting the following programming example)	Chapters 1–5, Section 8.1 of Chapter 8
PROGRAMMING EXAMPLE The Class `SavitchIn` (Optional)	Chapters 1–5, Section 8.1 of Chapter 8, section "Inputting and Outputting Numbers" of Chapter 7

If you wish to change the order of coverage, you can cover text files, Section 9.4, before covering any of the other material in this chapter. You can also delay coverage of some or all of this chapter.

9.1 Streams and Simple File I/O

> *Fish say, they have their stream and pond,*
> *But is there anything beyond?*
> **RUPERT BROOKE**, *Heaven*

You are already using files to store your Java classes and programs. You can also use files to store input for a program or to hold output from a program. However, in Java, the files that are commonly used for program input and output are a different kind of file known as *binary files*. In this section, we discuss binary files and how to perform simple file I/O using binary files.

file

In Java, file I/O, as well as keyboard/screen I/O, is handled by **streams.** A stream is an object that either delivers data to its destination, such as a file or the screen, or that takes data from a source, such as a file or the keyboard, and delivers the data to your program. The object `System.out` is the only output stream we have used so far. The class `SavitchIn`, which we have been using for input, behaves like an input streams (and in fact, has an input stream embedded in its definition). In this section, we discuss streams that connect your program to files. If at first you do not completely understand the notion of a *stream*, do not be concerned. As long as you understand how to do file I/O in Java, understanding the notion of a stream will come with time and experience.

stream

The Notion of a Stream

A **stream** is a flow of data. The data might be characters or numbers or bytes consisting of binary digits. If the data flows *into your program*, the stream is called an **input stream.** If the data flows *out of your program*, the stream is called an **output stream.** If an input stream is connected to your keyboard, then the data flows from your keyboard, and your program receive input from the keyboard. If an input stream is connected to a file, then data flows from the file, and your program will receive input from that file. In Java, streams are implemented as objects of special stream classes. The object `System.out` is an example of an output stream. The class `SavitchIn` is an example of an input stream class. You can also have streams that connect to files.

input stream
output stream

Why Use Files for I/O?

The keyboard input and screen output we have used so far deal with temporary data. When the program ends, the data typed in at the keyboard and the data left on the screen go away. Files provide you with a way to store data permanently. The contents of a file remain until a person or program changes the file. If your program sends its output to a file, the output file will remain after the program has finished running.

An input file can be used over and over again by many programs without the need to type in the data separately for each program. Files also provide you with a convenient way to deal with large quantities of data. When your program takes its input from a large input file, your program receives a lot of data without making the user do a lot of typing.

Introduction to Binary Files

All data in a file are stored as binary digits (or bits), that is, as a (probably long) sequence of zero/one digits. However, in many situations, we do not think of a file's contents as a sequence of binary digits. We often think of a file's contents as consisting of a sequence of characters. Files that are thought of as a sequence of characters and that have streams and methods to make the binary digits look like characters to your program and your editor are called **text files.** Files whose contents must be handled as sequences of binary digits are called **binary files.** Although it is not as technically precise and correct, it may be more informative to simply say that a text file

text files and binary files

contains a sequence of characters, whereas a binary file contains a sequence of binary digits. Your Java programs are stored in text files. The input and output files we will discuss in this section are binary files. Another way to phrase the distinction between binary files and text files is to note that text files are designed to be read by human beings and binary files are designed to be read by programs.

Most programming languages can handle both text file I/O and binary file I/O, but the designers of a language often favor either text files or binary files. One advantage of text files is that they are usually the same on all computers, so you can move your text files from one computer to another with little or no problems. The implementation of binary files usually differs from one computer to another. So, your binary data files ordinarily must be read only on the same computer and with the same programming language as the program that created that file. The advantage of binary files is that they are more efficient to process. Java favors binary files, but it gives its binary files some of the advantages of text files. In particular, the designers of Java made their binary files platform-independent; that is, with Java, you can move your binary files from one computer to another and your Java programs will still be able to read the binary files. This combines the portability of text files with the efficiency of binary files.

The one big advantage of text files is that they can be read from and written to by almost any text editor. With binary files, all the reading and writing to the file normally must be done by a program.

Binary files store data in the same way that they are stored in the computer's main memory (which we described in Chapter 1). Each data item, such as an integer, is stored as a sequence of bytes. Your Java program reads these bytes in very much the same way that it reads a data item, like an integer, from the computer's main memory.

The most commonly used stream classes for processing binary files are `DataInputStream` and `DataOutputStream`. Each of these classes have methods to read or write data one byte at a time. These streams can also automatically convert numbers and characters to bytes that can be stored in a binary file. They allow your program to be written as if the data placed in the file or read from the file were not just bytes, but were items of any of the Java primitive data types, such as *int*, *char*, *double*, and so forth. If you do not need to access your files using an editor, then the easiest and most efficient way to read and write data to files is to use `DataOutputStream` to write to a binary file and `DataInputStream` to read from the binary file. The next two subsections discuss these two stream classes in more detail.

Output to Files Using `DataOutputStream`

If you want to create files to store either `String` values or values of any of the primitive data types, such as *char*, *int*, and *double*, then you can use the stream class `DataOutputStream`. The files you create will be binary files and so they can only be read by another Java program. They cannot be read with a text editor. However, the programs are easy to write, the programs run efficiently, and the files can be moved from one computer to another and still be read by a Java program.

connecting a
stream to a file
Display 9.1 shows a program that writes integers to a binary file. Let's look at the details shown in that program. First, we need to take care of one technical

Display 9.1 Using DataOutputStream **to Write to a File**
....

We will give a better version of this program later in this chapter.

```java
import java.io.*;

public class DataOutputDemo
{
    public static void main(String[] args) throws IOException
    {
        DataOutputStream outputStream =
                new DataOutputStream(new FileOutputStream("numbers.dat"));
        int n;

        System.out.println("Enter nonnegative integers, one per line.");
        System.out.println("Place a negative number at the end.");

        do
        {
            n = SavitchIn.readLineInt();
            outputStream.writeInt(n);
        }while (n >= 0);

        System.out.println("Numbers and sentinel value");
        System.out.println("written to the file numbers.dat.");
        outputStream.close();
    }
}
```

Sample Screen Dialogue

```
Enter nonnegative integers, one per line.
Place a negative number at the end.
1
2
3
-1
Numbers and sentinel value
written to the file numbers.dat.
```

File numbers.dat **(after program is run)**

```
1
2
3
-1
```

Notice that the −1 is in the file. It does not have to be in the file, but in this program, we want it there as a sentinel value.

This is a binary file. You cannot read this file with your text editor.

detail. Any code that does file I/O in the ways we are describing can throw an
`IOException`, which is a way of saying that something has gone wrong with your
program I/O. In Section 9.2, we will discuss handling these exceptions. For this section, we will simplify things by basically ignoring the `IOExceptions` and assuming
that things do not go wrong. However, the compiler will not allow you to ignore
`IOExceptions` unless you add the clause *throws* `IOException` to the heading of
the `main` method as shown here:

```
public static void main(String[] args) throws IOException
```

If you have not yet read about exception handling, you can simply take this as a
"magic formula" that you are required to insert. However, this is not the best way to
account for these `IOExceptions` and so at some point you should read Section 9.2,
which describes better ways of handling these exceptions. Now, having postponed
our concerns about exceptions, let's discuss the other details in Display 9.1.

Note that program in Display 9.1 begins with the line:

import
java.io.*

```
import java.io.*;
```

This tells the Java compiler (and linker) that you will be using the `java.io` library,
which contains the definitions of the class `DataOutputStream` and the other file I/O
classes discussed in this chapter. Every program or class that does file I/O using any
of the techniques given in this chapter must contain the preceding import statement
near the beginning of the file.

Import Statement

Every program or class that does file I/O using any of the techniques given in this chapter must contain the following
statement near the beginning of the file.

```
import java.io.*;
```

This tells the Java compiler (and linker) that your program will be using the `java.io` library, which contains
the definitions of classes such as `DataOutputStream` and the other file I/O classes discussed in this chapter.

The output stream for writing to the file `numbers.dat` is created and named
with the following:

```
DataOutputStream outputStream =
    new DataOutputStream(new FileOutputStream("numbers.dat"));
```

The stream named `outputStream` is an object of the class `DataOutputStream`. It
has some similarity to the stream `System.out` in that it has methods for handling
program output. However `System.out` and objects of the class `DataOutputStream`
have output methods that have different names and that behave somewhat differently. Objects of the class `DataOutputStream` do not have a method named
`println`. However, as shown in Display 9.1, an object of the class `DataOutput-`
`Stream` does have a method named `writeInt` that can write a single *int* value to
a file, and it also has other output methods that we will discuss shortly. But first,
we need to explain the details in the above two lines that create and name the
stream object called `outputStream`.

The two lines

```
DataOutputStream outputStream =
    new DataOutputStream(new FileOutputStream("numbers.dat"));
```

connect the stream named `outputStream` to the file named `numbers.dat`. This connecting is often called **opening the file**. Note that the name of the file, in this case `numbers.dat`, is given as a `String` value and so is given in quotes. We will explain the words `new FileOutputStream` shortly, but for the moment, just think of the entire expression

opening a file

```
DataOutputStream Output_Stream_Name =
    new DataOutputStream(new FileOutputStream(File_Name));
```

as one difficult-to-spell operation that takes a *File_Name* as an argument, produces an output stream in the class `DataOutputStream`, and connects the stream to the named file. You can take this as one difficult-to-spell operation and still write working programs, but it will be more satisfying and more useful to understand a few more details.

File Names

The rules for how you spell file names depend on your operating system. They do not depend on Java. When you give a file name to a Java constructor for a stream, you are not giving the constructor a Java identifier. You are giving the constructor a string corresponding to the file name. Most common operating systems allow you to use letters, digits, and the dot symbol when spelling file names. Many operating systems allow other characters as well, but these are enough for most purposes. A suffix, such as `.dat` in `numbers.dat`, has no special meaning to a Java program. We are using the suffix `.dat` to indicate a binary file used as *data* for a Java program, but that is just a personal convention. It is not a rule you need to follow. You can use any file names that are allowed by your operating system.

Constructors for the class `DataOutputStream` create new streams in the class `DataOutputStream`. However, the class `DataOutputStream` does not have a constructor that takes a file name as an argument. If you try the following, you will get a compiler error message:

```
DataOutputStream outputStream =
    new DataOutputStream("numbers.dat"); //This is ILLEGAL!
```

The argument for the `DataOutputStream` constructor must be an output stream. It cannot be a string naming a file. Thus, when you connect a file to a stream of the class `DataOutputStream`, it must be a two-step process. First, you connect the file to another type of output stream that does work with a file name and then you connect this other output stream to a stream in the class `DataOutputStream`. For example, the following two lines from Display 9.1 create the output stream named `output-Stream` and connect it to the file `numbers.dat`:

```
DataOutputStream outputStream =
    new DataOutputStream(new FileOutputStream("numbers.dat"));
```

FileOutput-Stream

The class `FileOutputStream` is an output stream class with a constructor that accepts a file name as an argument. Thus,

```
new FileOutputStream("numbers.dat")
```

creates a new output stream in the class `FileOutputStream` and connects it to the file `numbers.dat`. But, streams in the class `FileOutputStream` do not have the output methods that we want, so we go one step further and connect this file output stream to a stream of type `DataOutputStream`, which has nicer output methods. It may help to note that

```
DataOutputStream outputStream =
    new DataOutputStream(new FileOutputStream("numbers.dat"));
```

is equivalent to

```
FileOutputStream middleman =
        new FileOutputStream("numbers.dat");
DataOutputStream outputStream =
        new DataOutputStream(middleman);
```

The only difference is that the first version does not bother to give the stream of type `FileOutputStream` the name `middleman`.

Connecting a Binary File to a Stream for Writing (Opening an Output File)

You create a stream of the class `DataOutputStream` and connect it to a binary file as follows:

Syntax:
```
DataOutputStream Output_Stream_Name =
    new DataOutputStream(new FileOutputStream(File_Name));
```

Examples:
```
DataOutputStream myOutputStream =
    new DataOutputStream(new FileOutputStream("myfile.dat"));
```

After this, you can use the methods of the class `DataOutputStream` to write to the file. ◻

A File Has Two Names

Every input and every output file used by your program has two names: the real file name that is used by the operating system and the name of the stream that is connected to the file. The stream name serves as a temporary name for the file that is used within your program. After you connect the file to the stream, your program always refers to the file by using the stream name. ◻

---

writeInt   Once a stream in the class `DataOutputStream` is connected to a file, you can write integers to the file with the method `writeInt`, as in the following line from Display 9.1:

```
outputStream.writeInt(n);
```

In Display 9.1, the preceding line writes the value of the *int* variable n to the file `numbers.dat`. If you look at the table in Display 9.2, you will see that there are sim-

Display 9.2 Some Methods in the Class DataOutputStream

public DataOutputStream(OutputStream streamObject)
This is the only constructor. If you want to create a stream using a file name, then you use

new DataOutputStream(*new* FileOutputStream(*File_Name*))

When used in this way, the FileOutputStream constructor and so the DataOutputStream constructor can throw an IOException.

public final void writeInt(*int* n) *throws* IOException
Writes the *int* value n to the output stream.

public final void writeLong(*long* n) *throws* IOException
Writes the *long* value n to the output stream.

public final void writeDouble(*double* x) *throws* IOException
Writes the *double* value x to the output stream.

public final void writeFloat(*float* x) *throws* IOException
Writes the *float* value x to the output stream.

public final void writeChar(*int* n) *throws* IOException
Writes the *char* value n to the output stream. Note that it expects its argument to be an *int* value, so you must do a type cast in order to actually write out a *char* value. For example:
outputStream.writeChar((*int*)'A');

public final void writeBoolean(*boolean* b) *throws* IOException
Writes the *boolean* value b to the output stream.

public final void writeUTF(String str) *throws* IOException
Writes the String value str to the output stream. "UTF" refers to a particular method of encoding the string. To read the string back from the file, you should use the method readUTF of the class DataInputStream.

public void close() *throws* IOException
Closes the stream's connection to a file. This method calls flush before closing the file.

public void flush() *throws* IOException
Flushes the output stream. This forces an actual physical write to the file of any data that have been buffered and not yet physically written to the file. Normally, you should not need to invoke flush.

ilar methods `writeLong`, `writeDouble`, and `writeFloat` that write numbers of other types to a file.

writeDouble

Notice that the program in Display 9.1 sends output to two different places by using two different output streams. The stream named `outputStream` is connected to the file `numbers.dat` and sends its output to that file. The other output stream is `System.out`. You are so used to using it that you might not think of `System.out` as an output stream, but it is an output stream that is connected to the screen. So output statements that use `System.out.println` send their output to the screen.

In Display 9.1, we made it look like the numbers in the file `numbers.dat` are written one per line in a human-readable form. That is not what happens. There are no lines or other separators between the numbers. Instead, the numbers are written in the file one immediately after the other, and they are encoded as a sequence of bytes in the same way that the numbers would be encoded in the computer's main memory. These coded *int* values cannot be read using your editor. Realistically, they can only be read by another Java program.

Text Files and Binary Files

Files that you write using an editor are called **text files**. Text files are sometimes also called *ASCII files* because they contain data encoded using the ASCII coding method (but, do not worry if you do not yet know what the ASCII encoding method is). When you write to a file using `DataOutputStream`, the file is a binary file. It is not a text file and you cannot read it with your text editor. Only another program can read a binary file.

---

closing a file

When your program is finished writing to a file, it should **close** the stream connected to that file. In Display 9.1, the stream connected to the file `numbers.dat` is closed with the statement:

```
outputStream.close();
```

The class `DataOutputStream`, and every other class for file output or file input streams, has a method named `close`. When this method is invoked, the system releases any resources used to connect the stream to the file and does any other housekeeping that is needed. If your program does not close a file before the program ends, then Java will close it for you, but it is safest to close the file with an explicit call to `close`.

final

Display 9.2 contains a list of some (but not all) of the methods in the class `DataOutputStream`. The reserved word *final* that appears in the description of many of these methods means that if you define a derived class with `DataOutput-Stream` as the base class, then you cannot redefine any of the methods that are marked *final*.[1]

---

final[1]

The reserved word *final* that appears in the description of many of the methods in Display 9.2/page 465 means that if you define a derived class, then you cannot redefine any of the methods that are marked *final*.

---

1. If you have not yet read about derived classes, you can safely ignore the word *final*.

Why Bother to Close a File?

If your program ends normally but without closing a file, the system will automatically close the file for you. So, why should you bother to close files with an explicit call to the method `close`? There are at least two reasons. First, if your program ends abnormally for some reason, then Java may not be able to close the file for you and the file could be left open with no program connected to it, and this can damage the file. The sooner you close a file, the less likely it is that this will happen. Second, if you program writes to a file and later reads from the same file, then it must close the file after is through writing to the file and reopen the file for reading. (Java does have a class that allows a file to be opened for both reading and writing, but we will not cover that in this book.)

That ends our description of the sample program in Display 9.1, but we still have not discussed all the methods of the class `DataOutputStream`, which we listed in Display 9.2. We do that next.

You can use a stream from the class `DataOutputStream` to output values of any primitive type and also to write data of the type `String`. Each primitive data type has a corresponding write method in the class `DataOutputStream`. We have already mentioned the write methods for outputting numbers. The method `writeChar` can be used to output a single character. The method `writeBoolean` can be used to output a single boolean value. For example, the following would output the character `'A'` followed by the boolean value *false* to the file connected to the stream named `outputStream`:

writeChar

write-Boolean

```
outputStream.writeChar((int)'A');
outputStream.writeBoolean(false);
```

The method `writeChar` has one possibly annoying property: It expects its argument to be of type *int*. So if you start with a value of type *char*, you must do a type cast before giving it to the method `writeChar`. To output `'A'`, you use `(int)'A'` as the argument to `writeChar`. To output the contents of a *char* variable named `symbol`, you use

```
outputStream.writeChar((int)symbol);
```

That takes care of outputting the primitive types. To output a value of type `String`, you use the method `writeUTF`. For example, if `outputStream` is a stream of type `DataOutputStream`, then the following will write the string `"Hi Mom"` to the file connected to that stream:

writeUTF for strings

```
outputStream.writeUTF("Hi Mom");
```

Of course, with `writeUTF`, or any of the write methods, you can use a variable of the appropriate type (in this case, `String`) as an argument to the method.

You may write output of different types to the same file. So, you may write a combination of, for example, *int* values, *double* values, and `String` values. However, mixing types in a file does require special care in order to make it possible to read them back out of the file. To read them back, you need to know the order in which the various types appear in the file, because, as you will see when we discuss the class `DataInputStream`, a program that reads from the file will use a different method to read data of each different type.

flush

Display 9.2 has one last method that we must discuss. Like all output streams that can be connected to a file, any stream object of the class `DataOutputStream` has a method named `flush`. We have not yet used `flush`, but you should be familiar with this important method. Like most programming languages, Java does not always send output immediately to its destination, such as a file, but sometimes it waits to send a larger package of data to the output destination. Thus, the output from a `writeInt` or a `writeUTF` may not be sent to the output file immediately. Instead, it might be saved and packaged with the output from the next write method invocation and then the output from both write method invocations might be sent to the file at the same time. This technique is called **buffering** and is done for efficiency reasons. The `flush` method sends all the pending data to their output destination. When you call the method `close`, that automatically calls the method `flush`. So, for most simple applications, you do not need to explicitly call the method `flush`. However, if you continue to program, you will eventually encounter situations where you want to use the method `flush`. The syntax for the method `flush` is illustrated by the following example:

buffering

```
outputStream.flush();
```

What Does "UTF" Stand For?

To write an *int* (when using the class `DataOutputStream`), you use `writeInt`; to write a *double*, you use `writeDouble`; and so forth. However, to write a string, you do *not* use `writeString`. You use `writeUTF`. There is no method called `writeString` in `DataOutputStream`. Why this funny name `writeUTF`? What does *UTF* stand for? *UTF* stands for *Unicode Text Format*. That is not a very descriptive name. Here is the full story:

Recall that Java uses the Unicode character set, a set of characters that includes many letters used in Asian languages and other languages whose character sets are very different from English. Most editors, undoubtedly including your editor, and most operating systems use the ASCII character set, which is the character set normally used for English and even for Java programs. The ASCII character set is a subset of the Unicode character set, so the Unicode character set has a lot of characters you do not need. There is a standard Unicode way of coding all the Unicode characters, but for English-speaking countries, it is not a very efficient coding scheme. The UTF coding scheme is an alternative coding scheme that still codes all Unicode characters but that favors the ASCII character set. The UTF coding method gives short, efficient codes for ASCII characters. The price is that it gives long, inefficient codes to the other Unicode characters. However, since you probably do not use the other Unicode characters, this is a good deal.

Some Details About `writeUTF` *(Optional)*

The method `writeInt` writes integers into a file using the same number of bytes, that is, the same number of zeros and ones, to store any integer. Similarly, the method `writeLong` uses the same number of bytes to store each value of type *long*. (But, the methods `writeInt` and `writeLong` use a different number of bytes from each other.) The situation is the same for all the other write methods, with the exception of `writeUTF`. All the write methods except for `writeUTF` write out the same number of bytes every time they write a value of their respective type. However, the method `writeUTF` uses differing numbers of bytes to store different strings in a file. Longer strings require more bytes than shorter strings. Now, this can present a problem to Java, since there are no separators between data items in a binary file. The way that

Java manages to make this work out is by writing some extra information at the start of each string. This extra information tells how many bytes are used to write the string, so readUTF knows how many bytes to read and convert.

The situation with writeUTF is even a little more complicated than what we discussed in the previous paragraph. We made a point of saying that the information at the start of the string code in the file tells how many *bytes* to read, *not how long the string is*. These two figures are not the same. With the UTF way of encoding, different characters are encoded in different numbers of bytes. However, all the ASCII characters are stored in just one byte, and you are undoubtedly using only ASCII characters, so this difference is more theoretical than real to you now. The box entitled **What Does "UTF" Stand For?** has some additional discussion of this variable length coding.

"Input" and "Output" Terminology

To avoid confusion, remember that the word *input* means that data move *into your program* (not into the file). The word *output* means that data move *out of your program* (not out of the file).

⚠ *GOTCHA* Overwriting a File

When you connect a stream to a file using the class DataOutputStream or most other output stream classes, you always produce an empty file. For example, consider:

```
DataOutputStream outputStream =
    new DataOutputStream(new FileOutputStream("numbers.dat"));
```

If there were no file named numbers.dat, then this will create an empty file named numbers.dat. If there already was a file named numbers.dat, then this will eliminate that file and create a new empty file named numbers.dat. So, if there were a file named numbers.dat before the preceding is executed, then all the data in that file would be eliminated. In Section 9.3, the subsection entitled **The** File **Class** tells you how to test to see if a file already exists so you can avoid accidentally overwriting a file.

Reading Input from a File Using DataInputStream

If you write to a file using DataOutputStream, you can read from that file using the stream class DataInputStream. Display 9.3 gives some of the most commonly used methods for the class DataInputStream. If you compare that table with the methods for DataOutputStream given in Display 9.2, you will see that corresponding to each output method for DataOutputStream, there is a corresponding input method in DataInputStream. For example, if you write an integer to a file using the method writeInt of DataOutputStream, then you can read that integer back with the method readInt of DataInputStream. If you write a number to a file using the method writeDouble of DataOutputStream, then you can read that number back with the method readDouble of DataInputStream, and so forth. Display 9.4/page 472 gives an example of using readInt in this way.

Display 9.3 Some Methods in the Class DataInputStream
••

DataInputStream(InputStream streamObject)
> This is the only constructor. If you want to create a stream using a file name, then you use

new DataInputStream(*new* FileInputStream(*File_Name*))

> When used in this way, the FileInputStream constructor and so the DataInputStream constructor can throw a FileNotFoundException.

public final int readInt() *throws* IOException
> Reads an *int* value from the input stream and returns that *int* value. If readInt tries to read a value from the file and that value was not written using the method writeInt of the class DataOutputStream (or written in some equivalent way), then the *int* value returned is a "garbage value" and further reading from the file is likely to be corrupted. If the read goes beyond the end of the file, then an EOFException is thrown.[a]

public final long readLong() *throws* IOException
> Reads a *long* value from the input stream and returns that *long* value. If readLong tries to read a value from the file and that value was not written using the method writeLong of the class DataOutputStream (or written in some equivalent way), then the *long* value returned is a "garbage value" and further reading from the file is likely to be corrupted. If the read goes beyond the end of the file, then an EOFException is thrown.[a]
>
> Note that it is not acceptable to write an integer with writeLong and later read the same integer with readInt or to write an integer with writeInt and later read it with readLong.

public final double readDouble() *throws* IOException
> Reads a *double* value from the input stream and returns that *double* value. If readDouble tries to read a value from the file and that value was not written using the method writeDouble of the class DataOutputStream (or written in some equivalent way), then the *double* value returned is a "garbage value" and further reading from the file is likely to be corrupted. If the read goes beyond the end of the file, then an EOFException is thrown.[a]

public final float readFloat() *throws* IOException
> Reads a *float* value from the input stream and returns that *float* value. If readFloat tries to read a value from the file and that value was not written using the method writeFloat of the class DataOutputStream (or written in some equivalent way), then the *float* value returned is a "garbage value" and further reading from the file is likely to be corrupted. If the read goes beyond the end of the file, then an EOFException is thrown.[a]
>
> Note that it is not acceptable to write a floating-point number with writeDouble and later read the same number with readFloat or to write a floating-point number with writeFloat and later read it with readDouble. Other type mismatches, such as writing with writeInt and reading with readDouble, are also not acceptable.

Display 9.3 Some Methods in the Class `DataInputStream`
•••

public final char `readChar()` *throws* `IOException`
    Reads a *char* value from the input stream and returns that *char* value. If `readChar` tries to read a value from the file and that value was not written using the method `writeChar` of the class `DataOutputStream` (or written in some equivalent way), then the *char* value returned is a "garbage value" and further reading from the file is likely to be corrupted. If the read goes beyond the end of the file, then an `EOFException` is thrown.[a]

public final boolean `readBoolean()` *throws* `IOException`
    Reads a *boolean* value from the input stream and returns that *boolean* value. If `readBoolean` tries to read a value from the file and that value was not written using the method `writeBoolean` of the class `DataOutputStream` (or written in some equivalent way), then the *boolean* value returned is a "garbage value" and further reading from the file is likely to be corrupted. If the read goes beyond the end of the file, then an `EOFException` is thrown.[a]

public final `String` `readUTF()` *throws* `IOException`
    Reads a `String` value from the input stream and returns that `String` value. If `readUTF` tries to read a value from the file and that value was not written using the method `writeUTF` of the class `DataOutputStream` (or written in some equivalent way), then the `String` value returned is a "garbage value" and further reading from the file is likely to be corrupted. If the read goes beyond the end of the file, then an `EOFException` is thrown.[a]

public void `close()` *throws* `IOException`
    Closes the streams connection to a file.

a. If you have not yet read about exception handling in Chapter 8, you can ignore the information about throwing exceptions for now.

    As was true in the case of output to a file, in this, our first discussion of input from a file, we will ignore any possible `IOExceptions` by adding the clause *throws* `IOException` to the heading of the `main` method as follows:

public static void `main(String[] args)` *throws* `IOException`

If you have not yet read about exception handling, you can simply take this as a "magic formula" that you are required to insert. However, this is not the best way to account for these `IOExceptions`, and so at some point you should read Section 9.2 which describes better ways of handling these exceptions. Now, let's move on to the other details in Display 9.4.

    Note that a file is opened for reading with `DataInputStream` in a manner similar to what you have already seen for `DataOutputStream`. In Display 9.4, the file `numbers.dat` is opened and connected to a stream named `inputStream` as follows:

```
DataInputStream inputStream =
    new DataInputStream(new FileInputStream("numbers.dat"));
```

Display 9.4 Using `DataInputStream` **to Read from a File**
••

```java
import java.io.*;

public class DataInputDemo
{
    public static void main(String[] args) throws IOException
    {
        DataInputStream inputStream
            = new DataInputStream(new
              FileInputStream("numbers.dat"));
        int n;

        System.out.println("Reading the nonnegative integers");
        System.out.println("in the file numbers.dat.");
        n = inputStream.readInt();
        while (n >= 0)
        {
            System.out.println(n);
            n = inputStream.readInt();
        }

        System.out.println("End of reading from file.");
        inputStream.close();
    }
}
```

We will giver a better version of this program later in this chapter.

Screen Output
(Assuming the program in Display 9.1/page 461 was already run with the dialogue shown there.)

```
Reading the nonnegative integers
in the file numbers.dat.
1
2
3
End of reading from file.
```

Notice that the sentinel value −1 is read from the file, but is not output to the screen.

••

Note that this is identical to what we used with DataOutputStream in Display 9.1/ page 461, except that we use the class DataInputStream instead of DataOutput-Stream and we use the class FileInputStream instead of FileOutputStream. The reason for needing FileInputStream is the same as the reason we needed File-OutputStream with DataOutputStream.

Also note that when you are through reading from a file, you should close the file with an invocation of the method close. The syntax and the reasons for closing a file read with DataInputStream are the same as what we described for DataOut-putStream.

close

Connecting a Binary File to a Stream for Reading
(Opening an Input File)

You create a stream of the class DataInputStream and connect it to a binary file as follows.

Syntax:
```
DataInputStream Input_Stream_Name =
        new DataInputStream(new FileInputStream(File_Name));
```

Examples:
```
DataInputStream myInputStream =
        new DataInputStream(new FileInputStream("myfile.dat"));
```

After this, you can use the methods of the class DataInputStream to read from the file.

Using DataInputStream, you may read input of different types from the same file. So, you may read a combinations of, for example, *int* values, *double* values, and String values. However, if the next data item in the file is not of the type expected by the reading method, then the result is likely to be a mess. For example, if your program writes an integer using writeInt, then any program that reads that integer should read it using readInt. If you instead use readLong or readDouble, then your program will misbehave. The case study **Writing and Reading a File of Records** shows a program that writes data of differing types to a file and it shows another program that reads the data.

reading
multiple types

⚠ GOTCHA Using DataInputStream with a Text File

Binary files and text files encode their data in different ways. Thus, a stream that expects to read a binary file, such as a stream in the class DataInputStream, will have problems reading a text file. If you attempt to read a text file with a stream in the class DataInputStream, then your program will either read "garbage values" or will encounter some other error condition. Similarly, you should not read from a binary file using a stream method that expects to read a text file. Although we have not yet discussed any, there are some methods in some stream classes that were designed to be used with text files.

? SELF-TEST QUESTIONS

1. Why would anybody write a program that sends its output to a file instead of sending its output to the screen?

2. How do you create an output stream of type `DataOutputStream` that is named `toFile` and is connected to a file named `stuff.data`?

3. Give three statements that will write the values of the three *double* variables x1, x2, and x3 to the file `stuff.data`. Use the stream `toFile` that you created as the answer to Question 2.

4. Give a statement that will close the stream `toFile` created as the answer to Question 2.

5. How do you create an input stream of type `DataInputStream` that is named `fromFile` and is connected to a file named `stuff.data`?

6. Give three statements that will read three *double* numbers from the file `stuff.data`. Use the stream `fromFile` that you created as the answer to Question 5. Declare three variables to hold the three numbers.

7. Give a statement that will close the stream `fromFile` created as the answer to Question 5.

▼ PROGRAMMING EXAMPLE *Reading a File Name from the Keyboard*

Thus far, we have written the literal file names for our input and output files into the code of our programs. We did this by giving the file name as the argument to a constructor when we connected the file to a stream. For example, we used the following in Display 9.4/page 472 to connect the file `numbers.dat` to the stream named `inputStream`:

```
DataInputStream inputStream =
    new DataInputStream(new FileInputStream("numbers.dat"));
```

However, you may not know what the file name will be when you write a program and so you may want to have the user enter the file name at the keyboard when the program is run. This is easy to do; simply have the program read the file name into a variable of type `String` and use that `String` variable in place of the file name. This technique is illustrated in the program in Display 9.5.

Notice that the program in Display 9.5 reads input from two different places. The class `SavitchIn` is used to read the file name from the keyboard. The stream named `inputStream` is connected to the file `numbers.dat` and reads its input from that file.

▲ GOTCHA *Defining a Method to Open a Stream*

The following looks like a fairly reasonable method to include in some class, but it has a problem:

Display 9.5 Reading a File Name

```
import java.io.*;

public class FileNameDemo
{
    public static void main(String[] args) throws IOException
    {
        System.out.println("Enter file name:");
        String fileName = SavitchIn.readLineWord();
        DataInputStream inputStream =
            new DataInputStream(new FileInputStream(fileName));

        System.out.println("Reading and summing the nonnegative");
        System.out.println("integers in the file " + fileName);
        int sum = 0;
        int n = inputStream.readInt();
        while (n > 0)
        {
            sum = sum + n;
            System.out.println(n);
            n = inputStream.readInt();
        }

        System.out.println("End of reading from file.");
        inputStream.close();
        System.out.println("The sum of the numbers is " + sum);
    }
}
```

In Section 9.2, we tell you how to eliminate the clause `throws IOException`.

Sample Screen Dialogue

(Assuming the program in Display 9.1/page 461 was run first, with the dialogue shown there.)

```
Enter file name:
numbers.dat
Reading and summing the nonnegative
integers in the file numbers.dat
1
2
3
End of reading from file.
The sum of the numbers is 6
```

```
//This method does do not what we want it to do.
public static void openFile(DataOutputStream streamName)
                                              throws IOException
{
    System.out.println("Enter file name:");
    String fileName = SavitchIn.readLineWord();
    streamName =
          new DataOutputStream(new FileOutputStream(fileName));
}
```

The method will compile fine and can be invoked, but it will not perform as you might hope. For example, consider the following. (Recall that *null* is a value that can be assigned to any variable of a class type. Although, the exact details of what *null* is do not matter here, you can find more information about *null* in Chapter 4.)

```
DataOutputStream outputStream = null;
openFile(outputStream);
```

After this code is executed, the value of `outputStream` is still *null*. The file that was opened in the method `openFile` went away when the method was over. The problems is a bit subtle and is unlikely to arise in very many situations, but this is one of those situations.

The problem has to do with how Java handles arguments of a class type. These arguments are passed to the method as a *memory address that cannot be changed.* The memory address normally names something that can be changed, but the memory address itself cannot be changed. Another (equivalent) way to think about this is to recall that an object variable, like the preceding `outputStream`, is a name. A method can change the contents of the file named by `outputStream`. For example, it can send output to the stream and so change the file connected to the stream. However, a method cannot change the stream name so that it names a different file. When you use *new*, you are changing `outputStream` so that it names a different file and that is not allowed.

Be sure to note that this is a very narrow restriction that applies in only very limited circumstances. Once a stream is connected to a file, you can pass the stream name as an argument to method and the method can change the file. Also note that this only applies to arguments to methods. If the stream name is a local variable or if the stream name is an instance variable, then you can open a file and connect it to a stream and this problem will not occur. (Of course, the local variable goes away when the method invocation ends, but that is to be expected with a local variable and should not be a problem.)

? SELF-TEST QUESTIONS

8. Give some Java code to create a stream of type `DataOutputStream`, name the stream `writer`, and connect it to the file whose name is stored in the `String` variable `theFile`.

9. Give some Java code to create a stream of type `DataInputStream`, name the stream `reader`, and connect it to the file whose name is stored in the `String` variable name `theFile`.

10. Write a complete Java program that will ask the user for a file name and output the first data item in that file to the screen. Assume that the first data item is a string that was written to the file with the method `writeUTF`.

9.2 Exception Handling with File I/O

The White Rabbit put on his spectacles. "Where shall I begin, please your Majesty?" he asked.
"Begin at the beginning," the King said, very gravely, "And go on till you come to the end: then stop."
LEWIS CARROLL, ALICE IN WONDERLAND

If you have not yet read the material in Sections 8.1 and 8.2 of Chapter 8 (which cover the basics of exception handling), then you should skip this section, and most of the rest of this chapter, until after you have covered that material.

Catching `IOExceptions`

`IOException` is a predefined exception class. Any code that does file I/O in the ways we are describing might throw an `IOException` when something happens to go wrong with the I/O processing. Such exceptions should not be ignored. You should not simply list `IOException` in a *throws*-clause of the method `main` (as we did in Section 9.1), but you should instead catch any possible `IOException` in a *catch*-block, even if the *catch*-block simply issues an error message and ends the program. In Display 9.6, we have rewritten the program from Display 9.1/page 461 so that it catches all `IOExceptions`.

`IO-Exception`

The program in Display 9.7/page 479 is a rewritten version of the program in Display 9.4/page 472. The only difference between this version and the version in Display 9.4 is that this version catches all exceptions that might be thrown. Notice that we inserted a separate *catch*-block for exceptions in the class `FileNotFoundException`. The class `FileNotFoundException` is another predefined exception class. An object of that class is thrown when a file is opened for reading input from the file, but there is no file with the name specified.

`File-NotFound-Exception`

The `FileNotFoundException` class is a derived class of the class `IOException`. So any *catch*-blocks that catch exceptions of the class `IOException` will also catch exceptions of the class `FileNotFoundException`. Thus, if we had omitted the *catch*-block for `FileNotFoundException`, then the program in Display 9.7 would still catch all exceptions, but we would not get as much information. By having a separate *catch*-block for the exception class `FileNotFoundException`, you ensure that you will get a message telling you when the named file is not found. If you only had the *catch*-block for `IOException`, then you would still get an error message if the named file was not found, but you would not know whether the error was due to the file not being found or due to some other I/O problem.

Display 9.6 Catching `IOException`**s with** `DataOutputStream`
••

```java
import java.io.*;

public class DataOutputDemoImproved
{
    public static void main(String[] args)
    {
      try
      {
          DataOutputStream outputStream =
              new DataOutputStream(new FileOutputStream("numbers.dat"));
          int n;

          System.out.println("Enter nonnegative integers, one per line.");
          System.out.println("Place a negative number at the end.");

          do
          {
              n = SavitchIn.readLineInt();
              outputStream.writeInt(n);
          }while (n > 0);

          System.out.println("Numbers and sentinel value");
          System.out.println("written to the file numbers.dat.");
          outputStream.close();
      }
      catch(IOException e)
      {
          System.out.println("Problem with output to file numbers.dat.");
      }
    }
}
```

This is an improved version of the program in Display 9.1/page 461.

As long as nothing unexpected happens, this program will perform the same as the program in Display 9.1/page 461. In particular, it will send the same output to the screen and the same output to the file `numbers.dat` as the program in Display 9.1. If something does go wrong, this program will output the message in the `catch`-block.

Display 9.7 Catching Exceptions with `DataInputStream`
• •

```java
import java.io.*;

public class DataInputDemoImproved
{
    public static void main(String[] args)
    {
        try
        {
            DataInputStream inputStream = new DataInputStream(
                                new FileInputStream("numbers.dat"));
            int n;

            System.out.println("Reading the nonnegative integers");
            System.out.println("in the file numbers.dat.");
            n = inputStream.readInt();
            while (n >= 0)
            {
                System.out.println(n);
                n = inputStream.readInt();
            }

            System.out.println("End of reading from file.");
            inputStream.close();
        }
        catch(FileNotFoundException e)
        {
            System.out.println("Cannot find file numbers.dat.");
        }
        catch(IOException e2)
        {
            System.out.println("Problem with input from file numbers.dat.");
        }
    }
}
```

This is an improved version of the program in Display 9.4/page 472.

Screen Output
(Assuming there is no file named `numbers.dat`.)

If nothing goes wrong, this program performs the same as the program in Display 9.4/page 472.

```
Cannot find file numbers.dat.
```

FileNotFoundException **Class**

If your program attempts to open a file for reading and there is no such file, then a FileNotFoundException is thrown. The class FileNotFoundException is a derived class of the class IOException. So, every exception of type FileNotFoundException is also of type IOException. In particular, a *catch*-block that catches exceptions of the class IOException will also catch exceptions in the class FileNotFoundException.

The EOFException **Class**

EOF-
Exception

Many, but not all, methods that read from a file will throw an exception of the class EOFException when they try to read beyond the end of a file. All of the DataInput-Stream methods shown in Display 9.3/page 470 throw an EOFException if they try to read beyond the end of a file.

As illustrated in Display 9.8, the class EOFException can be used to test for the end of a file when you are using DataInputStream. As illustrated in that sample program, the reading is placed in an "infinite loop," in this case, by using *true* as the boolean expression in the *while*-loop. The loop is not really infinite because when the end of the file is reached, an exception is thrown, and that ends the entire *try*-block and passes control to the *catch*-block. It is instructive to compare the program in Display 9.8 with the similar program in Display 9.7/page 479. The one in Display 9.7 tests for the end of a file by testing for a negative number. This is fine, but this means that you cannot store negative numbers in the file (except as a sentinel value). The program in Display 9.8 uses EOFException to test for the end of a file and so it can handle files that store any kind of integers including negative integers.

EOFException **Class**

If your program is reading from a file using any of the methods listed in Display 9.3/page 470 for the class DataInputStream and your program attempts to read beyond the end of the file, then an EOFException is thrown. This can be used to end a loop that reads all the data in a file. Other methods in other classes may also throw an EOFException when they try to read beyond the end of a file, but this is not true of all methods for reading from a file. You must check the documentation for each method you use to see if it will throw an EOFException. The class EOFException is a derived class of the class IOException. So, every exception of type EOFException is also of type IOException.

Checking for the End of a File

When reading a file, it is often the case that you want to read and process all the data in the file. The general outline of how your program might proceed is a loop of the form

Repeat the following until you get to the end of the file:
{
        read some data.
        process the data.
}

Display 9.8 Using EOFException *(Part 1 of 2)*

```java
import java.io.*;

public class EOFExceptionDemo
{
    public static void main(String[] args)
    {
        try
        {
            DataInputStream inputStream =
              new DataInputStream(new FileInputStream("numbers.dat"));
            int n;

            System.out.println("Reading ALL the integers");
            System.out.println("in the file numbers.dat.");
            try
            {
                while (true)
                {
                    n = inputStream.readInt();
                    System.out.println(n);
                }
            }
            catch(EOFException e)
            {
                System.out.println("End of reading from file.");
            }

            inputStream.close();
        }
        catch(FileNotFoundException e)
        {
            System.out.println("Cannot find file numbers.dat.");
        }
        catch(IOException e2)
        {
            System.out.println("Problem with input from file numbers.dat.");
        }
    }
}
```

> The loop ends when an exception is thrown.

Display 9.8 Using `EOFException` *(Part 2 of 2)*

Screen Output

(Assuming the program in Display 9.1/page 461 was run with the dialogue shown there.)

```
Reading ALL the integers
in the file numbers.dat.
1
2
3
-1
End of reading from
file.
```

Notice that when you use `EOFException`, *−1 is just like any other integer.* `EOFException` *allows you to have files that can contain any kind of integers.*

In order to implement this pseudocode, you need some way to test for reaching the end of the file. In Java, there are a number of different ways to test for the end of a file, depending on what stream is connected to the file and what method you use for reading. The commonly used methods to test for the end of a file all use one of the following three basic techniques:

1. Set up the input file so that it ends with a special value to serve as a sentinel value. Then your program can stop reading when the sentinel value is read. For example, a file of nonnegative integers could use a negative integer at the end as a sentinel value. In the subsection **Ending a Loop** of Chapter 3, we discussed using this technique for input from the keyboard. The same technique works for input from a file. Display 9.7/page 479 shows a program that uses this technique.

2. Throwing and catching an exception of the class `EOFException`. This is the technique we used in the program in Display 9.8/page 481.

3. Many of the methods for reading from a file return a special value when they try to read beyond the end of a file. None of the `DataInputStream` methods shown in Display 9.3/page 470 behave this way. So, if you are using `DataInputStream` for file input, this third possibility cannot be used. This technique is often used when reading from a text file, as discussed in Section 9.4/page 515.

⚠ *GOTCHA Forgetting to Check for the End of a File*

If your program makes no provisions for detecting the end of a file, then when the end of a file is reached, what happens will depend on the details of your program; but whatever happens, it will not be good. If your program tries to read beyond the end of a file, it may enter an infinite loop or it might end abnormally. Always be sure your program checks for the end of a file and does something appropriate when it reaches the end of the file. Even if you think your program will not read past the end of the file, you should provide for this eventuality just in case things do not go exactly as you planned.

▼ PROGRAMMING EXAMPLE Processing a File of Data

Display 9.9 contains a program that does some simple processing of data. It asks the user for two file names and then copies all the numbers in one file into the other file, but multiplies each number by 2 so that the numbers in the output file are all double the values in the input file. This is not a very complicated or interesting programming task, but it does show a simple example that employs a lot of standard programming techniques for handling file I/O. In particular, note that the variables for stream objects connected to the files are instance variables and that the task is broken down into subtasks assigned to various methods.

Note that all exceptions are caught, so there are no *throws*-clauses. Also note that we have made the *try*-blocks small, so that when an exception is thrown, it is caught in a nearby *catch*-block. If we had fewer *try*-blocks, it would be harder to decide what part of the code threw an exception.

◐ PROGRAMMING TIP Objects Should Do Their Own I/O

One of the principles of object-oriented programming is that objects are not simply passive collections of data, but are active things that should carry out whatever ac-

Display 9.9 Catching All Exceptions (Part 1 of 3)

```
import java.io.*;

public class FileProcessor
{
    /***********************************************************
     *Doubles the integers in one file and puts them in another file.
     ***********************************************************/
    public static void main(String[] args)
    {
        FileProcessor twoTimer = new FileProcessor();
        twoTimer.getInputFile();
        twoTimer.getOutputFile();
        twoTimer.timesTwo();
        twoTimer.closeFiles();
        System.out.println("Numbers from input file");
        System.out.println("doubled and copied to output file.")
    }
```

Display 9.9 Catching All Exceptions *(Part 2 of 3)*

```java
public void getInputFile()
{
    String inputFileName = getFileName("Enter input file name:");
    try
    {
        inputStream =
          new DataInputStream(
                          new FileInputStream(inputFileName));
    }
    catch(FileNotFoundException e)
    {
        System.out.println("File " + inputFileName
                                + " not found.");
        System.exit(0);
    }
}

public void getOutputFile()
{
    String outputFileName = getFileName("Enter output file name:");
    try
    {
        outputStream = new DataOutputStream(
                        new FileOutputStream(outputFileName));
    }
    catch(IOException e)
    {
        System.out.println("Error opening output file "
                                        + outputFileName);
        System.out.println(e.getMessage());
        System.exit(0);
    }
}

private String getFileName(String prompt)
{
    String fileName = null;
    System.out.println(prompt);
    fileName = SavitchIn.readLineWord();
    return fileName;
}
```

Display 9.9 Catching All Exceptions *(Part 3 of 3)*

```
    public void timesTwo()
    {
        int next;
        try
        {
            while (true)
            {
                next = inputStream.readInt();
                outputStream.writeInt(2*next);
            }
        }
        catch(EOFException e)
        {
            //Do nothing. This just ends the loop.
        }
        catch(IOException e)
        {
            System.out.println("Error reading or writing files.");
            System.out.println(e.getMessage());
            System.exit(0);
        }
    }

    public void closeFiles()
    {
        try
        {
            inputStream.close();
            outputStream.close();
        }
        catch(IOException e)
        {
            System.out.println("Error closing files "
                                    + e.getMessage());
            System.exit(0);
        }
    }

    private DataInputStream inputStream = null;
    private DataOutputStream outputStream = null;
}
```

> A real-life class might also have other methods that take data from the input file, transform the data in some way, and write the changed data to the output file.

tions need to be performed with the data. Thus, when we define classes, we often define input and output methods for the class. Before this chapter, the only input methods we could define obtained input from the keyboard, and the only output methods we could define sent their output to the screen. Now that you have learned about file I/O, you should also include methods for file input and file output whenever you define a class whose objects might be written to or read from a file.

As an example, we have rewritten the definition of the class Species from Chapter 4 (Display 4.15/page 214) so that it includes a method to send output to a binary file and a method to obtain input from a binary file. The class definition is shown in Display 9.10. (We have also taken this opportunity to add two constructors to the class definition. When we first defined the class Species, we had not yet learned about constructors.)

overloading

Notice that in the new class Species, the two names readInput and writeOutput are overloaded. Java decides which of the two definitions of readInput to use by checking the number of arguments. There is one definition that is used when the method readInput is called with no arguments and another definition that is used when the method readInput is called with an argument of type DataInputStream. If the readInput method is called with no arguments, then the input is taken from the keyboard. If the readInput method is called with an argument of type DataInputStream, then the input is taken from the file connected to the input stream. Java also decides which definition of writeOutput to use by checking the arguments. If the writeOutput method is called with no arguments, then the output goes to the screen. If the writeOutput method is called with an argument of type DataOutputStream, then the output goes to a binary file.

Notice that the methods readInput and writeOutput for writing to and reading from a file match in terms of the order of data types. The method writeOutput writes data to the file with

```
outputStream.writeUTF(name);
outputStream.writeInt(population);
outputStream.writeDouble(growthRate);
```

This writes a string, followed by an *int*, followed by a *double*. In order to read this data back out of the file, the data must be read as a string, followed by an *int*, followed by a *double*. This is exactly what the readInput method does. It reads a record with the following:

```
name = inputStream.readUTF();
population = inputStream.readInt();
growthRate = inputStream.readDouble();
```

Case Study   Writing and Reading a File of Records

task
specification

You have been hired by an international conservation group to write software to keep track of its records on endangered species. The group wants you to write software to store species records in a file and to display all the records for a specified file on a terminal screen.

Display 9.10 Species Class with Binary File I/O *(Part 1 of 3)*

```java
import java.io.*;

/***********************************************************
 *Class for data on endangered species.
 *This is a new, improved definition of the class Species,
 *which replaces the definition in Chapter 4.
 ***********************************************************/
public class Species
{
    public Species()
    {
        name = null;
        population = 0;
        growthRate = 0;
    }

    public Species(String theName, int thePopulation,
                                    double theGrowthRate)
    {
        name = theName;
        if (thePopulation >= 0)
            population = thePopulation;
        else
        {
            System.out.println("ERROR: can't have a negative population.");
            System.exit(0);
        }
        growthRate = theGrowthRate;
    }

    public void set(String newName, int newPopulation,
                                    double newGrowthRate)
    {
        name = newName;
        if (newPopulation >= 0)
            population = newPopulation;
        else
        {
            System.out.println("ERROR: can't have a negative population.");
            System.exit(0);
        }
        growthRate = newGrowthRate;
    }
```

Display 9.10 Species Class with Binary File I/O *(Part 2 of 3)*

<The methods speciesName, speciesPopulation, speciesGrowthRate, equals, and projectedPopulation are the same as in Display 4.15/page 214 >

> *The method name* readInput *is overloaded. With no argument, it reads its input from the keyboard. With an argument of type* DataInputStream, *it takes input from a binary file.*

```
/*****************************
 *Takes input from the keyboard.
 *****************************/
public void readInput()
{
    System.out.println("What is the species' name?");
    name = SavitchIn.readLine();
    System.out.println("What is the population of the species?");
    population = SavitchIn.readLineInt();
    System.out.println("Enter growth rate (percent increase per year):");
    growthRate = SavitchIn.readLineDouble();
}


/*****************************************************************
 *Precondition: The stream inputStream is connected to a file.
 *Each species record appears in the file as three items,
 *IN THIS ORDER: a String for the name, an int for the
 *population, and a double for the growth rate.
 *Action: Reads a record from the stream and resets the data
 *for the calling object. An attempt to read past the end
 *of the file will throw an EOFException.
 *****************************************************************/
public void readInput(DataInputStream inputStream)
                                            throws IOException
{
    name = inputStream.readUTF();
    population = inputStream.readInt();
    growthRate = inputStream.readDouble();
}
```

> *The method* readInput *throws an* EOFException *when it tries to read past the end of a file because* readUTF, readInt, *and* readDouble *each throw an* EOFException *when they try to read past the end of a file.*

Display 9.10 Species Class with Binary File I/O *(Part 3 of 3)*

The method name `writeOutput` is overloaded.
With no arguments, it sends output to the screen.
With an argument of type `DataOutputStream`,
it sends output to a binary file.

```
/*****************************
 *Sends output to the screen.
 *****************************/
public void writeOutput()
{
    System.out.println("Name = " + name);
    System.out.println("Population = " + population);
    System.out.println("Growth rate = " + growthRate + "%");
}



/***********************************************************
 *Precondition: The stream outputStream has been connected
 *to a file.
 *Action: A record of the species is written to the file
 *that is connected to outputStream. The record is written
 *as three items, IN THIS ORDER: a String for the name, an
 *int for the population, and a double for the growth rate.
 ***********************************************************/
public void writeOutput(DataOutputStream outputStream)
                                            throws IOException
{
    outputStream.writeUTF(name);
    outputStream.writeInt(population);
    outputStream.writeDouble(growthRate);
}




    private String name;
    private int population;
    private double growthRate;
}
```

file type and
class for data

You decide that the records should be stored in a binary file, since that is the most efficient kind of file to use. (At this stage, this is your only choice, since we have not yet covered classes that read and write to text files. But, using binary files would be a good choice even if you could use a text file.)

You decide to structure your software by using two classes, as well as the application program that will use these classes. One class is the class `Species`, which we defined in Display 9.10/page 487. This gives you a structure for the species records and a method to read and write species records to a binary file. The second class is a class with a method to create a file of records, a method to read a file of records and display them on the screen, and any auxiliary methods needed for these two tasks. You decide to call this class `SpeciesFiler`. The final program can then consist of an interface that invokes methods of the class `SpeciesFiler`.

data

You decide that the class `SpeciesFiler` should have the following instance variables to hold data:

> `fileName`: An instance variable of type `String` to hold a file name.
>
> `inputStream`: An instance variable of type `DataInputStream` to connect to files for reading input from a file.
>
> `outputStream`: An instance variable of type `DataOutputStream` to connect to files for writing output to a file.

actions

You decide that the class `SpeciesFiler` should have at least the following methods:

> `buildAFile`: A method that will ask the user for a file name and then fill the file with records read from the keyboard.
>
> `viewAFile`: A method that will ask the user for a file name and display the records in the named file to the screen.

You notice that both these methods have a common subtask, namely, obtaining a file name from the user. So, you decide to include a method for obtaining a file name from the user. Since this is just a helping method, you decide to make it a private method, so its definition will begin

getFileName

> *private* String getFileName(String prompt)

The code for `getFileName` is similar to other code we have seen and can be easily filled in. The class outline, as you have developed it so far, is shown in Display 9.11. Since it is routine, you fill in the code for the method `getFileName`.

buildAFile

Next you consider the method `buildAFile`. Since the class `Species` has a full complement of input and output methods, `buildAFile` can use an object of the class `Species` to obtain a record from the user and store it in the file. You thus write the following pseudocode for the method `buildAFile`:

```
fileName = getFileName("Enter name of file to hold records:");
outputStream =
        new DataOutputStream(new FileOutputStream(fileName));
Species oneSpecies = new Species();
```

Do the following while there are still records to be placed in the file:
```
{
    oneSpecies.readInput();
    oneSpecies.writeOutput(outputStream);
}
outputStream.close();
```

It is fairly routine to convert this pseudocode to Java code. The resulting definition is shown in Display 9.12. You realize that the user might overwrite a file if she or he gives the name of an existing file. So, you also add a warning to the user.

Next you turn your attention to the method `viewAFile`. You decide to separate the ordinary case from the exceptional cases. One important exceptional case is

`viewAFile`

Display 9.11 Outline of the Class `SpeciesFiler`
••

```
public class SpeciesFiler
{
    /**************************************************
    *Obtains a file name from the user and fills the
    *file with species records.
    **************************************************/
    public void buildAFile()
                <You still must complete the definition of buildAFile.>


    /**************************************************
    *Obtains a file name from the user and displays the
    *file content to the screen.
    *Precondition: The file must be a binary file of
    *the kind created by buildAFile.
    **************************************************/
    public void viewAFile()
                <You still must complete the definition of viewAFile.>


    private String getFileName(String prompt)
    {
        String fileName = null;
        System.out.println(prompt);
        fileName = SavitchIn.readLineWord();
        return fileName;
    }

    private String fileName = null;
    private DataInputStream inputStream = null;
    private DataOutputStream outputStream = null;
}
```
••

Display 9.12 The Method buildAFile **of the Class** SpeciesFiler
••

```
/***************************************************
*Obtains a file name from the user and fills the
*file with species records.
***************************************************/
public void buildAFile()
{
    System.out.println("This program will record the species records");
    System.out.println("you enter and store them in a file.");
    fileName = getFileName("Enter name of file to hold records:");
    System.out.println("If there already exists a file named "
                                                    + fileName);
    System.out.println("then all the data in that file will be lost.");
    System.out.println("OK to continue with the file "
                                            + fileName + "? (y/n)");
    char ans = SavitchIn.readLineNonwhiteChar();
    if ((ans != 'y') && (ans != 'Y'))
        System.out.println("File " + fileName + " not changed.");
    else
    {
        try
        {
            outputStream =
                new DataOutputStream(new FileOutputStream(fileName));

            Species oneSpecies = new Species();
            System.out.println("Ready to start entering records?(y/n)");
            ans = SavitchIn.readLineNonwhiteChar();
            while ((ans == 'y') || (ans == 'Y'))
            {
                oneSpecies.readInput();
                oneSpecies.writeOutput(outputStream);
                System.out.println("Enter another species?(y/n)");
                ans = SavitchIn.readLineNonwhiteChar();
            }
            outputStream.close();
            System.out.println("Species records written to the file "
                                                    + fileName);
        }
        catch(IOException e)
        {
            System.out.println("Error writing to file.");
        }
    }
}
```

••

when the user enters the name of a file that does not exist. You decide that if you process the ordinary case as if this would not happen and if the user does enter the name of a nonexistent file, then Java will throw a `FileNotFoundException`. So, you decide to write a method, called `viewAFileNoProblems`, and to invoke this method in a *try*-block. Thus, the method `viewAFile` can be defined as follows:

```
public void viewAFile()
{
    try
    {
        viewAFileNoProblems();
    }
    catch(FileNotFoundException e)
    {
        System.out.println("Cannot find a file named "
                                            + fileName);
    }
    catch(IOException e)
    {
        System.out.println("Error reading from file "
                                            + fileName);
    }
}
```

Even though you have not yet defined the method `viewAFileNoProblems`, you know that if the named file is not found, then it will throw a `FileNotFoundExcep-tion`, and if something else goes wrong it might throw an `IOException`.

You now turn your attention to the method `viewAFileNoProblems`. Obtaining the file name and connecting the file to a stream named by the instance variable `inputStream` is all routine. The part of the method definition that requires more attention is the input/output loop. That loop will continually read a record from the file and write it to the screen.

`viewAFile-NoProblems`

The heart of the loop body for reading one record from the file and writing it to the screen can be as follows (where `oneSpecies` is an object of the class `Species`):

```
oneSpecies.readInput(inputStream);
oneSpecies.writeOutput();
```

Whenever you design a loop, there are two main things that you need to con-sider: the loop body and a mechanism for ending the loop. You have already designed the heart of the loop body, but you still need a mechanism to determine how the loop will end. The pseudocode for the entire loop can be

loop design

Do the following until all records in the file have been read:
```
{
    oneSpecies.readInput(inputStream);
    oneSpecies.writeOutput();
}
```

To complete the Java code for this loop, you need some mechanism to determine when the end of the file is reached. In this case, you know that when the end of the

checking for end of file

file is reached, the method invocation `oneSpecies.readInput(inputStream)` will throw an exception in the class `EOFException` (because that is how we defined the method `readInput` of the class `Species` in Display 9.10/page 487). So, you terminate the loop when an `EOFException` is thrown. To do this, you write a loop that looks like an infinite loop, but you place it in a *try*-block to end the loop gracefully when an `EOFException` is thrown. So, your loop now looks like the following:

```
try
{
    while (true)
    {
        oneSpecies.readInput(inputStream);
        oneSpecies.writeOutput();
    }
}
catch(EOFException e)
{
    System.out.println("No more records in the file "
                                        + fileName");
}
```

slowing down the output

When you try out this loop in a test program, you see that there are some problems in how it displays data on the screen. If there are more records than can fit on one screen, they will go by so fast that the user cannot read the records. You need some way to stop the screen after each record is displayed. One easy way to stop the screen is to ask for some input after each record is displayed. But what input should you ask for? None is needed. The simplest thing to do is to ask the user to press the enter key (return key) when she or he is ready to read the next record. That simple input, of pressing the enter key, can be read as follows:

```
String junk = SavitchIn.readLine();
```

Thus, you can slow down the screen by using the following loop:

```
try
{
    while (true)
    {
        oneSpecies.readInput(inputStream);
        oneSpecies.writeOutput();
        System.out.println("Press Enter to see more.");
        String junk = SavitchIn.readLine();
    }
}
catch(EOFException e)
{
    System.out.println("No more records in the file "
                                        + fileName);
}
```

The string read into the variable `junk` will be the empty string, but you really do not care what string it is, since it is just discarded. The complete method definition for the method `viewAFileNoProblems` is shown in Display 9.13. That display also has the complete final definition of the class `SpeciesFiler`.

application
program

So far, you have simply developed a lot of tools. You have not even begun to write the application program that you contracted to write. However, with all these tools, it will be very easy to write the application program. All you need to do in the application program is present the user with a menu that chooses between an invocation of `buildAFile`, `viewAFile`, and quitting the program. So, you quickly (but carefully) write the program shown in Display 9.14.

? SELF-TEST QUESTIONS

11. The following appears in the program in Display 9.8/page 481:

```
try
{
    while (true)
    {
        n = inputStream.readInt();
        System.out.println(n);
    }
}
catch(EOFException e)
{
    System.out.println("End of reading from file.");
}
```

Why isn't this an infinite loop?

12. The method to input records from a file that we gave in Display 9.10/page 487 throws an exception in the class `EOFException` whenever it tries to reach past the end of a file, but the method definition begins

```
public void readInput(DataInputStream inputStream)
                                    throws IOException
```

Why doesn't it say *throws* `EOFException`?

13. Write a complete Java program that will read all the numbers in a binary file named `temperatures` and will write the numbers to the screen, one per line. Assume the file consists entirely of numbers written to it with the method `writeDouble`.

▼ ***PROGRAMMING EXAMPLE*** *A GUI Interface to Files (Alternative Ordering)*

You need to have covered Chapter 7 on the AWT in order to do this programming example. If you have covered Chapter 7, there is nothing unusually difficult about this example and there is no need to skip it.

In this programming example, we will present a GUI for building a file of records for endangered species and for viewing the records in such a file. We use

Display 9.13 A File-Handling Class *(Part 1 of 2)*

••

```java
import java.io.*;

/***********************************************************
 *A class to build files of species records and to display
 *the file contents on the screen. Uses the class Species.
 ***********************************************************/
public class SpeciesFiler
{
    /***********************************************
     *Obtains a file name from the user and fills the
     *file with species records.
     ***********************************************/
    public void buildAFile()
```
        <The rest of the method definition is the same as in Display 9.12/page 492.>

```java
    //Throws a FileNotFoundException if there is no file with the given name.
    private void viewAFileNoProblems() throws IOException
    {
        System.out.println("This program will display all the species");
        System.out.println("records contained in the file you specify.");
        fileName = getFileName("Enter name of file with records:");
        inputStream = new DataInputStream(new FileInputStream(fileName))
        Species oneSpecies = new Species();
        System.out.println("Records from the file " + fileName + ":");
        try
        {
            while (true)
            {
                oneSpecies.readInput(inputStream);
                oneSpecies.writeOutput();
                System.out.println("Press Enter to see more.");
                String junk = SavitchIn.readLine();
            }
        }
        catch(EOFException e)
        {
            System.out.println("No more records in the file "
                                            + fileName);
        }
        inputStream.close();
        System.out.println("File " + fileName + " put away.");
    }
```

••

Display 9.13 A File-Handling Class *(Part 2 of 2)*

```
/***************************************************
 *Obtains a file name from the user and displays the
 *file contents to the screen.
 *Precondition: The file must be a binary file of
 *the kind created by buildAFile.
 ***************************************************/
public void viewAFile()
{
    try
    {
        viewAFileNoProblems();
    }
    catch(FileNotFoundException e)
    {
        System.out.println("Cannot find a file named " + fileName);
    }
    catch(IOException e)
    {
        System.out.println("Error reading from file " + fileName);
    }
}

private String getFileName(String prompt)
    <The rest of the method definition is the same as in Display 9.11/page 491.>

private String fileName = null;
private DataInputStream inputStream = null;
private DataOutputStream outputStream = null;
}
```

the class Species in Display 9.10/page 487 to hold the record for one species and to write that record to a file (or to read such a record from a file). Our GUI class will have the same functionality as the class FileServer in Display 9.14/page 498, but will use a GUI interface developed using the AWT. The basic class for our GUI interface is called SpeciesGUI and is given in Display 9.15/page 500. When an object of this class is created and made visible, as in the main method of Display 9.15, it produces a window like the larger of the two windows shown at the end of Display 9.15. The user enters a file name in the text field and then clicks a button for the desired action: Either build a file of records with that name, or view all the records in the file of that name, or clear the text field to start over.

If the user makes an error, such as asking to see the records in a nonexisting file, then an error window, like the small window at the end of Display 9.15, is dis-

error window

Display 9.14 Application Program for Files of Species Records *(Part 1 of 2)*
••

```java
import java.io.*;

/***************************************************************
 *Program to store species records in a file and/or display all
 *the records in a file on a terminal screen.
 ***************************************************************/
public class FileServer
{
    public static void main(String[] args)
    {
        SpeciesFiler filer = new SpeciesFiler();
        System.out.print("This program can build and");
        System.out.println(" display files of species records.");

        char ans;
        boolean done = false;
        do
        {
            System.out.print("Enter choice: ");
            System.out.println(
                "B to build a file. V to view a file. Q to quit.");
            ans = SavitchIn.readLineNonwhiteChar();
            switch (ans)
            {
                case 'B':
                case 'b':
                    filer.buildAFile();
                    break;
                case 'V':
                case 'v':
                    filer.viewAFile();
                    break;
                case 'Q':
                case 'q':
                    done = true;
                    break;
                default:
                    System.out.println("That is not a valid choice.");
                    break;
            }
        }while ( ! done);
        System.out.println("File service closing down.");
    }
}
```

••

Display 9.14 Application Program for Files of Species Records *(Part 2 of 2)*

Sample Screen Dialogue

```
This program can build and display files of species records.
Enter choice: B to build a file. V to view a file. Q to quit.
B
This program will record the species records
you enter and store them in a file.
Enter name of file to hold records:
species.dat
If there already exists a file named species.dat
then all the data in that file will be lost.
OK to continue with the file species.dat? (y/n)
y
Ready to start entering records?(y/n)
y
What is the species name?
California Condor
What is the population of the species?
40
Enter growth rate (percent increase per year):
5
Enter another species?(y/n)
y
What is the species name?
Black Rhino
What is the population of the species?
100
Enter growth rate (percent increase per year):
2
Enter another species?(y/n)
n
Species records written to the file species.dat
Enter choice: B to build a file. V to view a file. Q to quit.
Q
File service closing down.
```

Display 9.15 GUI Interface for Species Record Processing *(Alternative Ordering) (Part 1 of 3)*

```java
import java.io.*;
import java.awt.*;
import java.awt.event.*;

/****************************************************************
 *Class for a GUI to store and retrieve species records from files.
 *Uses the classes Species, BuildFileGUI, ViewRecordsGUI, and ErrorWindow.
 ****************************************************************/
public class SpeciesGUI extends Frame implements ActionListener
{
    public static final int WINDOW_WIDTH = 300;
    public static final int WINDOW_HEIGHT = 200;

    public static void main(String[] args)
    {
        SpeciesGUI firstWindow = new SpeciesGUI();
        firstWindow.setVisible(true);
    }

    public SpeciesGUI()
    {
        setTitle("Species Filer");
        addWindowListener(new WindowDestroyer());
        setSize(WINDOW_WIDTH, WINDOW_HEIGHT);
        setLayout(new GridLayout(3, 1));

        Label instructions =
                new Label("Enter file name and choose action.");
        add(instructions);
        fileNameField = new TextField(20);
        add(fileNameField);

        Panel buttonPanel = new Panel();
        buttonPanel.setLayout(new FlowLayout());
        Button b = new Button("Build File");
        b.addActionListener(this);
        buttonPanel.add(b);
        b = new Button("View Records");
        b.addActionListener(this);
        buttonPanel.add(b);
        b = new Button("Clear");
        b.addActionListener(this);
        buttonPanel.add(b);
        add(buttonPanel);
    }
```

Display 9.15 GUI Interface for Species Record Processing *(Alternative Ordering) (Part 2 of 3)*

```java
    public void actionPerformed(ActionEvent e)
    {
        if (e.getActionCommand().equals("Build File"))
            buildFile();
        else if (e.getActionCommand().equals("View Records"))
            viewRecords();
        else if (e.getActionCommand().equals("Clear"))
            fileNameField.setText("");
        else
        {
            ErrorWindow ew =
                new ErrorWindow("Error. Start over.");
            ew.show();
        }

        repaint();
    }


    private void buildFile()
    {
        fileName = fileNameField.getText();
        fileNameField.setText(""); //For when the window returns.

        try
        {
            DataOutputStream outputStream =
                new DataOutputStream(new FileOutputStream(fileName));
            BuildFileGUI nextWindow =
                    new BuildFileGUI(fileName, outputStream);
            nextWindow.show();
        }
        catch(IOException e2)
        {
            ErrorWindow ew =
                new ErrorWindow("Error creating file " + fileName);
            ew.show();
        }
    }
```

Display 9.15 GUI Interface for Species Record Processing (Alternative Ordering) (Part 3 of 3)

```
    private void viewRecords()
    {
        fileName = fileNameField.getText();
        fileNameField.setText(""); //For when the window returns
        try
        {
            DataInputStream inputStream =
                new DataInputStream(new FileInputStream(fileName));
            ViewRecordsGUI nextWindow =
                        new ViewRecordsGUI(fileName, inputStream);
            nextWindow.show();
        }
        catch(FileNotFoundException e2)
        {
            ErrorWindow ew =
                new ErrorWindow("File " + fileName + " Not Found.");
            ew.show();
        }
    }

    private TextField fileNameField;
    private String fileName = null;
}
```

When this GUI starts, there is no error window present, and if all goes well, there will never be an error window shown.

Resulting GUI

```
┌────────────────────────────┬──┬──┐
│           Error            │  │ X│
├────────────────────────────┴──┴──┤
│ File species.bak Not Found.       │
│                                   │
│      ┌───────────────────┐        │
│      │        OK         │        │
│      └───────────────────┘        │
└───────────────────────────────────┘
```

The error window will probably be on top of the other window. We separated them so you could see both windows.

```
        ┌──────────────────────────┬────┬────┬──┐
        │      Species Filer       │    │    │ X│
        ├──────────────────────────┴────┴────┴──┤
        │ Enter file name and choose action.    │
        │                                        │
        │ ┌────────────────────────────────────┐│
        │ │ species.bak                        ││
        │ └────────────────────────────────────┘│
        │                                        │
        │ ┌───────────┐ ┌─────────────┐ ┌───────┐│
        │ │ Build File│ │ View Records│ │ Clear ││
        │ └───────────┘ └─────────────┘ └───────┘│
        └────────────────────────────────────────┘
```

played. These error windows are objects of another class named `ErrorWindow`. In reality, the error window would probably appear on top of the other larger window that is shown, but in Display 9.15, we have separated the two windows a bit so that you can clearly see both windows.

It requires a lot of code to create a good GUI interface, so this programming example is long. However, although it is long, it is not difficult to understand or even to design and code. The entire GUI display uses five classes: the class `SpeciesGUI` in Display 9.15; the class `ErrorWindow`, which we discussed briefly in the previous paragraph; the class `WindowDestroyer` from Display 7.2/page 332; and the two classes `BuildFileGUI` and `ViewRecordsGUI`. The class `WindowDestroyer` is the listener class we have always used to end an AWT display. If you click the close-window button in any of these windows, then a listener object of the class `WindowDestroyer` ends the entire GUI display, so that not just one window, but the entire GUI program ends. (It would be possible to design the GUI so that clicking the close-window button would only close one window and not end the entire GUI, but that would complicate an already long example.) Rather than clicking the close-window button, you would more often click some other button, and then a new window would be placed on top of (or would replace) the window currently visible on the screen. You already know about the class `WindowDestroyer`, since we have used it in every AWT program we have written. In this programming example, we will describe two of the new classes and leave the other two classes for Self-Test Questions. Since the answers to all Self-Test Questions are at the back of this chapter, we are ultimately giving you these other two classes as well, but we urge you to write them on your own before checking the answer at the end of this chapter.

close-window buttons

Let's first consider the class `SpeciesGUI` given in Display 9.15. The window title, the text field, the label for the text field, and buttons are placed in the window within the constructor in the same way as previous examples. The window listener for closing the window (an object of the class `WindowDestroyer`) is registered in the same way as we did in previous examples. Thus, the entire constructor, although long, is very routine. The new and interesting elements are in the method `actionPerformed`.

Species-GUI

action-Performed

The method `actionPerformed` receives the action event from a button click. If the user clicks the `"Build File"` button, then the file named in the text field is opened for writing and a new window is opened to handle the inputting of records. This new window is an object of the class `BuildFileGUI`. If the user instead clicks the `"View Records"` button, then the file named in the text field is opened for reading and a (different) new window is opened to display records. This new window is an object of the class `ViewRecordsGUI`. However, if there is any trouble opening the file, then an error window is shown instead of the window to build a file or the window to view records. The error window is an object of the class `Error-Window`. The constructor for `ErrorWindow` takes one string argument, which is the one-line error message that is displayed in the error window.

The class `BuildFileGUI` is shown in Display 9.16. Let's consider some details of how the class `BuildFileGUI` is used by the class `SpeciesGUI`. The action starts with an object of the class `SpeciesGUI`.

Display 9.16 GUI for Building a File of Records *(Alternative Ordering) (Part 1 of 4)*

••

```java
import java.io.*;
import java.awt.*;
import java.awt.event.*;

/************************************************************
 *Class for a GUI to store species records in a file.
 *Meant to be used as a helping class for the class SpeciesGUI.
 ************************************************************/
public class BuildFileGUI extends Frame implements ActionListener
{
    public static final int WINDOW_WIDTH = 400;
    public static final int WINDOW_HEIGHT = 300;

    public BuildFileGUI(String fileNameString,
                                  DataOutputStream outStream)
    {
        fileName = fileNameString;
        outputStream = outStream;
        setTitle("Build File");
        addWindowListener(new WindowDestroyer());
        setSize(WINDOW_WIDTH, WINDOW_HEIGHT);
        setLayout(new BorderLayout());

        Panel filePanel = new Panel();
        Label fileLabel = new Label("File Name");
        filePanel.add(fileLabel);
        fileNameField = new TextField(30);
        fileNameField.setText(fileNameString);
        filePanel.add(fileNameField);
        add(filePanel, "North");

        Panel recordPanel = new Panel();
        recordPanel.setBackground(Color.gray);
        recordPanel.setLayout(new GridLayout(3, 1));
        Label l;

        Panel namePanel = new Panel();
        l = new Label("Species Name");
        namePanel.add(l);
        speciesNameField = new TextField(30);
        namePanel.add(speciesNameField);
        recordPanel.add(namePanel);
```

••

Display 9.16 GUI for Building a File of Records *(Alternative Ordering) (Part 2 of 4)*
••

```
            Panel populationPanel = new Panel();
            l = new Label("Population");
            populationPanel.add(l);
            populationField = new TextField(10);
            populationPanel.add(populationField);
            recordPanel.add(populationPanel);

            Panel growthRatePanel = new Panel();
            l = new Label("Growth Rate (as percent)");
            growthRatePanel.add(l);
            growthRateField = new TextField(10);
            growthRatePanel.add(growthRateField);
            recordPanel.add(growthRatePanel);

            add(recordPanel, "Center");
            Panel buttonPanel = new Panel();
            buttonPanel.setLayout(new FlowLayout());
            Button b = new Button("Add Record");
            b.addActionListener(this);
            buttonPanel.add(b);
            b = new Button("Clear");
            b.addActionListener(this);
            buttonPanel.add(b);
            b = new Button("Done");
            b.addActionListener(this);
            buttonPanel.add(b);
            add(buttonPanel, "South");
        }

        //actionPerformed cannot throw IOException.
        public void actionPerformed(ActionEvent e)
        {
            if (e.getActionCommand().equals("Add Record"))
                enterNextRecord();
            else if (e.getActionCommand().equals("Clear"))
            {
                speciesNameField.setText("");
                populationField.setText("");
                growthRateField.setText("");
            }
```

<Definition of `actionPerformed` continued on page 506.>

••

Display 9.16 GUI for Building a File of Records *(Alternative Ordering) (Part 3 of 4)*

```
            else if (e.getActionCommand().equals("Done"))
            {
                try
                {
                    outputStream.close();
                    dispose();
                }
                catch(IOException e2)
                {
                    ErrorWindow ew =
                        new ErrorWindow("Error closing file.");
                    ew.show();
                }
            }
            else
            {
                ErrorWindow ew =
                    new ErrorWindow("Error. Start Over.");
                ew.show();
            }

            repaint();
        }

    private void enterNextRecord()
    {
        try
        {
            oneRecord.set(speciesNameField.getText(),
                    stringToInt(populationField.getText()),
                    stringToDouble(growthRateField.getText()));
            oneRecord.writeOutput(outputStream);
            speciesNameField.setText("record entered.");
            populationField.setText("");
            growthRateField.setText("");
        }
        catch(NumberFormatException e1)
        {//Incorrectly written number for population or growth rate.
            ErrorWindow ew =
              new ErrorWindow("Error: Incorrectly written number.");
            ew.show();
        }
```

<Additional *catch*-block in next part of display.>

Display 9.16 GUI for Building a File of Records *(Alternative Ordering) (Part 4 of 4)*
••

```
            catch(IOException e2)
            {
                ErrorWindow ew =
                        new ErrorWindow("Error writing to file.");
                ew.show();
            }
        }

    private static int stringToInt(String stringObject)
    {
        return Integer.valueOf(stringObject.trim()).intValue();
    }

    private static double stringToDouble(String stringObject)
    {
        return Double.valueOf(stringObject.trim()).doubleValue();
    }

    private Species oneRecord = new Species();
    private TextField fileNameField;
    private TextField speciesNameField;
    private TextField populationField;
    private TextField growthRateField;
    private String fileName = null;
    private DataOutputStream outputStream = null;
}
```

The windows will probably be one on top of the other, so only one is visible.

Resulting GUI

BuildFile-
GUI

Consider the GUI display produced by an object of the class SpeciesGUI and shown at the end of Display 9.15. When the GUI starts, there will not be any error window, only the larger window shown at the end of Display 9.15. The user enters a file name in the text field. When the user clicks the "Build File" button, this generates an action event e and sends this action event to the method actionPerformed. The method actionPerformed uses a nested *if-else*-statement to check e.getActionCommand(). Since, in this case, e.getActionCommand() equals "Build File", the method buildFile is invoked.

The method buildFile obtains the file name from the text field, clears the text field, and then executes the following *try*-bock:

```
try
{
    DataOutputStream outputStream =
        new DataOutputStream(new FileOutputStream(fileName));
    BuildFileGUI nextWindow =
        new BuildFileGUI(fileName, outputStream);
    nextWindow.show();
}
```

If there is any problem opening the file, then an IOException will be thrown and caught by the *catch*-block. The *catch*-block displays an error window. However, let's assume the file is opened successfully. In that case, a new object of the class BuildFileGUI is created, given the name nextWindow, and then displayed with the

show

show method. The show method is very similar to the method invocation setVisible(*true*), but the show method guarantees that the window will be on top of any other windows on the screen. This is important because the original window display does not go away, but just waits on the screen until the window nextWindow goes away. In this example, windows are created, placed on top of other windows, and then later are destroyed, allowing the underlying window to be available again to the user. When the following is executed, the screen display changes to the GUI shown at the end of Display 9.16.

```
nextWindow.show();
```

The new window will probably be right on top of the old window so that only one window is visible. We have shown the windows slightly out of alignment so you can see both windows.

Most of what is done by a GUI object of the class BuildFileGUI is routine and similar to things you have seen before. However, there is one thing that you may not have seen before. When the user clicks the "Done" button in the top window shown at the end of Display 9.16, this sends an action event to the method actionPerformed of the class BuildFileGUI. The method actionPerformed finds the right case in the nested *if-else*-statement and then does two things: It closes the file, and if the file closes without throwing an IOException, then it invokes the

dispose

method dispose as follows:

```
dispose();
```

This invocation of dispose is similar to setVisible(*false*). It makes the window go away. But it does not simply make it invisible so that it can later be made visible again. It actually destroys the window. Any future window for building a file will be a brand new window. However, the original window from the start of this entire process is under the window being destroyed and the original window that appeared at the very start of this entire GUI is again visible so that the screen looks like the GUI pictured at the end of Display 9.15/page 500, but without any error window present.

Be sure to notice that the method `actionPerformed` (in both classes shown in this example) always catches all exceptions. It does not have a *throws*-clause. Recall that you cannot declare any exceptions in a *throws*-clause of the method `actionPerformed`. All exceptions thrown in your definition of the method `actionPerformed` must be caught in that method definition. This is because the `ActionListener` interface completely specifies the interface for the method `actionPerformed` and you cannot change that interface. The interface for the method `ActionPerformed` does not specify any *throws*-clause, and so you cannot add a *throws*-clause.

action-
Performed

Frame **Methods** `dispose` **and** `show` *(Alternative Ordering)*

The method `dispose` takes no arguments. An invocation of `dispose` completely eliminates the object that invokes it. It is usually used to make a window go away.

The method `show` takes no arguments. An invocation of `show()` is like an invocation of `setVisible(true)`, but `show` also ensures that the window will be the top window and so visible to the user even if there are other windows on the screen.

? SELF-TEST QUESTIONS *(for Alternative Ordering Section)*

14. Write a definition for the class `ErrorWindow` to use in the preceding Programming Example. The screen display for an object of the class `ErrorWindow` should look approximately like the smaller window shown at the end of Display 9.15/page 500. When the user clicks the "`OK`" button, this results in an invocation of `dispose` so that the error window disappears. *Hint:* Use the error message string (that is given as an argument to the constructor) to construct a label and add it to the window.

15. Complete the previous Programming Example by giving a definition of the class `ViewRecordsGUI`. Use three text fields to display a single species record. When the window first comes up, it displays the first record in the file. (You can assume the file has at least one record.) Have a "`Next`" button that changes the display so that the next record in the file is shown. *Hint:* It will help to model much of the detail after the class `BuildFileGUI`.

9.3 More Classes for File I/O

An ounce of prevention is worth a pound of cure.
COMMON SAYING

In this section, we describe some additional classes that you might find handy when doing file I/O. You do not need to cover Section 9.2 on exception handling before reading this section. If you do not know about file path names, you can skip all the references to them. However, to get the most benefit from this section, you should first learn about file path names and learn how they are written on your system. (The details of file path names depend on the operating system you are using. They are not part of the Java language.)

The File Class

You can use the class named File to check properties of files. You can check things like whether or nor there is a file with a specified name and whether or not the file is readable. Display 9.17 gives a sample program using the class File. Notice that the File class is like a wrapper class for file names. A string like "treasure.dat" may be a file name, but only has string properties. It has no file-name properties. The object

```
new File("treasure.dat")
```

is not simply a string. It is an object that knows it is supposed to name a file.

Suppose you create a File object and name the object fileObject with the following code:

```
File fileObject = new File("treasure.dat");
```

exists

You can then use the method named exists to test whether there is any file with the name treasur.dat. For example,

```
if ( ! fileObject.exists())
    System.out.println("No file by that name.");
```

If there is a file with that name, you can tell if the operating system will let you read from the file with the method canRead. For example,

canRead

```
if ( ! fileObject.canRead())
    System.out.println("Not allowed to read from that file.");
```

Most operating systems let you designate some files as not readable or as only readable by certain people. This is a good way to check whether you or somebody else has inadvertently (or intentionally) made a file nonreadable.

Display 9.18/page 513 lists some of the methods in the class File.

When giving a file name, you may use either a simple file name, in which case it is assumed that the file is in the same directory (folder) as the one in which the program is run. You can also use a full or relative path name. A path name gives not only the name of the file, but also tells what directory (folder) the file is in. The way that you give path names depends on your particular operating system and you must write path names in the way that they are written in the operating system you are using.

path names

Display 9.17 Using the File Class *(Part 1 of 2)*

```
import java.io.*;

public class FileClassDemo
{
    public static void main(String[] args)
    {
        String name = null;
        File fileObject = null;

        System.out.println("I will show you the first string");
        System.out.println("in a file you name.");
        System.out.println("The first data item in the file");
        System.out.println("must be a string.");

        System.out.println("Enter file name:");
        name = SavitchIn.readLineWord();
        fileObject = new File(name);
        while ((! fileObject.exists()) || (! fileObject.canRead()))
        {
            if ( ! fileObject.exists())
                System.out.println("No such file");
            else if ( ! fileObject.canRead())
                System.out.println("That file is not readable.");
            System.out.println("Enter file name again:");
            name = SavitchIn.readLineWord();
            fileObject = new File(name);
        }

        try
        {
            DataInputStream fileInput =
                    new DataInputStream(new FileInputStream(name));
            System.out.println("The first string in the file is:");
            String firstString = fileInput.readUTF();
            System.out.println(firstString);

            fileInput.close();
        }
        catch(IOException e)
        {
            System.out.println("Problem reading from file.");
        }
    }
}
```

Display 9.17 Using the File Class *(Part 2 of 2)*
••

Sample Screen Dialogue

```
I will show you the first string
in a file you name.
The first data item in the file
must be a string.
Enter file name:
secrete.dat
That file is not readable.
Enter file name again:
dtionary.dat
No such file
Enter file name again:
dictionary.dat
The first string in the file is:
aardvark
```

••

Use of Path Names

You can use a full or relative path name for a file whenever Java calls for a string that is the file name. Thus, you can use a path name as an argument to the constructor for the class `File` or as an argument to any of the stream class constructors that accept a file name. However, the exact details on how you write the path name will depend on the operating system you are using.

A typical Windows path name is

```
D:\Work\Java\Programs\FileClassDemo.java
```

To create a `File` object from this and name the object `programFile`, you use

```
File programFile =
        new File("D:\Work\Java\Programs\FileClassDemo.java");
```

A typical UNIX path name is

```
/user/smith/home.work/java/FileClassDemo.java
```

To create a `File` object from this and name the object `programFile`, you use

```
File programFile =
    new File("/user/smith/home.work/java/FileClassDemo.java");
```

The exact details on path names will depend on what operating system you are using.

The Classes `FileInputStream` **and** `FileOutputStream`

We have used the stream class `FileInputStream` or `FileOutputStream` whenever we created a stream of the class `DataInputStream` or `DataOutputStream`. For example, the following were used in Display 9.17/page 511 and Display 9.1/page 461, respectively:

```
DataInputStream fileInput =
          new DataInputStream(new FileInputStream(name));
DataOutputStream outputStream =
      new DataOutputStream(new FileOutputStream("numbers.dat"));
```

We used the classes `FileInputStream` and `FileOutputStream` because they accept a file name as a constructor argument, such as the arguments `name` and `"numbers.dat"` in the preceding examples. Neither `DataInputStream` nor `DataOutputStream` accepts a file name as an argument. Thus, when you connect a `DataInputStream` to a file using a string name, you must take two steps. First, you create an object of the class `FileInputStream` with, for example, *new* `FileInput-`

Display 9.18 Some Methods in the Class `File`

∙∙

public boolean exists()
  Tests whether there is a file with the name used to create the `File` object.

public boolean canRead()
  Tests if the program can read from the file.

public boolean canWrite()
  Tests if the program can write to the file.

public boolean delete()
  Tries to delete the file. Returns *true* if it was able to delete the file. Returns *false* if it was unable to delete the file.

public long length()
  Returns the length of the file in bytes.

public String getName()
  Returns the name of the file. (Note this is not a path name, just the simple name.)

public String getPath()
  Returns the path name of the file.

Stream(name), and then you use this object of the class FileInputStream to create an object of the class DataInputStream with

```
DataInputStream fileInput =
                new DataInputStream(new FileInputStream(name));
```

Similarly, we produce a DataOutputStream from a file name in two steps using FileOutPutStream.

FileInputStream **and** FileOutputStream

In this book, we will use the classes FileInputStream and FileOutputStream for their constructors and nothing else. Each of these two classes has a constructor that takes a file name as an argument and another constructor that takes an object of the class File as an argument. We use these constructors to produce arguments for the constructors for stream classes such as DataInputStream and DataOutputStream. In what follows, there are two examples. The first uses a file name as an argument and the second uses an object of the class File.

```
DataOutputStream outputStream =
        new DataOutputStream(new FileOutputStream("stuff.dat"));

File fileObject = new File("stuff.dat");
DataInputStream inputStream =
        new DataInputStream(new FileInputStream(fileObject));
```

The constructor for FileInputStream can throw an exception in the class FileNotFoundException and that the constructor for FileOutputStream can throw an exception in the class IOException.

Since *new* FileInputStream(name) produces an input stream connected to the file named by the string in the variable name, why didn't we just use that stream instead of going on to create a DataInputStream? The reason is that the class FileInputStream does not have the nice input methods we want to use, like readInt, readDouble, and readUTF. The class FileInputStream does have methods for inputting raw bytes of data, but no methods that do the nice conversions to the Java types, such as *int*, *double*, and String. To get the nice methods in the class DataInputStream, we need to convert the FileInputStream to a DataInputStream. Whenever you chain streams together in this way, the resulting stream always has the methods of the last (i.e., leftmost stream named). For example, in

```
DataInputStream fileInput =
                new DataInputStream(new FileInputStream(name));
```

the stream fileInput has all the methods of the class DataInputStream, but does not have the methods of the class FileInputStream.

Similar remarks apply to why we do not simply use the class FileOutputStream, but instead go on to form a DataOutputStream.

Since we will only use the classes FileInputStream and FileOutputStream in arguments to constructors for stream classes such as DataInputStream and DataOutputStream, we do not really care what methods the class FileInputStream and FileOutputStream may or may not have, except for the constructor methods. We do care what constructors these classes have, since it is the constructors that we use with *new* in the preceding examples and similar cases. You already know that the classes `FileInputStream` and `FileOutputStream` each have a constructor that accepts a file name. Both `FileInputStream` and `FileOutputStream` also have constructors that accept an object of the class `File`. This can be handy when your program creates an object of the class `File` to represent a file. For example, in Display 9.19, we have rewritten the program in Display 9.17/page 511 so that the argument to `FileInputStream` is an object of the class `File`. Those two programs are completely equivalent.

When using `FileInputStream` and `FileOutputStream` in the ways we have described it, is important to note that the constructors for these classes can throw exceptions. The constructor for `FileInputStream` can throw an exception in the class `FileNotFoundException` and that the constructor for `FileOutputStream` can throw an exception in the class `IOException`.

? SELF-TEST QUESTIONS

16. Write a complete Java program that will ask the user for a file name, test if the file exists, and if the file exists, will ask the user if it should be deleted or not and delete it or not as the user requests.

17. Suppose you want to create an input stream and connect it to the binary file named `mydata.dat`. Will the following work? If not, how can you write something similar that does work?

```
DataInputStream inputStream =
                new DataInputStream("mydata.dat");
```

18. Does the class `FileInputStream` have a method named `readInt`? Does it have one named `readDouble`? Does it have one named `readUTF`?

19. Does the class `FileOutputStream` have a constructor that accepts a file name as an argument? Does the class `FileOutputStream` have a constructor that accepts an object of the class `File` as an argument?

20. Does the class `DataOutputStream` have a constructor that accepts a file name as an argument? Does the class `DataOutputStream` have a constructor that accepts an object of the class `File` as an argument?

9.4 Text File I/O

> *Proper words in proper places,*
>   *make the true definition of a style.*
> JONATHAN SWIFT, LETTER TO A YOUNG CLERGYMAN (JANUARY 9, 1720)

Binary files are more efficient than text files, but text files can be written to and read by people using a text editor. Java allows you to write programs that take input from a text file or send output to a text file. In this section, we will give a brief description of the most common way to do text file I/O in Java.

Display 9.19 Using a File Argument in a Constructor for `FileInputStream`

```java
import java.io.*;
public class FileClassDemo2
{
    public static void main(String[] args)
    {
        try
        {
            String name = null;
            File fileObject = null;

            System.out.println("I will show you the first string");
            System.out.println("in a file you name.");
            System.out.println("The first data item in the file");
            System.out.println("must be a string.");

            System.out.println("Enter file name:");
            name = SavitchIn.readLineWord();
            fileObject = new File(name);
            while (( ! fileObject.exists()) || ( ! fileObject.canRead()))
            {
                if ( ! fileObject.exists())
                    System.out.println("No such file");
                else if ( ! fileObject.canRead())
                    System.out.println("That file is not readable.");
                System.out.println("Enter file name again:");
                name = SavitchIn.readLineWord();
                fileObject = new File(name);
            }

            DataInputStream fileInput =
                new DataInputStream(new FileInputStream(fileObject));
            System.out.println("The first string in the file is:");
            String firstString = fileInput.readUTF();
            System.out.println(firstString);
            fileInput.close();
        }
        catch(IOException e)
        {
            System.out.println("Problem reading from file.");
        }
    }
}
```

In order to read this section, you do not need to have read the preceding sections of this chapter, although it might help if you read the introductory two paragraphs of Section 9.1, which appear on page 458. Before reading this section, you should have covered Chapters 1 through 6 and the basics of exception handling given in Section 8.1 of Chapter 8. You do not need Chapter 7 to understand this section. However, it would make this section more useful to you if you read the subsection of Chapter 7 entitled **Inputting and Outputting Numbers**.

Text File Output with `PrintWriter`

Writing output to a text file uses a method named `println` that behaves the same as `System.out.println`, but that is a method in the class `PrintWriter`. The class `PrintWriter` is the preferred stream class for writing to a text file. Display 9.20 contains a simple program that writes data to a text file.

PrintWriter

The program in Display 9.20 creates a text file named `out.txt` that can be read using an editor or can be read by another Java program using the class `BufferedReader`, which we will discuss in the next subsection. Notice how the file is *opened*:

```
PrintWriter outputStream =
        new PrintWriter(new FileOutputStream("out.txt"));
```

The preceding two lines connect the stream named `outputStream` to the file named `out.txt`. This connecting is called **opening a file**. Note that the name of the file, in this case `out.txt`, is given as a `String` value and so is given in quotes. You can think of the entire expression

opening a file

```
PrintWriter Output_Stream_Name =
        new PrintWriter(new FileOutputStream(File_Name));
```

as one difficult-to-spell operation that takes a *File_Name* as an argument, produces an output stream in the class `PrintWriter`, and connects the stream to the named file so that your program can send output to the file. The class `PrintWriter` has no constructor that takes a file name as its argument. So, we use the class `FileOutputStream` with the class `PrintWriter` in the way shown previously. If you have not already done so,

---

Connecting a Text File to a Stream for Writing
(Opening a Text File for Output)

You create a stream of the class `PrintWriter` and connect it to a text file for writing as follows.

Syntax:

```
PrintWriter Output_Stream_Name =
        new PrintWriter(new FileOutputStream(File_Name));
```

Example:

```
PrintWriter outputStream =
        new PrintWriter(new FileOutputStream("out.txt"));
```

After this, you can use the methods `println` and `print` to write to the file.

Display 9.20 Text File Output

```java
import java.io.*;
public class TextFileOutputDemo
{
    public static void main(String[] args)
    {
        PrintWriter outputStream = null;
        try
        {
            outputStream =
                    new PrintWriter(new FileOutputStream("out.txt"))
        }
        catch(IOException e)
        {
            System.out.println("Error opening the file out.txt.");
            System.exit(0);
        }

        System.out.println("Enter three lines of text:");
        String line = null;
        int count;
        for (count = 1; count <= 3; count++)
        {
            line = SavitchIn.readLine();
            outputStream.println(count + " " + line);
        }
        outputStream.close();
        System.out.println("Those lines were written to out.txt.");
    }
}
```

Sample Screen Dialogue

```
Enter three lines of text:
A tall tree
in a short forest is like
a big fish in a small pond.
Those lines were written to out.txt.
```

File `out.txt` (after program is run with given dialogue)

```
1 A tall tree
2 in a short forest is like
3 a big fish in a small pond.
```

You can read this file using a text editor.

then at some point you may wish to read the subsection **The Classes** `FileInput-` `Stream` **and** `FileOutputStream` to see why you must sometimes use this long expression to connect a stream, such as a stream of the class `PrintWriter`, to a file. However, you can simply view this as one difficult-to-spell operation and still write and understand Java programs.

When you open a text file as described in the previous paragraph, so that it is connected to a stream of type `PrintWriter`, that file opening can possibly throw an `IOException` and any such possible exception should be caught in a *catch*-block. (Actually it is the `FileOutputStream` constructor that might throw the `IOException`, but the net effect is that opening a file with the class `PrintWriter` in the way we have outlined can result in an `IOException` being thrown.)

Notice that, as illustrated in Display 9.20, the method `println` of the class `PrintWriter` works the same for writing to a text file as the method `System.out.println` works for writing to the screen. The class `PrintWriter` also has the method `print` and it behaves just like `System.out.print` except that the output goes to a text file. Display 9.21 describes some of the methods in the class `PrintWriter`.

`println`

Closing Text Files

When your program is finished writing to a file (or reading from a file), it should *close* the stream connected to that file by invoking the method named `close`.

Syntax:

  StreamName`.close();`

Example:

  `outputStream.close();`

▲ *GOTCHA* A `try`-*Block Is a Block*

Look again at the program in Display 9.20/page 518. It is not an accident or a minor stylistic concern that caused us to declare the variable `outputStream` outside of the `try`-block. If you were to move that declaration inside the `try`-block you would get a compiler error message. Let's look at the details.

Suppose you replace

```
PrintWriter outputStream = null;
try
{
    outputStream =
        new PrintWriter(new FileOutputStream("out.txt"));
}
```

with the following in Display 9.20:

Display 9.21 Some Methods in the Class `PrintWriter`
●●

`PrintWriter(InputStream streamObject)`
    This is the only constructor you are likely to need. There is no constructor that accepts a file name as an argument. If you want to create a stream using a file name, then you use

   `new PrintWriter(new FileOutputStream(File_Name))`

When used in this way, the `FileOutputStream` constructor and so the `PrintWriter` constructor can throw an `IOException`.

`public final void println(Object outputStuff)`
    Arguments can be strings, characters, integers, floating-point numbers, boolean values, or any combination of these connected with + signs. Outputs its argument to the file connected to the stream and ends the line.

`public final void print(Object outputStuff)`
    Arguments can be strings, characters, integers, floating-point numbers, boolean values, or any combination of these connected with + signs. Outputs its argument to the file connected to the stream but does not end the line. The next output will be on the same line.

`public void close()`
    Closes the streams connection to a file. This method calls `flush` before closing the file.

`public void flush()`
    Flushes the output stream. This forces an actual physical write to the file of any data that have been buffered and not yet physically written to the file. Normally, you should not need to invoke `flush`.

```
try
{
    PrintWriter outputStream =
        new PrintWriter(new FileOutputStream("out.txt"));
}
```

This looks innocent enough, but it makes the variable `outputStream` a variable that is local to the *try*-block, which would mean that you cannot use `outputStream` outside of the *try*-block. If you make this change and try to compile the changed program, you will get an error message saying that `outputStream` when used outside the *try*-block is an undefined variable.

    Remember a *try*-block is a block and so any variable declared in a *try*-block will be local to the *try*-block.

Text File Input with `BufferedReader`

Display 9.22 contains a simple program that reads data from a text file and writes them back to the screen. This is just a toy program to let you see how text file input works. The file `data.txt` is a text file that could have been created and written into with a text editor or could have been created by a Java program using the class `PrintWriter`.

Display 9.22 Text File Input

```java
import java.io.*;
public class TextFileInputDemo
{
    public static void main(String[] args)
    {
        try
        {
            BufferedReader inputStream = null;
            inputStream =
                new BufferedReader(new FileReader("data.txt"));

            String line = null;
            line = inputStream.readLine();
            System.out.println("The first line in data.txt is:");
            System.out.println(line);

            line = inputStream.readLine();
            System.out.println("The second line in data.txt is:");
            System.out.println(line);
            inputStream.close();
        }
        catch(FileNotFoundException e)
        {
            System.out.println("File data.txt not found.");
        }
        catch(IOException e2)
        {
            System.out.println("Error reading from file data.txt.");
        }
    }
}
```

File `data.txt`

```
1 2
buckle my shoe.
3 4
shut the door.
```

Screen Output

```
The first line in data.txt is:
1 2
The second line in data.txt is:
buckle my shoe.
```

Notice how the file is opened:

```
BufferedReader inputStream =
        new BufferedReader(new FileReader("data.txt"));
```

Buffered-
Reader

The class `BufferedReader` is the preferred stream class for reading from a text file.

As was true of the class `PrintWriter`, the class `BufferedReader` has no constructor that takes a file name as its argument, so we need to use another class, in this case, the class `FileReader`, to help with opening the file. The class `FileReader` will accept a file name (or an object of the class `File`) as a constructor argument and produce a stream that is a `Reader`. The constructor for `BufferedReader` will accept a `Reader` as an argument. `Reader` is an abstract class that includes all the streams with "Reader" in their name. However, rather than keep track of this rather complicated explanation, you can simply think of the following as one long, peculiarly spelled expression for connecting a text file to a stream of the class `Buff-eredReader` so that your program can read from the file:

```
BufferedReader Stream_Name =
        new BufferedReader(new FileReader(File_Name));
```

readLine

Notice that the method `readLine` of the class `BufferedReader` works the same for reading from a text file as the method `readLine` of the class `SavitchIn` works for reading a line of text from the keyboard. However, the class `BufferedReader` does *not* have any of the other read methods that are in the class `SavitchIn`, such as `readInt`, `readDouble`, and `readNonwhiteChar`. Display 9.23 describes some of the methods in the class `BufferedReader`.

Connecting a Text File to a Stream for Reading
(Opening a Text File for Reading)

You create a stream of the class `BufferedReader` and connect it to a text file for reading as follows.

Syntax:
```
BufferedReader Stream_Name =
        new BufferedReader(new FileReader(File_Name));
```

Example:
```
BufferedReader inputStream =
        new BufferedReader(new FileReader("data.txt"));
```

After this, you can use the methods `readLine` and `read` to read from the file. ∎

---

reading
numbers

Since `BufferedReader` has no methods like `readInt` that can read a number, the only way that you can read a number from a text file using the class `Buffere-dReader` is to read it as a string and then convert the string to a number. The techniques for converting strings to numbers are discussed in the subsection of Chapter 7 entitled **Inputting and Outputting Numbers** on page 376. The following optional subsection on the class `StringTokenizer` presents some other useful techniques to assist in processing strings, including string input that is read from a text file.

read method

The class `BufferedReader` does have a method, named simply `read`, that will read a single character. This method `read` is similar to the method `readChar` in

Display 9.23 Some Methods in the Class BufferedReader
••

BufferedReader(Reader readerObject)
    This is the only constructor you are likely to need. There is no constructor that accepts a file name as an argument. If you want to create a stream using a file name, then you use

new BufferedReader(*new* FileReader(*File_Name*))

When used in this way, the FileReader constructor and so the BufferedReader constructor can throw a FileNotFoundException.

public String readLine() *throws* IOException
    Reads a line of input from the input stream and returns that line. If the read goes beyond the end of the file, then *null* is returned. Note that an EOFException is not thrown at the end of a file. The end of a file is signaled by returning *null*.

public int read() *throws* IOException
    Reads a single character from the input stream and returns that character as an *int* value. If the read goes beyond the end of the file, then −1 is returned. Note that the value is returned as an *int*. To obtain a *char*, you must perform a type cast on the value returned. Note that an EOFException is not thrown at the end of a file. The end of a file is signaled by returning −1. (None of the "real" characters is returned as −1.)

public void close() *throws* IOException
    Closes the streams connection to a file.

_____

the class SavitchIn. There is, however, one complication. The method read returns a value of type *int* that corresponds to the character read; it does not return the character itself. Thus, to get the character, you must use a type cast as in, for example:

```
char next = (char)(inputStream.read());
```

If inputStream is in the class BufferedReader and is connected to a text file, this will set next equal to the first character in the file that has not yet been read.

The StringTokenizer **Class** *(Optional)*

When using the class BufferedReader to read input from a text file, you can read either entire lines or single characters. Often you would like to read words, but BufferedReader has no method that reads a single word. You can often realize something roughly equivalent to reading words by reading an entire line of text and then using the predefined class StringTokenizer to break the string into individual words.

    You can use the class StringTokenizer to break down a string into the separate words contained in the string. The following example illustrates a simple, but typical, way that the class is used:

```
StringTokenizer wordFinder =
                  new StringTokenizer("We love you madly.");
while (wordFinder.hasMoreTokens())
{
    System.out.println(wordFinder.nextToken());
}
```

This will produce the output:

```
We
love
you
madly.
```

The constructor (the part after the *new*) produces a new object of the class `StringTokenizer`. This object can produce the individual words in the string used as the argument to the constructor. These individual words are called **tokens.**

tokens

The method `nextToken` returns the first token (word) when it is invoked for the first time, it returns the second token when it is invoked the second time, and so forth. The method `hasMoreTokens` returns *true* as long as `nextToken` has not yet returned all the tokens in the string, and it returns *false* after the method `nextToken` has returned all the tokens in the string.

The class `StringTokenizer` is in the `util` (short for utility) package. So, any class or program that uses the class `StringTokenizer` must contain the following at the start of the file:

```
import java.util.*;
```

When the constructor for `StringTokenizer` is used with a single argument, as in the preceding example, then the tokens are substrings of nonwhitespace characters and the whitespace characters are used as the separators for the tokens. Any string of one or more whitespace characters is considered a separator. (Recall that whitespace characters are the blank, new line, and other symbols that print as whitespace if printed on paper.) Thus, in the preceding example, the last word is `"madly."`, including the period. This is because the period is not a whitespace character and so is not a separator. If you want to specify your own set of separator characters, rather than simply accept the default set consisting of the whitespace characters, then you give a second argument to the constructor when you set up the string tokenizer using *new*. The second argument is a string consisting of all the separator characters. Thus, if you want your separators to consist of the blank, new-line character, period, and comma, then you could proceed as in the following example:

```
StringTokenizer secondWordFinder =
        new StringTokenizer("Love you, madly.", " \n.,");
while (secondWordFinder.hasMoreTokens())
{
    System.out.println(secondWordFinder.nextToken());
}
```

This will produce the output:

```
Love
you
madly
```

Be sure to notice that the period and comma are not part of the tokens produced, since they are now token separators. Also, note that the string of tokens is the second argument to the constructor.

You can see another example of the use of the StringTokenizer class in the definition of the method readLineWord in the class SavitchIn given in Appendix 2. Some of the methods for the class StringTokenizer are summarized in what follows.

Some Methods in the Class StringTokenizer

public StringTokenizer(String theString)
Constructor for a tokenizer using whitespace characters to find tokens in theString.

public StringTokenizer(String theString, String delimiters)
Constructor for a tokenizer that will use the characters in the string delimiters as separators to find tokens in theString.

public boolean hasMoreTokens()
Tests if there are more tokens available from this tokenizer's string. When used in conjunction with nextToken, it returns *true* as long as nextToken has not yet returned all the tokens in the string; returns *false* otherwise.

public String nextToken()
Returns the next token from this string tokenizer. (Throws NoSuchElementException if there are no more tokens to return.)

public int countTokens()
Returns the number of tokens remaining to be returned by nextToken.

Testing for the End of a Text File

When using the class BufferedReader, if your program tries to read beyond the end of the file with either of the methods readLine or read, then the method returns a special value to signal that the end of the file has been reached. When readLine tries to read beyond the end of a file, it returns the value *null*. Thus, your program can test for the end of the file by testing to see if readLine returns *null*. This technique is illustrated in Display 9.24. When the method read tries to read beyond the end of a file, it returns the value −1. Since the *int* value corresponding to each ordinary character is nonnegative, this can be used to test for the end of a file. (If you have already read about binary files, then you will note that you check for the end of a file differently with text files than you do with binary files.)

Display 9.24 Checking for the End of a Text File *(Part 1 of 2)*

```
import java.io.*;

/****************************************************************
 *Makes storylines.txt the same as story.txt but with each line numbered.
 ****************************************************************/
public class TextEOFDemo
{
    public static void main(String[] args)
    {
        try
        {
            BufferedReader inputStream =
                new BufferedReader(new FileReader("story.txt"));
            PrintWriter outputStream =
                new PrintWriter(new FileOutputStream("storylines.txt"))

            int count = 0;
            String line = inputStream.readLine();
            while (line != null)
            {
                count++;
                outputStream.println(count + " " + line);
                line = inputStream.readLine();
            }
            System.out.println(count
                        + " lines written to storylines.txt.");

            inputStream.close();
            outputStream.close();
        }
        catch(FileNotFoundException e)
        {
            System.out.println("File story.txt not found.");
        }
        catch(IOException e2)
        {
            System.out.println("Error reading from file story.txt.");
        }
    }
}
```

Display 9.24 Checking for the End of a Text File *(Part 2 of 2)*

File `story.txt`

```
Once upon a time
there were three little
auto mechanics: Click,
Clack, and Joe.
```

File `storylines.txt` (after the program is run)

```
1 Once upon a time
2 there were three little
3 auto mechanics: Click,
4 Clack, and Joe.
```

Do not be concerned if your version of `storylines.txt` *has numbered blank lines after 4. That just means you had blank lines at the end of* `story.txt`.

Checking for the End of a Text File

The method `readLine` of the class `BufferedReader` returns *null* when it tries to read beyond the end of a text file. The method `read` of the class `BufferedReader` returns −1 when it tries to read beyond the end of a text file. Neither of these methods would throw an `EOFException`.

⚠ *GOTCHA* *Checking for the End of a File in the Wrong Way* **(Alternative Ordering)**

This Gotcha is only relevant if you have covered both binary files and text files.

Different file-reading methods (usually in different classes) check for the end of a file in different ways. Some throw an exception in the class `EOFException` when they try to read beyond the end of a file. Others return a special value, such as *null*, when they try to read beyond the end of a file. When reading from a file, you must be careful to test for the end of a file in the correct way for the method you are using. If you test for the end of a file in the wrong way, then one of two things will probably happen: Either your program will go into an unintended infinite loop or your program will terminate abnormally.

How can you tell whether or not a method for reading a file will throw an `EOFException` at the end of the file or return *null* or do something else? You must check the documentation or try a sample program. As a rule of thumb, if your program is reading from a binary file, then you can expect an `EOFException` to be thrown when reading goes beyond the end of the file. If you are reading from a text file, you can except that some special value, such as *null*, will be returned when your program attempt to read beyond the end of the text file, and you can expect that no EOFException will to be thrown with a text file.

▼ *PROGRAMMING EXAMPLE* *The Class* SavitchIn *(Optional)*

The class SavitchIn reads from the keyboard. It does not read from a text file. However, keyboard input is processed in the same way as text file input. You do not need to read the definition of the class SavitchIn to be able to read the rest of this book or to be able to learn the Java language. However, if you have read this chapter and a substantial part of Chapters 7 and 8, then you know enough to understand the definition of the class SavitchIn. The definition for the class SavitchIn is given in Appendix 2. In this subsection, we point out a few points that will make it easier for you to understand the code given there.

readChar   The class SavitchIn uses System.in.read to define the method readChar. System.in.read behaves the same as the method read in the class BufferedReader, except that System.in.read reads from the keyboard rather than reading from a text file. The code for the method readChar in SavitchIn is repeated in what follows:

```
public static char readChar()
{
    int charAsInt = -1; //To keep the compiler happy
    try
    {
        charAsInt = System.in.read();
    }
    catch(IOException e)
    {
        System.out.println(e.getMessage());
        System.out.println("Fatal error. Ending Program.");
        System.exit(0);
    }

    return (char)charAsInt;
}
```

Note that System.in.read returns an *int*, not a *char*. To obtain a *char* value, the code needs to do a type cast as shown in the preceding code.

readLine   The class SavitchIn uses the method readChar in the definition of the method readLine. The method readLine in SavitchIn behaves very much like the method readLine in the class BufferedReader. The code for the method readLine in SavitchIn is repeated in what follows:

```
public static String readLine() throws IOException
{
    char nextChar;
    String result = "";
    boolean done = false;
```

```
while (!done)
{
    nextChar = readChar();
    if (nextChar == '\n')
        done = true;
    else if (nextChar == '\r')
    {
        //Do nothing.  Next loop iteration will detect '\n'.
    }
    else
        result = result + nextChar;
}
return result;
}
```

The symbol '\r' is a special character called the **carriage return symbol**. You should already know about the next line symbol '\n'. Some systems simply use '\n' to denote the end of a line. Other systems use '\r' followed by '\n' to denote the end of a line. The method readLine checks for both possibilities.

The remaining methods use either readLine and/or readChar to do their reading from the keyboard. In order to understand these other methods, you should know how to convert strings to numbers, as described in the subsection of Chapter 7 entitled **Inputting and Outputting Numbers**. You also need to know the basics of exception handling covered in Chapter 8. The exception class NumberFormatEx-ception is thrown when one of the methods for converting a string to a number fails because the string is not a correctly written numeral.

? SELF-TEST QUESTIONS

21. Give some code that will create a stream named textStream that is a member of the class PrintWriter and that connects the stream to a text file named dobedo so that your program can send output to the text file dobedo.

22. Suppose you run a program that writes to the text file dobedo using the stream defined in Question 21. Give some code that will create a stream named inputStream that can be used to read from the text file dobedo in the ways we discussed in this section.

23. BufferedReader has a method named readLine that is essentially the same as the method readLine in the class SavitchIn, except that it takes its input from a text file. Does BufferedReader have any methods like readInt, readDouble, readWord, or readChar?

24. What happens when the method readLine in the class BufferedReader attempts to read beyond the end of a file.

Chapter Summary

- Files that are considered to be strings of characters and that look like characters to your program and your editor are called *text files*. Files whose contents must be handled as strings of binary digits are called *binary files*. When doing file I/O with a Java program, it is more common to use binary files, although it is possible to use text files.

- The class `DataOutputStream` is used to write output to a binary file. The class `DataInputStream` is used to read input from a binary file.

- When reading from a file, you should always check for the end of a file and do something appropriate if the end of the file is reached. The way that you test for the end of a file depends on the method you are using to read from the file.

- You can read a file name from the keyboard into a variable of type `String` and use that variable in place of a file name.

- The class `File` can be used to check to see if there is a file with a given name. It can also check to see if your program is allowed to read the file and/or allowed to write to the file.

- Your program can use the class `PrintWriter` to write to a text file and can use the class `BufferedReader` to read from a text file.

? ANSWERS to Self-Test Questions

1. If a program sends its output to the screen, the output goes away when (or soon after) the program ends. A program that sends its output to a file has made a (more or less) permanent copy of its output. Files provide you with a way to store data permanently. The contents of a file remain until a person or program changes the file. If your program sends its output to a file, the output file will remain after the program has finished running.

2.
```
DataOutputStream toFile =
    new DataOutputStream(new FileOutputStream("stuff.data"));
```

3.
```
toFile.writeDouble(x1);
toFile.writeDouble(x2);
toFile.writeDouble(x3);
```

4. `toFile.close();`

5.
```
DataInputStream fromFile =
    new DataInputStream(new FileInputStream("stuff.data"));
```

6.
```
double x1, x2, x3;
x1 = fromFile.readDouble();
x2 = fromFile.readDouble();
x3 = fromFile.readDouble();
```

7. `fromFile.close();`

8.
```
DataOutputStream writer =
        new DataOutputStream(new FileOutputStream(theFile));
```

9.
```
DataInputStream reader =
        new DataInputStream(new FileInputStream(theFile));
```

10.
```
import java.io.*;

public class FileNameExercise
{
    public static void main(String[] args) throws IOException
    {
        System.out.println("Enter file name:");
        String fileName = SavitchIn.readLineWord();
        DataInputStream inputStream =
            new DataInputStream(new FileInputStream(fileName));

        System.out.println("The first thing in the file");
        System.out.println(fileName + " is");
        String first = inputStream.readUTF();
        System.out.println(first);
        inputStream.close();
    }
}
```

11. Because when the end of the file is reached, an exception will be thrown and that will end the entire *try*-block.

12. Since `EOFException` is a derived class of `IOException`, every `EOFException` is also an `IOException`. So the *throws*-clause *throws* `IOException` accounts for any exceptions of type `EOFException`.

13.
```
import java.io.*;

public class TemperatureShow
{
    public static void main(String[] args)
    {
        try
        {
            DataInputStream inputStream =
                new DataInputStream(new FileInputStream(
                                            "temperatures"));
            double t;

            System.out.println(
                        "Numbers from the file temperatures:");
```

```
        try
        {
           while (true)
           {
              t = inputStream.readDouble();
              System.out.println(t);
           }
        }
        catch(EOFException e)
        {
           //Do nothing
        }

        System.out.println("End of reading from file.");
        inputStream.close();
     }
     catch(IOException e)
     {
        System.out.println("Problem reading from file.");
     }
   }
}
```

14.
```
import java.awt.*;
import java.awt.event.*;

/************************************************
 *Class to display an error message in a window.
 ***********************************************/
public class ErrorWindow extends Frame implements ActionListener
{
    public static final int WINDOW_WIDTH = 200;
    public static final int WINDOW_HEIGHT = 100;

    public ErrorWindow(String message)
    {
        setTitle("Error");
        addWindowListener(new WindowDestroyer());
        setSize(WINDOW_WIDTH, WINDOW_HEIGHT);
        setLayout(new BorderLayout());

        Label errorLabel = new Label(message);
        add(errorLabel, "Center");
```

```
        Panel recordPanel = new Panel();
        recordPanel.setBackground(Color.gray);
        recordPanel.setLayout(new GridLayout(3, 1));
        Label l;
        Button b = new Button("OK");
        b.addActionListener(this);
        add(b, "South");
    }

    //The default constructor is not needed for the
    //programming example, but it is nice to have.
    public ErrorWindow()
    {
        this("Error");
    }

    public void actionPerformed(ActionEvent e)
    {
        if (e.getActionCommand().equals("OK"))
            dispose();
    }
}
```

15.
```
import java.io.*;
import java.awt.*;
import java.awt.event.*;

/************************************************************
 *Class for a GUI to retrieve species records from files.
 *Meant to be used as a helping class for the class SpeciesGUI.
 ************************************************************/
public class ViewRecordsGUI extends Frame
                            implements ActionListener
{
    public static final int WINDOW_WIDTH = 400;
    public static final int WINDOW_HEIGHT = 300;

    public ViewRecordsGUI(String fileNameString,
                          DataInputStream inStream)
    {
        fileName = fileNameString;
        inputStream = inStream;
        setTitle("View Records");
        addWindowListener(new WindowDestroyer());
        setSize(WINDOW_WIDTH, WINDOW_HEIGHT);
        setLayout(new BorderLayout());
```

```
        Panel filePanel = new Panel();
        Label fileLabel = new Label("File Name");
        filePanel.add(fileLabel);
        fileNameField = new TextField(30);
        fileNameField.setText(fileNameString);
        filePanel.add(fileNameField);
        add(filePanel, "North");

        Panel recordPanel = new Panel();
        recordPanel.setBackground(Color.gray);
        recordPanel.setLayout(new GridLayout(3, 1));
        Label l;

        Panel namePanel = new Panel();
        l = new Label("Species Name");
        namePanel.add(l);
        speciesNameField = new TextField(20);
        namePanel.add(speciesNameField);
        recordPanel.add(namePanel);

        Panel populationPanel = new Panel();
        l = new Label("Population");
        populationPanel.add(l);
        populationField = new TextField(10);
        populationPanel.add(populationField);
        recordPanel.add(populationPanel);

        Panel growthRatePanel = new Panel();
        l = new Label("Growth Rate");
        growthRatePanel.add(l);
        growthRateField = new TextField(10);
        growthRatePanel.add(growthRateField);
        recordPanel.add(growthRatePanel);

        add(recordPanel, "Center");

        Panel buttonPanel = new Panel();
        buttonPanel.setLayout(new FlowLayout());
        Button b = new Button("Next");
        b.addActionListener(this);
        buttonPanel.add(b);
        b = new Button("Cancel");
        b.addActionListener(this);
        buttonPanel.add(b);
        add(buttonPanel, "South");

        getNextRecord();
    }
```

```java
public void actionPerformed(ActionEvent e)
{
    if (e.getActionCommand().equals("Next"))
        getNextRecord();
    else if (e.getActionCommand().equals("Cancel"))
        dispose();
    else
    {
        ErrorWindow ew =
            new ErrorWindow("Error. Start Over.");
        ew.show();
    }
    repaint();
}

private void getNextRecord()
{
    try
    {
       oneRecord.readInput(inputStream);
       speciesNameField.setText(oneRecord.speciesName());
       populationField.setText(
          Integer.toString(oneRecord.speciesPopulation()));
       growthRateField.setText(
         Double.toString(
           oneRecord.speciesGrowthRate()) + "%");
    }
    catch(EOFException e)
    {
        speciesNameField.setText("No More Records");
        populationField.setText("");
        growthRateField.setText("");
        try
        {
            inputStream.close();
        }
        catch(IOException e2)//The other catch-block does
        //not catch IOExceptions thrown in this try-block.
        {
            ErrorWindow ew =
             new ErrorWindow("Error closing file.");
            ew.show();
        }
    }
```

```
            catch(IOException e3)
            {
                ErrorWindow ew =
                    new ErrorWindow("Error reading from file.");
                ew.show();
            }
        }

    private Species oneRecord = new Species();
    private TextField fileNameField;
    private TextField speciesNameField;
    private TextField populationField;
    private TextField growthRateField;
    private String fileName = null;
    private DataInputStream inputStream = null;
}
```

16.
```
import java.io.*;

public class FileClassExercise
{
    public static void main(String[] args)
    {
        String name = null;
        File fileObject = null;

        System.out.print("Enter a file name and I will ");
        System.out.println("tell you if it exists.");
        name = SavitchIn.readLineWord();
        fileObject = new File(name);

        if (fileObject.exists())
        {
            System.out.println("I found the file " + name);
            System.out.println("Delete the file? (y/n)");
            char ans = SavitchIn.readLineNonwhiteChar();
            if ((ans == 'y') || (ans == 'Y'))
            {
                System.out.println(
                        "If you delete the file " + name);
                System.out.println(
                        "all data in the file will");
                System.out.println("be lost. Delete? (y/n)");
                ans = SavitchIn.readLineNonwhiteChar();
```

```
                    if ((ans == 'y') || (ans == 'Y'))
                    {
                          if (fileObject.delete())
                                System.out.println("File deleted.");
                          else
                                System.out.println(
                                          "Cannot delete file.");
                    }
                    else
                          System.out.println("File not deleted.");
                }
                else
                    System.out.println("File not deleted.");
            }
            else
                System.out.println("I cannot find " + name);
    }
}
```

17. It will not work because `DataInputStream` does not have a constructor with a parameter of type `String`. The correct way to accomplish the desired effect is

```
DataInputStream inputStream =
    new DataInputStream(new FileInputStream("mydata.dat"));
```

18. The class `FileInputStream` does not have any of the methods `readInt`, `readDouble`, or `readUTF`.

19. Yes to both.

20. No to both.

21.
```
PrintWriter textStream =
        new PrintWriter(new FileOutputStream("dobedo"));
```

22.
```
BufferedReader inputStream =
        new BufferedReader(new FileReader("dobedo"));
```

23. No, but the method `read` in the class `BufferedReader` can be used to read a single character and so is approximately equivalent to the method `readChar` in the class `SavitchIn`. However, the method `read` in the class `BufferedReader` returns its character as an *int* value and needs a type cast to make it into a *char* value.

24. It returns the value *null*. Note that it does not throw an `EOFException`.

? *PROGRAMMING EXERCISES*

•••

These exercises are written for binary files, but most of them can be adapted to use text files.

1. Write a program that searches a file of numbers and outputs, the largest number in the file, the smallest number in the file, and the average of all the numbers in the file. The output should go to the screen. The file should be a binary file that consists entirely of numbers of type *double* that were written using `writeDouble`. Do not assume that the numbers in the file are in any special order. Your program should obtain the file name from the user. Alternative version: If you have read Chapter 7 on the AWT, do this with a GUI interface.

2. Write a program that reads a file of numbers of type *int* and outputs all the numbers to another file, but without any repeated numbers. Assume that the input file is sorted from smallest first to largest last. After the program is run, the new file will contain all the numbers in the original file but no number will appear more than once in the file. The numbers in the output file should also be sorted smallest to largest. Your program should obtain both file names from the user. The files are binary files. Alternative version: If you have read Chapter 7 on the AWT, do this with a GUI interface.

3. Display 9.14/page 498 allows you to write records of endangered species to a file. Write another program that can search a file created by the program in Display 9.14 and show the user any requested record. The user gives the file name. The user then enters the name of the species and the program displays the entire record for that species or else it gives a message saying it has no record on that species. Allow the user to enter additional species names until the user says she or he is finished. Alternative version: If you have read Chapter 7 on the AWT, do this with a GUI interface.

4. Display 9.14/page 498 allows you to write records of endangered species to a file. Write another program that reads from a file created by the program in Display 9.14 and outputs the following information to the screen: the record of the species with the smallest population and the record of the species with the largest population. Do not assume that the records are in the file in any particular order. The user gives the file name. Use the version of the class for species given in Display 9.10/page 487 and use the input method in that species class definition. Alternative version: If you have read Chapter 7 on the AWT, do this with a GUI interface.

5. Display 9.14/page 498 allows you to write records of endangered species to a file. Write another program that reads from the file created by the program in Display 9.14 and outputs the records to another file. However, the records in the output file should not show the same population figure as in the input file, but should instead give the population as what it would be in 10 years given that species growth rate. You will want to use the method `projectedPopulation` of the class `Species`. Alternative version: If you have read Chapter 7 on the AWT, do this with a GUI interface.

Chapter 10

ARRAYS

10.1 ARRAY BASICS 541
Creating and Accessing Arrays 541
Array Details 545
Programming Tip Use Singular Array Names 547
The `length` Instance Variable 547
Gotcha Array Indexes Start with Zero 549
Programming Tip Use a `for`-Loop to Step Through an Array 549
Gotcha Array Index Out of Bounds 549
`ArrayIndexOutOfBounds-Exception` *(Alternative Ordering)* 551
Initializing Arrays 551

10.2 ARRAYS IN CLASSES AND METHODS 552
Case Study Sales Report 552
Indexed Variables as Method Arguments 559

Entire Arrays as Method Arguments 561
Gotcha Use of = and == with Arrays 564
Methods That Return Arrays 567

10.3 PROGRAMMING WITH ARRAYS AND CLASSES 570
Programming Example A Specialized List Class 570
Partially Filled Arrays 578
Searching an Array 579
Parallel Arrays 579
Gotcha Returning an Array Instance Variable 580

10.4 SORTING ARRAYS 587
Selection Sort 588
Programming Tip Correctness versus Efficiency 592

Chapter Summary 594
Answers to Self-Test Questions 594
Programming Exercises 599

ARRAYS

They stood at attention in a neat row, all with the same uniform, yet each with his own values.
WARREN PEACE, THE LIEUTENANT'S ARRAY

Introduction

An array is a special kind of object used to store a (possibly large) collection of data. An array differs from the other objects we have seen in two ways:

1. All the data stored in an array must be of the same type. For example, you might use an array to store a list of values of type *double* that record rainfall readings in centimeters or to store a list of objects of some class called Species that contain the records for various endangered species.

2. The only methods for an array object are a small number of predefined methods. Since arrays were used by programmers for many years before classes and objects (as we have used them) were invented, arrays use a special notation of their own to invoke those few predefined methods, and most people do not even call them methods.

In this chapter, we introduce you to arrays and show you how to use them in Java.

Prerequisites

Section	Prerequisite
Section 10.1 (omitting the following section)	Chapters 1–3
ArrayIndexOutOfBounds Exception (Alternative Ordering)	Chapters 1–3 and Section 8.1 of Chapter 8
Section 10.2	Chapters 1–5
Section 10.3 (more on arrays in classes)	Chapters 1–6 and Chapter 8
Section 10.4 (sorting)	Chapters 1–5

Section 10.4 on sorting does not require Section 10.3 and can be done after covering Sections 10.1 and 10.2. No material from Chapter 7 (AWT) or 9 (files) is required for any part of this chapter.

10.1 Array Basics

And in such indexes, although small pricks
To their subsequent volumes, there is seen
The baby figure of the giant mass
Of things to come.
WILLIAM SHAKESPEARE, TROILUS AND CRESSIDA

Suppose you want to compute the average temperature for each of the seven days in a week. You might use the following code:

```
int count;
double next, sum, average;
System.out.println("Enter 7 temperatures:");
sum = 0;
for (count = 0; count < 7; count++)
{
    next = SavitchIn.readLineDouble();
    sum = sum + next;
}
average = sum/7;
```

This works fine if all you want to know is the average, but suppose you want to also know which temperatures are above the average and which are below the average? Now, you have a problem. In order to compute the average, you must read in the seven temperatures, and you must do this before comparing each temperature to the average. Thus, in order to compare each temperature to the average, you must remember the seven temperatures. How can you do this. The obvious answer is to use seven variables of type *double*. This is a bit awkward, seven is a lot of variables to declare, and imagine doing the same thing for each day of the year instead of just each day of the week. Declaring 365 variables would be absurd. Arrays provide us with an elegant way to declare a collection of related variables.

An **array** is something like a long list of variables, but it handles the naming of the variables in a nice, compact way. Our array for this particular problem of seven temperatures will turn out to be, among other things, an easy way to create seven variables with the names temperature[0], temperature[1], temperature[2], temperature[3], temperature[4], temperature[5], and temperature[6]. As you will see, an array can be viewed as a list of variables each of which has a two-part name, one part is an identifier, like temperature, and the other part is an integer enclosed in square brackets, like [5]. Since the identifier is the same for each of the variables on the list, this will give us a uniform way to refer to all the variables on the list.

array

Creating and Accessing Arrays

In Java, an array is a special kind of object, but it is often more useful to think of an array as a collection of variables all of the same type. For example, an array to serve as a collection of seven variables of type *double* can be created as follows:

```
double[] temperature = new double[7];
```

This is like declaring the following to be seven variables of type *double*:

```
temperature[0], temperature[1], temperature[2], temperature[3],
temperature[4], temperature[5], temperature[6]
```

Note that the numbering starts with 0, *not* 1. Each of these seven variables can be used just like any other variable of type *double*. For example, all of the following are allowed in Java:

```
temperature[3] = 32;
temperature[6] = temperature[3] + 5;
System.out.println(temperature[6]);
```

But, these seven variables are more than just seven plain old variables of type *double*. That number in square brackets allows you to actually compute the name of one of these variables. You need not write an integer constant in the square brackets. You can use any expression that evaluates to an integer that is at least 0 and at most 6. So, the following is allowed:

```
System.out.println("Enter day number (0-6):");
int index = SavitchIn.readLineInt();
System.out.println("Enter temperature for day " + index);
temperature[index] = SavitchIn.readLineDouble();
```

indexed
variable

index

These variables with an integer expression in square brackets are referred to various ways. We will call them **indexed variables,** or **elements.** Some people call them **subscripted variables.** So, temperature[0], temperature[1], and so forth are indexed variables. The integer expression within the square brackets is called an **index** (or **subscript**). When we think of these indexed variables grouped together into one collective item, we will call them *an array*. So, we can refer to the *array* named temperature (without using any square brackets). As you will see, there are two different ways to view an array, like temperature:

1. You can view it as a collection of individual indexed variables like temperature[0], temperature[1], and so forth.

2. Alternatively, you can view it as one large composite object that has a number of different values all of the same type. In the case of our example array temperature, you can think of it as one object with seven values all of type *double*.

When programming with arrays, you need to be able to go back and forth between these two ways of viewing an array. We will discuss the first view here and discuss the second view later in this chapter when we discuss array parameters.

The program in Display 10.1 shows an example of using our sample array temperature as if it were seven indexed variables all of type *double*.

Note that the program can compute the name of an indexed variable by using a variable as the index, as in the following *for*-loop:

```
for (index = 0; index < 7; index++)
{
    temperature[index] = SavitchIn.readLineDouble();
    sum = sum + temperature[index];
}
```

Display 10.1 An Array Used in a Program *(Part 1 of 2)*
....

```
public class ArrayOfTemperatures
{
    /*********************************************************
     *Reads in 7 temperatures and shows which are above and
     *which are below  the average of the 7 temperatures.
     *********************************************************/
    public static void main(String[] args)
    {
        double[] temperature = new double[7];

        int index;
        double sum, average;
        System.out.println("Enter 7 temperatures:");
        sum = 0;
        for (index = 0; index < 7; index++)
        {
            temperature[index] = SavitchIn.readLineDouble();
            sum = sum + temperature[index];
        }
        average = sum/7;

        System.out.println("The average temperature is " + average);
        System.out.println("The temperatures are");
        for (index = 0; index < 7; index++)
        {
            if (temperature[index] < average)
                System.out.println(
                          temperature[index] + " below average.");
            else if (temperature[index] > average)
                System.out.println(
                          temperature[index] + " above average.");
            else //temperature[index] == average
                System.out.println(
                          temperature[index] + " the average.");
        }
        System.out.println("Have a nice week.");
    }
}
```

....

Display 10.1 An Array Used in a Program *(Part 2 of 2)*

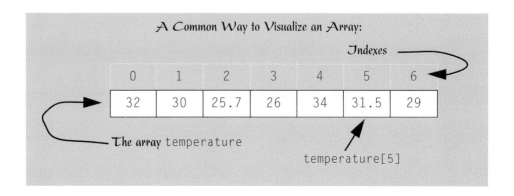

A Common Way to Visualize an Array:

Indexes

0	1	2	3	4	5	6
32	30	25.7	26	34	31.5	29

The array temperature

temperature[5]

Sample Screen Dialogue

```
Enter 7 temperatures:
32
30
25.7
26
34
31.5
29
The average temperature is 29.7428
The temperatures are
32.0 above average
30.0 above average
25.7 below average
26.0 below average
34.0 above average
31.5 above average
29.0 below average
Have a nice week.
```

Array Details

An array is created in basically the same way that an object of a class type is created, but there are some small differences in the notation used. When creating an array of elements of type *Base_Type*, the syntax is as follows:

> *Base_Type*[] *Array_Name* = new *Base_Type*[*Length*];

For example, the following creates an array named `pressure` that is equivalent to 100 variables of type *int*:

```
int[] pressure = new int[100];
```

As you might guess, the preceding can be broken down into a two-step process:

```
int[] pressure;
pressure = new int[100];
```

The type for the elements, in this example *int*, is called the **base type** of the array. The number of elements in an array is called the **length** of the array or the **size** of the array. So, this sample array `pressure` has length 100, which means it has indexed variables `pressure[0]` through `pressure[99]`. Note that since the indexes start at 0, an array of length 100, like `pressure`, will have *no* indexed variable `pressure[100]`.

The base type of an array can be any type. In particular it can be a class type. The following will create an array named `entry` that is equivalent to a collection of the three variables `entry[0]`, `entry[1]`, `entry[2]`, all of type `Species` (where `Species` is some class):

```
Species[] entry = new Species[3];
```

base type

length of an array

Declaring and Creating an Array

You declare an array name and create an array in basically the same way that you create and name objects of classes. There is only a slight difference in the syntax.

Syntax:

> *Base_Type*[] *Array_Name* = new *Base_Type*[*Length*];

Examples:

```
char[] symbol = new char[80];
double[] reading = new double[100];
Species[] specimen = new Species[80];
```

`Species` is a class.

Do not confuse the three ways to use the square brackets [] with an array name. First, the square brackets can be used to create a type name as in

```
int[] pressure;
```

Second, the square brackets can be used with an integer value as part of the special syntax Java used to create a new array, as in

```
pressure = new int[100];
```

square brackets []

The third use of square brackets is to name an element (also called an indexed variable) of the array, such as pressure[0] or pressure[3], as illustrated by the following two lines:

```
pressure[3] = SavitchIn.readLineInt();
System.out.println("You entered " + pressure[3]);
```

The integer inside the square brackets does not have to be an integer constant, such as 100 or 3. The expression inside of square brackets can be any expression that evaluates to an integer. For example, you can read in the length of an array from the keyboard, as follows:

reading an array length

```
System.out.println("How many temperatures will there be?");
int size = SavitchIn.readLineInt();
double[] temperature = new double[size];
```

A similar remark applies to the integer inside the square brackets in other situations. The integer can be given as any expression that evaluates to an appropriate integer, as in the following examples:

```
int point = 2;
temperature[point + 3] = 32;
System.out.println(
              "Temperature 5 is " + temperature[point + 3]);
```

Note that, in the preceding code, temperature[point + 3] and temperature[5] are the same indexed variable, because point + 3 evaluates to 5. The identity of an indexed variable, such as temperature[point + 3], is determined by the value of its index expression, not by what the index expression looks like.

Display 10.2 *Array Terminology*

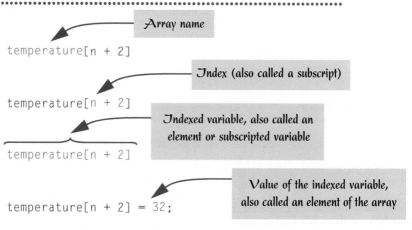

Display 10.2 illustrates some of most common terms used when referring to arrays. Notice that the word **element** has two meaning. An indexed variable is sometimes called an element. The value of an indexed variable is also sometimes called an element.

element

◑ PROGRAMMING TIP *Use Singular Array Names*

If you want an array to hold entries where each entry is an object of a class called `Species`, you might be tempted to use something like the following:

```
Species[] entries = new Species[20];//Legal but not nice.
```

Using a plural, like `entries`, makes sense since the array holds more than one element. However, programmers find that in many situations, it makes their programs read nicer if they use a singular form, like the following:

```
Species[] entry = new Species[20];//Nicer.
```

The reason that the singular form works better here is that, when the array name is used in some sort of computation, the name refers to only one element. The expression `entry[2]` is a single element of the array, as in a statement such as

```
System.out.println("The second entry is " + entry[2]);
```

If you had used the plural name `entries`, this would not read as well. It would be one of the following, both of which are awkward:

```
System.out.println("The second entries is " + entries[2]);//ugly
```

or

```
System.out.println("The second entry is " + entries[2]);//ugly
```

The use of singular names for arrays is not an absolute rule. There are situations in which it makes sense to use plural names. For example, if an array indexed variable contains the number of hours worked by employee number n, then the plural form `hours[n]` makes sense. The only sure test of whether to use a singular or plural name is to consider how an indexed variable would read in the context of your Java code.

The `length` Instance Variable

An array is a kind of object, and like other objects, it might have instance variables. As it turns out, an array has only one public instance variable, namely, the variable `length`, which is equal to the length of the array. For example, if you create an array as follows:

```
Species[] entry = new Species[20];
```

then `entry.length` has a value of 20.

The `length` instance variable can be used to make your program clearer by replacing a constant, like `20`, whose meaning may not always be obvious, with a meaningful name like `entry.length`. In Display 10.3 we have rewritten the program in Display 10.1/page 543 using the `length` instance variable.

Display 10.3 The `length` **Instance Variable**

●●

```java
public class ArrayOfTemperatures2
{
    /*********************************************************
     *Reads in 7 temperatures and shows which are above and
     *which are below  the average of the 7 temperatures.
     *********************************************************/
    public static void main(String[] args)
    {
        double[] temperature = new double[7];

        int index;
        double sum, average;
        System.out.println("Enter 7 temperatures:");
        sum = 0;
        for (index = 0; index < temperature.length; index++)
        {
            temperature[index] = SavitchIn.readLineDouble();
            sum = sum + temperature[index];
        }
        average = sum/7;

        System.out.println("The average temperature is " + average);
        System.out.println("The temperatures are");
        for (index = 0; index < temperature.length; index++)
        {
            if (temperature[index] < average)
                System.out.println(
                        temperature[index] + " below average.");
            else if (temperature[index] > average)
                System.out.println(
                        temperature[index] + " above average.");
            else //temperature[index] == average
                System.out.println(
                        temperature[index] + " the average.");
        }
        System.out.println("Have a nice week.");
    }
}
```

The dialogue is the same as in Display 10.1/page 543.

●●

The `length` instance variable cannot be changed by your program (other than by creating a new array with another use of *new*). For example, the following is illegal:

```
entry.length = 10;//Illegal!
```

▲ GOTCHA Array Indexes Start with Zero

In Java, the indexes of an array always start with 0. They never start with 1 or any number other than 0. This means that the last index number is not the length of the array, but one less than the length of the array. In a situation in which you normally think in terms of some other numbering scheme, you might need to adjust your code to reconcile the array indexes with the intuitive numbering. For example, you might want to think of the data stored in the array as being numbered starting with 1. For example, if employees are numbered starting with 1, then you might use code such as the following in a payroll program:

```
int[] hours = new int[100];
System.out.println("Enter hours worked for each employee:");
int index;
for (index = 0; index < hours.length; index++);
{
    System.out.println("Enter hours for employee " + (index + 1));
    hours[index] = SavitchIn.readLineInt();
}
```

With this code, employees are numbered 1 through 100, but their hours worked are stored in elements `hours[0]` through `hours[99]`.

◐ PROGRAMMING TIP Use a *for*-Loop to Step Through an Array

The *for*-statement is the perfect mechanism for stepping through the elements of an array. For example, the following *for*-loop from Display 10.3 illustrates how you can to step through an array using a *for*-loop:

```
for (index = 0; index < temperature.length; index++)
{
    temperature[index] = SavitchIn.readLineDouble();
    sum = sum + temperature[index];
}
```

▲ GOTCHA Array Index Out of Bounds

A very easy mistake to make when programming with arrays is to use an indexed expression that evaluates to an illegal array index. For example, consider the following array declaration:

```
double[] entry = new double[5];
```

Every index for the array `entry` must evaluate to one of the five integers: 0, 1, 2, 3, and 4. For example, if your program contains the indexed variable `entry[n + 2]`, then the $n + 2$ must evaluate to one of the five integers 0, 1, 2, 3, or 4. If an index expression evaluates to some integer other than 0 through one less than the length of the array, then the index is said to be **out of bounds** or **illegal**. If your program uses an index expression that is out of bounds, then your program (or class) will compile without any error message for the illegal index, but Java will complain when you run your program.

One common way that array indexes go out of bounds is when an array processing loop is iterated one too many times. This can happen with almost any kind of loop that deals with array indexes, but one very common example of this is a loop that fills an array. For example, when reading in a list of nonnegative numbers from the keyboard with a negative number as a sentinel value at the end, you might use the following:

```
System.out.println("Enter a list of nonnegative integers.");
System.out.println("Place a negative integer at the end.");
int[] a = new int[10];
int number = SavitchIn.readLineInt();
int i = 0;
while (number >= 0)
{
    a[i] = number;
    i++;
    number = SavitchIn.readLineInt();
}
if (number >=0)
{
    System.out.println("Could not read in all the numbers.");
    System.out.println("Only read in " + a.length + " numbers.");
}
```

If, however, the user enters more numbers than can fit in the array, this will produce an array index that is out of bounds. A better version of the preceding *while*-loop is the following:

```
while ( (i < a.length) && (number >= 0) )
{
    a[i] = number;
    i++;
    number = SavitchIn.readLineInt();
}
```

With this *while*-loop, the loop will end when the array is full.

Notice that in the preceding *while*-loop, we tested to see that the index i is strictly less than a.length. Since indexes start at 0, the last index is *not* a.length, but is one less than a.length. If you use <= instead of <, you may get an array index out-of-bounds error.

ArrayIndexOutOfBoundsException *(Alternative Ordering)*

This section is optional if you have not yet read the basics on exception handling in Chapter 8. If you have covered some of Chapter 8, you should not consider this section optional.

If your program attempts to use an array index that is out of bounds, then an ArrayIndexOutOfBoundsException is thrown and your program ends. This is not the sort of exception that you need to catch or need to declare in a *throws* -clause. This sort of exception indicates that there is something wrong with your code and what you need to do is to fix the mistake in your code.

Initializing Arrays

An array can be initialized at the time that it is declared. To do this, you enclose the values for the individual indexed variables in curly brackets and place them after the assignment operator, as in the following example:

```
double[] reading = {3.3, 15.8, 9.7};
```

The array length (size) is set to the minimum that will hold the given values. So, this initializing declaration is equivalent to the following statements:

```
double[] reading = new double[3];
reading[0] = 3.3;
reading[1] = 15.8;
reading[2] = 9.7;
```

If you do not initialize the elements of an array, then they will automatically be initialized to a default value for the base type. For example, if you do not initialize an array of integers, then each element of the array will be initialized to 0. However, it is usually clearer to do your own explicit initialization either by using the curly brackets as we just described or by some other method, such as the following *for* -loop.

automatic initialization

```
int[] count = new int[100];
int i;
for (i = 0; i < count.length; i++)
    a[i] = 0;
```

? SELF-TEST QUESTIONS

1. What output will be produced by the following code?

```
int i;
int[] a = new int[10];
for (i = 0; i < a.length; i++)
    a[i] = 2*i;
for (i = 0; i < a.length; i++)
    System.out.print(a[i] + " ");
System.out.println();
```

2. What output will be produced by the following code?

```
char[] vowels = {'a', 'e', 'i', 'o', 'u'};
int index;
for (index = 0; index < vowels.length; index++)
    System.out.println(vowels[index]);
```

3. What is the output produced by the following code?

```
double tide[] = {12.2, -7.3, 14.2, 11.3};
System.out.println("Tide 1 is " + tide[1]);
System.out.println("Tide 2 is " + tide[2]);
```

4. What is wrong with the following code to initialize an array b?

```
int[] b = new int[10];
int i;
for (i = 1; i <= b.length; i++)
    b[i] = 5*i;
```

5. Write a complete java program that will fill an array a with 20 values of type *double* read in from the keyboard, and will output the numbers in the array as well as how much each number differs from the last number in the input list. For example, if an array element is 2.0 and the last value in the input list is 5.0, the difference is 3.0. If an array element is 7.0 and the last value in the input list is 5.0, the difference is −2.0. Assume the users enter 20 numbers, one per line, from the keyboard. You need not give elaborate instructions to the user.

10.2 Arrays in Classes and Methods

A little more than kin, and less than kind.
WILLIAM SHAKESPEARE, *Hamlet*

Arrays can be used as instance variables in classes. Both an indexed variable of an array and an entire array can be an argument to a method. Methods can return an array value. In short, arrays can be used with classes and methods just like other objects. We begin with a case study that uses an array as an instance variable in a class.

Case Study *Sales Report*

task specification

In this case study, you will write a program to generate sales reports for a company's team of sales associates. The company wants to easily see which associate or associates have the highest sales and also wants to know how the sales of each associate compares to the average

You know that you will need to record a name and the sales figures for each associate. So, you design a class for a single sales associate that holds these two data items, does input and output, and has a reasonable complement of accessor methods. The class you design is shown in Display 10.4. This class definition is routine.

some data

Your program will use an array to keep track of the data on each sales associate. It will also need to record the average sales and the highest sales. So, you know you will need the following instance variables:

Display 10.4 Sales Associate Record Class

```
/*************************************
 *Class for sales associate records.
 *************************************/
public class SalesAssociate
{
    SalesAssociate()
    {
        name = "No record";
        sales = 0;
    }

    public void readInput()
    {
        System.out.print("Enter name of sales associates: ");
        name = SavitchIn.readLine();
        System.out.print("Enter associate's sales: $");
        sales = SavitchIn.readLineDouble();
    }

    public void writeOutput()
    {
        System.out.println("Sales associates: " + name);
        System.out.println("Sales: $" + sales);
    }

    public String theName()
    {
        return name;
    }

    public double theSales()
    {
        return sales;
    }

    public void reset(String newName, double newSales)
    {
        name = newName;
        sales = newSales;
    }

    private String name;
    private double sales;
}
```

```
private double highest;
private double average;
private SalesAssociate[] record;
```

You realize that you need to know the number of associates. This will be the same as record.length, but it will be good to have a separate well-named variable for the number of associates. So, you decide to also include the following instance variable:

```
private int numberOfAssociates; //Same as record.length
```

subtasks   The job of your program breaks down into three main subtasks:

Obtain the data.
Compute some figures (update the instance variables).
Display the results.

Thus, you know your program class will look like this

```
public class SalesReporter
{
    public static void main(String arg[])
    {
        SalesReporter clerk = new SalesReporter();
        clerk.getFigures();
        clerk.update();
        clerk.displayResults();
    }

            <More stuff needs to be added here.>

    private double highest;
    private double average;
    private SalesAssociate[] record;
    private int numberOfAssociates; //Same as record.length
}
```

All that remains is to design the three methods, getFigures, update, and displayResults (and to test and debug the program). You tackle the three methods in order.

getFigures   The input method getFigures is relatively straightforward, especially since you have an input method for objects of the class SalesAssociate. However, there are a couple of subtle points to worry about. You design the following basic input loop:

```
int i;
for (i = 0; i < numberOfAssociates; i++)
{
    System.out.println("Enter data for associate number " + (i+1));
    record[i].readInput();
}
```

You have handled one of the subtle points very nicely. The array indexes are numbered starting with 0 but the associates are numbered starting with 1, and so you have used `record[i]` for associate (i + 1) to adjust for this. But another problem remains.

When you test this loop, you get an error message saying something about a "null pointer." This problem is due to the fact that the base type of the array record is a class type. To see the problem, consider another situation first: Suppose you had the following code:

```
SalesAssociate a;
a.readInput();
```

This code would produce the same error message talking about a "null pointer." The problem is that the variable a is just a name, but does not yet name any object of the class `SalesAssociate`. The preceding code omitted the usual use of *new*. The code should be

```
SalesAssociate a;
a = new SalesAssociate();
a.readInput();
```

The indexed variable `record[i]` is also a variable of a class type and so it is also just a name. You need to use *new* before `record[i]` names an object that can be used with the method `readInput` (or any other method). Your code needs the following to be added:

```
record[i] = new SalesAssociate();
```

The complete definition of the method `getFigures` with this line inserted is shown in Display 10.5.

Next you turn your attention to the method `update`. You come up with the following code:

update

```
for (i = 0; i < numberOfAssociates; i++)
{
    sum = sum + record[i].theSales();
    if (record[i].theSales() > highest)
        highest = record[i].theSales();//highest sales figure so far.
}
average = sum/numberOfAssociates;
```

Now, this loop is basically OK, but you realize that the variables sum and highest must be initialized before the loop begins. You can initialize sum to 0, but what value do you use to initialize highest? Perhaps a negative number, since sales cannot be negative. However, you find out that sales can indeed be negative. If a customer returns goods that is considered a negative sales. However, you do know that the company always has at least one sales associate, and so you initialize both sum and highest to the sales for the first associate. This takes one case outside of the loop and places it before the loop as follows:

Display 10.5 Sales Report *(Part 1 of 3)*

```
/*******************************
 *Program to generate sales report.
 *******************************/
public class SalesReporter
{
    public static void main(String arg[])
    {
        SalesReporter clerk = new SalesReporter();
        clerk.getFigures();
        clerk.update();
        clerk.displayResults();
    }

    public void getFigures()
    {
        System.out.println("Enter number of sales associates:");
        numberOfAssociates = SavitchIn.readLineInt();
        record = new SalesAssociate[numberOfAssociates];
        int i;
        for (i = 0; i < numberOfAssociates; i++)
        {
            record[i] = new SalesAssociate();
            System.out.println("Enter data for associate " + (i + 1));
            record[i].readInput();
            System.out.println();
        }
    }
    /*********************************************
     *Computes the average and highest sales figures.
     *Precondition: There is at least one salesAssociate.
     *********************************************/
    public void update()
    {
        int i;
        double nextSales = record[0].theSales();
        highest = nextSales;
        double sum = nextSales;
        for (i = 1; i < numberOfAssociates; i++)
        {
            nextSales = record[i].theSales();
            sum = sum + nextSales;
            if (nextSales > highest)
                highest = nextSales;//highest sales figure so far.
        }
        average = sum/numberOfAssociates;
    }
```

Array object created here. (points to `record = new SalesAssociate[numberOfAssociates];`)

Already processed `record[0]`, *so the loop starts with* `record[1]`. (points to `for (i = 1; i < numberOfAssociates; i++)`)

Display 10.5 Sales Report *(Part 2 of 3)*

```
/*****************************************
 *Displays sales report on console screen.
 *****************************************/
public void displayResults()
{
    System.out.println("Average sales per associate is $" + average);
    System.out.println("The highest sales figure is $" + highest);
    System.out.println();
    int i;
    System.out.println("The following had the highest sales:");
    for (i = 0; i < numberOfAssociates; i++)
    {
        double nextSales = record[i].theSales();
        if (nextSales == highest)
        {
            record[i].writeOutput();
            System.out.println("$" + (nextSales - average)
                                      + " above the average.");
            System.out.println();
        }
    }

    System.out.println("The rest performed as follows:");
    for (i = 0; i < numberOfAssociates; i++)
    {
        double nextSales = record[i].theSales();
        if (record[i].theSales() != highest)
        {
            record[i].writeOutput();
            if (nextSales >= average)
                System.out.println("$" + (nextSales - average)
                                          + " above the average.");
            else
                System.out.println("$" + (average - nextSales)
                                          + " below the average.");
            System.out.println();
        }
    }
}

    private double highest;
    private double average;
    private SalesAssociate[] record;//Array object created in getFigures.
    private int numberOfAssociates; //Same as record.length
}
```

Display 10.5 **Sales Report** *(Part 3 of 3)*

Sample Screen Dialogue

```
Enter number of sales associates:
3
Enter data for associate number 1
Enter name of sales associates: Dusty Rhodes
Enter associate's sales: $3600

Enter data for associate number 2
Enter name of sales associates: Natalie Dressed
Enter associate's sales: $5000

Enter data for associate number 3
Enter name of sales associates: Sandy Hare
Enter associate's sales: $1000

Average sales per associate is $3200
The highest sales figure is $5000

The following had the highest sales:
Name: Natalie Dresses
Sales: $5000
$1800 above the average.

The rest performed as follows:
Name: Dusty Rhodes
Sales: $3600
$400 above the average.

Name: Sandy Hare
Sales: $1000
$2200 below the average.
```

```
highest = record[0].theSales();
double sum = record[0].theSales();
for (i = 1; i < numberOfAssociates; i++)
{
    sum = sum + record[i].theSales();
    if (record[i].theSales() > highest)
        highest = record[i].theSales();//highest sales figure so far.
}
average = sum/numberOfAssociates;
```

The preceding loop will work, but you realize that this code contains a repeated calculation. There are three identical method invocations of `record[i].the-Sales()`. You decide to only have one such invocation and store the result in a variables as follows:

```
int i;
double nextSales = record[0].theSales();
highest = nextSales;
double sum = nextSales;
for (i = 1; i < numberOfAssociates; i++)
{
    nextSales = record[i].theSales();
    sum = sum + nextSales;
    if (nextSales > highest)
        highest = nextSales;//highest sales figure so far.
}
average = sum/numberOfAssociates;
```

The complete final definition for the method `update` is given in Display 10.5.

The design of the final method `displayResults` only uses techniques that you have already seen and so we will not go over the details. The final method definition is shown in Display 10.5.

? SELF-TEST QUESTIONS

6. Write some Java code that will declare and an array named `entry` that has length 3, has `SalesAssociate` (Display 10.4/page 553) as its base type, and that is filled with three identical records. The records use name `"Jane Doe"` and sales of $5000. Use a *for*-loop.

Indexed Variables as Method Arguments

An indexed variable for an array `a`, such as `a[i]`, can be used anyplace that you can use any other variable of the base type of the array. So, an indexed variable for an array `a`, such as `a[i]`, can be an argument to a method in exactly the same way that any other variable of the array's base type can be an argument. For example, the program in Display 10.6 contains a program that illustrates the use of an indexed variable as an argument to a method.

Consider the method `average` that takes two arguments of type *int*. In the program Display 10.6, the array `nextScore` has base type *int*, so the program can

Display 10.6 Indexed Variables as Arguments

```
/*****************************************
 *A program to demonstrate the use of
 *indexed variables as arguments.
 *****************************************/
public class ArgumentDemo
{
    public static void main(String arg[])
    {
        System.out.println("Enter your score on exam 1:");
        int firstScore = SavitchIn.readLineInt();
        int[] nextScore = new int[3];
        int i;
        double possibleAverage;
        for (i = 0; i < nextScore.length; i++)
            nextScore[i] = 80 + 10*i;
        for (i = 0; i < nextScore.length; i++)
        {
            possibleAverage = average(firstScore, nextScore[i]);
            System.out.println("If your score on exam 2 is "
                                  + nextScore[i]);
            System.out.println("your average will be "
                                  + possibleAverage);
        }
    }

    public static double average(int n1, int n2)
    {
        return (n1 + n2)/2.0;
    }
}
```

Sample Screen Dialogue

```
Enter your score on exam 1:
80
If your score on exam 2 is 80
your average will be 80.0
If your score on exam 2 is 90
your average will be 85.0
If your score on exam 2 is 100
your average will be 90.0
```

use `nextScore[i]` as an argument to the method `average`, as in the following line from that program:

```
possibleAverage = average(firstScore, nextScore[i]);
```

The variable `firstScore` is an ordinary variable of type *int*. To help drive home the point that the indexed variable `nextScore[i]` can be used just like any other variable of type *int*, note that the program in Display 10.6 would behave exactly the same if the two arguments to the method `average` were interchanged so that the preceding invocation of `average` were replaced with the following:

```
possibleAverage = average(nextScore[i], firstScore);
```

Also, note the definition of the method `average`. That definition contains no indication that its arguments can be indexed variables for an array of *int*. The method `average` accepts arguments of type *int* and neither knows nor cares about whether those *int*s came from an indexed variable or a regular *int* variable or a constant *int* value.

There is one subtlety that applies to indexed variables used as method arguments. For example, again consider the method call:

evaluating
indexes

```
possibleAverage = average(firstScore, nextScore[i]);
```

If the value of `i` is 2, then the argument is `nextScore[2]`. On the other hand, if the value of `i` is 0, then the argument is `nextScore[0]`. The indexed expression is evaluated in order to determine exactly which indexed variable to use as the argument.

Be sure to note that an indexed variable of an array a, such as `a[i]`, is a variable of the base type of the array and when `a[i]` is used as an argument to a method, it is handled *exactly the same as any other variable of the base type of the array* a. In particular, if the base type of the array is a primitive type, such as *int*, *double*, or *char*, then the method cannot change the value of `a[i]`. On the other hand, if the base type of the array is a class type, then the method can change the object named by `a[i]`. This is nothing new. Just remember that an indexed variable, like `a[i]`, is a variable of the base type of the array and is handled just like any other variable of the base type of the array.

Array Indexed Variables as Arguments

An array indexed variable can be used as an argument anyplace that a variable of the array base type can be used. For example, suppose you have

```
double[] a = new double[10];
```

Then, indexed variables such as `a[3]` and `a[index]` can be used as arguments to any method that accepts a *double* variable as an argument.   ◻

Entire Arrays as Method Arguments

We have already seen that an indexed variable of an array can be used as an argument to a method. An entire array can also be used as a single argument to a method. The way that you specify an array parameter in a method definition is similar to the

---

When Can a Method Change an Indexed Variable Argument?

Suppose a[i] is an indexed variable of an array a and a[i] is used as an argument in a method invocation such as

```
doStuff(a[i]);
```

Whether or not the method doStuff can change the array element a[i] depends on the base type of the array a. If the base type of the array a is a primitive type, such as *int*, *double*, or *char*, then as with any argument of a primitive type, the method doStuff cannot change the value of a[i]. However, if the base type of the array a is a class, then the method doStuff can change the object named by a[i]. Note that there is nothing new here. The indexed variable a[i] is treated just like any other variable of the base type of the array. (To review the details on method arguments, see Chapter 4.)

---

way that you declare an array. For example, the method incrementArrayBy2 (which follows) will accept any array of *double*s as its single argument:

```
public class SampleClass
{
    public static void incrementArrayBy2(double[] a)
    {
        int i;
        for (i = 0; i < a.length; i++)
            a[i] = a[i] + 2;
    }
    <The rest of the class definition goes here.>
}
```

To illustrate this, suppose you have the following in some method definition:

```
double[] a = new double[10];
double[] b = new double[30];
```

and suppose the elements of the arrays a and b have been given values, then the following are both legal method invocations:

```
SampleClass.incrementArrayBy2(a);
SampleClass.incrementArrayBy2(b);
```

length of array arguments

There are a few things that we need to emphasize about array arguments. First, no square brackets are used when you give an entire array as an argument to a method. Second, a method can change the values in an array. This is illustrated by the preceding method incrementArrayBy2. Third, the same array parameter can be replaced with array arguments of different lengths. Note that the preceding

Array Parameters and Array Arguments

An argument to a method may be an entire array. Array arguments are like objects of a class in that the method can change the values in an array argument. A method with an array parameter is defined and invoked as illustrated by the following examples: (All the examples are assumed to be somewhere within a class definition.)

Examples (of formal array parameters):

```
public static void showArray(char[] a)
{
    int i;
    for (i = 0; i < a.length; i++)
        System.out.println(a[i]);
}

public static void reinitialize(int[] anArray)
{
    int i;
    for (i = 0; i < anArray.length; i++)
        anArray[i] = 0;
}
```

Examples (of array arguments):

```
char[] symbol = new char[10];
int[] a = new int[10];
int[] b = new int[20];

    <Some code to fill the arrays goes here.>

showArray(symbol);
reinitialize(a);
reinitialize(b);
```

Note that the arrays a and b have different lengths. Also, note that no square brackets are used with array arguments.

method `incrementArray` can take any length array as an argument. When you specify a parameter as an array parameter, you specify the type of the array elements, but you do not specify the length of the array.

Note that array arguments in method invocations are handled in basically the same way as class arguments in method invocations (although array parameters in method definitions have their own notation for specifying that the type of the parameter is an array type).

Array Types Are Reference Types

A variable of an array type only holds the address of where the array is stored in memory. This memory address is often called a **reference** to the array object in memory. For this reason, array types are often called *reference types*. A **reference type** is any type whose variables hold references (i.e., memory addresses), as opposed to the actual item named by the variable. Array types and class types are both reference types. Primitive types are not reference types.

The Method `main` Has an Array Parameter

The heading for the `main` method of a program is as follows:

```
public static void main(String[] args)
```

The part `String[] args` makes it look like `arg` is a parameter for an array of `String`s. Not only does it look like that, but it is in fact true that the method `main` does take an array of `String`s as an argument. But, we have never given `main` an array argument, or any other kind of argument, when we ran any of our programs. What is the story? As you know, an invocation of `main` is a very special sort of invocation. A default array of strings is automatically provided as a default argument to `main` when you run your program. It is possible to provide additional "string arguments" when you run a program and then those "string arguments" will automatically be made elements of the array argument that is automatically provided to `main`. However, we have no need for this feature and will not take the time to describe it.

⚠ GOTCHA Use of = and == with Arrays

assignment with arrays

Arrays are objects and so the assignment operator = and the equality operator == behave (and perhaps misbehave) the same way with arrays as with the kinds of objects we saw before discussing arrays. To understand how this applies to arrays, you need to know a little bit about how arrays are stored in the computer's main memory. The important point for this discussion is that the entire array contents (i.e., the contents of all the indexed variables) are stored together in one (possibly large) section of memory so that the location of the entire array contents can be specified by one memory address.

Now, recall that a variable for an object really contains the memory address of the object. The assignment operator copies this memory address. For example, consider the following code:

```
int[] a = new int[3];
int[] b = new int[3];
int i;
for (i = 0; i < a.length; i++)
    a[i] = i;
b = a;
System.out.println("a[2] = " + a[2] + " b[2] = " + b[2]);
a[2] = 2001;
System.out.println("a[2] = " + a[2] + " b[2] = " + b[2]);
```

This will produce the following output:

```
a[2] = 2 b[2] = 2
a[2] = 2001 b[2] = 2001
```

The assignment statement `b = a;` (in the preceding code) gives the array variable `b` the same memory address as the array variable `a`. So, `a` and `b` are two different names for the same array. Thus, when we change the value of `a[2]`, we are also changing the value of `b[2]`.

Because of the complications we discussed in the previous paragraph, it is best to just not use the assignment operator = with arrays (and similarly not use == with arrays). If you want the arrays a and b in the preceding code to be different arrays with the same values, then instead of the assignment statement

```
b = a;
```

you must use something like the following:

```
int i;
for (i = 0; i < a.length; i++)
    b[i] = a[i];
```

Note that the preceding code assumes that the arrays a and b have the same length.

The equality operator == tests two arrays to see if they are stored in the same place in the computer's memory. For example, consider the following code:

== with arrays

```
int[] a = new int[3];
int[] b = new int[3];
int i;
for (i = 0; i < a.length; i++)
    a[i] = i;
for (i = 0; i < a.length; i++)
    b[i] = i;

if (b == a)
    System.out.println("Equal by ==");
else
    System.out.println("Not equal by ==");
```

This produces the output

```
Not equal by ==
```

This is the output despite the fact that the arrays a and b contain the same integers in the same indexed variables. This happens because the arrays a and b are stored in different places in memory, and == tests for equal memory addresses.

If you want to test two arrays to see if they contain the same elements, then you can define an equals method for the arrays, just as you defined an equals method for a class. For example, Display 10.7 contains one possible definition of equals for arrays in a small demonstration class. There is not a uniquely correct definition of equals. The exact definition details depend on the application. Alternatively, you can simply write code to compare the two arrays element by element. For example, if the arrays a and b are arrays of *ints* of the same length, the following code could be used:

Display 10.7 Two Kinds of Equality (Part 1 of 2)

```
/***********************************************************
 *This is just a demonstration program to see how equals and == work.
 ***********************************************************/
public class TestEquals
{
    public static void main(String[] args)
    {
        int[] a = new int[3]; int[] b = new int[3]; int i;
        for (i = 0; i < a.length; i++)
            a[i] = i;
        for (i = 0; i < b.length; i++)
            b[i] = i;
        if (b == a)
            System.out.println("Equal by ==.");
        else
            System.out.println("Not equal by ==.");
        if (equals(b,a))
            System.out.println("Equal by the equals method.");
        else
            System.out.println("Not equal by the equals method.");
    }

    public static boolean equals(int[] a, int[] b)
    {
        boolean match;
        if (a.length != b.length)
            match = false;
        else
        {
            match = true; //tentatively
            int i = 0;
            while (match && (i < a.length))
            {
                if (a[i] != b[i])
                    match = false;
                i++;
            }
        }
        return match;
    }
}
```

The arrays a and b contain the same integers in the same order.

Display 10.7 Two Kinds of Equality *(Part 2 of 2)*

Screen Output

```
Not equal by ==.
Equal by the equals method.
```

```java
boolean match = true; //tentatively
int i = 0;
while (match && (i < a.length))
{
    if (a[i] != b[i])
        match = false;
    i++;
}
if (match)
    System.out.println("Arrays have the same contents");
else
    System.out.println("Arrays do not match");
```

Methods That Return Arrays

In Java, a method may return an array. You specify the returned type for a method
that returns an array in the same way that you specify a type for an array parameter. For example, Display 10.8 contains a slightly rewritten version of the program
in Display 10.6/page 560. The program in Display 10.8 performs pretty much the
same computation as the one in Display 10.6. However, in this new version (given
in Display 10.8), the various possible average scores are computed by the method
averageArray and returned as an array of scores (of type *double*).

Notice that a new array is created and then the new array is returned, as follows:

```java
double temp = new double[nextScore.length];
<Fill the array temp.>
return temp;
```

Display 10.8 A Method That Returns an Array

```
/*******************************************************
 *A program to demonstrate a method returning an array.
 *******************************************************/
public class ReturnArrayDemo
{
    public static void main(String arg[])
    {
        System.out.println("Enter your score on exam 1:");
        int firstScore = SavitchIn.readLineInt();
        int[] nextScore = new int[3];
        int i;
        for (i = 0; i < nextScore.length; i++)
            nextScore[i] = 80 + 10*i;
        double[] averageScore;
        averageScore = averageArray(firstScore, nextScore);
        for (i = 0; i < nextScore.length; i++)
        {
            System.out.println("If your score on exam 2 is "
                                    + nextScore[i]);
            System.out.println("your average will be "
                                    + averageScore[i]);
        }
    }

    public static double[] averageArray(int firstScore,
                                             int[] nextScore)
    {
        double[] temp = new double[nextScore.length];
        int i;
        for (i = 0; i < temp.length; i++)
            temp[i] = average(firstScore, nextScore[i]);
        return temp;
    }

    public static double average(int n1, int n2)
    {
        return (n1 + n2)/2.0;
    }
}
```

The sample screen dialogue is the same as in Display 10.6/page 560.

Returning an Array

A method can return an array. The details are basically the same as for any other returned type.

Syntax (for a typical way of returning an array):

```
public static Base_Type[] Method_Name(Parameter_List)
{
    Base_Type[] temp = new Base_Type[Array_Size]
    Statements_To_Fill_temp
    return temp;
}
```

The method need not be static and need not be public. The following are some of the other acceptable method headings:

```
public  Base_Type[] Method_Name(Parameter_List)

private static Base_Type[] Method_Name(Parameter_List)

private  Base_Type[] Method_Name(Parameter_List)
```

Example (Assumed to be in a class definition):

```
public static char[] vowels()
{
    char[] newArray = new char[5];
    newArray[0] = 'a';
    newArray[1] = 'e';
    newArray[2] = 'i';
    newArray[3] = 'o';
    newArray[4] = 'u';
    return newArray;
}
```

Are Arrays Really Objects?

Arrays behave very much like objects, and so we have chosen to call them *objects*. On the other hand, it is hard to come up with a commonly used name for the classes to which the arrays belong. Moreover, there is no notion of inheritance that can be used with arrays. For these reasons, many people say that arrays are not objects. So, are arrays objects or not? That really is a matter of definition, and there is no authoritative definition. So, whether we call them *objects* is a matter of convention. Arrays certainly are not values of primitive types. So, we can either call them objects or else consider them to be a new kind of data value. It turns out to be more convenient to simply consider them to be objects.

? SELF-TEST QUESTIONS

7. What output will be produced by the following code?

```
char[] a = new char[3];
char[] b;
int i;
for (i = 0; i < a.length; i++)
    a[i] = 'a';
b = a;
System.out.println("a[1] = " + a[1] + " b[1] = " + b[1]);
System.out.println("a[2] = " + a[2] + " b[2] = " + b[2]);
b[2] = 'b';
System.out.println("a[1] = " + a[1] + " b[1] = " + b[1]);
System.out.println("a[2] = " + a[2] + " b[2] = " + b[2]);
```

8. Give the definition of a method called showArray that has a single parameter for an array of chars and that writes a line of text to the screen consisting of the characters in the array argument written in order. Make it a static method. To test it, you can add it to any class, or better yet, write a class with a test program in the method main.

9. Give the definition of a method called halfArray that has a single parameter for an array of doubles and that returns another array of doubles that has the same length and that has each element divided by 2.0. Make it a static method. To test it, you can add it to any class, or better yet, write a class with a test program in the method main.

10.3 Programming with Arrays and Classes

The Moving Finger writes; and, having writ,
Moves on; nor all your Piety and Wit.
Shall lure it back to cancel half a line.
Nor all your Tears wash out a Word of it.
OMAR KHAYYAM, *The Ruba'iyat (Fitzgerald translation)*

In this section, we present some additional techniques for working with arrays. This section uses material on exception handling from Chapter 8. If you have not yet covered exception handling, you should skip this section and go on to Section 10.4. We begin with a programming example that illustrates some basic techniques.

▼ PROGRAMMING EXAMPLE A Specialized List Class

One way to use an array for a special purpose is to make the array an instance variable of a class and access it only through the class methods. This allows you to define classes whose objects are something like special-purpose arrays. The array is only accessed through the class methods and so you can add any checks and automatic processing that you want. In this programming example, we present an example of one such class.

In this example, we will define a class whose objects can be used for keeping lists of items, such as a grocery list or a list of things to do. The class will have the rather long name OneWayNoRepeatsList. (Long names are traditional in Java, but we did not choose a long name just to be traditional. All the short names, like *List*, *Table*, and so forth, already have a technical meaning in computer science and it could be confusing to use these short names for something other than their usual meaning.) The class OneWayNoRepeatsList will have a method for adding items to the list. An item on the list is a string, which in an application would say whatever you want the item to say, such as "Buy milk". This class has no method to change nor to delete a single item from the list. It does, however, have a method that lets you erase the entire list and start over again with a blank list. Each object of the class OneWayNoRepeatsList has a maximum number of items it can hold. At any time, the list might contain anywhere from zero to the maximum number of items.

An object of the class OneWayNoRepeatsList has an array of strings as an instance variable. This array holds the items on the list. However, you do not directly access the array. Instead, you use accessor methods. You can use *int* variables to hold a position in the list. One of these *int* variables is very much the same thing as an index, but positions are numbered starting with 1 rather than 0. For example, there is a method named entryAt that lets you recover the item at a given position. For example, if toDoList is an object of the class OneWayNoRepeatsList, then the following sets the string variable next to the entry at the second position:

```
String next = toDoList.entryAt(2);
```

There is no way to (directly) change an entry on the list. There is a method to add an entry to the end of the list and a method to erase the entire list, but those are the only ways that the list can be changed.

In Chapter 4 we discussed ADTs (abstract data types). The class OneWayNoRepeatsList is a good example of an ADT (although you do not really need the ADT material from Chapter 4 in order to understand this example). As we discussed in Chapter 4, an ADT is a data type defined so that the programmer who uses the data type need not know the details of how the data type is defined. If that is true of the class OneWayNoRepeatsList, then it makes sense to tell you how to use the class OneWayNoRepeatsList *before we give the definition of the class* OneWayNoRepeatsList. So, let's do that.

Display 10.9 contains a program that demonstrates how to use some of the methods for the class OneWayNoRepeatsList. Notice that there is a constructor that takes an integer argument. This integer specifies the maximum number of entries that can be placed in the list. Normally, the list will contain fewer than the maximum number of entries.

The method addItem adds a string to the list. For example, the following adds the string named by the variable next to the list toDoList.

```
toDoList.addItem(next);
```

If you look at the sample dialogue, you will see that "Buy milk." is added to the list twice, but that it only appears on the list once. If the item being added is already on the list, then the method addItem has no effect. This way the list has no repeats.

Display 10.9 Using the Class OneWayNoRepeatsList *(Part 1 of 2)*

```java
public class ListDemo
{
    public static void main(String[] args)
    {
        OneWayNoRepeatsList toDoList =
                            new OneWayNoRepeatsList(3);

        System.out.println("Enter items for the list, when prompted.");
        boolean done = false;
        String next = null;
        char ans;
        try
        {
            while (! done)
            {
                System.out.println("Input an entry:");
                next = SavitchIn.readLine();
                toDoList.addItem(next);
                System.out.print("More items for the list?(y/n): ");
                ans = SavitchIn.readLineNonwhiteChar();
                if ((ans == 'n') || (ans == 'N'))
                    done = true;
            }
        }
        catch(ListFullException e)
        {
            System.out.println("List is full.");
            System.out.println("Could not add: " + next);
        }

        System.out.println("The list contains:");
        int position = toDoList.START_POSITION;
        next = toDoList.entryAt(position);
        while (next != null)
        {
            System.out.println(next);
            position++;
            next = toDoList.entryAt(position);
        }
    }
}
```

null indicates the end of the list.

Display 10.9 Using the Class OneWayNoRepeatsList **(Part 2 of 2)**

Sample Screen Dialogue

```
Enter items for the list, when prompted.
Input an entry:
Buy milk.
More items for the list?(y/n): y
Input an entry:
Walk dog.
More items for the list?(y/n): y
Input an entry:
Buy milk.
More items for the list?(y/n): y
Input an entry:
Write program.
More items for the list?(y/n): y
Input an entry:
Go to movies.
The list is full. Could not add: Go to movies.
The list contains:
Buy milk.
Walk dog.
Write program.
```

You can use an `int` variable to step through the list from beginning to end. The technique is illustrated in Display 10.9. The following initializes an `int` variable so its value is the first position on the list:

stepping through a list

```
int position = toDoList.START_POSITION;
```

The defined constant `toDoList.START_POSITION` is simply another name for 1, but we use it because we are thinking of this as the start of the list, not as the number 1. You can recover the item at a given position with the method `entryAt`. For example, the following sets the string variable `next` equal to the string at the position (at the index) given by the variable `position`:

```
next = toDoList.entryAt(position);
```

To obtain the next item on the list, the program simply increments the value of `position` and repeats this sort of thing.

Display 10.10 `ListFullException`
•••

```
public class ListFullException extends Exception
{
    public ListFullException()
    {
        super("List Full Exception.");
    }

    public ListFullException(String message)
    {
        super(message);
    }
}
```

•••

The class `OneWayNoRepeatsList` uses two different methods to detect the end of the list, depending on the situation. The first situation occurs when you add to the list. If you try to add a new item to a list that is full, then a `ListFullExcep-tion` is thrown. This is illustrated by the *try*- and *catch*-blocks in Display 10.9. The class `ListFullException` is defined in Display 10.10 and is completely straightforward.

The other situation where you might encounter the end of the list is if you are reading from the items in the list from first to last, as in the following code taken from Display 10.9:

```
int position = toDoList.START_POSITION;
next = toDoList.entryAt(position);
while (next != null)
{
    System.out.println(next);
    position++;
    next = toDoList.entryAt(position);
}
```

Once the value of `position` is incremented beyond the last position in the list, there is no entry at the `position`, so we will define `toDoList.entryAt(posi-tion)` so that it returns the value *null* to indicate that there is no entry at the given position. Note that *null* is different from any real string and so *null* is an item that will not appear on any list. Thus, your program can test for the end of the list by checking for the value *null*.

The complete definition of the class `OneWayNoRepeatsList` is given in Display 10.11. The entries in a list are kept in the instant variable `entry`, which is an array of `Strings`. Thus, the maximum number of entries that the list can hold is

Display 10.11 An Array Wrapped in a Class *(Part 1 of 3)*

```
/************************************************************
 *An object of this class is a special kind of list. The list can only be written
 *from beginning to end. You can add to the end of the list, but you
 *cannot change individual entries. You can erase the entire list and
 *start over. No entry may appear more than once on the list. You can use
 *int variables as position markers into the list. Position markers are
 *similar to array indexes, but are numbered starting with 1 (one).
 ************************************************************/
public class OneWayNoRepeatsList
{
    public static int START_POSITION = 1;
    public static int DEFAULT_SIZE = 50;

    public OneWayNoRepeatsList(int maximumNumberOfEntries)
    {
        entry = new String[maximumNumberOfEntries];
        countOfEntries = 0;
    }

    /*****************************************************
     *Creates an empty list with a capacity of DEFAULT_SIZE.
     *****************************************************/
    public OneWayNoRepeatsList()
    {
        entry = new String[DEFAULT_SIZE];
        countOfEntries = 0;
    }

    /*********************************************************
     *Adds item. Throws a ListFullException if the list is full and item is
     *not already on the list. If item is already on the list, nothing happens.
     *********************************************************/
    public void addItem(String item) throws ListFullException
    {
        if (! onList(item))
        {
            if (countOfEntries == entry.length)
                throw new ListFullException("Adding to a full list.");
            else
            {
                entry[countOfEntries] = item;
                countOfEntries++;
            }
        }//else do nothing. Item is already on the list.
    }
```

Display 10.11 An Array Wrapped in a Class *(Part 2 of 3)*

```java
    public boolean full()
    {
        return (countOfEntries == entry.length);
    }


    public boolean empty()
    {
        return (countOfEntries == 0);
    }



    /*******************************************************
     *If the argument indicates a position on the list,
     *then the entry at that specified position is returned;
     *otherwise, null is returned.
     *******************************************************/
    public String entryAt(int position)
    {
        if ((1 <= position) && (position <= countOfEntries))
            return entry[position - 1];
        else
            return null;
    }



    /*********************************************
     *Returns true if position is the index of the
     *last item on the list; otherwise, returns false.
     *********************************************/
    public boolean atLastEntry(int position)
    {
        return (position == countOfEntries);
    }
```

Display 10.11 An Array Wrapped in a Class *(Part 3 of 3)*

```
/***********************************
 *Returns true if item is on the list;
 *otherwise, returns false.
 ***********************************/
public boolean onList(String item)
{
    boolean found = false;
    int i = 0;
    while ((! found) && (i < countOfEntries))
    {
        if (item.equals(entry[i]))
            found = true;
        else
            i++;
    }

    return found;
}

public int maximumNumberOfEntries()
{
    return entry.length;
}

public int numberOfEntries()
{
    return countOfEntries;
}

public void eraseList()
{
    countOfEntries = 0;
}



    //entry.length is the total number of items you have room
    //for on the list.  countOfEntries is the number of items
    //currently on the list.
    private int countOfEntries;//can be less than entry.length.
    private String[] entry;
}
```

entry.length. However, the list will not normally be full, but will typically contain fewer than entry.length entries. In order to keep track of how much of the array entry is currently being used, the class has an instance variable called countOfEntries. The entries are kept in the indexed variables, entry[0], entry[1], entry[2], through entry[countOfEntries − 1]. The values of the elements with indexes countOfEntries or higher are just "garbage values" and do not represent entries on the list. Thus, when you want to step through the items on the list, you stop at entry[countOfEntries − 1]. For example, in the definition of the method onList, there is a *while*-loop that steps through the array checking to see if the argument is equal to any of the entries on the list. The code only checks array elements with indexes less than countOfEntries. It does not check the entire array, because array entries at indexes greater than or equal to countOfEntries are not "on the list." So, the *while*-loop that checks to see whether item is on the list is

```
while ((! found) && (i < countOfEntries))
{
    if (item.equals(entry[i]))
        found = true;
    else
        i++;
}
```

The class OneWayNoRepeatsList has a few more methods than those we used in the demonstration program in Display 10.9. These extra methods are to make the class more useful for a wider variety of applications.

Note that although the array entry has indexes starting with 0, if you use an *int* variable as a position marker, such as the variable position in Display 10.9/ page 572, then the numbering starts at 1 not 0. The class methods automatically adjust the indexes, so when you want the item at location position, it gives you entry[position − 1].

Partially Filled Arrays

The array entry in the class OneWayNoRepeatsList in Display 10.11/page 575 is being used as a partially filled array. In some situations, you need some, but not all, of the indexed variables in an array, such as when the array entry contains the entries on a list and the list is not yet full. In these situations, you need to keep track of how much of the array has been used and how much is not currently being used. This is normally done with an *int* variable, like the instance variable countOfEntries in the class OneWayNoRepeatsList in Display 10.11/page 575. For example, the instance variable countOfEntries tells the methods that the list consists of the array elements with indexes 0 through countOfEntries − 1. This is diagrammed in Display 10.12. It is very important to keep track of how much of the array is currently being used, since the other array entries contain "garbage values" that do not represent anything. When accessing a partially filled array, you only want to access those elements in the first part of the array that contain meaningful values, and you want to ignore the "garbage values" in the rest of the array. Of course, as you add or delete entries from a partially filled array, the borderline between meaningful values and

Display 10.12 *A Partially Filled Array*

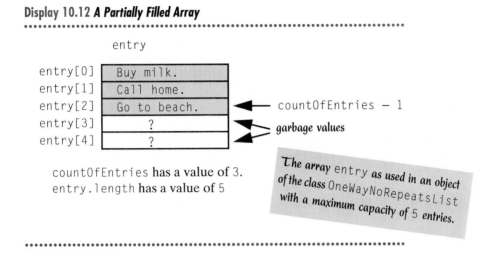

entry

entry[0]	Buy milk.
entry[1]	Call home.
entry[2]	Go to beach.
entry[3]	?
entry[4]	?

countOfEntries − 1

garbage values

countOfEntries has a value of 3.
entry.length has a value of 5

The array entry *as used in an object of the class* OneWayNoRepeatsList *with a maximum capacity of 5 entries.*

"garbage values" can move and this movement is recorded by changing the value of a suitable *int* variable, such as countOfEntries.

Searching an Array

The method onList of the class OneWayNoRepeatsList (Display 10.11, part 3, page 577) searches the array entry to see if the parameter item is in the array entry. This is an example of a *sequential search* of an array. The **sequential search** algorithm is very simple and straightforward: Your code looks at the array elements in the order from first to last to see if the sought-after item is equal to any of the array elements. (If the array is a partially filled array, the search stops when it reaches the end of the meaningful values.)

Parallel Arrays

You will sometimes want to have two different items associated with each index of an array. There are two commonly used ways to do this. One way is to make the base type of the array a class with two instance variables. Another way is to use two arrays with the same indexes. Two (or more) such arrays with the same indexes are called **parallel arrays** and are the topic of this subsection.

Consider the class OneWayNoRepeatsList shown in Display 10.11/page 575. Suppose you want to create a more versatile list that will let you check off items on the list. In that way, if the list is a list of things to do, you could check off the things that you did and then know which of the items on the list you had and had not done. One way to accomplish this is to use a pair of parallel arrays. The parallel arrays are the array entry, which is an instance variable of the class OneWayNoRepeatsList, and an array called checked, which is an array of boolean values, such that if entry[i] is "checked off" then checked[i] is set to *true*, and if entry[i] is not "checked off," then checked[i] is set to *false*. The technique is diagrammed in Display 10.13. How do you add an array (or any instance variable) to the class One-

Display 10.13 *Parallel Arrays*

	entry			checked
entry[0]	Wash car.		checked[0]	*true*
entry[1]	Study for exam.		checked[1]	*true*
entry[2]	Clean room.		checked[2]	*false*
entry[3]	Eat dinner.		checked[3]	*true*
entry[4]	Write letters.		checked[4]	*false*

If `checked[i]` is *true*, then `entry[i]` is checked off.

WayNoRepeatsList? You can define a derived class of the class OneWayNoRepeatsList and add one more array as an instance variable plus any needed new methods. We will do exactly that.

Display 10.14 contains the definition of a class called CheckList that is a derived class of the class OneWayNoRepeatsList and that has one added array called checked that serves the function diagrammed in Display 10.13. The definition of the class CheckList is relatively easy to understand once you understand the relationship between the parallel arrays checked and entry. (The array entry is inherited from the class OneWayNoRepeatsList.) A demonstration program that uses the class CheckList is shown in Display 10.15/page 583.

▲ *GOTCHA* *Returning an Array Instance Variable*

Consider the following accessor method that somebody might want to add to the class CheckList in Display 10.14:

```
public boolean[] theChecks()
{
    return checked;
}
```

Read the text to see what is wrong with this definition.

This definition looks innocent enough. It is pretty much like all the other accessor methods we have written for reading the data in a private instance variable. However, the fact that it is an array that is returned, instead of a primitive type, such as *int* or *double*, makes the situation very different. As we will see, the fact that this function returns an array and the fact that an array variable contains a reference (i.e., a memory address) means that this method provides a way to get around the designation *private*. This method allows programers to directly change the data in that private array instance variable named checked. Let's look at the details of the problem.

Suppose a programmer creates an object of type CheckList as follows:

```
CheckList myList = new CheckList();
```

Display 10.14 The Class CheckList *(Part 1 of 2)*

```
/****************************************************
 *A version of OneWayNoRepeatsList that allows you to
 *check off items on the list.
 ****************************************************/
public class CheckList extends OneWayNoRepeatsList
{
    public CheckList(int maximumNumberOfEntries)
    {
        super(maximumNumberOfEntries);
        checked = new boolean[maximumNumberOfEntries];
        clearChecks();
    }


    public CheckList()
    {
        super();
        checked = new boolean[DEFAULT_SIZE];
                          //DEFAULT_SIZE is inherited.
        clearChecks();
    }


    public void clearChecks()
    {
        int i;
        for (i = 0; i < checked.length; i++)
            checked[i] = false;
    }


    /*******************************************
     *Checks off entry at position of argument.
     *If position is not a legal position,
     *throws an ArrayIndexOutOfBoundsException
     *******************************************/
    public void checkEntry(int position)
    {
        if ((1 <= position) && (position <= numberOfEntries()))
            checked[position - 1] = true;
        else
            throw new ArrayIndexOutOfBoundsException(
                          "Invalid CheckList position");
    }
```

Display 10.14 The Class CheckList *(Part 2 of 2)*

```
/***********************************************
 *Returns true if entry at position is checked.
 *If position is not a legal position,
 *throws an ArrayIndexOutOfBoundsException
 ***********************************************/
public boolean entryIsChecked(int position)
{
    if ((1 <= position) && (position <= numberOfEntries()))
        return checked[position - 1];
    else
        throw new ArrayIndexOutOfBoundsException("Invalid CheckList position");
}


    private boolean[] checked;
    //true means the corresponding entry is checked.
}
```

Look at Display 10.13/page 580 to see the relationship between the array checked *and the array* entry *that is inherited from the class* OneWayNoRepeatsList.

Now suppose the programmer wants direct access to the private array instance variable checked in the object myList. The programmer should not be able to get such access. The qualifier *private* before the declaration of checked (in the class definition) was designed expressly to prevent such access. However, all that this sneaky (or maybe just careless) programmer needs to do in order to get access to the private array variable myList.checked is the following:

```
boolean[] a = myList.theChecks();
```

After the preceding is executed the array variable a contains the address of the array myList.checked. *So* a *is another name for the private array* myList.checked! So, our sneaky programmer can do anything she or he wants to the private array myList.checked by simply using the array name a. For example, suppose the programmer wants to do the following:

```
int i;
for (i = 0; i < myList.checked.length; i++)
    myList.checked[i] = true;//Illegal
```

Well, the programmer cannot do this, because the instance variable myList.checked is private and so the programmer cannot use the name checked, and the preceding code will produce a compiler error message. But, if the programmer is sneaky, she/he can do the following which means the exact same thing, since a is another name for myList.checked:

Display 10.15 Using the Class CheckList *(Part 1 of 3)*

```java
public class CheckListDemo
{
    public static void main(String[] args)
    {
        CheckList toDoList = new CheckList(10);

        System.out.println("Enter jobs to do, when prompted.");
        boolean done = false;
        String next = null;
        char ans;
        try
        {
            while (! done)
            {
                System.out.println("Input a job:");
                next = SavitchIn.readLine();
                toDoList.addItem(next);
                System.out.print("More items for the list?(y/n): ")
                ans = SavitchIn.readLineNonwhiteChar();
                if ((ans == 'n') || (ans == 'N'))
                    done = true;
            }
        }
        catch(ListFullException e)
        {
            System.out.println("List is full.");
            System.out.println("Could not add: " + next);
        }

        System.out.println("The list contains:");
        int position = toDoList.START_POSITION;
        next = toDoList.entryAt(position);
        while (next != null)
        {
            System.out.println(next);
            position++;
            next = toDoList.entryAt(position);
        }
```

Display 10.15 Using the Class `CheckList` *(Part 2 of 3)*

```java
            System.out.println("Do the things on your list and come back here.");
            System.out.println();
            System.out.println("OK, let's see what you did.");
            position = toDoList.START_POSITION;
            next = toDoList.entryAt(position);
            while (next != null)
            {
                System.out.print("Did you " + next + "? ");
                ans = SavitchIn.readLineNonwhiteChar();
                if ((ans == 'y') || (ans == 'Y'))
                    toDoList.checkEntry(position);
                position++;
                next = toDoList.entryAt(position);
            }

            System.out.println("You did the following:");
            position = toDoList.START_POSITION;
            next = toDoList.entryAt(position);
            while (next != null)
            {
                if (toDoList.entryIsChecked(position))
                    System.out.println(next);
                position++;
                next = toDoList.entryAt(position);
            }

            System.out.println("You still must do the following:");
            position = toDoList.START_POSITION;
            next = toDoList.entryAt(position);
            while (next != null)
            {
                if (!(toDoList.entryIsChecked(position)))
                    System.out.println(next);
                position++;
                next = toDoList.entryAt(position);
            }

        }
    }
```

Display 10.15 Using the Class CheckList *(Part 3 of 3)*

Sample Screen Dialogue

```
Enter jobs you need to do, when prompted.
Input a job:
Wash the car
More items for the list?(y/n): y
Input a job:
Study for exam
More items for the list?(y/n): y
Input a job:
Clean room
More items for the list?(y/n): y
Input a job:
Eat dinner
More items for the list?(y/n): y
Input a job:
Write letters.
More items for the list?(y/n): n
The list contains:
Wash the car
Study for exam
Clean room
Eat dinner
Write letters
Do the things on your list and come back here.

OK, let's see what you did.
Did you Wash the car? y
Did you Study for exam? y
Did you Clean room? n
Did you Eat dinner? y
Did you Write letters? n
You did the following:
Wash the car
Study for exam
Eat dinner
You still must do the following:
Clean room
Write letters
```

```
int i;
for (i = 0; i < a.length; i++)
    a[i] = true;
```

The arrays myList.checked and a are the exact same array!

Now, the preceding definition of the accessor method theChecks is not a suitable accessor method. So what should we do about providing an accessor method to the array checked? The first answer is that you do not need any accessor methods beyond those already in the class. The methods checkEntry, entryIsChecked, and clearChecks allow a programmer to do anything that legitimately needs to be done with a CheckList. It is, in fact, extremely unlikely that you would ever need an accessor method that returns an entire array instance variable. Unlikely, but not impossible.

Suppose that for some unusual reason you need to have the accessor method theChecks. The correct way to define the method is as follows:

```
public boolean[] theChecks()
{
    boolean[] temp = new boolean[checked.length];
    int i;
    for(i = 0; i < numberOfEntries(); i++)
        temp[i] = checked[i];
    return temp;
}
```

The array temp constructed in this method definition has the same entries as the array checked, but it is a different array. It is a copy of the array checked, but it is not the array checked itself. So, with this new definition of theChecks, the following is perfectly safe:

```
boolean[] a = myList.theChecks;
```

The programmer can change the array a, but that will have no effect on the array myList.checked. The array a is another name for the array temp constructed in the method definition; it is not a name for the array myList.checked. The array a is an identical copy of myList.checked, but is not the same array.[1]

If the array in question has a base type that is either a primitive type or the type String, this is pretty much the whole story, but if the base type of the array is a class type, then the problem does not go away that easily. If you have a private array instance variable with a class type as the base type, and you want an accessor method to return a safe copy of the array, you must not only copy the array, but must make a copy of each array entry. However, it is unlikely that you will need an accessor method that returns an entire array copy for a private instance variable whose base type is a class (other than the class String, which can be treated like a

---

1. You could argue that the arrays are not *identical* because we did not copy the garbage values at the end of the partially filled array checked. However, they are only garbage values. Moreover, if you really wanted to, you could also copy the garbage values, but there is no reason for that.

primitive type for this discussion.) So, we will not pursue this point any further. The problem is essentially the same as the problem we discussed in the subsection entitled **GOTCHA Instance Variables of a Class Type** on page 275 of Chapter 5, and as we said there, these kinds of problems are beyond the scope of this book. However, remember that if the base type of the private array instance variable is a primitive type or the type String, then you can use the techniques we gave before this paragraph and that will produce a safe copy of the array instance variable.

? SELF-TEST QUESTIONS

10. Suppose a is an array of values of type *double*. Write some code to display all the elements in a to the screen, one per line.

11. Suppose a is an array of values of type *double*. Suppose a is being used as a partially filled array that contains meaningful values in only the first numberUsed elements. (numberUsed is a variable of type *int* that contains the number of elements that contain meaningful values.) Write some code to display all the meaningful values in the array a.

12. Consider the array a from Question 11. Write some code that will add the number 42 to this partially filled array a. (*Hint:* You must update numberUsed. You can assume the array a is not full.)

13. Redo Question 12, but this time assume that you do not know whether the array a is full. If the array a is full, your code should output an appropriate message to the screen.

14. The program in Display 10.15/page 583 is quite long. It would be better to have some additional methods so that displaying lists can be done by a single method invocation. Define a derived class of the class CheckList that is called CheckListWithDisplay and that has a method that will display on the screen the entire list, another method that will display only the checked entries, and one method that will display only the unchecked entries. Rewrite the program in Display 10.15 so that it uses the class CheckListWithDisplay instead of the class CheckList.

10.4 Sorting Arrays

A place for everything and everything in its place.
ISABELLA MARY BEETON, *The Book of Household Management*

Suppose you have an array of values. You might want the array values to be sorted in some way. For example, you might want to sort an array of numbers from lowest to highest or from highest to lowest, or you might want to sort an array of strings into alphabetical order. In this section, we will discuss a simple sorting algorithm and give a Java implementation of that algorithm. We will present this algorithm as an algorithm to sort an array of values of type *int*. However, with only minor, obvious changes, it can be adapted to sort arrays of values of any type that can be ordered, such as an array of objects that represents employee records and that needs to be sorted by social security number.

Selection Sort

In this subsection, we discuss one of the easiest of the sorting algorithms to understand. This straightforward sorting algorithm is known as **selection sort**.

The algorithm will be implemented as a method that has an array of *ints* a as a parameter and that sorts the array a. The method will rearrange the values in the indexed variables of the array so that

```
a[0] <= a[1] <= a[2] <= ... <= a[a.length - 1]
```

The selection sort algorithm almost follows automatically from the specification of what we want the algorithm to do. We want the algorithm to sort an array named a. In other words, we want the algorithm to rearranging the values of the array so that a[0] is the smallest, a[1] the next smallest, and so forth. That specification leads to the following algorithm outline:

> *for* (index = 0; index < a.length; index++)
> **Place the** index^th **smallest element in** a[index].

(In this case, we count starting with 0, so the smallest element is the 0th smallest element, the next smallest is the "1th smallest," and so forth.)

We will implement the details of this algorithm using only the one array a. This means that we have no extra locations to store any of the array elements we are moving. The only way we can move an array element, without losing the array elements, is to have the element swap places with another element of the array. Any sorting algorithm that uses this sort of swapping of values is called an **interchange sorting algorithm.** So, our selection sort algorithm will be an interchanged sorting algorithm. Let's start with an example to see how the array elements are interchanged.

Display 10.16 shows how an array is sorted by interchanging values. The first picture is the array with its starting values. The smallest value in the array is the 3 in a[4]. So the value in a[4] needs to be interchanged with the value in a[0]. After that interchange, the smallest value is in a[0] where it belongs. The next smallest value is the 5 in a[6]. So, the value in a[6] needs to be interchanged with the value in a[1]. After that, the values in a[0] and a[1] are the smallest and next smallest values, which is what they should be in the final sorted array. The algorithm then interchanges the next smallest element with a[2], and so forth until the entire array is sorted.

pseudocode

This analysis produces the following pseudocode version of the selection sort algorithm:

<Text continued on page 591.>

Display 10.16 Sorting by Swapping Values

	a[0]	a[1]	a[2]	a[3]	a[4]	a[5]	a[6]	a[7]	a[8]	a[9]
	7	6	11	17	3	15	5	19	30	14

	7	6	11	17	3	15	5	19	30	14

	3	6	11	17	7	15	5	19	30	14

	3	6	11	17	7	15	5	19	30	14

	3	5	11	17	7	15	6	19	30	14

·
·
·

	3	5	6	7	11	14	15	17	19	30

Display 10.17 Selection Sort Class *(Part 1 of 2)*

●●

```
/***********************************************************
 *Class for sorting an array of ints from smallest to largest.
 ***********************************************************/
public class SelectionSort
{
    /***********************************************************
     *Precondition: Every indexed variable of the array a has a value.
     *Sorts the array a so that
     *a[0] <= a[1] <= ... <= a[a.length - 1].
     ***********************************************************/
    public static void sort(int[] a)
    {
        int index, indexOfNextSmallest;
        for (index = 0; index < a.length - 1; index++)
        {//Place the correct value in a[index]:
            indexOfNextSmallest = indexOfSmallest(index, a);
            interchange(index,indexOfNextSmallest, a);
            //a[0] <= a[1] <=...<= a[index] and these are the
            //smallest of the original array elements.
            //The remaining positions contain the rest of
            //the original array elements.
        }
    }

    /***********************************************************
     *Precondition: i and j are legal indexes for the array a.
     *Postcondition:
     *The values of a[i] and a[j] have been interchanged.
     ***********************************************************/
    private static void interchange(int i, int j, int[] a)
    {
        int temp;
        temp = a[i];
        a[i] = a[j];
        a[j] = temp;//original value of a[i]
    }
```

●●

Display 10.17 Selection Sort Class *(Part 2 of 2)*

```
/************************************************
 *Returns the index of the smallest value among
 *a[startIndex], a[startIndex+1], ..., a[a.length-1]
 ************************************************/
private static int indexOfSmallest(int startIndex, int[] a)
{
    int min = a[startIndex];
    int indexOfMin = startIndex;
    int index;
    for (index = startIndex + 1; index < a.length; index++)
        if (a[index] < min)
        {
            min = a[index];
            indexOfMin = index;
            //min is the smallest of a[startIndex] through a[index]
        }

    return indexOfMin;
    }
}
```

Selection Sort Algorithm to Sort an Array a

```
for (index = 0; index < a.length - 1; index++)
{//Place the correct value in a[index]:
    indexOfNextSmallest = the index of the smallest value among
                a[index], a[index+1], ..., a[a.length-1];
    Interchange the values of a[index] and a[indexOfNextSmallest].
    //a[0] <= a[1] <=...<= a[index] and these are the
    //smallest of the original array elements.
    //The remaining positions contain the rest of
    //the original array elements.
}
```

Notice that the *for*-loop ends with the last value of index equal to a.length − 2, even though the last index is a.length − 1. This is OK because when there is only one element left to be switched into position (namely, a[a.length − 1]), then that element must already be in the correct place. To see this just, note that when the algorithm gets all the elements except a[a.length − 1] correctly sorted, then the correct value for a[a.length − 1] is the smallest value left to be moved, and the only value left to be moved is the value that is already in a[a.length − 1].

Display 10.17 contains a class with a static method named sort that implements this selection sort algorithm. The method sort uses two private helping

indexOf-
Smallest

methods named `indexOfSmallest` and `interchange`. Once you understand the methods `indexOfSmallest` and `interchange`, it is easy to see that the definition of the method `sort` is a direct translation of our pseudocode into Java code. So, let's discuss the methods `indexOfSmallest` and `interchange`.

The method `indexOfSmallest` searches the following array elements and returns the index of the smallest of the following:

```
a[startIndex], a[startIndex+1], ..., a[a.length-1]
```

The method does this using the two local variables `min` and `indexOfMin`. At any point in its search, `min` is equal to smallest array value found so far and `indexOfMin` is the index of that value. Thus, among other things, `a[indexOfMin]` has the value `min`. Initially, `min` is set to `a[startIndex]`, which is the first value considered for `min`, and `indexOfMin` is set to `startIndex`. Then, each array element is considered in turn to see if it is a new minimum. After all the candidate array elements are checked, the method returns the value of `indexOfMin`.

inter-
change

The method named `interchange` will interchange the values of `a[i]` and `a[j]`. There is one subtle point in this definition. If you execute the code

```
a[i] = a[j];
```

then you will lose the value originally held in `a[i]`. So, before this is executed, the value of `a[i]` is saved in the local variable `temp`.

Display 10.18 contains a demonstration program that shows the selection sort class in action.

There are a number of well-known sorting algorithms, many of them more efficient (and more complicated) than selection sort. However, selection sort will suffice as an introduction to the general topic of sorting.

◑ PROGRAMMING TIP Correctness versus Efficiency

The selection sort algorithm is not the most efficient sorting algorithm known. In fact, it is significantly less efficient than a number of well-known sorting algorithms, but the selection sort algorithm is much simpler than these other algorithms. A simpler algorithm is less likely to have errors creep in when you code it. So, if you need to code a sorting algorithm in a hurry, it would be safer to use a selection sort (or some other simple algorithm). On the other hand, if efficiency is a major issue, you may wish to use a more complicated and more efficient algorithm. But, be aware that the more complicated algorithm will take longer to code, test, and debug. Efficiency can be a subtle topic. Remember, that getting the wrong result is always inefficient no matter how quickly your program can come up with the result.

? SELF-TEST QUESTIONS

15. How do you sort the following array using the class `SelectionSort`?

    `int[] myArray = {9, 22, 3, 2, 87, -17, 12, 14, 33, -2};`

16. How would you need to change the class `SelectionSort` so that it can sort an array of values of type *double* (rather than of type *int*)?

```
public class SelectionSortDemo
{
    public static void main(String[] args)
    {
        int[] b = {7, 5, 11, 2, 16, 4, 18, 14, 12, 30};

        System.out.println("Array values before sorting:");
        int i;
        for (i = 0; i < b.length; i++)
            System.out.print(b[i] + " ");
        System.out.println();

        SelectionSort.sort(b);

        System.out.println("Array values after sorting:");
        for (i = 0; i < b.length; i++)
            System.out.print(b[i] + " ");
        System.out.println();
    }
}
```

Screen Output

```
Array values before sorting:
7 5 11 2 16 4 18 14 12 30
Array values after sorting:
2 4 5 7 11 12 14 16 18 30
```

17. How would you need to change the class SelectionSort so that it can sort an array of values of type *int* into decreasing order, instead of increasing order?

18. If an array of *int*s has a value that occurs twice (like b[0] == 7 and b[5] == 7) and you sort the array using the method SelectionSort.sort, will there be one or two copies of the repeated value after the array is sorted?

Chapter Summary

- An array can be thought of as a collection of variables all of the same type. An array can also be considered a single object with a large composite value consisting of all of the elements of the array.

- Arrays are objects that are created with *new* just like the objects we discussed before this chapter (although there is a slight difference in the syntax used).

- Array indexed variables are numbered starting with 0 and ending with the number one less than the length of the array. If a is an array, then a[i] is an indexed variable of the array a. The index i must have a value greater than or equal to 0 and strictly less than a.length. If i has any other value, that is called an **array index out of bounds error** and will cause an error message when you run your program.

- An array indexed variable may be used as an argument to a method any-place that an argument of the base type is expected. An entire array may also be used as an argument to a method, but in that case, the method must have an array parameter.

- When an indexed variable is used as an argument to a method, it is treated just like any other argument of the base type. In particular, if the base type is a primitive type, then the method cannot change the value of the indexed variable, but if the base type is a class, then the method can change the element at the indexed variable.

- A method may return an array as the value returned by the method.

- When you only use part of an array, you normally store values in an initial segment of the array and use an *int* variable to keep track of how many values are stored in the array. This is called a partially filled array.

- When you wish to have two different values (possibly of different types) for each index of an array, you can use two arrays of the same length. Such arrays are called parallel arrays.

- An accessor method that returns an array corresponding to a private instance variable of an array type should be careful to return a copy of the array, and not to return the private instance variable itself.

- The selection sort algorithm can be used to sort an array of values, such as numbers sorted into increasing order or numbers sorted into decreasing order.

? ANSWERS to Self-Test Questions

1. 0 2 4 6 8 10 12 14 16 18

2.
   a
   e
   i
   o

u

3.
```
Tide 1 is −7.3
Tide 2 is 14.2
```

4. The *for*-loop references elements b[1] through b[10], but there is no element indexed by 10. The array elements are b[0] through b[9]. If included in a complete class or program, the code will compile without any error messages, but when it is run, you will get an error message saying an array index is out of bounds.

5. Write a complete java program that will fill an array a with 20 values of type *double* read in from the keyboard, and will output the numbers in the array as well as how much each number differs from the last number read. Assume the users enter 20 numbers, one per line, from the keyboard. You need not give elaborate instructions to the user.

```
public class Exercise
{
    public static void main(String[] args)
    {
        double[] a = new double[20];

        int index;
        System.out.println("Enter 20 numbers:");
        for (index = 0; index < a.length; index++)
            a[index] = SavitchIn.readLineDouble();

        System.out.println(
            "The numbers and differences from last number are:");
        for (index = 0; index < a.length; index++)
            System.out.println(a[index]
                + " differs from last by " + (a[19] − a[index]));
    }
}
```

You can use a[a.length − 1] in place of a[19].

6.
```
SalesAssociate[] entry = new SalesAssociate[3];
int i;
for (i = 0; i < entry.length; i++)
{
    entry[i] = new SalesAssociate();
    entry[i].reset("Jane Doe", 5000);
}
```

7.
```
a[1] = a b[1] = a
a[2] = a b[2] = a
a[1] = a b[1] = a
a[2] = b b[2] = b
```

8.
```java
public static void showArray(char[] a)
{
    int i;
    for (i = 0; i < a.length; i++)
        System.out.print(a[i]);
    System.out.println();//This line is optional.
}
```

9.
```java
public static double[] halfArray(double[] a)
{
    double[] temp = new double[a.length];
    int i;
    for (i = 0; i < a.length; i++)
        temp[i] = a[i]/2.0;
    return temp;
}
```

10.
```java
int i;
for (i = 0; i < a.length; i++)
    System.out.println(a[i]);
```

11.
```java
int i;
for (i = 0; i < numberUsed; i++)
    System.out.println(a[i]);
```

12.
```java
a[numberUsed] = 42;
numberUsed++;
```

13.
```java
if (numberUsed == a.length)
    System.out.println("List is full. Cannot add 42.");
else
{
    a[numberUsed] = 42;
    numberUsed++;
}
```

14.
```java
public class CheckListWithDisplay extends CheckList
{
    public CheckListWithDisplay(int maximumNumberOfEntries)
    {
        super(maximumNumberOfEntries);
    }
```

```
    public CheckListWithDisplay()
    {
        super();
    }
    public void displayAllEntries()
    {
        int position = START_POSITION;
        String next = entryAt(position);
        while (next != null)
        {
            System.out.println(next);
            position++;
            next = entryAt(position);
        }
    }
    public void displayCheckedEntries()
    {
        int position = START_POSITION;
        String next = entryAt(position);
        while (next != null)
        {
            if (entryIsChecked(position))
                System.out.println(next);
            position++;
            next = entryAt(position);
        }
    }
    public void displayNonCheckedEntries()
    {
        int position = START_POSITION;
        String next = entryAt(position);
        while (next != null)
        {
            if (!(entryIsChecked(position)))
                System.out.println(next);
            position++;
            next = entryAt(position);
        }
    }
}
```

The rewritten program is as follows:

```
public class CheckListWithDisplayDemo
{
    public static void main(String[] args)
    {
        CheckListWithDisplay toDoList =
                        new CheckListWithDisplay(10);
```

```java
System.out.println("Enter jobs to do, when prompted.");
boolean done = false;
String next = null;
char ans;
try
{
    while (! done)
    {
        System.out.println("Input a job:");
        next = SavitchIn.readLine();
        toDoList.addItem(next);
        System.out.print("More items for the list?(y/n): ");
        ans = SavitchIn.readLineNonwhiteChar();
        if ((ans == 'n') || (ans == 'N'))
            done = true;
    }
}
    catch(ListFullException e)
    {
        System.out.println("List is full.");
        System.out.println("Could not add: " + next);
    }

    System.out.println("The list contains:");
    toDoList.displayAllEntries();

    System.out.println(
            "Do the things on your list and come back here.");
    System.out.println();
    System.out.println("OK, let's see what you did.");
    int position = toDoList.START_POSITION;
    next = toDoList.entryAt(position);
    while (next != null)
    {
        System.out.print("Did you " + next + "? ");
        ans = SavitchIn.readLineNonwhiteChar();
        if ((ans == 'y') || (ans == 'Y'))
            toDoList.checkEntry(position);
        position++;
        next = toDoList.entryAt(position);
    }

    System.out.println("You did the following:");
    toDoList.displayCheckedEntries();

    System.out.println("You still must do the following:");
    toDoList.displayNonCheckedEntries();
    }
}
```

15.
```
SelectionSort.sort(myArray);
```

16. Just change the types for the array elements to *double*. You can simply replace all occurrences of *int* by *double*, *except for those occurrences of int that give the type of an index.* For example, you would replace

```
private static void interchange(int i, int j, int[] a)
```

with

```
private static void interchange(int i, int j, double[]
a)
```

Note that i and j are indexes and so they are still of type *int*.

17. All you need to do to make your code work for sorting into decreasing order is to replace the < with > in the following line of the definition of indexOfSmallest:

```
if (a[index] < min)
```

However, to make your code more readable, you should rename the method indexOfSmallest to something like indexOfLargest, rename the variable min to something like max, and rename the variable index-OfMin to something like indexOfMax. You should also rewrite some of the comments.

18. If an array of *int*s has a value that occurs twice and you sort the array using the method SelectionSort.sort, then there will be two copies of the repeated value after the array is sorted.

? PROGRAMMING EXERCISES

1. Write a program that reads in a list of *int* values one per line and outputs their sum as well as all the numbers read in with each number annotated to say what percentage it contributes to the sum. Your program will ask the user how many integers there will be, create an array of that length, and then fill the array with integers. A possible dialogue is

```
How many numbers will you enter?
4
Enter 4 integers one per line:
2
1
1
2
The sum is 6.
The numbers are:
2 33.3333% of the sum.
1 16.6666% of the sum.
1 16.6666% of the sum.
```

```
2 33.3333% of the sum.
```

Use a method that takes the entire array as one argument and returns the sum of the numbers in the array.

2. Write a program that will read in a line of text and output a list of all the letters that occur in the text along with the number of times each letter occurs. End the line with a period that serves as a sentinel value. The letters should be listed in alphabetical order when they are output. Use an array of `int`s of length 26, so each indexed variable contains the count of how many letters there are. Array indexed variable 0 contains the number of a's, array indexed variable 1 contains the number of b's, and so forth. Allow both upper- and lowercase letters as input, but treat uppercase and lowercase versions of the same letter as being equal. *Hints:* You will want to use one of the functions `toUpperCase` or `toLowerCase` in the wrapper class `Character` described in Chapter 5. You will find it helpful to define a method that takes a character as an argument and returns an *int* value that is the correct index for that character, such as `'a'` returning 0, `'b'` returning 1, and so forth. Note that you can use a type cast to change a *char* to an *int*, like `(int)letter`. Of course, this will not get the number you want, but if you subtract `(int)'a'`, you will then get the right index. Allow the user to repeat this task until the user says she or he is through.

Alternative version: If you have read Chapter 7 on the AWT, then do this with a GUI built using the AWT. The input line will be entered in a text field and will *not* require a period at the end. Use a text area for the output.

3. A **palindrome** is a string that reads the same forward and backwards, such as `"warts n straw"` or `"radar"`. Write a program that will accept a string of characters terminated by a period and will determine whether or not the string (without the period) is a palindrome. You may assume that the input contains only letters and the blank symbol. You may also assume that the input word is at most 30 characters long. Disregard blanks when deciding if a string is a palindrome and consider upper- and lowercase version of the same letter to be equal, so the following will be considered a palindrome by your program:

```
"Able was I ere I saw Elba"
```

Your program need not check that the string is a correct English phrase or word. The string "xyzczyx" will be considered a palindrome by your program. Include a loop that allows the user to check additional strings until the user requests that the program end. For this exercise, you should define a static method called palindrome that begins as follows:

```
/*****************************************************
 *Precondition: The array a contains letters and blanks in
 *positions a[0] through a[used - 1].
 *Returns true if the string is a palindrome and false otherwise.
 *****************************************************/
public static boolean palindrome(char[] a, int used)
```

Your program will read the input string into an array with base type *char* and call the preceding method with the array and one other *int* variable. The other *int* variable keeps track of how much of the array is used as described in the subsection entitled **Partially Filled Arrays**.

Alternative version: If you have read Chapter 7 on the AWT, then do this with a GUI built using the AWT. The input will be entered in a text field and will *not* require a period at the end. Do not send the output to the same text field as you used for the input. Use another text field. If you use the AWT, you may want the parameter to the method palindrome to be of type String, rather than *char[]*.

4. Design a class called BubbleSort that is similar to the class Selection-Sort given in Display 10.17/page 590. The class BubbleSort will be used in exactly the same way as the class SelectionSort, but the class BubbleSort will use the bubble sort algorithm.

The bubble sort algorithm goes through all adjacent pairs of elements in the array from the beginning to the end and interchanges any two elements that are out of order. This brings the array closer to being sorted. This procedure is repeated until the array is sorted. The algorithm in pseudocode is as follows:

Bubble Sort Algorithm to Sort An Array a

Repeat the following until the array a is sorted:
```
for (index = 0; index < a.length - 1; index++)
    if (a[index] > a[index + 1])
        Interchange the values of a[index] and a[index + 1].
```

The bubble sort algorithm is very efficient for sorting an array that is "almost sorted." It is not competitive to other sorting methods for most other situations.

5. Design a class called `InsertionSort` that is similar to the class `Selec-tionSort` given in Display 10.17/page 590. The class `InsertionSort` will be used in exactly the same way as the class `SelectionSort`, but the class `InsertionSort` will use the insertion sort algorithm.

   The insertion sort algorithm uses an additional array and copies elements from the array to be sorted to the other array. As each element is copied, it is inserted into the correct position in the array. This will usually require moving a number of elements in the array receiving the new elements. The algorithm in pseudocode is as follows:

Insertion Sort Algorithm to Sort An Array a

```
for (index = 0; index < a.length; index++)
        insert the value of a[index] into the array temp so that
        all the elements so far copied into the array temp are sorted.
Copy all the elements from temp back to a.
```

The array `temp` will be a local variable in the method `sort`. The array `temp` will be a partially filled array. So, when it is only partly filled, all the values will be at the beginning of the array `temp`.

Chapter 11

MULTIDIMENSIONAL ARRAYS AND VECTORS

11.1 MULTIDIMENSIONAL ARRAYS 604
Multidimensional-Array Basics 605
Gotcha Reversing Two-Array
    Indexes 609
Multidimensional-Array Parame-
    ters and Returned Values 609
Implementation of Multidimen-
    sional Arrays 610
Ragged Arrays *(Optional)* 613
Programming Example Employee Time
    Records 615

11.2 VECTORS 622
Using Vectors 622
Gotcha Vector Elements Are of Type
    `Object` 628
Comparing Vectors and Arrays 629
Gotcha Using `capacity` Instead of
    `size` 629
Programming Tip Use `trimToSize` to
    Save Memory 631
Gotcha Using the Method
    `clone` 631

Chapter Summary 634
Answers to Self-Test Questions 634
Programming Exercises 637

11

MULTIDIMENSIONAL ARRAYS AND VECTORS

··

> *Never trust to general impressions, my boy,*
> *but concentrate yourself upon details.*
> **SIR ARTHUR CONAN DOYLE,**
> **A *Case of Identity* (SHERLOCK HOLMES)**

Introduction

This chapter covers two additional array topics: multidimensional arrays and vectors. Multidimensional arrays are arrays that have more than one index. **Vectors** are objects that serve the same function as arrays, but with the added advantage that they can change length while your program is running. Section 11.1 on multidimensional arrays and Section 11.2 on vectors are completely independent of each other. Also, none of the material in the following chapters depends on this chapter. You may cover either one of the two sections in this chapter, or both sections, or neither.

Prerequisites

Section	Prerequisite
Section 11.1 (multidimensional arrays)	Chapters 1–5 and Chapter 10. (The material in Chapter 10 on exception handling is not required.)
Section 11.2 (vectors)	Chapters 1–6, Sections 8.1 and 8.2 of Chapter 8.

Section 11.2 on vectors makes only passing reference to throwing exceptions (Chapter 8), and could be read ignoring these references.

11.1 Multidimensional Arrays

> *Two indexes are better than one.*
> **FOUND ON THE WALL OF A COMPUTER SCIENCE**
> **DEPARTMENT WASHROOM**

It is sometimes useful to have an array with more than one index. For example, suppose you wanted to store the figures in Display 11.1 in some sort of array. The shaded part is just labeling. The nonshaded portion shows the actual entries. There are 60 entries. If you use an array with one index, then the array will have length 60 and it would be almost impossible to keep track of which entry goes with which index number. On the other hand, if you allow yourself two indexes, you can use one index

Display 11.1 A Table of Values

· ·

	Balances for Various Interest Rates Compounded Annually (Rounded to Whole Dollar Amounts)					
Year	5.00%	5.50%	6.00%	6.50%	7.00%	7.50%
1	$1050	$1055	$1060	$1065	$1070	$1075
2	$1103	$1113	$1124	$1134	$1145	$1156
3	$1158	$1174	$1191	$1208	$1225	$1242
4	$1216	$1239	$1262	$1286	$1311	$1335
5	$1276	$1307	$1338	$1370	$1403	$1436
6	$1340	$1379	$1419	$1459	$1501	$1543
7	$1407	$1455	$1504	$1554	$1606	$1659
8	$1477	$1535	$1594	$1655	$1718	$1783
9	$1551	$1619	$1689	$1763	$1838	$1917
10	$1629	$1708	$1791	$1877	$1967	$2061

· ·

for the row and one index for the column. This is illustrated in Display 11.2. Note that, as was true for the simple arrays we have already seen, we begin numbering indexes with zero rather than one. The Java notation for array elements with multiple indexes is also illustrated in Display 11.2. If the array is named `table` and it has two indexes, then `table[3][2]` is the entry in row number 3 and column number 2. Arrays that have exactly two entries can be displayed on paper as a two-dimensional table, and, therefore, are often called two-dimensional arrays. By convention, we think of the first entry as denoting the row and the second as denoting the column. More generally, an array is said to be an *n*-**dimensional array** if it has *n* indexes. Thus, the ordinary one-index arrays that we used up to now are sometimes called **one- dimensional arrays**.

Multidimensional-Array Basics

Arrays with multiple indexes are handled very much like arrays with a single index. To illustrate the details, we will take you through a Java example program that displays an array like the one in Display 11.2. The program is shown in Display 11.3. The array is called `table`. The name `table` is declared and the array is created as follows:

declarations

```
int[][] table = new int[10][6];
```

Display 11.2 Row and Column Indexes for an Array Named `table`

Row Index 3

indexes	0	1	2	3	4	5
0	$1050	$1055	$1060	$1065	$1070	$1075
1	$1103	$1113	$1124	$1134	$1145	$1156
2	$1158	$1174	$1191	$1208	$1225	$1242
3	$1216	$1239	$1262	$1286	$1311	$1335
4	$1276	$1307	$1338	$1370	$1403	$1436
5	$1340	$1379	$1419	$1459	$1501	$1543
6	$1407	$1455	$1504	$1554	$1606	$1659
7	$1477	$1535	$1594	$1655	$1718	$1783
8	$1551	$1619	$1689	$1763	$1838	$1917
9	$1629	$1708	$1791	$1877	$1967	$2061

`table[3][2]` has a value of 1262

Column Index 2

As you might expect, this is equivalent to the two steps:

```
int[][] table;
table = new int[10][6];
```

Note that this is almost identical to the syntax you used for the one-dimensional case. The only difference is that we added a second pair of square brackets in two places, and we gave a number specifying the size of the second dimension (i.e., the number of indexes in the second positions). You can have arrays with any number of indexes. To get more indexes, you just use more square brackets in the declaration.

indexed variables

Indexed variables for multidimensional arrays are just like indexed variables for one-dimensional arrays, except that they have multiple indexes each enclosed in a pair of square brackets. This is illustrated by the following *for*-loop from Display 11.3:

```
for (row = 0; row < 10; row++)
   for (column = 0; column < 6; column++)
      table[row][column] = balance(1000.00, row + 1, (5 + 0.5*column));
```

Display 11.3 Using a Two-Dimensional Array *(Part 1 of 2)*

```
/**********************************************************
 *Displays a two-dimensional table showing how interest
 *rates affect bank balances.
 **********************************************************/
public class InterestTable
{
    public static void main(String[] args)
    {
        int[][] table = new int[10][6];
        int row, column;
        for (row = 0; row < 10; row++)
            for (column = 0; column < 6; column++)
                table[row][column] = balance(1000.00, row + 1, (5 + 0.5*column));
        System.out.println("Balances for Various Interest Rates");
        System.out.println("Compounded Annually");
        System.out.println("(Rounded to Whole Dollar Amounts)");
        System.out.println("Years 5.00% 5.50% 6.00% 6.50% 7.00% 7.50%");
        System.out.println();
        for (row = 0; row < 10; row++)
        {
            System.out.print((row + 1) + "        ");
            for (column = 0; column < 6; column++)
                System.out.print("$" + table[row][column] + "   ");
            System.out.println();
        }
    }
```

A real application would do something more with the array `table`. *This is just a demonstration program.*

```
    /**********************************************************
     *Returns the balance in an account that starts with startBalance
     *and is left for the indicated number of years with rate as the
     *interest rate. Interest is compounded annually. The balance is
     *rounded to a whole number.
     **********************************************************/
    public static int balance(double startBalance, int years, double rate)
    {
        double runningBalance = startBalance;
        int count;
        for (count = 1; count <= years; count++)
            runningBalance = runningBalance*(1 + rate/100);
        return (int) (Math.round(runningBalance));
    }
}
```

Display 11.3 Using a Two-Dimensional Array *(Part 2 of 2)*
••

Sample Screen Dialogue

```
Balances for Various Interest Rates
Compounded Annually
(Rounded to Whole Dollar Amounts)
Years   5.00%  5.50%  6.00%  6.50%  7.00%  7.50%

1       $1050  $1055  $1060  $1065  $1070  $1075
2       $1103  $1113  $1124  $1134  $1145  $1156
3       $1158  $1174  $1191  $1208  $1225  $1242
4       $1216  $1239  $1262  $1286  $1311  $1335
5       $1276  $1307  $1338  $1370  $1403  $1436
6       $1340  $1379  $1419  $1459  $1501  $1543
7       $1407  $1455  $1504  $1554  $1606  $1659
8       $1477  $1535  $1594  $1655  $1718  $1783
9       $1551  $1619  $1689  $1763  $1838  $1917
10       $1629  $1708  $1791  $1877  $1967  $2061
```

The last line is out of alignment because 10 has two digits. This is easy to fix, but that would clutter the discussion of arrays with extraneous concerns.

••

Note that we used two *for*-loops, one nested within the other. This is a common way of stepping through all the indexed variables in a multidimensional array. If there had been three indexes, then we would have used three nested *for*-loops, and so forth for higher numbers of indexes. The illustration in Display 11.2 may help you to understand the meaning of the indexes in `table[row][column]` and the meaning of the nested *for*-loops.

As was true of the indexed variables for one-dimensional arrays, indexed variables for multidimensional arrays are variables of the base type and can be used anyplace that a variable of the base type is allowed. For example, for the two- dimensional array `table` in Display 11.3 an indexed variable, such as `table[3][2]`, is a variable of type *int* and can be used anyplace that an ordinary *int* variable can be used.

Declaring and Creating a Multidimensional Array

You declare a multidimensional-array name and create a multidimensional array in basically the same way that you create and name a one-dimensional array. You simply use as many square brackets as there are indexes.

Syntax:

Base_Type[ ]...[ ] *Array_Name* = new *Base_Type*[*Length_1*]...[*Length_n*] ;

Examples:

```
char[][] page = new char[100][80];
int[][] table = new int[10][6];
double[][][] threeDPicture = new double[10][20][30];
SomeClass[][] entry = new SomeClass[100][80];
```

SomeClass **is a class.**

▲ GOTCHA *Reversing Two-Array Indexes*

Suppose you have a two-dimensional array named `test` such that `test[i][j]` holds the grade that student i received on test number j. Now suppose student 1 received a 100 on test 1 and test 2; student number 2 received a 0 on tests number 1 and 2. Then you have:

```
test[1][1] == 100
test[1][2] == 100
test[2][1] == 0
test[2][2] == 0
```

If you confuse the indexes, you would give `test[1][2]` and `test[2][2]` to student number 2. So, student number 2 gets one 100 and one 0, which is a good deal for student 2, since she/he really got two 0's. On the other hand, student 1 would get the grades `test[1][1]` and `test[2][1]`. So, student 1 would also get one 100 and one 0, which is a big injustice, since student 1 really got two 100's. In both cases, the program will give very incorrect results.

Naming the indexes will help in many ways, but it is no insurance against this problem. If `studentNumber` and `testNumber` are both integer variables, then

```
test[studentNumber][testNumber]
test[testNumber][studentNumber]
```

are both valid expressions, but only one is likely to be correct for the task at hand. In this sort of situation, it pays to take Sherlock Holmes's advice: *Never trust to general impressions, my boy* (or girl), *but concentrate yourself upon details.*

Multidimensional-Array Parameters and Returned Values

Methods may have multidimensional-array parameters and may return a multidimensional array as the value returned. Again, the situation is similar to that of the

array arguments

one-dimensional case except that you use more square brackets. A two-dimensional array parameter is illustrated in Display 11.4. That program is a slight rewrite of the program in Display 11.3. Note that the type for the array parameter is `int[][]`.

returning an array

If you want to return a multidimensional array, then you use the same sort of type specification as you use for a multidimensional-array parameter. For example, the following method returns a two-dimensional array of `double`s:

```
/************************************************************
 *Precondition: Each dimension of startArray is at least the
 *value of size.
 *The array returned is the same as the size-by-size
 *upper left corner of the array startArray.
 ************************************************************/
public static double[][] corner(double[][] startArray, int size)
{
    double[][] temp = new double[size][size];
    int row, column;
    for (row = 0; row < size; row++)
        for (column = 0; column < size; column++)
            temp[row][column] = startArray[row][column];
    return temp;
}
```

Implementation of Multidimensional Arrays

In Java, multidimensional arrays are implemented using one-dimensional arrays. For example, consider the array

```
int[][] table = new int[10][6];
```

arrays of arrays

The array `table` is in fact a one-dimensional array of length 10 and its base type is the type `int[]`. In other words, multidimensional arrays are arrays of arrays.

Normally, you do not need to be concerned with the fact that multidimensional arrays are arrays of arrays. This detail is handled automatically by the compiler. However, there are a few occasions when you can profitably use your knowledge of this detail. For example, suppose you want to write a `for`-loop to fill a two-dimensional array with values. In the program in Display 11.4/page 612, we used the constants 6 and 10 to control the `for`-loops. It would be better style to use the `length` instance variable to control the `for`-loops. But when using the `length` instance variable, you need to think in terms of arrays of arrays. For example, the following is a rewrite of the nested `for`-loop in the `main` method in Display 11.4:

length

```
for (row = 0; row < table.length; row++)
    for (column = 0; column < table[row].length; column++)
        table[row][column] = balance(1000.00, row + 1, (5 + 0.5*column));
```

Let's analyze this nested `for`-loop in a bit more detail.

The array `table` is created with the following:

```
int[][] table = new int[10][6];
```

Multidimensional-Array Parameters

An argument to a method may be an entire multidimensional array. The syntax is almost identical to that of one-dimensional array parameters, except that more square brackets [ ] are used.

Examples (of multidimensional-array formal parameters):

```java
public static void showOneElement(char[][] a, int row, int column)
{
    System.out.print(a[row][column]);
}

public static void reinitialize(int[][] anArray)
{
    int row, column;
    for (row = 0; row < anArray.length; row++)
        for (column = 0; column < anArray[row].length; column++)
            anArray[row][column] = 0;
}
```

Examples (of array arguments):

```java
char[][] page = new char[100][80];
int[][] a = new int[10][20];
int[][] b = new int[30][40];
   <Some code to fill the arrays goes here.>
showOneElement(page, 5, 10);
reinitialize(a);
reinitialize(b);
```

length is explained in the subsection **Implementation of Multidimensional Arrays.**

Note that the arrays a and b have different dimensions. Also, note that no square brackets are used with array arguments.

(Preceding examples are in a method definition. All method definitions are assumed to be in the same class.)

Returning a Multidimensional Array

A method can return a multidimensional array value. The syntax is almost identical to that used to return one-dimensional arrays, except that more square brackets [ ] are used.

Syntax:

```java
public static Base_Type[]...[] Method_Name(Parameter_List)
Method_Body
```
You can use other modifiers instead of `public static`.

Example (assumed to be in a class definition):

```java
public static char[][] blankPage(
                   int numberOfLines, int charPerLine)
{
    char[][] newArray = new char[numberOfLines][charPerLine];
    int line, character;
    for (line = 0; line < numberOfLines; line++)
       for (character = 0; character < charPerLine; character++)
           newArray[line][character] = ' ';
    return newArray;
}
```

Display 11.4 A Multidimensional-Array Parameter

```
/***********************************************************
 *Displays a two-dimensional table showing how interest
 *rates affect bank balances.
 ***********************************************************/
public class InterestTable2
{
    public static void main(String[] args)
    {
        int[][] table = new int[10][6];
        int row, column;
        for (row = 0; row < 10; row++)
            for (column = 0; column < 6; column++)
                table[row][column] = balance(1000.00, row + 1, (5 + 0.5*column));

        System.out.println("Balances for Various Interest Rates");
        System.out.println("Compounded Annually");
        System.out.println("(Rounded to Whole Dollar Amounts)");
        System.out.println("Years 5.00% 5.50% 6.00% 6.50% 7.00% 7.50%");
        System.out.println();
        showTable(table);
    }

    /***********************************************************
     *Precondition: The array displayArray has 10 rows and 6 columns.
     *Postcondition: The array contents are displayed with dollar signs.
     ***********************************************************/
    public static void showTable(int[][] displayArray)
    {
        int row, column;
        for (row = 0; row < 10; row++)
        {
            System.out.print((row + 1) + "      ");
            for (column = 0; column < 6; column++)
                System.out.print("$" + displayArray[row][column] + "   ");
            System.out.println();
        }
    }
```

We will give a better definition of showTable later in this chapter.

The output is the same as in Display 11.3/page 607.

```
    public static int balance(double startBalance, int years, double rate)
```
<The rest of the definition of balance is the same as in Display 11.3/page 607.>
```
}
```

That means that `table` is actually a one-dimensional array of length 10 and each of the 10 indexed variables `table[0]` through `table[9]` are one-dimensional arrays of `int`s each of length 6. That is why the first *for*-loop is terminated using `table.length`. For a two-dimensional array, like `table`, the value of `length` is the number of first indexes, or equivalently the number of rows, or in this case 10. Now let's consider the second *for*-loop.

The 0th row in the two-dimensional array `table` is the one-dimensional array `table[0]` and it has `table[0].length` entries. More generally, `table[row]` is a one-dimensional array of `int`s and it has `table[row].length` entries. That is why the second *for*-loop is terminated using `table[row].length`. Of course, in this case, `table[0].length, table[1].length,...,table[9].length` all happen to equal 6.

You can use the fact that multidimensional arrays are arrays of arrays to rewrite the method `showTable` in Display 11.4. Notice that in Display 11.4, the method `showTable` assumes its array argument has 10 rows and 6 columns. That is fine for this particular program, but a nicer definition of `showTable` would work for an array of any two dimensions. In Display 11.5, we have redefined the method `showTable` so that its argument can be any two-dimensional array of `int`s with any number of rows and any number of columns.

Ragged Arrays *(Optional)*

Since a two-dimensional array in Java is an array of arrays, there is no need for each row to have the same number of entries. To phrase it slightly differently, different rows can have different numbers of columns. These sorts of arrays are called **ragged arrays**.

To illustrate what is involved, let's start with an ordinary, nonragged two dimensional array, created as follows:

```
int[][] a = new int[3][5];
```

This is equivalent to the following:

```
int[][] a;
a = new int[3][];
a[0] = new int[5];
a[1] = new int[5];
a[2] = new int[5];
```

The line

```
a = new int[3][];
```

makes `a` the name of an array of length 3, each entry of which is a name for an array of `int`s that can be of any length. The next three lines each create an array of `int`s of length 5 to be named by `a[0]`, `a[1]`, and `a[2]`. The net result is a two-dimensional array of `int`s with three rows and five columns.

The statements

```
a[0] = new int[5];
a[1] = new int[5];
a[2] = new int[5];
```

Display 11.5 The Method showTable **Redefined**

```
/*********************************************************
 *The array displayArray can have any dimensions.
 *Postcondition: The array contents are displayed with dollar signs.
 *********************************************************/
public static void showTable(int[][] displayArray)
{
    int row, column;
    for (row = 0; row < displayArray.length; row++)
    {
        System.out.print((row + 1) + "        ");
        for (column = 0; column < displayArray[row].length; column++)
            System.out.print("$" + displayArray[row][column] + "    ");
        System.out.println();
    }
}
```

This version of showTable will work for an array with any number of rows and any number of columns. In the program in Display 11.4/page 612, this version would behave the same as the version given in Display 11.4, but this version is more versatile and can be used in more different situations.

invite the question: "Do all the lengths need to be 5?" The answer is *no*. In what follows, we define a similar (ragged) array b in which each row has a different length:

```
int[][] b;
b = new int[3][];
b[0] = new int[5];
b[1] = new int[7];
b[2] = new int[4];
```

It is worth noting that after you fill the preceding array b with values, you can display the array using the method showTable as defined in Display 11.5. However, you could not display b using showTable if you instead defined showTable as we did in Display 11.4/page 612.

There are situations where you can profitably use ragged arrays, but most applications do not require ragged arrays. However, if you understand ragged arrays, you will have a better understanding of how all multidimensional arrays work in Java.

▼ **PROGRAMMING EXAMPLE** *Employee Time Records*

In this programming example, a two-dimensional array named hours is used to store the number of hours worked by each employee of a company for each of the five days Monday through Friday. The first array index is used to designate a day of the week and the second array index is used to designate an employee. The two-dimensional array is a private instance variable in a class named TimeBook shown in Display 11.6. The class includes a demonstration program in the method main that works for a small company with only three employees. The employees are numbered starting with 1 and the array indexes are numbered starting with 0, so an adjustment of minus one is sometimes needed when specifying and employee's array index. For example, the hours worked by employee number 3 on Tuesday is recorded in hours[1][2]. The first index denotes the second work day of the week (Tuesday), and the second index denotes the third employee. Days are numbered 0 for Monday, 1 for Tuesday, and so forth. Employees are numbered 1, 2, 3 but are stored in array index positions 0, 1, 2, and so you need to subtract one from the employee number to obtain the correct employee index.

The class TimeBook shown in Display 11.6 is not yet complete. It needs more methods to be a really useful class, but it has enough methods for the demonstration program in main. You can think of the definition in Display 11.6 as a first pass at writing the class definition. It even still has a stub for the definition of the method getHours. Recall that a stub is a definition of a method that can be used for testing, but which is not the final method definition. In Programming Exercise 1, you are asked to complete this class definition, but at this stage, it is complete enough to illustrate the use of the two-dimensional array hours, which is an instance variable of the class.

stub

The class TimeBook uses two ordinary one-dimensional arrays as instance variables, in addition to the two-dimensional array hours. The array weekHours is used to record the total hours worked in a week for each of the employees. The method computeWeekHours will set weekHours[0] equal to the total number of hours work by employee 1 in the week, weekHours[1] equal to the total number of hours work by employee 2 in the week, and so forth. The array dayHours will be used to record the total number of hours worked by all the employees on each day of the week. The method computeDayHours will set dayHours[0] equal to the total number of hours worked on Monday by all of the employees combined, will set dayHours[1] equal to the total number of hours worked on Tuesday by all of the employees, and so forth. Display 11.7/page 620 illustrates the relationships among the arrays hours, weekHours, and dayHours. In that display, we have shown some sample data for the array hours. These data, in turn, determine the values stored in weekHours and in dayHours.

Be sure to notice how the method computeWeekHours uses the array indexes of the two-dimensional array hours. There is a *for*-loop nested inside of a *for*-loop.

Display 11.6 Time Keeping Program *(Part 1 of 4)*

```
/***********************************************************
 *Class for a one week record of the time worked by each Employee.
 *Uses a five day week (Mon-Fri). main has a sample application.
 ***********************************************************/
public class TimeBook
{

    /***********************************************************
     *Reads hours worked for each employee on each day of
     *the week into the two-dimensional array hours. (The method
     *for input is just a stub in this preliminary version.)
     *Computes the total weekly hours for each employee and
     *the total daily hours for all employees combined.
     ***********************************************************/
    public static void main(String[] args)
    {
        TimeBook book = new TimeBook(3);
        book.getHours();
        book.update();
        book.showTable();
    }


    public TimeBook(int theNumberOfEmployees)
    {
        numberOfEmployees = theNumberOfEmployees;
        hours = new int[5][numberOfEmployees];
        //the 5 is for the 5 days Monday through Friday.
        weekHours = new int[numberOfEmployees];
        dayHours = new int[5];
    }
```

A real class would have more methods. We have only shown the methods used in `main`

```
    //This is just a stub.
    public void getHours()
    {
        hours[0][0] = 8;   hours[0][1] = 0;   hours[0][2] = 9;
        hours[1][0] = 8;   hours[1][1] = 0;   hours[1][2] = 9;
        hours[2][0] = 8;   hours[2][1] = 8;   hours[2][2] = 8;
        hours[3][0] = 8;   hours[3][1] = 8;   hours[3][2] = 4;
        hours[4][0] = 8;   hours[4][1] = 8;   hours[4][2] = 8;
    }
```

Display 11.6 Time Keeping Program *(Part 2 of 4)*

```java
public void update()
{
    computeWeekHours();
    computeDayHours();
}


private void computeWeekHours()
{
    int dayNumber, employeeNumber, sum;

    for (employeeNumber=1; employeeNumber <=numberOfEmployees; employeeNumber++)
    {//Process one employee:
        sum = 0;
        for(dayNumber = 0; dayNumber < 5; dayNumber++)
            sum = sum + hours[dayNumber][employeeNumber - 1];
            //sum contains the sum of all the hours worked
            //in one week by employee with number employeeNumber.
        weekHours[employeeNumber - 1] = sum;
    }
}


private void computeDayHours()
{
    int dayNumber, employeeNumber, sum;

    for (dayNumber = 0; dayNumber < 5; dayNumber++)
    {//Process one day's (for all employees):
        sum = 0;
        for (employeeNumber = 1;
                employeeNumber <= numberOfEmployees; employeeNumber++)
            sum = sum + hours[dayNumber][employeeNumber - 1];
            //sum contains the sum of all hours worked by all
            //employees on day dayNumber.
        dayHours[dayNumber] = sum;
    }
}
```

Display 11.6 Time Keeping Program *(Part 3 of 4)*

```
public void showTable()
{
    int row, column;
    System.out.print("Employee  ");
    for(column = 0; column < numberOfEmployees; column++)
        System.out.print((column + 1) + "    ");
    System.out.println("totals");
    System.out.println();

    for (row = 0; row < 5; row++)
    {
        System.out.print(day(row) + " ");
        for (column = 0; column < hours[row].length; column++)
            System.out.print(hours[row][column] + "    ");
        System.out.println(dayHours[row]);
    }
    System.out.println();

    System.out.print("Total  =  ");
    for (column = 0; column <  numberOfEmployees; column++)
        System.out.print(weekHours[column] + "  ");
    System.out.println();
}


//Converts 0 to "Monday", 1 to "Tuesday" etc.
//Blanks used to make all strings the same length.
private String day(int dayNumber)
{
    String dayName = null;

    switch (dayNumber)
    {
        case 0:
            dayName = "Monday   ";
            break;
        case 1:
            dayName = "Tuesday  ";
            break;
        case 2:
            dayName = "Wednesday";
            break;
```

> The method showTable can and should be made more robust. See Programming Exercise 1.

Display 11.6 Time Keeping Program *(Part 4 of 4)*

```
            case 3:
                dayName = "Thursday ";
                break;
            case 4:
                dayName = "Friday     ";
                break;
            default:
                System.out.println("Fatal Error.");
                System.exit(0);
                break;
        }

        return dayName;
    }

    private int numberOfEmployees;
    private int[][] hours;
        //hours[i][j] has the hours for employee j on day i.
    private int[] weekHours;
        //weekHours[i] has the week's hours work for employee i+1.
    private int[] dayHours;
        //dayHours[i] has the total hours worked by all employees.
        //on day i. Monday is 0, Tuesday 1, etc,
}
```

Screen Output

```
<In the final program, the stub getHours would be replaced with a real
method and there would then be an input dialogue here that obtains the
numbers of hours worked by each employee on each day.>

Employee   1   2   3    totals

Monday     8   0   9    17
Tuesday    8   0   9    17
Wednesday  8   8   8    24
Thursday   8   8   4    20
Friday     8   8   8    24

Total   =  40  24  38
```

The outer *for*-loop cycles through all employees, and the inner *for*-loop is executed once for each day of the week. The five days of the week (Monday through Friday) are represented by the five numbers 0 through 4. The inner *for*-loop (together with an initialization of the variable sum and a following assignment statement) is reproduced in what follows:

```
sum = 0;
for(dayNumber = 0; dayNumber < 5; dayNumber++)
    sum = sum + hours[dayNumber][employeeNumber - 1];
    //sum contains the sum of all the hours worked
    //in one week by employee with number employeeNumber.
weekHours[employeeNumber - 1] = sum;
```

Note that when computing the sum of the hours for one employee, the second index, which represents the particular employee, is held constant. This inner *for*-loop goes through all values of the first index and this way cycles through all the days for the single employee represented by the second index.

The method computeDayHours works in a similar way to compute the total number of hours worked by all employees on each day of the week. However, in this case, the inner *for*-loop cycles through the second index while the first index is

Display 11.7 Arrays for the Class TimeBook

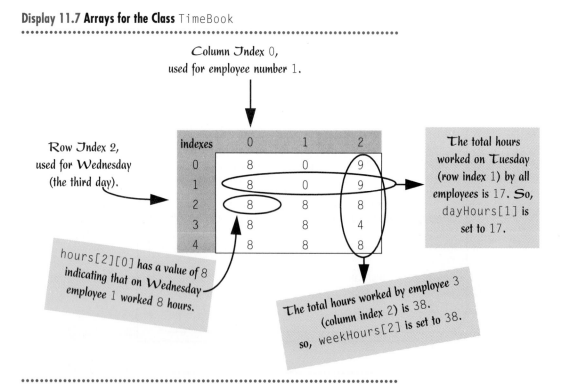

Column Index 0, used for employee number 1.

Row Index 2, used for Wednesday (the third day).

indexes	0	1	2
0	8	0	9
1	8	0	9
2	8	8	8
3	8	8	4
4	8	8	8

The total hours worked on Tuesday (row index 1) by all employees is 17. So, dayHours[1] is set to 17.

hours[2][0] has a value of 8 indicating that on Wednesday employee 1 worked 8 hours.

The total hours worked by employee 3 (column index 2) is 38. so, weekHours[2] is set to 38.

held constant. Or to phrase it another way, the roles of the employee index and the day of the week index are interchanged.

completing
class definition

The class `TimeBook` is not yet a finished piece of software ready to be saved and reused again and again. What is there is correct, but not yet complete. The method `getHours` is just a stub and needs to be replaced by a more generally applicable method that obtains hours from the user at the keyboard. The method `showTable` will not give a display as neat as the one in Display 11.6 unless all the hours have the same number of digits. The method `showTable` needs to be made more robust so that it will neatly display any combination of hours worked. Finally, the class `Time-Book` should have more methods so it will be a class that is useful in a wide range of situations. In Programming Exercise 1, you are asked to complete the definition of the class `TimeBook` in all of these ways. The version in Display 11.6 does, however, show all the essentials of using the two-dimensional array `hours`.

? SELF-TEST QUESTIONS

1. What is the output produced by the following code?

```java
int[][] testArray = new int[4][4];
int index1, index2;
for (index1 = 0; index1 < testArray.length; index1++)
    for (index2 = 0; index2 < testArray[index1].length; index2++)
        testArray[index1][index2] = index2;
for (index1 = 0; index1 < testArray.length; index1++)
{
    for (index2 = 0; index2 < testArray[index1].length; index2++)
        System.out.print(testArray[index1][index2] + " ");
    System.out.println();
}
```

2. Write code that will fill the array `a` (declared in what follows) with numbers typed in at the keyboard. The numbers will be input five per line, on four lines (although your solution need not depend on how the input numbers are divided into lines):

   ```java
   int[][] a = new int [4][5];
   ```

3. Write a method definition for a *void* method called `display` such that the following invocation will display the contents of the array `a` in Self-Test Question 2, and will display it in the same format as we specified for the input there (i.e., four lines of five numbers per line):

   ```java
   display(a);
   ```

   Your method definition should also work for two-dimensional arrays that have sizes other than 4 by 5. Make your method a static method that can be added to a class.

11.2 Vectors

"Well, I'll eat it," said Alice, "and if it makes me grow larger, I can reach the key; and if it makes me grow smaller, I can creep under the door; so either way I'll get into the garden...."
LEWIS CARROLL, *Alice's Adventures in Wonderland*

compared to arrays

Vectors can be thought of as arrays that can grow (and shrink) in length while your program is running. In Java, you can read in the length of an array when the program is run, but once your program creates an array of that size it cannot change its length. For example, suppose you write a program to record customer orders for a mail order house, and suppose you store all the orders for one customer in an array of objects of some class called `OrderItem`. You could ask the user how many items she or he will order, store the number in a variable called `numberOfItems`, and then create and name the array `item` with the following:

```
OrderItem[] item = new OrderItems[numberOfItems];
```

But, now suppose the customer enters `numberOfItems` items and then decides to order another item? There is no way to increase the array `item` by even one element. There are ways around this problem with arrays, but they are all rather complicated and all require creating a new array. Vectors serve the same purpose as arrays except that they can change length while the program is running. So, a vector could handle the customer's extra order without any problems.

which to use?

If vectors are like arrays but have the nice added feature of being able to change length, then why don't we just always use vectors instead of arrays? It often seems that every silver lining has a cloud, and that is true of vectors as well. There are two main problems with vectors: First, they are less efficient than arrays, and, second, the elements in a vector must be objects; they cannot be values of a primitive type, such as *int*, *double*, or *char*. For example, if you want a vector of *int*s, you must simulate this with a vector of `Integers`, where `Integer` is a wrapper class whose objects simulate *int* values. Thus, it is best to use arrays whenever you know that the length of the array does not need to change and to use vectors when the capacity of the vector will change often and by unpredictable amounts.

Using Vectors

Vectors are used very much the same way that arrays are used, but there are some important differences. First of all, the definition of the class `Vector` is not provided

java.util.*

automatically. The definition is in the package `jave.util`, and so, any code that uses the class `Vector` must contain the following, normally at the start of the file:

```
import java.util.*;
```

A vector is created and named in the same way as are objects of any class. For example,

```
Vector v = new Vector(20);
```

capacity

This makes v the name of a vector that has an *initial* **capacity** of 20 items. When we say that a vector has a certain capacity, we mean that it has been allocated memory for that many items, but if it needs more items, the system will automatically allocate more memory. By carefully choosing the capacity of a vector, you can (often) make your code more efficient, but it has no effect on what you can do with the vector. If you choose your capacity to be large enough, then the system will not need to reallocate memory too often, and so your program should run faster. On the other hand, if you make your capacity too large, you will waste storage. However, no matter what capacity you choose, you can still do anything you want with the vector. Other constructors, as well as most of the other methods for the class `Vector`, are described in Display 11.8. Which constructor you use can effect efficiency, but has no other effect on how the vector can be used.

Creating and Naming a Vector

An object of the class `Vector` is created and named in the same way as any other object.

Examples:
```
Vector v = new Vector();
Vector v2 = new Vector(30);
```

When a number is given as an argument to the constructor, that number determines the initial capacity of the vector.

Vectors can be used like arrays, but they do not have the array square bracket notation. If you would use the following for an array of strings a,

no square brackets

```
a[index] = "Hi Mom!";
```

then to do the analogous thing for a vector v, you would use

setElementAt

```
v.setElementAt("Hi Mom!", index);
```

If you would use the following for an array of strings a,

```
String temp = a[index];
```

then to do the analogous thing for a vector v, you would use

```
String temp = (String)v.elementAt(index);
```

The type cast `(String)` is needed because the base type of all vectors is `Object`. This point is discussed in more detail later in this chapter.

Accessing at an Index

If v is a vector, then elements can be accessed as follows:

Examples:
```
v.setElementAt("Here", index);//Sets the element
                              //at index to "Here".
String temp = (String)v.elementAt(index);//The expression
    //v.elementAt(index) returns the element at position index.
```

The `index` must be greater than or equal to 0 and *less than the current size of the vector* v.

Display 11.8 Some Methods in the Class `Vector`
••

Constructors

`public Vector(int initialCapacity, int capacityIncrement)`
   Constructs an empty vector with the specified initial capacity and capacity increment. When the vector needs to grow, it will add room for `capacityIncrement` more items.

`public Vector(int initialCapacity)`
   Creates an empty vector with the specified initial capacity. When the vector needs to increase its capacity, the capacity doubles.

`public Vector()`
   Creates an empty vector with an initial capacity of `10`. When the vector needs to increase its capacity, the capacity doubles.

Array-like Methods

`public final synchronized`[a] `void setElementAt(Object newElement,`
                                                    `int index)`
   Sets the element at the specified `index` to `newElement`. The previous element at that position is discarded. If you draw an analogy between the vector and an array `a`, then this is analogous to setting `a[index]` to the value `newElement`. The `index` must be a value greater than or equal to 0 and less than the current size of the vector. Throws `ArrayIndexOutOfBoundsException` if the `index` is not in this range.

`public final synchronized`[a] `Object elementAt(int index)`
   Returns the element at the specified index. This is analogous to returning `a[index]` for an array `a`. The `index` must be a value greater than or equal to 0 and less than the current size of the vector. Throws `ArrayIndexOutOfBoundsException` if the `index` is not in this range.

Methods to Add Elements

`public final synchronized`[a] `void addElement(Object newElement)`
   Adds the specified element to the end of the calling vector and increases its size by one. The capacity of the vector is increased if that is required.

---

[a] We have included the modifier *synchronized* for completeness, but it is of no consequence to what we are doing in this book and you can safely ignore it. The modifier *final* means that a derived class cannot change the definition of the method. (If you have not yet read about derived classes, you can ignore the word *final*.)

Display 11.8 Some Methods in the Class Vector **(Continued)**

··

`public final synchronized`[a] `void insertElementAt(Object newElement,`
                                              `int index)`

Inserts newElement as an element in the calling vector at the specified index. Each element in the vector with an index greater or equal to index is shifted upward to have an index one greater than the value it had previously. The index must be a value greater than or equal to 0 and less than *or equal to* the current size of the vector. Throws ArrayIndexOutOfBoundsException if the index is not in this range. Note that you can use this method to add an element after the last current element. The capacity of the vector is increased if that is required.

Methods to Remove Elements

`public final synchronized`[a] `void removeElementAt(int index)`

Deletes the element at the specified index. Each element in the vector with an index greater or equal to index is decreased to have an index one less than the value it had previously. The index must be a value greater than or equal to 0 and less than the current size of the vector. Throws ArrayIndexOutOfBounds-Exception if the index is not in this range.

`public final synchronized`[a] `boolean removeElement(Object`
            `theElement)`

Removes the first occurrence of theElement from the calling vector. If theElement is found in the vector, then each element in the vector with an index greater or equal to the theElement's index is decreased to have an index one less than the value it had previously. Returns *true* if theElement was found (and removed). Returns *false* if theElement was not found in the calling vector.

`public final synchronized`[a] `void removeAllElements()`

Removes all elements from the calling vector and sets its size to zero.

Search Methods

`public final`[a] `boolean contains(Object target)`

Returns *true* if target is an element of the calling vector; otherwise, returns *false*.

`public final`[a] `int indexOf(Object target)`

Returns the index of the first element that is equal to target. Uses the method equals of the object target to test for equality. Returns −1 if target is not found.

Display 11.8 Some Methods in the Class `Vector` *(Continued)*

●●●

```
public final synchronizedᵃ int indexOf(Object target,
                                                  int startIndex)
```
Returns the index of the first element that is equal to `target`, but only considers indexes that are greater than or equal to `startIndex`. Uses the method `equals` of the object `target` to test for equality. Returns −1 if `target` is not found.

```
public final synchronizedᵃ int lastIndexOf(Object target)
```
Returns the index of the last element that is equal to `target`. Uses the method `equals` of the object `target` to test for equality. Returns −1 if `target` is not found.

```
public final synchronizedᵃ Object firstElement()
```
Returns the first element of the calling vector. Throws `NoSuchElementException` if the vector is empty.

```
public final synchronizedᵃ Object lastElement()
```
Returns the last element of the calling vector. Throws `NoSuchElementException` if the vector is empty.

Memory Management (Size and Capacity)

```
public finalᵃ boolean isEmpty()
```
Returns *true* if the calling vector is empty (i.e., has size 0); otherwise, returns *false*.

```
public finalᵃ int size()
```
Returns the number of elements in the calling vector.

```
public finalᵃ int capacity()
```
Returns the current capacity of the calling vector.

```
public final synchronizedᵃ void ensureCapacity(int newCapacity)
```
Increases the capacity of the calling vector to ensure that it can hold at least `newCapacity` elements. Using `ensureCapacity` can sometimes increase efficiency, but its use is not needed for any other reason.

```
public final synchronizedᵃ void trimToSize()
```
Trims the capacity of the calling vector to be the vector's current size. This is used to save storage.

Make a Copy

```
public synchronizedᵃ Object clone()
```
Returns a clone of the calling vector. The clone is an identical copy of the calling vector.

The two methods `setElementAt` and `elementAt` give vectors approximately the same functionality that square brackets give to arrays. However, there is one important point that needs to be noted. The method invocation

```
v.setElementAt("Hi Mom!", index);
```

is *not* always completely analogous to

```
a[index] = "Hi Mom!";
```

The method `setElementAt` can replace any existing element, but unlike an array, you cannot use `setElementAt` to put an element at any higher index.[1] To set an element for the first time, you usually use the method `addElement`. The method `addElement` adds elements at index position 0, position 1, position 2, and so forth in that order. This means that vectors must always be filled in the order position 0, 1, 2, and so forth. But, your code can then go back and change any individual element, just as in an array.

---

addElement

Elements can be added to a vector using the method `addElement`. The elements are added to index positions 0, then 1, then 2, and so forth.

Examples:
```
v.addElement("Here");
v.addElement("There");
v.addElement("Everywhere");
```
The object `v` is a vector.

You can find out what indexes already have elements by using the method `size`. If v is a vector `v.size()` returns the size of the vector, which is the number of elements stored in the vector. The indexes of these elements go from 0 to one less than `v.size()`.

The Method `size`

The method `size` returns the number of elements in a vector.

Example:
```
for (index = 0; index < v.size(); index++)
    System.out.println(v.elementAt(index));
```
`v` is a vector and `index` is of type *int*.

---

1. Some implementations of Java may allow you to use `setElementAt` to add an element at the index equal to the size of the vector, i.e., at the first unused position, but we have seen implementations that do not allow this.

With arrays, the square brackets and the instance variable `length` are the only tools provided for you the programmer. If you want to use arrays for other things, you must write code to manipulate the arrays. Vectors, on the other hand, come with quite a large selection of powerful methods that can do many of the things you might need to write code to do with arrays. For example, the class `Vector` has methods to insert a new element between two elements in the vector. Most of these methods are described in Display 11.8/page 624.

base type

The base type of an array can be any type whatsoever. On the other hand, all vectors have the base type `Object`. In other words, in order to store an item in a vector, it must be of type `Object`. As you will recall, every class is a descendent class of the class `Object`. Thus, every object of every class type is also of type `Object`. So, you can add elements of any class type to a vector. In fact, you can even add elements of different class types to the same vector, but this is usually a dangerous thing to do. On the other hand, you cannot add elements of any primitive type,

primitive types

such as *int*, *double*, or *char*, to a vector.

If you want to do something equivalent to having a vector of elements of some primitive type, for example, the type *int*, then you must use the corresponding wrapper class, in this case `Integer`. You can have a vector of elements that are of type `Integer`. Wrapper classes are discussed in Chapter 5. We will not discuss them any further here.

Base Type of a Vector

All vectors have base type `Object`, but all classes are descendent classes of the class `Object`. This means that an element of a vector can be an object of any class, but you cannot have vector elements of a primitive type such as *int*, *double*, or *char*.

▲ *GOTCHA* Vector Elements Are of Type `Object`

The fact that an element added to a vector must be an `Object` has more consequences than you might at first think. Consider the following:

```
Vector v = new Vector();
String greeting = "Hi Mom!";
v.addElement(greeting);
System.out.println("Length is " + (v.elementAt(0)).length());
```

Read text to see what is wrong with this.

Although this may look fine, it will produce an error method telling you that the class `Object` does not have a method named `length`.

You might protest, `v.elementAt(0)` is of type `String` and so it does have a method named `length`. You are right, but Java does not know that `v.elementAt(0)` is of type `String`. It only knows it is an element of a vector, and all it knows about elements of a vector is that they are of type `Object`. You need to tell Java that `v.elementAt(0)` is of type `String` by using a type cast as follows:

```
(String)(v.elementAt(0))
```

So, the troublesome output statement needs to be rewritten to the following, which will work fine:

```
System.out.println("Length is " +
                         ((String)(v.elementAt(0))).length());
```

Comparing Vectors and Arrays

Vectors are used for the same sorts of applications as are arrays. So, how do you decide whether to use a vector or an array? They each have their advantages and disadvantages. The advantage of vectors is that they have very many built-in features. For example, a vector is automatically a partially filled vector. The method `size` keeps track of how much of the vector is filled with meaningful elements. This is illustrated in the sample program in Display 11.9. Vectors also have built-in methods to accomplish many of the common tasks that would require you to design your own code, if you were using arrays. For example, with vectors, you have a method to insert an element at any specified point in the vector, you have a method to delete an element from any place in the vector, and you have a method to test if an element is in the vector or not

Perhaps the biggest advantage of vectors over arrays is that vectors automatically increase their capacity should your program need room for more elements. Your program can determine the size of an array when the program is run, but once the array is created, the size cannot be changed. The size of a vector can change.

The advantage of arrays is that they are more efficient, that they have a very nice notation that uses the square brackets, and perhaps most importantly, the base type of an array can be of any type. The base type of a vector is always the type `Object`. This is not much of a disadvantage if you want to store objects of some class, but if you want to store values of a primitive type in a vector, then you need to use a wrapper class for the primitive type. With an array, you can simply make the primitive type the base type of the array.

▲ **GOTCHA** *Using* `capacity` *Instead of* `size`

In Display 11.9, we used the following code to print out the list of all strings in the vector `toDoList`:

```
int vectorSize = toDoList.size();
for (position = 0; position < vectorSize; position++)
    System.out.println((String)(toDoList.elementAt(position)));
```

Display 11.9 Vector Demonstration (Part 1 of 2)

●●●

```java
import java.util.*;


public class VectorDemo
{
    public static void main(String[] args)
    {
        Vector toDoList = new Vector(10);


        System.out.println("Enter items for the list, when
                prompted.");
        boolean done = false;
        String next = null;
        char ans;
        while (! done)
        {
            System.out.println("Input an entry:");
            next = SavitchIn.readLine();
            toDoList.addElement(next);
            System.out.print("More items for the list?(y/n): ");
            ans = SavitchIn.readLineNonwhiteChar();
            if ((ans == 'n') || (ans == 'N'))
                    done = true;
        }


        System.out.println("The list contains:");
        int position;
        int vectorSize = toDoList.size();
        for (position = 0; position < vectorSize; position++)

            System.out.println((String)(toDoList.elementAt(positi
            on)));
    }
}
```

●●●

Display 11.9 Vector Demonstration *(Part 2 of 2)*

●●

Sample Screen Dialogue

```
Enter items for the list, when prompted.
Input an entry
Buy milk.
More items for the list?(y/n): y
Input an entry
Wash car.
More items for the list?(y/n): y
Input an entry
Do assignment.
More items for the list?(y/n): n
The list contains:
Buy milk.
Wash car.
Do assignment.
```

●●

If we had mistakenly used the method `capacity` instead of `size`, we would be trying to write out garbage values. In this case, we are likely to find the error, because if we use `capacity` instead of `size`, then the program will end with a message saying it has thrown an `ArrayIndexOutOfBoundsException` (unless by coincidence the size and the capacity are equal).

◑ *PROGRAMMING TIP* Use `trimToSize` *to Save Memory*

Vectors automatically increase their capacity when your program needs them to have additional capacity. However, it may increase the capacity more than what your program requires. Also, when your program needs less capacity in a vector, the vector does not automatically shrink. If your vector has a large amount of excess capacity, you can save memory, by using the method `trimToSize` to shrink the capacity of a vector. If `v` is a vector, then an invocation of `v.trimToSize()` will shrink the capacity of the vector `v` down to the size of `v`, so that there is no unused capacity in `v`. Normally, you should only use `trimSize` when you know the vector will not later need its extra capacity.

▲ *GOTCHA* Using the Method `clone`

As was true of objects for other classes, and as is true for arrays, you cannot make a copy of a vector using the assignment statement. For example, consider the following code:

```
Vector v = new Vector(10);
<Some code to fill the vector v.>
Vector otherV;
otherV = v;
```

This code simply makes otherV another name for the vector v, so you have two names but only one vector. If you want to make otherV an identical, but different, copy of v, you use the method clone as follows:

```
Vector otherV = (Vector)v.clone();
```

Be sure to notice the type cast to the type Vector in the preceding line of code. That type cast is needed. Since the method clone returns a value of type Object, the following will produce an error message:

```
Vector otherV = v.clone();//Incorrect form
```

The reason that clone returns a value of type Object has to do with language features other than vectors and is a bit too complicated to explain here, but the way to cope with this inconvenience is clear and simple: just insert a type cast as shown in the preceding example.

A class can have a private instance variable of type Vector. However, private instance variables of type Vector have complications similar to those we discussed for private instance variables of an array type. Suppose you have a class with a private instance variable of an array type. In the subsection **GOTCHA Returning an Array Instance Variable** on page 580 of Chapter 10, we noted that to keep programmers from having direct access to the private array instance variables, your accessor methods should return a copy of the array. The exact same lesson applies to private instance variables of type Vector. An accessor method should not return the private instance vector itself, but should return a copy of the vector. To produce a copy of a vector you can use the vector method clone to produce a clone (i.e., a copy) of the private instance vector and return the clone.

Using the method clone, however, can be a bit complicated and produces a few pitfalls. First of all, the return type of the method clone is Object; it is not Vector. To see the problems that this can produce, suppose you have a private instance variable named v declared as follows:

```
class SampleClass
{
    ...
    private Vector v;
}
```

The following accessor method will produce a compiler error message when added to the class SampleClass:

```
public Vector getVector()
{
    return v.clone();
}
```

The problem is that v.clone is of type Object and needs a type cast to make it match the specified return value of Vector. One way to avoid the compiler error message is to write this accessor method as follows:

```
public Vector getVector()
{
    return (Vector)v.clone();
}
```

One other problem is a general problem frequently encountered with the use of the method clone with most classes, not just with the class Vector. If the objects stored in the vector do not themselves have a well-behaved clone method, then the clone of the vector will simply copy the memory addresses of the elements in the vector and not make copies of the elements in the vector. This can still allow for access of private data. The situation is similar to what we described for arrays of class in the subsection **GOTCHA Returning an Array Instance Variable** on page 580 of Chapter 10. Even if the other classes being used all have well-behaved clone methods, you may still need to do some extra work to get the accessor method in SampleClass to work correctly. The exact details are beyond the scope of this book, but you have at least been warned of the potential problems.

? SELF-TEST QUESTIONS

4. Can you use the method setElementAt to place an element in a vector at any index you want?

5. If you create a vector with the following, can the vector contain more than 20 elements?

```
Vector v = new Vector(20);
```

6. Give code that will output all the elements in a vector v to the screen. Assume that the elements are of type String.

7. This question is for those readers who have covered Section 10.4 of Chapter 10, which covers sorting. For this question, you will write a class for sorting strings into lexicographic order that follows the outline of the class SelectionSort in Display 10.17. However, your definition will use a vector of elements (all of which happen to be strings), rather than an array of elements of type *int*. For words, lexicographic order reduces to alphabetic order if all the words are in lowercase letters (or if all the words are in uppercase). You can compare two strings to see which is lexicographically first by using the String method compareTo. For strings s1 and s2, s1.compareTo(s2) returns a negative number if s1 is lexicographically before s2, returns 0 if s1 equals s2, and returns a positive number if s1 is lexicographically after s2. Call your class StringSelectionSort. *Hint:* Vector elements are of type Object, so if you want to use a String method, such as compareTo, with an element of the vector, you will need to do a type cast to a String. A test program you can use to test your class follows:

```
import java.util.*;

public class StringSelectionSortDemo
{
    public static void main(String[] args)
    {
        Vector b = new Vector();
        b.addElement("time");
        b.addElement("tide");
        b.addElement("clouds");
        b.addElement("rain");

        System.out.println("Vector values before sorting:");
        int i;
        for (i = 0; i < b.size(); i++)
            System.out.print(b.elementAt(i) + " ");
        System.out.println();

        StringSelectionSort.sort(b);
        System.out.println("Vector values after sorting:");
        for (i = 0; i < b.size(); i++)
            System.out.print(b.elementAt(i) + " ");
        System.out.println();
    }
}
```

Chapter Summary

- You can have arrays with more than one index. These are known as multi-dimensional arrays.

- A two-dimensional array can be thought of as a two-dimensional display with the first index giving the row and the second index giving the column.

- Multidimensional arrays are implemented in Java as arrays of arrays.

- Vectors can be thought of as arrays that can grow in length.

- The base type of all vectors is Object. Thus, the elements of a vector may be of any class type, but they cannot be of a primitive type.

? ANSWERS to Self-Test Questions

1.
```
0 1 2 3
0 1 2 3
0 1 2 3
0 1 2 3
```

2.
```
int[][] a = new int [4][5];
int row, column;
```

```
System.out.println("Enter numbers:");
for (row = 0; row < 4; row++)
    for (column = 0; column < 5; column++)
        a[row][column] = SavitchIn.readInt();
```

Alternatively, you could use

```
System.out.println("Enter numbers:");
for (row = 0; row < a.length; row++)
    for (column = 0; column < a[row].length; column++)
        a[row][column] = SavitchIn.readInt();
```

3.
```
public static void display(int[][] anArray)
{
    int row, column;
    for (row = 0; row < anArray.length; row++)
    {
        for (column = 0; column < anArray[row].length;
                                                column++)
            System.out.print(anArray[row][column] + " ");
        System.out.println();
    }
}
```

4. No. The index must be greater than or equal to 0 and less than the size of the vector. Thus, you can replace any existing element, but you cannot place the element at any higher index. This is unlike an array. If an array is partially filled to index 10, then you can add an element at index 20, as long as the array is that large. With a vector, you cannot add an element beyond the last used index.

5. Yes. The vector can contain more than 20 elements. The number 20 used as an argument to the constructor merely gives the initial memory allocation for the vector. More memory is automatically allocated when it is needed.

6.
```
int index;
for (index = 0; index < v.size(); index++)
    System.out.println(v.elementAt(index));
```

7.

```
import java.util.*;

/*************************************************
 *Class for sorting a vector of Strings lexicographically
 *(i.e., approximately alphabetically).
 *************************************************/
public class StringSelectionSort
{
    /****************************************************
     *Sorts the vector a so that a.elementAt(0), a.elementAt(1),...,
     *a.elementAt(a.size()-1) are in lexicographic order.
     *****************************************************/
    public static void sort(Vector a)
    {
        int index, indexOfNextSmallest;
        for (index = 0; index < a.size() - 1; index++)
        {//Place the correct value in position index:
            indexOfNextSmallest =
                          indexOfSmallest(index, a);
            interchange(index,indexOfNextSmallest, a);
            //a.elementAt(0), a.elementAt(1),...,
            //a.elementAt(index) are sorted. The rest of
            //the elements are in the remaining positions.
        }
    }


    /*****************************************************
     *Precondition: i and j are legal indexes for the vector a.
     *Postcondition: The values of a.elementAt(i) and
     *a.elementAt(j) have been interchanged.
     *****************************************************/
    private static void interchange(int i, int j, Vector a)
    {
        Object temp;
        temp = a.elementAt(i);
        a.setElementAt(a.elementAt(j), i);
        a.setElementAt(temp, j);
    }

    /****************************************************
     *Returns the index of the lexicographically first value among
     *a.elementAt(startIndex), a.elementAt(startIndex+1),...,
     *a.elementAt(a.size() - 1)
     *****************************************************/
    private static int indexOfSmallest(int startIndex, Vector
```

a)

```
    {
        String min = (String)a.elementAt(startIndex);
        int indexOfMin = startIndex;
        int index;
        for (index = startIndex + 1; index < a.size(); index++)
        if (((String)(a.elementAt(index))).compareTo(min) < 0)
        {
            min = (String)a.elementAt(index);
            indexOfMin = index;
        }
        return indexOfMin;
    }
}
```

? PROGRAMMING EXERCISES

1. The class TimeBook in Display 11.6/page 616 is not really finished. Complete the definition of the class TimeBook in the way described on page 621. In particular, be sure to add a default constructor, accessor methods to recover and change each of the instance variables, and each indexed variable of each array instance variable. Be sure you replace the stub getHours with a method that obtains values from the keyboard. You should also define a private method with two *int* parameters that will output the first *int* parameter in the number of spaces given by a second parameter. The extra spaces not filled by the first *int* parameter are to be filled with blanks. This will let you, for example, write each array indexed element in exactly four spaces (or however many spaces you want), and so will allow you to output neat rectangular displays of array elements. Be sure the main in Display 11.6 works correctly with these new methods. Also, write a separate test program to test all the new methods. *Hint:* To output an *int* value *n* in a fixed number of spaces, use Integer.toString(n) to covert the number to a string value and then work with the string value. This is discussed in the subsection **Integer, Double, and Other Wrapper Classes** on **page 255** of Chapter 5.

2. Write a class definition for a class called TicTacToe. An object of type TicTacToe is a single game of TicTacToe. Store the game board as a single two-dimensional array of *char*s with three rows and three columns. Include methods to add a move, to display the board, to tell whose turn it is (X or O), to tell if there is a winner, to say who the winner is, and to reinitialize the game to the beginning. Write a main for the class that will allow the user to play the game at the terminal and keyboard. Both players will sit at the keyboard and enter their moves in turn. Alternative version 1: This version will throw an exception if the move method causes somebody to win the game. This will allow the user to deal with a win in whatever way the user wants. For this version, define a new exception class. Alternative version 2: Do this with a GUI interface using the AWT package discussed in Chapter 7. Alternative version 3: Combine alternative versions 1 and 2.

3. Do Programming Exercise 4./page 601 in Chapter 10, except that in this exercise the class will sort a vector rather than an array. Assume the elements in the vector are all Strings. (*Hint:* Check out Self-Test Question 7./page 633.)

4. Do Programming Exercise 5./page 601 in Chapter 10, except that in this exercise, the class will sort a vector rather than an array. Assume the elements in the vector are all Strings. (*Hint:* Check out Self-Test Question 7./page 633.)

Chapter 12

RECURSION

12.1 THE BASICS OF RECURSION 640
Case Study Digits to Words 641
How Recursion Works 645
Gotcha Infinite Recursion 647
Recursive versus Iterative
    Definitions 651
Recursive Methods That Return a
    Value 653

12.2 PROGRAMMING WITH RECURSION 657
Handling Exceptions with
    Recursion *(Alternative
    Ordering)* 657
Case Study Binary Search
    (Alternative Ordering) 658

Chapter Summary 665
Answers to Self-Test Questions 665
Programming Projects 671

RECURSION

....

There are two kinds of people in the world, those who divide the world into two kinds of people and those who do not.
ANONYMOUS

Introduction

Many people believe that you should never define anything in terms of itself. That would be a kind of circularity, they say. However, there are situations in which it is both possible and useful to define a method in terms of itself. If you do it correctly, it need not even be circular (although that may take a little explaining). Java permits you to, in some sense, define a method in terms of itself. More precisely, a Java method definition may contain an invocation of the very method that is being defined. When a method definition contains an invocation of itself, the method is said to be **recursive**, and the general topic of these recursive methods is called **recursion.** In this chapter, we tell you about recursion.

Prerequisites

Section	Prerequisite
Section 12.1	Chapters 1–5
Section 12.2: There are only two subsections. They are independent and are listed below:	
Handling Exceptions with Recursion (Alternative Ordering)	Chapters 1–5 and Chapter 8
Binary Search (Alternative Ordering)	Chapters 1–5 and Chapter 10

12.1 The Basics of Recursion

This statement is false.
PARAPHRASING OF AN ANCIENT PARADOX

It often turns out that a natural way to design an algorithm involves using the same algorithm on one or more subcases. For example, here is an outline of an algorithm to search for a name in a phone book: Open the phone book to the middle of the book. If the name is on that page you are done. If the name is alphabetically before that page, then search the first half of the book. If the name is alphabetically after that page, then search the second half of the book. Searching half of the phone book is a smaller version of the original task of searching the entire phone book. As we will see, this sort of algorithm can be realized as a recursive Java method. More generally, whenever an algorithm needs to solve one subtask that is a smaller version of the entire algorithm's task, you can realize the algorithm as a Java recursive method. Of course, you must do this in the right way, or your Java code will produce problems, but the goal of this chapter is to show you that right way. We begin with a simple example to illustrate recursion in Java.

Recursive Call

If a method definition contains an invocation of the very method being defined, then that invocation is called a recursive call or recursive invocation.

Case Study Digits to Words

In this case study, you will write the definition of a method that takes a single integer as an argument and that writes out the digits in that integer as words. For example, if the argument is the number 223, then the method should output

```
two two three
```

The heading of your method will be

```
/************************************************************
*Precondition: numeral >= 0
*Action: The digits in numeral are written out in words.
*************************************************************/
public static void inWords(int numeral)
```

algorithm design

If the number is only a single digit, then you can use a long *switch*-statement to decide which word to use for a given digit. The method digitWord in Display 12.1 uses just such a *switch*-statement so that digitWord(0) returns "zero", digitWord(1) returns "one", and so forth. But, we still must consider the case of a number with more than one digit.

We now consider a number with more than one digit. There are lots of different ways to break this task down into subtasks. Some of them lend themselves to a solution using recursion and some do not. You will quickly learn which is which, but for this your first try, we will tell you one suitable decomposition into subtasks. One good way to decompose this task into two subtasks so that you can immediately solve one of the subtasks (and so that the other lends itself to the use of recursion) is

> Output all but the last digit as words.
> Output the word for the last digit.

The second subtask can be accomplished with a call to the method digitWord. The first subtask is a smaller version of the original problem. It is, in fact, the exact same problem as the one with which we started, except that the number in question is smaller. That means that the first subtask can be accomplished by a recursive call of the very method we are defining. (Well, this must be done with some care, but as you will see, it can be done this way.) This leads you to the following outline for an algorithm to use for the method inWords:

Display 12.1 Demonstrating Recursion *(Part 1 of 2)*

```
public class RecursionDemo
{
    public static void main(String[] args)
    {
        System.out.println("Enter an integer:");
        int numeral = SavitchIn.readLineInt();
        System.out.println("The digits in that number are:");
        inWords(numeral);
        System.out.println();

        System.out.println("If you add ten to that number,");
        System.out.println("the digits in the new number are:");
        numeral = numeral + 10;
        inWords(numeral);
        System.out.println();
    }

    /***********************************************************
     *Precondition: numeral >= 0
     *Action: The digits in numeral are written out in words.
     ***********************************************************/
    public static void inWords(int numeral)
    {
        if (numeral < 10)
            System.out.print(digitWord(numeral) + " ");
        else //numeral has two or more digits
        {
            inWords(numeral/10);                          recursive call
            System.out.print(digitWord(numeral%10) + " ");
        }
    }

    /***************************************
     *Precondition: 0 <= digit <= 9
     *Returns the word for the argument digit.
     ***************************************/
    private static String digitWord(int digit)
    {
        String result = null;

        switch (digit)
        {
            case 0:
                result = "zero";
                break;
```

Display 12.1 Demonstrating Recursion *(Part 2 of 2)*

```
            case 1:
                result = "one";
                break;
            case 2:
                result = "two";
                break;
            case 3:
                result = "three";
                break;
            case 4:
                result = "four";
                break;
            case 5:
                result = "five";
                break;
            case 6:
                result = "six";
                break;
            case 7:
                result = "seven";
                break;
            case 8:
                result = "eight";
                break;
            case 9:
                result = "nine";
                break;
            default:
                System.out.println("Fatal Error.");
                System.exit(0);
                break;
        }
        return result;
    }
}
```

Sample Screen Dialogue

```
Enter an integer:
987
The digits in that number are:
nine eight seven
If you add ten to that number,
the digits in the new number are:
nine nine seven
```

Algorithm for `inWords(numeral)`

`inWords(numeral` **with the last digit deleted**`);`
`System.out.print(digitWord(`**last digit of** `numeral) + " ");`

Now, consider a number with more than one digit, like 534. You want to divide 534 into the two numbers 53 and 4. As it turns out, you can accomplish this by doing integer division by 10. For example, 534/10 is 53 and 534%10 is 4. So, you can refine your algorithm to the following Java code:

```
inWords(numeral/10);
System.out.print(digitWord(numeral%10) + " ");
```

Well, it looks like you are done. It looks as if the following definition will work:

```
public static void inWords(int numeral)//Not quite right
{
    inWords(numeral/10);
    System.out.print(digitWord(numeral%10) + " ");
}
```

As the comment indicates, this will not quite work. It includes the right basic idea, but it has one big problem: The preceding definition assumes that the argument `numeral` is more than one digit long. You need to make a special case of numbers that are only one digit long. As we will see, unless this simple case is made to work correctly, no other case will work correctly. This leads you to rewrite the method definition as follows:

```
public static void inWords(int numeral)
{
    if (numeral < 10)
        System.out.print(digitWord(numeral) + " ");
    else //numeral has two or more digits
    {
        inWords(numeral/10);
        System.out.print(digitWord(numeral%10) + " ");
    }
}
```

The definition of the method `inWords` is now complete. Display 12.1/page 642 shows the method embedded in a demonstration program. However, before we leave this case study, let's discuss the method `inWords` a bit more.

The following recursive call of the method `inWords` occurs in the definition of the method `inWords`:

```
inWords(numeral/10);
```

Note that the argument `numeral/10` used in the recursive call is smaller than the parameter `numeral` that is used for the entire method definition. A recursive call solves a version of the original problem, but it is important that the problem solved by the recursive call be a "smaller" version of the original problem (in some intuitive notion of "smaller," which we will make clearer before this chapter ends.)

As you will see in the next subsection, the successful execution of a recursively defined method, such as inWords, requires that the simplest case be handled in a way that does not involve a recursive call. In the definition of inWords, this simplest case is handled as follows:

```
if (numeral < 10)
    System.out.print(digitWord(numeral) + " ");
```

Note that if the argument numeral is only one digit in length, then no recursive call is used.

How Recursion Works

Exactly how does the computer handle a recursive call? To see the details, consider the following invocation of the method inWords from Display 12.1/page 642.

```
inWords(987);
```

Although the definition of inWords contains a recursive call, the computer does nothing special to handle this or any other invocation of inWords. The computer plugs in the argument 987 into the method definition and executes the resulting code. Plugging in 987 for the parameter numeral in the method definition produces code equivalent to the following:

```
{//Code for invocation of inWords(987)
    if (987 < 10)
        System.out.print(digitWord(987) + " ");
    else //987 has two or more digits
    {
        inWords(987/10);
        System.out.print(digitWord(987%10) + " ");
    }
}
```

Just as with any other method invocation, the computer executes this code with the argument 987 plugged in for the parameter numeral. The computer first checks the boolean expression after the *if*. The boolean expression evaluates to *false*, because 987 is not less than 10. Since the boolean expression evaluates to *false*, the compound statement after the *else* is executed. Now, the compound statement after the *else* starts with the following recursive call:

```
inWords(987/10);
```

The rest of the computation cannot proceed until this recursive call is completed, So, the computer must stop what it is doing and make a side excursion to handle this new recursive call. So, the execution of the code for inWords(987) is suspended, and the computer works on the new recursive call inWords(987/10). After the computer completes the recursive call inWords(987/10), it will return to complete the interrupted computation of inWords(987).

The new recursive invocation, inWords(987/10), is handled just like any other method invocation: The argument 987/10 is plugged in for the parameter numeral in the method definition, and the resulting code is executed. Since 987/10 evaluates to 98, the computer plugs in 98 for the parameter `numeral` resulting in code equivalent to the following:

```
{//Code for invocation of inWords(98)
    if (98 < 10)
        System.out.print(digitWord(98) + " ");
    else //98 has two or more digits
    {
        inWords(98/10);
        System.out.print(digitWord(98%10) + " ");
    }
}
```

While executing this new code, the computer once again encounters a recursive call, specifically the recursive call `inWords(98/10);`. At that point, the preceding computation is suspended and the computer proceeds to the recursive call `inWords(98/10);`. Since 98/10 is equal to 9, 9 is plugged in for the parameter `numeral` in the definition of `inWords`, and the following code is executed:

```
{//Code for invocation of inWords(9)
    if (9 < 10)
        System.out.print(digitWord(9) + " ");
    else //9 has two or more digits
    {
        inWords(9/10);
        System.out.print(digitWord(9%10) + " ");
    }
}
```

Since 9 is indeed less than 10, the first part of the *if-else*-statement is executed. So, only the following is executed:

```
System.out.print(digitWord(9) + " ");
```

This is a stopping case, i.e., a case with no recursive calls. A quick look at the definition of the method `digitWord` shows that the preceding `System.out.println` causes the string `"nine"` to be written to the screen. The invocation of `inWords(98/10)` is now completed. At this point, the suspended computation, shown in what follows, can resume:

```
{//Code for invocation of inWords(98)
    if (98 < 10)
        System.out.print(digitWord(98) + " ");
    else //98 has two or more digits
    {
        inWords(98/10);  ◄──────────────
        System.out.print(digitWord(98%10) + " ");
    }
}
```

The computation resumes after the position indicated with the arrow, so the following is executed:

```
System.out.print(digitWord(98%10) + " ");
```

This causes the string `"eight"` to be output to the screen and this ends the invocation of the recursive call `inWords(98);`.

Stay with us dear reader. The process is almost over. Once the invocation of `inWords(98);` is completed, there is one suspended computation waiting to be completed, and it is shown in what follows:

```
{//Code for invocation of inWords(987)
    if (987 < 10)
        System.out.print(digitWord(987) + " ");
    else //987 has two or more digits
    {
        inWords(987/10); ◄─────────────────
        System.out.print(digitWord(987%10) + " ");
    }
}
```

The computation resumes after the position indicated by the arrow, and the following code is executed:

```
System.out.print(digitWord(987%10) + " ");
```

This causes `"seven"` to be written to the screen and the entire process ends. The sequence of recursive calls is illustrated in Display 12.2.

Note that the computer does nothing special when it encounters a recursive method call. It simply plugs in arguments for parameters and executes the code in the method definition, just as it does with any method invocation.

Successful Recursion

A definition of a method that includes a recursive invocation of the method being defined will not behave correctly unless you follow some specific design guidelines. The following rules apply to most cases that involve recursion.

* The heart of the method definition can be an *if-else*-statement or some other branching statement that leads to different cases, depending on some property of a parameter to the method being defined.

* One or more of the branches include a recursive invocation of the method. These recursive invocations should in some sense use "smaller" arguments or solve "smaller" versions of the task performed by the method.

* One or more branches should include no recursive invocations. These are the **stopping cases** (also known as the **base cases.**).

▲ *GOTCHA* *Infinite Recursion*

Consider the method `inWords` defined in Display 12.1. Suppose we had been careless and had defined it as follows:

```
public static void inWords(int numeral)//Not quite right
{
    inWords(numeral/10);
    System.out.print(digitWord(numeral%10) + " ");
}
```

Display 12.2 What Happens with a Recursive Call

`inWords(987);` **is equivalent to executing:**

```
{//Code for invocation of inWords(987)
    if (987 < 10)
        System.out.print(digitWord(987) + " ");
    else //987 has two or more digits
    {
        inWords(987/10);
        System.out.print(digitWord(987%10) + " ");
    }
}
```

Computation waits here for the completion of the recursive call.

`inWords(987/10);` **is equivalent to** `inWords(98);` **which is equivalent to executing:**

```
{//Code for invocation of inWords(98)
    if (98 < 10)
        System.out.print(digitWord(98) + " ");
    else //98 has two or more digits
    {
        inWords(98/10);
        System.out.print(digitWord(98%10) + " ");
    }
}
```

Computation waits here for the completion of the recursive call.

`inWords(98/10);` **is equivalent to** `inWords(9);` **which is equivalent to executing:**

```
{//Code for invocation of inWords(9)
    if (9 < 10)
        System.out.print(digitWord(9) + " ");
    else //9 has two or more digits
    {
        inWords(9/10);
        System.out.print(digitWord(9%10) + " ");
    }
}
```

This invocation does not cause another recursive call to be executed.

In fact, we almost did define it this way, until we noticed an omitted case. But, suppose we did not notice the omitted case and had used this shorter definition. If you go through the recursive call `inWords(987);` as we did in the previous subsection, you will see that the process never ends. Let's quickly trace the computation of this incorrect recursive method definition.

The method invocation `inWords(987);` (among other things) produces the recursive call `inWords(987/10);` which in turn is equivalent to `inWords(98);`. The invocation of `inWords(98);` produces the recursive call `inWords(98/10);` which is equivalent to `inWords(9);`. Since our incorrect version of `inWords` has no special case for one-digit numbers, the invocation of `inWords(9);` produces the recursive call `inWords(9/10);` which is equivalent to `inWords(0);`. Now the problem becomes apparent. The invocation of `inWords(0);` produces the recursive call `inWords(0/10);` which is equivalent to `inWords(0);`. So, the invocation of `inWords(0);` produces another invocation of `inWords(0);` which produces yet another invocation of `inWords(0);` and so forth forever (or until your computer runs out of resources). This is called **infinite recursion.**

infinite
recursion

The preceding shorter and incorrect definition of `inWords` is incorrect in the sense that it performs the wrong computation. However, it is not illegal. The Java compiler will accept this definition of `inWords` (and any similar recursive method definition that does not have a case to stop the series of recursive calls). However, unless your recursive definition is defined in such a way as to ensure that you do not get an unending chain of recursive calls, then when the method is invoked, you will get an infinite chain of recursive calls, causing your program to either run forever or to end abnormally.

In order for a recursive method definition to work correctly and not produce an infinite chain of recursive calls, there must be one or more cases that for certain values of the parameter(s) will end without producing any recursive call. These cases are called **base cases,** or **stopping cases.** The correct definition of `inWords`, given in Display 12.1/page 642, has one stopping case which is highlighted below:

stopping case
base case

```
public static void inWords(int numeral)
{
    if (numeral < 10)
        System.out.print(digitWord(numeral) + " ");
    else //numeral has two or more digits
    {
        inWords(numeral/10);
        System.out.print(digitWord(numeral%10) + " ");
    }
}
```

stopping case

These stopping cases must be designed so that they terminate every chain of recursive calls. A method invocation can produce a recursive invocation of the same method, and that invocation may produce another recursive invocation, and so forth for some number of recursive calls, but every such chain must eventually lead to a stopping case that ends with no recursive invocation. Otherwise, an invocation of the method might never end (or not end until the computer runs out of resources.)

A typical recursive method definition includes an *if-else*-statement or other branching statement that chooses between one or more cases that each include a recursive call of the method and one or more cases that each end the method invocation without any recursive invocation. Every chain of recursive calls must eventually lead to one of those stopping cases that do not involve any recursive calls.

The most common way to ensure that a stopping case is always reached is to make all the recursive invocations of the method use a "smaller" argument (in some intuitive sense of "smaller"). For example, consider the correct definition of inWords given in Display 12.1/page 642 and reproduced a few paragraphs back. The parameter to inWords is numeral. The parameter to the recursive invocation of inWords is the smaller value numeral/10. This way the recursive invocations in a chain of recursive calls each have a smaller argument. Since the correct definition of inWords has a stopping case for all "small" arguments, we know that eventually a stopping case is always reached.

Stack Overflow

When a method invocation leads to infinite recursion, your program is likely to end with an error message that refers to a "stack overflow." The term **stack** refers to a data structure that is used to keep track of recursive calls (and other things as well). Intuitively, a record of each recursive call is stored on something analogous to a piece of paper. These pieces of paper are intuitively stacked one on top of the other. When this "stack" becomes too large for the computer to handle, that is called a **stack overflow**. ∎

? SELF-TEST QUESTIONS

1. What is the output produced by the following program?

```
public class RecursionExercise
{
    public static void main(String[] args)
    {
        methodA(3);
    }

    public static void methodA(int n)
    {
        if (n < 1)
            System.out.println('B');
        else
        {
            methodA(n - 1);
            System.out.println('R');
        }
    }
}
```

2. What is the output produced by the following program?

```java
public class RecursionExercise2
{
   public static void main(String[] args)
   {
       methodB(3);
   }

   public static void methodB(int n)
   {
       if (n < 1)
           System.out.println('B');
       else
       {
           //The following two lines are the reverse of
           //what they are in Self-Test Question 1.
           System.out.println('R');
           methodB(n - 1);
       }
   }
}
```

3. Write a recursive method definition for the following method:

```java
/*********************************************************
*Precondition: n >= 1.
*Action: Writes out n of the symbol '#' on one line
*and advances to the next line.
*********************************************************/
public static void sharp(int n)
```

Note that the output advances to the next line after outputting the last
'#'. So,

```java
sharp(3);
```

is equivalent to

```java
System.out.println("###");
```

If you have trouble with this one, then first do it so that it does not
advance to the next line. For that simpler case, you need not worry about
the distinction between `print` and `println`. In the simpler case, you only
use `print` and never use `println`. After doing the simpler case, try to do
the exercise as stated.

Recursive versus Iterative Definitions

Any method definition that includes a recursive call can be rewritten so that it accomplishes the same task and does not use recursion. For example, Display 12.3 contains a rewriting of the program in Display 12.1/page 642, but this version has a
definition of `inWords` that does not use recursion. Both versions of `inWords` perform
the exact same action, i.e., the same output to the screen. As is true in this case, the

Display 12.3 Iterative Version of inWords
••

```java
public class IterativeDemo
{
    public static void main(String[] args)
    <The rest of main is the same as in Display 12.1/page 642.>


    /************************************************************
    *Precondition: numeral >= 0
    *Action: The digits in numeral are written out in words.
    ************************************************************/
    public static void inWords(int numeral)
    {
        int divisor = powerOfTen(numeral);
        int next = numeral;
        while (divisor >= 10)
        {
            System.out.print(digitWord(next/divisor) + " ");
            next = next%divisor;
            divisor = divisor/10;
        }

        System.out.print(digitWord(next/divisor) + " ");
    }


    /************************************************************
    *Precondition: n >= 0.  Returns the number of the form one
    *followed by all zeros that is the same length as n.
    ************************************************************/
    private static int powerOfTen(int n)
    {
        int result = 1;
        while(n >= 10)
        {
            result = result*10;
            n = n/10;
        }

        return result;
    }

    private static String digitWord(int digit)
    <The rest of digitWord is the same as in Display 12.1/page 642.>
}
```

The dialogue is exactly the same as in Display 12.1/page 642

••

nonrecursive version of a method definition typically involves a loop in place of recursion and so it is called an **iterative version**.

iterative version

A recursive version of a method definition is usually less efficient (i.e., runs slower and/or uses more storage) than an iterative definition of the same method. This is because of the overhead to the computer that results from keeping track of the recursive calls and suspended computations. Hence, you should confine your use of recursion to cases where it makes your code easier to understand. But, there are indeed cases where recursion can be a big aid to clarity.

Recursive Methods That Return a Value

Any kind of method may involve recursion. A recursive method can be a *void*-method or it can be a method that returns a value. You design a recursive method that returns a value in basically the same way as what we described for *void*-methods. The basic technique for defining a well-behaved recursive method definition that returns a value is as follows:

> The heart of the method definition can be an *if-else*-statement or some other branching statement that leads to different cases depending on some property of a parameter to the method being defined.

> One or more of the branches lead to cases in which the value returned is computed in terms of calls to the same method (i.e., using recursive calls). The arguments for the recursive calls should intuitively be "smaller."

> One or more of the branches lead to cases in which the value returned is computed without the use of any recursive calls. These cases without any recursive calls are called **base cases** or **stopping cases**. (Every chain of recursive calls should always end in one of these stopping cases.)

stopping case
base case

This technique is illustrated by the method numberOfZeros defined in Display 12.4. The method numberOfZeros takes a single *int* argument and returns the number of zeros in the number (when written in the usual way). For example, numberOfZeros(2030) returns 2 because 2030 contains two zero digits. Let's look at how the method numberOfZeros works.

The definition of the method numberOfZeros uses the following simple fact:

If n is two or more digits long, then the number of zero digits in n is
(the number of zeros in n with the last digit removed) plus one more, if that last digit is zero.

For example, the number of zeros in 20030 is the number of zeros in 2003 plus one for that last zero. The number of zeros in 20031 is the number of zeros in 2003 without adding anything, since the extra digit is not zero. With this in mind, let's go through a simple computation using numberOfZeros.

First, consider the simple expression:

```
numberOfZeros(0)
```

Display 12.4 A Recursive Method That Returns a Value
•••

```java
public class RecursionDemo2
{
    public static void main(String[] args)
    {
        System.out.println("Enter a nonnegative number:");
        int number = SavitchIn.readLineInt();
        System.out.println(number + " contains "
                                + numberOfZeros(number) + " zeros.");
    }

    /***********************************************
     *Precondition: n >= 0
     *Returns the number of zero digits in n.
     ***********************************************/
    public static int numberOfZeros(int n)
    {
        if (n == 0)
            return 1;
        else if (n < 10)//and not 0
            return 0;//0 for no zeros
        else if (n%10 == 0)
            return(numberOfZeros(n/10) + 1);
        else //n%10 != 0
            return(numberOfZeros(n/10));
    }
}
```

Sample Screen Dialogue

```
Enter a nonnegative number:
2001
2001 contains 2 zeros.
```

•••

(which might occur as the right-hand side of some assignment statement). When the method is called, the value of the parameter n is set equal to 0 and the code in the body of the method definition is executed. Since the value of n is equal to zero, the first case of the multiway `if-else`-statement applies; so the value returned is 1.

Next consider another simple expression:

```
numberOfZeros(5)
```

When the method is called, the value of the parameter n is set equal to 5 and the code in the body of the method definition is executed. Since the value of n is not equal to zero, the first case of the multiway `if-else`-statement does not apply. The value of n is, however, less than 10, so the second branch of the multiway `if-else`-statement applies and the value returned is 0. So, that's two simple cases that work out right.

Now let's look at an example that involves a recursive call. Consider the expression

```
numberOfZeros(50)
```

When the method is called, the value of n is set equal to 50, and the code in the body of the method definition is executed. Since this value of n is not equal to 0 and is not less than 10, neither of the first two branches of the multiway `if-else`-statement applies. However, n%10 (i.e., 50%10) is 0 and so the third branch applies. So, the value returned is

```
numberOfZeros(n/10)  + 1
```

which in this case is equivalent to

```
numberOfZeros(50/10)  + 1
```

which, in turn, is equivalent to

```
numberOfZeros(5)  + 1
```

But, we already decided that `numberOfZeros(5)` returns 0, so the value returned by `numberOfZeros(50)` is

```
0 + 1
```

(which is 1 and which is the correct value).

Larger numbers will produce longer chains of recursive calls. For example, consider the expression

```
numberOfZeros(2001)
```

The value of `numberOfZeros(2001)` is calculated as follows:

```
numberOfZeros(2001) is numberOfZeros(200) plus nothing
    numberOfZeros(200) is numberOfZeros(20) + 1
      numberOfZeros(20) is numberOfZeros(2) + 1
        numberOfZeros(2) is 0 (a stopping case)
```

When the computer reaches the stopping case `numberOfZeros(2)`, there are three suspended computations. After calculating the value returned for the stopping case, it resumes the most recently suspended computations to determine the value of `numberOfZeros(20)`. After that, the computer completes each of the other suspended computations, using each value computed as a value to plug into another suspended computation, until it reaches and completes the computation for the original invocation `numberOfZeros(2001)`. The suspended computations are completed as follows (which is like evaluating the preceding list of suspended computation *bottom to top*):

```
        numberOfZeros(2) is 0 (a stopping case)
      numberOfZeros(20) is numberOfZeros(2)  + 1, which is 0 + 1 == 1
    numberOfZeros(200) is numberOfZeros(20)  + 1, which is 1 + 1 == 2
  numberOfZeros(2001) is numberOfZeros(200) plus nothing ,
                                            which is 2 plus nothing  == 2
```

Thus, the final value returned by the invocation `numberOfZeros(2001)` is 2, which is correct because 2001 has two zero digits.

Recursion and Overloading

Do not confuse recursion and overloading. When you overload a method name, you are giving two different methods the same name. If the definition of one of these two methods includes a call to the other, that is not recursion. In a recursive method definition, the definition of the method includes a call to the exact same method with the exact same definition including the same number and types of parameters.

■

? SELF-TEST QUESTIONS

• •

4. What is the output of the following program?

```java
public class RecursionExercise4
{
    public static void main(String[] args)
    {
        System.out.println(mysteryValue(3));
    }

    public static int mysteryValue(int n)
    {
        if (n <= 1)
            return 1;
        else
            return (mysteryValue(n - 1) + n);
    }
}
```

5. Complete the definition of the following method. Your definition should be recursive. *Hint:* 10^n is $10^{n-1} * 10$ for $n > 1$.

```java
/****************************
 *Precondition: n >= 0
 *Returns 10 to the power n.
 ****************************/
public static int tenToThe(int n)
```

6. Complete the definition of the following method definition. Your defini-

tion should be recursive. It should use the same technique you used for Question 5 and should also have one more recursive case for negative exponents. *Hints:* 10^n is $1/10^{-n}$ for negative values of *n*. Also, if *n* is negative, then *–n* is positive. This one differs from Question 5 in that it also allows negative numbers as arguments.

```
/*******************************
 *Precondition: n can be any int.
 *Returns 10 to the power n.
 *******************************/
public static double tenToThe(int n)
```

12.2 Programming with Recursion

All short statements about programming techniques are false.
ANONYMOUS

The following two subsections are independent of each other, and no other material in this book depends on either subsection. Thus, you can do the subsections in any order, or choose one, or skip them both until later.

Handling Exceptions with Recursion *(Alternative Ordering)*
As you may well suspect, this subsection requires that you have already covered exception handling, which is done in Chapter 8.

One very common way of handling an exception is given by the following pseudocode outline:

```
try
{
    Try something and throw an exception if it fails.
}
catch(Exception_Class_Name e)
{
    Try again.
}
```

For example,

```
try
{
    System.out.println("Enter a positive number:");
    count = SavitchIn.readLineInt();
    if (count <=0 )
        throw new Exception("Input not positive.");
}
catch(Exception e)
{
    System.out.println(e.getMessage());
    System.out.println("Try again.");
    Start over from the beginning.
}
```

The only detail that is not given in Java code is the instruction

Start over from the beginning.

There is more than one way to accomplish this using Java code. One way is to embed the *try-catch*-block in a loop and use a boolean variable to decide if the loop must be repeated. However, a more intuitive and less awkward approach is to make this a method and to use recursion, as illustrated in Display 12.5.

In Display 12.5, we have used a new exception class (defined in Display 12.6) instead of using the predefined class Exception. This is not required, but is good technique.

The program in Display 12.5 simply requests a positive number and then does a countdown from that number. The number is entered using the method getCount. Notice that if the user enters a nonpositive number, an exception is thrown and then the method getCount is called recursively. This starts the input process all over again from the beginning. Thus, if the user enters another incorrect input, there will be another recursive call and the input will start yet again. This is repeated until the user enters a positive integer. Of course, in practice, an exception would seldom be thrown, but it will be thrown as often as is needed.

The program in Display 12.5 may seem to do a lot of extra work just to get a positive number. However, this is just a simple example to illustrate the technique. In many real situations, you already have all the details at hand and so the extra code will be quite modest. This is illustrated in Self-Test Question 7.

? SELF-TEST QUESTIONS

7. Look at the code for the method readLineInt of the class SavitchIn (Appendix 2 and also on the CD that comes with this book). It uses a loop to do something similar to what we did in Display 12.5. Rewrite the method readLineInt so that it uses recursion instead of a loop. This is a more realistic example of using recursion to do exception handling. (One reason we did not do this in the original definition of readLineInt is so that the code could be understood by students who had not yet covered recursion.)

Case Study Binary Search (Alternative Ordering)

This case study requires that you have already covered the basics about arrays given in Chapter 10.

In this case study, you will design a recursive method that tells you whether or not a given number is in an array of integers. If the sought-after number is in the array, the method will also tell you the index of where the number is in the array. For example, the array may contain a list of winning lottery tickets, and you might want to search the list to see if you are a winner. In Chapter 10, we discussed a method for searching an array by simply checking every array position. (See subsection **Searching an Array** on page 579 of Chapter 10.) The method you developed in this section will be much faster than that simple serial search we saw in Chapter 10. However, for this faster method to work, the array must be sorted.

Display 12.5 Exception Handling Using Recursion *(Part 1 of 2)*

```
public class CountDown
{
    public static void main(String[] args)
    {
        CountDown countDowner = new CountDown();
        countDowner.getCount();
        countDowner.showCountDown();
    }

    public void getCount()
    {
        try
        {
            System.out.println("Enter a positive number:");
            count = SavitchIn.readLineInt();
            if (count <= 0)
                throw new NonpositiveException();
        }
        catch(NonpositiveException e)
        {
            System.out.println("Input must be positive.");
            System.out.println("Try again.");
            getCount();//start over
        }
    }


    public void showCountDown()
    {
        int left;
        System.out.println("Counting down:");
        for (left = count; left >= 0; left--)
            System.out.println(left);
        System.out.println("Blast Off!");
    }


    private int count;
}
```

Display 12.5 Exception Handling Using Recursion *(Part 2 of 2)*

Sample Screen Dialogue

```
Enter a positive number:
0
Input must be positive.
Try again.
Enter a positive number:
-3
Input must be positive.
Try again.
Enter a positive number:
3
Counting down:
3
2
1
0
Blast Off!
```

Display 12.6 An Exception Class

```java
public class NonpositiveException extends Exception
{
    public NonpositiveException()
    {
        super("Nonpositive value.");
    }
    public NonpositiveException(String message)
    {
        super(message);
    }
}
```

We will assume that the array is sorted and completely filled. So, if the array is named a, then we know

task
specification

```
a[0] <= a[1] <= a[2] <= ... <= a[a.length - 1]
```

Often you want to know more than just whether or not an element is in an array. If the element is in the array, you often want to also know where it is in the array. For example, if you are searching for a winning lottery number, then the array index may serve as a record number. Another array indexed by these same indexes may hold phone numbers to call and arrange to claim your winnings. Hence, if the sought-after value is in the array, you will want your method to tell where it is in the array. Thus, you design your method to return an integer that gives the index of the sought-after number. If the number is not in the array, the method will return –1 to indicate that it is not in the array. Before you worry about the exact setup of the class and methods and connecting the method to an array, you first design some pseudocode to solve the search problem.

The algorithm you design will make use of the fact that the numbers in the array are sorted. Notice that, since the array is sorted, you can sometimes rule out whole sections of the array that could not possibly contain the number you are looking for. For example, if you are looking for the number 7 and you know that a[5] is equal to 9, then, of course, you know that 7 is not equal to a[5], but you know much more; you know that 7 is not equal to a[i] for any value of i that is greater than or equal to 5. Since the array is sorted, you know that

algorithm
design

7 < a[5] <= a[i] whenever i is greater than or equal to 5.

So all the elements a[i] for i greater than or equal to 5 need not be searched. You know that the sought-after value 7 is not among them, without needing to check them.

Similarly, if the sought-after number 7 were instead greater than a[5] (e.g., if a[5] were 3 instead of 9), then you could rule out all the elements a[i] with i less than or equal to 5.

Replacing 5 (in the preceding examples) with whatever index is in the middle of the array leads you to your first draft of an algorithm:

```
mid = approximate midpoint between 0 and (a.length - 1);
if (target == a[mid])
    return mid;
else if (target < a[mid])
    return the result of searching a[0] through a[mid - 1].
else if (target > a[mid])
    return the result of searching a[mid + 1] through a[a.length - 1].
```

Notice that the searching of subsegments of the array (in the two *else-if* cases) are smaller versions of the very task you are designing. Thus, the subsegments of the array can be searched with recursive calls to the algorithm itself.

The two pieces of pseudocode that correspond to recursive calls are

> return the result of searching a[0] through a[mid − 1].

and

> return the result of searching a[mid + 1] through a[a.length − 1]

There is, however, one complication. (Isn't there always?) In order to implement these recursive calls, you need more parameters. These recursive calls specify that a subrange of the array is to be searched. In the first case, it is the elements indexed by 0 through mid – 1. In the second case, it is the elements indexed by mid + 1 through a.length – 1. Thus, you need two extra parameters to specify the first and last indexes of the subrange of the array that is to be search. You call these extra parameters first and last. Using these parameters to specify the subrange to be searched, we can express the pseudocode more precisely as follows:

preliminary
pseudocode

> **Algorithm to search** a[first] **through** a[last]:
> mid = approximate midpoint between first and last;
> *if* (target == a[mid])
>   *return* mid;
> *else if* (target < a[mid])
>   return the result of searching a[first] through a[mid − 1].
> *else if* (target > a[mid])
>   return the result of searching a[mid + 1] through a[last].

If you want to search the entire array, you set first set equal to 0 and last equal to a.length – 1. Each recursive call will use some other values for first and last. For example, the first recursive call would set first equal to 0 and last equal to mid – 1.

You should always check that any recursive algorithm you write will not produce infinite recursion. Let's check whether every possible invocation of the algorithm will lead to a stopping case. Consider the three cases in the nested *if-else-*statement. In the first case, the sought-after number is found on the list, and there is no recursive call, and the process terminates. In each of the other two cases, a smaller subrange of the array is searched by a recursive call. If the sought-after number is in the array, the algorithm will narrow the range down smaller and smaller until it finds the number. But, what if the number is not anywhere in the array? Will the resulting series of recursive calls eventually lead to a stopping case if the number is not in the array? Well, unfortunately not, but that is not hard to fix.

Note that in each recursive call, the value of first is increased or the value of last is decreased. If they ever pass each other and first actually becomes larger than last, then we will know that there are no more indexes left to check and that the number target is not in the array. If we add this test to our pseudocode, we get the following more complete pseudocode:

Algorithm to search a[first] **through** a[last]:
mid = **approximate midpoint between** first **and** last;
if (first > last)
    return –1;
else if (target == a[mid])
    return mid;
else if (target < a[mid])
    return the result of searching a[first] **through** a[mid – 1].
else if (target > a[mid])
    return the result of searching a[mid + 1] **through** a[last].

complete
pseudocode

Next you need to translate this pseudocode algorithm into Java code. You decide that the method will be called search and it will be in a class called Array-Searcher. The class will have an instance variable to name the array and the array to be searched will be given that name by the constructor. The final code is shown in Display 12.7. A diagram of how the method performs on a sample array is given in Display 12.8/page 666.

coding

You realize that the method search has extra parameters that the user would always have to set equal to 0 and a.length – 1 to specify that the entire array is searched. You do not want the user to worry about this detail, so you add the method find, which allows the user to simply specify the target value and not worry about indexes. The method find simply calls the method search, but this saves the user a lot of bother. Since the method search is now just a helping method, you make it a private method.

find **versus**
search

A simple program that demonstrates how the class ArraySearcher works is given in Display 12.9/page 667.

When designing a recursive algorithm, you often need to solve a more general problem than the one you set out to solve. For example, consider the method search, which you designed to search an entire array. You needed to design it so that it could not only search the entire array, but so that it could search any sub-range of the array. This was necessary in order to be able to express the recursive subcases. It is very often true that when you are designing a recursive algorithm, you must make the problem a bit more general so that you can easily express the recursive subcases.

The binary search algorithm is extremely fast. In the binary search algorithm, you eliminate about half the array from consideration right at the start. You then eliminate a quarter, then an eighth of the array, and so forth. That means that most of the array need not be searched at all, and that saves a lot of time. For example, to search an array with 1000 elements, the binary search will only need to compare about 10 array elements to the target value. By comparison, a simple serial search could compare as many as all 1000 array elements to the target and on the average will compare about 500 array elements to the target.

efficiency

? *SELF-TEST QUESTIONS*

∙∙∙

8. Will the binary search algorithm work if the array is not sorted?

Display 12.7 Binary Search Class *(Part 1 of 2)*

```
/**************************************************************
 *Class for searching an already sorted array of ints.
 *To search the sorted and completely filled array b,
 *use the following:
 *ArraySearcher bSearcher = new ArraySearcher(b);
 *int index = bSearcher.find(target);
 *index will be given an index of where target is located
 *index will be set to -1 if target is not in the array.
 **************************************************************/
public class ArraySearcher
{
    /*********************************************
     *Precondition: theArray is full and is sorted
     *from lowest to highest.
     *********************************************/
    public ArraySearcher(int[] theArray)
    {
        a = theArray;//a is now another name for theArray.
    }


    /**************************************************************
     *If target is in the array, returns the index of an occurrence
     *of target. Returns -1 if target is not in the array.
     **************************************************************/
    public int find(int target)
    {
        return search(target, 0, a.length - 1);
    }


    //Uses binary search to search for target in a[first] through
    //a[last] inclusive. Returns the index of target if target
    //is found. Returns -1 if target is not found.
    private int search(int target, int first, int last)
    {
        int result = -1;//to keep the compiler happy.
        int mid;
        if (first > last)
            result = -1;
        else
```

Display 12.7 Binary Search Class *(Part 2 of 2)*

```
        {
            mid = (first + last)/2;

            if (target == a[mid])
                result = mid;
            else if (target < a[mid])
                result = search(target, first, mid - 1);
            else //(target > a[mid])
                result = search(target, mid + 1, last);
        }

        return result;
    }

    private int[] a;
}
```

9. Do the values in the array used with the constructor for `ArraySearcher` have to be all different, or is it OK to have repeated values?

10. Suppose you want the class `ArraySearcher` to work for arrays whose values are sorted from largest down to smallest instead of from smallest up to largest. How do you need to change the definition of `ArraySearcher`?

Chapter Summary

□ If a method definition includes an invocation of the very method being defined, that is called a **recursive call**. Recursive calls are legal in Java and can sometimes make a method definition clearer.

□ In order to avoid infinite recursion, a recursive method definition should contain two kinds of cases: one or more cases that include recursive call(s) and one or more stopping cases that do not involve any recursive calls.

□ Recursion can be a handy way to write code that says "if an exception is thrown, then start the whole process over again."

? ANSWERS to Self-Test Questions

1.
B
R
R
R

Display 12.8 Binary Search Example

●●●

`target` **is** 33

Eliminate half of the array:

Array contains:
a[0]=5 a[1]=7 a[2]=9 a[3]=13 a[4]=32 a[5]=33 a[6]=42 a[7]=54 a[8]=56 a[9]=88

mid = (0 + 9)/2 **(which is 4).**
33 > a[mid] **(that is,** 33 > a[4]**)**

So, if 33 **is in the array, then** 33 **is one of**
a[5]=33 a[6]=42 a[7]=54 a[8]=56 a[9]=88

Eliminate half of the remaining array elements:

If 33 **is in the array,**
then 33 **is one of**
a[5]=33 a[6]=42 a[7]=54 a[8]=56 a[9]=88

mid = (5 + 9)/2 **(which is 7)**
33 < a[mid] **(that is,** 33 < a[7]**)**

So, if 33 **is in the array, then** 33 **is one of**
a[5]=33 a[6]=42

Eliminate half of the remaining array elements:

If 33 **is in the array, then** 33 **is one of**
a[5]=33 a[6]=42

mid = (5 + 6)/2 **(which is** 5**)**
33 == a[mid] **So, we found** 33 **at index** 5.

33 *found in* a[5].

●●●

Display 12.9 Binary Search Demonstration *(Part 1 of 2)*

```
public class ArraySearcherDemo
{
    public static void main(String[] args)
    {
        int [] a = new int[10];
        System.out.println("Enter 10 integers in increasing order.");
        System.out.println("One per line.");
        int i;
        for (i = 0; i < 10; i++)
            a[i] = SavitchIn.readLineInt();

        System.out.println();
        for (i = 0; i < 10; i++)
            System.out.print("a[" + i + "]=" + a[i] + " ");
        System.out.println();
        System.out.println();

        ArraySearcher finder = new ArraySearcher(a);

        char ans;
        do
        {
            System.out.println("Enter a value to search for:");
            int target = SavitchIn.readLineInt();
            int result = finder.find(target);

            if (result < 0)
                System.out.println(target + " is not in the array.");
            else
                System.out.println(target + " is at index " + result);

            System.out.println("Again?(y/n)");
            ans = SavitchIn.readLineNonwhiteChar();
        }while ((ans == 'y') || (ans == 'Y'));

        System.out.println("May you find what you're searching for.");
    }
}
```

Display 12.9 Binary Search Demonstration *(Part 2 of 2)*

....

Sample Screen Dialogue

```
Enter 10 integers in increasing order.
One per line.
0
2
4
6
8
10
12
14
16
18

a[0]=0 a[1]=2 a[2]=4 a[3]=6 a[4]=8 a[5]=10 a[6]=12 a[7]=14 a[8]=16 a[9]=18

Enter a value to search for:
14
14 is at index 7
Again?(y/n)
y
Enter a value to search for:
0
0 is at index 0
Again?(y/n)
y
Enter a value to search for:
2
2 is at index 1
Again?(y/n)
y
Enter a value to search for:
13
13 is not in the array.
Again?(y/n)
n
May you find what you're looking for.
```

Note that the 'B' is the first output not the last output.

2.
```
R
R
R
B
```

Note that the 'B' is the last output.

3.
```
/***********************************************************
 *Precondition: n >= 1.
 *Action: Writes out n of the symbol '#' on one line
 *and advances to the next line.
 ***********************************************************/
public static void sharp(int n)
{
    if (n <= 1)
        System.out.println('#');
    else
    {
        System.out.print('#');
        sharp(n - 1);
    }
}
```

4. 6

5.
```
/****************************
 *Precondition: n >= 0
 *Returns 10 to the power n.
 ****************************/
public static int tenToThe(int n)
{
    if (n <= 0)
        return 1;
    else
        return ( tenToThe(n - 1)*10 );
}
```

6.

```
/*******************************
 *Precondition: n can be any int.
 *Returns 10 to the power n.
 *******************************/
public static double tenToThe(int n)
{
    if (n == 0)
        return 1;
    else if (n > 0)
        return (tenToThe(n - 1)*10 );
    else //n < 0
        return (1/tenToThe(-n));
}
```

7.

```
/**********************************************************************
*Precondition: The user has entered a whole number of type int on a line by
*itself, except that there may be white space before and/or after the number.
*Action: Reads and returns the number as a value of type int. The rest
*of the line is discarded. If the input is not entered correctly, then
*in most cases, the user will be asked to reenter the input. In particular,
*this applies to incorrect number formats and blank lines.
**********************************************************************/
public static int readLineInt()
{
    String inputString = null;
    int number = -9999;//To keep the compiler happy.

    try
    {
        inputString = readLine();
        inputString = inputString.trim();
        number = (Integer.valueOf(inputString).intValue());
    }
    catch (NumberFormatException e)
    {
        System.out.println(
            "Your input number is not correct. Your input number must be");
        System.out.println(
            "a whole number written as an ordinary numeral, such as 42");
        System.out.println(
            "Please, try again. Enter a whole number:");
        number = readLineInt();
    }

    return number;
}
```

8. No.

9. It is OK to have repeated values, as long as the array is sorted.

10. The multiway *if-else*-statement in the method `search` needs to have two comparison operators changed so that it reads as shown in what follows. No other changes are needed, but the comments should change to reflect the fact that the array is sorted largest to smallest.

```
if (target == a[mid])
    result = mid;
else if (target > a[mid])//Changed from < to >
    result = search(target, first, mid - 1);
else if (target < a[mid])//Changed from > to <
    result = search(target, mid + 1, last);
```

? PROGRAMMING EXERCISES

1. Write a recursive method definition for a method that has one argument of type *int* and returns the length of its argument (when written in the usual way). This will be a static method. You must allow for both positive and negative arguments. For negative arguments, the sign does not count as part of the length. So, –123 has length 3. Embed the method in a program and test it.

2. Write a recursive method definition for a method that has one parameter for an array of *int*s and that returns the sum of the elements in the array (i.e., the sum of the integers in the array). You can assume that every indexed variable of the array has a value. This will be a static method. Embed the method in a program and test it.

3. Write a recursive method definition for a method that has one parameter of type `String` and returns a *boolean* value. The method returns *true* if the argument is a palindrome and returns *false* otherwise. A palindrome is a string that reads the same forward and backward, such as `"radar"`. Disregard spaces and punctuations and consider upper- and lowercase versions of the same letter to be equal. So, for example, the following would be considered a palindrome by your method:

`"Straw? No, too stupid a fad, I put soot on warts."`

Your method need not check that the string is a correct English phrase or word. The string `"xyzczyx"` will be considered a palindrome by your method. This will be a static method. Embed the method in a program and test it.

Chapter 13

APPLETS AND HTML

13.1 **HTML 674**
HTML Basics 675
Programming Tip A Simple Document
Outline 676
Inserting Hyperlinks 680
13.2 **APPLETS 682**
Applet Basics 682
Running an Applet 684

Placing an Applet in an HTML
Document 686
Gotcha Using an Old Web
Browser 687
Programming Tip Converting an AWT
Application to an Applet 690

Chapter Summary 691
Answers to Self-Test Questions 691
Programming Exercises 691

13

APPLETS AND HTML
....

The web of our life is of a mingled yarn,
good and ill together.
WILLIAM SHAKESPEARE, *All's Well That Ends Well*

Introduction

All that has come before this chapter is important to learning how to program and is important to learning the Java language. However, we have not yet touched on the thing that initially made Java famous. Java became famous in large part due to its connection to the Internet. In this chapter, we describe a version of Java programs that can be run across the Internet. Applets are simply Java programs that are designed to run from a document (page) on the Internet. HTML is a language used to create Internet documents. A Java applet runs from within an HTML document, so we will say a bit about HTML before we discuss applets.

Prerequisites

Section	Prerequisite
Section 13.1	None
Section 13.2	Chapters 1–7 and Section 13.1

web browser

To really get much benefit from this chapter, you should know how to use a net browser such as the Netscape Navigator or Microsoft's Internet Explorer. All the constructs discussed in this chapter produce things to be viewed via a net browser. We will assume that you have used a web browser to read something across the Internet, but will not assume that you know how to create things to be viewed on the Internet. Most readers could get sufficient experience by simply playing with a net browser without any instruction or reading. To get the full benefit of this chapter, you should also understand how path names are used on your operating system so that you can name a file that is contained in a different directory (different folder).

13.1 HTML

You shall see them on a beautiful quarto page, where a neat rivulet of text
shall meander through a meadow of margin.
RICHARD BRINSLEY SHERIDAN, *The School for Scandal*

hypertext

Documents designed to be read on the Internet, or through a web browser whether or not they are on the Internet, are typically written in a language called **HTML**. HTML stands for **Hypertext Markup Language. Hypertext** is simply text that contains items that you can click with your mouse and that will send you to another document. These connections from document to document are called **links,** or **hyperlinks.** The documents themselves are often called **pages,** which is why a person's or a company's main location on the Internet is called a **home page.** The terms **HTML document** and **HTML page** mean the same thing and simply refer to a hypertext document created with the HTML language. HTML is not a full-blown programming language like Java. HTML is just a collection of simple commands that you can insert into a page of text to convert it to something that can be viewed on a web browser. The commands allow you to insert pictures and hyperlinks in the page. They also allow you to write editing commands that specify what is a main heading, what is a subheading, a paragraph beginning, and so forth. In short, most of HTML is simply a language for copy editing a manuscript so it can be viewed on the Internet.

home page

This is not really a book on HTML programming, so we will only give you a small taste of the language. This will allow you to design some very simple documents for the Internet (or just for your browser), but if you want to become an expert in HTML, you should eventually go on to a book dedicated entirely to HTML.

HTML Basics

Most HTML commands are of the form

> *⟨Command⟩*
> **Some text**
> *⟨/Command⟩*

For example, the following makes the phrase "My Home Page" a number 1 heading, which is the largest standard heading.

```
<H1>
My Home Page
</H1>
```

⟨H1⟩

Notice that the notation *⟨/Command⟩*, in this example *⟨/H1⟩*, is used to mark the end of the text to which the command applies.

You can have smaller heads, called number 2 heads (command H2), and even smaller heads, called number 3 heads (command H3), and so forth.

⟨H2⟩

HTML Is Not Case-Sensitive

We will write our HTML commands in uppercase letters. However, HTML does not distinguish between uppercase and lowercase letters in commands, and so the commands would behave the same if expressed in lowercase letters. (Any text to be displayed as text to be read by the person viewing the document will, of course, display uppercase letters in uppercase and lowercase letters in lowercase.) ◻

Some commands do not require that they be closed with a command of the form *⟨/Command⟩*. One such command is

⟨BR⟩

```
<BR>
```

which is a command to begin a new line. Another is

<P>

```
<P>
```

which is a command to begin a new paragraph.

    Commands in HTML are not absolute commands that determine the exact size of a portion of text, or even the exact line breaks. You give a command for a number 1 head and you can reasonably assume that it will be bigger than a number 2 head, but the browser will determine the exact size of the text. You can force a line break by inserting the **break command:**

break

```
<BR>
```

If you write a large piece of text (or even sometimes a small amount of text), the browser will insert line breaks where it determines it is necessary to fit on the screen and where it thinks it "looks good," and it will ignore your line breaks unless they are indicated with the <BR> command.

<CENTER>

    You can make some layout specifications. For example, anything between the commands <CENTER> and </CENTER> will be centered on the page when it is displayed. For example, the following will center the number 1 head we discussed earlier:

```
<H1>
<CENTER>
My Home Page
</CENTER>
</H1>
```

or, if you prefer, it can also be written

```
<CENTER>
<H1>
My Home Page
</H1>
</CENTER>
```

HTML File Names

An HTML file is a regular text file that you create and edit with a text editor, just the way you write a Java program. HTML files should end with .html, but otherwise can be named using the same rules as those for all other files on your system.

◐ *PROGRAMMING TIP A Simple Document Outline*

Display 13.1 contains an outline for a simple HTML document. That display also illustrates how you write comments in HTML. For example,

```
<!--Beginning of HTML document-->
```

comments

is a comment. A comment begins with <!-- and ends with -->. We have used comments to explain the new HTML commands, but a real document would not have

Display 13.1 Outline of a Simple HTML Document

```
<HTML> <!--Beginning of HTML document-->
<HEAD> <!--Begin the document head-->
<TITLE> <!--Begin document title. Used for browser "book marks"-->
Title of document.
</TITLE> <!--End document title-->
</HEAD> <!--End the document head-->
<BODY> <!--Stuff to appear on screen begins here-->
<H1>
First main heading.
</H1>
Maybe some text.
<H2>
First subheading.
</H2>
Probably some text.
<H2>
Second subheading.
</H2>
Probably some text.
<H1>
Second main heading.
</H1>
And then more of the same.
    . . .
</BODY> <!--Regular stuff ends here, but ADDRESS is displayed-->
<ADDRESS> <!--Optional, but normally used-->
The Email address of the person maintaining the page.
Also, the date of the last time the page was changed.
(You can actually put in whatever you want here, but the
  Email address and date are what people expect.)
</ADDRESS>
</HTML> <!--End of HTML Document-->
```

A real HTML document should not have this many comments.

this many comments, nor would it explain basic HTML commands as we have done here.

The beginning and end of the entire document is enclosed in the pair <HTML> and </HTML>. The head of the document is enclosed in <HEAD> and </HEAD>. The head is not displayed when the document is viewed, but does record certain information that is used by a browser. In our document, it only records a title (enclosed in <TITLE> and </TITLE>). The title is used as a name for the document. For exam-

<HTML>
<HEAD>

<TITLE>

Display 13.2 A Very Simple HTML Document

```
<HTML>
<HEAD>
<TITLE>
Java Club Home Page
</TITLE>
</HEAD>
<BODY>
<H1>
<CENTER>
Java Club
</CENTER>
</H1>

<H2>
Club Purpose
</H2>
<P>
A major goal of the club is to encourage
its members to become good programmers,
<P>
The club provides a setting where people who
like to program in the Java language can meet
and talk with other like-minded programmers.

<H2>
Meeting Times
</H2>
The first Wednesday of each month at 7 PM.
<H2>
Sun Microsystems Java Web Site
</H2>
<A HREF="http://java.sun.com">
Click here for the web site
</A>
</BODY>

<P>
<ADDRESS>
javaclub.somemachine@someschool.edu
<BR>
January 1, 1999
</ADDRESS>
</HTML>
```

Blank lines are ignored when the document is displayed, but they can make your HTML code easier to read.

Text may have different line breaks when displayed on your browser.

A new paragraph will always produce a line break and some separation.

This is explained in the subsection entitled **Inserting Hyperlinks.**

Display 13.3 Browser View of Display 13.2

Your particular browser will probably use this space for its trademark as well as
buttons for basic browser operations.

Java Club

Club Purpose
A major goal of the club is to encourage its
members to become good programmers.

The club provides a setting where people who like
to program in the Java language can meet and talk
with other like-minded programmers.

Meeting Times
The first Wednesday of each month at 7 PM.

Sun Microsystems Java Web Site
Click here for the web site.

javaclub.somemachine@someschool.edu
January 1, 1999

ple, a browser will let you set a bookmark at a document so you can return to the
document at a later time. The bookmark will be named by this title.

The part of the document that is displayed on the screen is divided into two
parts. The **body** (enclosed in `<BODY>` and `</BODY>`) is the real content of the doc- `<BODY>`
ument. The other displayed part is enclosed in `<ADDRESS>` and `</ADDRESS>`, and `<ADDRESS>`
is optional. It is used to give an Email address to contact the document's owner and
usually includes the date that the document was last modified.

A very simple HTML document is shown in Display 13.2. The display that would
be shown when this is viewed on a browser is shown in Display 13.3. Remember that
the exact line breaks, size of letters, and other layout details are determined by the
particular browser, and so might look a little different on your browser. The portion
that discusses the Sun Microsystems web site is explained in the next subsection.

Inserting Hyperlinks

Well this is all nice, but would hardly be worth the effort if an HTML document did not also contain some active elements. The key active element is a link that the person viewing the document can click to view another HTML document. The other document may be on the same computer, or thousands of miles away. These links are called **hyperlinks,** or simply **links.**

hyperlink

The syntax for hyperlinks is as follows:

```
<A HREF="Path_To_Document">
Displayed_Text_To_Click
</A>
```

For example, a link to the author's home page would be as follows:

```
<A HREF="http://www-cse.ucsd.edu/users/savitch">
Walter Savitch
</A>
```

Be sure to include the quotation marks as shown. This link can be included in any text and this part of the text will be underlined (or otherwise highlighted) by the browser. In this example, if the person viewing the document clicks the text `Walter Savitch`, then the browser will display the author's home page. You can insert this in any document in any part of the world, and it will take you to La Jolla, California with a click of your mouse.

Display 13.2 shows an HTML document that includes a link to the Java web site of Sun Microsystems. If you view this HTML document with a browser, it will look approximately like Display 13.3. If the user clicks the text that is underlined, the browser will display Sun Microsystems's Java web site. (That is, it will display the HTML document on the company's computer that gives information about Java.)

? SELF-TEST QUESTIONS

1. What is the difference between the commands `<H2>` and `<h2>`?

2. How do you insert a link to the home page

   `http://www.fool.com/`

Automatic Documentation with `javadoc`

The Java language comes with a program named `javadoc` that can automatically generate documentation for your Java classes. The documentation that is produced by `javadoc` is an HTML document that you read with a browser, just like any other HTML document. The program `javadoc` is described in Appendix 4.

Inserting a Hyperlink

The command for inserting a hyperlink is as follows. This may appear inside any text:

Syntax:

```
<A HREF="Path_To_Document">
Displayed_Text_To_Click
</A>
```

Example:

```
<A HREF="http://java.sun.com">
Sun Microsystems Java web site
</A>
```

Either a full or relative path name or a link to any place on the Internet may be used to name the document file with *Path_To_Document*. If the person viewing the document clicks the *Displayed_Text_To_Click*, then the document in the file *Path_To_Document* will be displayed.

Displaying a Picture

For what we are doing in this chapter, we do not need pictures, but you might want to put a picture in your document. The command to insert a picture is as follows:

Syntax:

```
<IMG SRC="File_With_Picture">
```

Example:

```
<IMG SRC="images/mypicture.gif">
```

Either a full or relative path name may be used to name the file with the encoded picture. Various picture-encoding formats are accepted.

URL

The name of an HTML document on the Internet is called a **URL,** which is an abbreviation for **Uniform Resource Locator.** The name is a kind of path name for the Internet system, a system that covers the entire globe. The hyperlinks we described in this section are all URLs, such as

```
http://java.sun.com
```

URLs are absolute path names to documents that can be anywhere on the globe. You can also use relative path names for links to HTML documents on your own computer.

URLs often begin with http, which is the name of the protocol used to transfer and interpret the HTML document (but now we are getting beyond the scope of this book).

13.2 Applets

An applet a day keeps the doctor away.
ANONYMOUS

The word *applet* sounds like it refers to a small apple, but it is supposed to sound like a *small application.* Thus, applets are just "little Java programs," in some sense of the word *little.* However, the character of applets comes not from their size, but from how and where they are run. Applets are Java programs that can be embedded in an HTML document and can be run using a browser that views the document. An applet is very much like an AWT windowing system, and if you understand the AWT, then you will find it very easy to write applets. In this section, we will assume that you are already familiar with the AWT as described in Chapter 7. We will show you how to write simple applets with the same functionality as the windowing systems we covered in Chapter 7 (the AWT chapter). If you go on to learn more about Java, and Java graphics in particular, then you can add graphics to your applets, but that topic is beyond the scope of this book.

Applet Basics

An applet is a derived class of the class `Applet` (actually, any descendent class, but typically a directly derived class). The class `Applet` is not in the AWT, so you need to import the `Applet` class as follows

`java.` `applet.*`

```
import java.applet.*;
```

When you are writing an applet, you will also need the AWT library, so your full list of import statements are likely to be the following:

```
import java.applet.*;
import java.awt.*;
import java.awt.event.*;
```

Although the `Applet` class is not officially in the AWT, it is conceptually in the AWT, and aside from that new import statement, you can think of the `Applet` class as being part of the AWT. To be very specific, the class `Applet` is a derived class of the AWT `Panel` class. Display 13.4 shows a part of the class hierarchy to help you put the class `Applet` in context. Note that an `Applet` is both a container and a component. Thus, you can add things to an applet and you can add an applet to other containers. In this book, we will only add things to an applet and will not add applets to other containers.

An applet class can be designed very much the same way you design a windowing system using the AWT. The main difference is that you derive an applet class from the class `Applet` instead of the class `Frame`. Other differences between an applet class and an AWT windowing class mostly consist of things that are omitted from the applet class definition.

Applets do not need the `setVisible` method nor the `show` method. Applets are embedded in HTML documents and it is the HTML document that displays the applet. For this reason, an applet also normally does not have a `main` method. A trivially simple applet is shown in Display 13.5. When this applet is viewed (typically within an HTML document), it will simply display the text

```
Testing 1, 2, 3.
```

Display 13.4 Placing Applets in the Class Hierarchy
● ●

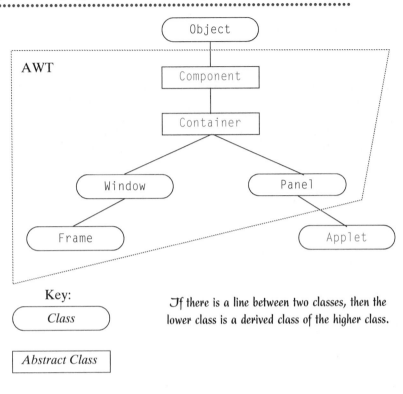

Key:

Class

*If there is a line between two classes, then the
lower class is a derived class of the higher class.*

Abstract Class

● ●

Note that an applet has a `paint` method, just like a `Frame` does, and that method   `paint`
serves the same basic purpose and is used in the same way as the `paint` method that
is used in a `Frame`.

Applets do not have titles, and so there is no need to use the `setTitle` method
in an applet. This is because applets normally go into HTML documents, and you
can insert the title in the HTML document that displays the applet. As we will see
in the next subsection, the HTML document also takes care of sizing the applet, so
you do not give any size instructions for an applet.

Applets do not normally use constructors, but they do use a method named
`init` that serves a similar purpose. When defining an applet, you place all the ini-   `init`
tializing actions, such as setting colors, adding buttons, adding text fields, and so
forth, in the method named `init`. The `init` method has no parameters.

Applets do not need to be closed with listeners, such as `WindowDestroyer`
shown in Display 7.2/page 332. When the HTML document is closed, that will automatically close the applet.

One way that applets differ from `Frame` classes is that an applet does not use
the same default layout managers as the class `Frame`. You should always explicitly
give layout mangers (with the `setLayout` method) when defining an applet.

Display 13.5 A Trivial Applet

```
import java.applet.*;
import java.awt.*;
import java.awt.event.*;

public class FirstApplet extends Applet
{
    public void paint(Graphics g)
    {
        g.drawString("Testing 1, 2, 3.", 10, 10);
    }
}
```

Applet View

```
        Testing 1, 2, 3.
```

The Applet **Class**

The Applet class is not officially part of the AWT, but for most practical purposes, it can be regarded as part of the AWT. The Applet class is a derived class of the AWT Panel class. This means, among other things, that an applet is both a container and a component. You can add things to an applet, in the same way that you add things to an AWT Frame. The definition of an applet normally contains the following import statements:

```
import java.applet.*;
import java.awt.*;
import java.awt.event.*;
```

For example, Display 13.6 contains an applet that will produce an adding machine window that is essentially the same as the one we produced in Chapter 7 (Display 7.17/page 382). The details are almost identical to those in the AWT class we defined in Display 7.17.

Running an Applet

applet viewer

The normal way to run an applet is from an HTML document, but if you want to test out an applet, you can run it using an *applet viewer.* An **applet viewer** is basically a program that automatically puts your applet in a simple HTML page and then runs

Display 13.6 An Applet Adding Machine *(Part 1 of 2)*

```java
import java.applet.*;
import java.awt.*;
import java.awt.event.*;

public class AdderApplet extends Applet implements ActionListener
{
    public void init()
    {
        setLayout(new BorderLayout());
        Panel buttonPanel = new Panel();
        buttonPanel.setBackground(Color.gray);
        buttonPanel.setLayout(new FlowLayout());
        Button addButton = new Button("Add In");
        addButton.addActionListener(this);
        buttonPanel.add(addButton);
        Button clearButton = new Button("Clear");
        clearButton.addActionListener(this);
        buttonPanel.add(clearButton);
        add(buttonPanel, "South");
        Panel textPanel = new Panel();
        textPanel.setBackground(Color.blue);
        inputOutputField = new TextField("Numbers go here.", 20);
        inputOutputField.setBackground(Color.white);
        textPanel.add(inputOutputField);
        add(textPanel, "Center");
    }

    public void actionPerformed(ActionEvent e)
    {
        if (e.getActionCommand().equals("Add In"))
        {
            sum = sum +
                stringToDouble(inputOutputField.getText());
            inputOutputField.setText(Double.toString(sum));
        }
        else if (e.getActionCommand().equals("Clear"))
        {
            sum = 0;
            inputOutputField.setText("0.0");
        }
        else
            inputOutputField.setText("Error in adder code.");

        repaint();
    }
```

Display 13.6 An Applet Adding Machine *(Part 2 of 2)*

```
private static double stringToDouble(String stringObject)
{
    return Double.valueOf(stringObject.trim()).doubleValue();
}


private TextField inputOutputField;
private double sum = 0;
}
```

The GUI display produced by this program is shown in Display 13.7.

it from there. However, an applet viewer makes it look like an applet is run just like any other program. If you are using an integrated environment that has a menu command called "Run" or "Execute," or something similar that you use to run an application program (i.e., to run an ordinary Java program), then you can probably run an applet just like you run an ordinary Java application program. Most environments will automatically call an applet viewer when your use them to run an applet class. If that does not work, you may have an applet viewer named (appropriately enough) `appletviewer`, which can be run as a one-line command. For example, the applet in Display 13.6 would be run as follows:

```
appletviewer AdderApplet.html
```

However, if you run an applet with a one-line command in this way, you may need to create an HTML document yourself (named `AdderApplet.html` in this example) and place the Applet in the HTML document. The details of placing an applet in an HTML document are described in the next subsection.

If you run the applet in Display 13.6 in an applet viewer, the result will look similar to Display 13.7.

Placing an Applet in an HTML Document

If you place the following command in an HTML document, then the document will display the adder window created by the applet in Display 13.6/page 685:

```
<APPLET CODE="AdderApplet.class" WIDTH=300 HEIGHT=200>
</APPLET>
```

This assumes that the HTML file and the file `AdderApplet.class` are in the same directory (same folder). If they are not in the same directory (same folder), then you would use an absolute or relative path name for the class `AdderApplet.class`. An expression such as the one previously displayed is often called an **applet tag.**

applet tag

Display 13.7 Display 13.6 Run with an Applet Viewer

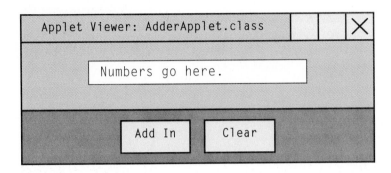

For example, Display 13.8 contains a sample HTML document that includes the applet given in Display 13.6/page 685. When displayed with a browser, this HTML document would look approximately as shown in Display 13.9.

Notice that when you place an applet in an HTML document, you give the name of the byte-code file that ends in `.class`, rather than the `.java` or other file name. Also, notice that you specify the width and height of the applet in this command and not within the applet class definition.

sizing an applet

Applets in HTML Documents

You place an applet in an HTML document as shown in what follows. You use the byte-code (`.class`) file of the applet. If the file is not in the same directory (same folder) as the HTML document, you can use either a full or relative path name to the applet file. The width and height are given in pixels.

Syntax:

```
<APPLET CODE="Name_Of_.class_File" WIDTH=Integer HEIGHT=Integer>
</APPLET>
```

Example:

```
<APPLET CODE="AdderApplet.class" WIDTH=300 HEIGHT=200>
</APPLET>
```

⚠ GOTCHA Using an Old Web Browser

Your web browser must be set up to run applets. The web browser does not use the same interpreter that is used to run an application. If you have an old web browser that is not set up for applets or that is only set up for applets from an earlier version of Java, then you may not be able to run applets from an HTML document, and this can be true even if Java applications run fine on your system. In such cases, all you can do is obtain a new browser.

Display 13.8 An HTML Document with an Applet

```
<HTML>
<HEAD>
<TITLE>
Budget Help
</TITLE>
</HEAD>

<BODY>
<H1>
The Budget Help Home Page
<BR>
Helpful Hints for a Balanced Budget
</H1>

<H2>
Pay off your credit cards every month.
</H2>

<H2>
Do not spend more than you earn.
</H2>

<H2>
Here is an adder to help you plan your budget:
</H2>
<APPLET CODE="AdderApplet.class" WIDTH=300 HEIGHT=200>
</APPLET>
<P>
</BODY>

<P>
<ADDRESS>
budgethelp@fleeceyou.com
<BR>
December 31, 1999
</ADDRESS>
</HTML>
```

Display 13.9 Browser View of Display 13.8

Your particular browser will probably use this space for its trademark as well as
buttons for basic browser operations.

The Budget Help Home Page
Helpful Hints for a Balanced Budget

Pay off your credit cards every month.

Do not spend more than you earn.

Here is an adder to help you plan your budget:

Numbers go here.

Add In   Clear

budgethelp@fleeceyou.com
December 31, 1999

◑ PROGRAMMING TIP *Converting an AWT Application to an Applet*

It is easy to convert an AWT application to an applet. In most cases, all that you need do is to follow the simple instructions that follow:

1. Add the following to the top of the program file:

   import java.applet.*;

   Typically, this means the file will begin with

   import java.applet.*;
   import java.awt.*;
   import java.awt.event.*;

2. Derive the class from the class Applet instead of deriving it from the class Frame. That is, replace *extends* Frame with *extends* Applet on the first line of the class definition.

3. Remove the main method. An applet does not need the things that are typically placed in main. An applet is automatically made visible and its size and location are determined by the HTML page from which it is run.

4. Remove all reference to listeners that close the window, such as WindowDe-stroyer shown in Display 7.2/page 332. When the HTML document is closed, that will automatically close the applet.

5. Replace all menu items with buttons or some other device. Applets do not have a menu bar and so cannot easily contain menus.

6. Replace the constructor with a method named init. The init method can be the same as the constructor, but with some items deleted. Delete any invocation of setTitle. (Applets have no titles, although you can put a title on the HTML page.) Delete any sizing or positioning of the window. (That is done by the HTML page from which the applet is run.) Be sure that you always explicitly specify a layout manager and do not rely on default layout managers. Applets require explicitly given layout managers.

7. Make an HTML page with an APPLET tag that refers to the byte-code (.class) version of the applet.

For example, the applet in Display 13.6 was obtained from the AWT application in Display 7.17/page 382 by following these rules.

? SELF-TEST QUESTIONS

3. Is the class Applet derived from a class in the AWT? If so, which class?

4. Do you normally include constructors in an applet class definition?

5. Is it normal for an applet class to have a main method?

6. When you list an applet in an HTML document, do you list the .java file or the .class file?

Chapter Summary

- ☐ Documents designed to be read across the Internet or through a web browser are typically written in a language called HTML. HTML stands for Hypertext Markup Language

- ☐ Applets are Java programs designed to be placed in and run from an HTML document.

- ☐ Applets are derived from the class `Applet` and are similar to AWT GUIs derived from the class `Frame`.

? ANSWERS to Self-Test Questions

1. None. HTML is not case-sensitive.

2.
```
<A HREF="http://www.fool.com/">
Any thing you want to say.
</A>
```

3. The class `Applet` is a derived class of the AWT class `Panel`. Among other things, that means that an `Applet` is both a `Component` and a `Container`.

4. Applet classes do not usually use constructors. However, they do use a method named `init` that serves a similar purpose.

5. Applet classes do not normally have a `main` method.

6. The `.class` file.

? PROGRAMMING EXERCISES

1. Design an HTML home page for yourself. Use your imagination to put in whatever you would like people to know about you or that you think they should know about you. Some possibilities are your name, your occupation or class schedule, where you go to school or work, your hobbies, your favorite quotation, how to reach you by Email, and/or anything you like. Note that your home page, as any home page, will consist of several files, each of which contains HTML documents. The hyperlinks allow the person viewing the document to move from one HTML document to another by clicking with a mouse. Variations: If you are in a class, ask your instructor whether or not you need to include an applet on your home page.

2. Convert the AWT application in Display 7.14/page 369 to an applet and place it in an HTML document.

Appendix 1
RESERVED WORDS

Reserved words are also called *keywords*. You may not redefine any of these reserved words. Their meanings are determined by the Java language and cannot be changed. In particular, you cannot use any of these reserved words for variable names, method names, or class names.

abstract	generic	rest
	goto	return
boolean		
break	if	short
byte	implements	static
	import	super
case	inner	switch
catch	instanceof	synchronized
char	int	
class	interface	this
const		throw
continue	long	throws
		transient
default	native	try
do	new	
double	null	var
		void
else	operator	volatile
extends	outer	
		while
final	package	
finally	private	
float	protected	
for	public	
future		

Appendix 2
SAVITCHIN

```java
import java.io.*;
import java.util.*;


/*************************************************************
 *Class for simple console input.
 *A class designed primarily for simple keyboard input of the form
 *one input value per line. If the user enters an improper input,
 *i.e., an input of the wrong type or a blank line, then the user
 *is prompted to reenter the input and given a brief explanation
 *of what is required. Also includes some additional methods to
 *input single numbers, words, and characters, without going to
 *the next line.
 *************************************************************/
public class SavitchIn
{

    /*********************************************************
     *Reads a line of text and returns that line as a String value.
     *The end of a line must be indicated either by a new-line
     *character '\n' or by a carriage return '\r' followed by a
     *new-line character '\n'. (Almost all systems do this
     *automatically. So, you need not worry about this detail.)
     *Neither the '\n', nor the '\r' if present, are part of the
     *string returned. This will read the rest of a line if the
     *line is already partially read.
     *********************************************************/
    public static String readLine()
    {
        char nextChar;
        String result = "";
        boolean done = false;
```

```
        while (!done)
        {
            nextChar = readChar();
            if (nextChar == '\n')
                done = true;
            else if (nextChar == '\r')
            {
                //Do nothing.
                //Next loop iteration will detect '\n'
            }
            else
                result = result + nextChar;
        }

        return result;
    }


    /**********************************************************
     *Reads the first string of nonwhite characters on a line and
     *returns that string. The rest of the line is discarded. If
     *the line contains only white space, then the user is asked
     *to reenter the line.
     **********************************************************/
    public static String readLineWord()
    {
        String inputString = null,
               result = null;
        boolean done = false;

        while(!done)
        {
            inputString = readLine();
            StringTokenizer wordSource =
                            new StringTokenizer(inputString);
            if (wordSource.hasMoreTokens())
            {
                result = wordSource.nextToken();
                done = true;
            }
```

```
        else
        {
            System.out.println(
                "Your input is not correct. Your input must");
            System.out.println(
              "contain at least one nonwhitespace character.");
            System.out.println(
                          "Please, try again. Enter input:");
        }
    }

    return result;
}


/***********************************************************
 *Precondition: The user has entered a number of type int on
 *a line by itself, except that there may be white space before
 *and/or after the number.
 *Action: Reads and returns the number as a value of type int.
 *The rest of the line is discarded. If the input is not
 *entered correctly, then in most cases, the user will be
 *asked to reenter the input. In particular, this applies to
 *incorrect number formats and blank lines.
 ***********************************************************/
public static int readLineInt()
{
    String inputString = null;
    int number = -9999;//To keep the compiler happy.
                       //Designed to look like a garbage value.
    boolean done = false;

    while (! done)
    {
        try
        {
            inputString = readLine();
            inputString = inputString.trim();
            number = (Integer.valueOf(inputString).intValue());
            done = true;
        }
```

```
            catch (NumberFormatException e)
            {
                System.out.println(
                            "Your input number is not correct.");
                System.out.println("Your input number must be");
                System.out.println("a whole number written as an");
                System.out.println("ordinary numeral, such as 42");
                System.out.println("Please, try again.");
                System.out.println("Enter a whole number:");
            }
        }

    return number;
}


/******************************************************************
*Precondition: The user has entered a number of type long on
*a line by itself, except that there may be white space
*before and/or after the number.
*Action: Reads and returns the number as a value of type
*long. The rest of the line is discarded. If the input is not
*entered correctly, then in most cases, the user will be asked
*to reenter the input. In particular, this applies to
*incorrect number formats and blank lines.
******************************************************************/
public static long readLineLong()
{
    String inputString = null;
    long number = -9999;//To keep the compiler happy.
                        //Designed to look like a garbage value.
    boolean done = false;

    while (! done)
    {
        try
        {
            inputString = readLine();
            inputString = inputString.trim();
            number = (Long.valueOf(inputString).longValue());
            done = true;
        }
```

```
        catch (NumberFormatException e)
        {
            System.out.println(
                        "Your input number is not correct.");
            System.out.println("Your input number must be");
            System.out.println("a whole number written as an");
            System.out.println("ordinary numeral, such as 42");
            System.out.println("Please, try again.");
            System.out.println("Enter a whole number:");
        }
    }

    return number;
}


/*************************************************************
*Precondition: The user has entered a number of type double
*on a line by itself, except that there may be white space
*before and/or after the number.
*Action: Reads and returns the number as a value of type
*double. The rest of the line is discarded. If the input is
*not entered correctly, then in most cases, the user will be
*asked to reenter the input. In particular, this applies to
*incorrect number formats and blank lines.
*************************************************************/
public static double readLineDouble()
{
    String inputString = null;
    double number = -9999;//To keep the compiler happy.
                        //Designed to look like a garbage value.
    boolean done = false;

    while (! done)
    {
        try
        {
            inputString = readLine();
            inputString = inputString.trim();
            number =
            (Double.valueOf(inputString).doubleValue());
            done = true;
        }
```

```
        catch (NumberFormatException e)
        {
            System.out.println(
                        "Your input number is not correct.");
            System.out.println("Your input number must be");
            System.out.println("an ordinary number either with");
            System.out.println("or without a decimal point,");
            System.out.println("such as 42 or 9.99");
            System.out.println("Please, try again.");
            System.out.println("Enter a whole number:");
        }
    }

    return number;
}


/*************************************************************
*Precondition: The user has entered a number of type float
*on a line by itself, except that there may be white space
*before and/or after the number.
*Action: Reads and returns the number as a value of type
*float. The rest of the line is discarded. If the input is
*not entered correctly, then in most cases, the user will
*be asked to reenter the input. In particular,
*this applies to incorrect number formats and blank lines.
**************************************************************/
public static float readLineFloat()
{
    String inputString = null;
    float number = -9999;//To keep the compiler happy.
                        //Designed to look like a garbage value.
    boolean done = false;

    while (! done)
    {
        try
        {
            inputString = readLine();
            inputString = inputString.trim();
            number = (Float.valueOf(inputString).floatValue());
            done = true;
        }
```

```
        catch (NumberFormatException e)
        {
            System.out.println(
                        "Your input number is not correct.");
            System.out.println("Your input number must be");
            System.out.println("an ordinary number either with");
            System.out.println("or without a decimal point,");
            System.out.println("such as 42 or 9.99");
            System.out.println("Please, try again.");
            System.out.println("Enter a whole number:");
        }
    }

    return number;
}


/**************************************************************
*Reads the first nonwhite character on a line and returns
*that character. The rest of the line is discarded. If the
*line contains only white space, then the user is asked to
*reenter the line.
**************************************************************/
public static char readLineNonwhiteChar()
{
    boolean done = false;
    String inputString = null;
    char nonWhite = ' ';//To keep the compiler happy.

    while (! done)
    {
        inputString = readLine();
        inputString = inputString.trim();
        if (inputString.length() == 0)
        {
            System.out.println(
                        "Your input is not correct.");
            System.out.println("Your input must contain at");
            System.out.println(
                        "least one nonwhitespace character.");
            System.out.println("Please, try again.");
            System.out.println("Enter input:");
        }
```

```
        else
        {
            nonWhite = (inputString.charAt(0));
            done = true;
        }
    }

    return nonWhite;
}


/**************************************************************
 *Input should consist of a single word on a line, possibly
 *surrounded by white space.  The line is read and discarded.
 *If the input word is "true" or "t", then true is returned.
 *If the input word is "false" or "f", then false is returned.
 *Uppercase and lowercase letters are considered equal. If the
 *user enters anything else (e.g., multiple words or different
 *words), then the user is asked to reenter the input.
 **************************************************************/
public static boolean readLineBoolean()
{
    boolean done = false;
    String inputString = null;
    boolean result = false;//To keep the compiler happy.

    while (! done)
    {
        inputString = readLine();
        inputString = inputString.trim();
        if (inputString.equalsIgnoreCase("true")
                || inputString.equalsIgnoreCase("t"))
        {
            result = true;
            done = true;
        }
        else if (inputString.equalsIgnoreCase("false")
                    || inputString.equalsIgnoreCase("f"))
        {
            result = false;
            done = true;
        }
```

```
        else
        {
            System.out.println(
                            "Your input number is not correct.");
            System.out.println("Your input number must be");
            System.out.println("one of the following:");
            System.out.println("the word true,");
            System.out.println("the word false,");
            System.out.println("the letter T,");
            System.out.println("or the letter F.");
            System.out.println("You may use either uppercase");
            System.out.println("or lowercase letters.");
            System.out.println("Please, try again.");
            System.out.println("Enter input:");
        }
    }

    return result;
}


/*****************************************************************
 *Reads the next input character and            that character     th
 *next read takes place on the same   in        th      this one   to
 *****************************************************************/
public static char readChar()
{
    int charAsInt = -1; //To keep the compiler happy
    try
    {
        charAsInt = System.in.read();
    }
    catch(IOException e)
    {
        System.out.println(e.getMessage());
        System.out.println("Fatal error. Ending Program.");
        System.exit(0);
    }

    return (char)charAsInt;
}
```

```
/*************************************************************
 *Reads the next nonwhite input character and returns that
 *character. The next read takes place immediately after
 *the character read.
 *************************************************************/
public static char readNonwhiteChar()
{
  char next;

  next =  readChar();
  while (Character.isWhitespace(next))
      next =  readChar();

  return next;
}



/*************************************************************
 *The following methods are not used in the text, except for
 *a brief reference in Chapter 2. No program code uses them.
 *However, some programmers may want to use them.
 *************************************************************/



/*************************************************************
 *Precondition: The next input in the stream consists of an
 *int value, possibly preceded by white space, but definitely
 *followed by white space.
 *Action: Reads the first string of nonwhite characters
 *and returns the int value it represents. Discards the first
 *whitespace character after the word. The next read takes
 *place immediately after the discarded whitespace.
 *In particular, if the word is at the end of a line, the
 *next reading will take place starting on the next line.
 *If the next word does not represent an int value,
 *a NumberFormatException is thrown.
 *************************************************************/
public static int readInt() throws NumberFormatException
{
    String inputString = null;
    inputString = readWord();
    return (Integer.valueOf(inputString).intValue());
}
```

```
/*************************************************************
 *Precondition: The next input consists of a long value,
 *possibly preceded by white space, but definitely
 *followed by white space.
 *Action: Reads the first string of nonwhite characters and
 *returns the long value it represents. Discards the first
 *whitespace character after the string read. The next read
 *takes place immediately after the discarded whitespace.
 *In particular, if the string read is at the end of a line,
 *the next reading will take place starting on the next line.
 *If the next word does not represent a long value,
 *a NumberFormatException is thrown.
 *************************************************************/
public static long readLong()
                 throws NumberFormatException
{
    String inputString = null;
    inputString = readWord();
    return (Long.valueOf(inputString).longValue());
}


/*************************************************************
 *Precondition: The next input consists of a double value,
 *possibly preceded by white space, but definitely
 *followed by white space.
 *Action: Reads the first string of nonwhitespace characters
 *and returns the double value it represents. Discards the
 *first whitespace character after the string read. The next
 *read takes place immediately after the discarded whitespace.
 *In particular, if the string read is at the end of a line,
 *the next reading will take place starting on the next line.
 *If the next word does not represent a double value,
 *a NumberFormatException is thrown.
 *************************************************************/
public static double readDouble()
                 throws NumberFormatException
{
    String inputString = null;
    inputString = readWord();
    return (Double.valueOf(inputString).doubleValue());
}
```

```
/*************************************************************
 *Precondition: The next input consists of a float value,
 *possibly preceded by white space, but definitely
 *followed by white space.
 *Action: Reads the first string of nonwhite characters and
 *returns the float value it represents. Discards the first
 *whitespace character after the string read. The next read
 *takes place immediately after the discarded whitespace.
 *In particular, if the string read is at the end of a line,
 *the next reading will take place starting on the next line.
 *If the next word does not represent a float value,
 *a NumberFormatException is thrown.
 *************************************************************/
public static float readFloat()
                      throws NumberFormatException
{
    String inputString = null;
    inputString = readWord();
    return (Float.valueOf(inputString).floatValue());
}



/*************************************************************
 *Reads the first string of nonwhite characters and returns
 *that string. Discards the first whitespace character after
 *the string read. The next read takes place immediately after
 *the  discarded whitespace. In particular, if the string
 *read is at the end of a line, the next reading will take
 *place starting on the next line. Note, that if it receives
 *blank lines, it will wait until it gets a nonwhitespace
 *character.
 *************************************************************/
public static String readWord()
{
    String result = "";
    char next;

    next =  readChar();
    while (Character.isWhitespace(next))
        next =  readChar();

    while (!(Character.isWhitespace(next)))
    {
        result = result + next;
        next =  readChar();
    }
```

```
    if (next == '\r')
    {
        next = readChar();
        if (next != '\n')
        {
            System.out.println(
                "Fatal Error in method readWord of class SavitchIn.");
            System.exit(1);
        }
    }

    return result;
}


//The following was intentionally not used in the code for
//other methods so that somebody reading the code could more
//quickly see what was being used.
/************************************************************
 *Reads the first byte in the input stream and returns that
 *byte as an int. The next read takes place where this one
 *left off. This read is the same as System.in.read(),
 *except that it catches IOExceptions.
 ************************************************************/
public static int read()
{
    int result = -1; //To keep the compiler happy
    try
    {
        result = System.in.read();
    }
    catch(IOException e)
    {
        System.out.println(e.getMessage());
        System.out.println("Fatal error. Ending Program.");
        System.exit(0);
    }
    return result;
}
}
```

Appendix 3
ASCII Character Set

· ·

Character number 32 is the blank. Only the printable characters are shown in the table.

32		56	8	80	P	104	h
33	!	57	9	81	Q	105	i
34	"	58	:	82	R	106	j
35	#	59	;	83	S	107	k
36	$	60	<	84	T	108	l
37	%	61	=	85	U	109	m
38	&	62	>	86	V	110	n
39	'	63	?	87	W	111	o
40	(	64	@	88	X	112	p
41	)	65	A	89	Y	113	q
42	*	66	B	90	Z	114	r
43	+	67	C	91	[	115	s
44	,	68	D	92	\	116	t
45	–	69	E	93	]	117	u
46	.	70	F	94	^	118	v
47	/	71	G	95	_	119	w
48	0	72	H	96	`	120	x
49	1	73	I	97	a	121	y
50	2	74	J	98	b	122	z
51	3	75	K	99	c	123	{
52	4	76	L	100	d	124		
53	5	77	M	101	e	125	}
54	6	78	N	102	f	126	~
55	7	79	O	103	g		

Appendix 4
javadoc

The Java language comes with a program named javadoc that will automatically generate HTML documents that describe your classes. This documentation tells somebody who uses your program or class what she or he needs to know in order to use it, but omits all the implementation details, such as the bodies of all method definitions (both public and private), all information about private methods, and all private instance variables.

In order to use javadoc to generate documentation for some classes, the classes must be in a package or packages. Packages are discussed in Chapter 5. You also need to have access to an HTML browser (a web browser) so that you can view the documents produced by javadoc. However, you do not need to know very much HTML in order to use javadoc. Chapter 13 contains more HTML than you need to know in order to use javadoc.

In this appendix, we will first discuss how you should comment your classes so that you can get the most value out of javadoc. We will then discus the details of how you run the javadoc program.

Commenting Classes for Use with javadoc

To get a more useful javadoc document, you must give your comments in a particular way. All the classes in this book have been commented for use with javadoc.

The program javadoc will extract the heading for your class as well as the headings for all public methods, and if the comments are done correctly, certain comments. No method bodies and no private items are extracted.

For javadoc to extract a comment, the comment must satisfy three conditions:

1. The comment must be *immediately preceding* a public class definition or a public method definition (or other public item).
2. The comment must be given by a /* and */ style comment and the opening /* must contain an extra *. So, the comment must be marked by /** at the beginning and */ at the end.
3. Each line of the comment must begin with an *.

Placing extra *'s is both allowed and common. Using a boxlike arrangement, as we have done in this book, will produce comments of the correct form. For example, if javadoc is run on the class SavitchIn in Appendix 2, the resulting HTML document can be viewed on a browser and will contain all the text shown in color in Appendix 2. None of the black text will be in the HTML document. The layout of the text will be a bit different than it is in the class definition file, but it will be similar.

You can insert HTML commands in your comments so that you gain more control over `javadoc`, but that is not necessary and may not even be desirable. The HTML commands in comments can clutter the comments when you look at the source file that contains the complete class definition.

Running `javadoc`

You run `javadoc` on an entire package. However, if you want to run it on a single class, you can make the class into a package simply by inserting the following at the start of the `.java` file for the class:

> `package` *Package_Name*;

Remember that the *Package_Name* should describe a relative path name for the directory containing the `.java` file for the class(es). The details on directory placement and package names are given in Section 5.5 of Chapter 5. (Directories are called *folders* in some operating systems. If your system has folders, they are the same as what we are calling *directories.*)

To run `javadoc`, you must be in the directory that *contains* the package directory, not in the package directory itself. To phrase it another way, you must be one directory above the directory that contains the class (or classes) for which you want to generate documentation. Then, all you need to do is give the following command:

> `javadoc -d` *Document_Directory Package_Name*

The *Document_Directory* is the name of the directory in which you want `javadoc` to place the HTML documents it produces. For example, *Document_Directory* can simply be the name of a subdirectory of where you are when you run the preceding command. The directory must already exist; `javadoc` will not create the directory for you.

For example, suppose you want to generate documentation for the class `SavitchIn` using `javadoc`. First, go to a directory on your CLASSPATH. (CLASSPATH is discussed in the subsection **Package Names and Directories** on page 280 of Chapter 5.) Create a subdirectory to hold a package; for example, you might call the subdirectory `ExtraSavitchStuff`. Place the file `SavitchIn.java` in the directory `ExtraSavitchStuff`, and place the following at the start of the file `SavitchIn.java`:

> `package` `ExtraSavitchStuff`;

You have now set up the package `ExtraSavitchStuff` so that it contains the class `SavitchIn`.

Next, create a directory to receive the HTML documents. For example, you might call this directory `SavitchDocs`. Make the directory a subdirectory of the same directory as the one containing `ExtraSavitchStuff`. (Do not make it a subdirectory of `ExtraSavitchStuff`.)

Finally, be sure you are in the directory such that both ExtraSavitchStuff and SavitchDocs are subdirectories of where you are, and give the following command:

```
javadoc -d SavitchDocs ExtraSavitchStuff
```

If you then look in the subdirectory SavitchDocs, you will see a number of HTML documents (files ending in .html). You can view these files using your browser. The HTML documents will describe the package ExtraSavitchStuff, including the class SavitchIn, which is probably all you have in the package.

If you wish, you can use the directory ExtraSavitchStuff in place of SavitchDocs so that both the source file SavitchIn.java and the HTML documents end up in the same directory.

This may seem like a lot of work just to get documentation consisting of the source file with some stuff deleted. However, if you are setting up the package as a library that can be imported into any class or program definition, then you need to do most of this work anyway. Moreover, once you get used to it, it's pretty easy, and best of all, it produces great documentation.

Adding the Icon Pictures

If you generate HTML documents the way we outlined, then you may find that your browser indicates that some art is missing. These are some standard icons used in the documentation for the predefined Java classes. If you can view the HTML documentation for predefined Java classes and there is no art missing, then you have these images. Look for them in a directory whose path name ends with

```
...\java\api\images
```

or

```
.../java/api/images
```

(depending on how your operating system writes path names).

The HTML documents generated by javadoc expects to find these pictures in a subdirectory called images. You can create a suitable subdirectory called images and copy all the picture files into this subdirectory.

Appendix 5
BEYOND PUBLIC AND PRIVATE

. . . .

We have always used one of the modifiers *public* and *private* before instance variables and before method definitions. Normally, those are the only modifiers you need, but there are two other possibilities that give restrictions whose severity is in between the two extremes of *public* and *private*. In this appendix, we discuss the modifier *protected* as well as the restriction that applies when you use no modifier at all.

If a method or instance variable is modified by *protected* (rather than *public* or *private*), then it can be directly accessed inside of its own class definition and it can be directly accessed inside of any class of which it is a parent (i.e., any class derived from it). If an instance variable or method definition is marked *protected*, then not only can it be accessed directly in the definition of any derived class, but it can also be accessed directly in any method definition for any class in the same package. That is the extent of the access. The *protected* method or instance variable cannot be directly accessed in any other classes. Thus, if a method is marked *protected* in class A and class B is derived from class A, then the method can be used inside any method definition in class B. However, in a class that is not in the same package as A and is not derived from A, it is as if the *protected* method were *private*.

The modifier *protected* is a peculiar sort of restriction, since it allows direct access to any programmer who is willing to go through the bother of defining a suitable derived class. Thus, it is like saying, "I'll make it difficult for you to use this, but I will not forbid you to use this." In practice, instance variables should never be marked *protected*. On very rare occasions, you may want to have a method marked *protected*. If you want an access intermediate between *public* and *private*, then the access described in the next paragraph is often a preferable alternative.

You may have noticed that if you forget to place one of the modifiers *public* or *private* before an instance variable or method definition, then your class definition will still compile. If you do not place any of the modifiers *public*, *private*, or *protected* before an instance variable or method definition, then the instance variable or method can be directly accessed inside the definition of any class in the same package, but not outside of the package. This is called **package access**, or **default access.** You use package access in situations where you have a package of cooperating classes that act as a single encapsulated unit. Note that package access is more restricted than *protected*, and that package access gives more control to the programmer defining the classes. If you control the package directory, then you control who is allowed package access.

Appendix 6
CLONING

. . . .

A clone of an object is (or at least should be) an exact copy of an object. The emphasis here is on both *exact* and *copy*. A clone should look like it has the exact same data values as the object being copied, and the clone should be a true copy and not simply another name for the object being copied. In Chapter 5 in Section 5.4 entitled **Information Hiding Revisited,** we discussed some of the problems involved in making copies of an object. You should read that section before reading this appendix.

A clone is made by invoking the method named `clone`. The method `clone` is invoked, just like any other method. The heading for the method `clone` is as follows:

```
public Object clone()
```

Although, the method `clone` returns a copy of an object of some class, it always returns it as an object of type `Object`. So, you normally need a type cast. For example, consider the class `PetRecord` in Display 5.12/page 269 of Chapter 5. After you make suitable additions to the class definition, you can make a copy of an object of type `PetRecord` as follows:

```
PetRecord original = new PetRecord("Fido", 2, 5.6);
PetRecord extraCopy = (PetRecord)original.clone();
```

Be sure to notice the type cast `(PetRecord)`.

The above invocation of `clone` (or any invocation of `clone`) will not work unless the class implements the `Cloneable` interface. Thus, in order to make the preceding code work, you must do two things. First, you must change the beginning of the class definition for `PetRecord` to the following:

```
public class PetRecord implements Cloneable
```

Second, you must add a definition of the method `clone` to the class definition. In the case of the class `PetRecord`, the method `clone` would be defined as shown in Display A6.1.

If the instance variables are all of types whose objects cannot be changed by its methods, such as the primitive types and the type `String`, then the above definition of `clone` shown in Display A6.1 will work fine. In that definition of `clone`, the method `clone` invokes the version of `clone` in the class `Object`, which simply makes a bit-by-bit copy of the memory used to store the calling object's instance variables. The *try-catch* blocks are required because the method `clone` can throw the exception `CloneNotSupportedException`, if the class does not implement the `Cloneable` interface. Of course, in these classes, we are implementing the `Clone-`

Display A6.1 Implementation of the Method `clone` **(Simple Case)**

```
public Object clone()
{
    try
    {
        return super.clone();//Invocation of clone in class Object
    }
    catch(CloneNotSupportedException e)
    {//This should not happen
        return null; //To keep the compiler happy.
    }
}
```

Works correctly if each instance variables is of a primitive type or of the type `String`. Does not work correctly in most other cases.

`able` interface so the exception will never be thrown, but the compiler will still insist on the `try-catch` blocks. There is a bit of detail to worry about here, but as long as each instance variable is either of a primitive type or of type `String`, then the definition of `clone` in Display A6.1 will work just fine and can simply be copied unchanged into your class definition.

If your class has instance variables of a class type (other than a class like `String` whose objects cannot change), then the definition of `clone` in Display A6.1 is legal, but it probably does not do what you want a `clone` method to do. If the class contains instance variables of some class type, then the clone produced will have a copy of the instance variable's memory address, rather than a copy of the instance variable's data. For a class like `String` that cannot be changed, this is not a problem. For most other classes, this would allow access to private data in the way we described in Chapter 5 in Section 5.4 entitled **Information Hiding Revisited**. When defining a `clone` method for a class that has instance variables of a class type (other than the type `String` or similar unchangeable class types), your definition of `clone` should make a clone of each instance variable of a changeable class type. Of course, this requires that those class types for the instance variables do themselves have a suitable `clone` method. The way to define such a `clone` method is illustrated in Display A6.2. Let's go over some of the details in that definition of that `clone` method.

Display A6.2 Outline of a Class with Cloning
••

```
public class Neighbor implements Cloneable
{
    public Object clone()
    {
        try
        {
            Neighbor copy = (Neighbor)super.clone();
            copy.pet = (PetRecord)pet.clone();
            return copy;
        }
        catch(CloneNotSupportedException e)
        {//This should not happen
            return null; //To keep the compiler happy.
        }
    }
```

<There are presumably other methods that are not shown.>

```
    private String name;
    private int numberOfChildren;
    private PetRecord pet;
}
```

••

The following line makes a bit-by-bit copy of the memory used to store the calling object's instance variables:

```
    Neighbor copy = (Neighbor)super.clone();
```

That sort of copy works fine for the instance variable `numberOfChildren`, which is of the primitive type `int`. It is also satisfactory for the instance variable `name` of type `String`. However, the value it gives to the instance variable `copy.pet` is the address of the `pet` instance variable of the calling object. It does not, as yet, give `copy.pet` the address of a *copy* of the calling object's `pet` instance variable. To change the value of `copy.pet` so that it names a copy of the calling object's `pet` instance variable, the `clone` method definition goes on to do the following:

```
    copy.pet = (PetRecord)pet.clone();
```

INDEX

Symbols

- - *see* decrement operator
! 90
!= 89
" 55
% 47
&& 88
    quick reference 90
* 36
*/ 64
    quick reference 67
+
    with strings 56
    used in System.out.println 38
++ *see* increment operator
/ 47
/* 64
    quick reference 67
// 64
    quick reference 67
< 89
<= 89
== 89
    dangers of 136
    with strings 91
    with class variables 209
> 89
>= 89
[] *see* array
{ 67
|| 90
    quick reference 91
} 67

A

A HREF 680
abs 244

Abstract data type *see* ADT
Abstract Window Toolkit *see* AWT
Accessor method 191
Action event *see* event, action
Action listener *see* listener, action
ActionEvent   *see* actionPerformed;
        event, action
ActionListener *see* listener, action
actionPerformed 354, 355–356
    quick reference 358
    throwing exceptions 430
add 349–350
    quick reference 351
addElement 627
    quick reference 624, 627
Adding machine GUI 379–385
<ADDRESS> 679
Address 5
addWindowListener
    quick reference 344
ADT 198–206
    implementation 200
    user interface 200
Algorithm 11–12
    quick reference 12
Ancestor 297
And *see* &&
Applet 16, 682–690
    converting an AWT application
        690
    init 683
    layout managers 683
    main 682
    no constructor 683
    placing in HTML document 686–
        687
        quick reference 687
    running 684–686
    sizing 687
    viewer 684

`Applet` 682
in class hierarchy 683
quick reference 684
see also applet 682
`appletviewer` 686
Argument 179
automatic type change 180
correspondence with parameters 182
primitive type 176–182
see also parameter
Arithmetic expression 46–48
parentheses in 47
spacing in 48
type of value returned 46
Arithmetic operators 46–48
Array 540–594
with = and == 564–567
argument 559–563
quick reference 561, 563
in assignment statement 564–565
base type 545
in a class 552–559, 570–578
creating 541–546
quick reference 545
declaring 541
quick reference 545
element 542, 547
equality 565–567
index 542, 549–551
out of bounds 549–551
indexed variable *see* variable, indexed
initializing 551
instance variable 580–587
length 545, 546, 547
multidimensional 604–621
declaring 605–606
employee time record example 615–621
implementation 610–613
indexed variable 606–609
parameter 609
quick reference 611
ragged *see* array, ragged
returned by method 610

quick reference 611
as an object 569
parallel 579–580
parameter *see* array, argument
partially full 578–579
ragged 613–615
returned by method 567–568
quick reference 569
searching 579
size *see* array, length 545
sorting *see* sorting
square brackets 545
see also array, creating; variable, indexed
subscript 542
terminology *quick reference* 546
ASCII 62, 468, 469
see also file, ASCII 469
table of characters 706
Assignment compatibilities 40–41
quick reference 41
Assignment statement 35–37
with an operator 37
quick reference 37
with class variables 207, 209
with quoted string 55
AWT 324–401
colors 343
coordinate system 336
hierarchy 350
multiple window GUI 495–509
number I/O 376–377
number input *quick reference* 378
number output *quick reference* 378
size units 334

B

Backslash 60
Base case *see* recursion, stopping
Base class 293
`private` instance variable 298–299
`private` method 299
quick reference 296
Beeton, Isabella Mary 587

Bera, Yogi 84
Berra, Yogi 327
Block 173–175
    quick reference 175
    see also compound statement
`<BODY>` 679
boolean 35
Boolean expression 88–91, 139–143
    parentheses in 90
Boolean input and output 144
boolean type 138–146
Boolean variable *see* variable, boolean
`BorderLayout` 352
`<BR>` 675, 676
brace *see* curly brackets
brackets
    curly *see* curly brackets
Branching statement 84–107
break
    in loops 124
        quick reference 126
    in switch 103
Browser 16, 674, 679, 687
    book mark 679
    not handling applets 687
Bubble sort 601
Buck 404
    passing *see throws*-clause
`BufferedReader` 520–528
    end of file 525–527
        quick reference 527
    methods 523
    opening a file 522
        quick reference 522
    reading numbers 522
Bug 14
Button 325, 346
`Button` class 353
    quick reference 354
Byte 5
byte 35
Byte code 8–9
    interpreter 8
    quick reference 8
    why it is called that 10

C

Calculator
    see also line oriented calculator
Call-by-reference 218
Call-by-value 179
Calling a method *see* invocation
Calling object 161
    omitting
        quick reference 238
`canRead` 510
    quick reference 513
`canWrite` 513
`capacity` vector method 626, 629
Carroll, Lewis 10, 63, 84, 206, 477, 622
Case sensitive 22
Casting *see* type casting
catch 409–412
    catch-block parameter 410
    multiple 427–431
catch-block *see catch*
`ceil` 244, 245
`<CENTER>` 676
Central Processing Unit *see* processor
char 35
Character
    ASCII *see* ASCII
    special 60–62
    Unicode *see* Unicode
`Character` 255, 256
    static methods 258
Character graphics 304–313
`CheckList` 579–582
Class 12, 13
    abstract 333
        quick reference 349
    base *see* base class
    child 297
    derived *see* derived classes
    inner 393–396
    parent 297
    wrapper *see* wrapper class
`ClassNotFoundException` 413
`CLASSPATH` 281–282
`clone` vector method 626

Code 7
  byte *see* byte code
  object *see* object code
  source *see* source code
Color 342
Colors *see* AWT, colors
Comma operator 121
Comment 64–65
  for `javadoc` 707–708
  quick reference 67
Compiler 6–7
  quick reference 7
Compiling
  Java class *see* compiling, Java
    program
  Java program 23, 156–157
Complete evaluation 143
Component 349
`Component` 349
Compound statement 95
  see also block
Concatenation 56
Constant 37
  naming 67–70
    quick reference 68
Constructor 267–274
  default 271–274
    omitting 274
    quick reference 274
  quick reference 274
Container class 345, 349–351
  quick reference 345
`contains` vector method 625
`countTokens` 525
CPU *see* processor
Curly brackets 67

opening a file 464
Debugging 14
  loops 135–137
Decrement Operator 53–54
`default` 103
default access 710
Default constructor *see* constructor,
    default
`delete` 513
Derived class
  constructor 300–301
  quick reference 296
  type of 302–304
Derived classes 293–295
Descendent 297
Digits to words case study 641–645
Directory 4, 280
Disk 3
Diskette 3
`dispose` 364, 508
  quick reference 509
Divide and conquer *see* top-down
    design
Division 47
  integer 47
DOS 6
dot 19
`Double` 255
`double` 34
  range 35
`do-while` 111, 113
  quick reference 113
`drawString` 330
  quick reference 337
Driver program 248, 250, 253
Dynamic binding 313–317

D

`DataInputStream` 469–473
  closing a file 473
  methods 470
  opening a file 471, 473
`DataOutputStream` 460–469
  closing a file 466
  methods 465

E

`E` 243
`e` in numbers 40
`elementAt`
  quick reference 624
`else`
  omitting 85
  see also `if-else`

Empty statement 122
Empty string 371
Encapsulation 201
End of file 480
ensureCapacity 626
EOFException 480
   quick reference 480
equals
   method 210–213
   String method 91–93
      quick reference 93
Equals *see* == *and* equals
equalsIgnoreCase 93
   quick reference 93
Error
   logic *see* logic error
   run-time *see* run-time error
   syntax *see* syntax error
Error message 14
Escape sequence 60
Event 325
   action 354–356
      quick reference 357
   firing 326
   handler 326
Event driven programming 325–327
Exception 404–453
   declaring *see* throws-clause
   defining exception classes 415–422
      quick reference 421
      when to 422, 435
   handling 405
   need not be caught 426–427
   overuse of 435
   predefined classes 413–414
   throwing 405
   uncaught 426
   when to throw 435
Exception 414
   quick reference 414
Execute 6
exists 510
   quick reference 513
exit 126
   quick reference 127

Expression
   boolean *see* boolean expression
   spacing in 48
extends 295

F

Field 157
File 4
   ASCII 466, 469
   binary 459–460
      input *see* DataInputStream 469
      output *see* DataOutputStream 460
   binary versus text 459, 466
   check for existence *see* exits
   check for readability *see* canRead
   check for writeability *see* canWrite
   closing 466
      why do it 467
   deleting *see* delete
   end of 480
   for a Java program 23
   GUI interface 495–509
   names 463, 464
      reading from keyboard 474
   opening 463
   path name *see* path name 510
   text 515–529
      closing 519
      reading from *see* BufferedReader
      writing to *see* PrintWriter
File class 510–515
   methods 513
File of records 486–495
   case study 486
FileInputStream 471, 513–515
   quick reference 514
FileNotFoundException 413, 477
   quick reference 480
FileOutputStream 464, 513–515
   quick reference 514
FileReader 522
final 68, 466

quick reference 466
finally 436
Float 255
float 34, 35
Floating point notation 40
Floating point number 34, 40, 44
floor 244, 245
Flow of control 84
FlowLayout 350, 351
flush 520
    quick reference 465
Folder *see* directory
for 118–121
    extra semicolon 121
    local variable 175
    quick reference 119
    with arrays 549
Format class 254, 283
Frame 328
    methods 344
Franklin, Benjamin 345

G

getActionCommand 356
getMessage 411, 417–422
    quick reference 413
getName 513
getPath 513
getText 368
    quick reference 371
Gosling, James 16
Gotcha 15
Graphical user interface *see* GUI
Graphics 330, 337
Greater than or equal *see* >=
Greater than *see* >
GridLayout 353
GUI 325
    quick reference 325

H

<H1> 675
<H2> 675
Hamlet 552

Hardware 2–4
hasMoreTokens 525
<HEAD> 677
Heading *see* <H1>, <H2>
HotJava 16
HREF 680
<HTML> 677
HTML 674–680
    comments 676
    file name 676
    inserting a hyperlink 680
        quick reference 681
    inserting a picture 681
    line break 676
    uppercase versus lowercase 675
.html 676
Hyperlink 680

I

I/O 71
Identifier 22
    quick reference 23
    spelling rules 22
    upper- and lowercase in 22
if-else 84–88
    multiway 97–98
        quick reference 101
    nested 97–98
implements 354, 362
import 280
    quick reference 281
Increment Operator 53–54
Indenting 65–67
Index
    in a string 56
indexOf
    method in String 58
indexOf vector method 625
Infinite Loop *see* loop, infinite
Infinite recursion *see* recursion, infinite
Information hiding 184–206
Inheritance 290–321
init *see* applet, init
Input
    echoing 78

keyboard 38, 74–78
`insertElementAt` 625
Insertion sort 601
Instance variables *see* variable, instance
int 33
  range 35
Integer 34
`Integer` 255
Interface 354, 358
Internet 674
Internet browser *see* browser
Internet Explorer 674
Internet, document *see* HTML 674
Interpreter 8
`intValue` 255
Invocation *see* method, invocation
`IOException` 413, 462, 477
`isEmpty` vector method 626
`isLowerCase` 258
`isUpperCase` 258
`isWhitespace` 258
Iterative version 653

J

Java
  history of 16
  how named 16
Java Virtual Machine 8
Java web site 680
`java.applet.*` 682
`java.awt.*` 328
`java.awt.event.*` 328
`java.util.*` 524, 622
`javac` 24
`javadoc` 202, 680, 707–709

K

Key word *see* reserved word
keywords 23
Khayyam, Omar 570

L

`Label` 372–373
  quick reference 373
Labeling components *see* `Label`
Language
  high level 6–7
  low level 6–7
`lastElement` vector method 626
`lastIndexOf` vector method 626
Late binding
  see dynamic binding.
Layout manager 350, 351–353
Lazy evaluation 143
`length`
  method in class `File` 513
  see also array, length
  method in `String` 57
Less than or equal *see* <=
Less than *see* <
Line oriented calculator 437–450
Linker 10
Linking 10
Listener 326
  action 354–356
    quick reference 357
  registering 331
`ListFullException` 574
Literal 37
Loan payoff example 113–116
Local variable *see* variable, local
Logic error 14
`Long` 255
long 35
Loop 107–137
  body 107, 128–129
  count controlled 130
  debugging 135–137
  designing 128–132
  do-while *see* *do-while*
  ending 130–132
  for *see* *for*
  infinite 116–117, 135
  initializing statements 129–130
  iteration 107
    zero times 110

nested 132
off-by-one error 136
sentinel value 131
statement 84
what kind to use 124
while see while

M

Macintosh 6
main 34, 239–240
Math class 243–245
max 244
Member 157
Memory
   auxiliary 3
   main 3
   secondary *see* memory, auxiliary
Memory address 208, 209
Memory location 3
Menu 325, 385–392
   quick reference 391
   bar 390
      quick reference 390
   item 389
   nested 390
   quick reference 390
Menu 389
MenuBar
   see menu, bar 390
MenuItem 389
Message 21
   error *see* error message
Method 12, 13, 161–168
   accessor 191
   body 164
   boolean valued 213–217
   calling method 235–237
   class 240
      see also method, static 240
   definition 163–171
      overiding *see* overriding
         method definition
      quick reference 170
      syntax summary 182–183
   heading 164

helping 239
invocation 161–163
   quick reference 21, 163
main 165
mutator 272
naming 168
recursive *see* recursion
static 240–243
   quick reference 241
testing 253–254
that returns a value 161–162
   quick reference 170
void 162–163
   quick reference 161, 170
Microsoft's Internet Explorer 674
min 244
Money output case study 246–252
Morison, Elting Elmore 2
Multidimensional array *see* array,
   multidimensional
Multiplication 36

N

Name *see* identifier
Naughton, Patrick 16
Net browser *see* browser
Netscape 16
Netscape Navigator 674
new 207
   in argument 342
      quick reference 342
   with arrays *see* array, creating
nextToken 525
Not equal *see* !=
Not *see* !
null 223
   quick reference 224
Null statement *see* empty statement
NumberFormatException 431–434
Numbers 39

O

Object 12, 13
   calling *see* calling object

creation 207
   see also `new`
`Object` 303
   quick reference 304
Object code 7
Object program *see* object code 7
Object-oriented programming 12–13
Off-by-one error 136
`OneWayNoRepeatsList` 570–578
OOP *see* object-oriented programming
Operating system 6
Operator
   arithmetic *see* arithmetic operator
Or *see* ||
Output
   screen 38, 71–73
Overloading 259–261
   interaction with automatic type conversion 264
      quick reference 265
   not on type returned 265
   quick reference 261
Overriding method definition 295–297
   quick reference 297

P

`<P>` 676
Package 279–282
   name 280–282
      quick reference 282
   quick reference 280
package access 710
`paint` 328, 336–337
   quick reference 338, 344
   versus `repaint` 346
Palindrome 600
Panel 365–367
   quick reference 367
Parameter
   actual 179
      see also argument
   as local variable 179
   class 217–220
      quick reference 220

comparing class and primitive type 220
   formal 179
   names
      choosing 185
   primitive type 176–182
      quick reference 181
   see also argument 182
Parentheses
   in arithmetic expressions 47
Path name 510–512
   quick reference 512
Payne, Jonathan 16
Peace, Warren 540
`Person` class 292
`PI` 243
Pixel 334
   quick reference 335
Polymorphism 259
Postcondition 187–188
`pow` 244
Precedence rule 48, 140, 142
Precedence rules 48
Precondition 187–188
`print`
   method of `PrintWriter` 519
      quick reference 520
`print` *see* `System.out.print` 72
`println`
   method of `PrintWriter` 519
      quick reference 520
`println` *see* `System.out.println`
`PrintWriter` 517–519
   closing a file 519
   methods 465, 520
   opening a file 517–519
      quick reference 517
Private 188
`private` 188–191, 239
   in base class *see* base class, `private`
   quick reference 190
Processor 3
Program 5
Programmer 17
`protected` 710

Pseudocode 11
  quick reference 12, 129
`public` 17, 188–190
  quick reference 190
Punch 385
`Purchase` class 194–198

Q

Quotes *see* string 60

R

`read`
  method of `BufferedReader` 522, 523
`read` method in `SavitchIn`
  source code 705
`readBoolean` 471
`readChar` 77, 471
  source code 701
`readDouble` 77, 469
  quick reference 470
  source code 703
`readFloat` 470
  source code 704
`readInt` 75, 469
  quick reference 470
  source code 702
`readLine` 75
  method of `BufferedReader` 522, 523
  source code 693
`readLineBoolean`
  source code 700
`readLineDouble` 74
  source code 697
`readLineFloat` 74
  source code 698
`readLineInt` 38, 74
  source code 695
`readLineLong` 74
  source code 696
`readLineNonwhiteChar` 74
  source code 699
`readLineWord`

  source code 694
`readLong` 470
  source code 703
`readNonwhiteChar` 77
  source code 702
`readUTF` 471
`readWord`
  source code 704
Recursion 640–665
  base cases *see* recursion, stopping case
  compared to overloading 656
  general technique outline 647
  infinite 647
  iterative version 651–653
  quick reference 641
  returning a value 653–656
  stopping cases 649, 653
Recursive method *see* recursion
Reference 206–220
`removeAllElements` 625
`removeElement` 625
`removeElementAt` 625
`repaint`
  quick reference 344
  versus `paint` 346
Reserved word 23
Reserved words
  list of 692
`return` 166–169
  in `void`-method 168–169
  quick reference 171
Returned value 38, 161
  quick reference 39
Roach infestation example 113–116
`round` 244, 245
Running
  Java program 9, 24
  program 6
Run-time error 14

S

Sales report case study 552–559
`SavitchIn` 23, 38, 74–78
  code explained 528–529

quick reference 76
source code 693–705
static methods 243
Screen 2
Secondary
memory *see* memory, secondary
Selection sort 588–592
Self-documenting
quick reference 64
self-documenting 64
Semicolon
extra in loop 121
Sentinel value 131
`setBackground` 340, 344
`setElementAt` 623
quick reference 624
`setForeground` 344
`setLayout` 350–351
`setSize` 330
quick reference 344
`setText` 371
quick reference 371
`setTitle` 340
quick reference 344
`setVisible` 331, 337–339
quick reference 339, 344
Shakespeare, William 279, 365, 458,
541, 552, 674
Sheridan, Richard Brinsley 674
`short` 35
Short-circuit evaluation 143
`show` 344, 508
quick reference 509
`size` 629
vector method 626, 627
quick reference 627
Software 2, 5–6
Sorting 587–592
see also specific sorting algorithms
Source code 7
Source program *see* source code
`Species` class 213
`sqrt` 244
Stack overflow 650
Statement 21
assignment *see* assignment

statement
branching *see* branching statement
compound *see* compound
statement
empty *see* empty statement
loop *see* loop, statement
nested 94–95
`static` 68
see also method, static 240
stepwise refinement
see top-down design
Stream 459
quick reference 459
`String` 55–62
string
quoted 55
see also `String`
`StringTokenizer` 523–525
stub 253
`Student` class 294
Style 63–70
`substring` 57
Sun Microsystems 16
`super` 300
calling object 302
quick reference 301
Swift, Jonathan 515
`switch` 101–104
controlling expression 103
quick reference 105
Syntax
error 14
quick reference 14
`System.exit` 332
`System.out.print` 72
quick reference 73
`System.out.println` 38, 71–73
quick reference 73

T

Testing
bottom up 253
see also loop, testing
see also method, testing
Text area 368–372

Text field 372
Text file *see* file, text
`TextArea` 368
    quick reference 371
    see also text area
`TextField` 372
    quick reference 371
    see also text field
`this` 169–171
    as method 301
        quick reference 302
    omitting 235–238
        quick reference 238
    quick reference 171
`throw` 409–410, 411
    multiple 427
    quick reference 410
Throwing an exception *see* `throw`
`throws`-clause 422–423
    in derived classes 427
    quick reference 426
`throw`-statement *see* `throw`
`<TITLE>` 677
Token 524
`toLowerCase` 57, 258
Top-down design 252–253
`toString` 256
`toUpperCase` 57, 258
Toy program 239
Tracing
    loop *see* variable, tracing 137
    variable 137
`trim` 57
`trimToSize` 626, 631
Truman, Harry 404
Truth tables 141
`try` 409
`try`-block *see* `try`
`try`-`throw`-`catch`
    quick reference 412
    see also `try`; `throw`; `catch`
Type 33
    class 33
    primitive 33, 34
Type casting 41
    quick re

U

Unicode 62
UNIX 6
URL 681
User 17
UTF 468, 469

V

Value returned *see* returned value
`valueOf` 256
Variable 30–32
    boolean 139–140
        ending a loop 144–146
    class 242
        see also variable, static 242
    class type 207–210
        quick reference 209
    declaration 32–34
        location of 33
        quick reference 33, 39
    global 173
    indexed 542
    initializing in declaration 44
        quick reference 44
    instance 157–160
    local 172–173
        in `for`-statement 175
        quick reference 173
    as memory location 32
    names 32
    static 242
    subscripted 43, 223
    uninitial
    val, static 240
`Vector` 622–633
    accessing at an index 623–627
        quick reference 623
    add element 624
    base type 628
        quick reference 628
    capacity 622–623
    constructor
        quick reference 624

creating 623
make a copy 626
memory management 626
remove element 625
search methods 625
size *see* `size`, vector method 627
`Vector`
methods 624–626
Vending machine program 49–51

W

Web browser *see* browser
while 108–110
quick reference 110
Whitehead, Alfred North 234
Whitespace 77, 258
Window 325, 327
listener 333
see also `Frame`
`Window` 333
`windowActivated` 334
`WindowAdapter` 331–332, 333
methods 334
`windowClosed` 334
`windowClosing` 332, 334
`windowDeactivated` 334
`windowDeiconified` 334
`WindowDestroyer` 330, 331–332
definition 332
`windowIconified` 334
`WindowListener` interface 362–365
`windowOpened` 334
Windows 6
Word
reserved *see* reserved word
World-wide web 16
Wrapper class 255–257
quick reference 255
`writeBoolean` 467
quick reference 465
`writeChar` 467
quick reference 465
`writeDouble` 466
quick reference 465
`writeFloat` 465, 466

`writeInt` 464–466
quick reference 465
`writeLong` 465
`writeUTF` 467–469
quick reference 465

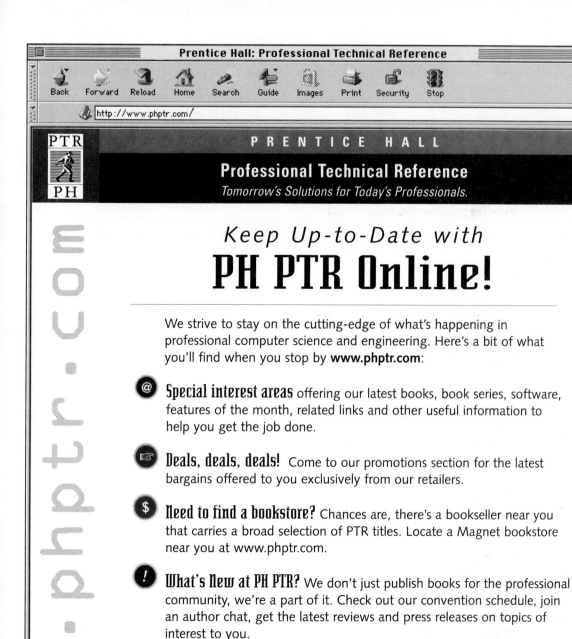

LICENSE AGREEMENT AND LIMITED WARRANTY

READ THE FOLLOWING TERMS AND CONDITIONS CAREFULLY BEFORE OPENING THIS SOFTWARE PACKAGE. THIS LEGAL DOCUMENT IS AN AGREEMENT BETWEEN YOU AND PRENTICE-HALL, INC. (THE "COMPANY"). BY OPENING THIS SEALED SOFTWARE PACKAGE, YOU ARE AGREEING TO BE BOUND BY THESE TERMS AND CONDITIONS. IF YOU DO NOT AGREE WITH THESE TERMS AND CONDITIONS, DO NOT OPEN THE SOFTWARE PACKAGE. PROMPTLY RETURN THE UNOPENED SOFTWARE PACKAGE AND ALL ACCOMPANYING ITEMS TO THE PLACE YOU OBTAINED THEM FOR A FULL REFUND OF ANY SUMS YOU HAVE PAID.

1.   GRANT OF LICENSE: In consideration of your purchase of this book, and your agreement to abide by the terms and conditions of this Agreement, the Company grants to you a nonexclusive right to use and display the copy of the enclosed software program (hereinafter the "SOFTWARE") on a single computer (i.e., with a single CPU) at a single location so long as you comply with the terms of this Agreement. The Company reserves all rights not expressly granted to you under this Agreement.

2.   OWNERSHIP OF SOFTWARE: You own only the magnetic or physical media (the enclosed media) on which the SOFTWARE is recorded or fixed, but the Company and the software developers retain all the rights, title, and ownership to the SOFTWARE recorded on the original media copy(ies) and all subsequent copies of the SOFTWARE, regardless of the form or media on which the original or other copies may exist. This license is not a sale of the original SOFTWARE or any copy to you.

3.   COPY RESTRICTIONS: This SOFTWARE and the accompanying printed materials and user manual (the "Documentation") are the subject of copyright. The individual programs on the media are copyrighted by the authors of each program. Some of the programs on the media include separate licensing agreements. If you intend to use one of these programs, you must read and follow its accompanying license agreement. You may not copy the Documentation or the SOFTWARE, except that you may make a single copy of the SOFTWARE for backup or archival purposes only. You may be held legally responsible for any copying or copyright infringement which is caused or encouraged by your failure to abide by the terms of this restriction.

4.   USE RESTRICTIONS: You may not network the SOFTWARE or otherwise use it on more than one computer or computer terminal at the same time. You may physically transfer the SOFTWARE from one computer to another provided that the SOFTWARE is used on only one computer at a time. You may not distribute copies of the SOFTWARE or Documentation to others. You may not reverse engineer, disassemble, decompile, modify, adapt, translate, or create derivative works based on the SOFTWARE or the Documentation without the prior written consent of the Company.

5.   TRANSFER RESTRICTIONS: The enclosed SOFTWARE is licensed only to you and may not be transferred to any one else without the prior written consent of the Company. Any unauthorized transfer of the SOFTWARE shall result in the immediate termination of this Agreement.

6.   TERMINATION: This license is effective until terminated. This license will terminate automatically without notice from the Company and become null and void if you fail to comply with any provisions or limitations of this license. Upon termination, you shall destroy the Documentation and all copies of the SOFTWARE. All provisions of this Agreement as to warranties, limitation of liability, remedies or damages, and our ownership rights shall survive termination.

7.   MISCELLANEOUS: This Agreement shall be construed in accordance with the laws of the United States of America and the State of New York and shall benefit the Company, its affiliates, and assignees.

8.   LIMITED WARRANTY AND DISCLAIMER OF WARRANTY: The Company warrants that the SOFTWARE, when properly used in accordance with the Documentation, will operate in substantial conformity with the description of the SOFTWARE set forth in the Documentation. The Company does not warrant that the SOFTWARE will meet your requirements or that the operation of the SOFTWARE will be uninterrupted or error-free. The Company warrants that the media on which the SOFTWARE is delivered shall be free from defects in materials and workmanship under normal use for a period of thirty (30) days from the date of your purchase. Your only remedy and the Company's only obligation under these limited warranties is, at the Company's option, return of the warranted item for a refund of any amounts paid by you or replacement of the item. Any replacement of SOFTWARE or media under the warranties shall not extend the original warranty period. The limited warranty set forth above shall not apply to any SOFTWARE which the Company determines in good faith has been subject to misuse, neglect, improper installation, repair, alteration, or damage by you. EXCEPT FOR THE EXPRESSED WARRANTIES SET FORTH ABOVE, THE COMPANY DISCLAIMS ALL WARRANTIES, EXPRESS OR IMPLIED, INCLUDING WITHOUT LIMITATION, THE IMPLIED WARRANTIES OF MERCHANTABILITY AND FITNESS FOR A PARTICULAR PURPOSE. EXCEPT FOR THE EXPRESS WARRANTY SET FORTH ABOVE, THE COMPANY DOES NOT WARRANT, GUARANTEE, OR MAKE ANY REPRESENTATION REGARDING THE USE OR THE RESULTS OF THE USE OF THE SOFTWARE IN TERMS OF ITS CORRECTNESS, ACCURACY, RELIABILITY, CURRENTNESS, OR OTHERWISE.

IN NO EVENT, SHALL THE COMPANY OR ITS EMPLOYEES, AGENTS, SUPPLIERS, OR CONTRACTORS BE LIABLE FOR ANY INCIDENTAL, INDIRECT, SPECIAL, OR CONSEQUENTIAL DAMAGES ARISING OUT OF OR IN CONNECTION WITH THE LICENSE GRANTED UNDER THIS AGREEMENT, OR FOR LOSS OF USE, LOSS OF DATA, LOSS OF INCOME OR PROFIT, OR OTHER LOSSES, SUSTAINED AS A RESULT OF INJURY TO ANY PERSON, OR LOSS OF OR DAMAGE TO PROPERTY, OR CLAIMS OF THIRD PARTIES, EVEN IF THE COMPANY OR AN AUTHORIZED REPRESENTATIVE OF THE COMPANY HAS BEEN ADVISED OF THE POSSIBILITY OF SUCH DAMAGES. IN NO EVENT SHALL LIABILITY OF THE COMPANY FOR DAMAGES WITH RESPECT TO THE SOFTWARE EXCEED THE AMOUNTS ACTUALLY PAID BY YOU, IF ANY, FOR THE SOFTWARE.

SOME JURISDICTIONS DO NOT ALLOW THE LIMITATION OF IMPLIED WARRANTIES OR LIABILITY FOR INCIDENTAL, INDIRECT, SPECIAL, OR CONSEQUENTIAL DAMAGES, SO THE ABOVE LIMITATIONS MAY NOT ALWAYS APPLY. THE WARRANTIES IN THIS AGREEMENT GIVE YOU SPECIFIC LEGAL RIGHTS AND YOU MAY ALSO HAVE OTHER RIGHTS WHICH VARY IN ACCORDANCE WITH LOCAL LAW.

YOU ACKNOWLEDGE THAT YOU HAVE READ THIS AGREEMENT, UNDERSTAND IT, AND AGREE TO BE BOUND BY ITS TERMS AND CONDITIONS. YOU ALSO AGREE THAT THIS AGREEMENT IS THE COMPLETE AND EXCLUSIVE STATEMENT OF THE AGREEMENT BETWEEN YOU AND THE COMPANY AND SUPERSEDES ALL PROPOSALS OR PRIOR AGREEMENTS, ORAL, OR WRITTEN, AND ANY OTHER COMMUNICATIONS BETWEEN YOU AND THE COMPANY OR ANY REPRESENTATIVE OF THE COMPANY